History of Wills, Testators and Their Families in Late Medieval Krakow

Later Medieval Europe

Managing Editor

Douglas Biggs (*University of Nebraska – Kearney*)

Editorial Board

Sara M. Butler (*The Ohio State University*)
Kelly DeVries (*Loyola University Maryland*)
William Chester Jordan (*Princeton University*)
Cynthia J. Neville (*Dalhousie University*)
Kathryn L. Reyerson (*University of Minnesota*)

VOLUME 23

The titles published in this series are listed at *brill.com/lme*

History of Wills, Testators and Their Families in Late Medieval Krakow

Tools of Power

By

Jakub Wysmułek

BRILL

LEIDEN | BOSTON

This is an open access title distributed under the terms of the CC BY-NC-ND 4.0 license, which permits any non-commercial use, distribution, and reproduction in any medium, provided no alterations are made and the original author(s) and source are credited. Further information and the complete license text can be found at https://creativecommons.org/licenses/by-nc-nd/4.0/.

The terms of the CC license apply only to the original material. The use of material from other sources (indicated by a reference) such as diagrams, illustrations, photos and text samples may require further permission from the respective copyright holder.

The translation and Open Access publication of the book was supported by the Polish Ministry of Science and Higher Education. The book received a financial grant (21H 17 0288 85) in the frame of National Programme for the Development of Humanities - 6 Round.

Cover illustration: *The Payment of the Tithes* (*The Tax-Collector*), also known as *Village Lawyer*, Pieter Breughel the Younger.

LC record available at https://lccn.loc.gov/2021012442
LC ebook record available at https://lccn.loc.gov/2021012443

Typeface for the Latin, Greek, and Cyrillic scripts: "Brill". See and download: brill.com/brill-typeface.

ISSN 1872-7875
ISBN 978-90-04-44816-2 (hardback)
ISBN 978-90-04-46144-4 (e-book)

Copyright 2021 by Jakub Wysmułek. Published by Koninklijke Brill NV, Leiden, The Netherlands. Koninklijke Brill NV incorporates the imprints Brill, Brill Hes & De Graaf, Brill Nijhoff, Brill Rodopi, Brill Sense, Hotei Publishing, mentis Verlag, Verlag Ferdinand Schöningh and Wilhelm Fink Verlag. Koninklijke Brill NV reserves the right to protect this publication against unauthorized use.

This book is printed on acid-free paper and produced in a sustainable manner.

CONTENTS VII

4   The Burgher Religiosity   238
  1   A Personal Relationship with God   242
    1.1   *Clergy*   242
      1.1.1   Confessors   242
      1.1.2   Preachers   247
      1.1.3   Other Clergy   250
    1.2   *Religious Objects in Wills*   252
      1.2.1   Rosaries   252
      1.2.2   Books and Paintings   254
      1.2.3   Expensive Symbols of Piety: Crosses and *Agnus Dei* Medallions   261
    1.3   *Participation in the* sacrum*: Personal Belongings Used for Religious Purposes*   263
  2   The Familial Dimension of Piety   270
  3   The Corporate Dimension of Burghers' Piety   280
  4   Parish Identity and Ties to Other Religious Institutions in the Medieval City   293
  5   Religion Civique – Communal Religiosity   300
    5.1   *Beguinages*   313
  6   Christian Duty   317
  7   Summary   322

Conclusion   326

Appendix   335
Glossary   364
Bibliography   366
Index of Places   400
Index of Names   401
Index of Subjects   402

Acknowledgements

When I started researching the topic of late medieval wills from Krakow, I was mostly interested in the details they offer regarding material culture and social relations in the city. I saw these acts as the lens through which I could perceive the everyday life of Krakow burghers. I also anticipated that the concentration of my efforts on the wills from one, relatively large urban centre would allow me to observe and track the changes occurring in the city over a longer period. However, I very quickly realised that the seemingly constant and unambiguous concept of the last will that I held differed significantly from the acts that I found in the sources – that is, in the documents and books created by the municipal offices of Krakow in the fourteenth and fifteenth centuries.

During my study of the source material, these questions multiplied, prompting me to change my perspective and, finally, to reorient radically the way I perceived the role and significance of 'testaments' in the process of transformation of late medieval urban society. As a result of this close source study, I moved from the initial questions concerning what people did with the wills, to questions about what these acts, in a metaphorical sense, did to people. From viewing wills as records of objects, people, and religious practices, I came to see them as potent tools of power that had a significant impact on the understanding of property ownership, family relations, and rivalry between secular and ecclesiastical authorities in the city. I hope that the questions posed and the answers I suggest will inspire other researchers to follow my path and to seek out the observed phenomena in sources created by citizens of other European cities of the period.

This intellectual adventure that I embarked upon a few years ago would not have been so fulfilling and satisfying without the friendly and professional help that I received from colleagues, friends, and family members. Among many of them, I wish to thank especially Agnieszka Bartoszewicz, the promoter of my doctoral dissertation, for her encouragement, useful suggestions and practical help with making the first steps in reading and analyzing medieval wills. During the later phase of the book development, I discussed many issues regarding my research and received thoughtful advice from Barbara Rosenwein, for which I am very thankful. The book would not have been completed without the unceasing support of my wife Ilona. Finally, I wish to thank Thomas Anessi who translated the book into English, and Pascal Porcheron who undertook the proofreading.

The book was originally published in 2015 in Polish, as *Testamenty mieszczan krakowskich* (*XIV-XV wiek*), by the Polish Historical Society (Polskie

Towarzystwo Historyczne) and Neriton Publishing House with the support of the Polish Ministry of Science and Higher Education. The translation into English and the Open Access publication of a revised and updated version of the book was possible thanks to a grant from the National Program for the Development of Humanities of the Polish Ministry of Education and Higher Education.

Figures, Graphs and Tables

Figures

1 The oldest woodcut picture of Krakow, Kazimierz and Kleparz, by Hartmann Schedl, *Liber Cronicarum* (1493) 353

2 Map of Wacław Grodecki (1535–1591). It was included in the first modern world atlas, *Theatrum Orbis Terrarum*, published by Abraham Ortelius in 1570 (1579) in Antwerp. "Cracovia" is depicted in the lower left corner of the map, in the Lesser Poland Voivodeship. Jakub Wojkowski, *CARTOGRAPHIA CRACOVIANA: Krakow i okolice na dawnych mapach — geoportal*. Krakow: Uniwersytet Rolniczy w Krakowie, Wydział Inżynierii Środowiska i Geodezji, 2020. dawnemapykrakowa.pl 354

3 Plan of the city of Krakow by Filip Lichocki, issued in 1787. The plan includes Krakow within the walls, together with Wawel hill, Stradom, Kazimierz and a fragment of Podgórze (called Jozefstadt at that time). Jakub Wojkowski, *CARTOGRAPHIA CRACOVIANA: Krakow i okolice na dawnych mapach — geoportal*. Krakow: Uniwersytet Rolniczy w Krakowie, Wydział Inżynierii Środowiska i Geodezji, 2020 dawnemapykrakowa.pl 355

4 Document of foundation as a 'testament,' issued by knight Zbylut for the Cistercian monastery in Łekno in 1153. State Archive of Poznan, Cystersi Łekno, sygn kl. Łekno D1 356

5 Will of Paszko vel Paulino Cavallo (1358), a Genoese-born councillor in Krakow and administrator of the Bochnia salt mines. National Archives in Krakow, Scabinalia Cracoviensia, 1300–1375, ms. no. 1, fol. 203. Photo: Malopolska Digital Library http://mbc.malopolska.pl/dlibra 357

6 Will of Nicholas Dambraw (1395), councilor of Krakow. Card with a will was pasted between the pages of the bench book. National Archives in Krakow, Scabinalia Cracoviensia, 1390–1397, ms. no. 3, fol. 188b. Photo: Malopolska Digital Library http://mbc.malopolska.pl/dlibra 358

7 Will and mutual bequest of Henry Woger and his wife Ursula (1400). National Archives in Krakow, Consularia Cracoviensia, 1392–1411, ms. no. 427, fol. 151. Photo: Malopolska Digital Library http://mbc.malopolska. pl/dlibra 359

8 Will of Michaelis of Nowa Wieś (Neudorff) (1418). National Archives in Krakow, Consularia Cracoviensia, 1412–1449, ms. no. 428, fol. 126. Photo: Malopolska Digital Library http://mbc.malopolska.pl/dlibra 360

XII FIGURES, GRAPHS AND TABLES

9 Will of Dorothy, widow of Little Jelge (1430). National Archives in Krakow, Scabinalia Cracoviensia, 1419–1430, ms. no. 5, fol. 210. Photo: Malopolska Digital Library http://mbc.malopolska.pl/dlibra 361

10 Will of Johannes Stolle of Głogów, the municipal notary (1451). National Archives in Krakow, Consularia Cracoviensia, 1459–1483, ms. no. 429, fol. 28–29. Photo: Malopolska Digital Library http://mbc.malopolska.pl/dlibra 362

11 Will of Barbara Putkinne (1456) and the first part of the will of John Swidniczer (1457), from *Liber Testamentorum*. National Archives in Krakow, Consularia Cracoviensia, 1427–1623, ms. no. 772, fol. 38–39. Photo: Malopolska Digital Library http://mbc.malopolska.pl/dlibra 363

Graphs

1 Number of extant wills from various sources from 1300 to 1550, by decade 104

2 Number of wills per type of book from 1427 to 1476, taking into account the assets of testators 107

3 Number of testators whose wills have survived to the present day and of those whose wills are only mentioned in the source material 108

4 Wills and other types of donations and dispositions 111

5 Wills made in each decade of the fourteenth and fifteenth centuries 113

6 Representatives of the municipal authorities among known Krakovian testators in the fourteenth and fifteenth centuries 127

7 Number of councillors and aldermen among known Krakovian testators in particular decades of the fourteenth and fifteenth centuries 127

8 Estimates of the wealth of the 25% of all testators who included dowers in their wills 164

9 Estimates of the wealth of all testators based on indirect information 164

10 Changes in the wealth of testators in the fourteenth and fifteenth centuries 166

11 Asset structure of female testators 166

12 Asset structure of all testators 167

13 Number of women and men among all Krakow testators in the fourteenth and fifteenth centuries 174

14 The amount bequeathed in dowers in the wills of Krakow's councillors 186

15 Amounts of dowers contained in the wills made by Krakow councillors and the wealthiest non-councillor Krakow's citizens 188

16 The number of testators who made wills before going on a pilgrimage 321

FIGURES, GRAPHS AND TABLES XIII

Tables

1   Records of *mortis causa* in Krakow sources from the years 1300–1500   8
2   Occupations of Krakovian testators in the years 1300–1500   133
3   Estimated distribution of the three social strata in Rostock, Stralsund, Lübeck, Wrocław, Torun, and Elblag   156
4   Dower records in Krakow wills   161
5   The number of women and men among Krakow testators in the years 1431–1470   174

Abbreviations

Advoc.	Advocatalia Cracoviensia, ms. no. 83
AMK	The National Archives in Krakow, Department III – Files of the City of Krakow (*Archiwum Narodowe w Krakowie, Akta miasta Krakowa*)
KDM	*Kodeks dyplomatyczny Małopolski*, vol. I-IV, ed. Franciszek Piekosiński, Krakow 1874–1876, 1887, 1905 (*Monumenta Medii Aevi Historica res gestas Poloniae illustrantia*, vol. 1, 9, 10, 17)
KDMK	*Kodeks dyplomatyczny miasta Krakowa*, vol. I-IV, ed. Franciszek Piekosiński, 1879–1882 (*Monumenta Medii Aevi Historica res gestas Poloniae illustrantia*, vol. 5, 7)
KDW	*Kodeks dyplomatyczny Wielkopolski*, vol. 1, ed. Ignacy Zakrzewski, Poznan 1877
KDWac.	*Kodeks dyplomatyczny katedry krakowskiej św. Wacława*, vol. I-II, ed. Franciszek Piekosiński, Krakow 1874, 1883 (*Monumenta Medii Aevi Historica res gestas Poloniae illustrantia*, vol. 1)
KH	"Kwartalnik Historyczny"
KHKM	"Kwartalnik Historii Kultury Materialnej"
SCAB.	*Księgi ławnicze krakowskie 1365–1376 i 1390–1397. Acta scabinalia Cracoviensia 1365–1376 et 1390–1397*, ed. Stanisław Krzyżanowski, Krakow 1904
SCAB. 4	AMK, Scabinalia Cracoviensia. Inscriptiones, ms. no. 4
SCAB. 5	AMK, Scabinalia Cracoviensia. Inscriptiones, ms. no. 5
SCAB. 6	AMK, Scabinalia Cracoviensia. Inscriptiones, ms. no. 6
SCAB. 7	AMK, Scabinalia Cracoviensia. Inscriptiones, ms. no. 7
SCAB. 8	AMK, Scabinalia Cracoviensia. Inscriptiones, ms. no. 8
SCAB. 9	AMK, Scabinalia Cracoviensia. Inscriptiones, ms. no. 9
CONS 427	AMK, Consularia Cracoviensia. Inscriptiones, ms. no. 427
CONS 428	AMK, Consularia Cracoviensia. Inscriptiones, ms. no. 428
CONS 429	AMK, Consularia Cracoviensia. Inscriptiones, ms. no. 429
CONS 430	AMK, Consularia Cracoviensia. Inscriptiones, ms. no. 430
LT	AMK, Liber Testamentorum. Testamenta in officio consulari Cracoviensi (1427–1623), ms. no. 772
NKiRMK	*Najstarsze księgi i rachunki miasta Krakowa od r. 1300 do 1400*, ed. Franciszek Piekosiński, Józef Szujski, Krakow 1878
PSB	"Polski Słownik Biograficzny" ('The Polish Biographical Dictionary')
Cod. Dipl. UJ	*Codex Diplomaticus Universitatis Studii Generalis Cracoviensis*, ed. Franciszek Piekosiński, vol. 1–3 (Krakow: sumptibus Universitatis, 1870–1880)

Introduction

> Run quickly to confession,
> Bring priests into your house,
> Cry for your sins, receive the sacrament,
> The body of Christ, consecrated oil!
> Give to the children your land and house;
> For the soul, give what you gained;
> Win friends with your possessions;
> They will put your soul in Heaven.
> Gather the creditor and the angry,
> Win them by pleas, pay all your debts;
> Lose not your soul for another's money
> And for this wrongly burn in hell.[1]
>
> > *Lament of a Dying Man* [*Skarga umierającego*], author unknown, trans.
> > Thomas Anessi

∴

The verses of the fifteenth-century poem *Lament of a Dying Man*, quoted in part above, include the late-medieval Catholic Church's prescriptions for a 'good death.' The dying man was to summon a priest, before whom he would make his final confession, repent his sins and receive the final anointing. In accordance with the custom of the day, he would also dispose of his possessions on his deathbed. His property – his house and fields – was to be given to his children, while his remaining worldly goods – his money and other movables of value – were to be shared between the clergy and the poor, two groups of 'expert' in the medieval formula for salvation. Mention is also made of the dying man's obligation to settle his earthly debts to his creditors.

Lament of a Dying Man was probably written in the latter half of the fifteenth century and contains ideas that appear in many fifteenth-century

---

1 This translation of *Lament of a Dying Man* (*Skarga umierającego*) is based on that of Michael Mikos, but has been slightly modified due to variations in the source text. The original is found in *Medieval Literature of Poland: An Anthology*, ed. & trans. Michael Mikos (New York: Garland Pub., 1992), 79–82. It can be found online at: http://staropolska.pl/ang/middleages/sec_poetry/Lament.php3 (accessed: 4 May 2019)

© JAKUB WYSMUŁEK, 2021 | DOI:10.1163/9789004461444_002
This is an open access chapter distributed under the terms of the CC BY-NC-ND 4.0 license.

didactic works in the *ars moriendi* (the Art of Dying Well) genre.[2] Such works were addressed to people from a broad range of social strata in the Polish Kingdom, and used rhyming verses written in the Polish vernacular to provide religious and social instruction on how to properly prepare for death. It is worth noting that the poem's protagonist is a man, a peasant, who as head of the family was the sole administrator of important hereditary immovable property – the family estate.

This act of last will was supposed to take place before an invited clergyman and the immediate family. If possible, debtors and creditors were also summoned and, often, friends and neighbours as well. The validity of this settling of accounts with one's worldly life was guaranteed by witnesses and the institutional authority of the Catholic Church, embodied by a member of the clergy. This act was performed orally and recorded in the memory of those present; when the donation to the Church was a large one, an entry was sometimes made in the parish records.

Based on the results of previous research, it can be assumed that despite the poem's didactic function, its description of the dying man's preparations accurately reflects what was then a preferred and widely disseminated model for preparing for death. Yet, it is worth noting that the word 'testament' is not mentioned anywhere in the above stanzas. There is no evidence that the dying man's resolutions were recorded in written form, or that among those present was a vogt,[3] alderman,[4] notary or some other secular administrative guarantor of the legitimacy of the resolutions.

This 'art of dying' relates to a world that was largely traditional, agrarian and illiterate. Alongside this world, however, a new model of urban life was emerging, one that was growing in significance economically and culturally, and in which the written word and the institutions of municipal self-government were considered the best means of safeguarding people's rights and security, and of ensuring the fulfilment of contracts and dispositions. This emerging model was reflected in the way in which the last will was understood and in the forms it took in the urban milieu. This was the setting in which the concept of the written will spread most quickly, first becoming a common practice among city-dwellers and later a part of municipal law. While at first wills mainly served the needs of an increasingly influential merchant class, they were later adapted to address those of craftsmen and domestic servants as well.

---

2   Maciej Włodarski, *Ars moriendi w literaturze polskiej XV i XVI w.* (Krakow: Znak, 1987), 14–63, 157–160.

3   See the Glossary: Vogt

4   See the Glossary: Bench court

INTRODUCTION

In my use of rural and urban milieus as categories, I treat them in some sense as ideal types. In doing so, my aim is not to deny the existence of a great wealth of diverse phenomena that testify to the ways in which these worlds were intertwined and the many intermediate forms of community life that lay between those found in a small village and a large city. I similarly juxtapose the 'good death' of a peasant and that of a merchant, and make comparisons between various legal institutions and social relations and practices. This allows us to discern – from among the diverse social practices discussed – the general direction and nature of the cultural changes that can be seen in historical sources.

In both the countryside and the city, death was largely defined by its religious aspects. Yet in Krakow, due to the presence of numerous clergy and religious orders, the range of pastoral offerings was much broader than was typical in a village, as was the level of knowledge among the city's inhabitants of the tenets of the Christian faith. Due to the evidence of general popularity of *ars moriendi* manuals in Poland and that time, it can be assumed that at least members of Krakow's elite were familiar with Christian teaching on the subject, either through rhymed poems that served a mnemonic function, or through sermons heard during Mass in one of the city's many churches.[5] Those townsmen who had studied at a university may also have had the chance to read one of the – sometimes richly illustrated – scholarly treatises on the subject, such as that attributed to Matthew of Krakow entitled *The Art of Dying, Collected from Various Scriptures, with Drawings, to Repel the Devil's Temptation to Every Christian's Death, Which Are Very Useful and Often Necessary.*[6]

These teachings, disseminated in urban communities through numerous channels, depicted the final moments on the death bed as decisive in terms of a sinner's potential salvation or eternal damnation. The fate of the dying person's soul rested in his own hands. In cities, the means most commonly promoted for ensuring salvation was the drawing up of a written will in which one's earthly obligations were settled and generous donations made as an act of charity. Such an act of expressing one's last will came to be seen as a Christian's

---

5 Krzysztof Bracha, *Nauczanie kaznodziejskie w Polsce późnego średniowiecza. Sermones dominicales et festivales z tzw. kolekcji Piotra z Miłosławia* (Kielce: Wydawnictwo Akademii Świętokrzyskiej w Kielcach, 2007), 162–165.

6 Authorship of the treatise, written around 1408–1410 and entitled *Ars moriendi ex variis scripturatum sententiis collecta cum figuris ad resistendum in mortis agone diabolice sugestioni valens cuilibet christifideli utilis ac multum necessaria,* is attributed to Matthew of Krakow, rector of Heidelberg University and a reformer of Jagiellonian University; cf. Włodarski, *Ars moriendi,* 23–24.

natural duty, which alongside the sacraments of confession, repentance and absolution, was to be fulfilled before death. Yet, if we look closely at the extant sources, we see that in the fourteenth and fifteenth centuries, when the 'art of dying' was being widely disseminated in late-medieval literature, wills were not yet a common phenomenon,[7] and the form of the written bequests they contained varied greatly; moreover, it is sometimes difficult to find in their content any traces of religious motivation. So, what were late-medieval last wills? For what purpose and by whom were they written? And, what is the most important, what impact did they have on the social reality and religious practices of their time?

This book is intended to answer these questions and many others. Despite the growing literature on wills, there are still frequent misunderstandings about the evolution of these acts, and a tendency to underestimate the role they played in the history of Europe. While wills have long been used in historical research, and have been viewed from a variety of perspectives, they have usually been used as evidence for some other phenomenon, such as the nature of religiosity, everyday life, material culture or family relations during a given period. Only very rarely have wills themselves been the subject of a deeper analysis, which considered their hidden functions and impact on social reality. For this reason, changes in the nature of wills and their social role have remained largely unexamined, seemingly self-evident. It is the first such comprehensive analysis of medieval Krakow wills, which covers the subject of socio-cultural role of wills and discusses in-depth the legal, social and economic background on which they were formed in the city. It is also a book that offers an original interpretation of these acts, shifting the readers popular perspective of what people did with them to, metaphorically, what these acts did with people. This book seeks to change the perception of these testamentary acts by treating the testamentary act itself as an important agent of historical social change – a 'tool of power.' The book's main thesis is that medieval testament was a legal instrument which on a macro level strongly influenced the process of expanding the scope of individual control over economic resources and on the micro level was used in order to expand the individual control on interpersonal relations with family members, friends, co-workers and fellow citizens.[8]

---

7 Hanna Zaremska, "Człowiek wobec śmierci. Wyobrażenia i rytuały," in *Kultura Polski średniowiecznej XIV–XV w.*, ed. Bronisław Geremek (Warszawa: Semper, 1997), 485–510.

8 As Mia Korpiola and Anu Lahtinen recently stressed: "Quickly, the individualistic potential of wills as a tool of crafting different property strategies became obvious. Within the boundaries of the law, the family became perceived more as "a descend group, a pool of potential heirs" to be moulded in accordance with the person's personal wishes. The will was thus a manifestation of power: the authoritative expression of the testator's last will (*ultima voluntas*).

INTRODUCTION

5

The will as a phenomenon defies universal definition. While its history has been influenced by the Church and eschatological conceptions propagated by the clergy, it also reflects wider social and cultural transformations, such as the expansion of cities, trade and the wider money and goods economy, the establishment of municipal law, the spread of literacy and the changes taking place in the structure of the burgher family. Taking into account these complex, dynamically changing social and cultural contexts, in the following chapters I analyse the nature and role of wills and the manner in which they functioned in the particular urban milieu of late-medieval Krakow. I relate the multidimensional history of the will, highlighting the diverse character of these legal acts, over a period of nearly two hundred years, from their appearance in medieval Krakow in the early fourteenth century, to the turn of the sixteenth century, by which time the form and legal foundations of the will were well established. In the book I also attempt to trace the evolution of the will from a purely religious act to one in which secular motives relating to family and property dominated, and from an act that required the presence of a clergyman and was part of the Canon law of the Catholic Church, to an act that took place in the presence of a city official and was regulated both by the laws and customs of a given urban centre and more generally by common law. In the first case, I propose using the term 'canonical will,' and in the second case, 'communal will.'

Subsequently, I ask a range of questions regarding the social characteristics of the group of testators, burghers from Krakow and visitors to the city. I analyse their positions within the social structure through an estimation of their wealth and their relations to power elites (the municipal authorities) as well as their occupations and places of origin. This information not only provides us with a better understanding of the reasons behind the creation of wills, but also casts light on the structure of urban society from a new angle. I also demonstrate the importance of wills as a tool for managing family and property relations in two distinctly different life situations – that of a rich merchant and a middle-class trader or artisan. Moreover, I put forward a thesis about the major role played by wills in the spread of a whole range of religious practices that contributed to the richness of late-medieval urban piety.

Although focused on a single urban centre – the city of Krakow – this book presents a generalizable model of the development of testamentary practices in Central and Eastern Europe, in a part of the continent that was beyond the direct influence of ancient Roman legal traditions, but which drew upon

---

That a person's last wil was to be fulfilled in accordance with the true intent of the testator became a leading principle in learned law – rendering it even more potent"; "Introduction," in *Planning for Death. Wills and Death-Related Property Arrangements in Europe, 1200–1600*, ed. Mia Korpiola, Anu Lahtinen (Brill, 2018), 18.

strong cultural and legal models that originated within the sphere of influence of the Holy Roman Empire. The relatively late urbanization of the eastern regions of Europe makes it possible to observe certain social phenomena through sources written *in statu nascendi* – i.e. at the moment these events occurred. Krakow seems to be extremely privileged in this respect because of the well-preserved state of its municipal books, including, in particular, the oldest known will, that of a burgess from Krakow, dating from 1303, for which, to the best of my knowledge, there is no equivalent in any other urban centre in Central and Eastern Europe.

The heart of the Kingdom of Poland was undoubtedly Krakow, with its royal court, bishopric, holy chapter, numerous monasteries and churches, and many visiting foreigners who influenced the dynamics of life in the city and contributed to its social and cultural diversity. Krakow was one of the largest and wealthiest cities in late-medieval Poland and an important trade centre for the entire Central European region.[9] The city's political, economic and religious importance spurred the intensive growth of its population and led to an associated increase in the level of wealth and occupational diversity among its inhabitants.[10] Krakow's role as a regional centre also meant that new currents in culture arrived here first, and only then spread to smaller affiliated population centres. One such example of the city's role and importance can be seen in wills, of which the earliest and best-preserved examples come from Krakow.

1   Definition of a 'Will'

The complexity of wills as sources is masked by their seemingly-straightforward purpose. Wills contain a wealth of details, and can be confusing, as it is

---

9   Jan Dąbrowski, "Krakow a Węgry w wiekach średnich," *Rocznik Krakowski* 13 (1911): 187–250; Feliks Kiryk, "Etos pracy (podstawy gospodarcze formowania się Krakowa lokacyjnego 1257–1333)," in *Krakow – dziedzictwo lokacji. Materiały sesji naukowej odbytej 21 kwietnia 2007 roku*, ed. Jan M. Małecki (Krakow: Towarzystwo Miłośników Historii i Zabytków Krakowa, 2008), 51–73; *idem*, "Związki Krakowa z Lwowem w późnym średniowieczu," in *Lwów. Miasto, społeczeństwo, kultura*, vol. 2, ed. Kazimierz Karolczak (Krakow: Wydawnictwo Naukowe Wyższej Szkoły Pedagogicznej, 1998), 9–39; Stanisław Kutrzeba, *Finanse i handel średniowiecznego Krakowa*, ed. Marcin Starzyński (Krakow: Wydawnictwo Avalon, 2009).

10   Maria Bogucka, Henryk Samsonowicz, *Dzieje miast i mieszczaństwa w Polsce przedrozbiorowej* (Wrocław–Warszawa–Krakow: Ossolineum, 1986) 114–118; Jerzy Wyrozumski, *Dzieje Krakowa. Krakow do schyłku wieków średnich* (Krakow: Wydawnictwo Lit., 1992), 314–396.

INTRODUCTION

often not clear what objects they are referring to. Personal and genealogical data are often incomplete, and we thus often have no clues about the identity of those mentioned or information about their relationship to the testator or to one other. Moreover, the motives of the testator are often obscured by the conventional structure and form of the bequests. We even face problems in attempting to define the 'testament' in relation to distinct concepts found in canon, municipal and common law, and to the wide spectrum of local testamentary practices. Attempting to define these detailed bequests, which varied greatly in both form and purpose, Steven Epstein stated that "[t]he will was an act made by an individual at a specific time and place, for personal motives."[11] This definition, despite its undoubted technical accuracy, is nevertheless applicable to almost every form of human activity, and therefore does not bring us any closer to understanding the specificity and uniqueness of the will as a legal and social phenomenon. Rather, it reveals the helplessness of the researcher in the face of this document, which eludes simple definition.

Despite the difficulties associated with defining wills, in order to reveal its intrinsic character, I have adopted a broad definition of the will as a gift made by an individual to another person, group of persons or institution, resulting in the transfer of rights to the bequeathed property after the death of that individual (and therefore various types of *donationes mortis causa* – both individual posthumous donations and wills in their full, 'mature' form – are taken into account here). In adopting such a definition, we are forced to consider a wide range of gifts, ranging from short pious bequests and mutual donations made between spouses (*mutuae donaciones*) to various types of donations to relatives and non-relatives. An analysis of late-medieval wills from Krakow confirms that all of these types of *mortis causa* bequests were made, and that the Krakow burghers referred to them in a quite free and inconsistent manner using the word 'testament.'

On the basis of the data contained in Table 1, it can be seen that the majority constitute different types of bequests which performed a function similar to that of wills in the full sense of the word (even when we take into account both all the surviving wills and references found in sources to ones that have not been preserved).[12] Due to the volume of source materials collected and the complex processes that led to the development of the communal will (which in its mature form became widespread only towards the end of the period

---

11   Stephen Epstein, *Wills and Wealth in Medieval Genoa, 1150–1250* (Cambridge (Mass.)–London: Harvard University Press, 1984), 38.

12   For more information on the variety of *mortis causa* and the ratio between them, see chapter 1, section 11, p. 104.

INTRODUCTION

TABLE 1   Records of *mortis causa* in Krakow sources from the years 1300–1500

Types of records	Number of records
Wills	537
Information about unpreserved wills	252
Single pious bequests	95
Individual donations to family members and other people	356
Mutual bequests of spouses	385
Records of dowers	79
Total	*1704*

being analysed here), our main focus will be on those bequests, considered as wills, with more complex provisions, which thereby reveal the most about the concept. The bequests considered as wills in the present book mainly include those, that indicate self-reflection on the part of the author and a desire to dispose of a significant portion of property for family or religious purposes.[13] However, it was impossible to avoid a certain arbitrariness in classifying the bequests into one group or the other, as not all of them are referred to as 'testaments' in the source materials.[14] This is especially true of bequests from the fourteenth century, when the concept of the will related primarily to religious donations, while 'secular' bequests were labelled with the Latin word *donatio* or the German term *Gemechte* or *Geschefft* (or similar terms that indicated their contractual nature).[15]

---

13   The present classification of collected wills was also guided by the opinion on the nature of wills expressed by Hanna Zaremska: "The thought of death prompts people to reflect on themselves in an orderly manner. This reflection induces them to go over the property they have acquired to date, to determine and hierarchically order the relationships with their relatives and loved ones, to establish heirs and to separate those they want to support from those they want to punish by disinheriting or disregarding them"; *eadem*, *Człowiek wobec śmierci*, 489.

14   See chapter 1, section 5, p. 60.

15   Cf. Jakub Wysmułek, "Wills as Testimony of Marriage Contracts in Late Medieval Krakow," in *Law and Marriage in Medieval and Early Modern Times, Proceedings of the Eight Carlsberg Academy Conference on Medieval Legal History 2011*, ed. Per Andersen, Kirsi Salonen, Helle Møller Sigh, Helle Vogt (Copenhagen: Djøf Forlag, 2012, 181–190; Otto Loening, *Das Testament im Gebiet des Magdeburger Stadtrechtes* (Breslau: M&G Marcus, 1906), 34–35.

INTRODUCTION

2   The Will – A Theoretical Perspective

The socio-historical research perspective I have chosen to adopt is intended to allow for a broad analysis of the phenomenon of the late medieval will, revealing its specificity and the role it played in the profound social and cultural transformations that were taking place during the period in question. The most important of them is the process of individualisation of society also associated with the birth of early forms of capitalism in late medieval cities. I formulated a working thesis about the importance of the will in the cultural transformation of city life, that is was an important factor in helping to bring about an increasingly individualised society. The use of wills and testaments related to, among other things, the expansion of the concept of private property, the formation of the nuclear family, and the increasingly widespread search for individual strategies of commemoration. The connection between these socio-cultural phenomena and the spread of the will as a concept in Poland suggests that it was an important factor in the historical process of individualisation, understood as a directed (though not linear) socio-historical progression towards "values, beliefs, attitudes and behaviour[s] [that] are increasingly based on personal choice and are less dependent on tradition and social institutions."[16] At the same time, we are dealing here with an apparent paradox. The increasingly clear distinction between the individual and his or her 'community of blood' (traditional family line and kinship groups) did not occur as a result of individuals distancing themselves from their group affiliations as such. This was rather a gradual process, based on conscious and voluntary choices made on a daily basis, which, as a consequence, established a new hierarchy of relations on the individual, group and institutional level. These choices were not conditioned by formal obligations related to the traditional law of kinship (*ius propinquitatis*), but on the basis of real-life practices. Shared experiences created the grounds on which mutual bonds of an emotional nature took root. The wealthy showed most interest in shaping their social group by means of their own wills. Initially, the urban elite were quite willing to make individual decisions regarding the division of property, and thus transform family relationships. This relationship between one's social position and a willingness to individually reshape the bonds and mutual obligations in one's existing network of social relations is clearly visible in the collection of wills from Krakow, as well as in sources from other cities in Central and Eastern Europe.

---

16   Peter Ester, Loek Halman, Rood de Moor, "Introduction," in *The Individualizing Society. Value Change in Europe and North America*, ed. Peter Ester, Loek Halman, Rood de Moor (Tilburg: Tilburg University Press, 1994), 7.

By extending an individual's control over their material world (in terms of the legal alienation of goods both during the owner's lifetime and after death), the will also became an instrument of power over one's relatives, friends and co-workers, the clergy, and others. A voluntary testamentary bequest was a gift that by its very nature demanded reciprocity,[17] even if only in some form of honouring or remembrance. It was also a disposition that could be revoked by the testator at any point during their lifetime. This meant that the potential future inheritance of property was often contingent on good relations being maintained between the testator and their friends and relatives. In this way, the assets accumulated by the testator became, through this unilateral disposition, a tool for the planning and shaping of both efforts to guarantee the welfare of one's soul, and the material and discursive commemoration of the testator among the living. It also became a powerful instrument for managing the testator's social relations with potential heirs later in life, and for ensuring one's influence on the lives of loved ones, even after death.[18]

Using categories taken from the social sciences, it can be said that a will, as a means of extending the scope of one's control over material goods, was therefore a tool for the transformation of economic capital accumulated during one's lifetime into social, symbolic[19] and 'eschatological' capital, involving, among other things, the guarantee of lifelong care by one's loved ones, the posthumous preservation of one's memory among the living, and the assurance of eternal life in heaven.

A will was likewise an instrument of power for institutions that sought to incorporate it into their rituals and cultural practices, and to place it under their exclusive legal jurisdiction. This was true, above all, of the Catholic Church, but later also of municipal authorities who competed with the Church hierarchy for control over the wills of members of the burgher estates.[20] The authorities

---

17   Marcel Mauss, *The Gift: The Form and Reason for Exchange in Archaic Societies*, trans. W.D. Halls (New York: W. W. Norton & Company, 1990 (1950)).

18   Worried about their family relations and the legitimacy of their actions, testators often tried to negotiate the content of their bequests with their heirs. In order to avoid future conflicts, the consent of their closest relatives to the testamentary dispositions was often required by the municipal authorities. However, a will could at least "potentially" be used as a tool against the "legal" heirs to property.

19   Pierre Bourdieu, "The Forms of Social Capital," in *Education, Culture, Economy and Society*, ed. A.H. Halsey, Hugh Lauder, Phillip Brown, Amy Stuart Wells (Oxford: Oxford University Press, 1997), 46–58.

20   Jakub Wysmułek, "Last Wills as Tool of Power. Development of Testamentary Practice in Krakow during Late Middle Ages," in *Planning for Death. Wills and Death-Related Property Arrangements in Europe 1200–1600*, ed. Mia Korpiola, Anu Lahtinen (Brill, 2018), 211–238.

INTRODUCTION   11

felt entitled to custody of burgher wills, in light of their sovereignty over the
city's property and the legal acts of its citizens. The question of whether testamentary dispositions were to be implemented as part of canon or municipal
law determined which institution would exercise control over the huge (on the
scale of the whole city) sums of money that were invested in various forms of
charity, pious gifts and commemoration. Institutional control over wills can
also be viewed as a means of building prestige, a symbolic presentation of the
city council's[21] sovereign power over the life and death of other burghers. For
the same reasons, up until the end of the Middle Ages, the church hierarchy
pointed to the leading role of its bishops and even the Holy See itself as granting it greater authority, in the event any disputes or problems arose in the
implementation of testamentary dispositions.

3   Source Base

The bequests contained in wills are extremely rich sources of information that
is private in nature – something rarely found in documents preserved from
medieval times.[22] At the same time, in the case of Krakow (and other large
medieval cities), these are what you might call 'mass sources,'[23] in the sense
that they are abundant and relatively similar in form. This allows us both to

---

21   See Glosary: City council
22   Regardless of the reasons for making last wills, whether alleged or stated by the testators
     themselves, wills express the wishes of townsmen from Krakow and as sources possess
     features that have led Winfried Schulze to label them "self-testimonies" (*Selbstzeugnisse*)
     or – following a well-known paper by the Dutch historian Jacques Presser – "ego-doc-
     uments," cf. "Ego-Dokumente. Annäherung an den Menschen in der Geschichte," *Selbst-
     zeugnisse der Neuzeit*, vol., Winfried Schulze (Berlin: De Gruyter, 1996); Rudolf Dekker,
     "Jacques Presser's Heritage. Egodocuments in the Study of History," *Memoria y Civilización*
     5 (2002), 13–37; Kaspar von Greyerz, "Ego-Documents. The Last Word?," *German History*
     28, 2010, no. 3, 273–282; Mary Fulbrook, Ulinka Rublack, *In Relation. The "Social Self" and
     Ego-Documents*, "German History" 28, no. 3 (2010) 263–272; Agnieszka Rosa, "Testamenty
     fordońskie jako egodokumenty mieszczańskie," *Kronika Bydgoska* 29 (2006), 41–72.
23   Martin Nodl did claim that testaments are not mass sources. While his arguments against
     the use of quantitative research methods on medieval wills to draw society-wide conclu-
     sions seem to me correct, the significant number of preserved wills from Krakow makes it
     possible to conduct quantitative research on the changing nature of the will itself, as well
     as its authors (i.e. testators). This was the aim of statistical studies in this paper; cf. Martin
     Nodl, "Středověký testament jako abnormalita," in *Pozdně středověké testamenty v českých
     městech. Prameny, metodologie a formy využití. Sborník příspěvků z konference uspořádané
     30. listopadu 2005 Archivem hlavního města Prahy a Historickým ústavem Akademie věd
     České republiky*, ed. Kateřina Jíšová, Eva Doležalová (Praha: Scriptorium, 2006), 73–85.

conduct qualitative research and to analyse the collected data by means of statistical methods.

The primary group of sources, i.e. those that made it possible to conduct this research on Krakow's wills, include bench court,[24] council and municipal books from 1301 to 1500. The initial period of the development of the will in the first half of the fourteenth century can be studied thanks to the preservation of the oldest known municipal book from Krakow, covering the years 1301–1375, in which cases heard by the bench court and the notes of the city council office were recorded.[25] Research on books from the fourteenth century was carried out on the basis of Franciszek Piekosiński's 1878 edition of *The Oldest Municipal Book [Najstarszaj księga miejskaj]*[26] and books of the Krakow bench court from 1365–1376 and 1390–1397, published in 1904 by Stanisław Krzyżanowski.[27]

Studies of sources from the late fourteenth century and fifteenth century were carried out mainly on manuscript sources. These included five books of the bench court from the years 1408–1476[28] (and bequests from another preserved book of the bench court from 1500),[29] as well as four council books from the years 1392–1500[30] (and the first part of the next council book containing entries from 1500).[31] Particular attention was paid to the oldest surviving book of wills, maintained by the Krakow city council. For the purposes of this study, the wills from the years 1427–1500, recorded in this book, formed the bulk of those analysed.[32] One will (from 1476) was also found in the oldest known book of the vogt's court.[33] A valuable document from 1485, a testamentary form written down by the Krakow viceroy Kacper Grosz, was found among a collection of loose parchment documents stored in the Acts of the City of Krakow in the State Archive in Krakow.[34]

---

24 See Glossary: Bench court

25 AMK, ms. 1; Bożena Wyrozumska, *Kancelaria miasta Krakowa w średniowieczu* (Krakow: Wydawn. Uniwersytetu Jagiellońskiego, 1995), 54–58; Agnieszka Bartoszewicz, *Piśmienność mieszczańska w późnośredniowiecznej Polsce* (Warszawa: Wydawnictwo Uniwersytetu Warszawskiego, 2012), 82–83.

26 NKiRMK.

27 SCAB..

28 AMK, ms. 4 (1408–1416), ms 5 (1419–1430), ms 6 (1431–1446), ms 7 (1447–1459), ms 8 (1459–1476).

29 AMK, ms 9 (1500).

30 AMK, ms 427 (1392–1411), ms 428 (1412–1449), ms 429 (1450–1483), ms 430 (1483–1500).

31 AMK, ms 431 (1500–1513).

32 AMK, ms 772; cf. Wyrozumska, *Kancelaria*, 92–93; Bartoszewicz, *Piśmienność*,109–110.

33 AMK, ms 83, fol. 8–9.

34 AMK, ms 779.

INTRODUCTION   13

This search was supplemented by documents published by Franciszek Piekosiński in *The Diplomatic Code of Lesser Poland*[35] and in *The Diplomatic Code of the City of Krakow 1257–1506*,[36] which is the source of the oldest known Krakow will, drawn up in 1303 by a burgher woman named Sulisława.[37] Documents published by Stanisław Kuraś and Irena Sułkowska-Kuraś in *The Małopolska Collection of Documents*[38] were also used. Valuable information about testators can be found in books of admissions to municipal law in Krakow published in 1913 by Kazimierz Kaczmarczyk.[39]

In total, 268 different testamentary dispositions were found in council books and in books of wills kept by the councillors[40] (84 in council books and 184 in the *Liber Testamentorum*), all but three of which date back to the fifteenth century. In addition, 264 testamentary bequests were contained in the books of bench courts (including the oldest preserved municipal book), 168 of which date back to the fifteenth century.[41] A search of sources created outside the main Krakow offices resulted in the discovery of just five burgher wills: one was entered in a book of the vogt's court,[42] and four survived in the form of documents.[43]

---

35   KDM.

36   KDMK.

37   KDMK, vol. 3, no. 368 (1303).

38   *Zbiór dokumentów małopolskich*, parts 1–18, ed. Stanisław Kuraś, Irena Sułkowska-Kuraś (Wrocław–Warszawa–Krakow: Zakład Nar. Im. Ossolińskich, Polska Akademia Nauk, 1962–1975).

39   *Księgi przyjęć do prawa miejskiego w Krakowie 1392–1506. Libri iuris civilis Cracoviensis 1392–1506*, ed. Kazimierz Kaczmarczyk (Krakow, Archiwum Aktów Dawnych Miasta Krakowa, 1913).

40   See Glosary: City council

41   Therefore, the claim made by Urszula Sowina, who stated that "in the Middle Ages and early modern period in Krakow, testamentary dispositions were usually recorded in the books of the bench court," is not true in regard of wills from fifteenth century. The state of preservation of sources from this period does not allow us to draw further conclusions about wills from the fourteenth century; cf. Urszula Sowina, "Testamenty mieszczan krakowskich o przekazywaniu majątku w późnym średniowieczu i we wczesnej nowożytności," in *Sociální svět středověkého města*, ed. Martin Nodl (Colloquia mediaevalia Pragensia, 5), (Praha:Filosofia, 2006), 175.

42   Will of the wife of Nicholas Zeidenhafter; *Advocatalia Cracoviensia*, ms no. 83, 8–9.

43   Two of them were individual documents stored in church archives (Sulisława's will of 1303 is stored in the archive of the Franciscans in Krakow, whereas the copy of Gotfrid Fattinante's will of 1393 was allegedly stored in the archives of the cathedral chapter in Krakow) and two were notarial deeds. The will of Claire Rolle of 1419 was published in KDMK, whereas the testamentary legacy of Nicholas Zarogowski was published in Cod. Dipl. UJ;; KDMK, vol. 3, no. 368; KDWac., vol. 2, no. 396; KDMK, vol. 3, no. 406; Cod. Dipl. UJ, vol. 3, no. 236, 17–18.

14   INTRODUCTION

The 537 bequests of last will discovered during the search of source materials were made by 447 testators, among which in 68 cases (13%) two versions of the act were found, in 16 cases (3%) – three, 5 cases (1%) – four, and 2 cases (0.4%) – as many as five different versions of the last will. Out of all the wills, 144 (37%) were made by 130 women.

In Krakow municipal sources, the wills of nine clergymen[44] were also found, of which only subsequent versions of the will of John Stolle from Głogów, a municipal notary and later altarist in St. Mary's Church,[45] were analysed in detail. Moreover, due to the strong ties between the testators and the Krakow burghers elites, the acts of last will of four persons formally belonging to the noble estate were also analysed. These included two Krakow councillors, Michael Lang, also known as *de Czirla*,[46] and Nicholas Zarogowski,[47] as well as Helena Leszczyńska[48] and Anna Obulczowa (the daughter of councillor George Orient).[49]

4   Subject Literature

In Europe research into medieval wills has a long tradition, thus I have chosen to mention here only those works which, either through their territorial proximity or thematic scope, are closely linked to the subject matter of this book.

Early studies on acts of last will, dating back to the latter half of the nineteenth century, are devoted primarily to the evolution of property rights. Worth noting here is the classic work *Ancient Law* (1861), written by the English historian and anthropologist Henry Maine.[50] Similar research was also conducted in Germany in the early twentieth century.[51] Particularly important from the

---

44   Sister Pauline, NKiRMK, no. 1524 (1344); Sister Elizabeth of Dornburg, NKiRMK, no. 1643 (1352); Nicholas Polner, a curate and altarist in St. Mary's Church in Krakow, CONS. 428, fol. 200 (1423); Theodoric Weinrich, a Krakow presbyter, KDMK, vol. 3, no. 432, 563–569 (1449); Nicholas Rybka, a cleric, CONS. 429, fol. 197 (1456); Magister Stephen Leipniger, LT, fol. 60 (1459); Hieronymus Gambicz, a cleric of Opatów, CONS. 429, fol. 373 (1466); Jacob Hoze, priest, LT, fol. 115 (1476).

45   SCAB. 6, fol. 186 (1439); SCAB. 6, fol. 187 (1439); SCAB. 6, fol. 267 (1442); CONS. 429, fol. 27–28 (1451); KDMK, vol. 3, no. 439, 574–576 (1454).

46   CONS. 428, fol. 341, 344 (1435).

47   CONS. 429, fol. 15–16 (1450); Cod. Dipl. UJ, vol. 3, no. 236 (1472); LT, fol. 129–131 (1482).

48   LT, fol. 53 (1458).

49   LT, fol. 147 (1489).

50   Henry Sumner Maine, *Ancient Law* (London: Oxford University Press, (1861) 1931).

51   Günter Aders, *Das Testamentsrecht der Stadt Köln im Mittelalter* (Köln: Verlag des Kölnischen Geschichtsvereins e.V. in Kommission bei Creutzer & Company, 1932).

INTRODUCTION   15

point of view of the subject under discussion is Otto Loening's 1906 study on
the role of the will in Magdeburg Law.[52]

Since the 1960s, interest in wills as historical sources has grown alongside
the spread of social and cultural history in European historiography.[53] Michael
M. Sheehan's works on early medieval English and Anglo-Saxon wills are particularly valuable.[54] In the 1980s, there was a rise in interest among historians in the social positions of testators and in the everyday life and material
culture of the Middle Ages emerging from bequests of last will.[55] Numerous
works were published, from which it is worth mentioning a few studies, such
as those of the Austrian historian Gerhard Jaritz, Hartmut Boockmann, from
Göttingen.[56] Paul Baur, who analysed wills from Konstanz;[57] Susanne Mosler-
Christoph, from Lüneburg;[58] Lucia Maestro, from Vienna;[59] and Johannes
Schildhauer, from Stralsund.[60]

The tradition in German historiography of researching the historical and
legal dimensions of wills was continued throughout the twentieth century.[61]

---

52   Otto Loening, *Das Testament*.

53   Ulrich Bach, *Das Testament als Literarische Form. Versuch einer Gattungsbestimmung auf
     der Grundlage englischer Texte* (Düsseldorf: Düsseldorfer Hochschulreihe, 1977).

54   Michael M. Sheehan, *The Will in Medieval England. From the Conversion of the Anglo-Sax-
     ons to the End of the Thirteen Century* (Toronto: Pontifical Institute of Mediaeval Studies,
     1963); *idem, Marriage, Family and Law in Medieval Europe. Collected Studies*, ed. James K.
     Farge (Cardiff: University of Toronto Press, 1996).

55   *Materielle Kultur und Religiöse Stiftung im Spätmittelalter. Internationales Round-Table-
     Gespräch Krems an der Donau, 26 September 1988*, ed. Gerhard Jaritz (Wien: Verlag der
     österreichischen Akademie der Wissenschaften, 1990); cf. Urs Martin Zahnd, "Spätmit-
     telalterliche Bürgertestamente als Quellen zu Realienkunde und Sozialgeschichte," *Mit-
     teilungen des Instituts für österreichische Geschichtsforschung* 96, 1988.

56   Hartmut Boockmann, *Leben und Sterben in einer spätmittelalterlichen Stadt. Über ein Göt-
     tinger Testament des 15. Jahrhunderts* (Göttingen: Hartmut Boockmann. Vandenhoeck
     & Ruprecht, 1983); Gerhard Jaritz, "Österreichische Bürgertestamente als Quelle zur
     Erforschung städtischer Lebensformen des Spätmittelalters," *Jahrbuch für Geschichte des
     Feudalismus* 8, 1984

57   Paul Baur, *Testament und Bürgerschaft, Alltagsleben und Sachkultur im spätmittelalterli-
     chen Konstanz* (Sigmaringen: Jan Thorbecke Verlag, 1989).

58   Susanne Mosler-Christoph, *Die materielle Kultur in den Lüneburger Testamenten 1323 bis
     1500* (PhD diss., Georg-August-Universität Göttingen, 1998).

59   Lucia Maestro, *Spätmittelalterliche Bürgertestamente in den Wiener Neustädter Rats-
     büchern als Quelle zur Alltagsgeschichte* (PhD diss. University of Vienna, 1995).

60   Johannes Schildhauer, *Hansestädtischer Alltag. Untersuchungen auf der Grundlage der
     Stralsunder Bürgertestamente vom Anfang des 14. bis zum Ausgang des 16. Jahrhunderts*
     (Weimar: Hermann Böhlaus Nachfolger, 1992).

61   Hans Lentze, "Das Wiener Testamentsrecht des Mittelalters," *Zeitschrift der Savigny-
     Stiftung für Rechtsgeschichte, Germanische Abteilung* 69/70 (1952/1953), 98–154, 159–229;

In addition, studies were carried out on the religious significance of acts of last will,[62] as were linguistic analyses.[63] In the late twentieth century, interest in the medieval family[64] and the position of women in urban settings increased among historians, represented in works by such authors as Linda Guzzetti,[65] Barbara A. Hanawalt[66] and Kathrin Pajcic.[67] Particularly noteworthy here is a very valuable analysis of wills from Cologne by Brigitte Klosterberg.[68] In recent years, numerous collections of wills have been made available to researchers in the form of catalogues or editions of collected sources, such as the publication

---

Johannes Kaps, *Das Testamentsrecht der Weltgeistlichen und Ordenspersonen in Rechtsgeschichte, Kirchenrecht und Bürgerlichem Recht Deutschlands, Österreichs und der Schweiz* (München: Verlag Christ Unterwegs, 1958); Harm Buss, *Letztwillige Verfügungen nach ostfriesischen Recht* (Göttingen: Verlag Ostfriesische Landschaft, 1963); Gerhard Hückstädt, *Der Testamentvollstrecker im deutschen Recht des Mittelalters* (PhD diss. Kiel, 1971); Gabriele Schulz, *Testamente des späten Mittelalters aus dem Mittelrheingebiet. Eine Untersuchung in rechts- und kulturgeschichtlicher Hinsicht* (Mainz: Selbstverlag der Gesellschaft für Mittelrheinische Kirchengeschichte, 1976); Henning Piper, *Testament und Vergabung von Todes wegen im braunschweigischen Stadtrecht des 13 bis 17 Jh.* (Braunschweig: Waisenhaus-Buchdruckerei und Verlag, 1960); Christian Neschwara, *Rechtsformen Letztwilliger Verfügungen in den Wiener Stadtbüchern (1395–1430). Eine Bilanz aufgrund der vorliegenden Edition bis 1417, Testamente aus der Habsburgermonarchie Alltagskultur, Recht, Überlieferung* (Wien: Böhlau, 2009); Lothar Kolmer, "Spätmittelalterliche Regensburger Testamente. Forschungsergebnisse und Forschungsziele. Regensburger Testamente im Vergleich", *Zeitschrift für Bayerische Landesgeschichte* 52 (1989): 475–500.

62   Marianne Riethmüller, *To troste miner sele, Aspekte spätmittelalterlicher Frömmigkeit im Spiegel Hamburger Testamente (1310–1400)* (Hamburg: Verlag Verein für Hamburgische Geschichte, 1994); Anneliese Mark, *Religiöses und karitatives Verhalten der Wiener Bürger im Spiegel ihrer Testamente (1400 bis 1420)* *(PhD diss. Innsbruck, 1976).

63   Andreas Bieberstedt, *Textstruktur, Textstrukturvariation, Textstrukturmuster. Lübecker mittelniederdeutsche Testamente des 14. und 15. Jahrhunderts* (Wien: Praesens Verlag, 2007).

64   Jack Goody, *The Development of the Family and Marriage in Europe* (Cambridge: Cambridge University Press, 1983); Ralph Houlbrooke, *Death, Religion, and the Family in England 1480–1750* (Oxford: Oxford University Press, 1998); *Marriage, Property and Succession*, ed. Lloyd Bonfield (Berlin: Duncker&Humblot, 1992); Rafael Ehrhardt, *Familie und Memoria in der Stadt. Eine Fallstudie zu Lübeck im Spätmittelalter* (Göttingen: Göttingen Niedersächsische Staats- und Universitätsbibliothek, 2001).

65   Linda Guzzetti, *Venezianische Vermächtnisse, Die soziale und wirtschaftliche Situation von Frauen im Spiegel spätmittelalterlichen Testamente* (Weimar: Verlag J. B. Metzler, 1998).

66   Barbara A. Hanawalt, *The Wealth of Wives. Women, Law, and Economy in Late Medieval London* (Oxford: Oxford University Press, 2007).

67   Kathrin Pajcic, *Frauenstimmen in der spätmittelalterlichen Stadt? Testamente von Frauen aus Lüneburg, Hamburg und Wien als soziale Kommunikation* (Würzburg: Königshausen u. Neumann, 2013).

68   Brigitte Klosterberg, *Zur Ehre Gottes und zum Wohl der Familie – Kölner Testamente von Laien und Kleriken im Spätmittelalter* (Köln: SH-Verlag, 1995).

INTRODUCTION   17

of wills from Brunswick (1314–1432) by Dietrich Mack,[69] from Hamburg (1351–1432) by Hans Dieter Loose,[70] and from Lüneburg (1323–1500) by Uta Reinhardt.[71]

In recent years, researchers of the medieval history of Bohemia (now the Czech Republic) and Hungary have also produced a number of works on wills. However, historians from these countries have focused primarily on the religious aspect of wills, as exemplified by the works of Judit Majorossa[72] and Kateřina Jíšova.[73] Important statements by Czech historians on the preservation of sources, research methodology, and the use of late medieval wills in historical research are found in a post-conference volume published in 2006.[74]

For many years, research on medieval wills was a marginal concern in Polish historiography. Wills were researched more extensively for the first time by Henryk Samsonowicz in his 1960 study of the burgher class in Gdańsk in the latter half of the fifteenth century.[75] However, his study focused primarily on economic issues. Then in 1976 a journal article by him made a major

---

69 Dietrich Mack, *Testamente der Stadt Braunschweig*, vol. 1–5 (Göttingen: Goltze, 1988–1990).

70 Hans Dieter Loose, *Hamburger Testamente, 1351 bis 1400. Veröffentlichungen aus dem Staatsarchiv der Freien und Hansestadt Hamburg* (Hamburg: Christians, 1970).

71 Uta Reinhardt, *Lüneburger Testamente des Mittelalters 1323 bis 1500* (Hannover: Hahn, 1996).

72 Judit Majorossy, *Church in Town. Urban Religious Life in Late Medieval Pressburg in the Mirror of Last Wills* (PhD diss., Budapest: Central European University, 1997); *eadem*, "Archives of the Dead. Administration of Last Wills in Medieval Hungarian Towns," *Medium Aevum Quotidianum* 48 (2003), 13–28; *Das Pressburger Protocollum Testamentorum 1410 (1427) – 1529*, vol. 1–2: *1410–1529*, ed. Judit Majorossy, Katalin Szende (Wien: Bohlau Verlag, 2010, 2014).

73 Kateřina Jíšová, *Testamenty novoměstských měšťanů v pozdním středověku* (PhD diss., Praha: Univerzita Karlova, 2008); *eadem*, "Charita, milosrdenství a spása duše v pozdně středověké Praze," in *Kaci, święci, templariusze*, ed. Błażej Śliwiński (Malbork: Muzeum Zamkowe, 2008), 139–190; *eadem*, "Testamenty pražských měšťanů v pozdním středověku. Religiozita, sociální rozvrstvení, majetkové a rodinné poměry novoměstských měšťanů (1421–1533)," in *Pierwsze polsko-czeskie forum młodych mediewistów. Materiały z konferencji naukowej, Gniezno 27–29 września 2005 r.*, ed. Józef Dobosz (Poznan: Instytut Historii UAM, 2007), 295–308; *eadem*, "Die Testamente der Elite von Krakau und Prag im Spätmittelalter," in *Elita władzy miasta Krakowa i jej związki z miastami Europy w średniowieczu i epoce nowożytnej (do połowy XVII wieku). Zbiór studiów*, ed. Zdzisław Noga (Krakow: Antykwa, 2011), 447–459.

74 *Pozdně středověké testamenty v českých městech*, ed. Kateřina Jíšová, Eva Doležalová.

75 Henryk Samsonowicz, *Badania nad kapitałem mieszczańskim Gdańska w II połowie XV wieku* (Warszawa: Uniwersytet Warszawski, 1960).

contribution to modern research on burgher acts of charity in the late Middle Ages.[76] However, Urszula Sowina can be considered the precursor of modern research on medieval wills in Poland. She devoted several valuable works to the topic,[77] the first of which, published in 1991, focusing on the townspeople of Sieradz[78] Very valuable is her article from 2006 discussing the source base of Krakow wills and examining formal and legal issues concerning the rules of inheritance in medieval Krakow.[79] In recent years studies of the role of the will in the medieval city have proliferated. It appears that in the case of most of these, attention has been focused primarily on the question of burgher religiosity in the light of the testamentary records of the *opera pietatis* (works of piety). This is true of much of Piotr Oliński's work, including an extensive monograph published in 2008 devoted to pious bequests from Prussian cities,[80] as well as numerous other articles of his.[81] Elżbieta Piwowarczyk, who shares similar interests, analysed Krakow wills in terms of their devotional records. Alongside some articles written on the basis of this research, and a few shorter

---

76 *Idem*, "Mieszczańska dobroczynność prywatna w Polsce późnego średniowiecza," in *Cultus et cognitio. Studia z dziejów średniowiecznej kultury*, ed. Stefan K. Kuczyński, Aleksander Gieysztor (Warszawa: Państwowe Wydawnictwo Naukowe, 1976), 505–511.

77 Urszula Sowina, "Testament pewnego kmiecia. Przyczynek do badań nad relacjami międzystanowymi w późnym średniowieczu i wczesnej nowożytności," in *Civitas & villa. Miasto i wieś w średniowiecznej Europie środkowej*, ed. Cezary Buśko (Wrocław–Praha: Instytut Archeologii i Etnologii PAN, 2002), 209–214; Urszula Sowina, Kazimierz Pacuski, "Testamenty mieszczan Krakowskich jako źródła do badań nad stronami rodzinnymi imigrantów w krakowskiej elicie władzy (Przykład Jana z Reguł na Mazowszu)," in *Elita władzy miasta Krakowa i jej związku z miastami Europy w średniowieczu i w epoce nowożytnej (do połowy XVII wieku). Zbiór studiów*," ed. Zdzisław Noga (Krakow: Antykwa, 2011), 433–446.

78 Urszula Sowina, "Najstarsze sieradzkie testamenty mieszczańskie z początku XVI w. Analiza źródłoznawcza," KHKM, 39, no. 1 (1991), 3–25.

79 Urszula Sowina, *Testamenty mieszczan krakowskich o przekazywaniu majątku,* 173–183.

80 Piotr Oliński, *Fundacje mieszczańskie w miastach pruskich w okresie średniowiecza i na progu czasów nowożytnych (Chełmno, Toruń, Elbląg, Gdańsk, Królewiec, Braniewo)* (Toruń: Wydawnictwo Naukowe Uniwersytetu Mikołaja Kopernika, 2008).

81 Piotr Oliński, "Mieszczanin w trosce o zbawienie. Uwagi o memoratywnych funkcjach fundacji mieszczańskich w wielkich miastach pruskich," in *Ecclesia et civitas. Kościół i życie religijne w mieście średniowiecznym*, ed. Halina Manikowska, Hanna Zaremska (Warszawa: Instytut Historii PAN, 2002), 347–361; *idem*, "Społeczne uwarunkowania zapisów testamentowych w średniowiecznym Elblągu," in *In memoriam honoremque Casimiri Jasiński*, ed. Jarosław Wenta, Piotr Oliński (Toruń: Wydawnictwo Naukowe Uniwersytetu Mikołaja Kopernika, 2010), 181–192; *idem*, "Fundacje i legaty religijne kobiet świeckich w wielkich miastach pruskich," in *Kobieta i rodzina w średniowieczu i na progu czasów nowożytnych*, ed. Zenon Hubert Nowak, Andrzej Radzimiński (Toruń: Wydawnictwo Uniwersytetu Mikołaja Kopernika, 1998), 143–160.

INTRODUCTION 19

texts,[82] in 2010 she published an extensive monograph devoted primarily to statistical analysis of Krakow's testamentary legacy on opera pietatis.[83]

Beata Możejko carried out an analysis of late medieval Gdansk wills, taking into account instructions for donations to relatives, alongside devotional records.[84] Rafał Kubicki,[85] in turn, analysed the characteristics of wills of the citizens of Elbląg. Bohdana Petryshak prepared an interesting discussion of the oldest medieval wills from Lviv.[86] It is also worth noting the writings of Bogdan Bobowski, who presented the wills of the burghers and nobility from *Weichbild Świdnicki*. His work covers the period from the first half of the fourteenth century up to the end of the first quarter of the seventeenth century. In his book on material culture, he presents the functioning of the will in the light of urban law and the significance of the will as an act of preparation for death and as a source for research on the burgher family.[87] A good example of the ever-more numerous, and often very detailed regional research on wills is an

---

82 Elżbieta Piwowarczyk, Piotr Tyszka, "Przyczynek do pobożności mieszczan krakowskich na podstawie XV-wiecznych legatów w Liber testamentorum (rkps 772)," *Nasza Przeszłość* 105 (2006), 7–42; Elżbieta Piwowarczyk, "Legaty na kościół i klasztor oo. Dominikanów w Krakowie (XIV–XV w.). Z badań nad pobożnością miejską," in *Mendykanci w średniowiecznym Krakowie*, ed. Krzysztof Ożóg, Tomasz Gałuszka, Anna Zajchowska (Krakow: Esprit, 2008), 485–503; Elżbieta Piwowarczyk, "Legaty na kościół Panny Marii (Mariacki) w Krakowie (XIV–XV w.). Przyczynek do badań nad religijnością miejską," *Rocznik Krakowski* 72 (2006), 5–23; Elżbieta Piwowarczyk, "Legaty testamentowe na kościół św. Anny (1400–1530). Z Krakowskich ksiąg miejskich," in *Studia z dziejów kościoła św. Anny w Krakowie*, ed. Zdzisław Kliś, Tomasz Węcławowicz (Krakow: Wydawnictwo UNUM, 2009), 73–89.

83 Elżbieta Piwowarczyk, *Legaty testamentowe ad pias causas w XV-wiecznym Krakowie* (Krakow: Drukarnia Akcydensowa) 2010.

84 Beata Możejko, *Rozrachunek z życiem doczesnym. Gdańskie testamenty mieszczańskie z XV i początku XVI wieku* (Gdańsk: Wydawnictwo Uniwersytetu Gdańskiego, 2010); Beata Możejko, "Gdański mieszczanin w obliczu śmierci. Zapisy testamentowe z II połowy XV w. (na podstawie księgi ławniczej)," in *Mieszczanie, wasale, zakonnicy*, ed. Błażej Śliwiński (Malbork: Muzeum Zamkowe w Malborku, 2004), 127–162.

85 Rafał Kubicki, "Kultura materialna w testamentach elbląskich z XV–początku XVI w.," KHKM, 58 no. 2 (2010), 197–210; *idem*, "Testamenty elbląskie z XIV–początków XVI w. Charakterystyka wraz z listą testatorów w układzie chronologicznym," *Rocznik Elbląski* 20 (2006), 199–208.

86 Bohdana Petryshak, "Sporządzanie testamentów we Lwowie w późnym średniowieczu — pisarze, ceny, okoliczności," *Kwartalnik Historii Kultury Materialnej*, 62, no. 3 (2014), 329–336.

87 Bogdan Bobowski, *Kultura materialna mieszczan Świdnicy i rycerstwa Weichbildu świdnickiego w świetle testamentów (od I połowy XIV do końca I ćwierci XVII wieku)* (Zielona Góra: Uniwersytet Zielonogórski, 2011); *idem*, "Testament w średniowiecznym prawie polskim," *Zeszyty Historyczne* 10, no. 10 (2009), 83–90.

20 INTRODUCTION

article by Ewa Wółkiewicz devoted to the last will of a burgher from the four-teenth century.[88] It is also worth noting the many linguistic studies on wills, useful in their detailed analysis, especially the collection of sketches by Józef Wiktorowicz.[89]

Since 2008, a research team from the Institute of History at the University of Warsaw, examining the history of old Polish culture, has carried out an extensive research project entitled "The Will as a Historical Source". The group has organised many international conferences, from which a number of papers have been published.[90] The most significant result of their years of work in this area was the publication of a series of catalogues of wills of city dwellers from areas of the Kingdom of Poland and the Grand Duchy of Lithuania from Middle Ages up the end of eighteenth century.[91]

---

88   Ewa Wółkiewicz, "Testament Anny Isenecher jako źródło do badań mikrohistorycznych. Próba ustalenia kręgu towarzyskiego śląskiej mieszczanki z XIV wieku," *Zeszyty Historyczne WSP w* Częstochowie, 6 (2000), 385–399. As examples of microhistorical research, we could include the following articles: Jan Tęgowski, "Testament ostatniego Piasta mazowieckiego," *Przegląd Historyczny*, 96 no. 1 (2005), 77–90; Wacława Szelińska, "Dwa testamenty Jana Dąbrówki. Z dziejów życia umysłowego Uniwersytetu Krakowskiego w połowie XV wieku," *Studia i Materiały z Dziejów Nauki Polskiej, seria A*, no 5 (1962), 1–40; Maria Koczerska, "Testamenty kanonika tarnowskiego i plebana Wszystkich Świętych w Krakowie," in *Ludzie, kościół, wierzenia. Studia z dziejów kultury i społeczeństwa Europy Środkowej (średniowiecze – wczesna epoka nowożytna)*, ed. Wojciech Iwańczak (Warszawa: Wydawnictwo DiG, 2001), 237–254; Franciszek Sikora, "Testament Przedbora z Koniecpola z roku 1460," *Studia Historyczne* 26, no. 2 (1983), 297–314; Maria Kowalczyk, "Testament biskupa Krakowskiego Floriana z Mokrska," *Studia Źródłoznawcze* 41 (2003) 65–70; Alicja Szymczak, Jan Szymczak, "Legaty testamentowe kanonika krakowskiego Adama z Będkowa z 1451 roku dla rodziny," in *Księga Jubileuszowa Profesora Feliksa Kiryka* (Krakow: Wydawnictwo Naukowe Akademii Pedagogicznej w Krakowie, 2004); Rościsław Żerelik, Testament Franciszka Koeckritza zwanego Faberem, pisarza miasta Wrocławia w latach 1542–1565, *Archaeologia Historica Polona* 7 (1998), 93–102; Wojciech Olszewski, "Testament jako źródło do badań życia miasta w średniowieczu," *Archaeologia Historica Polona* 7 (1998), 79–92.

89   Józef Wiktorowicz, *Krakauer Kenzleisprache. Forschungsperspektiven und Analysemethoden* (Warszawa: Zakład Graficzny Uniwersytetu Warszawskiego, 2011).

90   KHKM, vol. 58, 2010, no. 2; vol. 59, 2011, no. 3–4.

91   *Testamenty w księgach miejskich wileńskich z XVI i XVII wieku. Katalog*, ed. Kamil Frejlich, "Katalogi testamentów mieszkańców miast z terenów Korony i Wielkiego Księstwa Litewskiego do 1795 roku" (KTMM) 1 (Warszawa: Semper, 2017); *Testamenty mieszkańców miast Wołynia od końca XVI – do początku XVIII wieku. Katalog*, ed. Natalia Biłous, "KTMM" 2 (Warszawa: Semper, 2017); *Katalog testamentów mieszkańców Brześcia i Grodna od XVI do początku XVIII wieku*, ed. Natallia Sliż, "KTMM" 3 (Warszawa: Semper, 2017); *Testamenty mieszkańców lwowskich z drugiej połowy XVI i z XVII wieku. Katalog*, ed. Oksana Winnyczenko "KTMM" 4 (Warszawa: Semper, 2017); *Testamenty z ksiąg sądowych małych miast polskich do 1525 roku*, ed. Agnieszka Bartoszewicz, Krzysztof

INTRODUCTION   21

Research on medieval wills has also been supplemented by works on
bequests of last will from the sixteenth to the eighteenth century, including
numerous smaller studies (many published since the 1980s), which, following the *Annales* School of history, deal with the mentalities of various social
groups in the modern Republic of Poland. Works such as those by Katarzyna
Zielińska[92] and Andrzej Karpiński[93] need to be mentioned here. These were
innovative studies of the Polish context for the production of wills, exploring
social ties and religiosity. In addition, editions of wills from the time of the
Polish-Lithuanian Commonwealth (1569–1795), along with commentary, have
been produced by other Polish researchers, often as part of regional or microhistorical studies.[94]

Mrozowski, Maciej Radomski, Katarzyna Warda, ed. Agnieszka Bartoszewicz, "KTMM" 5
(Warszawa: Semper, 2017); Katalog testamentów z krakowskich ksiąg miejskich do 1550
roku, ed. Jakub Wysmułek, "KTMM" 6 (Warszawa: Semper, 2017); *Katalog testamentów
poznańskich z drugiej połowy XVI i z XVII wieku*, ed. Andrzej Karpiński, "KTMM" 7 (Warszawa: Semper, 2017); *Testamenty mieszczan warszawskich od XV do końca XVII wieku.
Katalog*, ed. Agnieszka Bartoszewicz, Andrzej Karpiński, Katarzyna Warda (Warszawa:
Semper, 2010).

92   Katarzyna Zielińska, *Więzi społeczne w połowie XVII wieku w świetle testamentów konsystorza pułtuskiego*, Przegląd Historyczny 77, no. 1 (1986), 45–59.

93   Andrzej Karpiński, "Zapisy pobożne i postawy religijne mieszczanek polskich w świetle
testamentów z drugiej połowy XVI i XVII wieku," in *Tryumfy i porażki. Studia z dziejów kultury polskiej XVI–XVIII wieku*, ed. Maria Bogucka (Warszawa: Państwowe Wydawnictwo
Naukowe, 1989), 204–233.

94   Małgorzata Borkowska, *Dekret w niebieskim ferowany parlamencie: wybór testamentów
z XVII–XVIII wieku* (Krakow: Znak, 1984); Stefan Krakowski, "Mieszczanie *Częstochowy
w* XVII wieku *w* świetle testamentów," *Ziemia Częstochowska* 5 (1965), 115–125; Grzegorz
Huszał, "Przygotowanie do śmierci w XVII w.," *Roczniki Humanistyczne* 31, no.2 (1983),
105–150; Waldemar Kowalski, "Testament daleszyckiego rajcy z 1637 roku," *Studia Kieleckie*
45, no. 1 (1985), 129–135; Sybill Hołdys, "Więzi rodzinne w świetle mieszczańskich testamentów z pierwszej połowy XVII wieku," *Studia Historyczne* 29, no.3 (1986), 347–357;
*Testamenty szlachty krakowskiej XVII–XVIII w. Wybór tekstów źródłowych z lat 1650–
1799*, ed. Alicja Falniowska-Gradowska (Krakow: Polska Akademia Umiejętności, 1997);
Urszula Augustyniak, "Wizerunek Krzysztofa II Radziwiłła jako magnata-ewangelika
w świetle jego testamentów," *Przegląd Historyczny* 81, no. 3–4 (1990), 461–477; Hanna
Żerek-Kleszcz, "Testamenty mieszczan pabianickich w XVII–XVIII wieku," *Pabianiciana* 1 (1992), 37–50; Maria Bogucka, "Testament burmistrza gdańskiego Hansa
Speymana z 1625 r.," in *Kultura średniowieczna i staropolska. Studia ofiarowane Aleksandrowi Gieysztorowi w pięćdziesięciolecie pracy naukowej*, ed. Danuta Gawinowa (Warszawa: Państwowe Wydawnictwo Naukowe, 1991), 587–597; Andrzej Pośpiech, *Pułapka
oczywistości. Pośmiertne spisy ruchomości szlachty wielkopolskiej z XVII wieku* (Warszawa:
Instytut Archeologii i Etnologii PAN, 1992); Małgorzata Aleksandrowicz-Szmulikowska,
*Radziwiłłówny w świetle swoich testamentów. Przyczynek do badań mentalności magnac-
kiej XVI–XVII wieku* (Warszawa: Semper, 1995); Jarosław Dumanowski, "Torunianin z

My research on the wills of Krakow burghers would not have been possible without the vast literature devoted to medieval Krakow. Among recent publications that proved particularly valuable and useful for the present book was a new monograph on the Krakow city council by Marcin Starzyński.[95] Starzyński's summary of research, along with his own findings, and his analysis of the role of the city council and its members in shaping Krakow's testamentary practices, were important reference points for this current study. My

---

wyboru. Z testamentu biskupa Stanisława Dąbskiego," *Rocznik Toruński* 26 (1999), 91–105; Jarosław Dumanowski, "'Pompa funebris'? Z testamentów szlachty wielkopolskiej XVIII w.," in *Wesela, chrzciny i pogrzeby w XVI–XVIII wieku. Kultura życia i śmierci*, ed. Henryk Suchojad (Warszawa: Semper, 2001), 315–322; Henryk Suchojad, "Wyposażenie siedzib duchownych i szlacheckich w świetle testamentów z XVII–XVIII wieku na terenie województwa sandomierskiego," in *Dwór polski. Zjawisko historyczne i kulturowe. Materiały V seminarium zorganizowanego przez Oddział Kielecki Stowarzyszenia Historyków Sztuki, Instytut Historii Wyższej Szkoły Pedagogicznej im. Jana Kochanowskiego w Kielcach oraz Kielecki Dom Środowisk Twórczych, Kielce 7–9 października 1999* (Warszawa: Stowarzyszenie Historyków Sztuki, 2000), 449–457; Henryk Suchojad, "Rozstanie ze światem doczesnym księdza Jakuba Grometiusa (1572–1651), plebana w Gnojnie (w świetle testamentu i towarzyszących mu dokumentów)," in *Wesela, chrzciny i pogrzeby*, 303–313; Jan Główka, "Testamenty mieszczan kieleckich z końca XVIII w. zwierciadłem epoki (w świetle księgi rady miejskiej Kielc 1789–1792)," in *Wesela, chrzciny i pogrzeby*, 323–332; idem, Podstawy prawne testamentów i inwentarzy pośmiertnych duchowieństwa katolickiego w Polsce w epoce potrydenckiej, *Archaeologia Historica Polona* 5 (1997), 203–210; idem, *Majątek osobisty duchowieństwa katolickiego w Koronie w XVII i XVIII wieku* (Warszawa: Wydawnictwo Instytutu Archeologii i Etnologii PAN, 2004); Tadeusz M. Trajdos, "Testament Stanisława Moniaka," *Rocznik Babiogórski* 4 (2002), 215–223; Jan Seredyka, *Testament Krzysztofa Moniwida Dorohostajskiego*, in *Aere perennius. Profesorowi Gerardowi Labudzie dnia 28 XII 2001 w hołdzie*, ed. Marceli Kosman (Poznan–Wrocław: Forum Naukowe, 2001), 115–129; Róża Dembska, "O testamencie w polskim prawie średniowiecznym," in *Studia z historii ustroju i prawa. Księga dedykowana profesorowi Jerzemu Walachowiczowi*, ed. Henryk Olszewski (Poznan: Printer, 2002), 57–71; Marek Górny, "W sprawie badania rodziny staropolskiej na podstawie testamentów," *Studia Historyczne* 30, no. 3 (1987), 487–494; Paweł Klint, "Testament Zofii ze Smoszowskich Pogorzelskiej z 1658 roku," *Genealogia. Studia i Materiały Historyczne* 13 (2001), 117–128; Otto Hedemann, *Testamenty brasławsko-dziśnieńskie XVII–XVIII wieku jako źródło historyczne* (Wilno: Księgarnia św. Wojciecha, 1935); Grzegorz Huszał, *Przygotowanie do śmierci*, 105–150; Jacek Krochmal, "Przemyskie testamenty staropolskie," *Rocznik Historyczno-Archiwalny* 6 (1989), 133–160; Jadwiga Muszyńska, "Testamenty mieszczan szydłowieckich z lat 1638–1645," in *Szydłowiec – z dziejów miasta*, ed. Jacek Wijaczka (Szydłowiec: Muzeum Ludowych Instrumentów Muzycznych, 1999), 133–160; Tomasz Wiślicz, *Zarobić na duszne zbawienie. Religijność chłopów małopolskich od połowy XVI do końca XVIII wieku* (Warszawa: Neriton, 2001); *Cui contingit nasci, restat mori. Wybór testamentów staropolskich z województwa sandomierskiego*, ed. Mariusz Lubczyński, Jacek Pielas, Henryk Suchojad (Warszawa: Semper, 2005).

95   Marcin Starzyński, *Krakowska rada miejska w średniowieczu* (Krakow: Tow. Naukowe "Societas Vistulana," 2010).

INTRODUCTION

research into the testators appearing in the oldest known Krakow municipal book was greatly assisted by the works of Jerzy Rajman,[96] Zbigniew Noga[97] and Feliks Kiryk,[98] among others.

Agnieszka Bartoszewicz's work on writing culture in late medieval Polish cities also proved invaluable for my own research. The rich source material she collects and analyses, in light of the latest research on the subject worldwide, allowed me to look at the will as an important factor in the process of popularization of writing, something which had a significant impact on late medieval people's lives.[99]

5   Structure of the Work

This study is divided into four chapters. In the first chapter, The Institution of the Will in Krakow in the Fourteenth and Fifteenth Centuries, the history of the will and its emergence in Polish lands and in Krakow itself is discussed. I look at the transformation of both the form of the last will and the role it played in urban society in the period under consideration.[100] This chapter also contains information about the place of wills in municipal law and the reasons for their being transcribed by the citizens of Krakow.

In the second chapter, The Economic and Social Structure of Testators, I present the family, property and social structures of testators, focusing primarily on distinguishing the group of testators from the rest of the urban community. I pay close attention to their social status, occupation and financial position. I also study testators who came to Krakow from different segments of the immigrant population. Following this I present the main determinants of social position for testators, through an analysis of bequests of last will.

In the third chapter, The Burgher Family as Depicted in Late-Medieval Wills, the family, legal and financial situation of testators is presented. It explains both the expectations they had of family life and the differences in the character of burgher families of different social and economic status.

---

96   Jerzy Rajman, *Krakow: zespół osadniczy, proces lokacji, mieszczanie do roku 1333* (Krakow: Wydawnictwo Naukowe Akademii Pedagogicznej, 2004).

97   Zdzisław Noga, *Elita władzy miasta Krakowa...*

98   Among others: Feliks Kiryk, "Migracje z miast małopolskich do elity władzy Krakowa w XIV-XVI wieku," in *Elita władzy miasta Krakowa*, ed. Zdzisław Noga, 181–190.

99   Agnieszka Bartoszewicz, *Urban Literacy in Late Medieval Poland* (Turnhout: Brepols, 2017).

100   The issue of the forms the will took in medieval Krakow was covered in exhaustive detail by Józef Wiktorowicz; *idem, Krakauer Kenzleisprache*

In the fourth chapter, Burgher Religiosity as Presented in Late-Medieval Wills, an attempt is made to characterise urban piety. Following up on numerous studies devoted to this issue, especially those of Elżbieta Piwowarczyk,[101] who focused on a statistical analysis of the data, this work attempts to present religiosity as a permanent and necessary social phenomenon. It explores the variety of forms of religiosity, from personal piety, through its functioning in the family, corporate and parish circles, to the phenomenon of *religion civique* and the participation of testators in the Christian pilgrimage movement.

The monograph ends with a conclusion which summarises the research findings and an annex containing a list of acts of last will from the fourteenth and fifteenth centuries found in Krakow sources.

---

101   Elżbieta. Piwowarczyk, *Legaty testamentowe.*

CHAPTER 1

The Institution of the Will

The emergence of the will in medieval Europe played a significant role in the social and cultural changes taking place during that era. An examination of the will's history as a social institution reveals it to be a multidimensional phenomenon which was both the cause and effect of many socio-cultural processes. The rediscovery of the ancient concept of the 'testament' was both a manifestation of the deepening Christianization of Europe and a significant driver in that process. However, the testament was only able to be so widely disseminated as a consequence of modernization and individualization processes already taking place in late medieval urban societies. Moreover, depending on the point of view adopted, one can see the will either as a factor undermining the existing family structure and traditional order of property rights,[1] or as a legal element complementing them, established to fulfil specific functions, including the regulation of one's earthly obligations and the salvation of the soul.[2] In order to learn more about the meaning of the will, its form and the role it played in various social and cultural processes in late-medieval Krakow (and other large cities in East-Central Europe), it is necessary to trace its history and examine the cultural and legal contexts in which it emerged.

The image of early medieval Germanic and Slavic tribal communities that emerges from an analysis of surviving collections of customary legal rights is one of fairly close-knit collectivities in which a dominant role was played by kinship groups. Patriarchal control and custody over the individual and his

---

1 Przemysław Dąbkowski agreed with the classical French legal historian Paul Violetta, who proposed the following: "The history of the will is a struggle between the rights of the family and the right to testamentary freedom"; Przemysław Dąbkowski, *Prawo prywatne polskie*, vol. 2 (Lwów: Drukarnia Uniwersytetu Jagiellońskiego, 1911), 75; "The will based upon the principle of the freedom to dispose of one's property according to one's wishes in the event of death shaped a new legal custom."; Bogdan Bobowski, *Kultura materialna mieszczan Świdnicy*, 38; cf. Kazimierz Kolańczyk, *Studia nad reliktami wspólnej własności ziemi w najdawniejszej Polsce. Rozporządzenia własnością ziemską do końca XIV wieku* (Poznan: Poznańskie Towarzystwo Przyjaciół Nauk, 1950), 71–75; Juliusz Bardach, *Historia państwa i prawa Polski do połowy XV wieku* (Warszawa: Państwowe Wydawnictwo Naukowe, 1957), 307–308.

2 Urszula Sowina, "Testamenty mieszczan krakowskich o przekazywaniu majątku w późnym średniowieczu i we wczesnej nowożytności," in *Sociální svět středověkého města*, ed. Martin Nodl, 173–183.

© JAKUB WYSMUŁEK, 2021 | DOI:10.1163/9789004461444_003
This is an open access chapter distributed under the terms of the CC BY-NC-ND 4.0 license.

property was exercised by the head of the family and other male relatives.[3] Ownership (mainly concerning real estate) was ancestral in nature, which meant that a person was only the user and beneficiary of property and not its owner. The goods inherited from one's ancestors were to be passed on to the next generation in as well-preserved a state as possible.[4] Along with the rise of private ownership of land and increasingly common transfers of real estate, the threat arose that family property would be diminished through transfers to third parties (alienation; primarily to Church institutions). The interests of relatives were safeguarded by medieval collections of laws grounded in the principle of 'the right of kinship' (*ius propinquitatis*).[5] The *Sachsenspiegel* (literally 'Saxon Mirror'), a compilation of customary laws that constituted one of the most significant sources of legal authority in Central and Eastern Europe, devotes a great deal of space to the rules for the inheritance of property. It clearly states that without the consent of his inheritors, no man could transfer their inheritance to a third party.[6] If a man attempted to do so, his heirs had the right to apply to the court for restitution of the unlawfully transferred property. If there were no direct heirs to the estate, it would pass on to the man's closest relatives, according to the legal principle that "goods circulate like blood," and thus, whoever was "closer by blood" was also "closer to the property."[7]

---

3 "For the Lombards, [...] it was the kinship group, its common property interests and its control over each of its members, that was of highest value. This was linked with the supremacy of the male head of the family and, particularly, the strict male guardianship (mund) over women and children. The individual was subjected to the group," Karol Modzelewski, *Barbarian Europe*, trans. Ewa Macura (Frankfurt am Main: Peter Lang, 2015), 76.

4 "[...] aput attavos nostros et patres ex antiquo statutum est, ut si quisquam de genere Polonorum vendiderit quodlibet patrymonium suum, eius heredes postmodum poterunt redimere [...]. Si quicquam possideo quod avus meus et pater mihi in possessionem reliquerunt, hoc est meum verum patrymonium"; *Liber Fundationis claustre Sancte Marie Virginis in Henrichow. Księga henrykowska*, ed. Roman Grodecki (Poznan: Instytut Zachodni, 1949), 280; Karol Koranyi, "Podstawy średniowiecznego prawa spadkowego," *Pamiętnik Historyczno-Prawn* 9 no. 2 (1930), 115.

5 Zygmunt Rymaszewski, *Prawo bliższości krewnych w polskim prawie ziemskim do końca XV wieku* (Wrocław–Warszawa–Krakow: Zakład Narodowy im. Ossolińskich - Wydawnictwo PAN, 1970), 172–172, 183–187.

6 "Absque heredum consensu et absque iudicio legali nemo suum proprius nec suos homines dare potest"; Jan Łaski, *Commune Incliti Polonie regni privilegium constitutionum et indultuum publicitus decretorum approbatorumque*, Krakow 1506, part 2, 209r–209v; "ane erven gelof [...] ne mut nieman sin egen [...] geven"; za: Karol Koranyi, *Podstawy średniowiecznego prawa spadkowego*, 117.

7 "Das gut rinnt wie das Blut" kamen die Blutsverwandten des engener Kreises der Hausgemeinschaft in den Genuß des Erbes; beim Fehler solcher bevorzugten Anwärter wurden die restlichen Verwandtschaftsmitglieder entsprechend dem Prinzip "Je näher dem Gut' berücksichtigt"; Paul Baur, *Testament und Bürgerschaft*, 12.

THE INSTITUTION OF THE WILL 27

The collective nature of property was an expression to some extent of the collective nature of identity, according to which a person was, first and foremost, a member of his or her family, and only then of other, larger community structures.[8]

A different level of importance was attached to movable goods, which originally designated one's personal equipment and belongings, such as weapons, tools, crockery, clothes and jewellery, as well as a person's livestock. Although it was land that determined a person's social status, the moveable goods one possessed were also symbols and determinants of one's wealth.[9] They had long been treated as private property, inseparable in principle from the person possessing them; according to the ancient adage, 'movables adhere to the bones' of their owner (in Latin *mobilia ossibus inhaerent*). This subjective nature of movable property was emphasized both by early medieval compilations of laws, according to which the theft of a living – or dead – person's possessions was just as severely punished as causing that person bodily injury, as well as by old pagan funeral customs, according to which the deceased took some of their personal belongings with them to the grave.[10] With the spread of Christianity, old burial traditions involving ritual cremation were replaced by the practice of burying the dead in the ground. Gifts stopped being placed in graves, and were instead given to the churches where the graves were now located. In this way, the Church's successful Christianisation of followers of the older pagan religion led to the transformation of their 'grave gifts' (*Totenteil* or *Totengabe*) into pious bequests meant to aid in the salvation of the deceased donor's soul (so-called *Seelgerät*).[11]

While a distinction between movable and immovable property is commonly found in medieval sources, a number of movables identified in land and municipal collections of rights also became classified over time as hereditary property. This was the case of the personal equipment and belongings of men (in German *hergewet*, in Latin *arma bellica*)[12] and women (in German *gerada*, in Latin *paraphernalia, suppellectilia* [...] *que ad mulieres pertineant* "accessories

---

8   "[...] Germanic law initially did not provide for the disposal of any real estate, while heirs had far-reaching rights. This stemmed from the structure of the Germanic family itself, which was based on family co-ownership of real estate"; Karol Koranyi, *Podstawy średniowiecznego prawa spadkowego*, 120.

9   *Ibid.*, 40.

10   *Ibid.*, 5–8, 46.

11   Gabriele Schulz, *Testamente des späten Mittelalters aus dem Mittelrheingebiet*, 3.

12   See Glossary: Hergewet

that belong to women"[13]),[14] which were supposed to be transferred into hands of their male or female relatives, respectively.[15] According to Magdeburg Law (*Magdeburgisches Weichbild*), a deceased husband's wife was to pass on to his male descendants his sword, his best saddled horse and best armour, as well as his *pulvinar bellicale* "military bed," which included a bed, two pillows, two sheets, a tablecloth, two bowls and a towel.[16] The hereditary property of a wife that was to be received by her daughter, and otherwise by her closest female relative, was much more extensive. Although in Łaski's Statutes these were defined as being only her sheep, dishes and the food in her home,[17] in the judgments of Magdeburg Law, translated into Polish in 1501,[18] these were described with much more precision as: the woman's silver and gold jewellery, cups, chalices, spoons, cupboards (in Latin *armarium*), wash-basins, cushions, sheets, pillows, tapestries, carpets for covering benches (In Latin *bancalis*) and beds and hanging on walls, tablecloths, towels, quilts, clothing, headscarves, chests, candlesticks, yarn, beer brewing kettles and books 'that women tend to read,' as well as a pot for melting wax, a mirror, scissors and other items commonly used by women.[19] In 1567, Bartłomiej Groicki, a notary at the High Court of Magdeburg Law in Krakow, described the *Weichbild* as follows:

> These things belong to the woman's movables [*gerada*] according to Magdeburg Law: all the woman's clothing, gowns and cloth cut for the clothing the woman typically wears and has power over; all gold and silver that is woven for the woman's clothing; all rings, buttons and pins, buckled belts, silk cloth, bracelets and necklaces, bed coverings, sheets, bath towels, curtains, lace curtains, beds, head-rests, pillows, table-cloths, bowls, brewery vessels to be leased, a wash-boiler, crates with lids, linen, washed and raw wool; books that women usually read; geese, ducks, sheep that are herded out to pasture.[20]

---

13   See Glossary: Gerada

14   Urszula Sowina, *Testamenty mieszczan krakowskich o przekazywaniu majątku*, 176–177.

15   In the collection of laws published by John Łaski there appears the phrase "De suppe-lectili, que ad mulieres pertinebat"; Jan Łaski, *Commune Incliti Poloniae regni privilegium constitutionum et indultuum publicitus decretorum approbatorumque, Libri duo*, part 1 (Krakow, 1506), 187r.

16   *Ibid.*, 187r.

17   *Ibid.*, 187r.

18   Michał Wiszniewski, *Historya literatury polskiej*, vol 5 (Krakow: Drukarnia Uniwersytecka, 1843), 151–163.

19   *Ibid.*, 237–238.

20   Bartłomiej Groicki, *Tytuły prawa majdeburskiego* (Warszawa: Wydawnictwo Prawnicze, 1954), 5.

THE INSTITUTION OF THE WILL   29

The gerada was described in a nearly identical fashion by Paul Szczerbic in 1581.[21]

The first major departure from the traditional principles of property inheritance was the development of the principle of excluding a so-called 'free portion' (*Freiteil*) from the inherited property. Calls to donate part of one's estate to the Church – that is, as the Church fathers worded it, to "include Christ among the heirs" of the deceased – began to be made in the late fourth century.[22] St. John Chrysostom determined the size of God's part of the inheritance to be from a half to one-third of the estate, while St. Augustine based the size of the part to be set aside for the Church on the number of sons the deceased possessed.[23] As the Church's power grew in the early Middle Ages, these appeals met with a more accommodating response. In spite of the established inviolability of family property in Christian Europe, the principle was adopted that, from a free one-third portion of an estate, it was possible to make an act of alms-giving called a *donatio mortis causa* "gift because of death."[24] Unlike other types of gift, the donation of the 'free portion' for alms-giving and for funeral preparations was legally valid even if the legal heirs opposed it.[25] In order to secure these pious bequests against the protests of relatives, from the fifth century onwards councils used the threat of excommunication against those who failed to fulfil the will of the deceased, while the bishops were obliged to oversee the donation of these goods.[26]

---

21   Paweł Szczerbic, *Ius municipale, to jest prawo miejskie majdeburskie, nowo z łacińskiego i z niemieckiego na polski język z pilnością i wiernie przełożone*, ed. Grzegorz Maria Kowalski (Krakow: Księgarnia Akademicka, 2011), 118–119.

22   Michael M. Sheehan, *The Will in Medieval England*, 11.

23   Karol Koranyi, *Podstawy średniowiecznego prawa spadkowego*, 194–195; Gabriele Schulz, *Testamente des späten Mittelalters aus dem Mittelrheingebiet*, 2; Paul Baur, *Testament und Bürgerschaft*, 12; Brigitte Klosterberg, *Zur Ehre Gottes und zum Wohl der Familie*, 53–54.

24   Harold Joseph Berman, *Law and Revolution. The Formation of the Western Legal Tradition* (*Cambridge-London: Harvard University Press, 2009*), Warszawa 1995, 288.

25   "Von diesem ursprünglich allein im Hinblick auf das Seelenheil verwendbaren Seelteil ist der Freiteil der Hinterlassenschaft des Erblassers zu unterscheiden, welcher sich aus der christlichen Caritaslehre Augustinscher Provenienz entwickelte und einen exakt quotierten Pflichtteil des Erbes für die Kirche als Vertreterin Christi auf Erden bezeichnet. Einer Zustimmung seitens des wartberechtigten Erben über diesen Teil seines Erbes bedurfte es hierbei nicht"; Paul Baur, *Testament und Bürgerschaft*, 12.

26   "The Church was not content to urge that these legacies be given; she even interested herself in their accomplishment. Councils of the fifth century excommunicated those who failed to distribute bequests in alms according to the wishes of the dead. The bishop became concerned with the supervision of the delivery of these legacies, and in time the laws of Justinian confirmed certain rights to him in this regard"; Michael M. Sheehan, *The Will in Medieval England*, 11.

Yet it was the will, following its rediscovery and reintroduction in medieval Europe at the turn of the eleventh and twelfth centuries, that proved itself to be the most effective instrument for ensuring a steady transfer of goods to an increasingly institutionalised Church.[27] The rediscovery of the will in the broad social consciousness of both the clergy and laity of that time was directly caused by the initiation of scholarly studies on Roman law led by a group of clerics and subsequently the creation of canon law based on it. Roman law carried with it an existing body of theory on the nature of the testament, its form and the types of goods which could be legally transferred in this way. It also provided the courts with tools to uphold and enforce testamentary dispositions.[28]

The testament, as it had been understood in medieval Europe since the mid-twelfth century, differed significantly in certain aspects from its ancient predecessor. Roman testaments relied primarily on the appointment of the head of the family, the *pater familias*, as its legal successor, which resulted, on the one hand, in the transfer of all goods to the heir and, on the other hand, in the exclusion of all other potential successors from them.[29] This freedom of the father of the family in disposing of private property was a generally accepted value, and it is easy to understand the surprise expressed by Tacitus in his description of the habits of Germanic tribes, where he states that they did not have wills, and that their only heirs and successors were their children.[30] The medieval testament, or 'last will' (*ultima voluntas*), both terms at that time were synonymous, was a collection of individual legacies for different persons and institutions (therefor often referred to in German literature as *Legatentestament*), and did not necessarily involve the designation of an heir to the estate or refer to the entirety of the deceased's property.[31]

---

27 "One of the many important developments that characterize the life of Europe during the last decades of the eleventh and whole of the twelfth centuries was the revival of the study of Roman civil law. In its wake came a considerable organization and adjustment of law, legal theory and practice. [...] The institutions that come to be better known was the testament, a legal act controlling the devolution of a testator's estate more efficiently than anything that the peoples of northern Europe had been able to devise"; *Ibid.*, 119–122.

28 "Roman law provided a theory of the testament and its nature, prescribed its forms and the limits of the property with which it might deal, and furnished a jurisprudence for the courts which controlled and enforced it"; *Ibid.*, 119.

29 Gabriele Schulz, *Testamente des späten Mittelalters aus dem Mittelrheingebiet*, 1–2.

30 Publis Cornelius Tacitus, *Germania*, trans. Tomasz Płóciennik, introduction and comments by Jerzy Kolendo (Poznan: Wydawnictwo Naukowe UAM, 2008), III, 20.

31 "Das deutsch-rechtliche Testament stimmte mit dem römischen Testament überein im Charakter als einseitig gefaßte, letztwillige Verfügung von Todes wegen sowie im Moment der Widerruflichkeit. Im Unterschied aber zum römischen Testament mußte

THE INSTITUTION OF THE WILL

31

The reception of Roman law and its gradual penetration into the codification of customary laws were important in ensuring wills their theoretical legal basis. However, the support of the Church as an institution was also a decisive factor in the adoption and dissemination of these acts. At the turn of the twelfth century, work was carried out with the help of the *Codex Justinianus* on the codification of the canons of the Church, which led St. Ivan of Chartres to revive the idea of the freedom to dispose of goods by means of a will.[32] With the *Decretum Gratiani* (c. 1140), the concept of the testament had established itself in the medieval Christian world. In his *Decretum* Gratian evoked the Roman concepts of the right to make alms from the testator's property and the freedom to choose the place of burial. Since then, the part of the property transferred to the Church was limited only by the Roman principle of the so-called *pars legitima*,[33] intended for the heirs of the deceased. The successors of Gratian went even further, increasing the power of bishops to defend their wills, while at the same time reducing the number of witnesses needed to recognise the legality of the will.[34] Under the threat of the most severe religious sanctions, Pope Alexander III defended the validity of wills made in the presence of two or three witnesses, proving in this respect the superiority of canon law over Roman law (which required either seven witnesses). In a letter (from 1171–1172) to the Bishop of Ostia, the Pope maintained that it was the law and custom of the Church to allow people to make wills at the end of their lives before the parish priest and two or three witnesses.[35] In other letters he emphasized the obligation of relatives and heirs to pay the debts of the

---

      das deutsch-rechtliche Vermächtnis nicht notwendigerweise eine Erbeneinsetzung enthalten und sah auch keine Einsetzung in das gesamte Vermögen des Erblassers vor, d. h. es kannte keinen Gesamtrechtsnachfolger. Vielmehr war es ein Legatentestament, d. h. ein Testament, welches auf eine Mehrzahl von Einzelvergabungen festgelegt war. Es stellte »eine mehr oder minder umfassende Aufzählung von Einzelyermächtnissen dar, wobei die Summe dieser Legate keineswegs dem Gesamtvermögen gleichzukommen« brauchte. Ein weiteres Charakteristikum ist es, daß gesetzlich geregelte Erbfolge und unbeschränkte Verfügungsfreiheit nebeneinander bestehen konnten"; Gabriele Schulz, *Testamente des späten Mittelalters aus dem Mittelrheingebiet*, 3–4; Brigitte Klosterberg, *Zur Ehre Gottes und zum Wohl der Familie*, 12; Paul Baur, *Testament und Bürgerschaft*, 13.

32   Michael M. Sheehan, *The Will in Medieval England*, 121–122.

33   Roman law, in Justinian's codification, provides for the division of property into three or four parts, at least one of which had to be passed on to legal heirs (the so-called *pars legitima*).

34   Michael M. Sheehan, *The Will in Medieval England*, 128.

35   Brigitte Klosterberg, *Zur Ehre Gottes und zum Wohl der Familie*, 53; Gabriele Schulz, *Testamente des späten Mittelalters aus dem Mittelrheingebiet*, 10–11.

32   CHAPTER 1

deceased[36] – later, bequests concerning the settlement of liabilities towards
debtors would become a permanent fixture of wills. The work of the decretal-
ists (a school of canon law interpretation which emphasised papal rulings on
matters of church discipline) and its support by church synods and by popes
in the twelfth-century led to the creation of the institution of the so-called
'canonical will,'[37] whose rules and form differed from those of Roman law. The
canonical will also differed from Roman wills in its function – providing a legal
basis for pious requests, and thereby facilitating them and ensuring their effective fulfilment for the benefit of the Church. In northern Europe, the testament
was for a long time a part of canon law rather than secular law and, therefore,
pious bequests constituted the major part of such acts and were the primary
motivation for creating them.[38]

1   Wills in Poland in the Twelfth and Thirteenth Centuries

In the Polish lands the notion of a last will, understood in the sense of the
canonical will, is already visible in bequests from the mid-twelfth century
onwards.[39] In the foundation charter of the Cistercian abbey in Łekno, issued
by Count (*comes*) Zbylut in 1153, a donation to the monastery of one of the

---

36   Michael M. Sheehan, *The Will in Medieval England*, 129.

37   "Das älteste Zeugnis für das Bestreben der Kirche, das kanonische Testament in
      Deutschland zu verbreiten, ist ein Beschluß der im Jahre 1266 in Bremen abgehaltenen
      Synode, die unter der Leitung des päpstlichen Legaten, des Kardinals Guido, stand.
      Gemäß diesem Beschluß wurde die »libera testandi facultas« der Laien, und zwar die
      kanonische Testamentsform gegen gewisse dawiderlaufende Statuten unter deutlichem
      Hinweis auf Lübeck in Schutz genommen"; Gabriele Schulz, *Testamente des späten Mit-
      telalters aus dem Mittelrheingebiet*, 11.

38   An important factor which contributed to such a strong support of the institution of the
      will by the Church authorities was the dispute with the secular authorities over the prop-
      erty of deceased clergymen, the so-called *ius spolii*. The will made it possible for the clergy
      to pass on their possessions according to their wishes, thus preventing them from being
      seized by a feudal lord. Casimir II the Just waived the right to *iuris spolii* in 1180, as the
      first ruler on the territory of Poland; Cf. Juliusz Bardach, Bogusław Leśnodorski, Michał
      Pietrzak, *Historia ustroju i prawa polskiego* (Warszawa: Lexis Nexis, 2000), 77; Gabriele
      Schulz, *Testamente des späten Mittelalters aus dem Mittelrheingebiet*, 8–9.

39   The oldest collection of Polish laws, written in the thirteenth century, provided only for
      the possibility of statutory inheritance, according to which sons inherited from their
      father, while daughters only had the right to a dower chosen by their father or broth-
      ers. In the absence of sons, the family property was to be transferred to prince, who was
      obliged to provide the daughters of the deceased with a dowdry on his behalf if they were
      to marry. This document, although compiled in the thirteenth century, applies to earlier

THE INSTITUTION OF THE WILL   33

villages he inherited was described as a 'testament.' For those who intended
to oppose this 'testamentary privilege' (*huius testamenti* [...] *privilegium*), the
document threatened punishment of 'eternal anathema' (*perpetui anathema-
tis*), resulting in the 'absorption of the living into hell' (*infernus eum vivum* [...]
absorbeat).[40] The word 'testament' was used in a similar context in High Duke
of Poland Mieszko III the Old's confirmation of the foundation of a Benedictine monastery in Mogilno (c.1143). In this case as well, those who sought to
undermine the donation were threatened with excommunication.[41]

Another interesting testamentary bequest is one made in 1190 by the knight
Dzierżko, brother of Wit, bishop of Płock. Before embarking on a crusade, he
donated his property to the nuns of the Abbey of Norbertine, which he himself had founded in the village of Busko.[42] However, he made this donation
dependent on the life path taken by his widow. If she re-married after his death,
she would receive just one village, while if she remained a widow, she would
have full possession of two villages and all of the servants and domestic staff,
and if she agreed to enter the Norbertine abbey he had founded, she would
also receive eight other villages and part of the village of Busko. However, if
she chose to join another order, she would receive only her robes.[43] In this

---

    times; Cf. *Najstarszy zwód prawa polskiego*, ed and rev. Józef Matuszewski (Łódź: Panst-
    wowe Wydawnictwo Naukowe, 1995), 85–87.

40   "Quapropter, huius mei devoti studii factive testamentum ne ulla umquam superior seu
    inferior persona prava machinatione ducere possit in irritum, sed ut integrum et inconvul-
    sum maneat in perpetuum, dominum Iohannem sancte Gneznensis ecclesie archipre-
    sulem, dominum Stephanum Poznaniensis ecclesie antistitem, dominum Mesiconem
    ducem, aliasque perplurimas personas sublimes ac humiles convocavi, ubi ab utroque
    episcopo coram astante multitudine sub perpetui anathematis obtentu confirmari votis
    omnium michi congaudentium impetravi: ut si quis in presens sive in posterum huius
    testamenti prevaricari presumpserit privilegium, superni iudicis sine misericordia sen-
    tentiam incidat, infernus eum vivum nisi resipuerit absorbeat"; KDW, vol. 1, no. 18 (1153).

41   "Fecique ego Mesco dux Polonie hoc meum confirmatorium testamentum super his
    omnibus tam scripto quam sigillo, tum etiam testimonio vero atque idoneo hic super-
    scripto, concedens non solum Radeow per Cuiaviam, sed et omnibus villis per Poloniam
    sancto Iohanni in Muglin spectantibus magnam ab omni meo iure meorumque succes-
    sorum in omnibus libertatem; confirmans hoc excommunicationis vinculo superiori, si
    quis hec post nos attemptaverit infringere quamdiu mundus steterit"; KDW, vol. 1, no. 33
    (1143?).

42   This was a women's order affiliated with the Norbertine monastery in Witowo, founded
    by his brother, Wit of Chotel, bishop of Płock; *Codex diplomaticus Poloniae*, vol. 1, no. 6,
    eds. Leon Rzyszczewski, Antoni Muczkowski, Antoni Zygmunt Helcel, Julian Bartosze-
    wicz (Warszawa: Drukiem Stanisława Strąbskiego, 1847), 15–16.

43   "In nomine patris et filii et Spiritus sancti. Ego Dirsco aduc [sic] vivens, offerens trado deo
    omnipotenti et beate Marie, fratribus et sororibus sub regula beati Augustini in Buzsk
    manentibus, quos de Vitov per manum meam adduxi, pro salute anime mee, bona mea

34 CHAPTER 1

document, written before the altar of the Blessed Virgin Mary in the church he had founded, Dzierżko stated that if any of his relatives tried to oppose his bequest, "Almighty God and his merciful mother Mary" would punish them.[44]

The number of pious donations of this kind began to increase significantly in the early thirteenth century. While they performed the same function as they had earlier – acting as a donation or bequest of real estate to religious institutions – they now began to be strictly defined as wills or testaments. For example, a *testamentaria dispositio* containing a bequest of villages and lakes to the above-mentioned Łekno Abbey dates back to 1216. In this document, apart from the donation of hereditary land, the donor, Świętosław (Svento-slaus) also bequeathed his other possessions to his wife and relatives. This act was made before the abbot, prior and other monks from the recipient monastery, who confirmed it with their seal and warned (just as was done in the Komes Zbylut donation mentioned above) "that those who opposed it would face 'anathema'."[45]

---

in hunc modum. Si uxor mea alteri viro nubere voluerit, Visloca ei detur; si in vidvitate, in habitu seculari permanserit, Viznicia sibi addetur; et in his duabus tantum permaneat, cum familia sua, servis videlicet et ancillis; cetera locus habeat. Si vero aliquando divina mediante clemencia, in prefato loco, habitum religionis suscipere voluerit, ut mihi sub iuramento quandoque promisit, omnes hereditates meas ei do: scilicet partem meam de Buzesk cum iumentis, Nosovo, Petrovo, Tuchapi, Bezdruovo, Rechovo, Viznica, Corenovo, Premislovo. Si autem in alio claustro habitum suscipere voluerit, de his omnibus supra dictis hereditatibus et de familia, de ceterisque bonis nichil penitus sibi detur, preter vestes quibus legitur"; *Ibid.*

44 "[...] set omnia non frater meus Episcopus Vitus, immo fratres et sorores supradicte religionis perpetuo iure obtineant. Hec autem dicta et scripta sunt in ecclesia beate Marie ante ipsius altare, sub testimonio solius dei et genitricis eius, dominique Johannis primi ibidem prepositi, facta ad eum confessione, et sacri corporis et sanguinis Christi de manu ipsius communione sumpta, dum ad bellum processi. Hec si dominus Episcopus V[itus] frater meus, vel aliqui alii cognatorum meorum immutaverint, deus omnipotens et mater pia virgo Maria vindicet in eis: sub cuius teslimonio sunt hec facta. Amen"; *Ibid.*

45 "[...] universis, quam etiam omnibus Luknensis ecclesie monachis tam presentibus quam posteris ego Sventoslaus notum facio, quia sanus mente meam villam Bracholino cum Jacubus integris claustro contuli. Zabicino et Moracino aliquis cognatorum pro pecunia vendat, qua videlicet pecunia creditoribus meis debita mea persolvantur, et quod residuum fuerit, pars pro Terra Domini et pars Romam mittatur. Uxori vero mee partem de Lukna que me attinet, Sedlez, Balosliw habebit, ut pro illis anniversarium mee depositionis singulis annis usque ad finem vite valeat observare. Post obitum ipsius, filii fratrum meorum ipsas villas dividant. Radgost vero nullo impediente libere pro se habebit, et reliquas villas post fluvium qui Uvira vocatur iacentes, pueris Drogomiri fratris mei senioris longe postea [sic] dabit, qui, seu filii ipsorum, cetera inter se dividant. Denique familiam meam, prout usque commisimus, uxor in memoria habeat. Et ne quispiam hoc in posterum mutare possit, scripto commendamus, sub testimonio Hugoldi abbatis,

THE INSTITUTION OF THE WILL

Duke Władysław Odonic used the term 'testament' to refer to an act endowing land to the Knights of St. John of Jerusalem (the Knights Hospitaller) in 1237 for the establishment of a monastery in Korytowo. The act contained language similar to that used by the Church fathers since the time of John Chrysostom in the fourth century: "Who would bequeath his earthly possessions to so many heirs and not make Christ an additional heir? From among all the possessions he secures for other people, a portion should be given to Him."[46]

Among other documents that have survived from the latter half of the thirteenth century are testamentary donations of real estate made by representatives of local elites,[47] the will of Princess Salomea of Krakow, who had been brought to Poland from Prague and who entered a monastery of Poor Clares (of the Order of St Clare),[48] and numerous other confirmations of testamentary donations.[49] Another interesting document is that concluding a dispute in 1258 between three relatives of a deceased palatine, Bogusz, and his widow Ludmiła, which was adjudicated by Duke Bolesław v the Chaste. Three knights (*milites*) – Świętosław, Simon and Chwalibóg – claimed that their relative could not transfer any inheritance to the Church or alienate it by any other means without their knowledge and consent or that of the Duke.[50] However, after reviewing the case, hearing witnesses' testimonies and consulting his barons (*barones*), the Duke decided that the last will and testament of the deceased was lawful and should be fulfilled. A strong defence of the will was voiced by the Bishop of Krakow Paul of Przemyków in the dispute between St. Kinga, Duke Bolesław the Chaste's widow, and his heir Leszek II the Black. Kinga,

---

Henrici prioris, Iacobi subprioris, Arperni, Leopoldi et Norberti sigillo nostro confirmamus, anathematisando eos qui huic deliberationi contradixerint. Anno Domini millesimo ducentesimo decimo sexto"; KDW, vol. 1, no. 88.

46   "Testamentum suum non bene disponit, qui terrenis tantum heredibus testatur et non facit Christum sue substantie conheredem: universa bona qui prestat hominibus, partem debet recipere prestitorum"; KDW, vol. 1, no. 202.

47   E.g., the will of *Comes* Lanchomir of 1271: "Anno Domini milessimo ducentesimo septuagesimo primo, decimo octavo Kalendas Februarii, ego comes Lanchomirus bona deliberatione habita, cupiens placere domino Jesu Christo, in mea ultima voluntate et condens testamentum delego et assigno beato Petro apostolorum principi ad ecclesiam Cruswiciensem villam meam que Procino nuncupatur"; KDW, vol. 1, no. 442.

48   KDM, vol. 1, no. 76 (1268).

49   There are at least three surviving documents of this kind issued by Prince Bolesław the Pious, and two issued by Prince Przemysł II; KDW, vol. 1, no. 354, 408, 446, 478, 540.

50   "[...] supradicti milites S. et C. et S. proposuerunt, quod cum ipsi essent veri consanguinei memorati palatini, ideo palatinus sine eorum connivencia et consensu ac domini terre, nullas hereditates posset alicui ecclesie in testamento legare, nec sub aliquo alio titulo alienare"; KDM, vol. 2, no. 454 (1258).

36   CHAPTER 1

who, like Salomea, entered the Poor Clares' monastery in Skała, bequeathed
to the order the income from customs duties she had inherited as well as
thirty villages with a significant total value of 20,000 *grivna* of pure silver.[51]
The bishop gave Duke Leszek the choice of recognizing the will or purchasing
the bequeathed property for the above-mentioned sum. If the new Duke did
not accept his decision, the bishop warned that he would defend the princess'
bequest with all his strength.[52]

2   Church Guardianship over Wills

The above examples of wills from the twelfth and thirteenth centuries share
several characteristic features. First, they were acts made by members of
the elites of several of the provinces and principalities of the Polish Kingdom in the times of its feudal fragmentation. This included princes or their
widows, palatines (*voivodes*) and local magnates. Of course, even before the
mid-twelfth century, a similar circle of elites was already interested in establishing new churches and abbeys. Since the thirteenth century, however, the
majority of these diverse pious bequests were referred to as wills, due in part
to the special protection these acts received from Church authorities. There
seems to be a clear link between 'testaments' and the evolution of canon law,
not only because of the pious purpose of these bequests, but also because they
contained the formulaic expression 'to include Christ among their heirs' and
threatened those who challenged them with the punishment of excommunication.

It also seems probable that there was a connection between the emergence
of the canonical will in Poland and the arrival of new religious communities.
This is indicated by the fact that the first mentions of wills are associated with
the coming of the Cistercians to Łekno[53] and the Norbertine nuns to Busko.
Later, thirteenth-century foundations which were also referred to as a 'testament and last will' (*testamentum et ultima voluntas*),[54] were connected with

---

51   See Glosary: Grivna

52   "Si uero sepedictus dux L. nullam predictarum ordinacionum uellet admittere, extunc
      nos una cum amicis nostris iusticiam ipsius domine contra quemlibet hominem uel per-
      sonam constanter promittimus deffensare"; KDM, vol. 2, no. 491 (1281).

53   The influence of the Cistercians on the freedom to transfer of property was also discussed
      by Kazimierz Kolańczyk; *idem, Studia nad reliktami*, 33.

54   KDM, vol. 2, no. 454 (1258).

THE INSTITUTION OF THE WILL

the arrival of the Franciscan[55] and Dominican[56] religious orders to Polish lands. Perhaps it was the members of these new mendicant orders who were responsible for introducing and popularising the institution of the will in these lands, which would have been in their own interests.[57] A strong link between wills and the Franciscan and Dominican orders established in the early thirteenth century is also indicated by a letter by Pope Innocent IV from 1245, addressed to members of these orders in Poland. He called on the authorities of both mendicant orders to ensure that donations made by testators as pious deeds (*in pios usus*), the purpose and recipient of which were usually left up to the will's executors, would be dedicated to the defence of the threatened Latin Empire.[58]

An essential factor in the adoption of this new form of donation was the support it received from state and ecclesiastical authorities, which safeguarded a testator's will from the challenges of heirs and relatives barred from

---

55 These include the testamentary bequests of blessed Salomea of Krakow and St. Kinga.

56 E.g. the testamentary bequest made by Segneus *heres de Cossek et de Plassow* of 60 *grivna* for the Dominicans; KDM, vol. 2, no. 595 (1329).

57 On the role of mendicant orders see *Wspólnoty zakonne w średniowiecznej Polsce* [Religious Communities in Medieval Poland] (Lublin: Wydawnictwo KUL, 2010), 120–134.

58 This letter was issued at a time when the political situation was getting increasingly complicated after the conquest of the Holy Land by Muslims in 1244 and shortly after the end of the first Council of Lyon. "Innocentius episcopus servus servorum Dei, dilectis filiis [...] priori Predicatorum et [...] ministro Minorum fratrum in Polonia, salutem et apostolicam benedictionem. Etsi ex suscepte servitutis officio cunctorum nobis cura imineat generalis, de succursu tamen imperii Constantinopolitani tanto propensius cogitare nos convenit, quanto ex hoc augmentum ortodoxe fidei, magnum Terre sancte subsidium, salus totius Christiani populi procurantur. Ad ipsius itaque imperii liberationem totis desideriis aspirantes, discretioni vestre per apostolica scripta in virtute obedientie districte precipiendo mandamus, quatinus ea, que relinquntur distribuenda in pios usus secundum arbitrium executorum testamentorum decedentium in Polonia et aliis locis ad que tuus fili prior prioratus et tua fili minister amministratio extenduntur, nisi prefata relicta ab ipsis testatoribus certis locis aut personis deputata fuerint vel de iure aliis debuerint, aut per predictos executores in usus huiusmodi sint conversa: fideliter per vos vel per aliquos de fratribus vestrorum Ordinum providos et discretos, quos ad hoc ydoneos esse noveritis, auctoritate nostra colligere, et apud aliquem tutum locum pro eiusdem imperii subsidio deponere cum omni diligentia procuretis, quantitatem ipsorum nobis postmodum rescripturi, contradictores per censuram ecclesiasticam appellatione postposita compescendo. Non obstantibus constitutione de duabus dietis, edita in Concilio generali, et indulgentia qua fratribus vestrorum Ordinum dicitur esse concessum, ne de causis que per litteras apostolicas commituntur eisdem, cognoscere teneantur, nisi de indulgentia huiusmodi expressam faciant mentionem. Quod si non ambo hys exequendis potueritis interesse, alter vestrum ea nichilominus exequatur. Datum Lugduni II Kalendas Octobris, pontificatus nostri anno tertio"; KDW, vol. 1, no. 247.

inheritance. Good examples of such protection include the above-mentioned judgment of the Duke of Krakow and Sandomierz Bolesław the Chaste, and Bishop Paul's opposition to Leszek Czarny's refusal to respect the will of his predecessor. An excellent example of the church's guardianship over such acts are the statutes issued in 1279 in Buda by Bishop Philip of Fermo, the papal legate for Hungary, Poland and Dalmatia. He devoted significant space to the principles to be followed in the drafting of wills, both by the clergy and laity, referring to the principle in canon law that testaments and acts of last will are under the jurisdiction of the office of the bishop. As a result, he enjoined both orders to submit their last wills to the priest of the parish to which they belonged, in the presence of trusted witnesses.[59] In the early fourteenth century, bishops in Krakow also began issuing decrees in their statutes concerning the drafting and fulfilment of wills.[60] The statutes issued by Bishop Nanker in 1320 contain an article referring to bequests of last will, but only those made by clergy. In it the bishop instructed deans that, upon learning that a parish priest or presbyter under their care was seriously ill, they were to send two or three priests to him who would witness and write down the will, and thereby secure the property of the dying person. Furthermore, a part of these goods were to be set aside for a proper funeral, presided over by the local chaplains and vicar, and a part to execute the will, i.e. pay off the debts and fulfil the pious bequests of the testator, while the remaining property would be set aside for the benefice of his successor. If a member of the laity attempted to forcibly seize something from the estate, the dean was to excommunicate them publicly in the name of Bishop Nanker, until he or she decided to return the property. Those who opposed the clergy were also threatened with a fine of one grivna of silver.[61] This decree was issued in response to a frequent cause

---

59   "De testamentis. Quum ad episcoporum spectat officium ut extreme legitime voluntates fidelium effectum mancipentur, precipimus et mandamus, ut tam clerici quam laici, quum sua voluerint condere testamenta vel ultimas voluntates, primum advocent parochie sacerdotem, et coram ipso et aliis idoneis testibus sua legitime ordinent testamenta vel ultimas voluntates"; KDW, vol. 1, no. 487.

60   On the statutes of the chapter of the Krakow cathedral and their sources, cf. Marek D. Kowalski, *Piętnastowieczne statuty kapituły katedralnej w Krakowie*, in *Polska i jej sąsiedzi w późnym średniowieczu*, eds. Krzysztof Ożóg, Stanisław Szczur (Krakow: Towarzystwo Naukowe Societas Vistulana, 2000), 233–253.

61   "Ne res clericorum, que bona sunt pauperum, usurpan, aut illicite contractari per manus violentas ymmo sacrilegas valeant laycorum, districte precipimus et mandamus, ut cum presbyter aliquis vel rector ecclesie graviter egrotari percipitur, quod de morte ipsius verisimiliter timeatur, decanus eius sine mora duos vel tres vicinos ad eum dirigat capellanos, qui res eius omnes et singulas diligenter conspiciant et conscribant, ut post eius mortem honeste sibi fiant exeque, et iuxta testamentum eius, quod racionabiliter et legitime

THE INSTITUTION OF THE WILL

of conflicts between church authorities and the lay patrons of church institutions, who claimed their right to the property of the deceased clergyman based on a traditional 'right of spoils' (*ius spolii*).[62]

Eleven years later, Bishop John Grot of Krakow also issued a statute referring to the making of wills in which he instructed that there was no duty more important than the fulfilment of the last will, whether it be that of an ill person or a healthy one, a clergyman or a lay person. The pastor or his deputy were to fulfil the deceased's requests concerning the place of burial, even if it was outside of the parish, and bequests made 'for the soul.' If anyone tried to oppose this, he would be deprived of the right to a Christian burial.[63] In a statute of

---

ordinatum existit, per ipsum solvantur debita, que contraxit, et per eum legata legitime dispensentur, pro successore quoque residuum conservetur. Ad cuius sepulturam laudabiliter peragendam, capellani vicarij, qui commode venire poterint, sine contradiccione accedere teneantur. Si quis autem patronus per potenciam secularem de talibus rebus recipere quidquam presumpserit, dictus decanus eum tamdiu auctoritate nostra excommunicet, et excommunicatum faciat per suos subditos publiee nunciari, donec ablata restituet, et pro temeritate commissa satisfaciat competenter. Contra dicentes in una marca argenti per superiorem proximum puniantur"; *Statuta synodalia episcoporum Cracoviensium XIV et XV saeculi e codicibus manu scriptis typis mandata additis statutis Vielunii et Calisii a. 1420 conditis (et ex rarissimis editionibus – etiam authenticis – nunc iterum editis)*, ed. Udalryk Heyzmann, Krakow 1875 (*Starodawne Prawa Polskiego Pomniki*, 4), 26.

62   This phenomenon was also present on German lands. Gabriele Schulz claimed it was associated with the development of the testament: "Eine sehr starke Einschränkung erfuhr diese Testierfreiheit jedoch durch das sogenannte Spolienrecht, d. h. durch das von verschiedenen Seiten, vor allem von weltlicher Seite beanspruchte Recht, nach dem Tode eines Klerikers dessen Hinterlassenschaft in Besitz zu nehmen. Gegen dieses Spolienrecht wandten sich immer wieder die Synoden. Sie waren bestrebt, »das Kirchengut seiner ursprünglichen Bestimmung zurückzugeben durch den freien Willen der einzelnen Kleriker, d. h. durch Aufhebung des Testamentsverbotes und Gewährung der vollen Testierfreiheit des Klerus über sein Eigentum, auch über das aus kirchlichen Einkünften erworbene Vermögen«. Die meisten Konzile in Deutschland, die gegen das Spolienrecht Stellung bezogen, haben zugleich den Klerikern die größtmögliche Testierfreiheit zugestanden. Es zeigt sich, daß das Spolienrecht letztlich den Ausschlag für die Testierfreiheit des Klerus auch über Einkünfte aus dem Kirchengut gab und damit dem Kleriker die Möglichkeit eröffnete, über sein gesamtes Vermögen frei zu verfügen. Es bestand aber trotz dieser vollen Testierfreiheit der Kleriker die Gewissenspflicht, den aus kirchlichen Quellen erworbenen Besitz der Kirche zu vermachen oder für fromme Stiftungen zu verwenden"; *eadem, Testamente des späten Mittelalters aus dem Mittelrheingebiet*, 8–9.

63   "Quia nichil est, quod magis debetur hominibus, quam ut eorum pija supreme voluntatis eulogia impleantur, igitur statuimus et ordinamus: ut si quisquam clericus vel laycus, sanus vel infirmus, cuiuscumque condicionis existat, pro anima sua aliquid disponere voluerit testamentum, aut testari, seu eciam eligere extra suam parrochiam sepulturam, rectorem parrochialis ecclesie, aut eius vicesgerentem, tamquam personam, que eius

40   CHAPTER 1

1331 the Bishop's guardianship was extended to the last wills of clerics as well as laity, to both healthy and sick people (*cuiuscumque condicionis existat*).

Bishop of Krakow Florian Mokrski treated the issue of the last will in a slightly different manner by insisting on their prior approval by a bishop before their execution. In his synodal statutes of 1373,[64] he addressed the people appointed as executors of wills, who at this time could be either from the clergy or laity. The Bishop declared that he had heard that some executors of the last will had used money and goods intended for pious bequests for other needs. Referring to the sanctions provided for in the 'sacred canons,' he stated that both the clergyman and the secular executor of the will should present the will to the bishop within a month in order to obtain his approval. The threat of excommunication was again used against those who tried to oppose this provision.[65]

One interesting statute proclaimed by Bishop Peter Wysz in 1396 referred to persons holding the title of public notary under a papal or imperial appointment. Pointing to the many injustices resulting from the actions of false notaries, he called on all *thabellionibus* (public notaries) to have their competence confirmed by the bishop's office. At the same time, he also delimited their role as follows: determining the beneficiaries of bequests to the church, courts, transactions, contracts, settlements and wills.[66] This order seems to

---

condicionem et conscienciam non creditur ignorare, et que sibi ministraverit ecclesiastica sacramenta, omnino advocet, et ipso presente pro anima leganda et testanda ordinet et disponet, et si voluerit, eligat sepulturam. Per cuius providenciam ipse testator dirigi poterit in hijs, que ad salutem anime sue pertinent, peragendis. Qui vero contrarium fecerit ex contemptu, ecclesiastica in fine careat sepultura, cuius eciam eleccio sit irrita ipso iure"; *Statuta synodalia episcoporum Cracoviensium,* ed. Udalryk Heyzmann, 40.

64   Bishop John Bodzanta had previously addressed the issue of wills in synodal statutes. However, in his statute *De testamentis per prelatos et canonicos Cracouiensis ecclesie faciendis,* he only discussed the implementation of the last wills of the prelates and canons of Krakow; *Statuta synodalia episcoporum Cracoviensium,* ed. Udalryk Heyzmann, 123.

65   "Fide dignis relatibus didicimus, quod nonnulli tam religiosi, quam clerici seculares et layci, pecuniam et alia bona, que per manus eorum testamentis decedencium debent iu usus pijos expendi, non dubitant alijs usibus applicare. Nos attendentes sacrorum canonum sancciones, quibus in omnibus pijs voluntatibus sit per locorum ordinarios providendum, statuimus: quod quocienscumque quisquam clericus vel laycus alicuius testamenti fuerit executor, illud testamentum infra unius mensis spacium nobis presentare fideliter teneatur, nostrum mandatum super execucione huiusmodi recepturus. Alias, si aliqui de bonis ipsis aliquid sibi retinuerint, seu retinere presumpserint, et non secundum voluntatem defuncti ipse distribuerint, testamentumque huiusmodi nobis non presentaverint, ut prefertur, excommunicacionis sentencie ipso facto eos volumus subiacere"; *Ibid.,* 40.

66   "Quoniam in negocijs et causis civilibus aliquando et in criminalibus, et quam plurimum in beneficialibus, in quibus bona fides et iustus tytulus requiritur, ac viciosus ingressus

THE INSTITUTION OF THE WILL   41

have been linked to broader action taken by the Church hierarchy against dishonest, under-educated and false public notaries. Similar acts were issued at that time by the Bishop of Płock, Jacob, and the Archbishop of Gniezno, Nicholas of Kurów.[67]

Similar prescriptions concerning the recognition and fulfilment of wills made by lay persons and priests, both 'in sickness and in health,' were included in the synodal statutes of Archbishop Nicholas Trąba, proclaimed in 1420. In them the Archbishop reaffirmed his earlier defence of the right to bequeath property on one's death bed and his right to act in the role of guardian to safeguard wills in accordance with canon law.[68]

The support for bequests of last will expressed both in the rulings of Piast princes and the Episcopal protection provided for in canon law most certainly played an important role in the spread of wills within and beyond the diocese of Krakow. The growing power of the papacy and the Pope's centralization of

---

debeat vitari, thabellionibus, tamquam servis publicis et scriniarijs, et eorum instrumentis ac scriptis autenticis, tam in iudicio, quam extra iudicium, in transaccionibus et in arbitrarijs que fiunt eciam ad instar iudiciorum, in testamentis et ultimis voluntatibus ac alijs contractibus diversis, et maxime in acceptacionibus et provisionibus ecclesiasticorum beneficiorum utimur probandis et improbandis"; *Ibid.*, 54.

67   Agnieszka Bartoszewicz, *Piśmienność mieszczańska*, 212.

68   "Ad hoc quod quedam in quibusdam partibus consuetudo, ymmo corruptela detestabilis observatur, videlicet quod tam laicus quam clericus, in lecto egritudinis constitutus, ultra certam summam iuxta loci illius consuetudinem limitatam nec piis locis nec personis ecclesiasticis pro anime sue remedio et salute aliqua possit ordinare legata: considerantes licet vicibus iam repetitis predictam consuetudinem et sacris canonibus et secularibus eciam legibus obviare, cum omnia iura clamant, quod ultima voluntas et ultimum hominis testamentum inviolabile perseveret, et nichil sit, quod magis hominibus debeatur, quam quod in extrema voluntate libera facultas existat, eandem consuetudinem Deo odibilem, animabus et moribus bonis inimicam auctoritate huius sacri concilii penitus reprobamus, firmiter statuentes, ut unicuique, quem iura a testamentorum non prohibent faccione, in sanitate vel in lecto egritudinis constituto, legandi, disponendi et ordinandi de bonis sibi collatis circa pia loca et personas ecclesiasticas, dummodo legitimos non pretereat successores, libera sit facultas. Volentes et precipientes districte, ut per locorum episcopos et ceteros prelatos iurisdicionem habentes universi clerici tam religiosi quam seculares et laici, impedientes defunctorum legata seu ultimas voluntates, per excommunicacionum in personas et interdicti in loca sentencias, canonica monicione premissa ferendas, ab huiusmodi impediments desistere compellantur; ad quorum execuciones et deblitas aggravaciones procedentes tempore faciendas episcopi et prelati, ad quos testamentorum defensio utroque iure suadente dinoscitur pertinere, benivolos se exhibeant et paratos, ne huiusmodi negligencia de eorum manibus in die districti iudicii requiratur"; *Statuty synodalne wieluńsko-kaliskie Mikołaja Trąby z r. 1420. Z materiałów przysposobionych przez B. Ulanowskiego*, eds. Jan Fijałek, Adam Vetulani (Krakow: Polska Akademia Umiejętności, 1951), 54–57.

the Church's bureaucratic apparatus, which was now able to provide effective support for the wills of not only clergy members, but also of lay people, were clearly also of major importance. The pious bequests contained in wills provided significant income for church institutions, and church guardianship over acts of last will guaranteed that they would be realized in line with the wishes and needs of the Church. It also safeguarded them against usurpation and misappropriation by laypersons, including powerful lords who had founded new private or parish churches and who possessed the 'right of patronage' (*ius patronatus*), relatives who in the absence of a will would have inherited a greater portion of the deceased's estate, and those chosen as executors of the will, who bore the bulk of the responsibility for the proper fulfilment of the will. The guardianship provided by the bishops of Krakow over wills is at times still visible in the fifteenth and early sixteenth centuries, however at that time they became increasingly secular affairs. There are indications that as late as the fifteenth century, some testators turned to an ecclesiastical court rather than a municipal court to authenticate their last will, placing greater trust in the former. For example, the Krakovian municipal notary John Stolle, when making his will in 1439, pointed out that if municipal councillors could not or did not want to carry out his bequests in full, he passed this duty on to Church authorities in Krakow: the bishop, the chapter and the church court.[69] The case of Stolle was to some extent exceptional because the testator was an ordained priest, but likewise in the will of the village administrator (*soltys*)[70] Peter Filipowski from 1460, it is mentioned that he revoked all his earlier wills, whether made before the bishop's court or elsewhere, before both clergy and laity.[71]

Another example of the Church's maintaining a form of jurisdiction over the provisions of the last will during this period can be found in a document dating from 1483. It is a notarial act drawn up by John, Bishop of Krakow, in which

---

69 "Item ap desim meyme testament icht hindernis entstunde is were von hern macht, adir von nicht beczalunge der czinse, adir von ander sache wegen, do von vorseumins geschege der gestifen mossen, do wedir dy patronen ratmanen nicht mochten adir nicht wolden, so czye ich alle dese bescheydunge mit foller macht an dy heylige Crakischer kirche an den erwidigen vatir den crakischen Bischoff, und an seyn Capitil, und Official, daz dy dovor raten, daz dis oppir meyner sawirn erbt, gote und seyner kirchen nicht entwand werde"; SCAB. 6, fol. 186 (1439).

70 See Glossary: Village administrator

71 "In primis revocat omnia et quelibet testamenta sua prius per eum sive coram reverendissimo domino episcopo Cracoviensi sive alias ubique facta, coram quibuscumque personis spiritualibus seu secularibus cassans omnia huiusmodi testamenta volens ipsa nullus roboris esse nec vigoris"; LT, fol. 66 (1460).

THE INSTITUTION OF THE WILL

he acted as a super-arbitrator in a dispute between the Castellan[72] of Wojnica, Paul Sborzeński, the executor of the last will of the Castellan of Wojnica's wife, Margaret Ossolińska, and both the altarist John Rusek and Ossolińska's heir, the late Nicholas Łowczowski.[73] Another interesting document is a slightly later ruling issued by Pope Alexander VI in response to a complaint from the executors of the will of bookseller John Klemesz. In it, the Pope recommended that the Krakovian canons assist in the fulfilment of the will.[74] Despite these late traces of intervention in support of wills by the Church hierarchy, it can be clearly seen that since the late fourteenth century, secular authorities increasingly treated last wills as falling within their purview, both incorporating them into common law (*ius commune*) and placing them under the supervision of secular courts, as we will see in the following chapters.[75]

3   Property Laws in Medieval Cities

The definition of the will contained in canon law clearly contradicted not only Polish land law, which was gradually being codified, but also so-called German town law, which played a crucial role in cities during this time. Like many other cities in the region, Krakow functioned under Magdeburg Law, which it officially adopted from Wrocław in 1257.[76] This already highly – though not

---

72   See Glossary: Castellan

73   AMK, Pergamyns., ms 334 (1483).

74   AMK, Pergamyns ms 377 (1503).

75   Paul Szczerbic's book from 1581 states that an infirmed individual cannot make a gift out of "fear of death" because they are no longer in control of themselves and thus "act in violation of the natural right" of their descendants. But he further states that: "Someone could argue against this article, and say that it is not good for many reasons. First, if this right were to be upheld, no man or woman would be able to pass on their possessions to anyone in ill health. No testament could do this. But this cannot be so, because everyone is free to make their own will according to their wishes. For it is stated in the law that if the descendant of the one who made a will does not fulfill it, then a bishop is to gather all the possessions, and to keep them at his disposal until the heir fulfills the wishes of their relative. And if the heir should satisfy the will of the deceased, then they are also free to give it to whomever they wish. The second reason is that this would mean the last will and testament would be rejected, which also cannot be so, because according to the law, everyone's last will is to be strictly observed. If someone gives anything for works of charity, then the descendant should carry out this bequest. And if the heir does not want to do so, then the testament should be executed or fulfilled by the bishop himself"; *idem, Ius municipale*, 215.

76   Jerzy Rajman, *Krakow: zespół osadniczy, proces lokacji, mieszczanie do roku 1333* (Krakow: Wydawnictwo Naukowe Akademii Pedagogicznej, 2004), 190–193; Jerzy Wyrozumski,

fully – developed and codified legal system consisted mainly of the aforementioned *Sachsenspiegel* (*Speculum saxonum*), i.e. a list of common laws from the territory of Saxony (divided into *landrecht* – land law, and *lehnrecht* – feudal law) and the *Magdeburg Weichbild* (*Ius municipale magdeburgense*), i.e. a collection of laws concerning the municipal political and court systems. If we take into account the fact that three *lokators*, and later vogts of Krakow, and many other burghers, originally came from Silesia,[77] and that already in 1308 a Latin version of the *Sachsenspiegel* (and German version of *Weichbild*) had been brought to Krakow from Wrocław, translated "for the city and its citizens" by a notary named Konrad of Opole, the initial close link between the legal system of Krakow and that developed in Silesian cities seems unquestionable.[78]

Dzieje Krakowa. Krakow do schyłku wieków średnich (Krakow: Wydawnictwo Literackie, 1992), 161–167; Marcin Starzyński, *Krakowska rada miejska w średniowieczu*, 23–28; Bogusław Krasnowolski, *Lokacje i rozwój Krakowa, Kazimierza i Okołu. Problematyka rozwiązań urbanistycznych*, in *Krakow. Nowe studia nad rozwojem miasta*, ed. Jerzy Wyrozumski (Krakow: Tow. Miłośników Historii i Zabytków Krakowa, 2007), 355–426; Jerzy Wyrozumski, *Lokacja czy lokacje Krakowa na prawie niemieckim?*, in *Ibid.*, 121–151.

77   Jerzy Rajman, "Mieszczanie z Górnego Śląska w elicie władzy Krakowa w XIV w.", in *Elita władzy miasta Krakowa i jej związki z miastami Europy w średniowieczu i epoce nowożytnej (do połowy XVII w.). Zbiór studiów*, ed. Zdzisław Noga (Krakow: Antykwa, 2011), 49–63; *idem*, *Krakow: zespół osadniczy*, 212–218; Jerzy Wyrozumski, *Dzieje Krakowa*, 171–172.

78   Konrad of Opole, who translated part of the *Sachsenspiegel* into Latin in 1308, "for the city and inhabitants of Krakow," did so, as he declared, both because he was inspired by God and because he was under orders to do it by the Bishop of Wrocław, so that the rights of the righteous would be protected and the unjust punished. He mentions Eike von Repkow, author of the *Sachsenspiegel*, but considers emperors Constantine and Charlemagne to be the true lawmakers because they were fulfilling God's will. Konrad of Sandomierz, author of the Latin translation of the *Landrecht* from the mid-fourteenth century, in contrast, considered the Holy Trinity and the Christian faith to be the true foundation of law. A collection of Chełmno laws dating back to the fifteenth century provides a direct link between the collection of town rights and their true author, God himself. It begins with the words that it was German law that God gave to Moses on Mount Sinai, and ends with the statement that "the words of German law, also known as Chełmno law, and which was spoken by God to Moses." By observing this law, "we can obtain the reward of eternal salvation." The divine authority of codified law and the religious sanctions associated with it are also expressed in the works of other translators and codifiers of urban and earthly laws; it is present in St. Thomas Aquinas' *Summa theologica*, as well as in the iconography of medieval collections of laws. Placing the image of Christ (initially ruling and later crucified) on the pages of legal codes acted as confirmation of the divine source and authority of the legal provisions contained in the acts. A characteristic example of this is the richly illuminated code of municipal rights created around 1505 by Balthazar Behem with a miniature depicting the crucified Christ; cf. Edward Potkowski, "Autorytet prawa w średniowieczu," in *Kultura prawna w Europie Środkowej*, ed. Antoni Barciak (Katowice:

THE INSTITUTION OF THE WILL   45

A detailed analysis of the preserved copies of those both sources of municipal law in medieval Poland allowed Maciej Mikuła to stress their mutual complementarity and describe the legal system as Saxon-Magdeburg Law. At the same time, he pointed out that it was *Weichbild* that played a major role in the legal practice of Polish cities as better suited to urban conditions.[79] However, both sources of legal code shared many features with traditional customary land law in their statutes governing the family and the rules of inheritance. Family blood ties and kinship played the most important role in both – the goods one possessed were to be inherited and passed on to the next generations in a customary order, "as the blood circulates."[80] The *Sachsenspiegel* and *Weichbild* allowed for the alienation of the hereditary estate, but only by an individual in good health who had obtained the consent of their relatives, i.e. by means of an *inter vivos* act. However, the type of will promoted by the Church allowed for donations also to be made on the death bed, which was expressly forbidden in the *Sachsenspiegel*, while in the *Weichbild* it was limited to the symbolic amount of three *solidi*.[81] These contradictions and the growing number of disputes in cities between the executors of wills and the legal heirs of the property bequeathed by the deceased, contributed to Pope Gregory XI issuing a bull in 1374 titled 'Saviour of the human race' (*Salvator humani generis*), in which he condemned 14 articles of the *Sachsenspiegel* (in the article named 'Against Magdeburg Law,' *Contra Ius Maydenburgense*), two of which concerned restrictions on the transfer of property. The first allowed for the transfer of movable property only by healthy persons who could hold a sword and shield in their

---

     Instytut Górnośląski, 2006), 15–34; *Miniatury z Kodeksu Baltazara Behema*, ed. Marcin Fabiański (Krakow: Wydawnictwo Karpaty, 2000).

79   Maciej Mikuła, *Prawo miejskie magdeburskie (Ius municipale Magdeburgense) w Polsce XIV-pocz. XVI w. Studium o ewolucji i adaptacji prawa* (Krakow: Wydawnictwo Uniwersytetu Jagiellońskiego, 2019), 178 (translated into English as *Municipal Magdeburg Law (Ius municipale Magdeburgense) in Late Medieval Poland. A Study on the Evolution and Adaptation of Law* (Medieval Law and Its Practice 30) (Leiden: Brill, 2021)); Zygmunt Rymaszewski, *Łacińskie teksty Landrechtu Zwierciadła Saskiego w Polsce: versio Vratislaviensis, versio Sandomiriensis, Łaski* (Studia nad Historią Państwa i Prawa, II, 15), (Wrocław: Zakład Narodowy im. Ossolińskich, 1975), 6; *idem*, "Miejskość czy wiejskość prawa Germanego w Polsce," *Zeszyty Naukowe Uniwersytetu Łódzkiego, Nauki Humanistyczno-Społeczne*, 69 (1970), 74–75.

80   "Ja naeher dem Blut, desto naeher dem Gut"; Uta Marquardt, "Görlitzer Testamente des 16. Jahrhunderts als Quelle sozialgeschichtlicher Untersuchungen," *Neues Lausitzisches Magazin* 123, no. 4 (2001), 34.

81   "De legationibus seu donis in lecto egritudinis. Nemo masculus; nec vlla mulier possent in loco egritudinis de bonis suis alicui vltra tres solidos dare, absque heredum consensu seu voluntate; nec mulier sine consensus mariti"; Jan Łaski, *Commune Incliti Poloniae, Libri duo*, vol. 1, 179r.

hands, while the second considered legal only those provisions that were made before a court and had the consent of the heirs.[82] The reason for the condemnation of the articles was the same: "These articles are erroneous because they prohibit alms, last wills, and pious acts."[83] Not only did municipal law initially not recognize wills, when it did, it expressed a clear hostility to them: according to the principle that the right to goods is possessed by he who can make use of them – that is, a healthy person – making donations on one's death bed was prohibited.[84] Moreover, according to the beliefs of the time, "a person's will was extinguished at the moment of death, and thus posthumous bequests could not yield legal consequences."[85] Thus, in the Pope's dispute with Magdeburg city law, his authority served to secure the freedom to bequeath property,[86] and a list of the condemned articles was included in the codification of the statutes and privileges of the Kingdom of Poland drawn up by John Łaski in 1506.[87] The papal bull was almost certainly published in the Kingdom of Poland shortly after its publication; for example, it is known that a list of forbidden articles

---

82   "Tredecimus articulus. Quod quicunque succinctus cum gladio clipeum tenens, non potest de lingo vel lapide pollicis vlnam quantum ad altitudinem habentem supra dextrarium scandere, talis non potest cedere, dimittere, vel infeudare, vel etiam mobilia bona alicui dare sic quod iste custoditus sit qui talia post mortem dantis expectat. Iste articulus est erroneus, inquantum elemosinas, testamenta, et alia pietatis opera prohibit. Quartusdecimus articulus est, Quod nullus sine licentia suorum heredum, sine Iudicio bannito, quod Saxonie dicitur, geheget ding, potest dare proprietatem suam, vel suos homine. Et sit alia daret alicui, heredes acquirent ista per iudicium, acsi dans illa mortuus esset. Isti duo articuli sunt erronei inquantum Elemosinas et alia pietatis opera prohibent"; *Ibid.*, 175r.

83   "Isti duo articuli sunt erronei inquantum Elemosinas et alia pietatis opera prohibent"; *Ibid.*

84   It was provided for in the thirteenth article of Magdeburg Law, which was supressed by Pope Gregory XI: "Quod quicunque succinctus cum gladio clipeum tenens, non potest de lingo vel lapide pollicis vlnam quantum ad altitudinem habentem supra dextrarium scandere, talis non potest cedere, dimittere, vel infeudare, vel etiam mobilia bona alicui dare sic quod iste custoditus sit qui talia post mortem dantis expectat"; *Ibid.*

85   Przemysław Dąbkowski, *Prawo prywatne polskie*, 67.

86   A major role in the Pope's condemning these articles was played by the Augustinian theologian Johannes Klenkok. In 1369, he wrote a work entitled *Decadikon* in which he condemned 10 articles of the *Sachsenspiegel*, which, in his opinion, restricted the Pope's power and were in conflict with "Christian law." These arguments were not accepted by the Bishop of Halberstadt, Albert, and in 1370 the municipal council of Magdeburg banished Johannes from the city. In 1372, he sent to Pope Gregory XI in Avignon an extended list of 21 articles of the *Sachsenspiegel* which he believed to be improper. On 8 April 1364, Gregory XI issued a bull condemning 14 of them; cf. Christopher Ocker, *Johannes Klenkok. A Friar's Life c. 1310–1374* (Philadelphia: American Philosophical Society, 1993), 42–69.

87   Łaski's Statutes also include King Alexander's confirmation of fourteen articles of Saxon and Magdeburg Law condemned by pope Gregory XI; Jan Łaski, *Commune Incliti Poloniae, Libri duo*, part 1, 174–174v.

THE INSTITUTION OF THE WILL 47

was found in a private textbook owned by an inquisitor residing in Krakow in the early fifteenth century.[88] However, we do not know how it was received, in particular by Krakow's municipal authorities.

The archaic bequests contained in the *Sachsenspiegel* concerning the ownership of goods did not simply become invalid. Writing down and codifying the law always eventually leads to its petrification, but, as these rules and norms became dated, they and their applications were not simply forgotten. Even that the handwriting nature of the legal codes allowed for a certain range of their modifications and adaptation to the contemporary needs, they definitely could not keep up with much more dynamic social changes.[89] As Henry Maine noticed "When primitive law has once been embodied in a Code, there is an end to what may be called its spontaneous development. Henceforward the changes effected in it, if effected at all, are effected deliberately and from without."[90] Jack Goody described broadly this phenomenon in his book *The Logic of Writing and the Organization of Society*. He referred, among others, to persuasive comment of Fritz Kern: "In contrast to the positive codified law, customary law 'quietly passes over obsolete laws, which sink into oblivion, and die peacefully, but the law remains young, always in the belief that is old. Yet it is not old... Statute law, on the other hand, cannot be freed from the letter of legal texts, until a new text has replaced an old one, even though life has long since condemned the old text to death; in the meantime the dead text retains power over life'."[91]

However, the dynamically changing nature of society and living conditions in the late medieval city required a departure from the archaic principles hitherto governing ownership and inheritance. Because capital investments in real estate and its sale were sources of income of the city, its elites needed to make existing rights concerning the ownership of property more flexible. Moreover, growing religious awareness, the influence of Mendicant orders, and the example provided by royal and magnate elite in terms of funding activities, strongly influenced the growing need among townspeople to make testamentary bequests. The above factors also influenced the process of distinguishing

---

88   "Twenty of the twenty-one articles, first reproved by Johannes Cleynkoc of the Orden of Hermits, and by master Berniger (i.e. Kerlinger) Walther of the Order of Preachers, and by Gregory XI, appear in collection of papal documents added to the handbook of an inquisitor of Krakow in the early fifteenth century"; Christopher Ocker, *Johannes Klenkok*, 63.

89   Maciej Mikuła, *Prawo miejskie magdeburskie*, 179–181.

90   Henry Sumner Maine, *Ancient Law*, 17.

91   Jack Goody, *The Logic of Writing and the Organization of Society* (Cambridge: Cambridge University Press, 1986), 127–171.

acquired goods from the rest of the estate – a phenomenon that had its roots in Polish lands as early as the early thirteenth century,[92] but which became widespread in urban jurisdictions over the following century.[93]

The division of property between hereditary and acquired goods is also found among the articles of the *Magdeburg Weichbild*. In an article concerning the principles for making bequests of dowers, it states that "every man who has a house subject to municipal law and in accordance with his last will can donate to his wife as a dower his hereditary goods (*priopriam hereditatem*), which he has the right to alienate from himself, as well as his other movables."[94] In another place in the *Weichbild*, it clearly states that "[a] man, being in good health, can pass on to whomever he wants only those movables and merchandise acquired through the joint work of the husband and wife."[95] With time, municipal law in Krakow adopted the principle of the free disposal of all acquired goods.[96] In bequests found in municipal books, mention of this principle can be found as early as the first half of the fourteenth century. For example, in one record from 1333, councillor Nicholas of Zawichost bequeathed

---

92   The document transferring the village of Udorz to the Monastery in Miechów in 1232 contains this remarkable statement: "enim dicte uille deuenit ad me tanquam aduenticia, non ad me perueniens ex paterna hereditate, et ob hoc ad suos non transferetur heredes"; KDM, vol. 2, no. 404 (1232).

93   "Only in the late thirteenth century, and initially only in town privileges, did differences develop in the legal treatment of *ervengut* [hereditary goods – J.W.] and *wunnenegut* [acquired goods – J.W.] in the Saxon law, adopted later also in land law. In some cases it was influenced by foreign laws, one would assume, considering the so-called 'Wrocław land law,' established in the mid-fourteenth century. Although it was strictly based on the *Sachsenspiegel*, it deviated from it on the issue of alienation of property, limiting the freedom of the owner to dispose of property without the permission of the heirs only to hereditary property, *anirstorben gut*. It is very likely that this was due to the influence of Polish law, which in the early thirteenth century, notably in Silesian sources, clearly emphasized the freedom of alienation for acquired goods, eliminating completely the possibility of intervention by the heirs. (etiam invitis amicis)"; Karol Koranyi, *Podstawy średniowiecznego prawa spadkowego*, 115–118; Cf. Przemysław Dąbkowski, *Prawo prywatne polskie*, 505.

94   "Etiam quivis vir habens mansionem infra ius municipal, ille sue contorali dare potest pro dotalicio suam propriam hereditatem, quam in posse habeat alienandi; et etiam in alys bonis suis mobilibus inquantum voluerit"; Jan Łaski, *Commune Incliti Poloniae, Libri duo...*, part 1, 178v.

95   "Si autem vir habuerit bona mobilia; aut mercimonia; que sibi propriis laboribus aut prospera fortuna accreverunt cum sua uxore; illa potest dare in valitudine vite sue cuicunque placet; cuiuslibet sine contradiction de Iure"; *Ibid.*, 183v.

96   "This fragment of the work [...] played a relatively important role in relaxing the principle of the non-transferability of immovable property in the event of death, which later also included free disposal of a certain portion of immovable property, or a certain kind of it"; Karol Koranyi, *Podstawy średniowiecznego prawa spadkowego*, 64.

THE INSTITUTION OF THE WILL   49

to the children of his son-in-law Hankon all his goods and the heritage he
"acquired through his work" (*que et quas proprijs laboribus conquisivit*), reserv-
ing for himself the right to use them as long as he was alive.[97] In the latter half
of the fourteenth century, one can observe the growing prevalence of declarations concerning the possession of goods acquired through one's work, as a
means of ensuring one's freedom to dispose of them by means other than the
principle of 'the circulation of blood.'[98] In a bequest from 1371, John of Eger
asks the municipal tribunal whether he could dispose of all of his goods in
accordance with his will, since he had acquired them through his work. The
tribunal replied in the affirmative.[99] In the following years, similar questions
appear more and more often on the pages of the books of municipal bench
court, which led to their being shortened into a universally applicable form.
For example, at the beginning of a bequest from 1395, there is only the following short note: *Mathias Breunchin requisivit in sentenciam etc…* "Mathias
Breunchin applied for the verdict etc."[100] which would be incomprehensible

---

97   "Eodem Anno et die Nycolaus de Zawichost coram iudicio bannito constitutus dedit et
      contulit pueris Hanconis dicti Zawichost generi sui omnia bona sua ac hereditates, que
      et quas proprijs laboribus conquisiuit, iure hereditario. Hijs enim bonis et hereditatibus
      iamdictus Nycolaus de Zawichost pueris predictis datis et resignatis coad uixerit, frui
      debet"; NKiRMK, no. 1141.
98   For example, in 1368 the alderman Nicholas Essenbach declared that all his property
      had been acquired through his work, so he ordered it to be passed on to his wife and her
      appointed guardians: "Nicolaus Essenbach constituit procuratores Nicolaum Stolczel (et)
      Nicolaum Grobnik uxoris sue et bonorum suorum omnium et requisivit in sua diffini-
      cione, ex quo omnia bona sua suis acquisivisset laboribus et hoc facto omnia dicta bona
      sua, in quantum prius ea moriretur, debet hereditarie super lucro et dampno ad tempora
      vite sue possidere, preter L mrc, que debent couterinis suis assignare, ipsa vero domina
      defuncta et bonis remanentibus eiusdem, domine filie sue Margarethe aut heredibus
      eius, preter XX mrc, que debent eidem domine Margarethe filie, alie X mrc. Debent
      assignari, residuum autem, quod fuerit, dicti tutores debent converti in usus infirmorum
      hospitalis, si vero fieri poterit ad pretorium Capelle debent assignari, isto expresso, quod
      dicta domina Katherina Petrum filium sororis sue circa se sibi ministrandi vite necessaria
      pro suo posse in quantum ipsam et scolas sequi voluerit ac sacros presbiteratos ordines
      mutari et ipsum in libris suis cum X mrc, volens dictus Nicolaus esse dominus bonorum
      suorum"; SCAB., no. 242 (1368); cf. Jacek Laberschek, *Mikołaj z Zawichostu*, in PSB, vol. 21
      (Wrocław–Warszawa–Krakow: Polska Akademia Nauk, Polska Akademia Umiejętności,
      1976), 152.
99   "Johannes de Egir requisivit a scabinis sentencialiter, ex quo omnia sua bona suis acqui-
      sisset laboribus, utrum cum eisdem posset facere, prout vellet; sentenciatum fuit hec
      posse fieri, ubi ipse domum in platea Castri contiguam domui Peszconis medici Petro
      Jordansmol perpetue resignavit"; SCAB., no. 603 (1371).
100   "Mathias Breunchin requisivit in sentenciam etc. tandem idem Mathias Breunchin omnia
      bona sua, que habet et habiturus fuerit, domine Margarethe conthorali sue legitime post

without knowing the context of this entry. The development of a permanent distinction between movable and immovable goods in the consciousness of Krakovians is also evidenced by the mention of the transfer of "all movable goods, hereditary property and immovable" (*omnia bona sua mobilia, heredi- taria et immobilia*),[101] and by a later clause which reads "all goods provided that they have been achieved through one's work."[102]

In the *ortyle*[103] (German *urteile*) i.e. judgements and legal clarifications of Magdeburg Law,[104] translated into Polish in the fifteenth century, the burgh- ers' doubts about whether they could dispose of their goods is addressed as follows: "A man can give his inheritance and all legally acquired goods to any person or to the church, or wherever and whenever he wishes in his will, and this is allowed by law."[105] The Magdeburg councillors' response is convincing evidence of the significant expansion of both the category of acquired goods and the right to dispose of them, which included wills at this point in time. Given the fact that these recommendations were addressed to burghers, who had often come to Krakow as immigrants and carried out numerous real estate transactions in the city, it is easy to imagine that in many cases the acquired goods could include almost all the property they possessed. Bequests con- cerning the transfer of property after the death of its owner, large numbers of which have been preserved in Krakow's municipal books, prove that the burghers often exercised this right.

---

mortem suam habenda cum plena faciendi et dimittendi facultate donavit, exclusis tantummodo C mrc. gr. prag., que statim post obitum ipsius in opera pietatis converti debebunt per subscriptos tutores et ipsa domina suum dotaliciuin renuncciavit; reservat dominium: tutores sunt: Swarczpeschko et Dauid Gunthir"; SCAB., no. 2155 (1395).

101 "Cristan murator omnia bona sua mobilia hereditaria et immobilia, que habet ad presens, domine Cristine consorti sue legitime libere contulit et donavit"; SCAB., no. 1579 (1392).

102 "Albertus de Auswinzin omnia bona sua, que elaboravit seu elaborabit, Katherine uxori sue cum faciendi et dimittendi facilitate resignavit"; SCAB., no. 1976 (1394).

103 See Glossary: Ortyle

104 In publishing these judgements, Michał Wiszniewski wrote: "In the library of the Academy of Krakow I found two collections, quite different from each other, of such judgments, or Urteils in German, written in the early fifteenth century at the latest. Apart from these two collections in the German language, I own a manuscript of a collection of judge- ments by jury members specializing in Magdeburg Law in the Polish language, rewritten by one scribe in 1501, as evidenced by his signature in red ink at the end, without any internal chronology. I compared these Polish judgements, with no specific dates, pub- lished here entirely in appendices, with a copy of the same Polish judgements made in 1533. This last manuscript with a slightly different spelling, with some German influences, is faithful to the original copy; it even repeats all its mistakes, and adds new, very serious ones"; *idem, Historya...*, 154–155.

105 *Ibid.*, 244.

THE INSTITUTION OF THE WILL   51

4   The Influence of Roman Law

Apart from the influence of the Church and the spontaneous development of municipal law, a third factor that played a significant role in the spread of the will in Krakow was Roman law, traces of which can be seen in the theory of civil law and in the practices of municipal courts. Of course, this did not concern classical Roman law, but "the medieval composition of glossaries and commentaries, for which the starting point was (often a misreading of) the Code of Justinian (*Codex Justinianeus*)."[106] The study of Roman law at European universities encouraged the incorporation of its concepts into the codification of local laws. At the University of Krakow, restored in 1400, Roman law was taught in as many as five faculties (i.e. the same number of faculties in which the liberal arts and medical sciences were taught).[107] There are echoes of some Roman law concepts in the *Sachsenspiegel* itself, although here they are of rather marginal significance.[108] However, the application of Roman law is barely perceptible in the documents created by municipal offices at that time, so it is difficult to state with confidence the extent to which the *Sachsenspiegel* reflects the influence of *ius civili* on municipal court systems, and to what extent these legal practices are unrelated.

The traces of the adoption in Krakow of principles taken from Roman law were fourteenth- and fifteenth-century glosses to Magdeburg.[109] However, the most important source of information came from Raymund Parthenopeus' treatise on law titled *Summa legum brevis levis et utilis*, written in the latter half of the fourteenth, or the early fifteenth, century. It is a concise lecture on the system of Roman law with some elements of canon law. *Summa* had a major influence on the practices of municipal courts, especially in cases that were not regulated in the *Sachsenspiegel*.[110] It was included in John Łaski's codification of 1506 because, in his opinion, it had long been considered an authoritative source in Polish towns and cities.[111] Łaski's opinion is confirmed by extant

---

106   Krystyna Bukowska, *Orzecznictwo krakowskich sądów wyższych w sporach o nieruchomości miejskie (XVI–XVIII w.)* (Warszawa: Państwowe Wydawnictwo Naukowe, 1967), 12.

107   Adam Vetulani, *Z badań nad kulturą prawniczą w Polsce piastowskiej* (Wrocław: Zakład Narodowy im. Ossolińskich, 1976), 207.

108   Krystyna Bukowska, *Orzecznictwo*, 12.

109   *Ibid.*, 9.

110   This was the task of Roman law according to the fourteenth-century gloss by von Buch; cf. *Ibid.*, 13.

111   "[...] quia eorum practica communiter fit in certis nostris locis ius Maidemburgense ac Theutonicum habentibus"; Jan Łaski, *Commune Incliti Poloniae, Libri duo*, part 1, 175.

sources.[112] There is ample evidence indicating that this work may have possibly been produced in the Kingdom of Poland, including the fact that the largest number of known surviving manuscript copies of *Summa* are located within the territory of the former kingdom.[113] One of the copies is in the possession of the municipal council of Poznan,[114] while another is found in the *Liber legum* code, stored in the Przemyśl city archive.[115] Dr. Raymund's work was most likely also known in Krakow,[116] and the legal regulations it contained could have been used by the local municipal judiciary.[117] Perhaps some representatives of the Krakow ruling elite, who would have had the education necessary to read it, might also have possessed copies of the work.[118]

Although there are no direct references to the principles of Roman law in the bequests in Krakovian council books or books of the municipal bench court, an analysis of the entries in these books allows us to see gradual changes in the basic concepts related to civil law (such as the nature of ownership of goods or the categories and laws relating to them).[119] Over the course of the slow process of transformation in these laws, one can observe:

> a desire to strengthen the position of the owner. The first step on this path was to move away from the German concept of wielding, which blurred the differences between ownership and other rights to things, in favour of

---

112 Adam Vetulani, "Fragment Summy Rajmunda w rękopisie warszawskim," *Czasopismo Prawno-Historyczne* 14, 1962, no. 2, 165–172.

113 Krystyna Kamińska, "Summa Rajmunda Partenopejczyka jako zabytek średniowiecznego prawa polskiego," *Czasopismo Prawno-Historyczne* 26, 1974, no. 1, 147–157.

114 It belonged to Matthias, a pharmacist, alderman and councillor from Poznan; Witold Maisel, "Poznanski rękopis Summy Rajmunda Partenopejczyka," *Czasopismo Prawno-Historyczne* 12, 1960, no. 2, 135–149.

115 According to Anna Łosowska this code: "had various functions. It could have been a convenient textbook for students, an interesting read for an educated clergyman, but also for a townsman who could write. It also might as well have served as a legal code kept on hand both in the municipal tribunal and in the municipal bench court." *eadem*, *Kolekcja 'Liber legum' i jej miejsce w kulturze umysłowej późnośredniowiecznego Przemyśla* (Warszawa–Przemyśl: Archiwum Państwowe, Przemyśl; Naczelna Dyrekcja Archiwów Państwowych, 2007), 258–269, 337.

116 "Raymundus Parthenopeus iuris utriusque doctor"; Jan Łaski, *Summe Raymundi de Iure*, in *idem*, *Commune incliti..., Registrum*.

117 Anna Łosowska, *Kolekcja 'Liber legum,'* 260–261; Bożena Wyrozumska, *Kancelaria miasta Krakowa w średniowieczu*, 102.

118 For example, counselor Stanisław Leymitter left three legal books; we also know that Herman, a doctor, kept his book collection in a locked chest, cf.: CONS. 429, fol. 368 (1465), CONS. 428, fol. 520, 534 (1449).

119 Krystyna Bukowska, *Orzecznictwo*, 33–36, 60–63, 109–113.

THE INSTITUTION OF THE WILL   53

Roman notions, which, by considering possession as a factual state corresponding to ownership, emphasized its independent and superior nature [...] The same objective is served by a progressive restriction of third parties' rights to immovable property [...] The adoption of the Roman theory of ownership is also linked to the restriction of the husband's rights in relation to the wife's property and of the guardian over the property of persons under his care.[120]

It seems, therefore, that the relationship between Krakow's municipal authorities and burgher last wills should also have been shaped by Roman law. The provisions on wills contained in Raymund Parthenopeus' aforementioned *Summa*, in which an exceptionally large amount of space is devoted to 'testaments,' provide valuable data in regard to this question. It provides definitions of wills and bequests and answers questions about who could make a will, what goods could be disposed in one, what part of a will a person had at his disposal, how many witnesses one needed to have, and who could act as a witness, as well as explaining the reasons for drawing up a will and how to write one.[121]

However, the explanations the *Summa* provides are somewhat ambiguous. For example, it states that "a will is the lawful disposition of one's goods after death in accordance with one's free will and common sense, and the appointment of an heir to them."[122] *Summa* here invokes the Roman principle of *nemo pro parte testatus* – nobody can inherit only part of an estate. The heir designated to receive the entire patrimony was in this sense expected to take the place of the deceased.[123] As defined in *Summa*, a will was limited to the transfer of a person's entire estate to a single individual, and a change in the provisions contained in the will was possible only as long as the testator was living. Bequests made orally, as well as those written on a plate, paper or parchment, with signatures or seals of witnesses, were all considered valid.[124] Yet,

---

120 *Ibid.*, 109–110.

121 Jan Łaski, *Summe*, no. 44–53, 60–61.

122 "De primo testamentum est voluntatis libere et sane mentis iusta sententia de eo quod quis post mortem suam fieri vult cum institutione heredis"; *Ibid.*, no. 44.

123 "Dixi de eo quod quis post mortem suam fieri vult; scilicet de universo patrimonio; quia nemo potest in parte testari; et quia ante mortem nemo potest sibi ex aliquo testamenti ius vendicare, dixi cum heredis institutione; quia heredis institutio est caput et fundamentum totius testamenti Et est institutio alicuius in locum suum statutio, qui persona defuncti et heredis una censetur"; *Ibid.*

124 "Due autem sunt species testamenti; una dicitur nuncupativa que sit per verba, alia inscriptis vel per instrumentum. Sed non est differentia si scribatur in tabulis vel papyro

54 CHAPTER 1

the above definition, taken directly from ancient Roman law, clearly differed from late medieval urban practices, a fact of which the author of the treatise must have been aware. A trace of such an awareness can be found in a section titled 'On the Solemn Will' (*De solenni testamento*).[125] He states that "according to the law [Roman law], there should be seven witnesses at the solemn will, who will sign it or affix their seal to it." Further on, however, the *Summa* distinguishes a 'private' or 'simple' will, a concept unknown to Roman law, for which only three witnesses are required for it to be recognised. He also mentions that canon law requires just two or three witnesses, indicating that any will could be made before just two or three witnesses. He also states that it is sufficient to have just one stamp – that of a prince or a city – affixed to the will for it to be considered credible.

Worth attention also are the rules for bequests contained in the section titled 'How Much Can Be Bequeathed' (*quantum testari possit*), which invoke an institution found in Roman law, that of a 'reserved share' of the estate, guaranteeing the right of heirs to receive a certain part of the deceased's estate.[126] In accordance with 'natural law' (*de iure naturalis*), if the father had four or less children, they were to divide equally one third of the estate, and if there were five or more children, they were to divide one half of all the deceased's goods among themselves. The remainder of the estate was considered the property of the father because he had acquired it through his own work. If he died without a will, this part of his estate was to be designated for pious bequests to benefit his soul. After citing these Roman and canonical principles, the author of *Summa*, however, stipulates that the rules applied should be in accordance with local customs:

> There are different customs in different places. There is one custom that a testator who is ill in body, but healthy in mind can freely dispose of his or her moveable goods. His real estate is divided equally between himself, his wife and all his children – and this is a good practice. There is

---

vel pergameno dummodo testibus signetur vel sigillis muniatur"; *Ibid.*

125   "De solenni testamento. In solenni testamento debent esse secundum leges septem testes viri honesti qui manibus suis se subscribant, vel sigilla sua appendant. Sed in privato et in simplici testamento requiruntur tres testes. Secundum vero canones duo vel tres, et in hac parte legibus derogatur que duo vel tres testes in omni testament suffitiunt. Si autem sunt proles tanto melius honestus et manifestius. Sufficit tamen aliqui in testamento unum Sigillum principis vel civitatis pro corroboratione testamenti. Et si sigillum propinquorum possit in testamento haberi esset utile et honestium Si vero non tunc extraneorum Sigilla suffitiunt ad eius firmitatem"; *Ibid.*, no. 51.

126   Krystyna Bukowska, *Orzecznictwo*, 99.

THE INSTITUTION OF THE WILL   55

another custom that a person can dispose of all his goods as he chooses, bequeathing more to one and less to another, though none of the children should be disinherited without cause. If [the] testator's children are adults, they should personally express their consent. Another custom says that goods which have been inherited from one's uncle, father or mother cannot be disposed of through a will, though personally acquired goods can be transferred by such means. There is another bad custom that a testator who is ill in body, but healthy in the mind cannot make a will. This violates all sense of justice, as in making a will one does not need a healthy body, but a healthy mind and good intent.[127]

In Krakovian wills one can see traces of all the customs mentioned above, apart from the last, which was condemned by both Raymund and Pope Gregory XI.[128] When drawing up deathbed wills, some burghers sought to limit their bequests to transfers of money to selected individuals and church institutions.[129] There were others (most often those without children) who, bedridden by illness, bequeathed their property to their wives, other relatives, or the Church.[130]

---

127   "Lex precepit liberis legittimis et naturalibus certam quantitatem rerum testari, quasi de iure naturalis eis debeatur. Hoc modo, si quattuor sunt aut pautiores tertiam partem omnium hereditatum, Si vero quinque sunt aut plures, tunc habebunt mediam partem totius paterne hereditatis, Reliqua substantia tota stat in voluntate patris usus, Quattuor aut infra dat natis iura trientem. Semissem vero dant natis quinque vel ultra. Arbitrium seruitur substantia cetera patris. Et non immerito, que ipse eas res elaboravit, ymmo si intestatus decederet. Adhuc anima sua partem suam habebit. Et nota quod semissem vel trientem isti nati debent inter se dividere, ita quod nulla iniuria fiat, et in his legatis debet consuetudo provinciarum servari, Sunt enim in diversis regionibus diverse consuetudines, Est tamen una consuetudo Quod testator sanus mente licet eger corpore de rebus mobilibus liberis suis secundum suum velle disponit. Res autem immobiles equaliter dividit inter se et suam uxorem, et cunctos liberos suos. Et est bona consuetudo, Est et alia consuetudo, Que de cunctis rebus suis potest disponere, prout vult uni plus alteri minus, uni hoc, alteri illud sic tamen quod legittimos liberos non debet sine causa exhereditate, in hereditate privare, vel preterire. Si autem habet puberes filios illorum consensus debet de honestate adesse. Alia iterum est consuetudo, Quod quis de rebus que perveniunt ab avo, vel a patre vel a matre liberis inuitis nihil testamentaliter disponeree potest. De rebus vero provectitiis vel adventitiis prout vult disponit. Est alia mala consuetudo, quod testator langvens corpore licet sit sanus mente bone racionis et mature deliberationis testamentum facere non possit. Quod est contra omnem iustitiam, quia in testamentis fatiendis non requiritur valitudo corporis, sed mentis sanitas et valitudo rationis"; Jan Łaski, *Summe*, no. 50.

128   In bulla *Salvator humani generis* from 1364; Jan Łaski, *Commune Incliti Poloniae, Libri duo*, part. 1, 175r.

129   E.g. CONS. 428, fol. 305 (1431).

130   E.g. LT, fol. 153 (1493).

56 CHAPTER 1

Traces of efforts to observe statutory provisions on the inheritance of hereditary property can be seen in, for example, challenges made to the act of last will of the councillor Stanisław Weingart. The last will, according to which the house and all other goods were intended for *opera pietatis* (a bequest 'for the soul'), and the sister of the deceased Osanna was completely disinherited, was challenged by this sister and her husband, the noble Bartholomeus of Górka, a notary for the land court in Krakow.[131]

One more section in the *Summa* on wills is worth quoting: 'The Reasons Why Wills Are Made' (*Quare fiunt testamenta*). The author first states that: "wills are made so that there are no quarrels or doubts about the legacy left after the testator's death." He then adds that "it often happens, however, that they lead to even greater hostility and murder." He goes on to quote the reasons that can motivate testators: "There are thus wills for holy places, for the salvation of their souls. They are also for wives, out of marital love.[132] They are also for children due to natural obligations towards them. They are also for relatives because of the union of blood. They are for the poor for the glory of God. They are also for servants for their service, etc."[133]

The reasons given by Raymund indicate that in his observations he distanced himself from both the classic perception of the will as an efficient tool for transferring control of one's estate to the chosen heir, and from the role prescribed to the will by the Church as an act securing for the deceased a path to salvation. The author of *Summa* was even critical of the very idea of a will, arguing that (perhaps unsurprisingly) it led to conflicts and even murders within the family. This remark, along with evidence from local customs (very close to practices known from Krakovian wills) prove that Raymund Parthenopeus had a good understanding of how the will functioned in the late

---

131 "Eodem anno sabato crastino sancte Barbare dominus Bartholomeus de Gorka tutorio nomine uxoris sue iam secundo arrestavit presens testamentum"; CONS. 428, fol. 406 (1439).

132 In his last will of 1494, salt-mine manager Michael Godzek left all his possessions to his wife Dorothy because she "worked faithfully with him and supported and served him with care and conscientiousness..." A year later, councillor Stanisław Przedbor similarly bequeathed all his possessions to his wife, because she "lived with him faithfully for 40 years in harmony and love"; LT, fol. 154–155.

133 "Quare fiunt testamenta. Testamenta fiunt, ne lites et controversie de hereditatibus a defuncto relictis post mortem testatoris oriantur, que tamen ut frequenter fiunt, ymmo qnandoque magne inimicitie et homicidia ex illis sequuntur. Fiunt etiam testamenta piis locis propter animarum salutem. Fiunt et uxoribus, propter coniugalem amorem. Fiunt filiis propter naturalem obligationem. Fiunt et propinquis propter sangvinis unionem. Fiunt pauperibus propter deum. Fiunt et famulis propter eorum obsequium etc."; Jan Łaski, *Summe*, no. 50.

THE INSTITUTION OF THE WILL 57

medieval city. However, the legal principles cited by him could also accurately depict the rules regulating the writing of wills wherever local city and land laws were silent about them, including fifteenth-century Krakow.

The legal regulation of wills in Krakow began only after the approval by Sigismund I the Old of the city's municipal statutes (*Willkür*) in 1530.[134] These statutes included an article guaranteeing spouses full freedom when making mutual bequests and an article containing the rules that applied to burghers when drawing up wills. All forms of wills previously deemed acceptable were recognised; this included both 'open' wills – personally witnessed by members of the municipal council or municipal bench court – and 'closed,' sealed wills brought to the municipal authorities for validation, as well as both wills made by healthy individuals and those made on the testator's deathbed. All provisions that were not in breach of the law had to be fulfilled. If any of the will's provisions was held to be contrary to the city's laws or ordinances, then only these parts were to be declared invalid, while the rest of the will should be executed. Although these privileges allowed only for movables to be disposed of on one's deathbed, they also allowed for the bequeathing of sums of money which were secured with real estate located within the city, which in practice allowed for the disposal of real estate in wills. An exception was also made for wills drawn up during times of plague, when the municipal administration did not function normally. It was possible at such times to confess one's last will before two or three members of a guild or other respected and trusted persons. After the testator's death, the witnesses were then to certify the will before the municipal council or bench court. The canonical requirement for two or three witnesses was thus limited to exceptional situations such as periods when a plague was in the city. Other wills were to be authenticated by a municipal bench court or council. This secularisation of wills and the laws regulating

---

134 The principles for bequeathing property were regulated in Hungary as early as in 1440. For the seven most important royal cities a code of rights, the *Codex authenticus iuris taverni-calis*, was issued at that time. Among other provisions, it provided for considerable freedom in disposing of one's acquired property and transferring inherited property to one's wife and children; cf. *Codex authenticus iuris tavernicalis*, ed. Martin Georg Kovachich (Buda: Kilian, 1803), 221–235; Katalin Szende, *Testaments and Testimonies. Orality and Literacy in Composing Last Wills in Late Medieval Hungary*, in *Oral History of the Middle Ages. The Spoken Word in Context*, ed. Gerhard Jaritz, Michael Richter (Krems: Medium Aevum Quotidianum; Budapest: Dept. of Medieval Studies, Central European University, 2001), 51; *Prawa, przywileje i statuta miasta Krakowa (1507–1795)*, vol. 1, ed. Franciszek Piekosiński (Krakow: Akademia Umiejętności Krakowskiej, 1885), no. 43, 59–64. A later translation of this act was published by Karol Mecherzyński; *idem, O magistratach miast polskich a w szczególności miasta Krakowa* (Krakow: D. E. Friedlein, 1845), 199–211.

them was also evident in the last article concerning them, which imposed sanctions on those who sought to challenge legally drafted burgher wills. From this point on, such individuals were to be punished for violating common law.

The description of wills in Bartłomiej Groicki's *Titles of Magdeburg Law* [*Tytuły prawa magdeburskiego*, 1567] is accompanied by a reference to a gloss to Magdeburg Law (published by Nicholas Jaskier in 1535), which states that:

> Common law thus instructs how to make a will: When someone wishes to bequeath his goods, it is necessary that he should do so in good health, and that it should be written in the presence of seven witnesses, to whom he would declare his wishes and confer his trust. Such a decision shall have force, and the witnesses to his wishes shall testify under oath, if necessary, before a court or some municipal office.[135]

Groicki then notes that: "In the making of wills, Krakovians follow a different custom. For a will to be valid, it must be made before an open court [*sąd gajony*] or council office." He also states that:

> And in many other cities, and generally everywhere, a system circumscribing wills is followed, that it is not made before witnesses. And it is better and safer before an office than before witnesses. Because an office, regardless of what happens, usually records the testament in its books or keeps it in its coffers (if it is submitted closed) until the death of the testator. And so even if some of those in the office die, the testament will be realised by others working in the deceased's position. If witnesses or anybody else die, nobody can take their place.[136]

He later paraphrases the entire contents of Krakow's municipal statutes of 1530.[137] According to Krystyna Bukowska, "Groicki's contribution was popularising the legal customs and regulations in force in Krakow, including the municipal statutes of 1530, which brought important changes in the area of inheritance law. Perhaps it was due to Groicki's publication of the municipal statutes that they became a model for other cities, which is often emphasized by Krakow's higher court in its case law."[138]

---

135   Bartłomiej Groicki, *Tytuły*, 178–179.
136   Bartłomiej Groicki, *Tytuły*, 186.
137   Bartłomiej Groicki, *Tytuły*, 187.
138   Krystyna Bukowska, *Orzecznictwo*, 108.

THE INSTITUTION OF THE WILL   59

In codifications of laws in the fifteenth and sixteenth centuries, there is a clear shift in how authority and oversight is exercised in regard to wills. While in the fourteenth century, power was exercised under canon law by the bishop, who could threaten excommunication as punishment for those who challenged wills, by the end of the fifteenth century, this offence began to be treated as a violation of public law. Just as Raymund had done earlier in his *Summa*, Bartłomiej Groicki, in the article 'The Testamentary Item to Which the Law Belongs,' confirms that a will "made before any secular office does not belong to church law, no one should have to answer for such a will before an ecclesiastical court, but in this law there should be reasonableness before which the will has been dropped."[139]

By the end of the fifteenth century, the will, which had previously been a religious act, had become a secular act under secular authority. According to Magdeburg Law, the municipal council was still forbidden to issue laws affecting canon law,[140] which probably resulted in a lack of municipal statutes regulating the principles for making wills in the fourteenth and fifteenth centuries.[141] It was not until the first half of the sixteenth century that the customs concerning wills were confirmed in Krakow. This transformation took place gradually, and the process itself can be observed only by analysing a broad span of time over two centuries. However, a more complete adoption of the principles of Roman law in the early sixteenth century enabled secular authorities to normalise the rules concerning wills in the light of common law (*ius commune*). It also made it possible to assert control over those legal acts that were often used to transfer both huge sums of money and large parcels of urban real estate, whose fate (and especially the taxes paid from them) for understandable reasons aroused particular concern among the municipal authorities. The rivalry between the Church and municipal authorities over the supervision of wills can be seen in the statutes of other cities in the region, for example, the Poznan municipal statutes. Even before 1462, it was forbidden for burghers in the city to make last wills in an ecclesiastical court (*iudicium spirituale*) on

---

139   Bartłomiej Groicki, *Tytuły*, 190.

140   "Was geistlich recht antrit und wertlich recht nicht ruret, do mogen sy nicht willekure uff seczen"; *Die Magdeburger Fragen*, ed. Jacob-Friedrich Behrend, Berlin 1865, I, I, II, as cited in Michał Patkaniowski, *Krakowska rada miejska w średnich wiekach* (Krakow: Towarzystwo Miłośników Historii i Zabytków Krakowa, 1934), 115.

141   The nature and the scope of the privilege the municipal council of Krakow refers to in the will of Gotfryd Fattinant are unknown: "secundum tenorem literarum Ciuitatis priuilegiarium"; KDWac., vol. 2, no. 396, 182–185 (1393).

60   CHAPTER 1

pain of a penalty of 100 grivna,[142] and in 1540, it became illegal to draw up a will with the help of public notaries, who were most often members of the clergy.[143] A similar rivalry is reflected in the decrees of the municipal council of the Hungarian town of Sopron. According to a municipal statute from 1418, wills made in the presence of clergy (as witnesses) were no longer to be considered valid.[144]

5   Property Bequests and Canonical Wills in Fourteenth-Century
      Krakow

The earliest known dispositions on the proper division of property after the owner's death, usually among members of the immediate family (i.e. *post mortem* donations), can be found on the first pages of the oldest surviving municipal book in Krakow. The oldest known testamentary disposition of this type was made by Wenzel Tschartek (Wacław Czartek) in 1302. He donated half of his house (*hof*) to his wife Juta, and the other half to his four children.[145] These donations reflect the gradual evolution of the rules concerning the right of ownership and the rules of inheritance and for making donations under Magdeburg Law.[146] The forms and names of these bequests varied. In German they were often referred to as *Schikung, Vormackung, Geschefft, Gestifte* or *Ordnungett*,[147] and thus by means of expressions that indicated their private,

---

142   "Item quicunque civis testamentum aliquod in agone sua, sive in sanitate sua, facere
      voluerit, ille non debet istud in iudicio facere spirituali, sed civili iudicio, coram con-
      sulate seu advocato et scabinis. Qui contra hoc fecerit, luet civitati centum marcas
      irremissibiliter"; *Wilkierze poznańskie*, vol. 1, *Administracja i sądownictwo*, ed. Witold
      Maisel (Wrocław–Warszawa–Krakow: Instytut Historii PAN, 1966), no. 59, 15–16.
143   "Testamente non coram officio civili, sed notariis publicis facta, irrita, inaniaque esse, a
      rege Sigismundo confirmatur"; *Ibid.*, no. 98, 31–32.
144   Katalin Szende, *Testaments and Testimonies*, 55.
145   "In disem selben dinge gab her wenzla Tschartek siner vrowe vern Iuten sinen hof halp,
      vnde daz ander halbe teil sinen kinden die her mit ir hat: claren vnde Nicolaus vnde
      Iohannes vnde Katherinen"; NKiRMK, no. 13.
146   Otto Loening, *Das Testament im Gebiet des Magdeburger Stadtrechtes* (Breslau: M&G
      Marcus, 1906), 23.
147   "Neben diesem aus dem römischen Recht stammenden Ausdruck testamentum kennen
      die deutschen Quellen des Magdeburger Rechtes eine ganze Anzahl deutscher Wörter
      für einseitige Verfügungen von Todes wegen. Am häufigsten findet sich der Ausdruck
      »bescheidung«, »bescheiden«. Ja es scheint, als ob dieser Ausdruck als technischer für
      testieren allein gebraucht worden ist; es ist mir jedenfalls keine Stelle bekannt, in der
      »bescheiden« auch von einer Vergabung gesagt wird. Ferner finden sich zur Bezeichnung
      von Testamenten Ausdrücke wie »schikung«, »vormackung«, »geschefft«, »gestifte«,
      »letzter wille«, »ordnungett« auch »seelgerethe« wird allgemein für Testament nicht nur

THE INSTITUTION OF THE WILL

semi-contractual nature. The books in which these bequests were made were referred to as *Gemächtebüche*.[148] Pious bequests not described in the sources as wills are described by means of expressions that still make reference to wills: *Letzte wille* 'last will'[149] and *Seelgerethe* 'bequests for the salvation of the one's soul.'[150]

Donations authenticated before a municipal bench court were used to transfer real estate to a spouse, children and, less frequently, to other relatives or the Church. It can be noted that, like Wenzel Tschartek's bequest, the oldest donations most often initially took the form of *inter vivos* bequests. Thus, in 1305, a woman named Merkelinne transferred her property to her four children before a municipal bench court.[151] A year later, a councillor known as Petzcholt von Rosenoue did the same, granting his two children 100 grivna each and half of his house.[152] Soon after, *post mortem* bequests began to appear in the oldest municipal book, the beneficiaries of which most often did not receive any inheritance from the wife's estate. For example, in three consecutive bequests made between 1314 and 1317, Tylus of Apkovicz, who was healthy in both body

---

für fromme Stiftungen verwendet. Auch Ausdrücke wie »bedenken« oder »geben an seinem letzten ende« oder »sin ding berichten« oder »setzen«, und andere mehr werden von einseitigen Verfügungen von Todes wegen gebraucht. Man darf jedoch nicht glauben, dass alle diese Ausdrücke nur für einseitige Verfügungen von Todes wegen angewendet werden. Wie man mit testamentum sowohl einseitige wie zweiseitige Verfügungen von Todes wegen bezeichnete, so verstand man unter den meisten der angegebenen Wörter ebenfalls nicht nur einseitige Verfügungen von Todes wegen. Viele von ihnen finden wir auch bei den Vergabungen wieder"; *Ibid.*, 34–35.

148 "Testaments- bzw. Gemächtebücher existierten hingegen in Städten des deutschsprachigen Raums wie Konstanz, Bern, Zürich, den österreichischen Kleinstädten und besonders Wien. Im Gegensatz zu der Überlieferungsform in Einzelurkunden bieten diese Testamentsbücher eine vollständige und lückenlose Dokumentation der Testamente eines bestimmten Zeitabschnitts. Neben diesen Formen der Testamentserrichtung sind vereinzelt Bürgertestamente in Notariatsregistern und Offizialatsakten überliefert worden"; Brigitte Klosterberg, *Zur Ehre Gottes und zum Wohl der Familie,* 45; cf. "Ein Großteil der Eintragungen im Gemächtebuch I bezieht sich auf innerfamiliäre erbrechtliche Auseinandersetzungen, welche dem Rat der Stadt Konstanz jeweils für einen strittigen Einzelfall zur richterlichen Entscheidung vorgelegt werden..."; Paul Baur, *Testament und Bürgerschaft,* 46.

149 E.g. SCAB. 7, fol. 82–83 (1450); 86 (1450).

150 E.g. CONS. 428, fol. 469 (1444).

151 "Die Merkelinne gap iren kindern ir erbe in einem voitdinge: pezolde vnde Thomas vnde Katherinen vnde Elsebeten, daz si alle glichen teil daran haben suln"; NKiRMK, no. 13.

152 "Petzcholdus von Rosenoue gab uf metzchen siner tochter den halben hof an des Borussen steynhuse, vnde darvber hundert march, vnde der ander tochyteren Elzben do bie den halben hof vnde hundert march, unde petere vnde hannus sinen Sunen dye hofe, do he inne voynnet, vnde ychlichem hundert march"; NKiRMK, no. 34.

62   CHAPTER 1

and mind – as the law required – transferred a home with a brewery to his wife Hedwig, giving her full right to dispose of it after his death.[153] Similarly, Michael Grebe bequeathed half of the family manor house (*curia*) to his wife Elczka, noting that if she died first, the property would remain at his disposal.[154] In a bequest from 1326 councillor Ulrich Tatar decided that in the event of his death, he would transfer to his wife Margaret his tenement building in Krakow, mines in Olkusz and all the other goods he owned in both of these cities.[155] Those townspeople who did not have natural heirs (i.e. children) often donated part of their property to the Church. Such a bequest was made in 1320 by Herman Kopka, who bequeathed half of his house to his wife, and half to the church "for the salvation of his soul."[156] In 1313, the butcher Ekel gave his wife his butcher's stall, which was to be sold after her death and the money used for religious purposes.[157]

In addition to the types of donations mentioned above, a new form of bequest appears in the book of the municipal bench court covering the years 1365–1376, the rapid proliferation of which may in some way be associated with the person of a notary named Nicholas and the operations of the municipal office.[158] These are so-called 'mutual donations' (*mutua donacio*), in which a husband and wife agreed on the reciprocal inheritance of property in the event of the death of one of them. The first bequest of this kind concerned the wealthy matron (*honoranda matrona*) Merlina Czeslarinne, who soon after her

---

153   "[...] iure hereditario publice resignauit taliter, quod Curiam predictam cum braseatorio et omnibus aliis attinenciis vendere possit et donare, cuicunque persone voluerit Et facere et dimittere cum dicta hereditate Et Curia, quidcumque sue placuerit voluntati"; NKiRMK, no. 290, 325, 455.

154   "Item Michael dictus grebe medietatem Curie sue videlicet illam partem, que es contra portam Visle, et insuper XXX marcas Grossorum domine Elczce sue vxori resignauit, sed si ipsa prius eo morietur, tunc predicta ad ipsius redire debent potestatem"; NKiRMK, no. 430, 431 (1317).

155   "Item feria sexta iudicium fuit in vigilia beati Stanislai (26. Septembris), tunc vlricus Tartharus coniugi sue Domine margarete Curiam suam et domum lapideam in Cracouia et omnia bona sua tam in ipsa cracouia, quam in ylcus cum foueis sachtis et omnibus partibus iure hereditario cum fundo resignauit taliter et sic, quam diu ipse viuit, dicta bona omnia in sua debent esse potestate"; NKiRMK, no. 847 (1326).

156   "Item feria sexta post conductum Pasce (n. Aprilis) iudicium fuit, tunc Hermannus dictus Kopka medietatem Curie sue tocius vxori sue resignauit, reliquam vero medietatem ad Ecclesias et ad alia loca et ad pias causas pro salute anime ipsius assignauit"; NKiRMK, no. 589.

157   Ekel then bequeathed half of his other slaughterhouse to his sister and her two children; NKiRMK, no. 284, 285.

158   This notary was involved in producing the first part of the collection of town privileges and statutes, drafted around 1375; cf. Bożena Wyrozumska, *Kancelaria*, 118.

THE INSTITUTION OF THE WILL   63

marriage to Jacob Tendirnal donated to him her house on Sławkowska Street, while he, in turn, bequeathed it to her *post mortem*.[159] Similar provisions soon began to be used in relation to all assets, as exemplified by an entry from 1371 in which Szczepan Oresnik bequeaths to his *Virtuosa domina* 'virtuous wife' Elizabeth and adult children all his movable and immovable goods, as well as six grivna to his not-yet-adult daughter (*puero*) Catherine as compensation. Elizabeth in turn bequeathed all these goods back to him in case she died before him. The contractual nature of this bequest is evidenced by an entry informing the reader of the issuance of two copies of this act.[160] Soon a simple formula for 'mutual bequests' was developed, which included a phrase about the exclusion from inheritance of all other relatives and family members not mentioned in the bequest.[161] These acts were a means of distributing goods and regulating their subsequent inheritance by a spouse (usually a wife), who after the disinheritance of other relatives, took possession of the entire estate. Some bequests briefly mention children, grandchildren or siblings to whom the spouse is to pass on a part of the property,[162] and sometimes there is an obligation to do so when a couple eventually have children.[163]

In sources from Krakow from the first half of the fourteenth century, especially in the oldest surviving Krakow municipal book,[164] the word 'tes-

---

159   "Honoranda matrona domina Merlina Czeslarinne, Peszcone de Sale pro tutore electo realiter et assumpto, presencialiter constituta domum suam ex opposito sancti Marci in platea Slaucoviensi fundamentaliter situatam Jacobo Tendirnal realiter et econverso dictus Jacobus domine Katherine uxori sue post mortem resignavit, interim tamen quoad vixerit wit illiusdem (esse) dominus atque heres"; SCAB., no. 15 (1365).

160   "Sczepan Oresnik omnia bona sua mobilia et immobilia, que habet vel fuerit habiturus, post mortem suam virtuose domine Elizabethconiuigi sue legitime et pueris suis resignavit, puero suo Katherine absolute VI mrc. Currentis monete eciam post mortem suam resignavit et econtra ipsa domina post ipsius mortem dicto suo marito omni modo, quo supra resignavit, et fiant due littere"; SCAB., no. 572.

161   E.g. "Nicolaus Gleywicz gladiator resignavit uxori sue omnia sua bona, exclusis omnibus amicis"; SCAB., no. 2227 (1396).

162   "Nicolaus Weydnow domine Margarethe conthorali sue in omnia bona sua hereditaria et mobilia equalem uni puerorum suorum post mortem suam tribuit porcionem, et si pueri morirentur, pars ipsorum ad dominam derivetur; si autem domina moriretur, extunc pars ipsius ad pueros devolvatur, exclusis omnibus amicis ipsius Nicolai"; SCAB., no. 2209 (1395).

163   "Niclos Jegirdorf et Dorothea ipsius Nico consors legitima, Johanne Czopchin sibi ibidem pro tutore recepto, omnia bona sua mobilia, hereditaria, que habent aut habituri fuerint, sibi invicem mutuo seu alterutrum, sub submissis condicionibus resignaverunt ita, si sine prole decederent, si autem pueros procrearent, tunc pueri consimilem porcionem debent habere et possidere, premissis non obstantibus"; SCAB., no. 1671 (1393).

164   This book contains entries from 1300 to 1375, but in the 1350s the number of entries decreases significantly, to just a few entries per year; NKiRMK.

64   CHAPTER 1

tament' occurs just a few times, usually in reference to the fulfilment of the
provisions of the will of the deceased. Nevertheless, among the other entries
in the book there are a fairly wide variety of property ordinances. It is clear
that for the burghers living in Krakow during this period, the term 'testament'
meant a pious bequest *ad pias causas* – for the salvation of the soul.[165] In this
regard, the form used in the oldest preserved will, that made in 1303 by a Krakovian burgher woman named Sulisława, is characteristic.[166] In both its form and
content, it represents an excellent example of a canonical will. It begins with
the invocation *In nomine Domini Amen,* followed by a formal legal statement
about the health and soundness of mind of the testator and then her disposal
of selected elements of her property, including a pious bequest for the rent
from a butcher's stall and a bread stall to be donated to benefit Franciscan and
Dominican monasteries and to fund the construction of the parish Church of
St. Mary for salvation of her soul and the souls of her family members.[167] In
order to better secure these bequests, she appointed as executor of the will the
Vogt of Krakow, Albert (who due to his public function had certain benefits
granted to him and his family). To make the document itself "unquestionable
and inviolable," the seals of both the Dominican convent, the guardian of the
local Franciscans, and of the municipal councillors were secured to it.[168]

Sulisława's will is extremely valuable not only because of its early date, but
also because it has been preserved in its original form. Although it is the only
fully preserved burgher testament from the first half of the fourteenth century,
it can be assumed that other wills drawn up by wealthy Krakovian burghers
were probably similar in form, both before and after 1303.[169] As has already

---

165   "The terms 'testament' and 'testamentum' as used in medieval sources have different
        meanings, in the general sense as dispositive documents, less frequently as ordinances
        of the last will, and more often as bases for the salvation of the soul"; Bogdan Bobowski,
        Kultura materialna, 20.

166   KDMK, vol. 3, no. 368, 493–494.

167   Bożena Wyrozumska, *Kancelaria*, 89–90.

168   "Vt autem hec ordinacio firma et inmobilis perseueret, presentem literam sigillis Religio-
        sorum virorum, videlicet prioris ordinis predicatorum, Guardiani ordinis minorum et
        honorabilium virorum ciuium cracouiensium feci roborari. Acta sunt hec in cracouia,
        Anno domini M.CCC. tercio, XIII kalendas Ianuarij"; KDMK, vol. 3, no. 368, 493–494.

169   "Die Geistlichkeit ist maßgeblich daran beteiligt, daß die Testamente auch in der Laien-
        welt Eingang finden. Die Vermächtnisse der Nichtgeistlichen lehnen sich in ihrer Form
        an die Klerikertestamente an. Wie diese sind sie im 13. Jahrhundert als Siegelurkunden
        ausgefertigt. Die Fülle der Testamenturkunden von Kleriker- wie von Laienseite setzt mit
        dem Beginn des 14. Jahrhunderts ein. Während die frühesten mittelrheinischen Laientes-
        tamente die Form der Siegelurkunde aufweisen, wählen die Kölner Bürger, die erst seit
        1300 testieren, zur Errichtung testamentarischer Verfügungen anfangs ausschließlich die

THE INSTITUTION OF THE WILL

65

been mentioned, the word 'testament' also appears in the oldest municipal book – albeit only nine times – each time in the context of bequests in opera pietatis.[170] In one bequest from 1313 we read that the son of the Krakovian councillor Henry of Racibórz divided his estate and gave half of his movable and immovable property to his wife and brother-in-law, while he described his donation of five 'bread stalls' (i.e. stalls on which bread was sold) to a Krakow hospital as a bequest for the salvation of his soul.[171] A will from 1321 includes a similar statement. Before going on a pilgrimage to Rome, Alusz, the widow of an alderman named Otton, made a last will before the court "for the salvation of her soul," in which she donated the significant sum of 32 grivna to St. Mary's Church, St. Stanislaus at Wawel Church, and *ad opus Ecclesie* of the Dominicans, as well as to a hospital and her brother Nicholas, who worked in it.[172]

Form der Schreinseintragung, d. h. die Eintragung in die Bücher des Schöffenschreins. Das ist verständlich, wenn man bedenkt, daß die Schreinseintragung die seit über 150 Jahren gebräuchliche und daher geläufige Form für jede Art von Verfügung war. Erst allmählich gehen dann auch die Kölner Bürger zum Gebrauch der Siegelurkunde über"; Gabriele Schulz, "Testamente des späten Mittelalters aus dem Mittelrheingebiet, 5–6; Walter Hoffman, Deutsch und Latein im spätmittelalterlichen Köln. Zur äußeren Sprachgeschichte des Kölner Geschäftsschriftums im 14. Jahrhundert," *Rheinische Vierteljahrblätter* 44, 1980, 146.

170   Henryk of Racibórz, NKiRMK, no. 286 (1313); Tymo the old, NKiRMK, no. 358 (1316); wife of Henryk Srolle, NKiRMK, no. 411 (1317); Wilhelm of Orient, NKiRMK, no. 477, 487 (1318); Alusza, widow of Otton, NKiRMK, no. 616 (1321); Konrad the brewer, NKiRMK, no. 750 (1325); Hedwig (*Heze*) the stallholder, NKiRMK, no. 1537 (1344); Paszko the salt mine owner, NKiRMK, no. 1692, 1693 (1361); Arnold de Caucina, the nuncio and papal collector, a scholastic from Krakow, NKiRMK, no. 1707 (1375).

171   "Item in eodem iudicio contestato Henricus dictus de Rathibor suam medietatem bonorum omnium inmobilium tam in civitate Cracovia, quam extra civitatem suo sororio Henconi dicto Vinrich civi Cracoviensi dedit, assignavit et resignavit cum fundo iure hereditario possidendam, cum universes fructibus ac pertinenciis quod cum bonis eisdem facere ac dimittere debeat, quidquid sibi placet. Item idem Henricus medietatem suam bonorum omnium mobilium sue consorti domine Marusse in eodem iudicio contestato dedit, assignavit et iure proprietatis resignavit, quod cum bonis eisdem mobilibus facere et dimittere debeat, quidquid sibi placet.Item idem Henricus pro salute anime ipsius testamentum faciens, legavit quinque bancas panum ad hospitale in Cracovia"; NKiRMK, no. 286.

172   "Item domina Allussa relicta Ottonis quondam Ciuis Cracouiensis, dum Romam ad limina beatorum Petri et Pauli apostolorum pergeret, in predicto Iudicio prouinciali tale pro salute anime sue testamentum fecit: Legauit igitur ad Capellam beate marie Virginis in Ciuitate Cracouia pro fabrica Grossorum denariorum XX marcas, Item legauit ad opus Ecclesie beati Stanizlay in Castro Cracouie Grossorum denariorum quatuor marcas, Item Legauit ad opus Ecclesie ffratrum Predicatorum quatuor marcas, Item Legauit infirmis ad hospitale denariorum grossorum tres marcas et Ibidem ffratri Nycolao vnam marcam, Et omnes agros suos, quos habuit ante Ciuitatem Cracouiam cum vniuersis vtilitatibus ac

66 CHAPTER 1

The identification of religious bequests with wills is also clearly visible in an entry from 1344 by a stall-owner named Heze. In it she obliges one of her daughters to pay 20 grivna "for testament" in return for the house she has received as her dowry, a requirement that should most certainly be understood as a pious bequest for the mother's soul.[173] Similarly, in other entries concerning the fulfilment of the wills of Krakovian burghers, the term 'testament' always indicates a bequest to a religious institution.[174] The majority of such acts, as in the case of Sulisława's will, which was stored in the archives of the Franciscan monks in Krakow,[175] were written down in the form of a document, in the presence of representatives of the churches and monasteries who authenticated them with their seals and gave the church's sanction to the decisions contained in them. Both the negligible number of such surviving wills, and negligible references to them in municipal books before the 1390s, as well as the custom of describing with the word 'testament' acts containing pious bequests for the salvation of the soul, suggest that other bequests of last will from that time which have not been preserved were most often made in accordance with the principles of canon law and were only occasionally additionally certified before the municipal court.[176]

---

prouentibus, Hanconi filio sue sororis in predicto resignauit Iudicio, Quod si reuersa non fuerit, quod extunc infra quatuor annos soluere debeat dictum testamentum de bonis adque agris predictis ad loca prescripta et ad Ecclesias memoratas"; NKiRMK, no. 616.

173   "Eodem Anno diuisio hereditatum et bonorum inter pueros Heze Institricis sane mentis facta erat, ita quod Katherine filie eiusdem cessit domus, que est sita contra predicatores, pro sua sorte taliter, quod eadem Vnica XX marcas grossorum daredebet pro testamento de eadem domo. Insuper dicta Katherina cum Marito et pueris eiusdem coram Consulibus et Iudicio Bannito abrenunciauit omni iuri, quod in alijs hereditatibus, rebus mobilibus habere possent, ita quod Salmiam Sororem eius et pueros Thome fratris eiusdem in hereditatibus et rebus mobilibus decetero nunquam inpetere debeat verbo penitus neque facto, sed ab eadem Katherina ab omni inpeticione liberi esse debent in antea et exempti in perpetuum"; NKiRMK, no. 1537.

174   For example, Marusza, the widow of alderman Wilhelm of Orient, said before the municipal bench court that her husband had made a will where he provided that one *grivna* of the annual rent for half of his manor house at Shoemaker's Street was to be donated to St. Mary's Church to fund candles, for the salvation of his soul; NKiRMK, no. 477, 487 (1318).

175   The Archive of the Province of the Franciscan Order in Krakow, ms G-I-2; cf. Dariusz Karczewski, "Miejsce krakowskiego klasztoru franciszkanów w strukturze czesko-polskiej prowincji zakonnej," in *Mendykanci w średniowiecznym Krakowie*, ed. Krzysztof Ożóg, Tomasz Gałuszka, Anna Zajchowska (Krakow: Esprit, 2008), 89.

176   This practice is evidenced indirectly by an entry in the Głogów municipal book from around 1386, according to which a person lying 'on their deathbed' could decide for himself whether to make a pious bequest before a priest or a secular court.: 'Der an sich

THE INSTITUTION OF THE WILL   67

The first known testament from Krakow, made from the testator's death
bed, was that of Paulino Cavallo (also known as Paszek), a Genoese-born councillor in Krakow and administrator of the Bochnia salt mines (1344–1358).[177]
His bequest was the first – and for some time the only – evidence of the later
practice of deathbed wills being drawn up in the presence of two or three
councillors called as witnesses.[178] The councillors, perhaps being aware of the
uniqueness of the situation, gave a detailed account of the circumstances in
which it occurred: "Councillor Paszek, being in ill health, requested that two
councillors come to him immediately, God willing, before whom he could make
his last will and testament. And two councillors came to him, Peter Winryk
and Nicholas Edeling, and witnessed his last will and testament, written and
sworn by Paszek on his oath and faith."[179] Afterwards the councillors recorded
the full text of the will "made in the moment of his death," in which Cavallo
distributed part of his possessions, making generous bequests to his relatives
and servants, and to clergy members, a hospital, and churches in Krakow. The
religious character of this will is indicated by, among other things, the fact that
there is no mention in these bequests of any of the properties he possessed,
which would have been due to the deceased's wife and children. This omission
suggests we may consider this will as a kind of 'canonical will,' made already
in the presence of city authorities and not representatives of the Church, what
was against the canon law.

The few mentions of testaments from the latter half of the fourteenth century up until the early 1390s continue to show that the testament was understood as a pious bequest made by a healthy man or woman in the municipal
court or before clergy from the churches and monasteries that were to receive

---

     bette todlich zelgerethe mag doz billichvorgangk in geystlichim rechte oder in wertlichim
     rechte'; za: Karol Koranyi, *Podstawy średniowiecznego prawa spadkowego*, 115.

177   Józef Piotrowicz, "Żupy krakowskie w pierwszych wiekach rozwoju, od połowy XIII do
     połowy XVI wieku," in *Dzieje żup krakowskich*, eds. Antoni Jodłowski et al. (Wieliczka:
     Muzeum Żup Krakowskich Wieliczka, 1988), 118; Marcin Starzyński, *Krakowska rada*, 233.

178   It can be assumed that the testator, who came from outside Krakow, played a significant
     role in this case.

179   "Pasco Zupparius protunc Consul rogauit instanter, ut dei intuitu duo de Consulibus ad
     ipsum venirent, qui interessent suo testamento et sue vltime voluntati, quod facere vellet
     in eadem infirmitate, Et constitutis apud eundem Pasconem duobus Consulibus, vide-
     licet Petro Winrici et Nicolao Edlingi talem suam vltimam voluntatem et testamentum
     conscriptam et factam per ipsum Pasconem sub Iuramento et fide protulerunt et ordi-
     narie conscriptam pronunciauerunt, ut subsequitur in hec verba"; NKiRMK, 1692 (1358).

68   CHAPTER 1

the bequest.[180] Apart from just one disposition,[181] the other mentions of testaments merely concern the fulfilment of their provisions,[182] or disputes arising from them.[183] A dispute between the three daughters of the late councillor Alex of Racibórz provides an indirect example of this practice.[184] The daughters were not only to divide up the large estate left by their father, carry out renovations on the family house, and distribute the items contained within it, but also collectively to fulfil the dispositions left by him in his will. As can be deduced from the content of these bequests, he ordered the repayment of a debt of 20 grivna he owed to his deceased sister, and bequeathed 75 grivna to establish an annuity payment for a chapel in St. Mary's Church.[185]

Another will, dated 1393, states explicitly that it was drawn up by an ailing man in the presence of Krakow municipal councillors, who had been called to him. This was the bequest of last will made by Gottfrid Fattinante, an administrator of the salt mines in Bochnia and Wieliczka, who, like Cavallo, came from distant Genoa.[186] At the beginning of the testamentary bequest,

---

180   The existence of this form of the will is indicated by a entry in the books of the Krakow municipal bench court from 1392 that mention Elena and Masza's claim to the household equipment and personal belongings (*omnia supellectilia rade dicta*) of their deceased sister Catherine (Czenke Katusze). However, their lawsuit was dismissed and the goods remained in the hands of Martin, the parish priest of Bodzanów, the executor of the deceased's will, who was to settle her debts and allocate the remainder of her estate to *opera pietatis*; SCAB., no. 1482 (1392).

181   There is a mention of seven *grivna* left in the 'trusted hands' (*ad manus fideles*) of Margaret Crenczlarinne by Margaret, 'mother-in-law of Nicholas Wronche,' who was about to embark on a pilgrimage to Rome, and in the event of her death, her son and daughter were to receive three *grivna* each, while one *grivna* was to be donated for the salvation of her soul; SCAB., no. 218 (1367).

182   SCAB., no. 933 (1374), 937 (1374), 1064 (1375), 1109 (1375), 1445 (1392), 1546 (1392).

183   SCAB., no. 1122 (1375), 1243 (1376), 1309–1311 (1391), 1502 (1392).

184   The fact that the testator Allexius was in fact the Krakow councillor Alex of Racibórz is indicated both by the years he held this function (1375 and 1379), the enormous estate listed in his will, including the tenement building at the Krakow old market square, and the fact that his sister Margaret was married to the wealthy Krakow councilor John Dobschicz, whose will was registered in the books of the municipal bench court; SCAB., no. 1309–1311 (1391), 2093 (1395).

185   "Item Hildebrandus notarius civitatis et Mathias Arnsberg presencialiter constituti recognoverunt publice, quomodo pueri seu filie condam Alexii videlicet A[gnes], B[arbara], illas quinquaginta marc, quas dictus olym Allexius in suo testamento pro capella ad beatam Virginem pro censu assignavit, in tribus partibus suis domus acialis eiusdem condam Allexii earum patris tenentur"; SCAB., no. 1311 (1391).

186   He came to Krakow from Genoese Kaffa on the Black Sea, where part of his family settled; cf. Józef Garbacik, *Gotfryd Fattinante*, in PSB, vol. 6 (Krakow: Wrocław–Warszawa–Krakow: Polska Akademia Nauk, Polska Akademia Umiejętności. 1948), 377–378.

THE INSTITUTION OF THE WILL

69

three councillors and a municipal notary testify that they had come to Got-tfrid at his special request to bear witness to his last will.[187] After making a number of bequests, Gottfrid chose as the executors of his last will (variously, in Latin, *procuratores, factores, actores et executores legitimos atque certos*) a doctor of Canon and Roman laws, Bishop of Krakow Peter Wysz of Radolin, Voivode[188] and Starost[189] of Krakow Spytek of Melszin, as well as "all present and future" Krakow municipal councillors. The will ended with an invocation by the councillors asking God to support them with his divine justice and mercy and noting that they had affixed the city seal to authenticate the document.[190] In this way they verified all the bequests contained in this document, which covered all of Gottfrid's assets. The councillors referred to an unspecified Krakow privilege to legitimize their actions – "written privilege of the city" (*literarum Ciuitatis priuilegiarum*).[191] This will was accepted by the councillors

---

187 "Nos Consules Ciuitatis Cracouiensis recognoscimus, quibus expedit, vniuersis, quod coram nobis, dum ad certum congregati fuissemus consilium, prouidi Nicolaus Bothmer, Nicolaus Sapnig et Nicolaus Dambrow nostri consortes consilij, necnon Petrus nostre Ciuitatis predicte Notarius, fideles et dilecti presencialiter constituti, sub fide et iuramento ipsorum infrascripta recognouerunt, pronunciauerunt et vniformiter protulerunt publice et expresse, quod cum auctoritate ofiicij consulatus nostri Famosum virum dominum Gottfridum Fattinantem de Ianua nostrum conciuem ex sua vocacione et rogacione speciali, vt sue voluntatis vltime disposicioni attendentes accessissent, idem Gottfridus licet debilis aliqualiter corpore, multa tarnen bona perfluens racione, voluntatem suam vltimam perpetuo duraturam, testando ac perpetuo et libere legando expressit atque constituit in hunc modum. Idem Gottfridus licet debilis aliqualiter corpore, multa tarnen bona perfluens racione, voluntatem suam vltimam perpetuo duraturam, testando ac perpetuo et libere legando expressit atque constituit in hunc modum"; KDWac., vol. 2, no. 396, 182–185 (1393).

188 See Glossary: Voivode

189 See Glossary: Starost

190 An entry from 1393 concerns the execution of this will by Sułek, who acted as a bishop's prosecutor, and the voivode and castellan of Krakow Spytko of Melsztyn. Further mentions of its execution in 1397 and 1398 can be found in the council book; SCAB., no. 1720; CONS. 427, fol. 166.

191 "Propter quod prefatus Gottfridus, prout predictorum presentis testamenti pronunciatorum relacione didicimus, nobis supplicauit pure ac humiliter propter Deum, quatenus diuine iusticie et misericordie intuitu presens suum testamentum ad maioris certitudinis euidenciam nostre ciuitatis authentico, sub quo omnia ratificata et confirmata et presertim legata et testata inconvulse secundum tenorem literarum Ciuitatis priuilegiarium perseuerent, ratificare, approbare et confirmare benignius dignaremur. Nos vero diligenter ac maturo inter nos tractato consilio, considerantes peticionem suam presentem fore iustam et honestam, angelis gratam, atque rem ipsam, pro qua petitur, ad laudem et honorem summi et omnipotentis Dei matrisque eius benedicte ac sanctorum Anthonij et Dorothee, de quibus supra, gloriosius pertinentem, perpendentesque nihilominus vniuersa omnia et singula suprascripta per premissum Gottfridum racionabiliter fore facta,

70   CHAPTER 1

for "the greater glory of God, His Mother and Saints Anthony and Dorothy"; it was also approved by the Bishop and Voivode, and was stamped with the city seal. It was thus fully secured against any attempt to overturn its provisions. This will testifies both to the expansion of burghers' rights to distribute their property, and to a new practice among wealthy Krakow burghers of making wills on their deathbeds in the presence of municipal councillors. From this point onward, the municipal council would increasingly encroach onto the competences of priests, who, in accordance with canon law, were at that time responsible for the protection of wills. It can be assumed that in the 1390s wills in Krakow lost their former religious character and changed from the 'canonical will' into something that can be described as a 'communal will.' It seems not to have been a coincidence either that the first two known wills drawn up by infirm individuals in the presence of municipal councillors belonged to influential mining officials (*żupnicy*) who had come to Krakow from Genoa. Although we know of no other wills from that period, it seems valid to hypothesize that wealthy Italians had a major influence on the evolution of testamentary practices in Krakow. The end of the fourteenth century was also in general a period of rapid change in the culture, economy and society of Krakow. It was a time of dynamic economic development in the city, and rapid influx of immigrants, the widening participation of burghers in written culture, and the growing influence of the Krakow municipal council, which was gradually trying to expand its jurisdiction over church institutions functioning within the walls of the city and the religious life of its inhabitants.[192]

6   Emergence of the Communal Will in Krakow

The number of wills and testamentary dispositions from the early 1390s preserved in municipal books is roughly equal to the number from the previous nine decades. In part, this rise in the number of bequests can be explained by the state of the sources themselves.[193] Nevertheless, we can also speak about a

---

disposita, testata, legata ac deifice ordinata, eadem in omnibus suis punetis, clausulis et distinccionibus approbamus, ratificamus et sigilli dicte ciuitatis appensione perpetuo confirmamus"; KDWac., vol. 2, no. 396 (1393).

192   Jerzy Wyrozumski, *Dzieje Krakowa*, 314–391; Agnieszka Bartoszewicz, *Piśmienność*, 70, 146–147; Halina Manikowska, "Religijność miejska," in *Ecclesia et civitas. Kościół i życie religijne w mieście średniowiecznym*, eds. Halina Manikowska, Hanna Zaremska (Warszawa: Instytut Historii PAN, 2002), 29–30; Marcin Starzyński, *Krakowska rada*, 116–132.

193   Contributing greatly most to this situation was the fact that the book of the municipal bench court from the years 1376–1391 did not survive to the present day.

THE INSTITUTION OF THE WILL

qualitative change in the form and function of wills in the late fourteenth century.[194] In 1393, the complete texts of wills began to be recorded in the municipal books (initially in the books of municipal bench courts), and we can see from these records how their content was changing.[195] There was a noticeable reduction in pious bequests, which gave way to dispositions concerning the distribution of property between close relatives, such as those safeguarding the rights of widows and children, and those regulating the rules of inheritance by children from first and second marriages. These and other secular motivations are more visible in fifteenth-century wills. This does not mean that pious bequests for the salvation of the testator's soul disappeared from the bequests. They remained a permanent element of many, but seemed to play only a minor role in them. For example, in that same year (1393), it was decided in the will of the alderman and later councillor John Ederer that his first wife, if she remained a widow and managed the remaining property well, could dispose of it up until the end of her life.[196] However, if she was unable to manage the estate, care for it was to be taken over by guardians specially chosen for this task. Next, the testator, probably seeking to avoid family disputes, ordered that his son would assume control of his part of the estate only after the age of 24, and that his widow, if she re-married, would receive a dower[197] of 150 grivna. In the event that his son died before reaching the age of maturity, the part of the estate set aside for him was to be used to make pious gifts of 20 grivna for the construction of Mogiła Abbey's cloister and ten grivna for the construction of the Church of St. Mary. John's brother, in turn, was to receive 40 grivna, while the remainder of the estate would be distributed to support charity work at the discretion and will of the executors.[198] The purpose of this will seems for

---

194   "In the late fourteenth century, separate accounting books were created from general council books; it is likely that at that time village adminstrators began keeping their own records. The need to keep records of privileges and announced judgements motivated the production of collections of copied documents. In the early fifteenth century, a separate section for additions to municipal law was also created from council books, and a little later, wills began to be entered into a separate manuscript [rather earlier – B.W.]. The municipal administration grew along with the development of the city and the expansion of the agendas of the local government, which was taking on an increasing number of responsibilities."; Bożena Wyrozumska, *Kancelaria*, 127.

195   The first of these belonged to Nicholas Strelicz, an alderman who later became a councillor; SCAB., no. 1645.

196   Józef Mitkowski, *Jan Ederer*, in PSB, vol. 6 (Krakow: Wrocław–Warszawa–Krakow: Polska Akademia Nauk, Polska Akademia Umiejętności, 1948), 201–202.

197   See Glossary: Dower

198   "Johannes Oderer antworte eyn czedilpapir, dorin her syn testament vnd lecztin willin yn geschrebin hatte, daz noch wortin luth alsus: ab mich got czu synem gnadin neme

72   CHAPTER 1

the most part not to have been saving the testator's soul, but rather providing economic security for his loved ones. The majority of other wills in the 1390s and in the following decades were similar in this respect.

We also learn from the municipal books that these acts were now being recorded in a new way. In them 39 wills have survived from the seven-year period between 1393 and 1400. Fifteen of them state that they were copied into the municipal books after having been originally written down on sheets of paper (*cedula papirea*) brought to the municipal authorities by the testators or executors of the wills. Moreover, in five cases the original notes (*notule*) have survived,[199] having been pasted between the pages of a book of the municipal bench court.[200] These surviving loose sheets make it possible to compare the original contents with the entries made in the book. An analysis of them shows the municipal notary modified very little when he recorded them in the municipal book, his interventions typically being limited to a short Latin, or German,[201] introductory sentence providing information about the testator,

---

vnd mein weip yn erem wittwenstule blebe siczczin, so sal sy mynes guttis eyne vrawe bleybin mit sampt mynem kinde bis an ir ende, alzo daz sy rechenunge tue alle jar den vormunden von dem gutte; is das sy das gut bessert, so sullin is ir dy vormunde lossin, wo sy ys nicht enbessirte, so sullen is dy vormunden nemen czu en vnde sullen de mete des bestin nemen vnd sullin muttir vnd kinde ere notdorf douon gebin; ab myn zon gewuchse vnd sein teile des guttis welde habin, dem sal man nichtis gebin, her kome denn czu XXIIII jaren; ab myn weip eren witwinstul vorruckitte, so sal man ir gebin vor morgingobe vnd vor allis, das sy angesterbin mochte von mynes kindes wegin, andirhalp hundert mrc. breitir groschin, vnd ab vnser hirre mynen zon czu synen gnodin neme, was da guttis bleibt, das sullin dy vormunde gebin, XX mrc. czur Mogil czum gewelbe des crucegangis, vnd ab dy vormunde sehen, das sich myn brudir Sigemunt welde neren vnd sich wol anlisse, so sullin em dy vormunde gebin XL mrc. gr. breitir, vnd czum gewelbe vnsir Vrawin bescheide ich X mrc. gr., waz dorebir blebe, das sullen sy gebin czu stege vnd czu wege vnd armen luthen douon [...] vnd sy kleiden douon vnd [...] der barmherczigkeit douon czu tun, doczu kyse ich Rudolfum vnd Petrum Brigir desir dinge czu vormunde, ab ir eyner abginge, das der eyne eynen andirn kyse, als erste, als sich das geborit, vnd dy hirschaft dirre gobin behalde ich mir, dy weile ich lebe"; SCAB., no. 1676.

199   The will of councillor Nicholas Dambraw includes the following note describing this kind of testamentary provision: "Nota quod Hermanno zuppario data est una littera notule prescripte, item domine Dambrynne data est una littera"; SCAB., no. 2210 (1395).

200   SCAB. 3, fol. 106a, 106b, 106c (1393); 140a, 140b (1394); 168a, 168b (1395); 188a, 188b, 188c (1395); cf. Agnieszka Bartoszewicz, "Języki wernakularne w testamentach mieszczan krakowskich XIV–XV w.", KHKM, 61, No 2 (2013), 251–261.

201   E.g. "Stano Mochaw presentavit cedulam papiream ad iudicium sub hac form"; SCAB., no. 1654 (1393) or "Martinus Junge presencialiter constitutus, sanus corpore, compos racionis, testamentum suum seu ultimam ipsius voluntatem in quandam cedulam ydeomate teuthonico conscriptam, presentavit, cuius tenor sequitur et est talis"; SCAB., no. 1816 (1393);

THE INSTITUTION OF THE WILL

his mental and physical health,[202] and his right to dispose of the property.[203] This was followed by an accurate transcription of the contents of the *notula*, usually written in the first person, and occasionally in the third person.[204] The slight differences found are generally limited to misspellings. Some wills from the fifteenth century note that they were transcribed from sheets of paper brought before the court, but in these cases the original *notule* themselves have not survived.[205]

In contrast to earlier periods, a significant number of these entries (20) were made in German – the mother tongue of many Krakovian burghers.[206] This change reflects the influence of making literal transcriptions of *notule* into municipal books and of the anonymous figure of the municipal notary who produced them. It is interesting that in at least one case – that of councillor Nicholas Dambraw – the will was written by the testator himself.[207] Nevertheless, the form and content of the dispositions made in it do not differ substantially from other extant wills from that period.

This sudden popularization of wills (or perhaps only of the practice of entering them into municipal books) may have been related to two successive major jubilee celebrations in Rome in 1390 and 1400.[208] The desire to participate in these massive ceremonies, fed by the indulgences promised by

---

     "Johannes Ederer antworte eyn czedilpapir, dorin her syn testament vnd lecztin willin yn geschrebin hatte, daz noch wortin luth alsus"; SCAB., no. 1676 (1393).

202   "Martinus Junge presencialiter constitutus, sanus corpore, compos racionis, testamentum suum seu ultimam ipsius voluntatem in quandam cedulam ydeomate teuthonico conscriptam, presentavit, cuius tenor sequitur et est talis"; SCAB., no. 1816 (1393).

203   "Utrum cum singulis suis bonis elaboratis et ceteris possit facere et dimittere iuxta libitum voluntatis et est ita sentenciatum"; SCAB., no. 1645 (1393).

204   Eg. the will of Hanco Czartke; SCAB., no. 2069 (1395).

205   Eg. the will of Dorothy, wife of Stanisław Homan, SCAB. 4, fol. 71 (1412); Nicholas Morsztyn, SCAB. 4, fol. 143 (1416); Peter Putko, SCAB. 6, fol. 158 (1438); Peter Warzigarnek, SCAB. 7, fol. 100 (1450); Ursula, the widow of Eustace, a municipal notary "edidit ultimam voluntatem et testamentum suum tali modo ut sequitur ex scedula sua convocata in almanico wulgari scripta," LT, fol. 148–149 (1489) and many others.

206   SCAB., no. 1641 (1393), 1654 (1393), 1676 (1393), 1755 (1393), 1773 (1393), 1774 (1393), 1816 (1393), 1894 (1394), 1931 (1394), 2041 (1394), 2042 (1394), 2069 (1395), 2070 (1395), 2093 (1395), 2210 (1395), 2354 (1396); CONS. 427, fol. 149 (1400), 151 (1400), 152 (1400), 157 (1400).

207   "Nicolaus Dambraw testamentum suum in carta papirea manu sua propria ydeomate theutonico conscriptum presentavit, cuius tenor sequitur in hec verba"; SCAB., no. 2210 (1395). A piece of paper glued between the pages of the book containing the will and testament of this councillor has also been preserved, and, as indicated above, was handwritten by him; SCAB. 3, fol. 188a, 188b (1395).

208   Halina Manikowska, *Jerozolima – Rzym – Compostela. Wielkie pielgrzymowanie u schyłku średniowiecza* (Wrocław: Wydawnictwo Uniwersytetu Wrocławskiego, 2008), 7.

the papacy and encouragement from the Church to express religious zeal in this way, prompted some of Krakow's inhabitants to embark on a pilgrimage to Rome. We find traces of this decision in several wills from that time. In 1396, municipal councillors in Krakow established the first book of wills, which unfortunately has not survived to the present day. This year can be regarded as the point when the changing attitude towards these acts was formalised. This was also most likely when the municipal council introduced as a permanent custom the visits of councillors to ailing burghers in order to witness their last will. This was connected, firstly, with the assumption of powers previously exercised exclusively by the clergy, and secondly, with the recognition by the municipal authorities of the form of the will made in "the moment of death" (*in articulo mortis*), which was contrary to a municipal law prohibiting donations to be made by those suffering from illness. Wills written in the presence of councillors had numerous canonical features, i.e. they could be made only in the presence of three witnesses – a mayor and two councillors – by people already on their deathbed; in most cases their content was clearly secular, even when they contained pious bequests.

This newly created book of wills was referred to as 'Book of Wills and Dowers' (*Liber Testamentorum et Dotaliciorum*) in the accounts of the municipal expenditures for that year.[209] The fact that it was written and maintained by municipal notaries until at least 1410 is known from a short note that precedes Bartek Hofer's will, published in the Krakow council book that year.[210] Its later fate and the number and nature of entries it contained are unknown, but we can nevertheless draw some conclusions about its content from its title, *The Book of Wills and Dowers*. The title indicates a seemingly inexplicable link between such two very different acts as the provisions of a will and bequests of a dower due to a wife in accordance with the marriage contract concluded by spouses.

The explanation of this connection may be found in the content of the survived wills from that period. At the turn of the fifteenth century, almost all

---

209   Expenditures for 1396 on *Pretorij necessaria* included two entries: "Item pro pergameno comparato ad libros testamentorum et dotaliciorum II mrc. XVI½ gr. Pragen" and "Item pro ligacione librorum testamenti et dotaliciorum I mrc"; "Registra perceptorum et distributorum civitatis Cracoviensis annorum 1390–1393, 1395–1405 nec non 1407–1410," ed. Franciszek Piekosiński, in *Libri antiquissimi civitatis Cracoviae saeculi decimi quinti*, pars posteriori (Krakow: Akademia Umiejętności, 1877), 313.

210   "Testamentum Bartken Hofer – Wir Johannes Borg, Petir Vochsczagil, Hartlib von Cluczke," and in other handwritting – "vide in libro testamentorum"; cons. 427, fol. 371; Bożena Wyrozumska, *Kancelaria*, 92.

THE INSTITUTION OF THE WILL

wills contained provisions confirming and guaranteeing the fulfilment of the obligations contained in marriage contracts. These provisions included, above all, confirmation of the amount of the dower promised to the wife and the rules for the distribution of property between the spouses (and their descendants) in the event of either of their deaths. At the end of the fourteenth century, Krakow's municipal books contain testimonies suggesting that at least some of the wills were made shortly after a first or second marriage.[211] The reason for their creation and authentication by the court seems to have been primarily the need to legally regulate the new properties and changed social situations of all the interested parties. This is evidenced both by the structure of the bequests, which often begin with a detailed description of the situation of one spouse in the event of the death of the other, a designation of his or her part of the estate and the rules for inheritance, followed by the instructions on how to proceed if children are born from the marriage. In his will the Krakow alderman and later municipal councillor Nicolaus Strelicz bequeathed his entire estate to his wife; however, he also stipulated that if children were born, she would be given a rich dower and a part of the estate equal to that received by the children.[212] Peter Puczk did the same, specifying the amount his wife had brought into the marriage, but also stipulating that the sum she was to receive after his death would be reduced if they were to have children.[213] In some wills, it was expressed explicitly that the bequest was being made to safeguard the rights of the testator's second wife and the distribution of property between her, their future children, and the children from the first marriage.[214]

The husband's responsibility for his wife as the administrator of their shared property meant that the most important part of the marriage contract was determining the size of the dower to which the woman was entitled after her husband's death. Originally performed orally in the presence of witnesses, this act later assumed a written form, reflecting the expansion both of the

---

211 Brigitte Klosterberg also notes these similarities, see: *eadem, Zur Ehre*, 207; for a more detailed discussion of the subject see Jakub Wysmułek, "Wills as Testimony of Marriage Contracts in Late Medieval Krakow," in *Law and Marriage in Medieval and Early Modern Times, Proceedings of the Eight Carlsberg Academy Conference on Medieval Legal History 2011*, eds. Per Andersen, Kirsi Salonen, Helle Møller Sigh, Helle Vogt (Copenhagen: DJØF Publishing, 2012), 181–190.

212 SCAB., no. 1645; cf. Jacek Laberschek, "Mikołaj Strzelicz," in PSB, vol. 45 (Warszawa–Krakow: Polska Akademia Nauk, Polska Akademia Umiejętności, 2007), 16–17.

213 "[...] ab ich sturbe ane fruchte [...] adir ap uns got fruchte gibt mitenandir"; SCAB., no. 2354.

214 E.g. the wills of Martin Junge, SCAB., no. 1816 (1393) and John Michilwicz, SCAB., no. 2070 (1395).

municipal bureaucracy and the municipal authorities' powers.[215] These developments are reflected in the resolutions of municipal councillors. For example, municipal statutes on weddings from the latter half of the fourteenth century (1378 and 1397) state that "if a man gives his wife a morning gift [*morgengabe*], he should come four days earlier to the councillors with his fiancée, relatives or alone and have the gift recorded so that in the future what was intended would come to be, and there would be no disputes among the relatives."[216] A later Krakow municipal statute from 1468 renewing "city resolutions compiled from earlier sources," extended this period to eight days after the wedding day.[217] Although there are references in Krakow's municipal books to dowers as early as the early fourteenth century, and the first entry containing a bequest calling for a dower to be paid from the husband's estate dates back to 1338, this type of entry was extremely rare. Nevertheless, in the late fourteenth century we can observe an interesting phenomenon in the records of the municipal offices, as bequests for the payment of dowers began to be associated with the idea of the 'testament.' Starting around this time, information about the size of the dower and the rules for dividing the estate among the heirs became fixed elements of late medieval wills. A characteristic example of this is the will of the Krakovian patrician John Bozemecz, whose last will states merely that his wife was to receive one third of his estate as a dower after his death.[218] An analogous bequest was made by the tailor Dinek, who bequeathed one third of his house to his wife Elisabeth (in the presence of his sisters and Elisabeth's legal guardian).[219] Other wills from this period also deal primarily with the size of the dower and the regulation of the distribution of property after the death of the husband. They do not contain any pious bequests, nor were any written down on the testator's death bed.

---

215 Richard H. Helmholz, *Marriage Contracts in Medieval England*, in *To Have and to Hold. Marrying and Its Documentation in Western Christendom, 400–1600*, eds. Philip L. Reynolds, John Witte (Cambridge: Cambridge University Press, 2007), 260–286.

216 *Najstarszy zbiór przywilejów i wilkierzy miasta Krakowa*, vol. 2, ed. Stanisław Estreicher (Krakow: Polska Akademia Umiejętności, 1936), no. 15.

217 KDMK, vol. 2, no. 334.

218 "Johannes Bozemecz testamentum suum condidit in hunc modum, ita videlicet, quod domina sua Agnes pro dotalicio et omnibus aliis terciam partem in omnia ipsius bona hereditaria et mobilia habere debet post mortem suam et tenere, reservat etc."; SCAB., no. 1914 (1394).

219 "Dinko sartor terciam partem domus sue in plathea sancti Floriani circa domum Jlkusserinne, presentibus Katherina, Agnete et Margareta filiabus suis et pro Nicolao Wislicia consencientibus, pro dotalicio et omnibus aliis ipsam concernere valentibus Elyzabeth conthorali sue resignavit; reservat dominium"; SCAB., no. 2278 (1396).

THE INSTITUTION OF THE WILL 77

In the light of the observations above, we can conclude that there are clear similarities between 'testaments' written in the late fourteenth century and both acts concerning donations to be made "in the event of death," records of dowers, and mutual bequests drawn up in the fourteenth and fifteenth centuries by Krakovian burghers. As the concept of the will took shape during this period, it came to include a variety of previously separate and independent donations and bequests, which now assumed a new, unified form. An example of the typical form in which a burgher's will was recorded in a late-fourteenth century municipal book is the entry for John Michilwicz's last will from 1395, which contains, according to my own classification:

1. *The circumstances in which the will was written.* The first sentence (in Latin) states that the document was written on a sheet of paper in German.

This is followed by the text of the will, written in the first person:

2. *Provisions of the dower.* Information about the amount of money that should be given to his wife and about the movables (gerada) that belong to her.

3. *Donations outside the equal division of the estate.* There is a donation of 30 grivna to a daughter from a previous marriage, to be made from the property allocated for division.

4. *Principles for the division of property between children*: "if God will give him [further] children with this or another wife, if there will be one," the remaining goods will be divided equally among any new children and the previously-mentioned daughter. However, if no further children are born, then this daughter will inherit everything.

5. *Protection of the power of the executors of the will over the children.* If one or more children do not heed the chosen executors (*vormunden*), the latter have the right to disinherit them and spend their share of the assets on pious bequests.

6. *A donation in opera pietatis.* If the testator survives his children, the executors of the will shall be entitled to sell his inherited property and other goods, and to distribute the money received among the poor according to their wishes.

7. *Designation of executors.* The appointment of four executors, indicating that if one of them dies, "as often happens," the others have the right to choose another in his place.[220]

---

220   This classification is based on the present author's own research and observations. Although there are numerous exceptions to this classification due to the great variety of such acts, it reflects the new nature of testamentary provisions in the late fourteenth cen-

78   CHAPTER 1

This formula, like that found in many other wills, consisted of seven individual bequests, most of which could also be made in the form of a declaration of last will or a traditional donation. Such instructions, which were sometimes referred to (but not always) as wills, were also combined with 'mutual bequests.' An example of securing a dower with a mutual donation is a bequest of 30 grivna made by John Steynbach on behalf of his wife Clare, who also bequeathed to her husband all of her goods.[221] Mutual bequests were also combined with bequests in opera pietatis, such as that made by Hensil Clingner and his wife Elisabeth, who bequeathed all their goods to each other in the event of the death of one of them, noting that if both of them and all their children died, their property should be transferred to the Church.[222] There are also more extensive mutual bequests concerning the provisions for the

---

tury: "Johannes Michilwicz testamentum suum in cedula papirea conscriptum ydeomate teutonico presentavit, cuius dispositio testamenti sequitur in hec verba: Ich bekenne das ich Katherin meyner elichin husfrawen gemorgengobt habe XXX mrg., dy sal se nemen noch meynem tode von meyner varnden habe, dorczu ir gerade, dy ir mit rechte geboren mag, also verre, als se, mich obirlebt, auch gebe ich Margarethen meyner tochter, dy ich vor gewinnen habe mit meyner ersten frawen Dorothea genant, XXX mrc. groschin in meyn gut erbe vnde varnde czuvor vs czu hebin vor allir teylunge, doch also, wurde mir got kinder geben mit desen frawen adir mit andirn, ap ich dy haben wurde, das dy czukunftigen kinder mit der vorgenanten Margriten myn guth vnd meyn erbe czu gleichim teile nemen sullen, vs genomen dy XXX mrg. dy Margaretha czuvor vs hebin sal, auch also, ap das got fugen wurde, das ich abeginge vnde nicht me kinder lisse, wenne dy vorgenannte Margarite, so sal dy selbe Margaretha meyn erbe vnd meyn gut, das ich lossen wurde noch meynem tode, gancz vnde gar hebin vnd nemen, vsgenomen dy vorgeschreben XXX mrg., dy ich Katherinen meyner husfrawen gemorge(n)gobt habe, doch das mit namen doryn genomen, was ich kinder wurde lossen noch meynem tode, ap der eyns adir me desen nochseschreben vormunden nicht gehorsam wurde seyn, das dy selbin Vormunden irkenten, das meyn guth an em nicht bestat were, so sullen se volle macht haben deme vngehorsamen kinde seyn gut czu entwenden vnde das teil wenden an dy werk der barmherczigkeit noch willin der vormunden vnde ap ich nicht kinder wurde lassen noch meynem tode, so gebe ich desen nochgeschrebenen vormunden volle macht meyn erbe czu vorkawfen vnde andir myn guth vnd das gelt czu geben armen leuthin, wo en das allirbeste geballen wirt; des mach ich mechtige schaffer Swarczpeschken, Petrum Girhardisdorf vnde Kunczonem Habirgeyst vnd Johannem vom Skawin, also ap eyner abeginge, wy ofte das geschege, das dy andern mogen czu en kysen, wer en gefallen wirt, doch wil ich eyn herre seyn meynis gutis, als vor"; SCAB., no. 2070.

221 "Johannes Steynbach domine Clare contorali sue post mortem suam XXX mrc. monete tunc currentis pro dotalicio suo et omnibus aliis, ipsam concernere valentibus, resignavit et ipsa sibi omnia bona econverso"; SCAB., no. 2358 (1396).

222 "Hensil Clingner omnia bona mobilia et immobilia uxori sue Elizabeth post mortem suam resignavit et econverso domina dicta viro suo eadem bona resignavit taliter, quod si dicti ambo morirentur cum pueris eorum, eadem debeant bona ad ecclesias converti"; SCAB., no. 727 (1372).

THE INSTITUTION OF THE WILL

inheritance of property by children and in the event that a spouse remarried, which brought them closer in form to wills from that period.[223] An example of the merging of this new formula for acts of last will with a mutual donation is the will of Ursula, Henry Woger's wife, made before she set off on a pilgrimage to Rome. She bequeathed to her husband half of the house and all of the household items and personal belongings in it, one quarter of her house to 'Dorothy,' a belt maker (probably a relative), and the remainder of her property to the executors of the will to be used for acts of charity. According to the formula, she retained the right to change the provisions of the will and disinherit all her other relatives.[224] In return, Henry bequeathed to her after his death all his movable and immovable goods, and also excluded all of his relatives from his will.[225]

In the late fourteenth century, a visible change took place among Krakovian burghers in their conception of the nature of wills and the reasons for making them. According to Agnieszka Bartoszewicz: "In the 1390s, Krakovian burghers began to build a new bureaucratic machinery: documents, produced independently, were obtained from various offices and officials, collected, and submitted in institutions associated with municipal, land and canon law."[226]

---

223 "Nicolaus Hungerkaste requisivit, in sentencia [...]. Idem Nicolaus domine Agneti consorti sue legitime domum suam in plathea Hospitalis, circa domum Nicolai Bochner relicte, post mortem suam contulit et donavit, ita quod ipsa domina pauperibus hospitalis sancti Spiritus in Cracovia dare debet II mrc. annis singulis, quamdiu vixerit et in viduitate permanserit, tenendam et omnia bona sua mobilia et suppellectilia domus omniaque parafernalia, que rade wlgariter dicuntur, tali condicione, quod si bona mobilia [ita bona] quemadmodum ipsius domine dotalicium, quod idem Nicolaus recongnovit facere XXX mrc., non forent, extunc in hereditate predicta, ipsa domina predictum dotalicium poterit recuperare, si autem ipsa domina maritum duceret, aut permittente domino moriretur, extunc domus predicta ad proximos dicti Nicolai, prout de iure debet, devolvatur, qui singulis annis III mrc. dabunt ad hospitale predictum et hoc XXX annis, quousque dicta domus pro XC mrc. fuerit persoluta; reservat dominium"; SCAB., no. 1967 (1394).

224 "Vraw Ursula cziende ken Rome hot ir testamenth gemacht und bescheyd noch irem tode heynrich woger irem Wirte dy helfte ires heusis, wo sy ynne wonit. Und alle ire vorinde habe und geczew und gerethe und was des ist und Vrawin Dorotheen gorliczynne desselbin hausis eyn Virteyl, und das obengen. virteyl und eyn Werk das Bodyn helt, gibt sy und bescheidit hern Casparn Krugiln und Petir Wochsczagil, dy sy kore czu vormundin, das sy das wendin sullin in dy Werk der Barmheczigkeyt, als sy en getrewit. Und behielt ir dy herschaft, dyweyle sy lebit ane vrunde wedirrede, dy se allhy enterbit"; CONS. 427, fol. 151 (1400).

225 "Item derselbige Heynrich Woger hat der egenanten Vrawin Ursulen seynen elichen Weybe al seyn gut beweglichs uud unbeweglichs das her hot adir habin wirt, czu kunftigen czeyt noch seyme tode czu habin bescheyden und gegebin und enterbit alle seyne vrunde unde mogin, das si nichsincht dorezu sullin habin, noch do wedir reden"; *Ibid.*

226 Agnieszka Bartoszewicz, *Piśmienność*, 241.

80 CHAPTER 1

This phenomenon and the influence of notaries employed in the Krakow city registry were most likely the forces that led to a standardised formula for making acts of last will and pious bequests to be carried out after one's death. The burgher communal will that came into being in the late fourteenth century combined the prescriptions for: the bequest of a dower; donations to be given to selected family members, relatives and servants; a marriage contract designating the role and place of the wife after the death of her husband; pious bequests for the salvation of the testator's soul; and the selection of executors to carry out these bequests, with the power to decide about the deceased's children and property left in their care. Sometimes the communal will would include some kind of reciprocal clause in the form of a bequest transferring all property to the spouse.

These changes are part of a clearly visible process by means of which the Krakow municipal council assumed responsibility for, and control over, wills. The first information we have about the actions taken by the city authorities in this area comes from a municipal statute approved in 1342 by Casimir the Great. It stipulates that a seriously ill individual, or one going on either a distant or overseas journey or pilgrimage, could,[227] in the presence of three councillors, choose legal guardians for his underage children and transfer to them custody of his whole estate.[228] In this municipal statute there is no mention of testaments as such (which were still in general subject to canon law),[229]

---

227 A mention of pilgrimages, distant journeys and overseas travels indicates that a strong interest in its publication was expressed by city elites, who preferred to bequeath their considerable wealth to their friends and to local communities rather than to their relatives, who often lived far away; cf. Marcin Starzyński, "Patrycjat krakowski w aktach Kamery Papieskiej z XIV w. (ze studiów nad udziałem kupiectwa krakowskiego w międzynarodowym transferze finansów)," in *Elita władzy miasta Krakowa*, 333–378.

228 "Que Statuta, Constitutiones atque Arbitria predicta scribuntur in hec verba. Si contingeret, quod homo ita infirmus efficeretur, quod timendum esset de vita sua, vel si proponeret visitare limina sanctorum aut recipere se ad vias longinquas, vel ultra mare, Ille potest coram tribus Consulibus eligere tutores vnum vel plures pro pueris suis, vel pro propinquiribus suis amicis, qui etatem non haberent, et pro omnibus suis rebus mobilibus et immobilibus, quemcumque voluerit, sive sint amici vel Extranei, et hij debent habere plenam auctoritatem et posse, sicut ad hoc essent nati; Et quod idem infirmus sit circa bonam racionem. Et si propinquires illius vellent hoc destruere, non possunt, quousque pueri perveniunt ad Annos quindecim. Sed si femellam infra istos Annos nubere contingeret, tunc Maritus eius ipsius tutelam accipiet hoc statuto non obstante"; KDMK, vol. 3, no. 25.

229 This thesis was put forward by Bożena Wyrozumska, who believed this statute granted townsmen the right to dispose of all their property. Moreover, she states that: "The council appears to have displayed usurpatory tendencies, since it ruled that the last will could only be made before a councilor"; *eadem, Kancelaria*, 89–90.

THE INSTITUTION OF THE WILL

81

but it does mention the practice of the municipal council assuming custody of orphans and their inherited property. This municipal statute significantly limited the rights of more distant family members to be granted responsibility for non-adult relatives and their property, in favour of trusted individuals who were not necessarily related.

In the late fourteenth century, three important factors influenced the formation of the customs and laws that guided the making of wills over the next century. First, during this period wills began to be entered into the books of the municipal bench court and into council books in their entirety, using the wording found on the transcribed statements brought to court.[230] Second, the municipal council introduced the practice of authenticating wills drawn up in its presence,[231] and of having two or three councillors visit the infirm with a municipal notary in order to write down and secure dispositions of last will,[232] which may have been connected with the privilege invoked in the 1393 will of Gottfrid Fattinante of Genoa.[233] Third, the first book of wills was published, which has not survived to the present day.

The rights guaranteed by the councillors are likely to have been relatively new. In the will of councillor Nicholas Wierzynek the younger, drawn up in

---

230 Since the book of the municipal bench court covering the 1376–1390 period has been lost, it is uncertain whether this custom existed earlier; however, the beginnings of this practice is indicated by the fact that in the book of the municipal bench court for 1390–1397, townspeople's wills were first fully recorded only in 1393.

231 For example, the will of George Dubrawka was made in this manner in 1398. "Georgius dubrawka sanus corpore et racionis compos, testamentum suum in nostri presencia consilii disposuit in hunc modum, et primo domine hancze, conthorali sue racione ipsius dotalicii et ceterarum omnium porcionum ipsam in bonis suis concernenium equalem uni suorum puerorum tribuit porcionem. Et quamdiu ipsa hanca in viduitate sua permanserit, debet omnium bonorum dicti Georgii fore domina et eisdem utifrui. Constituit Petrum Kaldherberge bonorum suorum et puerorum tutorem, reservans dominium, quoad vixerit in humanis"; CONS. 427, fol. 106 (1398).

232 "Swantag polonicalis licet debilis corpore multum tamen bona perfruens racione in domo habitacionis sue coram dominis Iacobo Mordbir et Ioh. Puswange consulibus testamentum voluntatis sue ultime condidit in hunc modum, videlicet quod universa et singula bona sua hereditaria et mobilia, quibuscunque nominibus appellentur, que habet aut habiturus est quomodolibet in futurum, domine Barbare conthorali sue legitime post mortem suam habenda dedit, contulit et donavit, exclusis omnibus amicis suis et propinguis, quos de dictis bonis suis omnibus inibidem exhereditavit. Litera est data"; Ibid.

233 "Propter quod prefatus Gottfridus, prout predictorum presentis testamenti pronunciatorum relacione didicimus, nobis supplicauit pure ac humiliter propter Deum, quatenus diuine iusticie et misericordie intuitu presens suum testamentum ad maioris certitudinis euidenciam nostre ciuitatis authentico, sub quo omnia ratificata et confirmata et presertim legata et testata inconvulse secundum tenorem literarum Ciuitatis priuilegiarium perseuerent, ratificare, approbare et confirmare benignius dignaremur"; KDWac., vol. 2, no.396.

1426 before the council, it was noted that: "it is a privilege of the city that the testament and last will of anyone, regardless of how much he possesses, can be made before councillors with the same power and effectiveness as if it had been solemnly sworn before the municipal bench court."[234] In the same year, Margaret, widow of Nicholas Glezer, brought to the court "the complete and incontestable will of her deceased husband, with a seal affixed to it by municipal councillors, in which it was stated that this Nicholas Glezer, husband of this Margaret, made his testamentary dispositions before the councillors, in accordance 'with the privilege of the city' (*iuxta quod est privilegium Civitatis*)." [235] In light of the above, it seems convincing that in the early fifteenth century there existed a now lost privilege or municipal statute in which the municipal council of Krakow reserved the right to write down and authenticate the wills of burghers – acts which, according to a verdict by aldermen in Magdeburg, could only be carried out by a municipal bench court.[236] Perhaps we are again dealing with the same privilege invoked in Gottfrid Fattinante's will from 1393.

7   Open and Closed Wills in the Fifteenth Century

The social and cultural changes taking place in the fifteenth century, including the dynamic development of the municipal chancellery, and the initiatives introduced by councillors in Krakow, did not lead to the full standardisation

---

234   "Dominus Nicolaus Wirzing unus ex nostras presessaribus et senioribus consulibus plena sanitate integra tam in corpore quam mencie iuxta quod est privilegium Civitatis quod quidquod coram Consulibus sic quantumlibet eciam sorte habet esset vel totam vim et omne eandis efficaciam habere debet sicut si cum omni solempnitate coram bannito Judicio publice agetur fecit et disponuit in Consulatu testamentum suum sive ultimam voluntatem in hunc modum"; CONS. 428, fol. 231.

235   "Domina Margaretha relicta Nicolai Gleser posuit in Judicium literam testamenti eiusdem olim viri sui sanam et integram et omni prorsus suspicione carentem emanatam a dominis Consulibus Cracoviensis et sigillo appendenti eiusdem Civitatis sigillatam In quam ibidem plane et expresse continebatur quod dictus Nicolaus Gleser maritus dicte domine Margarethe testamentaliter eorum dictis dominis Consulibus disposuit iuxta quod est privilegium Civitatis"; SCAB. 5, fol. 121 (1426).

236   The Magdeburg court's judgements include a description of a mutual will made by two Krakow students that was to be executed in the event of one of their deaths, made before a municipal notary and witnesses "under canon law and custom." After many years, one of them married, and when the other one fell seriously ill, he went to him with councillors and witnesses to confirm the earlier agreement, which he did. After his death, however, the relatives of the deceased challenged the will, and the aldermen in Magdeburg confirmed that such a transfer could only be made before the municipal bench court; Michał Wiszniewski, *Historya*, 228–229; cf. Bożena Wyrozumska, *Kancelaria*, 90.

THE INSTITUTION OF THE WILL

of Krakow's testamentary practices. Although, due to the loss of the city's oldest book of wills, the number of extant acts of last will from the first half of the fourteenth century is unclear, the wills that were entered in the books of the municipal bench court and council books, or which have survived as a separate document, indicate that they continued to display a high level of diversity, both in terms of their function and content, as well as in the formula used. First, there remained a great deal of uncertainty as to what a 'testament' was and what rights were connected with it. This can be seen in, among other places, a bequest from 1405 made by the councillor Lucas Bochner before setting off on a long journey.[237] In the council book it is written that Lucas, being healthy in body and mind, chose two burghers as executors of his will, which he described as a *geschefte testament und zelgerethe,* that is, as a will in the form of secular dispositions and a donation for the soul of the testator. He also instructed the executors to carry out everything indicated for them to do in the will, which had been written down on paper and sealed. This bequest was therefore evidence of the making of so-called 'closed wills,' which were written by a public notary, a privately hired scribe or, occasionally, by the testators themselves, and then sealed and left for the executors to open before the municipal council or municipal bench court after the testator's death.[238] Examples of this practice can also be found in many other last wills from the fifteenth century. One characteristic example is an entry in the books of the municipal bench court in 1435 concerning the will of Jost the Bowyer. The aldermen testified that they had been visited by Paul the Bowyer, brother of the deceased, his widow Catherine and son Hensel, and three representatives of the bowyers' guild. From the text we also learn that the will was brought to the office by guildmasters and members of Jost's immediate family merely to have its contents authenticated before the court.[239]

---

237 "Lucas Bochner mit gezundem leibe und guter vornunfft hat gekorn gesaczt und gemacht dy erbarn Casparn Krugiln und Nicolaum Platener czu vormunden schaffern und zundirlichen vorwesern, alzo das se seyn gescheffte testament und zelgerethe, ab an em off dem wege icht geschege, vorwesen, volbrengen und schaffen sullen czutun und czulasen In allir mose und weyse, als se in eyme papirn brife den her en vorsegilt antwortin wirt, werden finden beschrebin"; CONS. 427, fol. 240 (1405).

238 Gabriele Schulz, *Testamente des späten Mittelalters aus dem Mittelrheingebiet,* 5–6.

239 "Bekant haben dy nochgeschrebene personen, daz Jost bogner seyn testament und leczten willen mit guter vornunft gemacht hot vor in nochlaute eyner czedil dy sy uns entwerten in gehegte bank, als, Paul Bogener seyn geborner bruder, Katherina seyne eliche hawsfraw, Hansel seyn son, Meistir Crebis der Bogener, Jungprews der bogener und Peter bogener, und haben dyselben seyne nesten, als seyn bruder, seyn son und seyne hawsfraw dasselbe Testament und schirkunge seyns leczten willens voryowortit gelibt geannemit und ofgenomen in allen stucken das von worte czu worte also lautit"; SCAB. 6, fol. 108 (1435).

84   CHAPTER 1

In most cases, testators who wrote down their wills (often with the help of a third party, perhaps an individual who dealt professionally with the written word, such as a municipal or public notary), out of fear of attempts to override their decisions, chose to certify them before the municipal bench court or council during their lifetime. This was the decision taken by John Wole who, being healthy in body and mind (as he himself declared) and in accordance with custom, asked if he could dispose of his non-inherited goods in accordance with his will,[240] and then presented his 'testament' written down on a sheet of paper to aldermen.[241] An interesting bequest in this respect is one made in 1435 by Nicholas Opoczko and his wife Dorothy. They gave each other a house at Sławkowska Street and all their other remaining goods, while excluding all other relatives.[242] On the adjacent page there is a full transcription of a mutual bequest in German, copied from a sealed letter. In it we read that Nicholas, being healthy in body and mind, asked if he could dispose of the non-inherited goods he had acquired in accordance with his will, since he had no children or other legal heirs, and that the court ruled that he could dispose of these goods, in accordance with the law. Following this was a mutual bequest of a house and other goods between a husband and wife.[243] These entries show both what

---

240   This recurring phrase may be not only a standard formula, but also a trace of some kind of official ritual.

241   "Hannus Wole bey guter vornunft und gesundem leibe frogte im rechtem ap her mit seynen wolgewonnen gute das in nicht anirstorben ist, tuen mag und lossen noch seinem bestin willenund do im das durch uns geteilt was, hot her seyn testament und in eyn czedil vorschreiben geentwert dy also laute"; SCAB. 7, fol. 32 (1448).

242   "Nicolaus Opoczka Dorothee uxori sue legittime, domum suum in platea Slavkoviensi sitam in qua manet et omnia alia bona sua mobilia et immobilia quecumque habet et que habebit resignavit, Excludens omnes et singulos suos consangwineos et amicos. Reservans sibi dominium quamdiu ipsi viverit. Similiter econverso ipsa domina Dorothea per Michaelem aurifabrum resignavit predicto viro seu marito suo legitimo omnia bona sua mobilia et immobilia quecumque habet aut habebit excludens omnes consangwineos et propinquos, et reservaavit sibi ipsa eciam dominium quamdiu vivet"; SCAB. 6, fol. 110.

243   "Der irbar man Nicolaus Opoczka unser mitburger keiginworticlich steende gesund des leibes und guter vornunft frogende im rechten ap her mit seym wolgewonnen gute das her mit seyns selbis erbt gewonnen hot und das in von nymande angeerbt noch andirstorben ist, tuen und lossen mochte noch seyme willen, so her keyn kind hot adir elichen erben dorczu, und von uns hir of sulche orteylliche bestetigunge horende, daz her das wol tuen mochte von rechtis wegen, hot of sulch unser ortil und bestetigunge seyn haws of der Slawkischen gasse in deme her wonet mitsampt alle andern seyme gute und habe erblich und farnde beweglich und unbeweglich, das her hot und ummer gewynnet keyns ausgenomen, der irben frawen Doroyhee seyner elichen hawsfrawen noch seyme tode czu haben erblich und mit volkomener macht czu tuen und czu lossen vorreicht und ofgegeben. Und slos aus und schid aus dovon gancz und gar alle seyne frunde, nesten

THE INSTITUTION OF THE WILL   85

a letter sealed by aldermen looked like, in this case one in which a burgher couple made a mutual donation, and indicate that municipal books usually contain abbreviated versions of the recorded acts. Other Krakovian burghers, such as John Phert, whose will was preserved in five different versions, also had their bequests authenticated. In an act confirmed before aldermen in 1445, Phert revoked his previous will and asked about his right to dispose of his acquired property. After obtaining a satisfactory answer, he handed over a sheet of paper with a new act of last will written on it.[244] Wills were also often authenticated in court by people going on a longer journey or pilgrimage, such as Michael Molner in 1444.[245]

A list of fees charged by the municipal notary for his services, entered into the pages of the council book in 1435, also indicates that the custom of councillors and (later) aldermen visiting the sick was a common practice. We find the following entry: "For going to [witness] a will – 6 groszy [*Wenn man geet czu Testamente 6 gr*]." This entry both confirms the municipal notary's participation in visits by members of the municipal council "to a will," and indicates that a slightly higher fee than usual was charged for writing the will down

---

     und mogen, und behild im dy herschaft dy weyle her lebit, und frogte ortil und recht. So her keiginwortig stunde und seyner hawsfrawen sulche gobe tete, und ir also ofgebe, ap is bund und kraft sulde haben, ader was do recht were, und dorof habe wir czu bestetigunge eyn sulch ortil und recht ausgesprochen, daz sint der czeyt daz her keiginwortig steet mit gesundem leibe und mit guter vornunft und mit wolbedochtem mute und seyner hawsfrawen ofgibt seyn haus und alle seyn gut als obene, und slewst aus dovon alle seyne nesten mogen und frunde, so sal is bund und kraft haben von rechtis wegen, und dy ofgobe enpfing dyseben fraw durch Michil Goltsmed unser mitbruder obgenanten den sy ir dorczu gerichticlich czu vormunde nam, und dokegen hot dyselbe fraw Dorothea durch denselben iren vormunden deme obgenanten iren manne Nicolao Opoczka hinwedir ofgegeben allis das sy hot adir ummer gewynnet is were beweglich adir unbeweglich, und wy man das genommen mochte noch irem tode czu haben, und slos aus dovon alle ire nesten mogen und frunde, und behilt ir ouch dy herschaft dy weyle sy lebt, und das ist abir mit ortil bewert, und durch uns bestetigilt alse recht ist noch forma des gerichtis als obene"; SCAB. 6, fol. 111.

244   "Hannus Phert revocavit testamentum quod prius fecit in tote et confecit aliud testamentum ut sequitur infra. Hannus Phert gesund des leibes und seyner vornunft steende, frogte umb ortel und recht, ab her mit seyme direrbtin und wolgewonnen gutte tuen mochte und lossen noch seyme willen do wart em gerichtlich ausgesprochen daz her tuen mochte und lossen noch seyme direrbtin und gewonnen gutte noch seyme willen. Do legte her vor uns in gehegte ding eyne czedil, dy von worte czu worte lauth also"; SCAB. 6, fol. 342.

245   "Michil Molner unsir miteburger gesunt seynes leibis mit gutter vornunft wellinde besuchen dy heiligen Czwelfboten sinte Peter sinte Paul czu Rome seyn Testament und lecztin willen beschreben in eyner czedil hot nedirgelag, dy von worte czu worte lauth also"; SCAB. 6, fol. 321.

86 CHAPTER 1

in the patient's home. In other articles of the municipal statute, it is stated that the municipal notary is entitled to one *grosz* for an entry made before the municipal bench court and four groszes for a letter written on parchment before the municipal bench court or council, unless it is a letter containing a privilege or a 'large will' (*grosse Testament*), for which a larger sum of money could be collected.[246]

The list of notarial fees from 1435 suggests that the term 'large will' was used in reference to wills made in the form of documents written down on parchment and often stamped by city authorities. The few wills preserved in this form clearly reveal their religious character, and that their form was still strongly influenced by that of the 'canonical will.' This is most clearly visible in Claire Rolle's will from 1419.[247] Written down on parchment by the public notary John Stolle of Głogów,[248] 'the will' (*tabula testament*) begins with the invocation [*I*]*n nomine Domini amen,* which, apart from in this will, appears only in Sulisława's will from 1303 and in the testaments of clergy members, such as that of the Krakovian presbyter Theodoric Weinrich, written in 1449.[249] Next, the date was placed in accordance with the form used in notarial documents. It is then noted that:

> [I]n the city of Krakow, in the presence of a notary and the following personally appointed witnesses [priests from churches to be gifted by the testator] Claire, widow of Jacob Rolle, in her home, being healthy in body and mind, guided by fervent piety, wishing to devote her goods to the worship of God, which is the most befitting of the works of charity, and out of thanksgiving and love for the beloved supplier and donor of all goods, and for the salvation of the souls of her and her deceased

---

246   "Von Scheppinbrifen und Ratisbrifen of permynt IIII gr. Ausgenomen grosse testament adir Vorrichtbrife, do von mag her me nemen [...]. Wenn man geet czu Testamente VI gr"; CONS. 428, fol. 348.

247   At the time of writing her will, she had been for many years the widow of the wealthy Krakow bowyer Jacob Rolle, whose will was entered in the book of the municipal bench court in 1392; SCAB., no. 1425.

248   John Stolle signed the document as a priest from the diocese of Wrocław, and certified it with his personal notarial seal: "Et ego Iohannes Nicolai Stolle de Glogouia maiori, Clericus wratislauiensis diocesis, publicus Imperiali auctoritate Notarius, dicte voluntatis disposicioni interfui vna cum testibus iam nominatis hic supra, et eam totaliter et omnimode in sensu quidem, sicut supra hic notatum est, loquente domina predicta et scedulam exhibente, tunc ibidem audita percepi et uidi, et manu mea in hanc formam scripsi, Signo meo et nomine solitis consignatam"; KDMK, vol. 3, no. 406; for more on John Stolle, see Bożena Wyrozumska, *Kancelaria*, 121.

249   KDMK, vol. 3, no. 368, 493–494 (1303), no. 406, 532–534 (1419), no. 432, 563–569 (1449).

THE INSTITUTION OF THE WILL 87

husband, who died without making a will,[250] other than leaving to her the making of pious bequests, which were to be made and allocated from her property...[251]

In accordance with this declaration, numerous pious bequests are then mentioned, including the bequest of a tenement building to establish a new foundation to maintain the altar to Mary Magdalene in St. Mary's Church. The testament ends with a noteworthy statement: "she wishes that in order for this disposition of her will to be confirmed and better secured as a testament or legacy, or at the least, as a legal codicil, or any donation from her last will, or in accordance with the law, the current circumstances, or what is customary, that all of these things be made a public document by me as a notary."[252] This provision not only signals the existence of uncertainties concerning the legal underpinnings of wills and the means for ensuring the

---

250   Jacob Rolle left behind a provision in which he bequeathed all of his possessions to his wife, obliging her to donate 100 *grivna* to help the poor. It is possible that his widow decided to secure the salvation of her husband's soul only many years later in her will. This bequest indicates that as recently as the early fifteenth century, the will was primarily considered a religious act; cf. "Jacobus Rolle domine Clare eius consorti legitime post mortem suam universa bona sua hereditaria et mobilia, que habet et postmodum habuerit, exclusis omnium suorum propinquorum contradiccionibus, si et inquantum ipsa domina vidua permanserit, libere resignavit, de quibus bonis centum marcas infirmis in hospitali et aliis pauperibus debet distribuere cum effectu, si autem de novo maritum contraxerit, extunc tutores infrascripti eidem domine centum sexagenas donate debent cum plena faciendi et dimittendi facilitate, debent eciam eidem tutores domine Katherine eius filie, Johannis Reyman consorti legitime, similiter centum marcas donare et effectualiter post dicte domine Clare obitum assignare. Tutores Nicolaus Gemlich et Johannes Frienstat; premissis"; SCAB., no. 1425 (1392).

251   "In nomine domini amen. Anno nativitatis eiusdem millesimo quadringentesimo decimo nono, Indiccione duodecima, Pontificatus sanctissimi in christo patris et domini, domini Martini diuina prouidencia pape quinti anno secundo, Veneris die duodecima mensis May, hora vesperorum, In ciuitate Cracouiensi, In presencia mei notarij et testium infrascriptorum personaliter constituta honesta domina Clara relicta Iacobi Rolle, In domo sua, sana corpore et bone racionis, zelo pietatis ardenter cupiens facultates suas ad cultum diuini numinis disponere, quippe qui saluberrimum sit operum caritatis, ac pro gracia et amore amantissimi datoris et remuneratoris omnium bonorum et in remedium et salutem anime sue atque dicti quondam eius mariti, qui decedens testamentum aliud non fecit, nisi quod ipsum disponendum eius fideli reliquit voluntati, Voluit dari et mandauit de bonis suis"; KDMK, vol. 3, no. 406, 532–534 (1419).

252   "Et hanc suam voluntatis disposicionem ualere uoluit ut testamentum vel legatum aut saltim iure codicillorum, aut donacionis cuiusuis ultime uoluntatis, aut prout alias de iure uel de facto uel de consuetudine melius subsistere poterit et valare, petens sibi super his a me Notario fieri publicum Instrumentum"; *Ibid.*

88   CHAPTER 1

implementation of their provisions, but also reflects a utilitarian approach in
the legal recommendations it makes. Broad-ranging similarities between the
form of this will and the purpose for writing it down and those of other wills
preserved as notarial instruments, both the last wills of clergy members, like
that of presbyter Theodoric Weinrich,[253] and those of the gentry, like the last
will (made in Lublin) of the Starost[254] of Brodnica, Francis Gliwicz from Krakow.[255] It seems, however, that for burghers, both those who were members of
the elite and ordinary members of Krakovian society, it was usually sufficient
for wills to be made in the form of a document produced before a municipal
council or bench court in a much more abbreviated form.

Some burghers, especially during epidemics of infectious diseases, made
their wills not in a closed form or openly in the town hall, but in private in the
presence of their friends, neighbours, or fellow members of guilds or brotherhoods. In 1443, ten masters from the furriers' guild appeared before the municipal council to testify on behalf of their fellow tradesmen that the late guild
member John Baumgart had given,[256] "as a testament" for building and funding a new chapel in St. Mary's Church, 40 grivna, which was owed to him by
Nicholas Schretil. Accordingly, the furriers' guild secured the money from the
debtor and used it to fund the chapel.[257] Similarly, in 1475 three senior members of the salt merchants' guild (*sallicide*) testified that the deceased Peter
Romanus owed fifteen florins to Martin Swetcz from Mazovia.[258] In the *Liber*

---

253   KDMK, vol. 3, no. 432, 563–569 (1449).
254   See Glosary: Starosta
255   "Et Ego Iohannes Andree de Gorzicze Clericus Poznaniensis diocesis, Notarius publicus
      Imperiali auctoritate, Reuerendissimi in christo patris et domini, domini Iohannis dei gra-
      cia Episcopi Cracouiensis Causarumque et facti huiusmodj coram sua peternitate Scriba,
      Quia predictis Testamenti siue Codicilli reposicioni, testium Induccioni, Recognicioni,
      Peticioni, confirmacioni et ratificacioni, Alijsque omnibus et singulis premissis, dum sic
      vt premittitur agerentur et fierent, vna cum prenominatis testibus interfui, Eaque omnia
      et singula premissa sic fierj vidj et audiui, Ideo presentes Confirmacionis literas siue pre-
      sens publicum Instrumentum manu mea propria scriptum confeci et in hanc publicam
      formam redegi, Signo et nomine meis solitis et conswetis vnacum appensione Sigilli dicti
      dominj Episcopi Cracouiensi et de eius mandato speciali consignans, In fidem et testi-
      monium omnium et singulorum premissorum"; KDMK, vol. 3, no. 474, 624–626 (1484); for
      more about the Brodnica *starost* Francis Gliwicz from Krakow and the 'Old Horse' coat of
      arms, cf. Feliks Kiryk, *Zarys dziejów osadnictwa*, in *Dzieje Olkusza i regionu olkuskiego*, vol.
      1, eds. Feliks Kiryk, Ryszard Kołodziejczyk (Warszawa, Państ. Wydaw. Naukowe, 1978), 107.
256   "Niclas Cleynhoze, Thomas Czan, Niclas Czipser, Antonius Meilner, Petir Ar, Petir Kauf-
      man, Mathis Schretil, Lazarus Poneczky, Bartholomeus Tretkopi John Konynsky seniors
      pellificum"; CONS. 428, fol. 466 (1443).
257   *Ibid.*
258   CONS. 429, fol. 543 (1475).

THE INSTITUTION OF THE WILL 89

Testamentorum there is a bequest from 1482, a time of plague, which states explicitly that the tailor John Biały, being healthy in body and mind, made his testament before the elders of his guild. A year later, the will was placed in the book of wills, most likely as a result of the actions of the executors of the will.[259] The following year, John Wilki and Martin, two guards of the city's gates testified before the council that they were witnesses to the will made by John the Master, who chose Benedict the furrier as his will's executor. These two witnesses testified before the council to the honesty of Benedict, who was accused of misappropriating the money, claiming that he had properly carried out the provisions of the last will, giving the money to monasteries and brotherhoods in Krakow and to a woman. This entry shows that John's will was not authenticated before any office, and that its authenticity could be attested to only by means of oral testimony.[260]

8   Fifteenth-Century Wills "Made in Sickness and in Health"

Magdeburg Law theoretically only allowed people who were healthy in body and mind to dispose of movable and immovable property before the municipal bench court. However, in the late fourteenth century, Krakow councillors started the practice of visiting sick burghers to witness their last will and guarantee its fulfilment. In order to safeguard wills made in the presence of council envoys – usually the mayor and two or three other councillors – they were recorded in council books, including special 'books of wills' that were kept by the municipal council. One of the first examples of this practice is the fifteenth-century will of Dorothy Pauswanginne, written in 1405. The entry concerning this act begins with the statement that Dorothy's will was written down "word for word" in the council book by order of the municipal councillors. It reads as follows:

> We Nicholas Bochner, John Borg, Peter Meinhard, Nicholas Platener and Matthias Arnsberg, councillors of the city of Krakow, declare to all those who so require, that sitting here before us on the council, councillors Hartlip von Klucze, *John* Czopchin and *John* Falkinberg testified that at our

---

259   "Byaly Jan sartor condidit testamentum suum ultime voluntatis die dominica in vigilia divisionis appostolorum Anno Domini MCCCCLXXX secundo, sanus mente eger Corpore presentibus senioribus artificii videlicet Johanne Mroczek, Jarosch, Stari Niclos, Laurencio Prazak et Girzik quos executores testament constituit"; LT, fol. 133–134 (1482).

260   CONS. 429, fol. 762 (1483); cf. Bożena Wyrozumska, *Kancelaria*, 91.

90 CHAPTER 1

request and by virtue of their council office [*von unser bevelunge in crafft ires Ratampts*] they went to Dorothy, widow of John Pauswang. Dorothy, being of sound mind, in the presence of these councillors and through her chosen guardian John Ederer made and disposed her testament, a bequest for the soul and the last will...[261]

It follows that as early as 1405 council "visits to the sick" were perceived as a normal part of a councillor's obligation. In later years, the testimonies entered in the council books often contained information about sending to the sick three councillors "at special request," who wrote down the testimony of a person's last will and then brought it to the full council for authentication.[262] This practice soon acquired the authority of antiquity, as seen in a passage in the will of Margaret Glezerinne (the above-mentioned widow of Nicholas Glezer) from 1428. The visit of three members of the municipal council to the sick woman was described as 'the old custom of our city' (*alder gewonheit und haldunge unser Stat*).[263] The same term was used in this context in the bequests of Erhart Eigilwart, an alderman from Augsburg, in 1431,[264] and of the former Košice burgher John Czenmark in 1436.[265]

---

261 "Tenor litere testamenti domine Dorothee Pauswanginne de verbo ad verbum hic notatis est ad mandatum dominorum. Wir Niclos Bochner, Hannos Borg, Petrus Meynhard, Niclos Platener und Mathias Arnsberg Ratmannen der Stat Cracovia Bekennen allen den is notdurft ist,daz vor uns in siczczinden Rate, die ersamen Hartlib von Klucze, Johannes Czopchin und Johannes Falkinberg unsir mitRatmannen und eyrgenossen habin offimberlich und eyntrechticlich bekant daz alz se von unser bevelunge in crafft ires Ratampts, czu der erbarn frawen Dorothean Johannis Pauswangin witwen gegangen woren, do hat diselbe fraw Dorothea vor en alz Ratmannen, mit wolbedochtem mute und guter vornunfft, durch Johannem Ederer iren doselbist gekornen vormunden Ir testament zelgerethe und leczten willen, gemacht geschickit, gescifftit und geordnit in zotener weyse"; CONS. 427, [. 241 (1405).

262 Such an annotation can be found in the wills of Young Peter the tanner (Jung Petir rufficerdus), CONS. 427, fol. 354–355 (1409); Stanisław Leytman the younger, CONS. 428, fol. 23 (1414) and Michael the butcher (smersneyder), CONS. 428, fol. 120 (1419).

263 "Wir Peter Fetter, Jorge Swarcz, Wilhelm Willand, Peter Grazer, Dithrich Weynrich, Bernhard vom Brige, Hannus Hoze und Nicolaus Alberti Ratmanne der Stat Cracow Bekenne offintlich mit desim brifem daz als dreye aus uns gesant und gegangen weren von des ratis wegen als her Peter Fetter, her Jorge Swarcz und her Peter Graser czu der irbarn frawen Margrit Glezerynne czu verhoren ir testament und schicunge ires leczten willen, noch alder gewonheit und haldunge unser Stat, do hot dyselbe fraw Margrith Glezerynne in krangheit leggende ader bey guter vornunfft wesende ir testament vor In gemacht und lossern beschreiben als sy vor uns bekant haben in sulcher worten und also"; CONS. 428, fol. 243.

264 CONS. 428, fol. 305.

265 CONS. 428, fol. 354.

THE INSTITUTION OF THE WILL   91

An interesting phenomenon that seems to have occurred sporadically during this period was the making of wills by ailing burghers in the presence of Krakow aldermen. The fact that this situation was exceptional is evidenced by the fact that only a few wills have survived to our times that are known to have been written down in such circumstances. The first mention of this kind can be found in the will of Anna, widow of the councillor John Bartfal.[266] In an entry from 1419 it is noted that councillor John Plesner, when he was still a alderman, along with the aldermen Nicholas Bastgert and Nicholas Szwarczhensil, testified together with vogt Nicholas Schaffer, that due to Anna's illness, they had held an open court (*iudicium bannitum*) in her house, before which she bequeathed through her chosen guardian John Plesner three grivna in rent to St. Mary's Church.[267] It is worth noting that this act of last will was entered into the council book, and not into the book of the municipal bench court, probably at the request of John Plesner who she had chosen as the executor of her will. The precedent-setting character of this case was probably influenced by the nature of the disposition, which was a generous bequest to St. Mary's Church, an institution supported by the city authorities. The social position occupied by the widow of an influential Krakow alderman was probably also not without significance.

Information about another will, made in a similar fashion, but this time entered into the book of the municipal bench court, dates back to 1466. Like Anna Bartfalowa, Bartholomeus Graudencz was also closely associated with the city authorities, having served for many years in Krakow as a alderman. In this case as well, aldermen testified that they went to the sick man's house, where, together with mayor Hartlip Parchwicz, they held an open court (*gehegt ding*).[268] Before them Bartholomeus distributed his extensive estate between his wife Margaret and the children of Nicholas Dittrich and gave an account of his debts and liabilities.[269] Interestingly, in both of the above acts the word

---

266   He is listed as John from Bardiow in the register of the Krakow councillors compiled by Marcin Starzyński; Marcin Starzyński, *Krakowska rada*, 247.

267   "Johannes Plessener noster Consul alias Scabinus, Johannes de Sale, Nicolaus Bastgerth, et Nicolaus Swarczhensil tunc eciam scabini Regognoverint sub iuramento ipsorum, Quod cum ipsi cum Nicolao Schaffer Advocato, Judicium in domo habitacionis domine Anne Relicte Johannis Bartfal propter ipsius corporis debilitatem bannunssent tunc dicta domina Anna dicto Johannes Plessenen pro tutore recepto coram eodem iudicio banito III mrc census terragii perpetui in et super domo Ilkusserinne in plathea sancti Floriani sitis fratrum ad sanctam Mariam Ecclesie parochialis Cracoviensi resignasset iure hereditario"; CONS. 428, fol. 123 (1419).

268   See Glossary: Bench court

269   "Wir Scheppin der Stat Cracow bekennen offintlich mit desim brife das wir of sunderliche begerunge und bete des Erbern Bartholomei Grawdencz unsirs libin mitbruders geruchtin czu im In seyn haws czugeen do selbist wir komende der do leginde was In

'testament' itself is not used. It does appear, however, in a bequest made in similar circumstances a year later by Nicholas Wishube. The aldermen here testified that together with mayor Hartlip Parchwicz, "at the special request" of Nicholas, they held court in the sick man's house. It may be assumed that the granting of the act as a "testament and last will" was related to the fact that (unlike Graudencz) Nicholas Wishube made many pious bequests to benefit churches and hospitals in the Krakow agglomeration.[270] The book of the municipal bench court from the same year also contains the will of the Mayor of Krakow, the aforementioned Hartlip Parchwicz, in whose house court was held by the Vice-Vogt (*untervogt*)[271] Michael Opoczko and the aldermen Matthias Apteker, John Gartner and Nicholas Gobil. This bequest of last will was entered onto the pages of the book in a slightly different form than the previous ones. Only at the end of the entry does information appear that it was written down in the home of the ailing Parchwicz.[272] All three wills mentioned above come from the years 1466–1467, when a great plague was rife in Krakow, which may in part explain the special measures taken by the aldermen and their assumption of duties that had previously been the responsibility of the municipal council. Few testaments have survived that were written down in the presence of Krakow aldermen and contain an annotation that they were made by infirm individuals. It seems, however, that in this regard the 1466 plague could have been a transformational event that changed the municipal bench court's approach to wills. This is indirectly indicated by the bequest of last will of the merchant John Raisser from Memmingen (southern Germany),

---

crangheit in seynen Stuben also of seine begerunge wir eyn not gehegt ding gehegit habin In welchim dinge der Ersame her Hartlip Parchwicz unsir foit sas, der obgenante Bartholomeus Grawdencz wy wol her swachis leibes gewest ist, idach seiner guttir vornunft gebrawchende doselbist vor unsirm gehegtim dinge sitczende hot eyne solche gobe und bekentnis gegebin und geton hot"; SCAB. 8, fol. 246.

270 "Wir Scheppin der Stat Crakow bekennen offintlich mit desim brife das wir of sunderliche bete und begerunge des Erbern Nicolai Wishubes unsirs mitburgers geruchtin czu im In seyn haws czu geen Also do wir komende woren der do leginde was In seynem hawse of seyne begerunge doselbist wir eyn not gehegt ding gehegit habin, In welchim gehegtim dinge der Ersame her Hartlip Parchwicz unsir foit ses der obgenante Niclos Wishube wy wol her swachis leibis gewest ist idach wesinde bey guttir seynir fornunft und mit wol bedochtim mutte vor dem selbin gehegtim unsirn notdinge her seyn Testament und schickunge seynes lecztin willes also gemacht hot"; SCAB. 8, fol. 250 (1467).

271 See Glossary: Vice-Vogt

272 "Hec omnes recogniciones et ___ prout superius continent ___ ___ per dictum Hartlip infirmium et langwentem in domo habitacionis ipsius ubi ad ipsius peticiones Judicium Bannitum per Scabinos est celebrantum"; SCAB. 8, fol. 269 (1467).

THE INSTITUTION OF THE WILL   93

who came to Krakow in 1476. The holding of a session of the municipal bench court at the house where he was staying was this time described as 'our custom' (*unsir gewonheit*).[273] Moreover, unlike in previous wills, where they were simply referred to as open courts (*iudicium bannitum,* or *gehegt ding*), here the expression *notding* is used,[274] i.e. a 'extraordinary court' (*iudicium necessarium*), that is, a court hearing called in special and urgent situations.

What were initially exceptional, for aldermen – the occasional hearing and recording of the last wills of members of the city elite – became with time an increasingly frequent practice (especially during epidemics, when council members often left the city walls). The extraordinary jurisdictions of municipal bench courts included cases requiring immediate intervention. It is surprising, however, that although the concept of an extraordinary court existed in Magdeburg Law from at least the fourteenth century,[275] it was used for the first time in the context of the last will of an ailing individual only in the latter half of the fifteenth century.[276] It seems that to some extent this phenomenon

---

273   "Wir Mattis Apteker etc. Scheppin der Stad Crakow bekennen offintlich mit desim briffe vor allen und iczlichen dy en sehen ader leszin das so wir off sunderliche bete und beger des Erbarn und Czuchtigen Hannus Rayssir von Mammyngen czu ym gegangen weren in das haws des namhaftigen herren Sebastiani Fogilwedirs unsirs mitburgirs in seyn gemach do her sichet und in crangheyt gelegen hot czu vorhorchen seyn Testament und schickunge seynis letczsten willen und do selbist noch unsir gewonheit vor em eyn notdingt gehegit hatten. So hot do selbist vor uns in gehegtdinge das der Erbar Stanislaus Steynbach unsir ffoyt sasz der selbe Hannus Raysir in crangheit leginde und swachen des leibis ydoch bey guttir voller vornunft wesinde mit wolbedochten mutte und mit gancz vorsatcz und willen seyn testament gemacht in sulchir geschicht also her noch folgit"; SCAB. 8, fol. 598–599.

274   See Glossary: Bench court

275   "In practice there ocurred incidents requiring the court's immediate intervention. In view of the fact that high and ordinary courts were held only on certain dates, Magdeburg Law created a type of court convened on an ad hoc basis, called a *notding*" Witold Maisel, *Sądownictwo miasta Poznania do końca XVI w.* (Poznan: Wydawnictwo naukowe PWN, 1961), 30–31; According to Witold Maisel (referring to Wiktor Friese), townspeople were given permission to appoint such a court in the location privilege of Poznan as early as the mid-thirteenth century. The term *notding* as a court of emergency to judge the case of a 'guest' or person embarking on a journey is also used in the Code of Magdeburg Law of 1389.: "Ap man gesten notding hegen sal adir burgir kegen gaste," *Ibid.*

276   One of the Magdeburg judgements sent to Krakow in 1382, includes a mention that John Czetirwange, a Krakow townsman, made his last will and testament before an emergency court (*notding*), which was later confirmed during regular proceedings of the bench court. According to this note, however, it was made by a man who was physically and mentally fit. It may have been connected with a plan expressed by John in 1373 to embark on a pilgrimage; cf. SCAB.K, no. 812. According to the Magdeburg bench court's decision,

94   CHAPTER 1

can be associated with a growing understanding of Magdeburg Law and a more faithful adherence to its letter.[277] It is also possible that the dissemination of wills among broader circles of urban society – connected with a growing sense of danger from the plague in the latter half of the fifteenth century – resulted in a gradual transfer of jurisdiction over wills into the hands of the bench court and hearings conducted by the emergency court.[278]

The growing importance of making and authenticating wills before the municipal bench court in the latter half of the fifteenth century is also indicated by the bequest of last will of the municipal notary Christopher Rebentcz, who, before going to Wrocław in 1481, drew up an act of last will before the municipal bench court "in accordance with city law" (*noch der Stat recht*), but confirmed it before the municipal council only after returning from the journey.[279] A similar situation also occurred in the case of Peter Schepcz's will from 1483. The document, handwritten by the testator, was later authenticated by him before the municipal bench court, but it was only after his death that the chosen executors decided to enter it into the *Liber Testamentorum*.[280] However, the absence of two books of the municipal bench court from the years 1476–1500 makes it impossible to fully confirm these observations on the basis of primary source materials.

---

     such a provision could not be questioned by the wife of the deceased; *Kodex Pilźnieński ortylów magdeburskich. Odbitka z II tomu Sprawozdań Wydz. Hist. Fil. Akad. Umiejętn.*, ed. Władysław Wisłocki (Krakow: Akademia Umiejętności, 1874), 60–64.

277   This phenomenon can be observed in the growing number of testamentary bequests made and confirmed – in accordance with Magdeburg Law – before a municipal bench court, rather than before the municipal council, as well as in the wills found in the late fifteenth-century *Liber Testamentorum*, including references to the council's privilege to accept and confirm these documents, which may point to attempts made at this time to contest this law.

278   In his description of the functioning of extraordinary bench courts, Witold Maisel referred only to examples from the sixteenth century; cf. *idem, Sądownictwo*, 80–81.

279   CONS. 429, fol. 693.

280   "Herren Ulricus Jeczinbergir und Stanislaus Lanthman gekorne vormunde Petri Schepcz Testament dem got gnade legeten vor uns vedir des selben Petri Schepcz Testament welche her bey gesunde leibe und seynir eygen hant geschriben hat und vorsigilt in unsir gerichte den Scheppen ingelegit hat In sulcher weyse, worde got obir yn etwas todis halbe thuen das is bunt und craft sulle haben sam is in der Scheppen buch wen geschreben noch ynnehaldunge unsir Scheppen bucher begereten von uns das is solte werden gelesen und dorch uns mit unsirm buche och worde bestetigit welchis gelesen wart in keginwortikeit der obgenanten czwir vormunde und Petri des obgenanten Petri Schepcz Eldistir zon und lawtet von worte zu worte"; LT, fol. 137 (1483).

THE INSTITUTION OF THE WILL

9   Formula for Wills from 1485

An extremely important, though quite late, example of an attempt to standardise the formula used in acts of last will written in Krakow is the following testamentary form, which has survived to the present day.[281] It was written on a single sheet of paper in German, probably in 1485:

> Jesus, Mary. In the name of our Lord Jesus Christ. Because almighty God has made human nature weak, so that man cannot escape death and the hour of death comes to him unseen, so that man must always be ready to accept the hour of death, just as he appeared in this world, and so man should distribute and pass on his goods which God has lent him, so that by God's grace he can allocate them for the salvation of his soul. With this in mind, I, P.K., a burgher from Krakow, with careful consideration and goodwill, being healthy in body, in accordance with which I can dispose I make this act of last will with careful consideration and in good faith, so that I have not made any other will after it, in all respects the best protective form known and in accordance with the law, as I could have done and disposed of, every regulation point by point, as follows:
>
> First of all, because almighty God has made me mortal and in death I will depart, I thus entrust my soul to almighty God and his mother Mary and all the heavenly lords, and my body to the earth, where it should be buried according to the Christian rite, should be commissioned for love for almighty God and for the salvation of my soul.
>
> If, after my death, my children are to assume my legacy, remaining in love and friendship, and none of them shall demand anything more, then I the sole father of all my children and sole owner of all my possessions, which I can legally dispose of according to my will and judgement, shall share and dispose of it, and it is my last will, that all my movable and immovable goods, which God has lent me, in all places and confines where they may be found, which I shall leave behind me, in its entirety should fall to my heirs in accordance with these instructions, which I have written with my own hand and confirmed with my seal. Just as if it had been made before a council meeting or before a municipal bench

---

281   Elżbieta Piwowarczyk did not recognize this document as a testamentary form, and instead considered it to be an actual will: "in the ruling of a Krakow councillor using only the initials P.K., in the early sixteenth century."; *eadem, Legaty testamentowe ad pias causas,* 69.

96 CHAPTER 1

court. Then, I bequeath for works of charity, etc., and other things. For this I choose executors.

These dispositions are issued in the form of a testament by me, P.K., and thus made and recorded, I give them to councillors (or aldermen) of the city of Krakowto keep and safeguard during my lifetime and to have executed without objections by any persons, while after my death it is to be given to my children and heirs in their or their guardians' presence, and they are to confirm it. And it will be additionally safeguarded in the municipal book in order for it to have authority and force in all matters.

As long as I shall live, in all these matters I retain the power to change, improve, increase or reduce anything in accordance with my will.

Testament made in German [Lat.].[282]

---

282 "Jesus Maria. In dem nam unsers herren Jesu Cristi. So der Almechtigen gott dy menschliche nature sweblich geschossen hot also das der mensch dem tode nicht entgeen mag und ym dy stunde des todis geen verborgen hot auff das das der mensch alle czeit bereit sey dy stunde des todes an zu nehmen So her von diste werlt gefundert wirt Auch das der mensch zeyne gutte dy ym gott vorlihen hott, also vorschafferbenen und ferschaffen sal, das her der durch gotis genode von seinir sele selikeyt enlangen mochte Das betrachtunde, hab Ich P K burger zu Crake mit gutten czeitigen vor rote, auch wol bedochtem wille, gesunt des leibes do ich das wol gethon mocht awss rechte vornunfft und redlichen vorsachen mich dorczu bewegende dass meyn geschofft an stadt meynes leczten willes, so ich keyn andern testament noch dem machen worden In aller besten brefftigensten und bestendigensten form undemunge weise und recht so ich ynnee tun kann und mag, gemacht und geordent hab, Setcz schaff und verorden von stuck zu stuke als her noch folgt. Czum ersten so der almechtigen gott mich von diste immortall erfordert, und ich mit todt abgegangen bin, so befel ich meyne zele dem almechtigen got und seiner werder mutter Marien und dem gancze hymelschen here, und meynen leichnam zu der erden welchs mit cristliches erberkeyt sal bestalt werden dem allmechtigen gotte zu lebe und meyner zele selikeyt; Item das noch meynen tode meyne kinder und erben ader erb nehmen in eynikeit libe und fruntschafft bliben und eyns das ander nicht hett vorummb anzulangen Zo ich eyn vattir allen meynen kinder und eyn her meynes wolgewonen guttis byn und hab folkomener gewalt von rechte der mit zu thuen und zu lossen noch meynen eille und besten erkantnisse, so shikich und schaff und ist das men leczten will, das alle meyne habe und gutte dy mir gott verlihen hott, ligende und farende in allen orten und enden vor dy gefunden werden dy ich noch mir lossen worde keyns ausgenomen nich hynden an gesatcz sollen von meynen linden und erben also angenomen werden in kunfft dists geschefftis welches ich mit meyner eygener handt geschreibh hab und mit meynen pitschaffte vormacht und vorsigelt Gleich sam ys vor gesassenen rote adir vor gerichte gemacht werre her noch folget. Item in dy werk der barherczikeit vorschaff etc. tem ander dinge etc. Dornoch executores und vormunden; Diss gescheffte und ordenunge an stadt eynes testamentis von mir P K also gemacht und geschriben gib ich dem ersamen rote (ader dem scheppen) der stadt Croke zu behalden und zu bewonen bey meynen lebetagen zu meynen gutten willen und ys wider __ben um von yne zu fordenen und zu namen von ich will an allen hindernisse irkeynen menschen Sunder noch meynen tode sal ys gegeben werden meynen kindern und erben so sy das kegenwertigdurch

THE INSTITUTION OF THE WILL

This form was written by the hand of the long-time deputy notary of Krakow Kacper Grosz.[283] The initials P.K. on the form, however, may also refer to the author of the original will, which provided the model for the municipal notary. Interestingly, there is not a single will from Krakow with an equally extensive invocation and preamble or such flowery phrasings. We thus do not know whether the original was the work of a Krakow burgher, or whether it came from another source.[284] The question therefore remains open as to whether this formula is evidence of an attempt by the municipal chancellery to introduce in Krakow an expanded form of the burgher will, with a formula modelled on wills drawn up in the form of notarial instruments. It is also possible that some wills drawn up as a written document in the latter half of the fifteenth century were similar in form, but were entered into the municipal book or *Liber Testamentorum* in a significantly simplified form. As early as 1888 Bolesław Ulanowski noted that:

> Anyone who has read our court books has often met with the expression at the end of a bequest: ut in forma. This means that the notary did not adorn the act with all the stylistic accessories, but summarising it briefly in the court protocol, confined himself to drawing on the relevant formula for such a matter. If, on the basis of a court bequest, it was appropriate to issue a document (*litteram iudicialem*), then the relevant formula would have been used in its entirety.[285]

In the case of wills, it was also the custom of municipal notaries to simplify the documents presented to them for authentication. This phenomenon is evident in the case of Kunil Gluk's will. His last will has survived both on the original sheet of paper and in the form of an entry in the book of the municipal bench court from 1394. In rewriting the original text, the municipal notary omitted a very short promulgation of the act, leaving only the first and last name of

---

      sich ader iren vormunden und in abwesen durch eyn iren anwelden gefordenen und hei-schen werden Idoch das ys bestetiget wirt und in stadt buch ingeschriben das is bundt und krafft haben solde allenhalben; In dem allem behalde ich mir dy herschafft dy weile ich lebe das zu wandeln zu bessern zu meren zu mynden noch meynen wille und wol gefallen; Testament in wulgari faciendis"; AMK, ms 779.

283   Agnieszka Bartoszewicz, *Piśmienność*, 147–148.

284   Kacper Grosz allegedly spent some time in Venice, but it is not known for what purpose; *Ibid.*, 148.

285   *Libri Formularum saeculi XVmi*, ed. Bolesław Ulanowski, Krakow 1888 (Starodawne Prawa Polskiego Pomniki, 10), VI.

98   CHAPTER 1

the testator.[286] A similar course of action was recommended by Bartholomeus Groicki in the mid-sixteenth century. In *Titles of Magdeburg Law*, published in 1567, he stated that the form of the will was unimportant, as long as nothing in it was "in violation of the law, statutes (*Willkür*)[287] or the rules of propriety."[288] He continued, however, to include sample forms written in Polish of wills made openly before the city office, as well as of closed ones submitted to city authorities for authentication after the testator's death.[289] He also included a form written in Latin for entering a closed will into city books.[290] Containing only the most basic information, the text was devoid of invocations and religious preambles. This reflected a desire to avoid disputes between heirs and facilitate official confirmation of the will's conformity with the laws of the city and their privileges.[291]

---

286   "Wissit liben herren das ich Kunil Glóke bekenne das ich gemorgingobt habe meyne eli-
       chym weybe Cloren L marg und dorczu geb ich yr X marg das ys wem LX marg noch
       meyme tode in meyne guter ab do icht oberigis bleibit _er do czu recht worde habin dem
       folgis ys sy den das __s got eyn frocht bescherte. Ipsa prius consensit. Reservat dominium,"
       SCAB. 3, fol. 140b; cf. "Kunil Geluke cedulam papiream, in quo testamentum suum ac ulti-
       mam ipsius voluntatem ydeomate teutonico conscripserat presentavit, cuius cedule tenor
       sequitur in hec verba: Ich Kunel Glucke bekenne, das ich gemorgengabt habe meyme eli-
       chen weibe Cloren L marg. vnd dorczu geb ich ir X marg, das is wern LX marg noch meyme
       tode in meyne guter, ab do icht oberigis bleybit, wer dorczu recht wurde haben dem folge
       is, ys sey denne, das vns got eyne frucht bescherte; in quam donacionem ipsa domina
       presencialiter constituta consensit; reservat sibi dominium, quamdiu vitam duxerit in
       humanis"; SCAB., no. 1931 (1394); cf. Agnieszka Bartoszewicz, *Języki wernakularne*
287   See Glossary: Willkur
288   "Every person can make their own testament according to their own wishes, both one
       made publicly before an authority and a private one, presented to authorities only so it
       does not go against the law, municipal statutes and good practices. After all, a testament
       made before an office is a kind of model which may provide a model for other testa-
       ments"; Bartłomiej Groicki, *Tytuły*, 190.
289   "This *summa* may be a closed will"; *Ibid.*, 191.
290   "This will be the formulation of a closed will recorded by a notary, if such will is submitted
       to an office"; *Ibid.*, 193–194.
291   "Coram hoc iudicio personaliter comparens famatus N. sanus mente et corpore, cupiens
       removere omnes controversias et dissensione, si quae post decessum suum ex hac vita
       inter suos haeredes de bonis per eum relinquendis quavis ratione oboriri possintm,
       exhibuit eidem iudicio testamentum suum clausum sigilloque suo obsignatum, volens, ut
       iuxta illius tenorem de rebus suis disponeretur, atque postulans illud vigore privilegiorum
       civitati huic concessorum aut iuris ordine confirmari. Quod quidem confirmatum est
       hac lege, si et in quantum nihil intro contineatur, quod Iuri Maydeburgensi et plebiscitis
       civitatis huius repugnaret. Dans et concedens haeredibus suis omnibus et in aliquorum
       absentia praesentibus aut his et his executoribus vel tutoribus N.N. plenam et sufficientem
       potestatem ac authoritatem, ut post decessum suum ex hac vita ad eorundem instantiam
       et petitionem testamentum hoc possit aperiri, publice legi, actisque iudiciariis inscribi

THE INSTITUTION OF THE WILL

99

The form from 1485 represents a type of closed will written down as a separate document which was popular in Krakow from at least the late fourteenth century. The will was first written down by hand (often by a professional notary) and confirmed with a stamped seal, and then submitted to the municipal council or bench court, which held it for safekeeping. The document was opened only after the testator's death, when its beneficiaries learned about the provisions it contained and the natural heirs were required to confirm them in the presence of the municipal authorities. Then, to better safeguard the will, its text was entered in an abbreviated form into the municipal book. The formula used in it was very important because it also indicated the testators' right to have all of their possessions, whether movable or immovable, remain at their disposal. The absence of a reference to a division between hereditary and acquired property suggests that this formula allowed for the disposal of both categories of property. The heirs were left only with the requirement to confirm the will's provisions before the court. The principles for bequests of property made in this form were therefore similar to those expressed in the Krakow municipal statute of 1530.[292] Another important issue was the right to authenticate wills before both the municipal council office and bench court, which also brings this form closer to Krakow's testamentary practices.

10   *Liber Testamentorum* from 1450

A significant number of the wills of Krakovian burghers analysed in this study were found on the pages of the oldest surviving book of wills, established by the municipal council in 1450. This date is indicated by an inscription found on the first page: "Here begins the Book of Wills established by order of the councilors."[293] It should be noted, however, that of the 22 acts of last will from 1427–1449 recorded on the book's first thirteen pages, some have been entered in non-chronological order. Another eleven pages of the book have been left blank, and it is only on page 26 that wills begin to be listed in chronological order, starting with the entries from 1451. This order is disrupted only by the will of the tanner John Milde, written on page 25 and made in 1452 before the

---

absque quarumvis personarum contradictione et impedimento. Dominium tamen sibi opse testator ac plenam facultatem reservavit in his omnibus, quo advixerit, testamentum hoc suum a iudicio rursus accipiendi, mutandi, cassandi in toto vel in parte, aliudque condendi, quandocunque voluerit"; *Ibid.*, 193–194.

292   Cf. Section 4.

293   For unknown reasons, the remainder of this entry was blurred; LT, fol. 1.

municipal bench court in front of Szewska Gate, which was entered into the book "by order of the councillors selected by him as executors."[294] On this basis, it can be concluded that although the book was established in 1450, the municipal councillors and the municipal notary did not begin using it until the following year.

The book was kept until 1623. Up to the end of 1500, as many as 188 different bequests of last will were recorded on its pages. It is worth mentioning here the probable reason for the establishment of a new book of wills. The year 1450 was exceptional because it had been declared a Jubilee year by Pope Martin V in his bull *Immens et Innumerabilia*, which resulted in a wave of pilgrimages to Rome. The 'eternal city,' with its relics and indulgences, attracted thousands of pilgrims from all over Europe.[295] Numerous traces of preparations for the journey to the tombs of St. Peter and Paul can also be found in sources from Krakow. In 1450, a record number of twenty five wills and other 'in the event of death' bequests were recorded in the books of the municipal bench court and council.[296] The pilgrimages to Rome made during the Jubilee year, and the hopes and fears associated with them, generated in people a need to address their earthly and spiritual obligations. This clear interest in testamentary bequests, especially among the city's social elites, was probably the primary factor in the city authorities' establishment of a new book of wills (after the previous *Liber Testamentorum* in Krakow had been filled up or lost).[297]

The form of the entries in the book of wills in the fifteenth century does not differ fundamentally from the previously discussed acts entered into bench court or city council registers. These included both extensive acts of

---

294   "Testamentum Johannis Milde cerdonis conditum coram Bannito Judicio ante valvam sutorum et ex mandato dominorum Consulum hic notatum est quia ipsi per dictum Milde electi sunt in tutores presentis testamenti." Below the will there is also a note concerning its execution: "Item anno domini MCCCCLIIII Domus predicta consilio et voluntate dominorum Consulum vendita et resignata es tut in libro Scabinorum, Mathie Brotke"; LT, fol. 25.

295   For Wrocław: "Sources indicate that jubilee pilgrimages started to gain popularity by the mid-fifteenth century at the latest – the largest number of entries mentioning the *Romwege* in municipal records (six each) were made in 1450 and 1475"; Halina Manikowska, *Jerozolima – Rzym – Compostela*, 7–8, 247–253.

296   In the *Liber Testamentorum* itself there are no entries from 1450; they only begin the following year; LT, fol. 26.

297   The fact that there was a discontinuity in the keeping of the first and second registers of wills is indicated indirectly by the rapid increase in the number of surviving acts of last will since the 1430s; see chapter 1, section 11, p. 104.

THE INSTITUTION OF THE WILL   101

last will, for example the last will of John Sweidniczer from 1457,[298] as well
as short donations,[299] statements on the appointment of guardians for a wife
and children or the executors of the last will,[300] and mutual bequests.[301] The
wills recorded in these books were made in person by healthy people standing
before the municipal council,[302] or by the infirm in the presence of councillors

---

298 "Wir Ratmanne der Stat Cracow Bekannen offintlich mit destin brise, Wy das dy Ersamen
    hern als Walcherus keznig of dy czeit Burgermeister Johannes Pitczen Jacobus Weger
    Jarosch Scharley und Martinus Belze unsirs Ratis mitbrudere In unsirs Ratis befelunge
    und in craft unsir hantfesten gegangen woren czu dem Ersamen hern Johanni Sweid-
    niczer unsirs Ratis mitbruder der in crangheit lag czu vorhoren und czu vorstere seynen
    leczten willen und schikunge seynes testaments und sy noch solcher vorhochunge und
    unsir befelunge, Wedirkomende in sitczenden Rat bekannende, Wy das der obgenante
    her Johannes Sweidniczer, Wy wol her crang gewest were Idach mit wolbedochtem mutte,
    und bey ganczer guttir vormmist seynen leczten willen und testament eigintlich in sol-
    chen worten als hernoch folgit gemacht geordint, und beslossen hette"; LT, fol. 39–45
    (1457).
299 "Anno etc. XXXII feria secunda diei sancti Mathie apostoli Scharf peter Institor pauper
    fecit testamentum coram dominis Consulibus Cuncze korsner et Johanne Crancz. Anne
    uxori sue legavit omnia bona sua que habet post mortem suam habenda cum plena
    faciendi et dimittendi potestate Exclusis omnes suos consangwineos propinquos et ami-
    cas. Sin autem ipse supervivent moriente uxore extunc ipse mulieris quam sua habere
    cum plena potestate ut super exclusis eciam omnibus propinquis et amicis eiusdem uxo-
    ris. Et in hanc ordinacionem testamenti Anna prefata praesentialiter constituta plena-
    rie consensit suscipiens eam pro grato Neutraparcium reservavit dominorum"; LT, fol. 3
    (1432).
300 "Anno etc. XXXVI ipso die Invencionis sancte crucis Mathias Engil nomine uxoris sue
    elegit Tutores petrum bogner, Johannem Phert et Johannem Litwanum aurifabros Cives
    Cracovie, Quos supradictos dictus Mathias ut dictam suam uxorem Margaretam et filios
    eius tuerentur et providentur eisdem sicut veri et legittimi Tutores In omnibus causis et
    negocys ipsorum Excludens omnis et singulos consangwineos et propinquos tam suos
    quam uxoris sue quantis Iuris est voluitque in casu si aliquis aut aliqui dictorum Tutorum
    decederent, quod superstites meliori kosilio et concorditer alium seu alios loco ipsius seu
    ipsorum eligerent sit quod dictum numerus integer remaneret. Et hot fecit de consensu
    uxoris sue tunc presentis petuitquedominos Consules Quod predictam electionem Tuto-
    rum ratam haberent et confirmarent. Ad predicta stans uxor sua ad omnia singula immu-
    nit et consensit presentibus dominis Petro Graser et Wilhelmo Wylanth"; LT, fol. 3 (1436).
301 "Feria VI ante Viti Anno 1482. Nicolaus Graudencz frisz und gesunt mit seynen gutten
    willen stehende vor uns hot alle seyne gutter bewegliche und unbeweglich dy her itczunt
    hot und her nochmols haben wirt Anne seynir hawsfrawen noch seynen tode zu haben
    ofgegeben und vorreichit und her wedir Anna obgenanten hot alle guttir beweglich und
    unbeweglich dy sy itczunt hot und her nochmols haben worde Nicolao Graudencz yren
    elichen manne noch yren tode zu haben ofgegeben und abegetreten awsslisende alle yre
    nesten frunde und mogen an beyden teylen Behaldende yn dy herschaft dy weyle sy leben
    dys zu wandeln und weddirczuruffen wen sy wellen"; LT, fol. 129 (1482).
302 "Anno domini Millesimo CCCCLVI feria quinta post Vitalis Hannos Lode Coram Consu-
    lam fecit suum Testamentum in hunc modum. Hannos Lode unsir mitburger wellende

102 CHAPTER 1

who came to their house.[303] Many wills were 'closed,' in other words, they had been previously written in person (in a few cases) or by a notary,[304] and afterwards authenticated by the testator or the executors of the will. It seems that the desire to record one's will in the *Liber Testamentorum* was associated with the special prestige of this book and the accompanying sense of better safeguarding the act of last will by placing it under the authority of the municipal council. This confidence continued up to the end of the fifteenth century, when the number of wills entered into council books (including the *Liber Testamentorum* itself) decreased, while the number of bequests made and secured by aldermen increased.

In 1476 Stephen Eichorn and his wife Margaret made an act (in German *gemechte*) comprising both a will and a mutual donation. In this act, they provided for the mutual inheritance of a house on Wiślna Street. After their deaths this house and other movables were to be divided into three parts and passed on to their designated relatives. In addition, both bequeathed 100 florins for the payment of annual rent for a German 'preacher' in St. Mary's Church.[305] Later, in 1482, it was added to the council book in a different hand that Stephen Eichorn had revoked this entry in order to have it included in the book of wills.[306] In fact, in that same year, a bequest appeared in the *Liber Testamentorum*, in which he revoked all his previous wills, stripped his previously chosen guardians of power and announced his intent to choose new ones, making his

---

czyen wedir dy ungetrawen finde der Cristenlichen glawbins dy Turken vor sitczendem Rate machende seyn testament frisch und gesint bey guttir vornumft in solchen worten. Czum irsten gebe ich Margarethe meyner Hawsfrawen hundirt ungerische gulden noch meynem tode czu haben. Item meynem bruder Niclos Loden czu Pilsen czeen gulden dy sal sy haben wenne sy mondig wirt. Item in das Spital czu Cracow czeen gulden, und behalde mir desis testamentes hirschaft czu wandiln dy weyle ich lebe, und kyse czu awsrichtunge des Matis Paschken, Hannos Frankensteyn, und Niclas Menteler"; LT, fol. 37 (1456).

303 "Anno domini Millesimo quadringentesimo LX quinto sabato ante Invocavit Dominus Johannes Beme in stuba domus sue habitationis consedensque cum dominis Infrascriptis ad eum missis licet corpore debili usu tamen bone et perfecte racionis suum fecit testamentum in fornace cum dominis sedens videlicet domino Johanne Wirsznik, magistro Curium, Paulo Newburger, Johanne Mozancz et Johanne Teschner, tale condidit et sue ultime voluntatis disposicionem seu testamentum prout sequitur"; LT, fol. 86 (1465).

304 E.g. the will of Peter Schepcz; LT, fol. 137 (1483).

305 "Stephan Eichorn und Margaretha seine hausfrawe unsir mitteburgir, haben eyn sulche gemechte macht von allen iren guttirn beweglich und unbeweglich keyne awsgenomen, und iren testament und schickunge ires letczen willen gesunt und bey guttir vornunft wesinde, also das"; CONS. 429, fol. 557.

306 "Anno 1482 Steffan Eichorn revocavit hot totam volens ut esse utqui in libro testamentorum"; CONS. 429, fol. 558.

THE INSTITUTION OF THE WILL   103

will before the municipal bench court.[307] In this case, it is not clear why the testator revoked his previous wills and, ultimately, despite his announcement, chose not to make a new act in the book of wills, though the expression of such a need is characteristic in itself.[308] In the case of a will personally written by Peter Schepcz, his executors decided that, in addition to entering it into the book of the municipal bench court, the act of last will should also be confirmed by an entry in the book of wills.[309] Entering the text of a will into more than one official book gave the impression that it was better safeguarded.

The same situation occurred seventy years earlier, in 1413, when Nicholas Czeginkop's will was entered into the book of the municipal bench court. His last will was first written on a sheet of paper in the presence of two councillors who came to him while he was sick, after which, at the order of the municipal council, it was written on parchment in the form of a document. In the end, the executors of the will "for its better protection" brought it before the municipal bench court, while the aldermen entered it into their book, where it survived to the present day. A similar need to authenticate an act of last will by aldermen can be found in a will from 1408. John the Wheelwright (*stelmecher*), who bequeathed all his property to his wife and daughter before the municipal council, asked his legal representative to confirm this act before the vogt and aldermen.[310]

The bench court's jurisdiction over wills became so strong over time, that in wills from the 1480s and 1490s city privileges are invoked that seem to justify wills being made in the presence of visiting councillors. For example, in the

---

307 "Steffan Eichorn stehende vor uns hat weddirruffen alle testament dy her gemacht hette bis of den hewtigen tag welllnde dy machtlosz seyn benemende seyn vormunde dy macht dy her vormols gekoren hat und her wirt andir kysen und testament machen vor gehegtindinge"; LT, fol. 133.

308 Due to a lack of books of the nunicipal bench court from 1476 to 500 it is not known whether Stephen Eichorn kept his promise.

309 "Herren Ulricus Jeczinbergir und Stanislaus Lanthman gekorne vormunde Petri Schepcz Testament dem got gnade legeten vor uns vedir des selben Petri Schepcz Testament welche her bey gesunde leibe und seynir eygen hant geschriben hat und vorsigilt in unsir gerichte den Scheppen ingelegit hat In sulcher weyse, worde got obir yn etwas todis halbe thuen das is bunt und craft sulle haben sam is in der Scheppen buch wen geschreben noch ynnehaldunge unsir Scheppen bucher begereten von uns das is solte werden gelesen und dorch uns mit unsirm buche och worde bestetigit welchis gelesen wart in keginwortikeit der obgenanten czwir vormunde und Petri des obgenanten Petri Schepcz Eldistir zon und lawtet von worte zu worte"; LT, fol. 137 (1483).

310 "[...] reservans sibi dominium quamdiu vixerit et constitutus Hartlibum de Clucze in procuratorium ad predictum resignacionem in bannito proximo iudicio coram advocato Scabinis confirmandam"; CONS. 427, fol. 328 (1408).

bequest of last will of Wojtek the Armourer (*plathner*) from 1487, the document is described as having been made "by virtue of privileges, etc., according to the custom of the office,"[311] and that of Barbara, daughter of Michael Unger, from 1491, "by virtue of the city's privileges" (*vigore privilegiorum Civitatis*).[312] For some reason, after almost a century of writing wills in the presence of representatives of the municipal council, the need arose once again to emphasise the rule of law, citing privileges and city customs. Although we may only be dealing with the style of a single municipal notary,[313] these phenomena generally indicate that a process of change was underway in terms of who was authorised to draw up and certify wills, a competence which had rested with the municipal council since the late fourteenth century, and with the municipal bench court in the late fifteenth century.

11 The Number of Wills in Krakow from 1300 to 1500

Graph 1 illustrates the increasing popularity of the will as an institution and changes in the burgher class' perception of it in the fourteenth and fifteenth centuries. The lines indicate both the number of preserved wills in total and the number found in particular types of sources, including books of the municipal bench court, council books, the *Liber Testamentorum* and other sources. The shape of this graph was largely influenced by the state of preservation of these sources. The books of the municipal bench court from the years 1376 to 1390 are

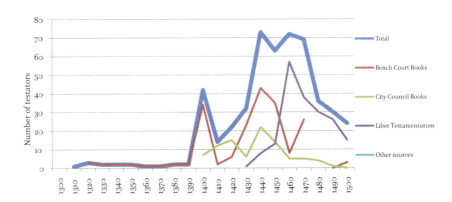

GRAPH 1   Number of extant wills from various sources from 1300 to 1550, by decade

---

311   LT, fol. 143.
312   LT, fol. 149.
313   The municipal notary John Heydeke worked in the municipal office during the period from 1481 to 1500; Bożena Wyrozumska, *Kancelaria*, 125–126.

THE INSTITUTION OF THE WILL

105

missing, so it is unclear whether the sudden increase in the number of wills in the 1390s was preceded by increases in previous decades. Similarly, the absence of the books of the municipal bench court from the turn of the fourteenth and early fifteenth centuries and from the last 24 years of the fifteenth century significantly blurs the image obtained from this data. Yet, even bearing these limitations in mind, two very important phenomena can still be identified. First, the significantly lower number of wills from the years 1400 to 1430 coincides roughly with a period covered in the first book of wills, which has been lost. The reason for this apparent interval of approximately 20 years between the first and second book of wills cannot be determined today with certainty, but it can be assumed that this gap is related to the exclusive nature of this book. It seems that the first, lost *Liber Testamentotum et Dotaliciorum* was even more elite in character than the second, surviving book of wills. After either its completion or destruction, only a few bequests of last will were entered each year into the books of the council and municipal bench court (this can be seen in the diagram below), which were maintained parallel to one another. This situation changed during the Jubilee year in Rome in 1450, and the growing number of burghers who sought to authenticate their act of last will before leaving on a pilgrimage to the 'holy city.' The second phenomenon is related to the surviving *Liber Testamentorum*. On the one hand, after its introduction in 1450, the number of wills entered in council books in Krakow declined significantly, which shows that the municipal council consistently held to the practice of entering such acts in the *Liber Testamentorum*. On the other hand, there are interesting correlations between the book of wills and the wills recorded in the books of the municipal bench court. The number of wills in the latter dramatically decreased with the establishment and maintenance of the *Liber Testamentorum* from 1450 to 1460, but started to increase again from 1460 to 1476, a time when the number of entries in the *Liber Testamentorum* was declining. The absence of the books of the municipal bench court from the years 1476 to 1500 does not allow for unequivocal confirmation of this tendency, but there is good reason to believe it: this includes the rapidly decreasing number of wills in the *Liber Testamentorum* in the last quarter of the fifteenth century, the lack of wills written in council books, and the large number of wills found in books of the municipal bench court in the years 1500 to 1550.[314]

---

314   From the beginning of the sixteenth century, the number of surviving wills definitely increases. The number of wills recorded on the pages of bench court book from 1500–1513 is considerably higher than in the preceeding years, both in council and bench court books. For example, among the 16 wills for the year 1501, 13 are recorded in the bench court book. Similarly, in the year 1502, from a total of 15 surviving wills, 13 are found on the pages of the bench court book, and the other two in the 'Liber Testamentorum.' The

106   CHAPTER 1

This graph also confirms that the municipal bench court had been gradually assuming authority over wills since the 1470s. The reasons for this shift are not entirely clear; however, as already suggested, it is possible to point out a few phenomena that might be relevant in this respect. One of these was a developing sophistication in municipal legal system and growing knowledge of its fundamentals among the urban elites, which led to a more careful delineation of the functions and responsibilities of different municipal authorities.[315] This is indirectly proven by judgements relating to wills issued by the Higher Court of Magdeburg Law at the Castle of Krakow. Because the city of Krakow had its own privileges and local customs, the judgments of the court were usually addressed to other towns and villages in the 'Lesser Poland' region (*Małopolska*).[316] They often emphasized the legal principle derived from Magdeburg Law of the legality of wills being authenticated before a municipal bench court.[317] A better knowledge of Magdeburg Law (extended to include verdicts [*ortyle*][318] and attached Romanistic Glosses, i.e. legal opinions [*glossy*]), even if this was limited to the local authorities and municipal notaries, could have translated into a growing tendency to certify wills before this municipal organ.

Yet, the role of other factors cannot be overlooked. The municipal council, which, at the turn of the fourteenth and fifteenth centuries, sought to assume authority over wills (drawn up in the vast majority of cases by members of the urban elite) for reasons of prestige, and in order to oversee the religious activities of city inhabitants, may have lost interest in them and their broad dissemination, particularly given that, during a time of plague, the Krakow custom of representatives visiting the sick was simply dangerous for health and life. In the second half of fifteenth century, as the fear of plague increased, so did

---

total number of surviving wills from 1300–1550 was calculated by myself in *Katalog testamentów z krakowskich ksiąg miejskich do 1550 roku* (Warsaw: Semper, 2017).

315   Urszula Sowina has noted that "in medieval and early modern Krakow, testamentary dispositions were registered primarily in the books of the municipal bench court – the body responsible for private law, including provisions and decisions concerning the means for transferring property"; *eadem, Testamenty mieszczan krakowskich o przekazywaniu majątku*, 175.

316   Among the 61 cases concerning wills from 1456 to 1511 in which the Higher Court of Magdeburg Law at the Krakow Castle ruled, just one, dating from 1502 and referring to a Krakow townsman is indirectly connected with a will; *Decreta iuris supremi Magdeburgensis castri Cracoviensis. Rechtssprüche des Oberhofs des deutschen Rechts auf der Burg zu Krakau*, vol. 2: *1481–1511*, eds. Ludwik Łysiak (Frankfurt am Main: V. Klostermann, 1997), no. 881.

317   Michał Wiszniewski, *Historya*, 228–229.

318   See Glossary: Urteil

THE INSTITUTION OF THE WILL 107

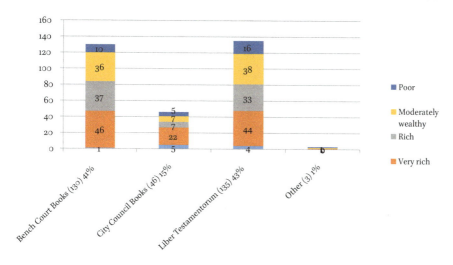

GRAPH 2   Number of wills per type of book from 1427 to 1476, taking into account the assets of testators.[320]

the reluctance to fulfil this onerous duty.[319] It is unsurprising that it was only in the latter half of the fifteenth century that it was underscored in the text of a will that it had been written during a time of plague (*temporis pestilentia*). The plague afflicted the inhabitants of the city several times during the period under consideration, the most tragic of which seems to have been the plagues of 1466 and 1482, i.e. during the changes concerning the control over wills discussed above.

From 1427 to 1476, i.e. from the first will entered in the extant first book of *Liber Testamentorum*, to the last date of the final entry in the last extant fifteenth-century book of the municipal bench court, 322 acts of last will have survived. In Graph 2 above, which shows the number of wills preserved in particular types of books, we can see an interesting phenomenon: there is a certain balance in both the number (140 to 133 records of last will) and the social position of the people whose wills were included in the books of the municipal bench court and in the book of wills. However, if we take into account both the entries in council books and in the *Liber Testamentorum* itself, we can notice

---

319   Urban elites tended to leave the city to escape epidemics; Andrzej Karpiński, *W walce z niewidzialnym wrogiem. Epidemie chorób zakaźnych w Rzeczypospolitej w XVI–XVIII wieku i ich następstwa demograficzne, społeczno-ekonomiczne i polityczne* (Warszawa: Neriton, 2000), 82.

320   The division based on the economic status of the townspeople applied here is discussed in more detail in Chapter 2, Sections 5–9 on the economic stratification of Krakow testators.

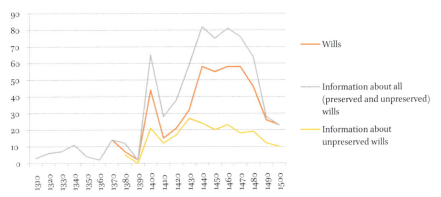

GRAPH 3 Number of testators whose wills have survived to the present day and of those whose wills are only mentioned in the source material.

that in the five decades covered, the municipal office maintained a numerical advantage over the bench court in terms of registering and authenticating Krakovian burghers' bequests of last will. As we can see in Graph 1, this situation began to change only in the latter half of the 1460s.

Another key issue significantly affecting the perception of the will as a social and cultural phenomenon in the lives of Krakow's burghers is the question of its prevalence in Krakovian society and the representativeness of the surviving wills in relation to all the wills written down in this city during the analysed period. In order to answer these questions properly, all references to the burgher wills were collected from municipal books, including both those relating to surviving wills and those referring to wills that have been lost. The results of this research were quite surprising, as can be seen Graph 3.

The graph shows three types of collected information: that relating to all testators in Krakow, to those whose wills have survived to the present day, and to those whose bequests of last will have been lost. In the years 1390–1435, the lines indicating the number of wills surviving and lost reflect similar trends indicating a rapid growth, then decline and finally a gradual increase in the number of wills made by Krakovian burghers. This data confirms observations mentioned earlier about the state of preservation of the sources. In the 1430s, the two lines rapidly diverge from each other, indicating a significant change in the ratio of extant wills to lost wills, in favour of the former. This graph therefore also confirms the 1430s as the probable end of the functioning of the first, lost book of wills. Only the absence of books of the municipal bench court from the last quarter of the fifteenth century and the declining number of wills entered onto the pages of council books during that period leads the two lines to once again converge.

These studies also allow us to draw certain conclusions concerning the popularity of the will as an institution in late medieval Krakow. Even taking

THE INSTITUTION OF THE WILL

into account the aforementioned incomplete preservation of sources in the city and the lack of reference to those wills which did not require confirmation before the municipal court because they did not involve the disposal of real estate (apart from that which fell under the traditional rules of inheritance), it must be assumed that the number of all wills written down in Krakow was not large. In the period during which the books of both the city council and the bench court have been best preserved, i.e. 1440 to 1476, the number of references to wills that have been lost represents only half of the number of surviving wills. Even if one takes into account the factors mentioned above, which lead to an underestimation of the number of wills that have been lost, the number would still not be much higher. These observations make it possible to assert that the will as a phenomenon was to a large degree elite in nature and extremely limited in its prevalence, being of interest primarily to individuals from the richest burgher families in Krakow. The will in late medieval Krakow should therefore be treated as a manifestation of 'high culture' in a medieval city, rather than as an element typical of the community as a whole. Despite the growing number of people who became interested in the will as a means of settlement of accounts at the end of their life, it did not lose its elite character during the period under examination. This act remained strongly associated both with participation in writing culture, which was still an elite sphere in the late medieval city, and with the culture of written law and its increasing codification.[321] Agnieszka Bartoszewicz, who has conducted studies on the writing culture of small and medium towns in late medieval Poland, argues that the spread of the practice of making wills influenced the development of pragmatic literacy among burghers.[322]

Wills, commonly referred to as 'testaments,' which are extended dispositions in the event of death, are the principally analysed sources in this book. However, fourteenth- and fifteenth-century municipal books include records of many other individual bequests which served a similar function and were written for similar reasons. For example, there are various bequests made 'between the living' (*inter vivos*) i.e. taking place during the one's life that, nevertheless, could serve a role similar to 'gifts because of death' (*donationes mortis causa*). They consisted of single pious bequests for opera pietatis (95 of them) and *post mortem* bequests for selected family members (356). Mutual bequests (385) also played an important role, often replacing written wills, but also sometimes complementing them. Much less numerous were the separate provisions for

---

321 As opposed to traditional customary law, which was to a greater extent a part of popular culture; cf. Leopold Pospíšil, *Anthropology of Law. A Comparative Theory* (New Haven: Harper & Row, 1974), *passim*.

322 Agnieszka Bartoszewicz, *Piśmienność*, 255.

wives, aimed at securing the position of the widow after the death of her husband (79). The fact that information on the provisions of dowers in marriage contracts has been preserved much more often in testaments than in the form of separate entries in city books, and that testators often decided to increase their value significantly in their bequests of last will, clearly indicates the affinities between these two types of acts.[323] There was not always a sharp line between wills and acts appointing guardians (*tutores*) for property, wives and children during the absence and after the death of the husband. For example, during the plague in 1467, councillor John Gartner made a bequest before the municipal bench court in which he chose as guardians for his wife Barbara and children, councillor Martin Chmiel and future alderman John Kunisz the Furrier (to whom he left the right to choose another guardian in the event of the death of one of the two listed), and also testified that he owed 100 grivna to his wife.[324] Just as wills of this kind were occasionally inscribed in the *Liber Testamentorum*, they were also made in the same circumstances: during epidemics of plague,[325] and before a long journey or war.[326] The situation was similar for testimonies made by burghers concerning the handling of debts and liabilities in the event of their death. Some of these types of testimonies entered into council books were not treated as wills, while wills that essentially contain only information on debts and liabilities have survived. This is the case, for example, with the bequest in the council book of 1439. The mayor, along with the two councillors sent in the name of the municipal council, went to the house of councillor John Slepkogil, who in their presence testified to debts amounting to 575 grivna. He outlined how they were to be paid, and declared that his wife Agnes did not possess any of his property, and that he had no rights to her silver or any other movable property, thus protecting her from liability for his financial obligations.[327]

All this gives the impression of great chaos, and of inconsistencies and a lack of a means for formally defining the character of such acts and what

---

323   Cf. Section 6, p. 70.

324   SCAB. 8, fol. 269.

325   E.g. the disposition of Anna Gliwiczowa from 1465, CONS. 429, fol. 365; of John Gartner from 1467, SCAB. 8, fol. 269 or of Wilhelm Megirszheimer of Dinkelsbühl (*von Thunkilspul*) from 1482, LT, fol. 135–136.

326   E.g. Adam Czech 'ad expedicionem transiens' in 1410, CONS. 427, fol. 376; John Stochse the gunsmith 'iturus ad expedicionem contra prutenos' in 1433, CONS. 428, fol. 317; Stanisław the cartwright 'volens proficisci contra Thurcos' in 1464, LT, fol. 81.

327   CONS. 428, fol. 397.

THE INSTITUTION OF THE WILL

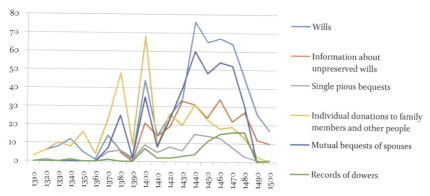

GRAPH 4 Wills and other types of donations and dispositions

distinguished them from one another.[328] Although the present book primarily analyses bequests that are more extensive in nature, during searches of source materials other, shorter bequests were also collected. The chart below outlines the different types of acts mentioned above, together with the number of wills and references in sources to lost wills in various decades of the fourteenth and fifteenth centuries. What can be seen here, above all, is that most of these (mainly donations to family members and mutual bequests) reflect the same upward and downward trends that are also observed in wills. This reflects to a certain extent the state of preservation of the source materials (especially books of the municipal bench court), but it also seems to reflect similarities in the nature of these bequests. It is also interesting to note that individual donations to family members declined significantly as wills proliferated during the fifteenth century.

In total, during the two-hundred-year period analysed, more than two thousand different kinds of bequests of a dispositive nature related to death and preparations made for it were registered (in this context, one can also include bequests of marriage dowers drawn up after marriage; see Graph 4). This number, although it is still not comparable with the number of preserved records of last will from large urban centres in Western Europe, stands out significantly when compared to the number of wills from cities in the Central European region.[329]

---

328 "When examining *mortis causa* dispositions made on the basis of municipal law, one has to take into account limitations caused by the lack of precise terminology that would have made it possible to distinguish them from alienation through acts made between the living."; Krystyna Bukowska, *Orzecznictwo*, 93.

329 Paul Baur, *Testament und Bürgerschaft*, 30; Martin Nodl, "Středověký testament jako abnormalita," in *Pozdně středověké testamenty v českých městech. Prameny, metodologie*

12   The Reasons for Writing Wills

A cursory review of surviving last wills shows the influence of epidemics and other external factors on the number of wills recorded; however, more can be seen by analysing the number of wills made in specific decades of the fourteenth and fifteenth centuries. Graph 5 provides a breakdown by year of surviving wills found in different types of municipal book. The chart indicates that in most years during this period no more than five bequests of last will were made. Given Krakow's size, this small number of acts of last will allows us to assume that they were most often made for purely personal reasons. There are only a few years in which the number of wills exceeded ten, which seems to indicate that these rises were motivated by extraordinary circumstances. The most important of these were epidemics of infectious diseases (marked in Graph 5 on the lower axis of the graph with black squares) and years of Jubilee (marked with red squares), which encouraged numerous pilgrimages from Krakow to Rome. This correlation is most evident in the wills made during the Jubilee year of 1450, the plague epidemic of 1466–1467, the subsequent Jubilee year of 1475, and the plague epidemic of 1482–1483. In the last case, however, the lack of books of the municipal bench court prevents us from properly assessing the scale of this phenomenon (the same is true for the plague epidemic of 1494–1497). Two other years in which an equally large number of wills was recorded – 1439 and 1458 – are noteworthy. In both cases, there is a surge in the number of wills.[330] Although surviving wills do not reveal the causes of this steep rise, in the first case, it may reflect the impact of major fires that in 1439 engulfed houses on Shoemaker's Street, Szczepańska Street, Jewish Street and St. Nicholas street in the city suburbs.[331] However, it is worth noting the lack of a similar increase in the number of wills in other periods in the fifteenth century, during which

---

a formy využití. Sborník příspěvků z konference uspořádané 30. listopadu 2005 Archivem hlavního města Prahy a Historickým ústavem Akademie věd České republiky, eds. Kateřina Jíšová, Eva Doleželová (Praha: Akademie věd České republiky, 2006), 73–85.

330   There are eight surviving wills from 1438, 18 from 1439, and seven from 1441. Similarly, there are eight extant bequests of last will from 1457, 15 from 1458, and eight from 1459; see the list of wills in the Annex of the present book.

331   "Urbs Cracoviensis eo anno duplex incendium pertulit: unum feria quarta quatuor temporum Penthecostes, quo tres platee: Sutorum, Sancti Stephani et Iudeorum, aliud vicesima tercia Iulii, quo platea Sancti Nicolai et suburbia eius conflagrunt"; *Joannis Dlugossii Annales Seu Cronicae Incliti Regni Poloniae: Lib. 11 et Lib. 12, 1431–1444* (Warszawa: Wydaw. Naukowe PWN, 2001), 206; cf. *Jana Długosza kanonika krakowskiego Dziejów polskich ksiąg dwanaście*, vol. 4, trans. Karol Mecherzyński, ed. Alexander Przeździecki (Krakow: Drukarnia W. Kirchmayera, 1869), 574.

THE INSTITUTION OF THE WILL 113

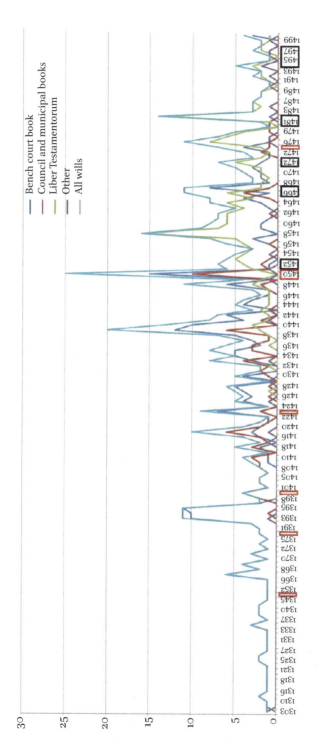

GRAPH 5   Wills made in each decade of the fourteenth and fifteenth centuries.

time there were equally severe or more serious natural disasters that struck Krakow. A decrease in the number of wills is recorded in the city both during and after the great earthquake of 1443, and following the fires of 1455 and 1462. There is also no correlation between the number of wills and the great flood that inundated the city in 1475.[332]

The motivations for writing wills, sometimes given by testators in the *arenga* (preamble) of these acts, are most often spiritual or family-related. In the first case, wills served as a vehicle for making pious bequests intended to ensure the salvation of the donor's soul; this role came from the very concept of the so-called 'canonical will' and from individual bequests for the soul, called *seelgerethe* in German. For example, in 1440 a professional court plenipotentiary named Lawrence made a will, as he himself wrote, "out of his love of God and for the rescue of his soul" (*Ich Lorencz vorreder mache meynament gote czu lobe und meyner zele czu hulfe*).[333] As seen in the *arenga* of various wills, these acts also provided instructions for the distribution of assets and the principles for the peaceful mutual co-existence of the testator's close relatives, after his death. This is mentioned in the will of councillor George Lange from 1497: "George Lange, our fellow councillor, healthy in body and mind, standing before the council today, made his last will and provided for the division of his wealth, so that after his death there would be no disputes between his wife and children."[334] Although such annotations began to appear in testaments only at the end of the fifteenth century, there is no doubt that these same reasons had led people to make such acts much earlier. The majority of wills took both of these aspects into account, as is clearly indicated by the will of councillor Nicholas Zarogowski, who "in order to ensure the salvation of his soul, standing before the council, handed over his will, written on a piece of paper, and his bequests of last will, asking that they be accepted and confirmed by the councillors, so that later there would be no disputes between his sons, daughters and wife."[335] Burghers' reasons for writing down their wills also included making preparations before a long journey military campaign, or pilgrimage,

---

332 Stanisław A. Sroka, "Klęski elementarne w Krakowie," *Rocznik Krakowski* 67, 2001, 13–18.

333 SCAB. 6, fol. 213.

334 "Der Ersame herr Georgius Lange unsirs Rathismitbruder frisch und gesunt mit wolbedochtem mute hic ym sitczendem Rathe auschinde hewt dy ferlickeit der czeit hat gemacht seynen leczten willen und schickunge seynir habe of das noch seynen tode czwuschen seynir hawsfrawen und seynir kindern nichtis czwetracht irstunde"; LT, fol. 155–156.

335 "Famosus dominus Nicolaus Zarogowsky confrater noster sanus mente et corpore non coactus nec compulsus sed de bona voluntate volens providere saluti anime sui coram nobis stans Testamentum suum et ultime voluntatis disposicionem in cartis scriptum reposuit petens id a nobis suscipi et actis nostris confirmari ne in post inter filios et filias ac uxorem suam aliqua lis sive discordia fiat"; LT, fol. 128–131 (1482).

THE INSTITUTION OF THE WILL   115

all of which were associated with the risk of loss of life.[336] Here too, family
and religious reasons tended to play an equally important role. The aforementioned councillor Nicholas Zarogowski gave an interesting explanation for the
writing of his will in 1450 before going on a pilgrimage to Rome. He wrote that
he made it "so that his successors would not make mistakes."[337]

The answer to every question about what guides peoples' actions or decisions lies somewhere within three levels of human consciousness: the conscious, subconscious and unconscious mind. If we want to delve deeper into
the motives that guided testators in Krakow, we can assume that the hidden
psychological factors involved included efforts to attain prestige in a given
social group, and sympathies and antipathies felt towards family members and
other people close to them. Factors of which they would not be conscious, or
only weakly aware, include the natural fear of death and their psychological
defence mechanisms to suppress it, and the desire to ensure they would be
remembered in the future.[338] To these two groups of factors creating a need in
people to write down an act of last will, we can also add the internal desire to
improve themselves and make redress for actions they felt violated their personal moral codes. A good example of this is a bequest in the will of Gottfrid
Fattinante from Genoa, in which the testator clearly states that as a councillor
and steward of the municipal treasury, a lack of vigilance in the decisions he
made or funds he disbursed could have caused harm to the city, and therefore
"in this hour of compensating and repaying debts" (*in horum recompensam ac
satisfaccionem debitam*) he bequeathed to the city of Krakow the significant
sum of 600 grivna to be paid to its creditors.[339]

---

336   E.g. CONS. 429, fol. 676 (1480), 693 (1481); CONS. 427, fol. 376 (1410); CONS. 428, fol. 317
       (1433); LT, fol. 81 (1464); NKiRMK, no. 616 (1321); CONS. 428, fol. 513 (1448); SCAB. 8,
       fol. 575 (1475).

337   "Ego Nicolaus Zarogowsky ob anime mee salute proponens limina beatorum Petri et Pauli
       in hoc Jubilei visitare accidente casu si me interim ab hac luce migrare contingeret primi-
       tus testamentum meum coram dominatoribus nostris facio et statuo in hac forma ut suc-
       cessors mei errore non pertirbentur"; CONS. 429, fol. 15–16.

338   Otto Gerhard Oexle, "Die Gegenwart der Lebenden und der Toten. Gedanken über Memo-
       ria," in *Gedächtnis, das Gemeinschaft stiftet*, ed. Karl Schmid (München-Zürich: Verl. Sch-
       nell & Steiner, 1985).

339   "Ceterum quia pretactus Gottfridus quondam distributor peccuniarum Ciuitatis
       Cracouiensis et legalis Consul extiterat, et si ex sua negligencia in consulendo, di-
       stribuendo seu exaccionem exsoluendo aliquos errores commisisset, ex quibus ipsi ciui-
       tati damna aliqua euenissent, ideo in horum recompensam ac satisfaccionem debitam
       predicte Ciuitati Cracouiensi quingentos florenos aur veri debiti duci Russie mutuatos
       et concessos, pro quibus Gocze Czeyn predictus et Martinus Varschow fideiusserunt,
       prout in eorumdem desuper confectis patet uteris, et apud Henricum Schuler centum
       marcas predicte Ciuitati Cracouiensi perpetuo contulit atque dedit"; KDWac., vol. 2, no.
       396, 182–185 (1393).

CHAPTER 2

The Socio-economic Position of Testators

1   Social Characteristics of the Late Medieval City

In the 1420s, the Bishop of Poznan, Stanisław Ciołek, wrote the following, in a song of praise to Krakow: "City of Krakow, your citizens united" (*Cracovia civitas, Te civium unitas*).[1] Later, an anonymous fifteenth-century preacher added that if burghers did not create unity, they should not be called burghers, but rather peasants, arguing that Christ, as a burgher himself, greatly valued *unitas*.[2] This ideal of unity among the citizenry was also commonly found among the members of the urban municipality, especially in regards to outside groups or foreign influences – both inside and outside the city walls. When correspondence was exchanged or negotiations conducted with other cities, and when homage was paid to the majesty of the royal power, the Krakow community spoke formally with one voice. For example, in 1425 the city swore an oath of allegiance to King Władysław Jagiełło which begins *Nos consules et tota civitas Cracoviensis...*[3] Yet differences of social and financial position, occupation, ethnicity, family line, place of origin and cultural capital were visible almost everywhere. These differences defined the needs and opportunities of the city's inhabitants, and thus their social and religious practices, as well.

In a community, various factors affect the unity and sense of collective identity of its members. The first of these is certainly the feeling of power that derives from belonging to this community. The bigger, richer and stronger the community, the greater and stronger this feeling becomes. Belonging is here a

---

1   Stanisław Ciołek, *Pochwała Krakowa* [In Praise of Krakow] in *Codex Epistolaris Vitoldi Magni Ducis Lithuanie 1376–1430*, ed. Antoni Prochaska (Krakow: Acad. Literarum, 1882), 1057–1058, 1057–1058.

2   "Et Christosomus dicit postquam rex celorum orbis terre natus est secundum carnem cepit esse concivis non villanus. Quia civitas dicitur civium unitas, quam unitatem Christus summe dilexit et nunc diligit. Unde ubicumque cives non sunt unanimes non menciuntur dici cives, sed villani, quia non sunt concordes"; as in Krzysztof Bracha, *Nauczanie kaznodziejskie w Polsce późnego średniowiecza. Sermones dominicales et festivales z tzw. kolekcji Piotra z Miłosławia* (Kielce: Wydawnictwo Akademii Świętokrzyskiej w Kielcach, 2007), 271.

3   For example, the city of Krakow swore an oath of allegiance to King Władysław Jagiełło, his son Władysław, and in the event of their childless deaths, to Princess Hedwig; *Codex epistolaris saeculi decimi quinti*, vol. 1, ed. Anatol Lewicki (Krakow: Akad. Umiejętności, 1891), no. 67 (1425).

© JAKUB WYSMUŁEK, 2021 | DOI:10.1163/9789004461444_004
This is an open access chapter distributed under the terms of the CC BY-NC-ND 4.0 license.

THE SOCIO-ECONOMIC POSITION OF TESTATORS

source of happiness and pride, even if one plays a relatively marginal role in the community. As a community is weakened, one's identification with it can likewise become the source of a sense of weakness or inferiority. The cohesiveness of any given community is maintained by collective rituals celebrating its unity and hierarchies. These include shared holiday celebrations, processions that provide an opportunity to manifest one's identification with the community and position within it,[4] and traditional feasts and gatherings that play an elementary, archaic role, of inducting individuals into a circle of friends, family, clan or a wider social group. These shared celebrations also serve a most important function; they are a means of sustaining *memoria* – the memory of a community's history and its deceased members.[5] On the other hand, community is first built through mutual utility – through giving and receiving. In this way, a network of commitments is created; that is, bonds that join people together by means of the eternal principle of reciprocity and the debt an indebted individual owes to their benefactor. In traditional societies, a donation has not so much an economic dimension as a social, moral and religious one.[6] Like a will, a larger pious foundation is a form of gift, if not to the community as a whole, then at least to a specific group of people. It is a means of identifying with the community, a proof of one's trust in it and concern for it, and a testament to one's hope that this generous gift will be repaid. For giving is never a sign of indifference or neutral in character. It creates a social bond, but it is also a form of symbolic violence.[7] One must either succumb to the expectation of reciprocity or reject the gift, which is seen as an insult; an affront to the donor and a renunciation of friendship.

---

4   "In other words, a procession, with its established order, symbolic stations, songs and a whole scenario, expressed the most important concepts of urban theology, and communicated to its participants that the city was a common good, that it was – according to a metaphor by Wilhelm of Auvergne – a shared creation of free and united citizens who lived in a wonderful environment by means of mutual agreement."; Jacques Rossiaud, *Mieszczanin i życie w mieście*, in *Człowiek średniowiecza*, ed. Jacques Le Goff, trans.. Maria Radożycka-Paoletti (Warszawa–Gdańsk: Świat Książki, 1996), 225 (J. Rossiaud, *Le Citadin*, "L'Homme medieval," ed. Jacques Le Goff, Seuil 1989); cf. Hanna Zaremska, "Procesje Bożego Ciała w Krakowie w XIV–XVI wieku," in *Kultura elitarna a kultura masowa w Polsce późnego średniowiecza*, ed. Bronisław Geremek (Wrocław: Zakład Narodowy im. Ossolińskich, 1978), 25–40, 25–40.

5   Otto Gerhard Oexle, "Memoria und Memorialüberlieferung im frühen Mittelalter," *Frühmittelalterliche Studien*, vol. 10, 1976; idem, "Die Gegenwart der Lebenden und der Toten. Gedanken über Memoria," in *Gedächtnis, das Gemeinschaft stiftet*, ed. Karl Schmid (München-Zürich: Verl. Schnell & Steiner, 1985).

6   Marcel Mauss, *The Gift: The Form and Reason for Exchange in Archaic Societies*, trans. W.D. Halls (New York: Routledge, 1990 (1950)).

7   Pierre Bourdieu, *The Logic of Practice* (Cambridge: Cambridge University Press, 1990), 122–134.

People's place in the community in which they live, their position and prestige are partly a matter of perspective. Everyone evaluates himself or herself from the point of view of his or her own values, prestige and power. This position is evaluated differently by one's own family, neighbours, members of social or professional groups to which one belongs, and members of other communities. In culturally homogeneous and traditional rural communities, due to the limited number of members, similarities in the way they live and work, and their fundamental self-sufficiency, there is no need to create more extensive social structures than those determined by personal prestige and wealth. A fundamental feature of a large city in almost every age is that new immigrants coming from smaller towns and the countryside had to face its social, professional, financial, class, and even ethnic, linguistic and religious diversity. In this much larger and much more complex community, a person's place was largely determined by his belonging to one or more communities that were either secular or religious in nature (and most often containing elements from both). These groups were of a formal, corporate or devotional character, or based on informal ties of friendship, neighborhood, kinship and personal interests, and comprised the complex social structure of the medieval city. The principle of group solidarity, and the identity based on it, did not necessarily differ much from that already found in rural environments. In the city, however, unlike in rural areas, social groups were more often voluntary associations than natural communities.[8] Where wealth is based on money and not on land inherited, where personal activity is more important than inherited honours, people have a greater part to play in making personal decisions, selecting which groups they wish to be members of, and defining their role within these groups.

The medieval city was also a world of paradoxes and contradictions. In their search for sources of authority, its inhabitants often turned to 'old customs,' even though modernizing forces were considerably stronger in urban areas. In the city, more than anywhere else, money meant power, even as poverty was venerated, especially voluntary poverty. Finally, in a relatively small area lived a community in which there were enormous income disparities, where

---

8   In the well-known division between Community (Gemeinschaft) and Society (Gesellschaft) Ferdinand Tönnies referred to the earlier work of J.G. Bluntschli and R. Bradter: "...Wherever urban culture flourishes, 'Society' also appears as its indispensable medium. Country people know little of it. On the other hand, everyone who praises rural life has pointed to the fact that people there have a stronger and livelier sense of Community. Community means genuine, enduring life together, whereas Society is a transient and superficial thing. Thus Gemeinschaft must be understood as a living organism in its own right, while Gesellschaft is a mechanical aggregate and artefact.", Ferdinand Tönnies, *Community and Civil Society*, ed. Jose Harris (Cambridge: Cambridge University Press, 2001), 19

THE SOCIO-ECONOMIC POSITION OF TESTATORS

alongside rich merchants who lent money to the king, lived impoverished people with very modest resources. Nevertheless, in the urban *communitas* the evangelical ideal of modesty and the notion of the equality of its members were still alive.

How, then, in this complex social structure, in which the determinants of position were such disparate values as humility, charity and piety, on the one hand, and ostentatious wealth and wasteful consumption, on the other, can we designate the place of those who chose to write a will? Does the social standing of the testators explain how they used wills to express, maintain or advance their own position?

It seems the answers should be sought both in the social categories used by medieval burghers and in the meaning they assigned to them. The preserved sources may bring us closer to an understanding of the structure of the social and cultural groups that included medieval Krakovian testators.

Wills are rarely used as sources in research on urban societies. This is due to a number of methodological problems, the most important of which are undoubtedly their diverse nature and their unrepresentativeness in relation to urban society as a whole. Yet, they contain a great deal of valuable information about the property and family relations of burghers that is found nowhere else. In the present chapter, devoted to an analysis of the groups to which Krakow testators belonged, an attempt has been made to overcome these difficulties in order to make the most of the potential inherent in these sources. At the same time, understanding who the people were who decided to write their acts of last will should also help us better understand their role and the reasons why these documents were written.

2 Categories of Urban Social Subdivisions

When describing urban society, historians often refer to a classic tripartite model, comprising the patricians, the common citizens (in Polish – *pospólstwo*), and plebeians (*plebs*) – the poorest social stratum in the city.[9] Of these three

---

9 Andrzej Karpiński, *Pauperes. O mieszkańcach Warszawy XVI i XVII wieku* (Warszawa: Państwowe Wydawnictwo Naukowe, 1983); Jan Ptaśnik, *Miasta i mieszczaństwo w dawnej Polsce* (Warszawa: Państwowe Wydawnictwo Naukowe, 1949), 87; Maria Bogucka, Henryk Samsonowicz, *Dzieje miast i mieszczaństwa w Polsce przedrozbiorowej* (Wrocław–Warszawa–Krakow: Zakład Narodowy im. Ossolińskich, 1986), 138–156; Jacek Wiesiołowski, "Biedni, bogaci, przeciętni. Stratyfikacja społeczeństwa polskiego w końcu XV w.," in *Biedni i bogaci. Studia z dziejów społeczeństwa i kultury ofiarowane Bronisławowi Geremkowi w sześćdziesiątą rocznicę urodzin* (Warszawa: Państwowe Wydawnictwo Naukowe, 1992), 145–154.

groups, however, only the common citizens has any foundation in the sources, as a translation of the Latin expression *communitas civium* – civic community.[10] Synonyms are the Polish terms *komuna* (commune) and *gmina* (community) derived from the German word *gemeynde*, which has the same meaning. The concepts of patrician and plebeian were borrowed from ancient Rome – and thus far from the realities of medieval cities – where conflicts often broke out between the privileged and politically disadvantaged strata of society.[11] These are therefore not terms used by medieval townsmen themselves. In reality, a basic division between 'us and them' dominated,[12] with any collectivity being defined by its opposition to some other group. Roman Czaja rightly points out that most information about how the social system was perceived was connected with social conflicts.[13] When a municipality had to deal with people from outside it, such as representatives of other cities, states or territorial authorities, it acted as a homogeneous community of citizens, as a communitas. However, when conflicts broke out within the community, it usually broke down into two camps, a community of citizens (in German *gancze gemeyne*) and councillors exercising power over them (*di libin herren*), as was the case after the anti-Jewish pogrom of 1407.[14] Earlier, in 1368, when the municipal council was accused of mismanaging the finances of the community, and its citizens demanded a means to control the municipal authorities, Casimir III the Great ordered the community to elect representatives to the council, half from craftsmen (in Latin *a populo mechanico*) and half from the commonalty and merchants (*a populo civili ac mercatorum*).[15] In this case, it seems that the conflict was between craftsmen and merchants, as it had been in 1418, when as a result of a complaint from the city community (in German *gemeynde*),

---

10   Jan Ptaśnik, *Miasta i mieszczaństwo*, 87.

11   "In 1516 Christoph Scheuerl (1481–1542), a lawyer and humanist, used the Roman term 'patricia' to accentuate the antiquity of the families ruling Nuremberg. In the seventeenth century, the term 'Patriciat' became widely used in Germany to refer to the people who ruled cities, and in the mid-nineteenth century the term was also used to refer to powerful elites in medieval cities."; Roman Czaja, *Grupy rządzące w miastach nadbałtyckich w średniowieczu* (Toruń: Wydawnictwo Naukowe Uniwersytetu Mikołaja Kopernika, 2008), 18.

12   Ludwik Stomma, *Od 'czarnej legendy' do kategorii 'swój – obcy,'* in idem, *Antropologia kultury wsi polskiej XIX wieku oraz wybrane eseje* (Łódź: P. Dopierała, 2002), 40.

13   Roman Czaja, *Grupy rządzące*, 66–67.

14   Hanna Zaremska, *Żydzi w średniowiecznej Polsce. Gmina krakowska* (Warszawa: Instytut Historii PAN, 2011), 471.

15   Jan Ptaśnik, *Miasta i mieszczaństwo*, 89; Marcin Starzyński, *Krakowska rada miejska w średniowieczu* (Krakow: "Societas Vistulana," 2010), 68.

THE SOCIO-ECONOMIC POSITION OF TESTATORS

a special, 16-person organ was established at the request of King Władysław Jagiełło to consult the council, consisting of eight representatives of merchants and eight representatives of Krakow's guilds (*achte von deme Kaufmanne und achte von den Czechen*).[16] Without the consent of these representatives of the community, the council had no right to issue or impose new taxes, and had to report to them on the city's finances.[17] A similar symbolic division of the urban community occurred in 1462, after the murder of Andrew Tęczyński, when his brother and Castellan of Krakow, John Tęczyński, named as guilty parties both members of the municipal council and representatives of the community, i.e. senior merchants and craftsmen (*universum consulatum cum senioribus mercatorum et mechanicorum civitatis citari fecit*).[18]

Among the basic symbolic divisions used by people at that time was the opposition between the urban municipality and an increasingly independent municipal council – that is between the rulers and the ruled. Another was a division within the communitas based on profession – between merchants and craftsmen, or those whose work involved bookkeeping and trade, and those who worked with their hands. Although the difference between a merchant engaged in international trade and a market stallholder was as great as the difference between a goldsmith and a local tanner, these basic distinctions were considered functional by contemporaries. Inaccurate as they may be, as models which shaped the popular imagination and social expectations of the time, it is important we take them seriously.

In Middle Ages, an occupation involving trade was associated with the intellect and accounting, while the crafts were seen primarily as forms of physical labour. Along with the disparities in the economic capital, these differing social attitudes towards specific types of work and the practices they involved influenced the social value assigned to them. The increasing employment of accounting and written culture among members of the merchant class and the nature of their work, which required the establishment of trading companies, frequent travel, dealing with money and managing financial affairs, and cooperating with people whose social class (estate) or status differed from their own, resulted in the development of a new way of thinking – a merchant's mentality – among this social class. This mentality was characterized by an ability to calculate and plan, to manage people and goods, and to participate

---

16   KDMK, vol. I, no. 111.

17   Jan Ptaśnik, *Miasta i mieszczaństwo*, 91; Marcin Starzyński, *Krakowska rada*, 79.

18   *Codex epistolaris saeculi decimi quinti*, vol. 2, ed. Anatol Lewicki (Krakow: Akad. Umiejętności, 1891), 214.

in the written culture.[19] At the same time, the merchant class was becoming increasingly prosperous, with ever more wealth concentrated in their hands. These factors greatly influenced the adoption and spread of writing wills among the merchant class, who now emulated members of the highest social strata in the city in drawing up acts of last will and creating foundations.

The craftsman's way of thinking was probably much more 'local-collectivist' in nature. After a journeyman completed his 'journeyman years' (*wanderjahre*) and chose a city in which to settle, he usually stayed there, becoming part of the local parish, guild and neighborhood structures. Both the limited prospects for social advancement offered by working in a small craft workshop and a low level of involvement in written culture caused craftsmen to be closely tied to a specific part of the urban communitas. Based on the differences between these characterological types, it can be said that while the merchant sought to emphasize his own personal social position and increase the distance between himself and other inhabitants of the city, medieval urban craftsmen were guided by the ideals of moderation and equality among the burgher class.[20] Nevertheless, influenced by the practices of the upper classes, over time the practice of writing a will came to be seen as a proper way to bid farewell to loved ones and to the temporal world, and became a common practice among Krakow's craftsmen too.[21]

The value of structural models of urban communities, like those above, should not be underestimated, as they also express the manner in which particular social groups conceived of themselves and others. Moreover, the way in which a community and its boundaries were defined affected how power was exercised in the city and who was denied this privilege. We can expect that members of the ruling elite tended to think more often in terms of the interests

---

19 Agnieszka Bartoszewicz, *Piśmienność mieszczańska*, 240–267; *eadem*, "Piśmienność mieszczańska w późnośredniowiecznej Polsce," in *Historia społeczna późnego średniowiecza. Nowe badania*, ed. Sławomir Gawlas (Warszawa: DiG, 2011), 275–292; Jerzy Kaliszuk, *Przemiany społecznych funkcji pisma w późnym średniowieczu. Programy badawcze i ich rezultaty*, in *ibidem*, 169–188; vol. Jurek, *Pismo w życiu społecznym Polski późnego średniowiecza*, in *ibidem*, 203–232.

20 Aron J. Gurevich, *Kupiec*, in *Człowiek średniowiecza*, 323–331 (A. J. Gurevich, *Le Marchand*, "L'Homme medieval," ed. Jacques Le Goff, Seuil 1989); Jacek Wiesiołowski, *Socjotopografia późnośredniowiecznego Poznania* (Poznan: Państwowe Wydawn. Nauk., 1997), 29.

21 "It is hard to deny the fact that lower-status groups often imitated the cultural practices of higher status groups. Explaining this imitation is rather more difficult. The lower groups may have done this because they wanted to rise socially, or to appear to have risen socially, because they accepted the 'cultural hegemony' of the upper classes. On the other hand, they may have imitated the habits of their so-called 'betters' as an affirmation of equity with them.", Peter Burke, *Popular Culture in Early Modern Europe*, New York, Ashgate 2009, 15.

THE SOCIO-ECONOMIC POSITION OF TESTATORS

of the communitas as a whole as well as to act in ways that enhanced their own prestige and that of their family.[22] Such actions included making generous bequests to city churches, especially for the founding of altars, perpetual masses, and private chapels, which not only commemorated the founder and his family, but also served the entire community. On the other hand, Krakovian burghers made pious bequests for work that served the public good, including the maintenance of city roads, bridges and city walls, which reveal something about the sacred dimension of the city, the urban community and its institutions.[23] The activity of most burghers, who were prevented from participation in the broader political life of the municipality, was focused instead on concerns of smaller social groups functioning within the urban community, such as their immediate family, guilds, fraternities, and their neighborhood and parish communities. This narrower field of social contacts, limited financial means, and the craftsman's ideals of moderation and equality meant that those institutions closest to the burghers were the main beneficiaries of the provisions of their last wills.

The changes taking place in urban culture during the late Middle Ages resulted in the social elevation of the professions of the merchant and craftsman. The merchant profession, which had been earlier burdened by an association with the sin of usury, now acquired social and religious acceptance.[24] As the concept arose of profit as 'compensation' for the merchant who lent money for his lost time and the risk he assumed, monetary transactions lost their previous, unambiguously negative, connotation. Belief in Purgatory, and the resulting conviction that it was possible to actively seek salvation through the prayerful support of others, led to the development of various forms of charitable activity.[25] In the words of historian Jacques Le Goff, "[i]t is also clear that, in parallel with a certain social and spiritual promotion of the merchant, the management of money benefited from a shift in the ideas and practices of the Church which, it seems, wished to assist the people of the Middle Ages in their desire to safeguard their money and their lives, that is, both their earthly

---

22   Janusz Sztumski, *Elity – ich miejsce i rola w społeczeństwie* (Katowice: "Śląsk," 1997), 45–46.

23   Marek Słoń, *Religijność komunalna w Europie środkowej późnego średniowiecza,* in *Zbožnost středověku,* ed. Martin Nodl, Krzysztof Bracha, Jan Hrdina, Paweł Kras (Praha: Filosofia, 2007) (Colloquia mediaevalia Pragensia, 6), 9–21.

24   Jacques Le Goff, *Money and the Middle Ages* (Cambridge: Cambridge University Press, 2012), 20–22.

25   "It was manifested in special care paid to the body which, like the body of the suffering Christ, was destined to rise from the dead"; *ibidem,* 99; cf. Stanisław Bylina, *Człowiek i zaświaty.* Wizje kar pośmiertnych w Polsce średniowiecznej (Warszawa: Instytut Historii PAN, 1992), 115–135.

124 CHAPTER 2

wealth and their eternal salvation."[26] The growing importance of money both in the everyday life of the city's inhabitants and in the policies pursued by the rulers caused property to become an increasingly important (though still not the sole) determinant of one's social position. From that time on, the amount of property one owned, and thus the urban tax revenue it generated, differentiated the city's inhabitants into distinct categories with different obligations towards the urban community.

Physical labour, previously seen as a punishment – a consequence of original sin – underwent a similar evolution in the late Middle Ages. A man who worked in a workshop with his hands became a disciple of both St. Joseph and Jesus himself, who was supposed to have worked as a carpenter in his youth. Church teachings about God's creation of the world prompted comparisons with the heavy burden of human fate: "The man who worked thus became a co-worker with God in his construction of a world which struggled to live up to the expectations of its Creator."[27] Guild organizations, which became increasingly prevalent in the fourteenth and especially fifteenth centuries in Krakow,[28] not only oversaw the work of craftsmen and organized their social life, but also provided a strong base of support for enhancing the social prestige of their members. The larger and stronger the guilds were, the greater the importance of their members in the city.[29] They provided a link between the city authorities, dominated by merchants, and the internally diversified community of craftsmen. It is therefore not surprising that prestigious, well-established guild masters were chosen by testators to act as executors of their wills or to assume the role of guardians for their underage children; moreover, in some cases, testators chose to have their last wills attested before Krakovian

---

26   Jacques Le Goff, *Money and the Middle Ages*, 149.

27   *Ibidem*, 71.

28   Jerzy Wyrozumski, *Dzieje Krakowa. Krakow do schyłku wieków średnich* (Krakow: Wydawnictwo Literackie, 1992), 331–371; Hanna Zaremska, *Bractwa w średniowiecznym Krakowie. Studium form społecznych życia religijnego* (Wrocław–Warszawa–Krakow: Instytut Historii PAN, 1977), 24–30.

29   Mateusz Goliński, *Socjotopografia późnośredniowiecznego Wrocławia* (Wrocław: Wydawn. Uniwersytetu Wrocławskiego, 1997), 463; Jerzy Wyrozumski, *Dzieje Krakowa*, 331–371; Feliks Kiryk, Porządek cechowy w lokacyjnym Krakowie, in *Krakow. Studia z dziejów miasta*, ed. Jerzy Rajman (Krakow: Wydawn. Nauk. Akademii Pedagogicznej, 2007), 76–86; Zdzisław Noga, *Grupy zawodowe i przepływy międzygrupowe w Krakowie i miastach województwa Krakowskiego w średniowieczu*, in *Człowiek w średniowieczu*, ed. Alicja Szymczakowa (Łódź: Wydawnictwo Uniwersytetu Łódzkiego, 2009), 253–263; Stanisław Herbst, *Toruńskie cechy rzemieślnicze. Zarys przeszłości* (Toruń: Nakładem Cechów toruńskich, 1933); Henryk Samsonowicz, "Cechy rzemieślnicze w średniowiecznej Polsce. Mity i rzeczywistość," PH, vol. 75, 1984, no. 2, 551–567.

THE SOCIO-ECONOMIC POSITION OF TESTATORS

craftsmen. In the latter case, the craftsmen's role was formally limited to being witnesses to the transmission of the dying person's last will, though their status as senior guild members was undoubtedly an additional guarantor of the will's implementation.[30]

Apart from merchants (including stallholders) and craftsmen, there was a third, broad but fairly elusive, category of city inhabitant – the urban poor.[31] Their numbers can only be generally estimated, and they were usually not actively involved in the local community. They did not own real estate in the city, and were tied to it only insofar as they could find a way to support themselves there. However, when their economic situation or that of the city deteriorated, or when unforeseen political or social circumstances arose, it was easy for them to leave the city walls, and either return to their home villages and towns, or move on in search of success in other large urban centres. This habit made them appear like a liquid mass of outsiders in the eyes of the city and its authorities. Of course, the status of a guild journeyman was different from that of an unskilled worker or a maid, or that of a beggar, thief or prostitute. It seems, however, that the social bonds between the poor were stronger than those tying them to other citizens of the city with whom and for whom they worked, not so much due to the occupations they were engaged in, but perhaps above all because of their lack of material wealth.[32] Due to their low social status, they were also excluded from the burgher culture that was forming, as well as its ethic, social order and the forms of piety associated with it.[33] A will was a tool allowing one to dispose of one's property, and thus to maintain control over its fate, even after one's death. A lack of means and the costs associated with making a will economically excluded broad groups of

---

30   CONS. 428, fol. 466 (1443); CONS. 429, fol. 543 (1475); LT, fol. 133–134 (1482); as well as, for example, the will of Emerancza Długoszowa of 1508; The National Archives in Krakow, Wills and testaments, ms 779.

31   "Therefore, tax registers do not include those permanent citizens of cities who did not enjoy burgher privileges, i.e.: apprentices, students, servants, hired workers, beggars and others who did not own property. Thus, municipal tax registers leave out a significant part of the urban population – the poor, who, for example, constituted 16% of Hamburg inhabitants in 1451, 20% in 1487, 20%, and 24% in 1538. It was discovered that at the turn of the fourteenth and fifteenth centuries only about 20% of the inhabitants of the Baltic cities had burgher privileges."; Antoni Czacharowski, "Ze studiów nad strukturą społeczną mieszczaństwa toruńskiego na przełomie XIV/XV wieku," *Acta Universitatis Nicolai Copernici: Historia* 9 (1973), 90.

32   Bronisław Geremek, *Litość i szubienica. Dzieje nędzy i miłosierdzia* (Warszawa: Czytelnik, 1989), 74–86.

33   Norbert Schindler, *Ludzie prości, ludzie niepokorni... Kultura ludowa w początkach dziejów nowożytnych*, trans. Barbara Ostrowska (Warszawa: Wiedza Powszechna, 2002), 33–36.

city dwellers from becoming potential testators. Moreover, culturally it is no surprise that the urban poor of the period, who owned little property, rarely made wills: the growing phenomenon of the will was integral to the formation of a burgher culture aspiring to greater rationality, anchored in the ownership of material goods.[34]

3 Municipal Authorities as Testators

Affluent members of the burgher community with ties to the municipal authorities were the people primarily responsible for the introduction of the practice of making pious bequests for Church institutions and the dissemination of wills as a means of enabling such religious foundations, in the first half of the fourteenth century. Subsequently, in the late-fourteenth and fifteenth centuries, members of this same social group were those most interested in, and prepared for, the disposal of their property and establishment of rules of inheritance that would protect their estate from dispersion. Although the social elite of Krakow was certainly not limited to representatives of the city authorities, it was nevertheless members of councillors' families, endowed with the prestige of a governing authority, who had the greatest influence on the adoption and spread of new cultural trends and legal solutions in Krakow, including the increasing prevalence of the communal will.

Among the 457 Krakow burghers whose wills have survived to this day, 34 were aldermen, and another 71 were councillors. Representatives of the municipal authorities constituted nearly a quarter of all Krakovian testators. If we add to this the eighteen women who appear in wills as the wives and widows of aldermen and councillors, we find that members of these two groups comprise more than a quarter of all known Krakovian testators from the fourteenth and fifteenth centuries. It can be assumed that among those preparing written acts of last will, the final number of people associated with the circles of power, i.e. including all the widows of councillors and aldermen (including those who remarried, and whose new spouses were not city officials) and their children, sons-in-law and daughters-in-law, must have been much higher.

As can be seen from Graph 6, the share of city officials among all known Krakovian testators decreased steadily over the course of the fourteenth and fifteenth centuries. In the first half of the fourteenth century, they constituted

---

34 "Modern, specifically occidental capitalism grew out of relatively rationally administered, specifically occidental, urban organisations..." Max Weber, *Economy and Society*, trans. Keith Tribe (Harvard: Harvard University Press, 2019), 373

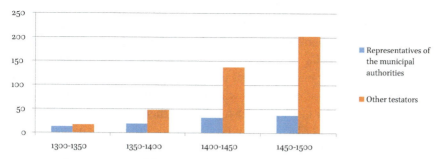

GRAPH 6 Representatives of the municipal authorities among known Krakovian testators in the fourteenth-fifteenth centuries.

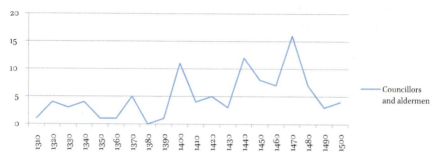

GRAPH 7 Number of councillors and aldermen among known Krakovian testators in particular decades of the fourteenth and fifteenth centuries.

as much as 43% of all testators, while in the latter half only 28%; in the first half of the fifteenth century, they constituted as much as 19% of all testators, and in the latter half only 15%.

There are also visible fluctuations in particular decades of the fourteenth and fifteenth centuries in the number of councillors and aldermen whose records of last will have survived to our times (Graph 7).[35] The most interesting of these are the sharp increases in their number over three decades: 1391 to 1400 (11), 1431 to 1440 (12) and 1461 to 1470 (16).

Although wills are usually more affected by individual, local factors than others, there are some broader social and cultural trends worth considering here. In each of the three 'peak' moments mentioned above, slightly different reasons seem to have prompted members of the elite among Krakow's authorities to write down their last wills. The number of Krakovian wills written during the 1390s (44) that have been preserved is exceptionally large, especially in comparison with previous decades. At that time, the reasons for writing wills,

---

35   In this study, the date when the will was first written by each person is taken into account.

128 CHAPTER 2

and the form they took, changed significantly: the Krakow municipal council assumed a form of patronage over burgher wills, establishing the first book of wills and introducing as a standard practice (German *Gewonheit*) councillors going to sick burghers to witness the declaration of their last will. Consequently, a new form of communal will was becoming institutionalized. The municipal authorities' new approach to wills and their 'promotion' of the practice of writing an act of last will can be seen in such things as the significant number of wills made by councillors and aldermen during this decade (especially since all of these wills were written by healthy individuals).

The years 1431–1440, when as many as twelve Krakow councillors and aldermen wrote their wills, were also a period from which a significant number of all wills have been preserved. We are probably dealing here with a distortion of research data due to the absence of the first book of wills. It seems possible, therefore, that this steep increase in the number of wills recorded during this period is a reflection of their ceasing to be recorded in the missing first *Liber Testamentorum*, which likely occurred some time in the 1430s. This hypothesis is supported by the fact that we are not dealing at this time with a specific type of written will, e.g. during an illness or before a pilgrimage, but with various types of bequests of last will recorded both in books of the bench court and in council books.

However, the preservation of as many as sixteen wills made by representatives of the municipal authorities between 1461 and 1470 is mainly due to two important events that took place during this decade. The first was the murder of Andrew Tęczyński in 1461 and the related trial, conviction and execution of three Krakow councillors: Stanisław Leymitter,[36] Jarosz Szarlej and Konrad Lang, in January 1462.[37] The second event linked to this increase in the writing of acts of last will was an epidemic of plague in Krakow in 1466 and 1467, when as many as seven councillors and aldermen made such dispositions.[38]

The decrease in the number of wills made by representatives of the ruling elite from the 1470s onwards is related to a general decrease in the number of wills written in Krakow, due, among other things, to the loss of one or two

---

36   Sławomira Pańków, "Stanisław Leymitter," in PSB, vol. 17 (Wrocław–Warszawa–Krakow: Polska Akademia Nauk, Polska Akademia Umiejętności, 1971), 263.

37   Stanisław Leymitter, LT, fol. 81; Jarosz Szarlej, LT, fol. 73–74; Konrad Lang, LT, fol. 72–73; Marcin Starzyński, *Krakowska rada*, 89–96.

38   Bartholomeus Graudencz, SCAB. 8, fol. 246; John Kunisz, SCAB. 8, fol. 273; John Czarny, SCAB. 8, fol. 300–301; Jacob Wilkowski, CONS. 429, fol. 372; Hartlip Parchwicz, SCAB. 8, fol. 269; Paul Ber, SCAB. 8, fol. 270–271; John Gartner, SCAB. 8, fol. 269.

THE SOCIO-ECONOMIC POSITION OF TESTATORS

books of the bench court from the end of the sixteenth century and a significant decrease in the number of wills entered in council books at that time.

Among the more than 100 wills written by members of Krakow's municipal authorities, the wills of the three above-mentioned Krakow councillors, who were held responsible for the death of Andrew Tęczyński, deserve special attention due to the exceptional circumstances under which they were written.[39] These men, who were among the most influential citizens of Krakow, were suddenly imprisoned and charged with the capital crime of murder. While awaiting trial in the prison located in the Krakow City Hall, they wrote their wills in accordance with the prevailing practice and notions of a 'good death.'[40]

Stanisław Leymitter, the first to write his will, did so before the final verdict was passed on 7th January 1462. On July 16th 1461, when the murder of Tęczyński occurred, Leymitter was serving as the city's mayor, which probably assured a guilty plea and left him with no hope of avoiding execution. Compared to other councillors, his situation was made even worse by the fact that he was the *homo novus* in the group of councillors. Although he had sat on the municipal bench court since as early as 1454, he was not co-opted to the town council until 1461.[41] The will Leymitter made was traditional in form.[42] In the first part, he makes bequests to opera pietatis,[43] to which he allocated 70 florins, and then bequeathed to his wife Sophie 600 florins as a dower, secured by his estate. Later in his will, he gave to his brother (perhaps his younger brother) Paul an annual payment of ten grivna "for food and clothing," which he would receive for the rest of his life. At the end of the will, he listed and donated the debts he owed and sums owed to him, along with an inventory of the lead he traded in, to his children – the heirs of the rest of the estate. He confirmed having settled accounts with his brother Nicholas, most likely his business partner, and chose as executors of the will John Wierzynek and his brother-in-law Andrew Czeringer.

---

39   Marcin Starzyński, *Krakowska rada*, 89–96; Janusz Kurtyka, *Tęczyńscy. Studium z dziejów polskiej elity możnowładczej w średniowieczu* (Krakow: Secesja, 1997), 373–374.

40   Stanisław Leymitter did so on January 7, 1462, Konrad Lang and Jarosz Szarlej declared their last wills during the night of January 8; cf. Marcin Starzyński, *Krakowska rada*, 94.

41   *Ibidem*, 93, 284.

42   Sławomira Pańków, Stanisław Leymitter, 263.

43   20 florins toward the construction of the Church of the Blessed Virgin Mary, 30 florins for the building of St. Bernard's; five florins for food for poor patients of the 'big hospital' of the Holy Spirit; five florins for poor patients of the hospital of St. Hedwig in Stradom; five florins for food for lepers, men and women, both at St. Leonard's and St. Valentine's; LT, fol. 81.

Jarosz Szarlej's will is much longer and is rich in interesting information. The career of this renowned councillor (who had held this office since 1455) was likewise interrupted in 1462 by the murder of Andrew Tęczyński.[44] On the night of the eighth of January, he was detained together with other accused councillors, and wrote down his last will while in prison in the town hall.[45] The nature of this will is reminiscent of other acts of last will written by people whose illness took them by surprise during the course of their day-to-day lives. In addition to dispositions aimed at safeguarding his family's future, a major part of the will consists of a list of debts and sums owed. Szarlej bequeathed 200 fines to his wife, increased in his will by another 100 fines. He also owned a house at the market square, which his wife had inherited from her father, as well as half of another house at the market square, houses at Sławkowska and St. Florian Streets, and a cloth stall at the market square. The fact that trade in cloth was one of his main income sources is evidenced by the provisions of his will, and in particular by information about a debt owed by King Kazimierz Jagiellończyk of 400 grivna for cloth purchased from the councillor. It is interesting to note that after listing his debtors and creditors, and distributing his movable property, real estate, and clothing and personal items among his children, the testator, who was awaiting his fate on 'death row,' decided to make a pious bequest of only a few grivna.[46]

Also interesting is the will of the third convicted councillor – Konrad (*Cuncze*) Lang, son of the Krakovian alderman and councillor Nicholas Lang[47] and brother of another Krakovian testator and councillor from Krakow, Stanisław Lang.[48] Having been raised in a well-rooted Krakovian elite family, Konrad first sat on the municipal bench court from 1442 to 1451, and was then elected councillor, and held this office until 1462.[49] To his second wife, Hedwig,[50] he bequeathed 400 florins as a dower, stipulating that every florin should be counted as 28 Czech *groschen*.[51] He then distributed his movables

---

44   Marcin Starzyński, *Krakowska rada*, 89–94.

45   LT, fol. 73–74.

46   He bequeathed two grivna to the monastery in Częstochowa, two grivna to the Bernardine monastery in Krakow and ordered 30 Gregorian masses to be celebrated for his soul in the monastery in Mogiła.

47   Marcin Starzyński, *Krakowska rada*, 93, 278.

48   LT, fol. 117 (1476); Marcin Starzyński, *Krakowska rada*, 286.

49   Marcin Starzyński, *Krakowska rada*, 278.

50   She was already married to him in 1451 when she bequeathed her hereditary possessions to him before the municipal council, and in turn, provided for a dower for her in his will before the court; SCAB. 7, fol. 112, 165, 169.

51   "[...] den gulden gerechend umb acht und czwenczig groschen bemische"; LT, fol. 72.

THE SOCIO-ECONOMIC POSITION OF TESTATORS   131

and properties, clearly distinguishing what his wife and children should receive.[52] In a clear effort to avoid family quarrels and protect his wife from potential disputes with her stepchildren, he guaranteed her the right to live in their house and have one bedroom and one dining room in it (In German *eyne kemnot und stube*) for as long as she remained a widow. He also divided his property between the children of his first and second marriage and allocated some of his household furnishings (perhaps as a *hergewet* – the hereditary property due to a man) to his oldest, already independent son, Lawrence. Konrad, like Jarosz Szarlej, owned a company (*geselschaft*) with his brother Stanisław and entrusted him with the settlement of the money they shared. He also did not leave out his nephew Michael (*Michno*), to whom he bequeathed a horse, a coat and a robe.[53] Faced with death, this extremely wealthy testator allotted to pious bequests only a robe, a tunic and a fur, recommending that they be sold and used *in dy werk der barmherczikeit,* leaving the choice of recipients at the discretion of the executors of the will.[54] He ended the will with a listing of his debts and debts owed to him, part of which were to be found in a register he kept, and the names of the executors of the will: his brother Stanisław, his son-in-law Jacob, and Matthias the apothecary.[55]

The wills of the three executed Krakow councillors described above are extremely similar in both form and content to the last wills made by other Krakow burghers. All of them naturally differ in the specifics of the bequests, the family situation of the testators, and the pious bequests made. However, they do not contain anything that would indicate the dramatic situation of the city officials, who were imprisoned and facing death. If the unusual circumstances surrounding the writing of these wills was not already known to us, there would be little cause to focus our attention more closely on them. Knowledge of context such as this, not explained in the testamentary form and not preserved in any other source materials relating to the bequests, undoubtedly provides valuable information indicating how various external circumstances could have impacted the making of final bequests in wills.

---

52   The testator even specified which of the silver cups and spoons should be given to the wife and which to his children; LT, fol. 72.

53   "Item so gebe ich Michno meynes bruders son das czelden pfert und den newfarben mantil mit mardern und dy olstene schawbe"; LT, fol. 72.

54   "Item dy marderynne schawbe, und den bruen rog mit mardern und das czobelyn futter, das allis sal man vorkeuffen, und das gelt In dy werk der barmherczikeit gebin noch dirkentnis der vormunden"; *ibidem*.

55   LT, fol. 73.

It also seems important that there are no fundamental differences in the content and form of the wills written by city officials and generally unrelated wealthy individuals. However, it can be observed that sitting on a bench court on the municipal council could undoubtedly have had an impact on the need to write a will, as these municipal bodies clearly supported the production of such legal documents.

4   Occupational Structure of Testators

The source materials on Krakovian testators analysed in this study allow for a determination of the profession of a significant number of these individuals. Their professions can be discerned by a study of the use of nicknames, by information contained in the wills themselves, and by data from various entries in Krakow's municipal books.[56] On this basis, the professions of 235 testators of both sexes were identified,[57] which accounts for 51% of all the burghers whose wills were analysed.[58] The identified persons represent 53 professions found in greatly varying numbers in medieval Krakow (Table 2). On the one hand, numerically dominant are crafts and trades (35, i.e. 66%) represented by only one, two or three individual testators during the analysed two hundred years; on the other hand, merchants and stallholders as a group represented as many as 65 testators (28%).

In the group of crafts discussed above, the occupational structure is similar to that in other cities in the region. Among Krakovian testators, in Poznan, for example, a decided majority comprises those engaged in the most prestigious crafts. Based on his research on medieval Poznan, Jacek Wiesiołowski placed stallholders and goldsmiths among the wealthiest burghers, alongside

---

[56]   Proving particularly useful were annual censuses of guildmasters recorded on the pages of council books. The first, incomplete list of guild masters from 1398 included only the guilds of butchers (*arvinatorum*), weavers (*textorum*), cutlers (*cultellifabrorum*) and belt makers (*cingulatorum*); CONS. 427, fol. 103.

[57]   Wives and widows of members of these professions were also included in the respective categories.

[58]   In the course of the study, 457 testators who were Krakow burghers were identified. Among those there were also several foreign merchants who decided to make their wills in the city due to illness or other life-threatening circumstances. However, 11 people were excluded, since their short mutual bequests or donations, made e.g. due to travel plans or plague, could also serve as a last will; these were significantly different in form from other wills. There were also 10 excluded wills of clergymen who left their wills in town books through their roots, connections and family ties.

THE SOCIO-ECONOMIC POSITION OF TESTATORS

TABLE 2   Occupations of Krakovian testators in the years 1300–1500

Occupation	Number of testators
Merchants and stallholders (*mercator, kaufman, institor, kromer*)	64
Goldsmiths (*aurifaber, goltsmed*)	14
Belt makers (*cingulator, gortler*)	10
Sellers of fustian fabric (*parchanista, parchener*)	9
Innkeepers (*tabernator, kreczmer*)	9
Brewers and maltsters (*braxator, braseator, melczer*)	8
Butchers (*carnifex, fleischer*)	8
Tailors (*sartor, schneider*)	7
Shoemakers (*sutor, schuster*)	7
Bowyers (crossbow makers) (*arcufex, bogner*)	6
Bakers (*pistor, becke*)	6
Armourers and bladesmiths (*torrifex, helmsmed, plathnerz*)	5
Fish sellers (*allecista, heringer, senior in foro piscium*)	5
Capmakers (*pileator, hutter*)	4
Furriers (*pellifex, korsner*)	4
Sausage Makers' (*arvinator, smersneyder*)	4
Scribes and notaries (*notarius, schreiber*)	4
Salt merchants (*salicida*)	4
Coopers (*doleator, botener*)	3
Pewter makers and bell-founders (*cantrifex, kannengisser, cuprifaber, ruffifusor, rothgisser, pixidarius*)	3
Blacksmiths (*faber, parvifaber, smed*)	3
Bathhouse owners (*balneator, bader*)	3
Cutlers (*cultellifaber, messirsmed*)	3
Leatherworker (*corrigiator, rymer*)	3
Servants (*servitor, vigil, dyner, circulator*)	3
Tanners (*cerdo, gerber, rufficerdo, rotgeber*)	3
Apothecaries (*apothecarius, apteker*)	2
Professional court deputies (*prolocutor, vorreder, vorsprecher*)	2
Embroiderers (*haftarius, zaidenhafter, hafter*)	2
Purse makers (*bursifex, perator, beutler*)	2
Painters (*pictor, moler*)	2
Minters (*monetarius, monczer*)	2

TABLE 2   Occupations of Krakovian testators in the years 1300–1500 (*cont.*)

Occupation	Number of testators
Soap makers (*smigmator*)	2
Carriage-builders (*currifex, stelmecher*)	2
Weavers (*textor, weber*)	2
Salt mines administrators (*supparius*)	2
Customs officials (*teloneator*)	1
Dyers (*tinctor, farber*)	1
Potters (*figulus, topper*)	1
Barbers (*barbitonsor, barbirer*)	1
Needle makers (*acufex, noldener*)	1
Equerries (*marstelle*)	1
Sword makers (*gladiator, zarwechter*)	1
Millers (*molendinator, molner*)	1
Bricklayers (*murator, mewrer*)	1
Oil makers (*oleator, olslager*)	1
Silver malters (*cremator*)	1
Glovers (*cirothecarius*)	1
Saddlers (*sellator, zatheler*)	1
Joiners (*mensifex, teschner*)	1
Glaziers (*vitreator, glezer*)	1
Candle makers (*luminator, sweszniczka*)	1
Coat makers (*menteler*)	1

furriers, brewers, doctors, butchers and tailors.[59] A similar hierarchy among professions can be found in Wrocław, where at the turn of the fourteenth and fifteenth centuries innkeepers and some stallholders were among the richest burghers, and rich in comparison to many craftsmen – such as butchers, bakers, shoemakers, weavers, maltsters, goldsmiths and furriers. At the same time, a profession's prestige was also influenced by the strength of its guild.[60]

59   Jacek Wiesiołowski, *Socjotopografia*, 30–53.

60   "This is no coincidence, but rather a source of their strength. Apart from prestige and wealth, the evaluation of the profession was based on 'political' factors, the position in the commune expressed in terms of numbers and its economic importance"; Mateusz. Goliński, *Socjotopografia*, 462–463.

THE SOCIO-ECONOMIC POSITION OF TESTATORS   135

In German cities, such as Brunswick, Wartburg, Goslar and Göttingen, cloth cutters, weavers, tanners, shoemakers, goldsmiths, bakers and stallholders were among the most important groups of burghers.[61] Studies on the social structure of medieval Toruń carried out by Tomasz Jasiński and Krzysztof Mikulski indicated similarities with the occupational hierarchy presented above. At the turn of the fourteenth and fifteenth centuries in Toruń, brewers, saddlers, goldsmiths and wheelwrights were among those practicing the most highly valued crafts.[62]

4.1   Merchants and Stallholders

Analysis of the data presented in Table 2 above leads to interesting conclusions concerning the prevalence of the institution of the will among particular professional groups. The most common occupational group among testators was undoubtedly merchants. Because of the blurred and rather arbitrary boundary between merchants and stallholders, the two activities were treated together in this research. Some testators involved in trade were poor stallholders, such as Peter Chromy,[63] or from the middle-class, such as Stanisław Kulek,[64] but the vast majority were wealthy or very wealthy members of the upper social strata of Krakovian burghers. Among the testators on a list from 1410 were both elders of merchant guilds (in Latin *seniores mercatorum*),[65] the aldermen and, later, councillors like Nicholas Glezer,[66] and Paul Homan,[67] as well as many others who served as elders of the stallholders guild (*seniores institorum*), such as councillors Peter Hirszberg, John Weinke and Stanisław Streicher, and alderman Matthias Opoczko. This group also includes foreign merchants, such as John Raisser from Memmingen, Wilhelm Megirszheimer from Bavarian

---

61   Dietrich Denecke, *Sozialtopographie und sozialräumliche Gliederung der spätmittelalter-lichen Stadt*, in *Über Bürger, Stadt und städtische Literatur im Spätmittelalter*, ed. Josef Fleckenstein, Karl Stackmann (Göttingen: Vandenhoeck & Ruprecht, 1980), 180–183.

62   After a period of economic crisis resulting from the Thirteen Years' War, in the latter half of the fifteenth century there was a sudden change in the direction and logistics of how trade was done, which also affected the property structure of Toruń's craftsmen. At that time, bakers, brewers and representatives of leather crafts (mainly furriers) gained importance and wealth; vol. Jasiński, "Z zagadnień topografii społecznej średniowiecznego Toru-nia, part 1: Stare Miasto," 'Zapiski Historyczne' 48, no. 3 (1983), 132–133; Krzysztof Mikulski, *Przestrzeń i społeczeństwo Torunia od końca XIV do początku XVIII wieku* (Toruń: Wydaw. Uniwersytetu Mikołaja Kopernika, 1999), 133.

63   CONS. 429, fol. 16–17 (1450).

64   LT, fol. 93 (1468).

65   CONS. 427, fol. 361, 377 (1410).

66   SCAB. 4, fol. 66b (1412); SCAB. 5, fol. 121 (1426).

67   SCAB. 5, fol. 79 (1423).

Dinkelsbühl (Thunkilspul, near Nuremberg) as well as Erhart Eigilwart from Augsburg, who settled in Krakow.[68] Also qualifying as stallholders were many burghers who bequeathed stalls in their will, as well as their wives and their widows, such as Catherine, wife of the senior stallholder Peter Bedlka, who in her will mentioned two stalls she owned in the city;[69] Łazaria, the rich owner of a cloth stall and wife of Nicholas Slop;[70] and the first testator in Krakow (whose will has survived to our times) Sulisława, who had a stall, a butcher's stall, and a bread stall.[71] Although it is unlikely that all of these individuals were personally involved in trading from these stalls, which were sometimes owned by them only as a form of capital investment, it seems that the business activity of renters – consisting of carrying out investments, obtaining loans and the renting itself – was much closer to the types of work performed by a merchant and stallholder than to those of a craftsman.

The number of people among Krakovian testators who profited from commercial and credit transactions was in fact much higher than the number of actual stallholders recorded, perhaps even twice as high, given that most members of Krakow's elite had multiple sources of income and some craftsmen also traded in real estate, made loans, and set up their own trading companies. It can also be assumed that for a significant portion of Krakow's wealthy citizens who were outside circles of power, regardless of their designated profession, trading activities comprised at least one of a number of sources of income. A good example of such professional mobility is Simon the needle-maker (in German *noldener*), whose profession and limited participation in the city's official public life indicate that he most likely did not possess much property. Simon held the position of an elder of the blacksmiths guild in 1463, near the end of his life.[72] There are few mentions of him apart from information that in 1448 he bought a house at Szczepańska Street worth 150 grivna from the executors of Peter Eichler's will.[73] If he had not left three versions of his will,[74] it would have been difficult to believe that he was one of Krakow's richest burghers, who, alongside his work as a craftsman, was also engaged in trading and lending activities.

---

68   SCAB. 6, fol. 205 (1440); SCAB. 6, fol. 188 (1439); SCAB. 6, fol. 174 (1439); LT, fol. 108–109 (1473); SCAB. 8, fol. 598–599 (1476); LT, fol. 135–136 (1482); CONS. 428, fol. 305 (1431).

69   SCAB. 4, fol. 41 (1411).

70   LT, fol. 87 (1464).

71   KDMK, vol. 3, no. 368 (1303).

72   CONS. 429, fol. 327.

73   SCAB. 7, fol. 60.

74   CONS. 429, fol. 16 (1450); LT, fol. 55 (1458); SCAB. 8, fol. 69 (1461).

THE SOCIO-ECONOMIC POSITION OF TESTATORS

Simon made his first bequest of last will in the Jubilee year of 1450. Before making a pilgrimage, he made a simple bequest of all his possessions to his two daughters and wife Dorothy. He named Sigismund the butcher and Paul Brower the furrier as the executors of the will.[75] Eight years later, he made another will before councillors who came to him to witness the document, in which he bequeathed everything to his second wife Catherine, including 100 florins as her previously promised dower.[76] He also gave 300 florins for pious deeds, of which 200 were to be donated to St. Bernard's Church.[77] This time the executors of the will were the future alderman and councillor Nicholas Gobil and two elders of the blacksmiths guild, Stanisław Schilling and Nicholas Wogisgeringe. Three years later Simon made his third will, this time before a municipal bench court.[78] He once again bequeathed to his wife Catherine a dower of 100 florins as well as the contents of a stall (in German *cromgerethe*, but not the craft tools – *werkgeczew*), as well as valuable items and household equipment pledged to him.[79] This time he confined himself to bequeathing nearly 100 florins for pious deeds,[80] but in this version of his will he included additional relatives, who were to receive 20 florins "if they arrived within a year and a day." As executors of the will, he again chose the same two elders of the blacksmiths guild, Schilling and Wogisgeringe, to whom he allocated two florins each for carrying out the aforementioned dispositions.

---

75   CONS. 429, fol. 16.

76   LT, fol. 55.

77   "10 florins to the Blessed Virgin Mary Church for the construction of the church; two grivna to the Hungarian Chapel of St. Francis for the brotherhood; two grivna to the main hospital for the poor for food; 10 florins to St. Hedwig for the sick; 10 florins to All Saints for construction; 10 florins to St. Francis for construction; 12 florins to St. Valentine for food for the sick; 10 florins to St. Leonard for food for lepers; 20 florins to Corpus Christi in Kazimierz for construction; four grivna to St. Stephen for construction; 10 florins to St. Mark for construction"; CONS. 429, fol. 16.

78   SCAB. 8, fol. 69 (1461).

79   Among the items pledged with him he mentioned a gold-plated belt, two gold rings worth altogether 12 florins, 12 silver spoons pledged for eight florins and a chalice from the so-called Hungarian chapel [!] pledged for six grivna.

80   "10 florins to the Blessed Virgin Mary for construction; 10 florins to the Hospital of the Holy Spirit for food for poor patients; 20 florins to the brotherhood of St. Bernard for their needs; and another 20 florins to build their monastery; 10 florins to St. Francis for construction of the monastery; and I give 20 florins to my relatives who will come within a period of a year and a day, in accordance with the law of next of kin. If none of the relatives comes during this time, the 20 florins will be added to the sum for construction of the Blessed Virgin Mary Church; 10 florins for *czu wegin und czu stegin*; two grivna to St. Valentine; two grivna to leprous women; two grivna to leprous men at St. Leonard"; SCAB. 8, fol. 69.

Apart from burghers, who can generally be described as merchants and stallholders, the table above also includes people trading in specific types of goods, such as sellers of fabrics (fustian), among whom were nine guild elders, including two councillors John Sweidniczer[81] (one of the richest burghers in Krakow) and John Beme,[82] and an influential cloth and silk merchant Nicholas Dolsky (alias Swob);[83] five fishmongers, among whom three were distinguished as 'elders of fish market' (*seniores in foro piscium*);[84] four salt merchants (Polish *prasol*), whose considerable wealth can be inferred, for example in the cases of John Włosaty and Michael Godzek,[85] on the basis of the high fees paid by them during the adoption of municipal law.[86] Taking into account these groups of occupations as well, the number of merchants and stallholders identified among testators can be estimated to be no less than 84 persons (36%).

One example of a wealthy Krakow fishmonger is John Czarny, who served as the *senior in foro piscium* from 1459 to 1465.[87] Later in his career, in 1466,[88] he was nominated as a alderman and served in this function from 1467 to 1474.[89] His appointment as commander of the tower over the New Gate (Latin *Novam Valvam*) in 1473 can be seen as an expression of his social prestige.[90] In 1465, in a will made before the municipal bench court, he bequeathed the significant sum of 100 grivna to his wife.[91] He also sought to secure the future of his wife after his death, requiring his children to give her a sunny room and a free table at which she could sit in the dining room under the window by the heater. In

---

81 The example of John Sweidniczer clearly shows just how misleading the simple classifications of the professional activities of burghers based on their nicknames or their guild functions were. His will of 1457 alone provides evidence of the great variety of financial and trade activities undertaken by this wealthy townsman. His most important sources of income included international trade in lead, cloth, iron, copper, wine and salt; cf. CONS. 428, fol. 402 (1439); LT, fol. 39–45 (1457); *senior parchanorum*, 1438, CONS. 428, fol. 384; cf. Danuta Molenda, *Polski ołów na rynkach Europy Środkowej w XIII–XVII wieku* (Warszawa: Instytut Archeologii i Etnologii PAN, 2001), 104–106.

82 LT, fol. 86–87 (1465); *senior parchanorum*, 1436, 1439, 1443, CONS. 428, fol. 352, 399, 456.

83 LT, fol. 143–144 (1487); *senior parchanorum*, 1468, 1472, 1475, 1478, 1480, CONS. 429, fol. 404, 463, 527, 606, 653.

84 Martinus Weyner, LT, fol. 68–69 (1461); Czarny John, SCAB. 8, fol. 223 (1465); Duchon, CONS. 429, fol. 382 (1466).

85 They both wrote their wills in 1494; LT, fol. 154.

86 They paid 36 and 24 groszy, respectively; cf. Book of Admissions, no. 8747, 347 i no. 6399, 213.

87 CONS. 429, fol. 227, 359.

88 SCAB. 8, fol. 262.

89 SCAB. 8, fol. 371, 473, 482, 483, 501–502, 509.

90 CONS. 429, fol. 485.

91 She was supposed to be paid these 100 grivna by the children of the testator (probably from his first marriage), and until they did, they should pay her rent out of that amount; CONS. 429, fol. 227, 359.

THE SOCIO-ECONOMIC POSITION OF TESTATORS

139

addition, the children were to meet all her other needs.[92] Later on in the will he gave his two sons Adam and Pawel 100 florins each, then divided the rest of the estate in equal parts among all his children, explaining that his daughters Hedwig and Barbara had already left the house, and had already received a similar amount of money as a dowry. Most of these dispositions were repeated by the testator in the second version of his will, which he had drawn up while serving as a alderman.[93] In this version, however, he left his entire house, located behind his butcher's stall, to his wife for life, as well as repeating his earlier bequest of 100 grivna to her as a dower. Interestingly, in 1475 the sons of John Czarny, Adam and Paul, made a mutual bequest of all their possessions, claiming that they had earned everything they had from their own work and not inherited anything, and therefore could exclude their relatives from any inheritance. This decision was confirmed in court by their father, who added that he owed them 100 florins for cloth.[94] Information about John's death and the execution of his testamentary dispositions is found in the record for the following year – 1476.[95]

4.2 Goldsmiths and Belt Makers

The second and third group of professions most commonly found among testators (24 persons – 10%) are the closely-related professions of goldsmith and belt maker (belts were very often decorated with silver ornamentation and sometimes even gold plated). These guilds represented the richest and most prestigious group of Krakovian craftsmen. A certain affinity and mutual ties between the representatives of these trades can be seen in the example of the Pferd family, in which there were two members named John. One of them was a goldsmith, and the other, a belt maker from Zittau.[96] It is not known exactly how the two were related, but it is notable that Agnes Pferdinne, who originally came from this family, was the wife of a belt maker named Nicholas, who had the nickname *Goldener*.[97] He also made his will shortly after Agnes's death, after entering into a new marriage with 'Magdalene.'[98]

---

92   If the testator's children wished to sell the house, they could only do so if they granted the widow the conditions specified in the will ("dassy den freyen willen und dy gebunge dy ich ir benumit habe yn meynem hawse sal sy haben und genissen als oben und sust sal das haws nicht vorkowft warden"); CONS. 429, fol. 227, 359.

93   SCAB. 8, fol. 300–301.

94   SCAB. 8, fol. 641, 642.

95   CONS. 429, fol. 569.

96   Jerzy Pietrusiński, *Złotnicy krakowscy XIV–XVI wieku i ich księga cechowa* (Warszawa: Inst. Sztuki Polskiej Akad. Nauk, 2000), 390.

97   LT, fol. 59 (1459).

98   LT, fol. 68 (1460); CONS. 429, fol. 250 (1459).

140   CHAPTER 2

Although he was never a member of the city council or bench court, the goldsmith John Pferd was a very influential burgher, as evidenced by the fact that his wife Margaret was the daughter of the alderman and Krakow councillor Peter Pelczer the furrier.[99] In the town books, one can find information about the professional and social career of this testator, who in 1422, 1427, 1431, 1434 and 1439 served as an elder in the goldsmiths guild,[100] and in 1430 was elected as a defense commander of the Jewish Tower (in Latin *capitanus Turri Judeorum*).[101] John Pferd left behind an exceptionally large number of surviving wills (as many as five, from 1423, 1425, 1439, 1445 and 1445[102], which provide us with a relatively good knowledge of his property and family status. He drew up the first of these acts of last will in 1423 before leaving on a pilgrimage to Rome. In it he bequeathed to his wife Margaret 200 grivna, while another 100 grivna and the tools of his craft were to be divided up between his mother Catherine and the offspring of his siblings (he mentions his nieces and nephews).[103] Two years later, after returning from his pilgrimage and (probably) after his mother's death, he made another will in which he bequeathed a total of 120 grivna to more distant family members such as his cousin Sophie, from the Upper Silesian town of Niemodlin (in German Falkenberg).[104] In 1439, in the third version of his will, he confined himself to securing a dower for his wife and making provisions for his sister, adult niece, two underage nieces and maid, allocating 150 florins for this purpose, and the rest to opera pietatis.[105] When, six years later in 1445, he made another version of his will, it no longer mainly featured bequests to his family, but detailly planned pious bequests, for which he allocated 138 florins. From among the members of his large family, he now included only his sister from Niemodlin, to whom he bequeathed 50 florins, and his wife, who became the beneficiary of most of the estate, and whose dower of 200 grivna was increased by another 100 grivna; she also received a house at the market square and all its furnishings.[106] In the same year, the testator changed his will once again, probably out of fear that his relatives might challenge the will in court. This will, made before the municipal bench court, was more of a mutual bequest, in which the testator bequeathed to his

---

99   SCAB. 5, fol. 109; Marcin Starzyński, *Krakowska rada*, 276–277.
100   CONS. 428, fol. 183–184, 233, 288, 325, 352, 399.
101   CONS. 428, fol. 272.
102   CONS. 428, fol. 198; SCAB. 5, fol. 109; CONS. 428, fol. 403; SCAB. 6, fol. 338; SCAB. 6, fol. 342.
103   CONS. 428, fol. 198.
104   SCAB. 5, fol. 109.
105   CONS. 428, fol. 403.
106   SCAB. 6, fol. 338.

THE SOCIO-ECONOMIC POSITION OF TESTATORS 141

wife a larger dower and secured it with his home on the market square; she, in turn, left him the same property along with her dowry in the event that she died first. They both disinherited their relatives from their common property.[107] The wills left by John Pferd show both the growing wealth of the burghers and the gradually decreasing share allocated to relatives in their inheritances. His initial, large estate was enlarged thanks to his marriage to the daughter of the wealthy future councillor Peter Pelczer. His business and family connections allowed him later to buy a house on the market square, and to enlarge it in 1431.[108] This was a visible trace of his social position.[109]

4.3 Food-Related Crafts

Those engaged in food-related crafts among Krakovian testators included those involved in the production and sale of beer (brewers, maltsters and inn-keepers) as well as bakers and butchers (in total 35 people – 15%). For the most part, they were middle-class and wealthy burghers, though none of them were aldermen or councillors. The professional activities of the owners of butcheries and malt-houses, who sold their products in Krakow's taverns and markets, shared features with those performed by both stallholders and craftsmen, who sold the goods they produced. Butchers were often the most rebellious social group in medieval towns, perhaps because of their borderline position between merchants and craftsmen. Hanna Zaremska, in her description of the relations between religious fraternities and urban elites, noted:

> Cooperation between brewers and butchers was an expression of an alliance among a group of rich people who did not differ in material terms from the merchant families who ruled the city. Conflicts caused by their exclusion from the ruling class led these craftsmen to launch armed protests against the authorities, and in times of 'social tranquility' to seek other ways to satisfy their ambitions.[110]

---

107 SCAB. 6, fol. 342.
108 That year he bought a half of a house at the market square from Anna, wife of Stanisław Morsztyn, which was located next to his own property at the market square.; SCAB. 6, fol. 18.
109 Cf. Jerzy Pietrusiński, *Złotnicy krakowscy*, 387–390.
110 They were initiators or participants in the majority of revolts against the municipal authorities and merchants supporting them, e.g. in Wrocław in 1408, Gdańsk, Toruń and Poznan; Janusz Tandecki, *Struktury administracyjne i społeczne oraz formy życia w wielkich miastach Prus Krzyżackich i Królewskich w średniowieczu i na progu czasów nowożytnych* (Toruń: Uniwersytet Mikołaja Kopernika, 2001), 82–88; Edmund Cieślak, *Walki ustrojowe w Gdańsku i Toruniu oraz niektórych miastach hanzeatyckich w XV w.* (Gdańsk: Gdańskie

An example of a – not particularly wealthy – representative of the food-related crafts was Martin Masarz. In 1415, he bequeathed before the municipal bench court all of his movable and immovable property to his wife Catherine and son John Schirmer, except for his "butcher's shop" (*thugurium arminale vulgariter Smerhutte*), which was to be run by Catherine as long as she remained a widow, and then reserved for Martin's grandson.[111] In 1419, "lying in sickness," Martin revoked before councillors all his previous bequests and donations, leaving to his son John all his movable and immovable property, except for 10 grivna, which he intended as – an unusually small – dower for his wife. The value of the total Martin's real estate is not known, but the dower bequest indicates that the economic position of this testator could not have been too high. However, we can speak of a social advancement in the case of his son John, who in 1416 and then in 1421 held the position of elder in the butcher's guild.[112]

4.4 Clothing-Related Crafts

Among the crafts represented by a relatively large number of Krakovian testators were the traditionally rich guilds of tailors and furriers and of capmakers (a total of 15 people – 6%). The majority of tailors occupied a high social position. The richest of them appears to have been Peter of Pyzdry, called as a "tailor to the Queen," and later a councillor and court vogt.[113] Apart from the valuable real estate he owned, further proof of his importance in the city was the fact that his son-in-law was Jacob Sweidniczer, brother of John Sweidniczer, one of the most influential patricians in Krakow. Peter earlier bequeathed to his wife a dower of 250 grivna, then increased it in his will to an impressive 700 grivna. In addition, there are wills of other wealthy townspeople who were engaged in tailoring crafts, such as the councillors John Teschner, Jarosz Clothier and John Biały.[114] Estates only slightly smaller were most likely owned by the tailor John Tifnaw, who concluded a form of marriage contract (*gemechte*) with his wife in 1441,[115] and Elizabeth, the widow of the deceased tailor Philip, who owned a house on Pig Street.[116]

---

111   Towarz. Nauk, 1960), 20–21; Antoni Gąsiorowski, "Walki o władzę w Poznaniu u schyłku wieków średnich," KH, vol. 82, no. 2 (1975), 256–259; Hanna Zaremska, *Bractwa*, 105.

111   SCAB. 4, fol. 124.

112   The value of this butcher's shop is difficult to estimate, but the mere fact of its possession indicates the relatively stable financial and professional position of this burgher; CONS. 427, fol. 88, 159.

113   LT, fol. 4 (1442); Marcin Starzyński, *Krakowska rada*, 274–275.

114   SCAB. 8, fol. 577 (1475), LT, fol. 151–152 (1492), LT, fol. 133–134 (1482).

115   Together they bequeathed as many as 100 grivna (50 each) for the salvation of their souls. Furthermore, after John's death, his widow was supposed to receive 50 grivna from her father's inheritance and 40 grivna from the dower she was entitled to; SCAB. 6, fol. 227.

116   CONS. 429, fol. 55 (1452); SCAB. 7, fol. 312 (1457).

THE SOCIO-ECONOMIC POSITION OF TESTATORS   143

Four identified furriers were undoubtedly part of Krakow's elites. Matthias Paszke was an elder of the furriers guild in the years 1436, 1438, 1447, 1453, 1455 and 1457,[117] and in 1460 he was elected as a senior stallholder.[118] In addition, from 1440 to 1469, he sat on the bench court at least thirteen times, and in 1469 was elected for the first time to the municipal council, on which he also appears in the censuses of 1476 and 1477.[119] John Kunisz[120] and Michael Graser,[121] before they were elected to the municipal bench court, held the office of elders of the furriers guild for many years, while John Baumgart's position as head of this guild is evidenced by his house on the market square and his kinship ties with the Morsztyn family.[122]

Two masters of the capmakers guild, Nicholas Tunkel and Matthias Hutter, and two widows of former guild elders, Hedwig Granoszowa and Anna Mazerinne, were part of much less wealthy circles among Krakovian burghers.[123] They owned properties located on the side streets of Krakow,[124] and their bequests were clearly different in size from those of the above-mentioned tailors and furriers.

4.5   *Metalworking and Armour-Making Crafts*[125]
Surprisingly, there is also a large representation of crafts related to the production of weaponry, such as bowyers (crossbow-makers),[126] armourers, bladesmiths and at least one gunsmith (Latin *pixidarius*) belonging to the

---

117   *Senior pellificum*, 1436, CONS. 428, fol. 352; 1438, CONS. 428, fol. 384; 1447, CONS. 428, fol. 497; 1452, CONS. 429, fol. 44; 1455, CONS. 429, fol. 114; 1459, CONS. 429, fol. 227.

118   CONS. 429, fol. 265.

119   LT, fol. 108 (1473); Marcin Starzyński, *Krakowska rada*, 289.

120   SCAB. 8, fol. 273 (1467); LT, fol. 126 (1481).

121   LT, fol. 34 (1455).

122   SCAB. 6, fol. 215 (1440); CONS. 428, fol. 466 (1443).

123   SCAB. 6, fol. 149 (1437), SCAB. 7, fol. 13 (1447); SCAB. 5, fol. 157b (1428); SCAB. 6, fol. 168 (1438); LT, fol. 5 (1440); LT, fol. 145 (1487); LT, fol. 30 (1453).

124   Matthias Hutter had a house on St. Florian Street, and Hedwig Granoszowa owned one on *twergasse* next to the house of the poor (bursa pauperorum); Anna Mazerinne, widow of John Mazer, had a house on Wiślna Street next to the gate; SCAB. 5, fol. 157b (1428); SCAB. 6, fol. 168 (1438); LT, fol. 5 (1440); LT, fol. 135 (1487); SCAB. 6, fol. 335 (1445).

125   Division adopted from: Janusz Sztetyłło, "Rzemiosła metalowe wraz z uzbrojeniem," in *Historia kultury materialnej Polski w zarysie*, vol. 2: *Od XIII do XV w.*, ed. Anna Rutkowska-Płachcińska (Wrocław–Warszawa–Krakow: Zakład Narodowy im. Ossolińskich, 1978), 73–108.

126   Jan Szymczak, "Od samostrzelników do grzebieniarzy w Krakowie, czyli rzecz o zmierzchu znaczenia kuszy na przełomie XV i XVI wieku," in *Aetas media, aetas moderna. Studia ofiarowane profesorowi Henrykowi Samsonowiczowi w siedemdziesiątą rocznicę urodzin*, ed. Agnieszka Bartoszewicz, Wojciech Fałkowski, Halina Manikowska, Antoni Mączak, Karol Modzelewski (Warszawa: Instytut Historyczny Uniwersytetu Warszawskiego, 2000), 122–128.

bell-founders guild (a total of thirteen people – 5.5%). We can speak of an extreme affluence in the case of the aforementioned bladesmith Thomas Zarwechter, who served as a guild elder and then became an alderman (in 1448 and again in 1450),[127] after which he was quickly promoted to the office of Krakow councillor (1452–1466).[128] Perhaps the secret of his quick social advancement, quite unusual for his profession, is connected with his marriage to the rich widow of Mark the innkeeper in 1440.[129]

Although craftsmen from the tinsmiths and bell-founders guilds are not primarily associated with the production of weapons, John Stochse, a gunsmith whose nickname indicates his specialisation in the production of firearms, was a member of precisely this guild. The four versions of his will allow us to examine closely his property and family status.[130] He served, with some interruptions, for many years – from 1415 to 1459 – as an elder in the guild of tinsmiths and bell-founders.[131]Although he owned only a wooden house on Hospital Street, his significant wealth is indicated by his generous bequest for his wife's dower, which he increased to 140 grivna, and the fact that in his will we find a clear symbol of wealth and social prestige – a precious gold-plated belt.[132]

We can speak of moderate wealth in the case of most of those among the four armourers and five bowyers among the Krakovian testators. Besides Jacub Rolle and his wife Claire, who stood out in this respect,[133] the other persons were middle-class members of the urban community. For example, Jost the bowyer (in German *bogner*) made a bequest for his wife's dower of 30 grivna and Henczil the bowyer (in Latin *arcufex*) 50 grivna, while everyone associated with Krakow's armourers guild – Nicholas Fridil the armourer (in German *plathner*),[134] Wojtek the armourer,[135] Catherine wife of Fricz the armourer[136]

---

127   *Senior gladiatorum*, 1433, CONS. 428, fol. 315.

128   Marcin Starzyński, *Krakowska rada*, 278.

129   CONS. 428, fol. 412 (1439); SCAB. 6, fol. 209 (1440).

130   CONS. 428, fol. 317 (1433); LT, fol. 30 (1453); LT, fol. 33 (1454); LT, fol. 51 (1458).

131   For example, in 1437 he belonged to the guild: *Cuprifusorum, cantrifusorum et messing-sloer,* but in 1447 *Cantrificum Rufifusorum* and in 1454 *Cantrificum Ruffifusorum*; CONS. 428, fol. 370 (1437); CONS. 428, fol. 497 (1447); CONS. 429, fol. 84 (1454).

132   CONS. 428, fol. 317 (1433); LT, fol. 30 (1453); LT, fol. 33 (1454); LT, fol. 51 (1458).

133   He bequeathed as many as 160 grivna as a dower for his wife, and after his death the widow, Claire gave the house 'behind the slaughterhouses' to found a perpetual mass at St. Mary's Church, and also made pious bequests worth more than 100 grivna; SCAB., no. 1425 (1392); KDMK, vol. 3, no. 406, 532–534 (1419); SCAB. 5, fol. 31 (1420).

134   CONS. 428, fol. 317 (1433).

135   LT, fol. 143 (1487).

136   SCAB. 6, fol. 74 (1434); SCAB. 6, fol. 361 (1446).

THE SOCIO-ECONOMIC POSITION OF TESTATORS

and Anna wife of the helmet maker (in German *helmsmedinne*)[137] – were all owners of wooden houses on the prestigious Grodzka Street.

4.6   Professionals of the Written Word

Among Krakovian testators, professions requiring a formal education are relatively well represented (eight persons – 3%).[138] These include the wills of three municipal notaries: John Stolle,[139] Eustace and Christopher Rebentcz,[140] as well as the public notary and later councillor Nicholas Zarogowski,[141] the municipal deputy notary (in German *undirstatschreiber*) Nicholas Newmaister,[142] two professional court plenipotentiaries Peter Streicher and Lawrence[143] and, to a lesser extent, the pharmacist Paul Tanneman and Dorothy, widow of the

---

137   SCAB., 1641 i 1642 (1393).

138   "Apart from the notary employed in the municipal office, there were also other professional writers who could edit a document or letter, read and translate more or less complicated texts, and explain the complexities of law"; Agnieszka Bartoszewicz, *Piśmienność* (2012), 193.

139   KDMK, vol. 3, no. 406, 532–534 (1419 r.); SCAB. 6, fol. 186 (1439); LT, fol. 61–63 (1459); CONS. 429, fol. 693 (1481); Bożena Wyrozumska, *Kancelaria miasta Krakowa w średniowieczu*, 121–124; Agnieszka Bartoszewicz, *Piśmienność* (2012), 163–165.

140   "People in 'intellectual professions' were an important, perhaps even the most important group from the point of view of research on urban literacy: notaries employed in offices and courts, as well as by private individuals, then book copyists, tutors, court attorneys, and finally – doctors and pharmacists who required professional knowledge in their work. [...] All these people had one thing in common – they made money using a pen and were engaged in one or more of the above-mentioned professions. On the other hand, they differed in terms of wealth, social prestige, level of education and social rank"; Agnieszka Bartoszewicz, *Piśmienność* (2012), 36–37.

141   CONS. 429, fol. 15–16 (1450); LT, fol. 129–131 (1482); The fact that Nicholas Zarogowski held the position of public notary was mentioned in Elżbieta Piwowarczyk, *Legaty testamentowe ad pias causas,* 502. A version of his last will and testament from 1472 is kept in the archives of Jagiellonian University; cf. *Codex diplomaticus Universitatis Studii Generalis Cracoviensis*, vol. 2, ed. Feliks Piekosiński (Krakow: sumptibus Universitatis, 1870–1880), no. 236.

142   Although in the Old Polish period there were such terms as *podpisek* and *pisarczyk* 'junior writer,' such a translation of the term *undirstatschreiber* in the medieval period would mean a major departure from the source terminology; cf. Krzysztof Skupieński, "Notariusze i notariat w średniowiecznej Polsce," in *Kultura piśmienna średniowiecza i czasów nowożytnych. Problemy i konteksty badawcze*, ed. Piotr Dymmel, Barbara Trelińska (Res Historica, 3), (Lublin: Wydawn. Uniwersytetu Marii Curie-Skłodowskiej, 1998), 169–170; SCAB. 7, fol. 120 (1451).

143   CONS. 428, fol. 125 (1419); SCAB. 6, fol. 184 (1439).

pharmacist Stanisław.[144] All the municipal notaries who made wills had significant assets at their disposal, numbering in the hundreds of grivna.[145] The Krakow's deputy notary Nicholas and his wife Salomea made a mutual bequest that for the 300 grivna he had received from her as a dowry, he would leave her half of his entire estate, which therefore had to be worth at least 600 grivna.[146] The pharmacist Paul Tanneman also had a very large estate,[147] and also owned a house on the market square.[148] The situation of two professional court plenipotentiaries from Krakow, however, was more complex. As A. Bartoszewicz explains:

> The entries in the municipal books of seemingly all urban centers prove the popularity of the institution of the legal plenipotentiary. Apart from their clients in court, and the burghers, nobles, peasants and clergy they represented before municipal offices, these lawyers also often represented absent parties or accompanied clients during a trial (*prolocutor, prelocutor, procurator, causidicus*), wielding a general or limited power of attorney in a specific case. In many cases, such functions were entrusted to relatives and neighbors.[149]

In contrast to medium-sized and small towns, in Krakow a group of professional court deputies was established in the mid-fourteenth century. Peter and Lawrence were not the only ones to appear as *prolocutores* in fifteenth-century municipal books, but they certainly appeared most frequently in them.[150]

---

144 SCAB. 6, fol. 113 (1435); SCAB. 7, fol. 303–304 (1457); SCAB. 8, fol. 466 (1472); SCAB. 8, fol. 501–502 (1473); LT, fol. 105 (1472).

145 On the earnings, sources of income and social status of municipal notaries cf. Agnieszka Bartoszewicz, *Piśmienność* (2012), 152–165; Jacek Wiesiołowski, *Socjotopografia*, 124–128; Bożena Wyrozumska, *Kancelaria*, 25–27.

146 SCAB. 7, fol. 120.

147 Agnieszka Bartoszewicz, *Piśmienność* (2012), 62–64; Jacek Wiesiołowski, *Socjotopografia*, 124–128.

148 In his will of 1435, his bequests do not yet indicate his wealth; only entries in the books of the bench court made 38 years later indicate the significant wealth he had accumulated over the course of his long life; SCAB. 6, fol. 113 (1435); SCAB. 8, fol. 501–502 (1473).

149 Agnieszka Bartoszewicz, *Piśmienność* (2012), 198; Józef Rafacz, *Zastępcy stron w dawnym procesie polskim* (Krakow: Gebethner & Wolff in Komm, 1923), 14–37.

150 Another very active court proxy in Krakow was Rafał from Wielopole (also known as Rafał from Krakow), at the turn of the fifteenth and sixteenth centuries, but there is no information about what he left in his will; cf. Agnieszka Bartoszewicz, *Piśmienność* (2012), 199–202.

THE SOCIO-ECONOMIC POSITION OF TESTATORS

Prolocutor Lawrence appeared in municipal books for the first time in 1419, when he acted as the plenipotentiary for the parson of Pobiedziska in the will of Peter, a Krakow bathhouse owner.[151] He then appeared in several dozen entries in both books of the bench court and in council books. He served in court as a guardian or executor of wills.[152] In 1420, perhaps after his marriage, he bequeathed all of his property to his wife Margaret.[153] Four years later, he bought from Michael Krzykawski[154] a tenement building on Wiślna Street, next door to the bishop's manor house.[155] For reasons unknown to us, in 1434 the deputy vogt John Hering, acting on behalf of Lawrence, gave this house to the man's wife, Margaret, and a year later the property was sold to the Krakow municipal council.[156] In that same year, Lawrence bought a house on Bracka Street from councillor Francis Neorza (guardian of the widow and children of a certain Paschek) for 122 grivna.[157] The coincidence between these dates leads to the conclusion that this transaction with the Council had been previously agreed upon. After obtaining consent from the bench court to dispose of his acquired goods, in 1439 he drew up the first version of his will.[158] He ordered the sale of a house at Bracka Street, paid 50 grivna to his wife from the dowry he had received,[159] and confirmed the mutual bequest they had made together with her,[160] while the rest of the money from the sale of the house and other goods was to be used for works of charity (in German *werg der barmherczikeit*). Noteworthy are the 20 grivna for "my brothers for the altar [?] to Corpus Christi in the Church of St. Francis" and the five grivna for the brothers to pay for food

---

151 SCAB. 5, fol. 2.

152 Eg.: SCAB. 5, fol. 25, 32, 74, 96, 108, 117, 137, 144, 158a, 174; SCAB. 6, fol. 15, 18, 22, 35, 66, 70, 83, 86, 96, 97, 117, 120, 123, 152, 166, 194, 201, 205, 209, 212, 214, 218, 224, 233, 245, 254, 261; CONS. 428, fol. 317, 381.

153 SCAB. 5, fol. 22.

154 Michael Krzykawski must have been a relatively wealthy and respected town citizen, since in 1412 he was the an elder of the salt merchants' guild (*salsatorum*); CONS. 428, fol. 5. Moreover, in 1421 he was mentioned as the keeper of the padlocks for the chains closing Wiślna Street (*Secuntur qui habent seras ad cathenas statuarum in platheis...*); CONS. 428, fol. 164; and, in 1422, he was appointed commander of one of the town's defence towers (CONS. 428, fol. 164); CONS. 428, fol. 188.

155 SCAB. 5, fol. 93.

156 SCAB. 5, fol. 117.

157 *Ibidem.*

158 SCAB. 6, fol. 184.

159 "L mrc gemeyner muncze das gebe ich ir hewte vor gehegtim dinge"; SCAB. 6, fol. 184.

160 "[...] und den brif do wir inne enander of gegeben haben der sal bey craft bleiben und macht haben"; *ibidem.*

148   CHAPTER 2

and running a bathhouse.[161] This probably concerns the brotherhood of the
so-called Hungarian Chapel in the Franciscan church, with which the testator
must have been associated. The remaining amounts, totalling 43 grivna, were
paid to various church institutions in Krakow and the surrounding area.[162] He
also ordered six grivna be given to his confessor Jacub Stegen from the castle
(*of dem hawse*)[163] and ten grivna to his wife's nephew. After his wife's death,
everything she left behind was to be used to pay for charitable works. He chose
as executors the aforementioned priest Jacob Stegen, Stanisław the pharmacist and John, the owner of a bathhouse in Piasek, and his wife. However, in
1440, a year later, he drew up a new will "for the glory of God and the salvation of his soul" (*gote czu lobe und meyner zele czule hulfe*).[164] In it he repeated
most of his previous pious bequests, this time making a donation to the fraternity at the Church of the Blessed Virgin Mary and allocating a total of just
24 grivna to 'pious works.'[165] It seems this was associated with the fact that
the duty to care for the soul of the deceased was placed in the hands of his
wife Margaret.[166] Based on his bequests, we can see that the value of his estate
was close to the amount for which he bought the house on Bracka Street, i.e.
about 120 grivna, although perhaps we should also add to this the value of

---

161   "Item so bescheide ich czu dem heiligen leichnam czu sinte Francisco meynen brudern
      XX mrc czu dem gebewde und V marg den brudern daz man do von machit eyn essen und
      czu dem bade"; SCAB. 6, fol. 184; Kazimierz. S. Rosenbaiger, *Dzieje Kościoła OO. Francisz-
      kanów w Krakowie w wiekach średnich* (Krakow: Zakład Narodowy im. Ossolińskich, 1933),
      76; Hanna Zaremska, *Bractwa*, 80–83.

162   "20 grivna for the construction of St. Mary's Church, 10 grivna to the Dominicans of the
      Holy Trinity for food and their bathhouse, five grivna to the hospital of the Holy Spirit for
      food, five grivna to poor leprous women from St. Valentine's Hospital near Krakow and
      five grivna to poor leprous men from St. Leonard's Hospital near Kazimierz"; SCAB. 6, fol.
      184 (1439).

163   The phrase *of dem hawse* was also used in relation to the Higher Court of Magdeburg Law
      at the Krakow castle and, for example, to vicars of the Wawel Cathedral (*vicarien of dem
      hawse*); cf. SCAB. 6, fol. 178 (1439), 262 (1442). "Item so bescheide ich unsern Beich vater
      her Jocob Stegen of dem hawse VI mrc of das daz her got vor uns bete in der messe"; SCAB.
      6, fol. 184 (1439).

164   SCAB. 6, fol. 213.

165   He left 10 grivna to the Franciscans for the construction of their church, five grivna to
      the brotherhood of the Blessed Virgin Mary ("Item der Bruderschaft czu unser Frawen
      czu stewir des dinstis unser liben frrawen V marg"), three grivna to lepers from outside
      Krakow for construction or other needs, three grivna to lepers from outside Kazimierz for
      construction or other needs, three grivna for poor patients at Krakow hospital for food;
      SCAB. 6, fol. 213.

166   "[...] befele is Margarethe meyner hausfrawen in deme getrawen das ich czu irre trew
      habe, daz sy meynir zele dovon getrewlich gut tuen sal"; SCAB. 6, fol. 213.

THE SOCIO-ECONOMIC POSITION OF TESTATORS 149

clothing and other personal belongings that were not mentioned in any versions of his will.

Although Peter Streicher, a court plenipotentiary, held functions similar to Lawrence in the city, he was undoubtedly less wealthy. His weaker position is indicated both by the smaller number of cases recorded in the municipal books (from 1411 to 1437) in which he appeared,[167] and by his more modest estate, which we learn about mainly in his will, written in 1418, when five councillors came to the ailing burgher.[168] Most of the bequests mentioned in the will were to be given to the testator's brother "Matthias, a carpenter from Pilzen." The donation was made up of cash deposited with a certain John Teuderneuder and items of clothing and weaponry, listed in detail.[169] In addition, all Streicher's silver, which was also under the care of John Teuderneuder, was to be used for the creation of a chalice to be donated to the monastery of St. Mark. Peter also testified that when he married his wife, he did not bequeath any dower money to her, so, as he lay sick, he decided to give her his best blue gown and half of his house on Mirror Street (in German *Spiegler Gasse*, in Latin *Platea Specultorum*) in Krakow.[170] The other half of the house was to be leased out for rent, and after her death, part of this property was to be given to his brother Matthias. From the entry preserved in the Krakow municipal book of the bench court, we learn that Peter's house, located alongside Mirror Street, was burdened by a rent of sixty groszy, which reduced the value of the property itself, which was probably not very high.[171]

---

167 SCAB. 4, fol. 43, 53, 60, 90; SCAB. 5, fol. 21, 75, 121, 172; SCAB. 6, fol. 92, 99, 113, 141.

168 That will was probably copied to the council book from the first book of wills, which was not preserved, as indicated by the beginning of the entry: "Copia Testamenti Petri Prolocutoris. Petir Fochsczagil, Michil Neudorff, Caspar Bozmecz, Petris Fetter i Petrus Kaldherberg Rathmannen der Stat Cracow Bekenne allen den is notdorfft wirt seyn, das in unsers Rathis keginwortikeit, die ersamen Georgius Morrensteyn czu der czeit Burgermeister und Johannes Faber unser Rathman und eitgenosen und haben bekant offinbar und mit laute, das als sie von unser bevelunge in krafft unsers und ihres Rathampts czu Petro vorspreche seyne meynunge czu vorhoren gegangen weren, do hette her derselbe Petrus vor en seyn Testamenth und lecztin willen gemacht und geschikit in sulche weyse"; CONS. 428, fol. 125.

169 "Czu dem irsten eynen swarczen Rok mit Weysen Lempinern undirsatter, eyne swarczen mantil desselben gewandis, eynen Roten mantil, eynen gefutirtin, eynen grunen Breslichen Rok, eyn groen Engilischis gewandis Rokmit czweliche gefutirte, czwer swert, czwee brostblech, eynen ysenhut, eyn par eyserinen hanczken, eyne swarcze kogil, eyne rote mocze, und drey par hozen"; *ibidem*.

170 "[...] off seyne leczte fart genomen, die seyne sele faren sulde, das her ir keynen pfening noch pfeningis wert gemorgengobit hette, wenne her betwungen werre mit dem rechten dorczu sie czu nemen"; *ibidem*.

171 SCAB. 5, fol. 10.

150   CHAPTER 2

4.7   Other Crafts

The remaining thirty crafts listed in Table 2 were represented by only one, two or three testators each. Therefore, in these cases one can speak both of their incidental character and the fact that they comprise most of the 'typical' craft occupations, including coopers, blacksmiths, cutlers, tanners, wheelwrights, weavers and carpenters. The relatively low number of representatives of these crafts among testators indicates that their decision to write a will was more likely influenced by personal factors and exceptional circumstances than by their belonging to a particular professional or social group. The presumed affiliation of people in this group with a particular craft is often indicated only by their nickname or surname. This was the case with the wealthy Dorothy Stelmecherinne (the surname meaning 'wife of a wheelwright'), who owned two houses at St. Florian Street and two stalls,[172] or Margaret Glezerinne, widow of counciller Nicholas Glezer (meaning 'glazier').[173] As in the case of the above-mentioned professions, many of the 58 people representing these 31 professions belonged to a kind of 'craftsmen's elite,' and had for many years served as elders in their guilds and confraternities.[174] The unique position they held in their social and professional environment and their related ambitions to participate in writing culture and in the founding and religious activities of the municipal elite seems to have led them to be more interested than their fellow guild members in settling accounts with their loved ones and with God by means of a will.

In many cases, it is likely that individual and chance circumstances also determined that some relatively poor craftsmen are found among the group of testators under discussion. An interesting example is undoubtedly the Krakow's citizen Martin the bricklayer. His will, made before the town council, was entered into the *Liber Testamentorum* in 1464.[175] The first mention of him comes from 1446, when he bought a house on St. John Street for 40 grivna from Andrew Radwanowicz;[176] in the same year, he also obtained city citizenship,

---

172   SCAB. 6, fol. 202 (1440), 225 (1441).
173   CONS. 428, fol. 243 (1428).
174   For example, Stephen the furrier, who left two versions of his will, served as an elder of the guild of Krakow furriers in the years 1410, 1415, 1429 and 1437; cf. CONS. 427, fol. 357; CONS. 428, fol. 70–72, 246, 370. Nicholas Czeginkop was an elder of the guild of German shoemakers in the years 1403 and 1417; cf. CONS. 427, fol. 173–174; CONS. 428, fol. 96–98, and Nicholas Clingsor was elected as an elder of the bakers' guild in the years 1431, 1433 and 1435; cf. CONS. 428, fol. 288, 315, 336.
175   LT, fol. 82.
176   SCAB. 6, fol. 351, 356.

THE SOCIO-ECONOMIC POSITION OF TESTATORS   151

paying a relatively sizable fee of 17 *skojecs* (i.e. 34 groszy).[177] In his will, which he made before leaving on an expedition against the Turks, he bequeathed a dower of 15 grivna to his wife Margaret (secured by his house by the Gate of St. Nicholas),[178] together with all his household goods and personal belongings (in Latin *suppellectilibus et parafernalibus*). If, however, his wife died before him, her son from her first marriage was to receive 10 grivna. Martin also made a bequest of five grivna to St. Nicholas Church (most likely his parish church) and another five grivna to the Polish Brotherhood in this church. The second part of this will is very interesting. In it he points out that if his uncle (*avunculus*) the noble John Banczelski came to Krakow and obtained city citizenship, he would have the right to live in this house and would have preemptive rights to its purchase.[179] Martin chose as executors John Raciborski the blacksmith, John Orł the dyer, and Nicholas the municipal carpenter (Latin *carpentarius civitatis*) – people who, by virtue of their profession, could have been suburban burghers, like the testator himself. The figure of Martin the bricklayer is extremely interesting both because of his participation in the military expedition against the Turks and because of his blood ties to nobility. One ambiguity here is the readiness expressed in the will to respect relatives' right of inheritance, which in Martin's case manifests itself in his imposing conditions on his uncle to come to the city and obtain city citizenship, which would have merely given him preemptive rights in the purchase of Martin's house outside the city, worth around 25 grivna.

4.8   Summary: Trade and Handicraft

As can be seen from this analysis, the dominant position among testators was held by people engaged in trade, although clear professional classifications here are very difficult to make, even when the burghers served as elders or

---

177   Book of Admissions, no. 5649.

178   "[...] ante walvam sancti Nicolai circa ortum Orientin sita" – the expression 'ante valvam' suggests that the house was located within the city walls, but the specifying comment 'circa ortum Orientin sita' points to its suburban location. It is probably the garden next to St. Nicholas' Church, the ownership of which was transferred for 20 grivna from councilor Marek, a needle maker (*noldenfesser*), to councilor George Orient together with a house, barn and half a grivna for rent to support this church in 1442; SCAB. 6, fol. 261.

179   "Ita tamen si nobilem Johannem Banczelszky dicti Martini avunculum advenire contingerit et Ius Civitatis conquesierit, liberum sit ei in eadem domo demorari et eadem non alteri quam uni ex concivibus vendendi. Et omnia testata atque legata prout super descripta sunt expedire et solvere cum effectum, Si autem domum ipse Johannes habere noluerit, extunc executores, ipsius infranominati plenam et omnimodam proprietatem habebunt domum prememoratam vendendi et de pecuniis disponendi iuxta testamentaliter legata ipsius conmissaet descripta solvendi"; LT, fol. 82.

152   CHAPTER 2

masters in their guilds. In terms of the social advancement that seems to have occurred among a significant portion of testators, it is clear that changing one's occupational affiliation was possible, including one's belonging to a given guild. This was often reflected in the abandonment of handicrafts in favour of commercial activity, with burghers usually making such a change in an effort to diversify their sources of income. For many craftsmen, their handicraft and commercial activity were intrinsically linked. The social position they held, between the patricians and commoners, between trade and the crafts, often led to tensions, and even to outbreaks of social unrest. However, it is significant that the main participants in these events tended to be same professional groups: butchers, maltsters and brewers, as well as goldsmiths, furriers, tailors and cloth makers.[180] It seems that these members of the urban community could be counted among the most socially mobile individuals, and the one's with the greatest chances of crossing group and class lines (if not in the first, then in the second generation).

5   The Financial Situation of Krakovian Testators

There are two categories of sources which allow us to assess with a high degree of accuracy the financial situation of Krakow's burghers: the city's *szos* tax

---

180   As Henryk Samsonowicz noted, "of greater importance for the shaping of power in the city was the fight between the opposition and the Patrician council. Since the mid-fourteenth century, they had been a permanent part of urban life in Central Europe. This was not a struggle between two classes; it was an attempt by people and groups that were growing wealthy quickly and trying to gain access to power and its benefits"; Maria Bogucka, Henryk Samsonowicz, *Dzieje miast*, 163–167; Hanna Zaremska, on the other hand, while describing the aspirations of wealthy representatives of Krakow's craftsmen, wrote: "They placed their chapels in the main churches. They started brawls over their place in processions […]. The statutes of their guilds often mention the importance of a decent appearance and proper clothing. Butchers, goldsmiths, furriers, cloth makers – the aristocracy of 'producers' – their organizations were associated with the main churches, while others relied on communities in their own parish churches"; *eadem, Bractwa*, 102–106; more on social conflicts in the late medieval and early modern cities of the Kingdom of Poland cf. Ryszard Szczygieł, "Wpływ konfliktów wewnętrznych w miastach polskich XV–XVI wieku na zmiany struktur społecznych," in *Stare i nowe struktury społeczne w Polsce*, vol. 1: *Miasto*, ed. Irena Machaj, Józef Styk (Lublin: Uniwersytet Marii Curie-Skłodowskiej, 1994), 40–41; *idem*, "Konflikty społeczne w miastach Królestwa Polskiego w XV i XVI wieku związane z dostępem do władz miejskich," *Sium* 7, 35–42; Janusz Tandecki, *Struktury administracyjne i społeczne*, 82–88; Edmund Cieślak, *Walki ustrojowe*, 20–21; Antoni Gąsiorowski, *Walki o władzę*, 256–259.

THE SOCIO-ECONOMIC POSITION OF TESTATORS

register and records of the size of dowers contained in marriage contracts.[181] In the first case, unfortunately, the szos registers for medieval Krakow, which would enable relatively precise research on the 'socio-topography' of the city and the asset diversity of its inhabitants, have not been preserved.[182] We do have, however, the municipal statute (German *Willkür*) announced in 1385 by the municipal council concerning the rules for the collection of this tax from Krakow's burghers.[183] The tax rate was based on a burgher's wealth, taking into account his real estate, capital, and receivables, as well as the location of his home and his livelihood.[184] Stanisław Kutrzeba distinguished three bases for the city's annual income: a land and residential property tax, a tax on profits from trade and production activities, and a tax on assets.[185] In the first case, a fee was charged based on the size and location of a parcel of land owned within the city walls. On the basis of a so-called 'city plot' (in German *ein gantczer hof*), measuring 36 cubits wide and 72 cubits long, a fee was collected based on its location in relation to the market square. For parcels on the market square itself, one paid 24 groszy, for a parcel up to the first junction (*krewtcze*) from the market square – 16 groszy, and for plots located between the first junction and the city walls – 12 groszy.[186] Such evidence of the differing values of urban property is an important prerequisite for assessing the wealth of testators who owned houses in particular parts of the city. Anything that might have been used as an element of exchange or trade or provide some other source of income was taken into account when taxing such property. Horses, cattle, pigs, grain and meat were excluded from these goods and were instead classified as personal property that was kept for "a hard times" (*farende habe* [...] *czu schlechter notdorfft*); also excluded were objects usually classified as the personal property of a woman (*gerada*) or man (*hergewet*), described in the municipal statute as items for personal use, like 'jewellery.' The third part of

---

181 Jacek Wiesiołowski, "Stratyfikacja mieszczaństwa polskiego w późnym średniowieczu," in *Struktura feudální společnosti na území Československa a Polska do přelomu 15. a 16. stoleti*, ed. Ján Čierny, František Hejl, Antonín Verbík (Praha: Ústav československých a světových dějin Československé akademie věd, 1984), 278; Antoni Czacharowski, *Ze studiów*, 89–90.

182 Marcin Starzyński, "Nad średniowiecznymi księgami rachunkowymi miasta Krakowa," *Roczniki Historyczne* 74 (2008), 165–178.

183 KDMK, vol. 2, no. 277.

184 Jacek Wiesiołowski, *Stratyfikacja mieszczaństwa polskiego*, 279.

185 Stanisław Kutrzeba, *Finanse i handel średniowiecznego Krakowa*, 69.

186 A judgement of this kind also included changes in the size of the plot, and its enlargement or reduction in relation to its original size. The tax depended on what part of a standard urban plot they constituted (*noch deme das erbe kleyn ader grosz were*). Neither the size nor the structure of the house on the plot were taken into account. It was probably included in the property tax, which was ½ grosz for each grivna, i.e. 48 groszy.

the szos was a 12 groszy tax on shops (*von der kauffkammern*), and 6 groszy on stalls (*von der cremen*), butchers' stalls (*von der fleischbencken*) and 'benches' (*von dem tissche*). Those who had neither "inherited property" nor assets worth more than 12 grivna were to pay based on their point of sale. This tax was therefore primarily intended to tax the poorest city inhabitants who, lacking any major assets, made a living from retail trade. This is also an important source of information about the 'poverty line' in Krakow in the late fourteenth century. These rules for the taxation of burghers remained in use with only minor changes throughout the Middle Ages.[187]

6 Social Structure in Other Cities and Towns

Given the lack of szos registers for Krakow, a valuable reference would be the comparative studies of late medieval Wrocław conducted by Mateusz Goliński.[188] In the latter half of the fourteenth century, Wrocław councillors introduced a new tax system under which the property tax was five times less than that in Krakow (only one grosz for each 10 grivna), while the money invested in rents was subject to a tax of as much as one grosz for each grivna in rent.[189] Testifying to the divisions within the Wrocław municipality was the principle introduced between 1357 and 1374 that the richest of the burghers (regardless of the

---

187 Stanisław Kutrzeba, *Finanse i handel*, 66–67.

188 The rules for assessing the *szos* there was like those used in Krakow. They included taxes on real estate and property, but the profession declared by burghers was also taken into account. As in Krakow, taxed goods did not include household appliances, clothes, jewellery or weaponry, as well as reserves of food, meat, beer and grain stored by the owner for their own use. This similarity is hardly surprising given the strong ties between the two cities and the Magdeburg Law governing both of them; Mateusz Goliński, *Socjotopografia*, 290–291.

189 Such a tax regulation clearly affected the richest part of the city's population, who invested their money in trade and collected rent paid for city property. This intention is also evidenced by the system of non-taxable property thresholds, differentiated "according to the size of the capital needed to set up a workshop in this profession," merchants were exempt from taxation of the first 100 grivna, rich stallholders – 30, innkeepers – 20, and craftsmen – 10. The list of these exemptions reflects in itself the awareness that the variability of wealth among the city's inhabitants depended on the way they made their living. This hierarchy is also emphasized by another component of the *szos* collected in Wrocław: the *de opere* tax that was paid on the basis of one's occupation. According to the 1384 tax tariff, merchants were to pay 24, innkeepers 12, stallholders 6, butchers 12, bakers, weavers, shoemakers, tanners, maltsters, coopers, blacksmiths, tailors, spinners, hat makers, bathhouse owners, glaziers 6, furriers, purse makers, cobblers, cutlers, locksmiths, belt makers, linen merchants 4, and other crafts 2 groszy each; *ibidem*.

THE SOCIO-ECONOMIC POSITION OF TESTATORS 155

activities they were engaged in), in other words those who owned property[190] worth at least 240 grivna, would settle their obligations to the city in person in the town hall, while other taxpayers would be visited by town officials in their homes, in accordance with the existing practice. At the same time, burghers who did not reach this 240-grivna ceiling had the szos tax they were to pay reduced by half (0.5 grosz for each ten grivna of property owned and 0.5 grosz for each grivna in rent). This – quite complicated – tax system was aimed at the legal separation of two social groups that lived within the urban community. Rich burghers were charged a higher tax, but at the same time, they were allowed to make a private, 'dignified' settlement and payment of their obligations. This also reflected the ideological balance between the few 'honourable' inhabitants of the city (approximately 6.7% of the total) and 'ordinary' burghers, because both classes of tax were supposed to generate the same level of revenue for the city despite the disparity in wealth between the two groups.[191]

The layered, 'pyramidal' structure of late medieval urban society is also evidenced by research carried out on the inhabitants of other large cities in the Hanseatic region. Roman Czaja compared the military burdens imposed on the city of Elbląg's burghers in the early fifteenth century with data on their real estate in 'land books.'[192] This allowed him to classify the burghers into three strata, each of which was divided into an upper and a lower group. In the early fifteenth century, Elbląg's population "had a wealth structure typical of Hanseatic cities sustained by long-distance trade" and was characterised by a relatively large group of wealthy burghers (14%–4% in the upper and 10% in the lower group) and a significant group of middle-income burghers (28%–18% in the upper and 10% in the lower), while the largest group was comprised of the poorest burghers (58%). In the latter half of this century, the gap in property ownership between burghers in the different strata widened significantly, with

---

190 Considered was taxable property, without the above-mentioned tax exemption, which meant, in the case of e.g. merchants and stallholders, a minimum of 340 and 270 grivna, respectively; *ibidem.*

191 A comparison of estimated numbers of both categories of taxpayers – about 209 representatives in the higher tax group (citizens) and about 2900 taxpayers, men and women, in the lower group (6.7% to 85% of the population identifiable in sources) gives an idea of the diversity in terms of wealth among the inhabitants of Wrocław. An Average wealthy burgher paid almost 17 times higher taxes than their average fellow resident from a lower tax class, while the differences between the their property and income must have been even higher; *ibidem*, 301.

192 Roman Czaja, *Socjotopografia miasta Elbląga w średniowieczu* (Toruń: Wydawn. Adam marszałek, 1992), 38.

the poorest group of burghers now accounting for 64% of Elbląg's population.[193] This reconstruction is supported by similar models of the wealth structures of other fifteenth-century Hanseatic cities.[194]

A list of the citizens of Toruń's military obligations to the Teutonic Order (a Catholic military and religious order founded in 1192 in Acre and settled from 1226 in Prussia) was used by Antoni Czacharowski to study the wealth structure of the city's society at the turn of the fourteenth century.[195] From this he identified four subgroups among the "wealthiest groups of Toruń's society." The first and most affluent group – comprising 19% of the sample – consisted mainly of wealthy merchants, including representatives of the patricians, but also a few of the richest craftsmen (a saddler, a goldsmith and a tailor) and one innkeeper. The second group in terms of wealth included 36% of all taxed individuals and consisted of less wealthy merchants, rich craftsmen (such as tinsmiths, blacksmiths, goldsmiths, armourers) and nineteen innkeepers. The third group – 20% – consisted mainly of craftsmen (furriers, saddlers, goldsmiths, glaziers, tinsmiths and some bakers) and innkeepers. The fourth group, which included 25% of all the persons mentioned, was in actuality much more numerous, as it also included poor craftsmen who were not mentioned by name in the census. It was made up of bakers, wheelwrights, shepherds, belt makers and 26 stallholders.[196]

The data collected from relevant literature on the subject and presented in Table 3 show significant differences between the estimated size of the

TABLE 3   Estimated distribution of the three social strata in Rostock, Stralsund, Lübeck, Wrocław, Torun, and Elblag

	Upper strata	Middle strata	Lower strata
Rostok	7%	38%	55%
Stralsund	12%	32%	56%
Lübeck	18%	30%	52%
Wrocław	15,8%	84,2%	
Toruń	18,7%	29,3%	52%
Ebląg	14%	28%	58%

---

193   *Ibidem*, 42–45.
194   Approx. 7, 38 and 55% respectively for Rostock in 1430, 12, 32 and 56% for Stralsund 1405–1409, and about 18, 30 and 52% for Lübeck in 1460; as in Roman Czaja, *Socjotopografia*, 45.
195   Antoni Czacharowski, *Ze studiów*, 89–96.
196   *Ibidem*, 94.

THE SOCIO-ECONOMIC POSITION OF TESTATORS

social strata in particular cities. They are related both to the different research methodologies adopted and to the different types of sources available to the researchers. The specificity and size of each of these cities is also of no less importance.[197] Taking into account the reservations above, it seems justified, however, to adopt a model of a large late-medieval city in which the upper strata was formed by about 10–15% of its inhabitants, the middle strata by about 30%, and the lower strata by about 55–60%. The complicated nature of the actual social relations means that this division into layers is something of a simplification, but it allows us to see the vertical structure of wealth in urban society and the significant differences in terms of the level of affluence among these particular groups, which are traditionally referred to as patricians, commoners and plebeians. Social divisions based on financial status determined in large part both the social prestige and self-identification of individuals: only the richest burghers and their close relatives had access to holding municipal offices, the nature of one's work determined the 'nobility' of one's profession, personal wealth determined the burden of city taxes and therefore the individual support of the city's finances, and sumptuary laws restrained individuals from making inordinate displays of wealth through their choice of attire.

7 Wealth and Social Status

The divisions between the rulers and the ruled, as well as between large-scale trade and small-scale handicraft resulted in enormous differences in wealth among Krakovian burghers.[198] In no other environment was 'hard cash' such a key to social advancement as in the city:

> With some exceptions (Jews or foreigners), material conditions always take precedence over social status, determining levels of respect or contempt. With certain periodic exceptions, money makes it possible to move from craftsmanship to the world of business, to gain entry into the

---

197 There was a much smaller higher stratum in Rostock and Lübeck, compared to other cities listed on this table, probably due to the fact that it only contains the richest burghers, so-called patricians, who made up the upper group of the upper strata in the six-group division. The upper lower group was included in the wider middle stratum.

198 "Differences in status, origin, social status, or, in short, qualitative differences, created social divisions which overlapped with property divisions. Moreover, the urban social model was still bourgeois and the basic factor influencing social diversification was money"; Jacques Rossiaud, *Mieszczanin i życie w mieście*, 191 (J. Rossiaud, *Le Citadin*).

Hanseatic League, to markets, to a place among the rich, and finally even into the ranks of the city elite.[199]

In the late medieval Kingdom of Poland, it was even common for the wealthiest Krakovian burghers to be raised to the rank of nobility.[200]

The data emerging from analyses of tax records from other late-medieval towns in the region can only serve as a reference point for research on Krakow's inhabitants. The lack of a source base allowing for easy comparisons means that in principle the only type of sources enabling an even fragmentary reconstruction of the social structure in the city are records reflecting marital contracts that were concluded there, i.e. dower records. It is assumed in the literature that these records provide a relatively faithful picture of the economic situation of the spouses involved, smoothing out short-term rises and falls in the wealth of the townspeople or their exemption from rent payments, which could affect, for example, the szos register for particular years.[201] The usefulness of these source records for research on the social structure of the city was proven by Jacek Wiesiołowski, who used the example of late medieval Poznan. In *libri resignationes* from the years 1430–1499, he found over 2000 dower records made by Poznan's burghers. This allowed him to carry out an exemplary study of the city's social hierarchy and socio-topography.[202] His research showed that over this period, the median value of bequests changed little, increasing from fifteen to 24 grivna at the end of the century.[203] At the same time, the arithmetic mean of bequests grew almost continuously from 22 to 65 grivna, an indication of the growing stratification of wealth and the increase in the concentration of wealth in the hands of the richest burghers during the fifteenth century.[204]

In municipal sources from Krakow we find only occasionally entries concerning the means for securing the money promised to future wifes. For the

---

199   *Ibidem.*

200   Zdzisław Noga, *Krakowska rada miejska w XVI wieku. Studium o elicie władzy* (Krakow: Wydawnictwo Naukowe Akademii Pedagogicznej, 2003).

201   This phenomenon is indicated, for example, by szos registers from Kazimierz in Krakow from the years 1385–1387, where 353, 406 and 338 people paid the szos tax. Also in Olkusz, in the years 1455–1456, there were 197 and 110 szos taxpayers. Significant differences in the number of burghers taxed were also found in Lviv in the years 1406–1417; cf. Jacek Wiesiołowski, *Stratyfikacja mieszczaństwa polskiego*, 280; Danuta Molenda, *Dzieje Olkusza do 1795 roku*, in *Dzieje Olkusza i regionu olkuskiego*, 171.

202   Jacek Wiesiołowski, *Socjotopografia*

203   *Ibidem*, 16.

204   *Ibidem*, 15–25.

THE SOCIO-ECONOMIC POSITION OF TESTATORS 159

years 1300–1500, only eighty bequests of this type were found in municipal books (both in books of the bench court and city council). At the same time, most of these dowers were very high (100–200 grivna), and in some cases dowers were given in the form of real estate, a house, a stall or a garden (or part of one), whose value is difficult to estimate precisely.

8   Dower Records in Krakovian Wills

A lack of sufficient sources makes it impossible to conduct detailed research on the social structure of Krakow. It seems, however, that dower bequests fulfilled a function similar to that of burgher wills. Confirmation of the amount of the dower promised to a wife and the rules for the division of property between spouses (and their descendants) in the event of the death of one of them – evidence of marriage contracts that had been concluded – constituted a frequently occurring element in burgher wills. The fact that the municipal authorities merged these two forms of documents is evidenced by, among other things, information that in 1396 the Krakow municipal council established the first, now-lost book of wills, referred to as *Liber Testamentorum et dotaliciorum* – the book of wills and dowers.[205]

Research has allowed us to identify 125 wills containing information about the amount of a dower due to a wife, constituting about 25% of all acts of last will, and 37% of those wills written by men. For the majority of the remaining 63% of wills, the widow's economic security usually consisted of a bequest for a specific part of the testator's estate (usually one-half, one-third, or a part equal to that received by each of the children) and bequests of property as a dower, with no indication of its estimated value, which made it impossible to use it for this purpose.

Limitations related to the statistical use of dower bequests for assessing the wealth, and thus the social position, of testators can in part be compensated for by prosopographic research on selected individuals. Despite widely shared views on the fundamental usefulness of dower bequests in research on the social structure of late medieval cities, it should be stressed that the amount given as a dower in each case varied according to a wide range of factors, including some very obvious ones, such as the economic situation of the husband's

---

205   *Registra perceptorum et distributorum civitatis Cracoviensis annorum 1390–1393, 1395–1405 nec non 1407–1410*, ed. Franciszek Piekosiński, in *Libri antiquissimi civitatis Cracoviae saeculi decimi quinti*, pars posteriori, Krakow 1877, 313. The fact that the book was still in use in 1410 is proven by an entry in the council book; CONS. 427, fol. 371.

and wife's families, as well as whether it was their first or successive marriage, or whether either of them had received an inheritance from their parents or relatives. Moreover, the difference between a will made in the municipal book shortly after marriage and a will written at a dying man's bedside was often a reflection of the passage of time, during which the property and personal and social positions of the spouses could have changed significantly. The emotional relations between them greatly influenced the final dispositions made to one or both of them. An example of this is undoubtedly the frequently enlarged dowers, so-called *dotalicium*, which sometimes increased the amount due to the wife after the death of her husband by two- or three-fold. However, the institution of the dotalicium itself shows that the initial amount of the dower, which was a very important part of the marriage contract, was remembered and probably sometimes secured in writing, and any increase was usually added to the initial amount.[206]

Since one quarter of all the preserved wills constitute a relatively representative source base, these were compared with the data collected by Jacek Wiesiołowski for fifteenth-century Poznan. The aim of this exercise was to determine the wealth and, consequently, the social position occupied by this group of testators. To some extent, the results of this analysis should also be representative of the entire group of Krakow testators from the fourteenth and fifteenth centuries, who were divided into six income groups according to the model proposed by Wiesiołowski.[207]

The data collected in Table 4 allow us to see the exceptionally stratified nature of testators' wealth throughout the entire period under study. Upper upper-income testators were responsible for at least half of all the acts of last will produced, and together with lower upper-income testators account for as

---

206   Bartłomiej Groicki wrote about an unspecified but pledged security of the dower in the latter half of the sixteenth century. He considered this practice a fraud committed by women who "cast aside their fear of God, shame, faith and marital duty, having forgotten their children's children, dared to oppose their consciences and evidence, to demand large sums of money which had never been promised them at the time of their marriage; Thus they deprived their children or their husbands' friends out of a large part of their hereditary goods contrary to God's will, claiming this promised dower from their husbands' property"; *idem, Tytuły prawa majdeburskiego* (Warszawa: Wydawnictwo Prawnicze, 1954), 62.

207   Each of them was divided into a higher and a lower group. "The convertibility of the six groups and the flexibility of the system are the factors that justify this division. The two groups in the upper strata allow for a precise definition of phenomena among urban patricians, the diversity of the Poznan populace is reflected in the three groups encompassing average burghers (the entire middle strata and the upper group of the lower strata), while all of the plebs, which are rarely mentioned in the sources, belong to the lower part of the lower layer"; *idem, Socjotopografia,* 13.

TABLE 4 Dower records in Krakow wills

	Wills with record of dower	Upper upper-income (>100 grivnas)	Lower upper-income (61–100 grivnas)	Upper middle-income (31–60 grivnas)	Lower middle-income (20–30 grivnas)	Upper lower-income (10–19 grivnas)	Lower lower-income (<10 grivnas)
until 1350	1	-	1	-	-	-	-
1351–1400	21	11	2	8	-	-	-
1401–1450	39	21	8	6	2	2	-
1451–1500	64	25	22	6	9	2	-
	125	57	33	20	11	4	0
	(100%)	(46%)	(26%)	(16%)	(9%)	(3%)	(0%)

much as 72% of all the wills analysed (90 out of 125). 25% of these acts of last will (31 out of 125) were written by representatives of the middle-income (upper and lower groups), and only in four cases (3%) were testators from the lower-income groups. If, in line with Wiesiołowski's proposal, we apply this division to the traditional tripartite model of urban society, which differentiates between patricians, the general population (commoners) and plebeians, this means that representatives of the city's elite wrote almost three quarters of all the wills under discussion, while members of the financially and socially diverse general population made one quarter of the wills, and only in four cases (3% of all wills) can we assume that the testators were from among the poorest burghers, and thus classified as plebeians. In this group, however, there are very few people whose dowers were less than ten grivna, which would qualify them as belonging to the poorest group of Krakovian burghers.

9   Estimates of Testators' Wealth

The wealth of Krakovian testators, and thus the social class they belonged to, was examined above in the case of the one quarter of those whose wills contained dower bequests. A closer examination of the almost 447 testators whose wills have survived to the present day required, however, more detailed prosopographic studies. These made it possible to estimate burghers' assets based both on data contained in the wills themselves and from indirect information found in Krakow's municipal books. When assessing the wealth of each individual, the most important criteria, apart from the above-mentioned dower bequests, included: bequests of money and rent made in wills, properties owned and their location within the city or outside of it, the functions performed on the municipal council, family and geographical origin, occupation and other sources of income.

On the basis of the collected data, the testators were divided according to the previously adopted six-part division, into groups conventionally named the very rich (corresponding to the upper upper-income group), the rich (corresponding to the lower upper-income group), the moderately well-to-do (upper middle-income group), those of modest means (lower middle-income group), and the poor (upper lower-income group). As the above analysis of the dower bequests shows, during the period under study, nobody from among the poorest burghers (those from the lower low-income group) are found among Krakovian testators. Due to the marginal occurrence of wills made by people who, according to Wiesiołowski, would represent a burgher of average means –
civis medianus (one who would find himself between the upper lower-income

THE SOCIO-ECONOMIC POSITION OF TESTATORS

and lower lower-income groups), the differences between wealthy burghers is more visible in this division.

These groups of testators could be defined using the above criteria as follows:

- the poor: dower bequests between ten and nineteen grivna; cash donations of up to 20 grivna; wooden houses on the city's side streets and outside the city; craftsmen belonging to poor guilds, journeymen, servants, residents of the suburbs and their close relatives and immediate family (wives, children, stepchildren, sons-in-law);
- those of modest means: dower bequests between 20 and 30 grivna; cash donations between 20 and 50 grivna; wooden houses on the city's side streets; guild craftsmen, occasionally elders but of less important guilds, and their close relatives and immediate family (wives, children, stepchildren, sons-in-law);
- those moderately well-to-do: dower bequests between 31 and 60 grivna; cash donations between 50 and 100 grivna; wooden houses, real estate on important 'gate' streets in the city, but also on the streets leading off of these streets; guild elders and wealthy craftsmen and their close relatives and immediate family (wives, children, stepchildren, sons-in-law);
- the rich: dower bequests between 61 and 100 grivna; cash donations between 100 and 250 grivna; tenement buildings and other properties in the city on important, 'gateway' streets; aldermen on the bench court, long-time elders in Krakow's wealthy guilds and their close relatives and immediate family (wives, children, stepchildren, sons-in-law);
- the very rich: dower bequests over 100 grivna; cash donations over 250 grivna; tenement buildings and real estate on the market and out to "the first junction"[208] or more than one house in various parts of the city; members of the municipal council and bench court; born into councillor's families and the wealthiest merchant families.

---

208 "Another division of the space of Krakow were three zones of property tax, based on their rates. This division is found in the De exactione civili 'schoss' judgement from 1385. It defines the tax rates applicable in particular zones, as well as their limits. The first zone included the houses located at the market square, where the tax rates were the highest. The second zone consisted of buildings situated at the market blocks, but separated from the first group by currently non-existant streets running among them, and from the third one by major crossstreets. There the rates were slightly lower. The third zone included the area stretching from the so-called first junction (*das erste kreucze*), i.e. the first block of the street leading from the market square to the walls. The tax was lowest there"; Piotr Tyszka, *Obraz przestrzeni miejskiej Krakowa XIV–XV wieku w świadomości jego mieszkańców* (Lublin: Wydawnictwo Uniwersytetu Marii Curie-Skłodowskiej, 2001), 221–229.

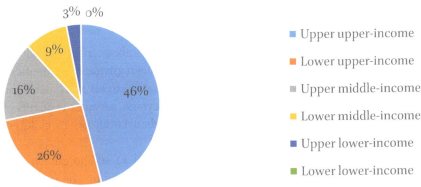

GRAPH 8   Estimates of the wealth of the 25% of all testators who included dowers in their wills

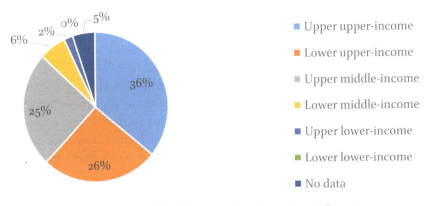

GRAPH 9   Estimates of the wealth of all testators based on indirect information

The rules discussed above for assessing the so-called szos tax indicate (based on the tax levied on poor stallholders) that the 'poverty line' was considered to include those whose estate had a value of less than twelve grivna (they only paid tax on the place of sale as part of the szos tax).[209] According to the above system of division, the poor peddler would be classified as being in the lower lower-income group. Such poor burghers do not, however, appear among Krakovian testators – at least from what is possible to determine on the basis of surviving wills.

As can be seen from Graphs 8 and 9, estimates of the assets of all the individuals whose wills have been preserved largely coincide with the calculations made for the 125 persons who mentioned in their wills the sum of the dower

---

209   Stanisław Kutrzeba, *Finanse i handel*, 69.

THE SOCIO-ECONOMIC POSITION OF TESTATORS   165

they bequeathed to their wives. Even if we were to take into account the 5% of individuals for whom source information is insufficient even to allow us to estimate their wealth, and include them in the lowest strata of the urban community,[210] 62% of all wills would have been made by those from the upper strata, about 30% by persons from the middle section, and only a small percentage would have been made by those from the lower strata. At the same time, the assets of all testators are undoubtedly somewhat underestimated due to the caution exercised in analysing the source references, which in many cases have been preserved in a fragmented state.

The data collected largely confirms the elite social status of Krakovian testators. The vast majority originated from a narrow circle of the richest Krakovian burghers, from among people whose entire estate is difficult to value, but who made dower bequests to their wives many times greater than those of middle-income and lower-income burghers. The income diversity seen among the testators extends along a wide scale, ranging from ten grivna to 1800 florins (about 1350 grivna). It also indicates a growing stratification in terms of wealth among Krakovian burghers. In the first half of the fourteenth century, the largest (and only) dower bequest was 100 grivna; over the next 50 years, 250 grivna; in the first half of the fifteenth century, 750 grivna; and in the latter half of this century, it reached the aforementioned 1800 florins, or 1350 grivna. Nevertheless, representatives not only of Krakow's financial elite and wealthy craftsmen, but also some of the poorer inhabitants of Krakow, made the decision to write a will.

Changes that took place among testators during the analyzed period are presented in the chart below. The initial dominance of wills made by the richest Krakow burghers, usually city officials, council members and aldermen or their close relatives, can be seen here. Over the next fifty years, this initial bias towards wealthy burghers is balanced by a growing number of middle-class testators. Interestingly, Graph 10 clearly shows that, starting in the latter half of the fourteenth century, there is a gradual increase in the number of lower-income testators. Although on a personal level, the making of a last will was decided primarily by individual factors, the collected data testifies to the gradual dissemination of written last will dispositions in wider circles of urban society.

---

210   Although among them there may also have been some testators who were much more affluent than average; it seems that their absence in Krakow's municipal books indicates their negligible social significance, and since there were no registered commercial transactions on their part, they could not have been wealthy.

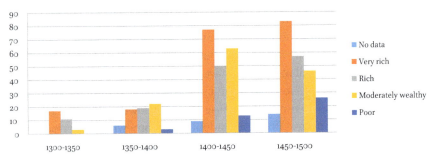

GRAPH 10   Changes in the wealth of testators in the fourteenth and fifteenth centuries.

The breakdown of the wealth of female testators seen in Graph 11 and 12 below, is likewise interesting. These represent members of the same social groups as male testators, but they are to a much greater extent middle-income, and less often very rich burghers. A small shift of just a few percent can be seen over time in each of the three richest social groups. The most significant factor in female Krakovian burghers' decision to write a will appears to have been their becoming widows. Both the need to dispose of part of the property owned by the married couple and the limited possibilities for capital accumulation by unmarried widows were conducive to their pauperisation if they did not re-marry.[211] The relative lack of wealth among these women was also influenced by the custom and legal principle (not always respected) that real estate – the most valuable property in terms of capital accumulation – was to

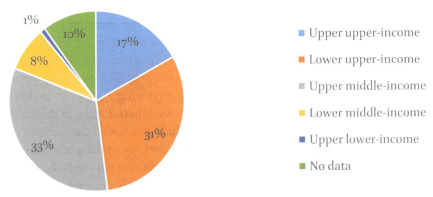

GRAPH 11   Asset structure of female testators

---

211   Consequently, the evaluation of a widowed woman's wealth on the basis of the goods she possessed usually indicated a poorer social circle than the one to which she actually belonged. This factor may have had an impact on the possibly underestimated social position of some of them; Andrzej Karpiński, *Kobieta w mieście polskim w drugiej połowie XVI i w XVII wieku* (Warszawa: Instytut Historii PAN, 1995), 206–207.

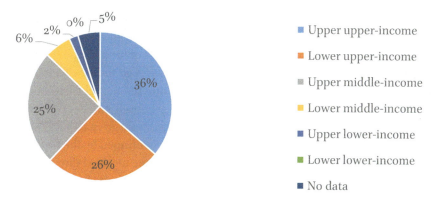

GRAPH 12   Asset structure of all testators

be inherited by sons and other male members of the family, while women were expected to leave the home with the money and valuables they had inherited from their deceased husbands, usually in the form of a dower. It can therefore be assumed that in many cases the economic position of a widow-testator did not reflect her real social position.

10   Characteristics of Particular Social Groups

10.1   *Impoverished Testators*

Only ten testators whose records of their last will have survived to this day have been classified as poor burghers, i.e. those belonging to the poorest group.[212] Out of these testators, there were eight men and two women. Amongst the men, there was a butcher, a baker, a stallholder, a bricklayer, a shoemaker, a fustian cutter, a servant at Wawel Castle, and in one case, no information has survived to indicate his occupation. For one female testator, the nickname *textrix* indicates she worked as a weaver, while another is represented only by her first name and her husband's first name (Anna Gregorinne). Four of these male burghers made dower bequests in their wills: three for ten grivna each and one for fifteen grivna. The possessions of the remaining four male testators were estimated on the basis of their bequests and a small number of entries in municipal books.

---

[212]   In relation to the system proposed by Jacek Wiesiołowski with three social class layers, each of which was divided into an upper and a lower group, the category of 'poor burgher' corresponds to the lower upper social group.

The baker Piots Ossuch, who made his will during an illness in 1445, noted that Barbara, his daughter from his first marriage, had already been married off and should get one third of the proceeds from the sale of his house, but only if she so requested, while the remaining proceeds should go to his wife and his daughter Martha.[213] He had bought the house behind the Rogacka bathhouse in 1428 from the councillor Bernard of Brzeg (who himself had been given it in a court settlement) and declared that he was owed eight grivna for it.[214] The fact that this was the actual value of the property is confirmed by the fact that in 1449 Barbara, the daughter of the now deceased Peter, received three grivna from her stepmother, in accordance with her father's will, which represented the money she had been promised from the sale of the aforementioned house.[215] It can therefore be assumed that since the value of the house was 8–9 grivna, the value of the baker's other assets was not much higher.

Among all the fourteenth- and fifteenth-century acts of last will, there is only one made by a journeyman – Johnny from the goldsmiths' guild (in Latin *artificii aurificum familiaris*), who together with Martin the bricklayer, set out in 1464 on a campaign against the Turks. According to his will, written on a piece of paper, he also had a relatively valuable estate. He left to the guild a sword and six silver skojecs worth together eighteen florins, thirteen silver grivna and all his clothes and other things, which in the event of his death were to be divided into three parts between his brother, sister and pious deeds. He gave his goldsmiths' tools to his relative Wojtek. This will proves that even the goldsmith Johnny, who had not yet started a family, and did not have a house in the city (he probably lived with his master), already had assets worth at least 30 grivna.

10.2   *Testators of Modest Means*

Although in terms of the wealth found within the city's overall social structure, burghers of modest means[216] corresponded most closely with Krakow's commoner class, to which the average burgher (Latin *civis medianus*) belonged, such individuals comprised only about 6% of all testators. They made dower bequests in the region of 20–30 grivna, which is two or three times higher than the amounts recorded by burghers who belonged to the poor, but also two or three times lower than those characteristic of the more affluent burghers of average means.

---

213   LT, fol. 9.
214   CONS. 428, fol. 169.
215   CONS. 428, fol. 528.
216   Corresponding to the lower middle group in the six group division.

THE SOCIO-ECONOMIC POSITION OF TESTATORS

Among twelve of the 32 individuals (37.5%) for whom dower bequests were known to have been made, five secured them with 30 grivna, two allocated 30 florins (i.e. 22.5 grivna) and five with 20 grivna each. This category also includes a relatively large number of women – eleven (34%), of whom nine were already widows at the time of the writing of their will. In addition, of the 32 wills made by both sexes, seven people (22%) made wills before going on a pilgrimage (including all four of those who made wills from the latter half of the fourteenth century). It seems that the nature of these provisions was conducive to the disclosure in the wills of only part of the property owned, the rest having to be spent on travel expenses. The wealth of the remaining nine male testators (21%) was estimated on the basis of their bequests and a few entries in municipal books.

John Panzira, elected in 1438, 1451 and 1454 as an elder in the shoemaker's guild, was included among the group of poor citizens.[217] In his will, written in 1458, before councillors who had come to his home, he gave his second wife Catherine a dower of 30 grivna secured by a wooden house at the corner of St. John Street (opposite St. John's Church).[218] Due to his stipulation that if his wife did not receive this money, she had the right to lease all his movable and immovable property, it can be assumed that the value of the house was about 30 grivna. In order to secure her future existence, he not only gave her his shoemaker's bench, but also allowed her to work as a shoemaker even after his death, until she found a new husband to take care of her. He also allowed his son-in-law Maciek Bozanczin to live in half the house until John's children from his first marriage reached adulthood. They were to be the final heirs to the house and the shoemaking bench, as well as to other movables, clothing and weapons. A debt of less than six grivna was to be paid after the sale of the first wife's clothing. Two shoemakers were chosen as executors of the will, one of whom was then an elder in the shoemaker's guild. A year later, Catherine, who was now married to Nicholas Mikulka, received the house on St. John Street from the executors and guardians of her first husband's children.[219]

10.3 Moderately Well-Off Testators

Among moderately well-off testators (corresponding to the upper middle-income group) were burghers whose assets and social position placed them above those representing the statistical *civis medianus*. They constituted a large portion of all testators, approximately 25%. They made dower bequests

---

217 CONS. 428, fol. 384; CONS. 429, fol. 23, 84.
218 LT, fol. 50.
219 Then she sold it to the furrier Nicholas Wolfram; SCAB. 8, fol. 369.

170   CHAPTER 2

of between 31 and 60 grivna, which was two to three times the amount pledged by lower-income burghers. Among this group were many wealthy craftsmen and members of older guilds, as well as stallholders, inn-keepers, bathhouse owners and even attorneys.

Among the testators who left relatively numerous entries in municipal books (along with three versions of his last will) was Nicholas Topler. In the will he made in 1450, he divided his personal belongings between his mother and wife Catherine; these included his most valuable clothing (fox fur-lined coats, two newly-dyed tunics and two belts, one of which was gold-plated), cloth (20 ells) and four silver spoons and bowls. He ordered the remaining goods belonging to him to be given after his death to his relatives.[220] The nature of this bequest suggests that it could have been made, like many other wills in that particular year, before Nicholas's pilgrimage to Rome. His first wife died shortly after his return to Krakow, and in 1455 he made a mutual bequest with his new wife, Margaret.[221] Another will made by Nicholas Topler dates to 1461, when he went on another pilgrimage to Rome.[222] This time, apart from valuable personal property, he also listed a tenement building on Sławkowska Street and a debt of 60 grivna owed by his sister Barbara, and secured by her house on St. Florian Street. The siblings had inherited these valuable properties after the death of their mother (as Nicholas explains in another document). Before setting off once again, he entrusted his sister and her husband Kacper with the care of his only child,[223] his daughter Ursula, and financially secured the future of his third wife Catherine, bequeathing her a dower of 60 florins (45 grivna) and noting that when he took her for his wife, he received 50 florins from her, of which he still owed her 34 florins.[224] Moreover, he placed in a box the valuable moveable goods meant to be given to his child and deposited them with his sister, leaving the rest of his household furnishings for his wife's use. Nine years later, Nicholas made a third version of his will, written before councillors when he was lying in a state of infirmity.[225] This last will had a different character from the previous ones, since the first part of it was taken up by a list of debtors and creditors, followed by confirmation of a dower bequest to his wife Catherine

---

220   CONS. 429, fol. 16.

221   SCAB. 7, fol. 218.

222   LT, fol. 69.

223   This was probably Caspar Topeler, an elder of the tanners' guild in 1459, 1461, 1466 and 1468; CONS. 429, fol. 227, 287, 370, 404.

224   He gave her his yellow marten-lined coat (*de coftir*) toward repaying this amount, and he was supposed to return the rest if he came back from his pilgrimage.

225   LT, fol. 99–100.

of 60 florins, absent from earlier versions of the will. Nicholas ordered that two silver spoons and a silver belt be given to St. Bernard's Church and used to make a chalice and a patena (i.e. a plate used in the ceremony of the Eucharist). The will ended with a bequest of rent for his niece and the donation of two houses at Sławkowska and St. Florian Streets to Ursula's daughter.

It is worth noting Nicholas Topler's presumed participation in two pilgrimages to Rome and his three marriages. It can also be assumed that although he had a relatively large estate, he did not achieve much professional or social success in his life. He did not act as the elder of any of Krakow's guilds, and his property did not increase as a result of his actions, but only after his mother inherited a significant sum.

10.4   *Wealthy Testators*

The testators included in the group of rich burghers represented the city's economic and social elite. The amounts of bequests written to wives were usually round sums of 100 florins or 100 grivna, indicating that the value of the testator's entire property was likely at least two or three times higher. In this group, one can already find many aldermen, especially those who had not yet been able to join the city council. There were also many rich guild masters in this group, mainly representatives of profitable professions, such as merchants, goldsmiths, stallholders, furriers, innkeepers and fish merchants, but there were also pressmen, tailors, butchers, shoemakers, captains, wheelwrights and archers.[226] Among the 137 testators included in this group there were also 36 women (26% of the total), most often the well-secured widows of wealthy Krakow burghers.

A typical example of a rich burgher is the goldsmith Nicholas Brenner.[227] After obtaining citizenship in Krakow in 1440, he was listed in the book of records of new citizens as a goldsmith from Paczków near Nysa. His identity was certified by Krakow guild elders, and he paid a significant fee of one grivna to become a citizen.[228] Soon afterward he married the widow of the deceased goldsmith Pawel Brenner.[229] Nicholas must have had previous contact with the goldsmiths of Krakow, since they vouched for him. This is also proven by the fact that five years later he was elected as an elder of the goldsmiths' guild in Krakow.[230] He also held this prestigious position in later years (1448, 1450,

---

226   The hierarchy of professions in the discussed group of crafts is similar to that in other towns of the region.

227   Jerzy Pietrusiński, *Złotnicy krakowscy*, 594–599.

228   "Niclas Brenner de Paczke aurifaber h.i. Pro littera fideiusserunt seniores in brevi, dedit 1 mrc"; Books of Admissions, no. 5071, 161.

229   Jerzy Pietrusiński, *Złotnicy krakowscy*, 594.

230   CONS. 428, fol. 477.

1455, 1458, 1460 and 1464).[231] By the end of his life, his social position in the city had improved such that in 1462 he was elected to the municipal bench court.[232] However, soon afterwards (in 1464) he fell ill and "lying on his mortal bed" (German *tot bette*), he gave his last will to the councillors who had come to his home.[233] Using the security of half of his house, he confirmed a previously made bequest of 100 florins for his wife Barbara's dower. He donated his remaining property to his son Lorenzo. This brief bequest for his family was preceded by a detailed list of all the debts and receivables he had not managed to settle before his death, and which he left to his wife. This entry is an extremely interesting source of information both about the items he produced and about their intended recipients (including the nobleman John Kobiliński, the canon John Długosz, the voivode of Lublin Dobek, the voivode of Tarnów and the voivode of Krakow John Tęczyński).[234] The presence of these figures testifies to the fact that this testator was one of the most valued goldsmiths not only in Krakow itself, but also in the whole region, and that his social and financial standing improved thanks to his exceptional professional skills.[235]

10.5   *Extremely Wealthy Testators*

The last and largest group of testators is made up of people counted among the richest and most influential spheres of Krakow's society. Representatives of this social group, often identified with the patrician class,[236] are estimated to have comprised only a few percent of the city's overall population, but made as many as 36% of all preserved bequests of last will. Among the testators from this group, as many as 69 people were councillors on the Krakow municipal council (45%), while the remaining male testators consisted of close relatives of councillors and rich aldermen. There were many merchants, including several who came to Krakow from other urban centers, sometimes very distant ones (such as Wilhelm Megirszheimer of Dinkelsbühl, John Raisser of Memmingen or Erhart Eigilwart of Augsburg).[237] There were also Krakow's writers (Eustace the municipal notary, John Stolle of Głogów, Nicholas Newmeister

---

231   CONS. 428, fol. 511; CONS. 429, fol. 3, 114, 196, 264, 347.

232   CONS. 429, fol. 119.

233   LT, fol. 83–84.

234   From spoons and plates to gold-plated belts and stripes to crosses, monstrances and chalices; LT, fol. 83–84.

235   The testator's death in the same year is evidenced by an entry in the council book in which the council gave Barbara's widows precedence before all his creditors to claim her dower from the estate of the deceased; SCAB. 8, fol. 187.

236   Roman Czaja, *Grupy rządzące*, 16–18.

237   LT, fol. 135–136 (1482); SCAB. 8, fol. 598–599 (1476); CONS. 428, fol. 305 (1431).

THE SOCIO-ECONOMIC POSITION OF TESTATORS

municipal deputy notary, and Christopher Rebentcz)[238] whose wealth was equal to that of the richest citizens of Krakow. Among the factors proving their financial and social position, we can first mention the public functions they served on the municipal council and the municipal bench court, the bequests of dowers of considerable size (from 100 to 1350 grivna in the case of the richest of them, John Sweidniczer) and real estate located on prestigious plots near the city market square and in its vicinity. This group, due to its elite character, seems to be the most interconnected. Its characteristic feature was its participation in the culture of writing and wide reception of the practice of preserving a last will in writing. In many cases, wills made by a husband, his widow, his son or daughter have been preserved.[239]

11   Female Testators

Since the first wills appeared in Krakow, female testators have been found among those who made them.[240] Although in the fourteenth century, testators were most often men – considered the rightful managers of property and goods – over time the number of women in this group grew and, as in other large urban centers, during the course of the two centuries under study here, constituted almost 30% of the total.[241] Graph 13[242] shows how the number of female testators evolved in relation to the number of surviving wills.

---

238   LT, fol. 61–63 (1459); SCAB. 6, fol. 186, 187, 267; CONS. 429, fol. 27–28; KDMK, vol. 3, no. 439 (1439, 1442, 1451, 1454); SCAB. 6, fol. 186, 187, 267; CONS. 429, fol. 27–28; KDMK, vol. 3, no. 439 (1439, 1442, 1451, 1454; SCAB. 7, fol. 120 (1451); CONS. 429, fol. 693 (1481).

239   The well-known Morsztyn family is a good example of this, where the wills of Nicholas (1416 – SCAB. 4, fol. 143), John (1450 – CONS. 429, fol. 12), Stanisław (1450 – SCAB. 7, fol. 86) and George (1500 – LT, fol. 161–164) have been preserved, as well as the wills of people linked to this family, e.g. councilorcou John Pitchen (LT, fol. 45), who was Stanisław's father-in-law, while his brother-in-law was the municipal notary Eustace (LT, fol. 61–63), or John Baumgart, a furrier (SCAB. 6, fol. 215; CONS. 428, fol. 466).

240   KDMK, vol. 3, no. 368 (1302).

241   Similar proportions are found in medieval wills from other towns in the region, e.g. in Konstanz, in the period from 1368 to 1542 women made 31.7% of all the preserved wills, and in Bratislava – 38%. However, these proportions tend to vary from 20 to more than 50% depending on the town, the size of the preserved collections of wills and when they were written; cf. Paul Baur, *Testament und Bürgerschaft*, 61–68; *Das Pressburger Protocollum Testamentorum 1410 (1427) – 1529*, vol. 1, ed. Judit Majorossy, Katalin Szende (Fontes rerum Austriacarum, Österreichische Geschichtsquellen, 3, Fontes Iuris), (Wien: Bohlau Verlag), 3–10.

242   In Graph no. 6, in cases where the testator made more than one will, the date of the first will was taken into account.

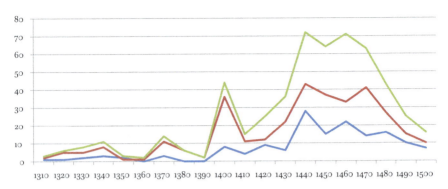

GRAPH 13   Number of women (blue) and men (red) among all Kraków testators (green) in the fourteenth and fifteenth centuries

This continuing dominance of male testators was natural in the medieval city, reflecting the culture and social dynamics of the day, according to which a married woman was subordinated to her husband, who managed their common property. Nevertheless, the comparison of the number of female and male testators from the period 1431–1470 brings interesting results. These results are based on the source database of municipal bench and council books, both of which have survived for this period.

Table 5 shows that in the discussed period the percentage of women among all testators was over 50%, and in some decades it even reached 65% and 67%. It is a valuable testimony of the similar participation of (usually wealthy) men and women in the group of Krakow testators. On this basis, it can be concluded that in the period of relative dissemination of wills among Krakow burghers, gender seemed not to play a major role.

TABLE 5   The number of women and men among Krakow testators in the years 1431–1470

Years	Women (N)	Men (N)	Percent of women among testators
1431–1440	28	43	65%
1441–1450	15	37	41%
1451–1460	22	33	67%
1461–1470	14	41	34%
Total	79	154	51%

THE SOCIO-ECONOMIC POSITION OF TESTATORS

12   Immigrant Testators

12.1   *Immigration and the City's Population*

The image of large medieval cities that emerges from demographic research presents local metropolises as sick and weak organisms, 'consuming' large numbers of their inhabitants (due to high mortality rates) and thriving only thanks to a constant influx of new settlers from the countryside and smaller population centers. In the words of Jacek Wiesiołowski, "Medieval cities are considered to be giant places of extinction for their inhabitants, where the population cannot even sustain its own numbers, and where growth is totally dependent on high rates of migration."[243] This phenomenon must also be taken into account when analysing the socio-occupational structure of Krakow. It is worth noting, however, that this refers to the population of the city as a whole, which itself was highly diverse in every respect, including in the fertility and mortality of its members. Studies of the development of pre-industrial cities point to a fundamental difference between two categories of inhabitants, permanent residents (i.e. burghers born in cities and immigrants who stayed in them permanently) and those who stayed there for a short time, for example because they were too poor to stay permanently.[244] One theory derived from historical demographics proposes that it was the increase in mortality and lower fertility among immigrants that contributed to the negative birth rate in medieval cities.[245] The essence of this distinction is the assumption that the living conditions and social roles available to newcomers made it difficult for them to start a family and attain a stable living situation, which in consequence contributed to lower birthrates and worse conditions for raising a child than among the city's permanent residents. It can be assumed, however, that it was mainly difficult living conditions, a problem experienced by the majority

---

243   Jerzy Wiesiołowski, *Socjotopografia*, 235.

244   "The permanent residents, consisting of natives and some immigrants, lived out their lives in the city – married, had children and died – and enjoyed some measure of natural increase. The temporary immigrants who came to the cities, on the other hand, were preponderantly artisan journeymen and servants, and people of that status could seldom marry by the standards of early modern society. Given the high mortality conditions of the times, they contributed their due share of deaths to the vital registers of the cities, but as illegitimate fertility was substantially lower than legitimate, deaths outnumbered births by a very large amount"; Allan N. Sharlin, "Natural Decrease in Early Modern Cities. A Reconsideration," 'Past and Present' 79 (1978), 127, as in Jan de Vries, *European Urbanization 1500–1800* (Cambridge (Mass.): Harvard University Press, 1984), 181.

245   Jan de Vries, *European Urbanization*, 185.

176   CHAPTER 2

of both newcomers and permanent residents of cities, that had the greatest impact on this phenomenon.

12.2 Newcomers to the City

The origin and family ties of Krakovian testators can be determined on the basis of three sources: a nickname indicating the place of origin of the person concerned; entries in the books of records of new citizens, in which the place of origin of a new citizen was sometimes noted; and finally, the contents of wills, in which the testator's parents or siblings living in other cities were sometimes mentioned, or bequests made (or foundations established) for hospitals and parish churches located in other communities.[246]

Nicknames containing place-names are most commonly found in wills made in the first half of the fourteenth century, when Krakow's elites had close ties with Wrocław and cities in Upper Silesia and Małopolska, a fact reflected in people's names.[247] Among the testators were Krakow residents originally from Racibórz,[248] Cieszyn,[249] Żary,[250] Głogów,[251] Kluczbork,[252] Olkusz[253] and Rożnów.[254] Later, the practice of including one's hometown in one's name began to decline, especially among wealthy burghers, in favour of professional nicknames and a newly emerging form of family name – surnames. Despite this, in the fifteenth century, the origins of burghers who had come to Krakow from elsewhere is sometimes indicated by their surname, e.g. John Willusch from Zator,[255] Nicholas Klausnicz a fustian maker from Nowy Torun[256] or Gregory from Nowy Sacz.[257]

Of the 256 fifteenth-century male testators whose wills have survived to the present day, as many as 87 (i.e. 34%) are found in the book of admissions to

---

246   Urszula Sowina, Kazimierz Pacuski, *Testamenty mieszczan Krakowskich jako źródła do badań nad stronami rodzinnymi imigrantów w Krakowskiej elicie władzy (Przykład Jana z Reguł na Mazowszu)*, in *Elita władzy miasta Krakowa i jej związki z miastami Europy w średniowieczu i epoce nowożytnej (do połowy XVII wieku). Zbiór studiów*, ed. Zdzisław Noga (Krakow: Antykwa, 2011), 433–445.

247   Jerzy Rajman, *Mieszczanie z Górnego Śląska w elicie władzy Krakowa w XIV w.*, in *Elita władzy miasta Krakowa*, 49–80.

248   Henryk of Racibórz; NKiRMK, no. 286 (1313).

249   Nicholas of Cieszyn; NKiRMK, no. 1189 (1336).

250   Herman of Żary; NKiRMK, no. 1190, 1325 (1336).

251   Sydelman of Głogów; NKiRMK, no. 1352, 1397 (1340).

252   Gertrude, a widow of Nicholas from Kluczbork; NKiRMK, no. 1548 (1345).

253   Frederick of Olkusz; NKiRMK, no. 106 (1310).

254   Peczold of Rożnów; NKiRMK, no. 34 (1306).

255   CONS. 427, fol. 46 (1394).

256   LT, fol. 94 (1468).

257   SCAB. 8, fol. 29 (1460).

THE SOCIO-ECONOMIC POSITION OF TESTATORS

municipal law (*Libri iuris civilis*) in Krakow, i.e. among the burghers obtaining city citizenship.[258] Another 74 testators were found to have acted (sometimes several times) as guarantors of persons being granted citizenship in Krakow, which indicates that they had already done so. On the basis of this data it can be concluded that a significant number of testators, at least one third of them, were immigrants who had arrived in Krakow from elsewhere, and who then, following a variety of different paths, merged into the city's urban society. What is more, among the group of 89 burghers, as many as 17 of them served as Krakow councillors. This proves that the city's elites were quite open to 'foreigners' who possessed significant economic and cultural capital. Social capital, in turn, was usually acquired by newcomers by marrying Krakow citizens belonging to this elite.[259]

Although books of records of new citizens are a very valuable source for research on the medieval society of Krakow, they inform us only about a certain segment of the people who came to the city. While the purchase of a house was not officially required to obtain citizenship in Krakow, and sometimes even members of the poor were allowed to receive such a status (in such cases, the councillors granted them exemptions or reductions of fees)[260] only a small percentage of all immigrants to Krakow were interested in obtaining citizenship in the city. The greatest interest was expressed by those who would benefit directly from such a change. These were most often merchants and craftsmen, for whom citizenship in the city would give them the right to join a guild or be granted trade privileges made to Krakovians.[261] It is therefore not surprising that the ownership status of testators who had the right to obtain citizenship reflected basic tendencies observed within the group as a whole: 39 newcomers (45%) can be described as very rich, fifteen (17%) as rich, 26 (30%) as well-off and only seven (8%) as poor. Again, the rich and very rich – representatives of the upper class – constitute the vast majority of all 87 testators considered

---

258 In some cases, there are some doubts as to whether the note in the Book of Admissions relates to a given testator or just a person with a similar name and nickname. This problem mainly concerns townspeople with popular names, such as John, Peter, Matthias or Nicholas, with nicknames indicating their occupation.

259 The concept of economic, cultural and social (and symbolic) capital was developed by Pierre Bourdieu; cf. *idem, The Forms of Social Capital*.

260 "In fourteenth- and fifteenth-century Krakow (1392–1485), many people, i.e. 58 people, defined as servants (*servitor, famulus*) became citizens of the city, as well as four janitors in the years 1401–1503, and fourteen people generally referred to as *laborator* in the same period"; Stanisław Gierszewski, *Obywatele miast Polski przedrozbiorowej* (Warszawa: Państwowe Wydawn. Naukowe, 1973), 38. Neophytes, Jews, Lithuanians and Ruthenians were usually also exempted from the fees; cf. Books of Admissions, XVIII.

261 Stanisław Gierszewski, *Obywatele miast*, 36.

178   CHAPTER 2

here. Similar conclusions can be drawn from an analysis of the fees paid for citizenship. The tax rate charged depended on one's wealth and, as mentioned above, ranged from nine to 60 groszy. Among the 87 testators who obtained Krakow citizenship, in 27 cases we know the amount of their fees. These were in the range of sixteen to 72 groszy,[262] with an arithmetic mean of 37.5 groszy, and a median sum of 36 groszy.

In nearly every case, the decision to emigrate meant a radical change in one's living situation. Newcomers to Krakow had to work hard to build up their social position from scratch, unless a foundation had been laid earlier by previously existing trade or family contacts (which appears to have been the case for at least some of those who came to Krakow from the surrounding area and for merchants engaged in long-distance trade). For many immigrants, the easiest way to assimilate and make a career in their new environment was to get married. While married burghers such as John Raczko *de Brunen* brought their wives to Krakow from their hometowns,[263] poorer immigrants who lacked the support of relatives, friends or co-workers in the city had a harder time finding a marriage partner than the *cives* who were born in the city.[264] This problem affected both men and women alike. However, it can be assumed that the majority of newcomers were men who were expected to be more mobile than women in a traditional society such as this one. One of the most reliable ways to find a place within the city's social structure was to marry into a Krakovian burgher family. However, the marriage market must have been characterised by a relatively higher demand than supply of potential 'good wives.'[265] And, as Rossiaud points out, "Money undoubtedly facilitated integration, but it was not able to solve all one's problems. Even if he possessed the same level of property as a local burgher, the immigrant did not have the same network of contacts or the same opportunities for employment, admission to a guild, or participation in public life as the native-born, who put before him all sorts of legal and practical obstacles."[266] Urban history studies confirm that these two

---

262   It was not until 1436 that the practice of recording the amounts paid by citizens was established; Books of Admissions, XIV–XV.

263   "Johannes Raczko de Brunen i.h. Matis Pasko et Nickel Edrer pro littera et eius uxore huc in duodecim septimanis sub pena X mrc et perdicione iuris civilis., ballistam dedit"; Books of Admissions, no. 5578 (1445).

264   Jan de Vries, *European Urbanization*, 186–197.

265   This phenomenon seems to have been occurring despite estimates by German historians indicating a larger share of women than men in Hanseatic cities; Henryk Samsonowicz, "Zagadnienia demografii historycznej w rejonie Hanzy w XV–XVI w.," *Zapiski Historyczne* 28, no. 4, 523–554.

266   Jacques Rossiaud, *Mieszczanin i życie w mieście*, 187 (J. Rossiaud, *Le Citadin*).

THE SOCIO-ECONOMIC POSITION OF TESTATORS   179

tendencies often coexisted; protectionist policies favouring the sons of local citizens were bolstered by legal and financial obstacles placed before immigrants that could be easier or harder to overcome, depending on the city's need for labour.[267] Rich and well-off immigrant-testators who through their resourcefulness, wealth and family influence, found their future wives in Krakow, gradually blended into the city's fabric after their marriage. Some married rich widows, such as Paul Newburger, the future Krakow alderman and councillor, who took Krakow citizenship after marrying the widow of councillor Tilman de Bruch.[268] A. Bartoszewicz gives the following example: "After his marriage to Ursula Hoze, the career of Eustace, deputy notary of Krakow from 1451, began almost immediately: in 1454 he became the head of the municipal chancellery, and obtained city citizenship;[269] he then entered the circle of Krakow patricians, began trading in lead from Olkusz, and accumulated considerable wealth."[270] The social successes of other famous Krakow *litterati* were also often associated with marriages to wealthy widows.[271]

The time immigrants spent in the city before they wrote their wills also testifies to how rooted they had become in the city. The differences in this respect are, of course, enormous and depend on many individual factors, ranging from whether the wills were made a few years before obtaining citizenship or made a few decades later. However, both the arithmetic mean and the median in both cases amount to as much as a 21-year difference between acquiring citizenship and the writing of a will,[272] which indicates both the old age of a large portion of the testators and the long years they spent in Krakow.

Despite the testators having lived in Krakow for many years, in many wills one can find traces of old family ties, whether professional or purely emotional, connecting testators with their former home towns. In many cases, siblings who remained in the family's hometown were included in the will. For example, the wealthy burgher John Lode, who became a citizen of Krakow in 1446, paying a fee of as much as one grivna to obtain citizenship,[273] bequeathed in 1456 ten

---

267   Stanisław Gierszewski, *Obywatele miast*, 48.
268   "Paulus Newburger maritus relicte Tilmanni de Bruch h.i. Pro littera portanda ad festum Pasce fideiussit Tawbinfelt et Sweydniczbir"; Books of Admissions, 136.
269   The municipal notary Eustace, when accepting the municipal charter of Krakow in 1455, was exempted from such a fee.; cf. "Eustachius notarius civitatis i.h. Prius litteram portabit,nichil dedit"; Books of admissions, no. 6255.
270   Agnieszka Bartoszewicz, *Piśmienność* (2012), 183.
271   *Ibidem.*
272   In the case of testators who left several versions of their last will, only the date of the first one was considered.
273   Books of Admissions, no. 5670.

florins to his brother Nicholas Lode from the Małopolska town of Pilzen, which he was to receive when he grew up.[274] John Baumgart, who became a citizen of Krakow in 1412,[275] bequeathed in his will of 1440 part of his estate to his sister in Dresden.[276] The wealthy Ambrose Czockeling did the same, and in 1451 gave his sister and her children from Wrocław 50 florins.[277]

In his will, Paul Ber, a long-time alderman and later Krakow councillor, wrote very clearly about his ties with his family in Głogów. This burgher, whose 'good fortune' in the process of obtaining citizenship was guaranteed by the alderman Bartholomew Graudencz,[278] bequeathed in his will of 1467 to his sister Anna part of the money due to him from the family house in Głogów, where this Anna still lived.[279] Moreover, he gave the Głogów local parish Church of St. Nicholas a chasuble and a large new missal, "so that these two things could be used every day to remember and comfort the souls of my parents and relatives whose bodies lay in rest there."[280] This clearly testifies to the sense of community he felt with both his family and his former parish church.

Signs that testators maintained attachments to religious communities to which they once belonged are present in many other cases, as well. Although the numerous churches in Krakow are usually the primary beneficiaries in their last wills, burghers also made donations to former parish churches and hospitals in their hometowns. This was the case with John Sweidniczer, who obtained Krakow citizenship in 1417. He sold his house in Świdnica in order to establish a fund for a new altar with a substantial annuity (twelve to fourteen grivna) in the local parish church. He also decided to make a donation to the monastery Church of the Holy Cross in Świdnica (belonging to the Knights of the Cross with the Red Star) and the Franciscan Church of the Blessed Virgin Mary in Toruń, where his brother Jacob and perhaps other relatives lived.[281]

Krakovian testators from Wrocław also took into consideration in their wills places of worship with which they were formerly associated. In 1439,

---

274   LT, fol. 37.

275   Books of Admissions, no. 2335.

276   "[...] meynir swestir Barbara dy czu Drezen in der Stat wonet und ir elicher man ist genant Michel Richter"; SCAB. 6, fol. 215.

277   LT, fol. 26.

278   Books of Admissions, no. 5690.

279   SCAB. 8, fol. 270–271.

280   "Ouch bescheyde ich ken Grosglogow yn dy pharkirche zu sinte Niclos eyne kamiche kasel dy beste undir czween dy ich gereyt habe und das grosse newe Missale das man dy czwestucke alle tage notczen sal zu eyme gedechtnisse und troste meyner elden und frunden zelen, der leythnam derselbist rasten"; SCAB. 8, fol. 270–271.

281   LT, fol. 39–45 (1457).

THE SOCIO-ECONOMIC POSITION OF TESTATORS 181

Margaret, widow of alderman Nicholas Slepkogil, bequeathed twelve and a half grivna to Wrocław councillors for an altar in the Corpus Christi chapel in the parish church at the Wrocław market square.[282] John Kletner, a rich burgher from Wrocław who later served as a alderman and councillor in Krakow and who obtained Krakow citizenship in 1448, bequeathed in his will in 1460 the handsome sum of 500 grivna to his sister Barbara from Wrocław, and also left detailed instructions for making pious bequests. He left 200 florins in the 'trusted hands' of Henry Hemmerdeye in Wrocław, which was to be used to support charitable work at St. Barbara's Hospital, or another beneficiary of Henry's choice.[283] Another 400 florins owed to him were to be donated to fund construction of St. Catherine's Church in Wrocław, and especially – in accordance with the testator's wishes – the construction of its nave.

The rich stallholder Martin Streicher, who came from Brzeg, and John Schultis (also known as Thob Johan), one of the richest patricians in Krakow, both made generous bequests. Streicher bequeathed an annuity of three grivna to the local hospital in Brzeg.[284] In the first version of his will, made in 1443, John Schultis used the huge sum of 66 grivna (collected in rent in Wrocław) to make various bequests: he bequeathed ten grivna each to St. Anthony's Church in Brzeg, to his local parish church and to the parson's household in Brzeg, and used the remaining 36 grivna and 32 groszy in rent for the foundation of a perpetual sung mass at one of the altars for the salvation of his soul.[285] In a second will, made eight years later, he repeated his previously made pious bequests.[286]

Some testators also mentioned their native cities because they still owned property in them, presumably inherited from their immediate families. This was true in the case of John Reinczka, who came from Olkusz. Four years after he obtained Krakow citizenship in 1458,[287] following an illness he made a will in which he stated that his wife could live in their house in Olkusz until her death (if she remained a widow).[288] A similar provision was included in the last will and testament of Stanisław Czolek in 1479. He granted to his brother Nicholas Koth possession for life of his property in Zator, but after Nicholas's death, it was to be given to Stanisław's heirs.[289] The origin of Nicholas, the

---

282   CONS. 428, fol. 398.
283   LT, fol. 67.
284   LT, fol. 5–6 (1440).
285   LT, fol. 7–8.
286   LT, fol. 31.
287   "Johannes Reynczke de Ilkus i.h. Et l. Dedit 1/2mrc"; Books of Admissions no. 6413.
288   LT, fol. 76 (1462).
289   LT, fol. 121 (1479).

owner of the Jewish bathhouse, who obtained citizenship in Krakow in 1446, is suggested by his ownership of real estate in the town of Robczyce. The mention in his will of 1453 of people from nearby Pilzno (Nicholas Jangueski and Matthias łaziebnik) indicates that after leaving Robczyce, Nicholas could have lived for some time in a larger city, and only at the end of his life moved to the capital, Krakow.[290]

Often, however, a testator and his closest relatives were also able to leave their hometown in search of opportunity both closer and farther away. A good example of this is the will of John Tile, who mentioned relatives (*frunde*) living in various places: Dominik Czop with his son John from Sandomierz (*Czudmir*), a relative named Merlin, the daughter of Crotinpfulis from Racibórz (*Rathibor*), and the daughter of Andrew Ruswormos from Ząbkowice Śląskie (*Frankinsteyn*).[291]

12.3 Cultural Capital of Newcomers

On the basis of the examples given above, it can be seen that the strong ties connecting Krakow and Silesia in the first half of the fourteenth century continued to be maintained later. Świdnica, Brzeg, Głogów and – above all – Wrocław were all cities from which a significant part of Krakow's rich burghers and even its power elites were recruited. These wealthy and influential burghers were also most interested in maintaining ties with their former towns, where their property, family members and former parish churches, as well as the remains of their ancestors, still remained. However, there is also no shortage among the testators of influential Krakow burghers coming from other, often quite distant population centres, such as John Raisser from Bavarian Memmingen,[292] Erhart Eigilwart from Augsburg,[293] or Gotfrid Fattinante from Genoa.[294]

Behind the rapid social advancement of wealthy immigrants in large cities were undoubtedly previously established business contacts and considerable wealth. However, we cannot ignore a less obvious factor: their cultural capital. This meant knowing what behaviour was 'proper' and how to behave in particular places and circumstances, and how to talk to different people. Norbert Elias' research on the phenomenon of the 'civilisation process' showed how the social norms for a good education were shaped in the Middle Ages, and in

---

290   LT, fol. 29.
291   SCAB. 4, fol. 144d (1416).
292   SCAB. 8, fol. 598–599 (1476).
293   CONS. 428, fol. 305 (1431).
294   KDWac., vol. 2, no. 396, 182–185 (1393).

THE SOCIO-ECONOMIC POSITION OF TESTATORS

subsequent centuries.[295] Legal principles for proper dress (e.g. anti-sumptuary laws,[296] and bans on walking around the city without a head-covering, as laid down in the municipal statutes),[297] and behaviour in the town hall, at a fraternity meeting or at the church,[298] as well as at the table,[299] were resources of cultural knowledge, without which it was impossible to function in a group. While first generation immigrants from villages and small towns who came to Krakow had to assimilate many of these rules and certainly would not have felt comfortable, the more sophisticated citizens of large German or Italian cities who came to Krakow could use their cultural capital in their relations with the citizens of Krakow and in their efforts to penetrate its elite social circles. This was probably the case with Italian newcomers, who initially took lucrative positions as royal miners, served the king, and engaged in large amounts of international trade,[300] as well as the Rhineland Germans, who from the mid-fifteenth century eagerly came to Krakow. The Krakow councillor and secretary of King Sigismund I, Louis Decius, proudly describes the process by which his compatriots from Wissemburg come to Krakow: "Reinfred arrives in Krakow, and having found financial success and respect here greater than in his former homeland, he brings in his relatives and friends."[301] Cultural capital was at least as important as material capital in making immigrants valuable partners. The same rules seemed to apply elsewhere. Antoni Gąsiorowski describes a similar situation in Poznan, discussing the successful career and rapid promotion of a newcomer to the city, George Bock, as follows:

> Bo[c]k with his merchant and banker individuality, shaped in the conditions of a big city like fifteenth-century Gdańsk, surpassed all his partners in Poznan, both in terms of his significance as a merchant and his influence with the municipal government. The history of his career, however,

---

295 Norbert Elias, *Przemiany obyczajów w cywilizacji Zachodu*, trans. Tadeusz Zabłudowski (Warszawa: Państwowy Instytut Wydawniczy, 1980).

296 KDMK, vol. 1, no. 21; KDMK, vol. 2, no. 259, 334, 352; *Najstarszy zbiór przywilejów i wilkierzy miasta Krakowa*, vol. 2, ed. Stanisław Estreicher, no. 12.

297 KDMK, vol. 2, no. 334.

298 *Ibidem*.

299 *Obyczaje w Polsce. Od średniowiecza do czasów współczesnych*, ed. Andrzej Chwalba (Warszawa: Państwowe Wydawnictwo Naukowe, 2004), 60–63.

300 Stanisław Kutrzeba, Jan Ptaśnik, "Dzieje handlu i kupiectwa krakowskiego," *Rocznik Krakowski* 14, 1910, 96–108.

301 *Ibidem*, 73.

184

shows how easy it was to make a career in a city like Poznan for an important newcomer who had come from a big city center.[302]

It seems that, soon after their arrival in Krakow, less wealthy burgher-testators tended to engage in the crafts, and not trade, and often lost contact with their hometowns. However, knowing that their relatives still remained in their hometowns, many had fearful thoughts about how their relatives' rights of inheritance might compromise the financial security of their immediate family. It can also be assumed that most of these immigrants came from nearby cities, towns and even villages – from these places wealthy peasant youths, the sons of members of the rural elite, came to Krakow.[303] It can also be assumed with a high probability that Krakow attracted moderately well-to-do peasants and the rural poor. As a large city – with a market, hospitals and almshouses – it offered greater chances of earning money and food than could have been expected in the countryside, even in periods of food shortages. However, these sorts of immigrants did not usually try to obtain Krakow citizenship, to which they probably did not even aspire. It is even less likely that they would write their wills in Krakow, relying instead on the traditional rules of inheritance of property, or giving only oral instructions concerning their assets.[304]

Jacek Wiesiołowski's estimates, which used 1.5 children per burgher family as the fertility rate indicator in medieval Poznan, brought him to the conclusion that the demographic growth of the city was possible only with a significant influx of immigrants, who constituted 60% of the city's population in each generation.[305] Even if the number of children in the average Krakovian burgher family was higher and the percentage of immigrants living there slightly lower than in Poznan, the population of medieval Krakow must still have consisted to a large extent of immigrants, constituting a colourful

---

302 Antoni Gąsiorowski, "Ludność napływowa w strukturze społecznej późnośredniowiecznego Poznania," *Studia i Materiały do Dziejów Wielkopolski i Pomorza*, 11, no. 2(22) (1975), 11–25.

303 *Ibidem.*

304 Studies on migration from rural to urban areas in the Old Polish period indicate that the rule that "the larger the city, the smaller the number of people of rural origin had a chance to enter the ranks of citizens. Conversely, in large cities, peasants were more likely to be accepted as labourers than in small towns, while the urban poor were more likely to be accepted as 'loose' people. After all, the struggle for the labour force between the feudal lords and big cities continued. There is no available research for medieval Krakow concerning the size of peasant immigration and what part of it was granted citizenship, but it was probably proportionately smaller than in fifteenth-century Poznan, where about 1/3 of all people granted town rights originated from rural areas"; Stanisław Gierszewski, *Obywatele miast*, 111; Antoni Gąsiorowski, *Ludność napływowa*, 13–15.

305 Jacek Wiesiołowski, *Socjotopografia*, 236.

THE SOCIO-ECONOMIC POSITION OF TESTATORS 185

mosaic of people of varying levels of wealth, engaged in many different professions, and representing a variety of cultural groupings that had different places within the life of the city. Only 10% of those who obtained citizenship in Poznan in the years 1443–1445 left any trace in other sources, which means that "the vast majority of these burghers did not make a career in the city, did not conduct any property transactions (which would have been reflected in the completely preserved resignation books), [and] did not attain a municipal office such as the guild seniority, not to mention a place on the bench court or the municipal council."[306] Martin Nodl, who studied the society of medieval Stříb at the turn of the fourteenth and fifteenth centuries, stated that only one third of immigrants settled in the town permanently. Only those who stayed in the city for more than ten years had a chance to gain higher material status and move to a higher tax group.[307] This significant mobility among the poorest inhabitants of the city is confirmed by the changes in the number of taxpayers in Kazimierz in the years 1385–1387: "The set of property owners is relatively stable, and the whole burden of the changes falls mainly on the poorer strata, especially those who have no possessions, who respond quickly to a changing economic situation or a downturn, and during such times either leave the city or are drawn to it."[308]

13 Determinants of Testators' Social Position

13.1 *Economic Capital*
From what we know about the composition of the Krakow municipal council, a large amount of economic capital was a *conditio sine qua non* for applying for a seat on the council. This condition was fulfilled by all of the 66 councillors whose wills have survived in municipal books to the present day (which is about 21% of all 325 known councillors up to the end of the fifteenth century).

Graph 14 reveals certain patterns in the dower bequests found in councillors' wills, indicating to some extent the distribution of wealth among them. Three main thresholds can be distinguished: up to 200 grivna – nine bequests (most of them before the 1430s); from 200 to 450 grivna – thirteen bequests (from the 1430s to the end of the century) and from 450 to 1350 grivna – four

---

306 Antoni Gąsiorowski, *Ludność napływowa*, 18.
307 Ewa Wółkiewicz, *Migracje do miast średniowiecznych w świetle ksiąg przyjęć do prawa miejskiego*, in *Miasto czyni wolnym. 790 lat lokacji Opola (ok. 1217–2007)*, ed. Anna Pobóg-Lenartowicz (Opole: Polskie Towarzystwo Historyczne, 2008), 52.
308 Jacek Wiesiołowski, *Stratyfikacja mieszczaństwa polskiego*, 278.

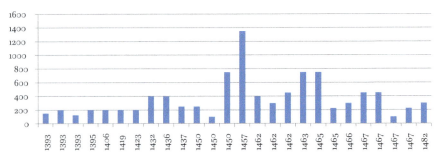

GRAPH 14 The amount bequeathed in dowers in the wills of Krakow's councillors

bequests. It should be noted, however, that the table above includes the largest dowers present in the wills made by each individual. When he made his first will before councillors in 1439, councillor John Sweidniczer left his wife Anna 600 grivna, as well as 200 grivna for the dower promised to her before their wedding (which probably took place around 1417, when he obtained city citizenship) and an additional 400 grivna as an expansion of the dower.[309] In 1447, he revoked the will,[310] and in 1456 provided a dower for his second wife Agnes, giving her 600 florins, which was to be added to the 1000 florins that she had brought into the marriage (she had been a widow with her own children).[311] Later that year, John, stricken with illness, called for councillors and once again revoked all his previous wills, this time leaving his wife Agnes 1800 florins for her dower as well as the money she had brought into the marriage.[312] This is also the case with another very wealthy councillor, John Teschner, who in his testament of 1453 revoked all the bequests and donations he had previously made to his wife and gave her a dower of 800 florins "for her faithful service" and allowed her to live in his corner house for the rest of her life.[313] However, nine years later, in 1462, he testified before councillors and in the presence of his brother-in-law, John Turzon of Levoča:

> [I]n accordance with the call of the holy Christian Church, he went with his wife Martha to her home city of Levoča, and there, before councillors

---

309 CONS. 428, fol. 402.
310 *Ibidem*.
311 CONS. 429, fol. 137.
312 This will is dated 1457 in *Liber Testamentorum*, but other provisions related to the execution of his will indicate that Sweidniczer died in 1456; LT, fol. 39–43; CONS. 429, fol. 160, 163, 167, 172, 173, 174, 176, 178, 180, 192, 194,195, 210, 212, 213, 218, 221, 229, 246, 247, 249, 261–262, 274, 279, 310, 328, 338.
313 CONS. 429, fol. 71.

THE SOCIO-ECONOMIC POSITION OF TESTATORS   187

in that city, bequeathed to her a dower of 600 florins; today, in present-
ing this letter, he was informing [the councillors] that he was adding an
additional 400 florins to the dower. Therefore, after his death she was to
receive 1000 florins secured by all his assets, with no objections permitted from his relatives.[314]

As the examples above show, the amount of the dower varied depending on
when it was made, the financial status of the testator, the social and financial
position of the wife's family, and whether or not the testator had remarried
after the death of his previous wife. However, it is also worth noting that testators and notaries writing down their wills usually tried to adhere to the principle of indicating both the amount of the dower promised before the marriage
and the amount that had been added to it (in Polish *przywianek*).

On the other hand, among the testators, we find many burghers whose large
dower bequests and considerable wealth were still not enough to qualify them
for a seat on the municipal council. In Graph 15, which lists the amounts of
the dowers bequeathed by wealthiest testators, we can see that the group of
very rich burghers included, apart from the aforementioned 26 councillors,
32 other Krakovian burghers. Among the rich burghers (corresponding to
the lower upper-income group in Jacek Wiesiołowski's classification) we find
another 32 citizens of Krakow who made dower bequests of between 60 and
100 grivna. These figures do not provide a basis for estimating the total size of
these groups, nor for assessing what part of them were Krakow councillors, but
they do point to the existence of a relatively broad and varied group of very
wealthy Krakovian burghers who were never officials in the municipal government. To investigate further who they were and how their wealth compared to
councillors,' the sizes of their dower bequests have been compared with those
made by councillors.

In most cases, the dowers contained in the wills of non-councillors are similar in size to those of Krakow councillors. The vast majority of non-councillors
(27 individuals) bequeathed between 150 and 300 grivna, while only five of
them left their wives more than 300 grivna (compared to ten councillors who
made such provisions). As a result, there is a smaller range than in the councillors' group, yielding a mean value of 239 grivna, and a median value of 200
grivna. While in the case of the non-councillor burghers we are dealing with
a fairly homogeneous group, in most cases they were no less wealthy than the
group of councillors.

---

314   CONS. 429, fol. 338.

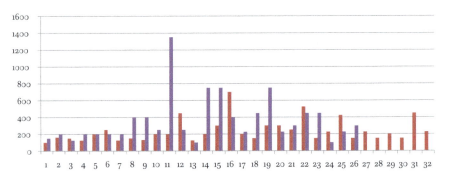

GRAPH 15   Amounts of dowers contained in the wills made by Krakówcouncillors and the wealthiest non-councillor Krakow's citizens

The most prominent people in the non-councillor group are the five individuals whose dowers amounted to more than 300 grivna. In order to better illustrate their social position, references to them contained in municipal books are presented below:

1. Erhart Eigilwart, of Augsburg, who served on the bench court in 1418 and 1421, was a merchant who had ties to Wrocław and the prosecutor Conrad Goczcze of Augsburg. In 1422 he was entered into the municipal book as elder of stallholder guild (*senior institorum*). The preserved will was made by Eigilwart while ill in 1431.[315]

2. John Schultis, *alias* Thob Johan, who probably came from Brzeg, was a alderman in Krakow (in 1419, 1421, 1424, 1426 and 1428) and one of the richest merchants in the city, trading with Košice, Lviv and Wrocław. In 1406, he was among those few who paid the special royal tax for the armed expedition to Lithuania (he paid the relatively small amount of four grivna).[316] In 1421, he was mentioned as a person who held the keys and padlocks to the chains that closed off the ends of the streets leading to the market,[317] which means that he owned a house on a prestigious corner plot by the market. In 1422 he was elected the commander of the tower above the New Gate (in Latin *Nova Valva*) on the city walls.[318] He founded his own chapel and altar in St. Mary's Church. After his death, he

---

315   CONS. 428, fol. 305. Erhart Eigilwart (Egilbart) is mentioned in the book of records of a new citizens only once, as a guarantor for Jost Reborr in 1417; cf. Books of Admissions, no. 3049.
316   CONS. 427, fol. 270.
317   CONS. 428, fol. 165.
318   CONS. 428, fol. 188.

THE SOCIO-ECONOMIC POSITION OF TESTATORS 189

was entered into the Book of the Dead of the Brotherhood of the Blessed Virgin Mary (as was his son John, who also left a will).[319]

3. Sylwester Sweidniczer, brother of John Sweidniczer, was one of the richest fifteenth-century Krakovian burghers. He obtained Krakow citizenship in 1439, after paying an entrance fee of one grivna, backed by his father-in-law Nicholas Scholwicz, a Krakow councillor. In 1451, after the death of Scholwicz, and his wife's receipt of an inheritance from her father, he secured a dower of 200 grivna for her. In 1452, when he was ill, he raised the amount of dower 700 florins. He owned a house at the market square. He was a cloth merchant.[320]

4. Eustace Statschreiber became Krakow deputy notary in 1451, but obtained citizenship only in 1454 and was then appointed the municipal notary. He traded in lead from Olkusz. He married Ursula, daughter of councillor John Hoze and the widow of Nicholas Schirtel. In 1453, in a mutual bequest, she gave him all the rights to the inheritance from her parents and sisters, while he secured this inheritance with his own estate and left her a dower as well.[321] The will, written on his sickbed, was entered in the *Liber Testamentorum* in 1459.[322]

5. Peter Schepcz was a Krakow alderman (1481–1483) and son-in-law of Peter Pelczer (son-in-law of John Sweidniczer).[323] In 1477, after the death of his father-in-law, his wife Hedwig gave her inheritance from her father to him.[324] In 1482, he made his own will, which he later confirmed before the bench court. In it, he included many carefully thought out pious bequests and divided his property between his daughter Dorothy and second wife, also named Dorothy, who was pregnant at the time.[325] He

---

319 Józef Mitkowski, "Księga zmarłych bractwa kościoła Panny Marii w Krakowie (wiek XIV–XVIII)," *Studia Historyczne* 11, no. 1 (1968), 85.

320 LT, fol. 28–29; Books of Admissions, 4995, 158; CONS. 429, fol. 35; SCAB. 6, fol. 303.

321 SCAB. 7, fol. 165, 173.

322 LT, fol. 61–63; cf. Bożena Wyrozumska, *Kancelaria*, 123; Agnieszka Bartoszewicz, *Piśmienność* (2012), 164, 183.

323 Bequest of a dower for Sweidniczer's daughter in 1443; SCAB. 6, fol. 293.

324 CONS. 429, fol. 585.

325 A total of 66 florins: "I give 10 florins to the hospital for food for the poor; five florins to poor pupils for food; five florins to St. Valentine for food for the poor; 10 florins to St. Hedwig for food for the poor; 10 florins to St. Bernard for food for the monks; four florins to St. Leonard for food for the poor; two florins to the poor lunatics (*torichten*) for food; two florins to the imprisoned for food (*gefengene in den stogk*); two florins to St. Francis for Gregorian masses, for food; two florins to St. Trinity for Gregorian masses (for the salvation of the soul); two florins to the monks at St. Catherine for Gregorian masses; one florin

owned the following properties in Krakow: a house at the market square, another house on St. Florian Street, and half a pharmacy. In his will he also made many pious bequests. He entrusted guardians to settle all his liabilities with the help of his accounting book and other notes. After his death, in order to validate his will, it was entered into the *Liber Testamentorum*, and his son, also called Peter Schepcz, confirmed its validity.[326]

Of these five Krakovian burghers, all with considerable estates, none were councillors. Three were aldermen (two of them only held the position for 2–3 years), one was a municipal notary, and one was a brother of the very influential councillor John Sweidniczer. Peter Schepcz and Eustace the notary had connections with the families of councillors. But the most notable thing they had in common was the fact that they were all engaged in long-distance trade. Although they were not members of the municipal council, and did not belong to the Krakow elite, they were nonetheless part of the same social circle. It is possible that what prevented them from becoming councillors was the fact that they all appear to have come from outside of Krakow: Apart from Peter Schepcz, whose origin is unknown, the remaining four testators came from other cities and had to build their social capital from scratch when they relocated to Krakow.

The data presented above suggests that the city's ruling elite was significantly diversified in terms of wealth and individual prestige. The council, like the entire town population, had its own structure. The council was led by a few of the most influential individuals, notable for their wealth, business transactions and connections. The remaining councillors comprised a less diversified group, similar in wealth to other prosperous Krakow residents. This confirms the assumption that wealth (economic capital), although an important factor determining the social position of testators, was certainly not synonymous with a place on the council. It seems fair to assume that this kind of social advancement was determined by other factors, which, in the language of Pierre Bourdieu, can be described as cultural, social and symbolic capital.[327]

13.2 *Cultural Capital – Education*

In late medieval Krakow, the university elite had long been legally and socially distinct from Krakow's burghers. Although members of the *Studium Generale*

---

to the monks of the monastery of the Blessed Virgin Mary for Gregorian masses; one florin to the monks at St. Mark for Gregorian masses; 10 florins for the altar of the Virgin Mary (*der tofele der Juncfraw Marien*)"; LT, fol. 137–140.

326 *Ibidem.*

327 Pierre Bourdieu, *The Forms of Social Capital*, 46–58.

THE SOCIO-ECONOMIC POSITION OF TESTATORS

enjoyed great authority, because they were subject to church law they were considered to be more like clergymen than townspeople. Despite their mutual connections with town citizens, like priests and monks they were not of the same community as the city's other citizens, at least not from the perspective of the authorities, because they were not subject to their jurisdiction and were not bound by the same legal norms as other inhabitants. Over the course of the late fifteenth century, however, due to the university's close ties with the city, the growing number of influential burghers' sons among the student population, and changing cultural trends – often associated with the Renaissance, broadly defined – the representatives of academia began to play an increasingly important role within the upper strata of civil society.[328] As early as in 1393, Gotfrid Fattinante from Genoa chose the Krakow bishop, a doctor of Canon and Roman laws Peter Wysz from Radolin, as one of the executors of his will.[329] Similarly, in 1439, as one of the executors of his will John Sweidniczer appointed Doctor of Canon law Nicholas from Brzeg.[330] In 1484, the validity of Francis Gliwicz's will was confirmed by the Krakow canon and John Starzechowski, a doctor of canon law.[331] In 1468, the first councillor from the university was the dean and rector of the university, the noble astrologer and doctor of medicine Peter Gaszowiec. It seems, however, that of much greater importance to Krakow's ruling elite was the university professor John of Reguła, who assumed the office of councillor in 1482.[332] As a councillor, he visited the sick who wanted to record their last will.[333] His strong ties with the city are also evidenced by the fact that his will was included in the *Liber Testamentorum*.[334] His future son-in-law, Lukas Noskowski from Mazowsze, who was

---

328   Antoni Gąsiorowski, "O mieszczanach studiujących na Uniwersytecie Krakowskim w XV wieku," in *Aetas media, aetas moderna*, 653–663.

329   "Constituit insuper sepedictus dominus Gotfridus ac prefecit Reuerendum virum dominum Petrum de Radolina virum utique elegantissimum, iuris vtriusque doctorem ac ad Cracouiensem ecclesiam predictam postulatum, ac Magnificum Spitconem Palatinum et Capitaneum, necnon Consules Ciuitatis eiusdem predictos, qui sunt aut fuerint in futurum, presentis sui testamenti ac voluntatis sue vltime suos veros procuratores, factores, actores et executores legitimos atque certos"; KDWac., vol. 2, no. 396.

330   CONS. 428, fol. 402.

331   KDMK, vol. 3, no. 474.

332   Zdzisław Noga, *Urzędnicy miejscy Krakowa*, part 2: *1500–1794* (Krakow: Wydawnictwo Naukowe Uniwersytetu Pedagogicznego, 2008), XXI.

333   In 1482 he probated the will of Susan Mathis Beckinne, in 1484 that of Catherine Jorge Goltsmidinne, in 1487 that of Hedwig Granoszowa, in 1492 that of Jarosz the tailor, and in 1493 that of George Monczer; LT, fol. 135, 142–143, 145, 51–152, 153.

334   For more on John from Reguły and his will cf. Urszula Sowina, Kazimierz Pacuski, *Testamenty mieszczan krakowskich jako źródła*, 433–446.

born in Nałęcz, assumed the post of councillor in 1520, after finishing his university studies.[335] In the sixteenth century, the number councilors who were 'doctors' increased to sixteen, ten of whom received the title in medicine and six in law. This trend continued in other centuries, which corresponds to the situation in many other European cities, including Cologne (where, however, it was primarily doctors of law who joined the ranks of the city's elite power structures).[336] Meanwhile, the number of sons from wealthy Krakow families who were enrolled as students was growing.[337] The growing social significance of a university education can be observed in the biographies of many of the most influential burghers, future Krakow councillors, in the late-fifteenth century, who were enrolled as students at the University of Krakow.[338]

13.3 Social Capital – Quarter Captains, Tower Commanders and Administrators

A burgher's importance, and the level of respect they commanded in society, was determined in large part by their participation in the official structures of government, the municipal council and the municipal bench court, and was also bolstered by membership of a guild as an elder (as discussed earlier in the chapter). Many testators served in these prestigious offices, which, alongside

---

335 Zdzisław Noga, *Krakowska rada*, 142–143.

336 *Ibidem.*

337 "[...] data concerning social status of the matriculated were only found for 83 persons. Among them, 57 students came from families that were part of the highest elite of the Krakow patriciate. Their fathers or relatives were members of the council, and their families acquired their financial position through trade, leasing salt mines and Krakow town tariffs. The most numerous families were the Morsztyn family (11 people), the Szwarc family (five people), the Krupka family (five people), and the Salomon family (six people). Three students each came from the Arnsberg, Koczwar, Teszner, Genkner families, while two each came from the Borek, Turzon, Bar, Scholtis and Kuncz families. Only one representative of the Becks, Bems, Brendelers, Brigers, Wiewiórkas, Noldenfessers, Longpeters, Orienths and Wolframs was confirmed in the university records. This is certainly not the entire list of all the members of the Krakow patricians who were ever admitted to the university. Among the remaining 26 persons, whose fathers' occupations were determined with more or less certainty, there is no prevailing profession. They include sons of tailors, furriers, shoemakers, belt makers, goldsmiths, herring traders, maltsters, fat producers, merchants, bag makers, cutlers and wheelwrights"; Krzysztof Boroda, *Studenci Uniwersytetu Krakowskiego w późnym średniowieczu* (Krakow: Wydawnictwo Avalon, 2010), 122–124.

338 The *Album studiosorum Universitatis Cracoviensis* features, among others, Kasper Gengner in 1462, John Kisling in 1463, Kasper Ber in 1470, John Haller since 1482, and, in the late fifteenth century, Jphn Turzon, Nicholas and Peter Solomon, George and John Morsztyn; Zdzisław Noga, *Krakowska rada*, 146–148.

THE SOCIO-ECONOMIC POSITION OF TESTATORS

a burgher's financial situation, provides the best indication of their social position within the city. However, apart from these high stations, Krakovian testators also held other, less frequently mentioned city offices, that likewise testified to their social capital.

One interesting group in Krakow was the 'quarter captains' (in German *Virtilsleute*, and in Latin *Capitaneos quartalibus, Seniores quartalium, Quartalenses*, or *Hominum quartaliorum*), who were chosen for this office by the municipal council.[339] In the first entry containing information about them (from 1396) in council books, it is noted that they were chosen 'by the streets' (*per platheas*).[340] This may indicate that they were both residents of a given street and representatives of it in matters delegated to them by the municipal council. This is indicated by the above-mentioned entry, which states that particular streets in each quarter of the city were the responsibility of specific people. For example, in the pottery quarter, Langseidel was responsible for Franciscan Street; Bozemecz for Wiślana Street; Grudner for Jewish Street and John Voit for Shoemaker's Street.[341] During the period up to 1500, information is given only fourteen times about the selection of quarter captains (in the years 1396, 1419, 1421, 1422, 1425, 1426, 1430, 1441, 1452, 1461, 1464, 1469 and 1473); however, on the basis of these entries and other notes in which they are mentioned, it can be assumed that in one form or another this function was performed by these persons throughout this period. Their task was to adjudicate simple disputes related to urban plots of land, the buildings on them, and the walls and canals that separated them from one another.[342] As many as 43 Krakow testators as well as nine people who wrote wills that have been lost are found on lists of quarter captains in council books. In addition, it has been possible to identify the names of six quarter captains who made separate dower bequests for their wives, six who made mutual bequests with their wives, one

---

339 CONS. 427, fol. 68.

340 "Capitaneorum ad quartalia Civitatis per platheas singulas constituti, feria secunda proxima post festum Beatorum Viti et Modesti martirum. Anno domini MCCCXCVI nunc currente per dominos consules Anni illiusdem"; CONS. 427, fol. 68.

341 "Quartale Castrense: In plathea Castrj a Circulo usque ad Ecclesiam Sti Petri Tylo Zatheler, Henricus Parchowicz; et ab Ecclesia Sti Petri ulterius usque ad Valuam: Iacussius maritus Wercholmine, Petrus Cadner; Quartair figulorum: In plathea minorum, Langseidel, Wysle: Bozemecz Iudeorum Grudner, Sutorum Hannus Voyt; Quartale Slawcoviense: Stephanus, Hannus de Scawin, Slavcoviensis: Oderberg Iohannis, Hano Hesse et Iorge Deuczulrich; Quartale Carnificum: Floriani, Miczko Smersneyder et Tempilvelt, Hospitalis Valhenne; Carnificum: Degin et Petir Bemisch"; CONS. 427, fol. 68.

342 E.g. the case of a wall between two houses built by Peter Graser, CONS. 428, fol. 274; the case of the gutter between the houses of Hannus Borg and Wilhelm at Bracka Street, CONS. 428, fol. 319.

who made a bequest to his wife, and one who made a pious bequest. All in all, the above-mentioned group accounted for nearly half of all the people we know who held this function. Among them were 32 Krakow councillors (those sitting at the time on the municipal council or as aldermen on the bench court), fourteen further aldermen and 20 other influential burghers, most of whom were recruited from among wealthy Krakovian guild elders. The institution of quarter captain, which probably did not have any major significance for or influence on the shape of the city's political order, is, however, an interesting example of the existence of a kind of informal urban elite, which was not limited solely to councillors and aldermen. As a group exercising certain judicial powers, quarter captains were chosen from among rich and influential burghers, including both those who also sat on the municipal council and bench court, as well as others who were not members of these bodies. Initially, *capitanei quartalium* may have been meant to represent the citizenry of Krakow as a whole. For example, among all those serving as quarter captains in 1396, two acted as representatives of the Krakow community (as opposed to the city council) in 1408 after an anti-Jewish pogrom.[343] A preliminary analysis of quarter captains as a group shows an ever-increasing number of councillors holding this position year to year.[344] In result, over the course of the fifteenth century, this municipal function was dominated by the city council.

Another valuable example of a group of individuals invested with special trust (and thus social prestige) by the burghers are those who were responsible for crucial elements of the city's defence: the iron chains securing Krakow's streets (an element of the security system inside the city) and the towers in the city walls. In the first case, in 1421, 63 people are listed (two of these have been crossed out) as having been entrusted with padlocks to the chains securing particular streets in the city. This group includes both councillors and aldermen, as well as people who did not hold these positions (including some of the above-mentioned quarter captains).[345] Although the first (lost) book of wills was probably still being kept at that time, we have information about the wills made by some of these people and, in individual cases, the wills themselves, which were entered in the books of the bench court.[346]

---

343   Peter Cadner, Peter Valhenne and John Steynbach, who was a quarter guard in 1422; CONS. 427, fol. 278, 311.

344   There were no councilors among the quarter captains in 1396 and 1419, although some were wealthy; in 1441 councilors comprised at least half of them, and in 1473 most of them.

345   "Secuntur qui habent seras ad cathenas statuarum in platheis"; CONS. 428, fol. 164.

346   E.g. of Nicholas Opoczko, SCAB. 6, fol. 110, 111 or alderman and councillor Ederer (Oderer), SCAB.,1676.

THE SOCIO-ECONOMIC POSITION OF TESTATORS   195

Valuable information has been preserved in council books about commanders of city towers and gates (*capitanei turrum et valvas Civitatis*),[347] including lists of commanders of city towers from the years 1410, 1414, 1422, 1430 and 1473.[348] In the event of danger, two or four (perhaps depending on the size of the area) trusted burghers from among Krakow's citizenry were entrusted with commanding the defence of a tower and the adjacent parts of the walls. In the census of 1473, it is indicated which parts of Krakow's walls should be guarded by craftsmen from specific guilds.[349] The appointed tower commanders, however, were not acting as representatives of the guild, but – as in the other cases discussed above – belonged to an elite group of burghers endowed with the highest level of authority and trust within the city, and who were often members of the municipal council, bench court or influential Krakovian families. It is worth noting that although in the 1410 census current or former councillors constitute the vast majority of such individuals, they are only found sporadically in later censuses – for example, in 1430 there were four councillors, and in 1473 none. However, in each of the five preserved entries, one can easily find many people who made wills or other types of bequests in the event of their death.

An individual's social capital can also be evidenced by prestigious functions performed in their religious community, such as holding the office of parish treasurer (in Latin *vitricus ecclesiae*) or church and hospital lay administrator (*provisor*), having patronage over a chapel or altar in a church, or serving in a senior position in one of Krakow's religious brotherhoods.[350] Records of numerous wills written by such councillors have survived. These include wills by Kacper Krugil, the Carmelite Monastery's treasurer, Peter Graser, the administrator of the Holy Spirit Hospital (he also made a mutual bequest with his wife and donated rent to the brotherhood in the Church of the Holy Virgin Mary) and Peter Kaldherberg, the treasurer of St. Mary's Church. The administrator of this church was the alderman Michael the goldsmith (*Michil goltsmed* or *Michael aurifaber*), whose will has survived to our times. The very wealthy burgher Bartholomew Melczer, one of the administrators of the Holy Spirit Hospital, who in 1425 also served as its treasurer, also made a testamentary

---

347   The first of the preserved lists date back to 1410 and was probably written following the outbreak of the Polish-Teutonic War: "Feria secunda die sancte Egidii 1410, Nota infrascripti sunt ad Turres Civitatis et valvas Capitanei electi"; CONS. 427, fol. 378.

348   CONS. 427, fol. 378; CONS. 428, fol. 66, 188–189, 272; CONS. 429, fol. 485.

349   CONS. 429, fol. 485.

350   Agnieszka Bartoszewicz, *Warta, społeczeństwo miasta w II połowie XV i na początku XVI wieku* (Warszawa: Wydawn. Fundacji Historia pro Futuro, 1997), 131.

bequest to his wife and stepdaughter. In Krakow, as in many other large cities in late medieval Europe, the municipal council began in the latter half of the fourteenth century to assume its authority over the city's religious institutions. This was connected, on the one hand, with the growing independence of the municipal authorities, and, on the other, with the perception of the city community and its market, stalls, gates, and churches as a single organism, whose functioning the councillors worked to ensure and maintain. In the literature on the subject, it is common to describe this phenomenon as *religion civique*,[351] 'urban religiosity,'[352] or 'communal religiosity.'[353] During the fifteenth century, the council managed to assert its sole guardianship over urban churches, and thus the position of treasurer or administrator in the city's churches was usually held by designated councillors.[354]

14   Changes in Social Position

Statistical research on the wealth and social position of testators enables a better understanding and characterisation of the group of Krakow burghers who for various reasons showed the most interest in drawing up an act of last will. The image obtained from a reconstruction of Krakow's social structure reflects quite well the domination of the richest burgher-testators over their less wealthy fellow-townsmen. This kind of analysis, however, does not help us recognize or understand the dynamic character of the 'social position' occupied by such individuals over the course of their lives or the multi-faceted nature of the factors that influenced it. Only a closer look at individual wills and an

---

351   Trevor Dean, *The Towns of Italy in the Later Middle Ages* (Manchester: Manchester University Press, 2000), 63–71.

352   Halina Manikowska, *Religijność miejska*, in *Ecclesia et civitas. Kościół i życie religijne w mieście średniowiecznym*, ed. Halina Manikowska, Hanna Zaremska (Warszawa: Instytut Historii PAN, 2002), 11–34.

353   Marek Słoń, *Religijność komunalna*, 9–21.

354   Church treasurers among the councillors included Nicholas Gemlich (the treasurer of the 'New Monastery'), Kacper Krugil (Carmelite Monastery), Martinus Belze and Nicholas Kezinger (St. Bernard's Church), Peter Graser (Hospital of the Holy Spirit) and Peter Kaldherberg and Nicholas Zalcz, who were treasurers at the Blessed Virgin Mary Church at the market square in Krakow. Other aldermen and burghers who acted as church treasurers and administrators included John Smed, Alex, Nicholas carpentarius, Bartholomeus Melczer, Michael the goldsmith and Nicholas Kazimirski; CONS. 427, fol. 401 (1411), 405 (1411), 409 (1411); CONS. 428, fol. 467 (1444); CONS. 429, fol. 324 (1463), 568 (1476); SCAB. 4, fol. 70 (1412); SCAB. 5, fol. 97 (1424), 106 (1425); SCAB. 6, fol. 245 (1441), 281 (1443), 357 (1446); SCAB. 8, fol. 293 (1466).

THE SOCIO-ECONOMIC POSITION OF TESTATORS

attempt at a partial reconstruction of the lives of those who made them can reveal the weaknesses of using dower bequests as the sole means for determining the social status of Krakovian burghers. It also allows us to see that while we rarely encounter a situation in which an individual suddenly experiences social advancement or a decisive decline in standing, transition to a higher or lower status in terms of wealth during a burgher's lifetime was quite common. Both quantitative and qualitative research have their limitations and weaknesses, so it seems that only a combination of these two research methods will allow us to obtain a richer and more nuanced picture of the social reality of late medieval Krakow.

14.1   *The Dower and Level of Wealth*

Although in most cases dower bequests seem to provide a good indication of the financial situation of Krakovian burghers, like other types of sources, they cannot be approached uncritically. An interesting case here is the last will of the shoemaker Nicholas Mewsil in which the dower bequest does not seem to accurately reflect the testator's wealth or the amount of inheritance due to the wife. Mewsil's will was entered into the *Liber Testamentorum* in 1458.[355] Defined by the councillors as 'our citizen' (*unsir mitburger*), Mewsil obtained Krakow citizenship on Christmas Eve 1415,[356] and as early as 1422 served as an elder in the Krakow shoemakers guild.[357] He also held this position in 1434 and 1439.[358] In 1425, he bought from John Weigant a house on Wide Street, next to the Dominican monastery.[359] He sold this property in 1436 (the house was already rented at that time for 36 groszy to the Church of All Saints).[360] In 1456, it was reported that he owned a house on St. Florian Street.[361] Moreover, in municipal books he appears once (in 1431) as a guarantor for the wife of another shoemaker from Krakow,[362] twice as a witness in a case related to the care of orphans (1435 and 1441)[363] and once as the court representative of Anna Weinbrotinne, widow of the shoemaker John Weinbrot.[364] Given this high level of social activity, it is surprising the testator's last will and testament

---

355   LT, fol. 54.
356   Books of Admissions, no. 2878, 80.
357   CONS. 428, fol. 183.
358   CONS. 428, fol. 325, CONS. 428, fol. 399.
359   SCAB. 5, fol. 111.
360   SCAB. 6, fol. 133.
361   SCAB. 7, fol. 257.
362   SCAB. 6, fol. 5.
363   SCAB. 6, fol. 116; CONS. 428, fol. 438.
364   CONS. 429, fol. 55.

198 CHAPTER 2

contains a bequest of only ten grivna as a dower for his wife Margaret, which was to be paid to her from the sale of her inheritance "or other acquired goods."[365] In addition, she was to receive all the family's household furnishings. The rest of the estate was to be divided between his wife, his son Gabriel and his daughter Appolonia, with the exception of a shoemaker's bench and related equipment, which was intended for his daughter Justine. The will was confirmed by his wife Margaret, son Gabriel and daughter Justine, together with her husband George Fleischenbrot.[366] In the light of other information gathered about this testator, it can be assumed that such a small bequest in the will may be a trace of the low level of affluence of Nicholas Mewsil at the time he married Margaret (perhaps shortly after obtaining citizenship of the city in 1415). The forty-three years that had passed since then and information we have about his life testify to his social and economic advancement, while the actual bulk of the inheritance his wife Margaret was to receive came from the third of the estate that she was to be given.

The case of the maltster and innkeeper John Specht is an example of how the size of the dower could depend on the wealth of the wife's family and the emotional factors binding her to her spouse, rather than on the economic situation of the testator himself. After obtaining Krakow citizenship in 1424, Specht was listed as a maltster from the Lower Silesian town of Przemków.[367] His move to Krakow might have been facilitated by another, perhaps related, John Specht, who became a Krakow citizen in 1417, and in 1423 and 1425 was already serving in the position of elder in the belt makers guild.[368] The first mentions of the malster John Specht in municipal books date back to 1433 and 1435, when he appeared in a census of guild elders as one of the chosen elders of the innkeepers guild.[369] His quick integration into the structure of Krakow society and his professional advancement allowed him to buy a house in 1437 on a plot located on the corner of Hospital Street.[370] Two years later, in 1439, he is listed as being a elder in the maltsters' guild.[371] At about that time, now a respected citizen of the city, he began to act as both the executor of the wills of Margaret

---

365   "[...] also dassy meyn erbe do ich ynne wone noch meynem tode vorkewfen sollen, und von dem gelde adir aus ander meynen gewissen guttern folgen sal"; LT, fol. 54.

366   What is remarkable here are the unusual names of Mewsil's children: Appolonia, Gabriel and Justine, which in a way point to his broader intellectual horizons.

367   Book of Admissions, no. 3684, 105.

368   SCAB. 5, fol. 193, 217.

369   CONS. 428, fol. 316, 336.

370   SCAB. 6, fol. 137.

371   CONS. 428, fol. 399.

THE SOCIO-ECONOMIC POSITION OF TESTATORS

Lechlerinne (1439 and 1442),[372] innkeeper Peter Warzigarnek (1450)[373] and Margaret Grobniginne (1460),[374] and as the attorney of Barbara Fornalin during the sale of her house (1442).[375] When in 1451 the councillors detected fraud being committed by innkeepers serving beer, he was appointed as a trusted individual to be one of the commissioners investigating the quality of the city's beer.[376] He may also have gone on a jubilee pilgrimage to Rome in 1450, the year in which he made his last will before the municipal bench court, together with other burghers who were going on pilgrimages. In the will, he bequeathed all his possessions to his wife Barbara and son John, to be divided equally, and stated that if his son died childless first, his property should be given to his more distant relatives after his wife's death.[377] The testator returned safely from the pilgrimage, but it seems that soon afterwards he had to deal with the death of his son, because four years later, in 1454, he and his wife Barbara bequeathed all of their property to one another in the event of the death of one of them.[378] However, John also survived his wife Barbara, and after some time, now quite old, remarried, this time to a Margaret, who is mentioned in his will of 1466. This was a notable year because during it Krakow was stricken by plague, which sowed terror among its inhabitants. John Specht, most likely out of a fear of dying – though he was apparently not ill himself – decided to write his will before other councillors.[379] He divided most of his estate among Krakow's hospitals (five florins for St. Valentine's, ten florins for St. Hedwig's and 30 florins for St. Spirit's) and for food for the Bernardine brothers (20 florins). However, he bequeathed only 20 grivna to his wife, Margaret, and did not mention any other relatives save for his nephew, Melchior the shoemaker (*Malchar des schuster*), who he made an executor of his will. One year after the epidemic ended, however, he revoked the will on account of having sold the house on Hospital Street (to the alderman and later councillor Paul Ber).[380] The last version of John Specht's will was made (this time before the bench court) in 1469.[381]

---

372 SCAB. 6, fol. 183; SCAB. 6, fol. 271.

373 SCAB. 7, fol. 100.

374 LT, fol. 66–67.

375 SCAB. 6, fol. 265.

376 CONS. 429, fol. 25.

377 SCAB. 7, fol. 81.

378 SCAB. 7, fol. 195.

379 LT, fol. 88; this situation was quite exceptional, as the will of a burgher who was still alive was recorded in the *Liber Testamentorum*.

380 SCAB. 8, fol. 310. In 1468, he also annulled the will before the councilorcouas a precaution; LT, fol. 88.

381 SCAB. 8, fol. 373.

In accordance with law and custom, he asked whether he could dispose of his acquired (and not inherited) property according to his will and, after obtaining approval from the bench court, handed over to them his will written on a piece of paper. In it he repeated part of his previous will's provisions, giving his wife 20 grivna as a dower and making bequests to the same institutions he had previously endowed. This time, however, after the sale of the house, his pious bequests were much more generous. He contributed once again mainly to Krakow's hospitals: 30 florins to the women in Holy Spirit, 30 florins to the poor in St. Hedwig's, 10 florins to the poor in St. Valentine's and ten florins to St. Leonard's Hospital. He also donated to the Bernardines (40 florins for food), and the Bernardine Sisters from St. Agnes (10 florins for food). In this version of the will he also included the children of his nephew Melchior, to whom he bequeathed 20 florins, provided that Melchior would help him and work for him (*her dy notczen und do mitte arbitten sal*). Other relatives were excluded from the inheritance. John Specht died at a very old age, as evidenced by the fact that it was not until 1476 that his wife Margaret received from the will's executors the 20 grivna due to her. Specht's story is both an interesting example of a burgher's life and the social advancement he made, as well as providing proof of the extent to which in certain justified cases the dowry no longer reflected the social and financial status of the testator. Having married once again, this time to a woman who was poorer than himself, John Specht was legally obliged merely to secure for her a relatively modest dower (which corresponded to the dowry she brought to the marriage). It can be assumed that due to a lack of strong emotional ties with his new wife, he chose to focus his bequests on Church institutions and his more distant relatives than to use his money to secure the economic situation of his wife after his death.

Due to the nature of the dower itself, as a form of compensation and security for the dowry provided earlier by the wife, a new marriage to either a better- or poorer-situated spouse could change its amount. However, there is no shortage of examples where even in the case of a marriage to the same woman, especially in the absence of offspring – the natural heirs to the estate – the size of the dowry could be increased significantly. A good example of this is the figure of John Lode, who made his first will in 1439 before going on a pilgrimage to Rome.[382] Arguing that this step was intended to avoid family disputes about the property he would leave behind, he bequeathed to his wife Margaret 50 florins, and to his underage brother Nicholas ten florins, along with all his

---

382   The date of the will is unknown. It could have been written in 1439, according to its place in the *Liber Testamentorum*, but in several cases, in the first part of the book, the order of the registered wills is distorted; LT, fol. 10.

THE SOCIO-ECONOMIC POSITION OF TESTATORS   201

personal belongings. He donated the rest of his property to St. Mary's Church, Holy Spirit Hospital, the Franciscan brotherhood,[383] and to help 'poor people.' In 1454 John and Margaret made a mutual bequest of all of their goods,[384] and two years later, in 1456, John Lode, "going to the Turks who did not know the Christian faith" and counting on the possibility of death among these 'heathen,' this time bequeathed as much as 100 florins to his wife Margaret, and ten more florins to his brother Nicholas Lode of Plzeň, when he reached adulthood. Of the previous pious bequests, there remained only the donation of ten florins to the Krakow hospital. It may be assumed that in this case, the doubling of the dowry to his wife Margaret was not connected with a corresponding doubling of the testator's estate, but, above all, with their lack of children and the husband's entrusting the salvation of his soul to his wife (as evidenced by the much more modest pious bequests made in the second version of the will).

14.2   *Social Mobility*

In analysing the social position of Krakovian testators, one's efforts can be frustrated by encounters with enigmatic and incomplete information about the assets contained in wills or by an over-reliance on the size of dower bequests. It is likewise risky to base one's work on a single will produced by a given individual as a means of determining his or her economic and social capital. In the case of those testators for whom prosopographic research yields a larger volume of data, one generally sees changes in their social position over the course of their lives.[385]

Social advancement can be seen, for example, in the case of the poor oil seller John Noga. In 1442, he bought from Peter the oil seller a house behind St. Stephen's Church with a rent of sixty groszy,[386] and then, in the same year, bequeathed a dower of 30 grivna to his wife Dorothy.[387] When he wrote his will in 1464, he already owned two houses behind St. Mark's Church,[388] one of which was shared with his son by his second wife, Catherine, while the other was sold for 60 grivna by the executor of his son's will (who was also called John Noga the oil seller).[389]

---

383   This refers to the brotherhood in the so-called Hungarian chapel in St. Francis Church; Hanna Zaremska, *Bractwa*, 81–83.

384   SCAB. 7, fol. 195.

385   Roman Czaja, "Społeczna mobilność jako paradygmat badań nad patrycjatem i grupami kierowniczymi w średniowieczu," in *Elita władzy miasta Krakowa*, 9–21.

386   SCAB. 6, fol. 258.

387   SCAB. 6, fol. 269.

388   SCAB. 8, fol. 177.

389   CONS. 429, fol. 545.

202 CHAPTER 2

Szymek from Jewish Street can also be counted among the group of Krakow burghers who became wealthy as a result of their own labour. He confirmed his will before a bench court, where, according to custom, he asked if "he could dispose of his earned wealth in accordance with his will, namely, if he wishes, to give one child more than to others or to another, depending on his merits" (*uni puero plus dando quam aliis vel alio iuxta erga eum plus merito*). After receiving a positive answer from the bench court, he handed over his will, written on a piece of paper, which was then entered into the court's book.[390] He began with a bequest of ten grivna to his wife Dorothy, to which he added 20 more grivna and secured this with his property, in particular his house on Jewish Street and by the garden in front of Szewska Gate. This significant increase in the size of the dower (*melioracio dotalicii*) was justified by the fact that her money helped to pay off the house rent of two grivna, with which it had been burdened. Szymek bequeathed 20 grivna to each of his three children, who were also to inherit in equal parts what remained after the sale of the property. This will was accompanied by an interesting note, which shows that after the testator's death the widow was repaid 30 grivna by Stanisław, a son from Szymek's first marriage. The note also states that Stanisław gave 20 grivna to Dorothy, Szymek's daughter, and five grivna to Barbara, a maid not mentioned in the will. The testator, despite his initial low social status (which may be indicated by the ten grivna he originally bequeathed as a dower), significantly increased his estate, since in his will he had assets worth almost 100 grivna (of which his wife was entitled to 30). Information about the testator's second marriage and the fact that his new wife (perhaps from her dowry or inheritance money) had paid off the encumbrance against their home also sheds more light on this will. The increase in her dower was equal to the amount needed to pay off the rent. This will is undoubtedly an interesting example of how successive marriages could contribute to the accumulation of economic capital, even among relatively low-income burghers. While entering into a favourable marriage could significantly influence the social advancement of even a not-very-wealthy burgher, in the case of wealthy individuals belonging to the social elite, it must have had an even more significant impact.[391]

---

390 SCAB. 8, fol. 202.

391 The previously mentioned alderman Peter Schepcz is a good example. The goods he inherited from his first wife, Dorothy, are evidenced by the very valuable clothes and ornaments mentioned in his will. These were supposed to be given to his daughters from his first marriage. The assets brought by his second wife Jadwiga point to the very large dowry she received, which was at least the equivalent of the dower she was given. What is more, after they married, Peter came into even more wealth when his wife Hedwig received an inheritance from her parents from the town hall in 1477; cf. LT, fol. 137–140; CONS. 428, fol. 585.

THE SOCIO-ECONOMIC POSITION OF TESTATORS

Analysing the wills described above, we see the dynamic and complex nature of the position occupied by an individual within a social group and the many elements affecting this situation which are difficult to discern by means of quantitative research. A highly significant factor influencing the accumulation of economic capital among burghers was their successive – very often two or three – marriages. Well-considered marriage contracts played a greater role primarily among members of Krakow society's upper class (as evidenced by, among other things, the size of dower bequests entered into municipal books), but there is no doubt that for less wealthy burghers this could also have provided a means by which to significantly increase their wealth and thus improve their social situation.[392]

The gathered data indicate that wills as 'tools of power' could have played an important role in the burgher's individual strategies of securing and improving their social position. A variety of testamentary practices, including securing marriage contracts, management of goods accumulated during lifetime, disinheriting distant relatives, as well as popular reciprocal clauses between spouses, allowed and supported the accumulation of goods within urban families. All of these testamentary practices had an impact on a general social mobility in the city. However, as indicated by the analyzed wills, these 'tools' were used primarily by members of the most privileged groups, in which the surplus of capital facilitated its further multiplication.

The complexity of Krakovian wills, written for various reasons, in different ways and during different periods during the lifetime of the testator, means that any estimates of individuals' financial situation and comparisons made between wills must be made with great care. In only a few cases have several versions of the wills written by a single burgher been preserved; more cases like these would have made it possible to better understand both the circumstances surrounding the writing of wills in this period and the changes in the economic and social situations of the testators involved.

---

392   Zdzisław Noga, *Grupy zawodowe*, 253–263.

CHAPTER 3

The Burgher Family

1 Family and Marriage in the Light of Law and Tradition

The family, the most basic and enduring form of community, has always functioned as part of a wider social system and reflected the changes this system underwent over time. The size, shape and meaning of the family and the bonds between its members were influenced by an ongoing process of social, economic and cultural change. In the Middle Ages, the Church played a modernizing role in this respect: Christianity's adoption of a new, relatively coherent set of moral and formal concepts, values and principles greatly impacted all aspects of social life, giving rise to what is commonly termed Latin civilization.[1] Among the spheres in which the Church made a strong effort to exert greater control was the family and familial and marital relations. Yet, paradoxically, through its efforts to enshrine and sanctify the affective dimensions of the institution of marriage, the Church contributed greatly to a lessening of the importance of blood relations, and thus to the dissolution of the traditional family model, based on kinship.[2] It did so, on the one hand, by rejecting the means conventionally used to maintain strong, cohesive family kinship bonds, including adoption, cohabitation, inbreeding and the marrying of widows of deceased family members.[3] Meanwhile, one the other, it cherished and sanctified the affective and consensual aspect of marriage,[4] supporting both the right of women to inheritances and of every man to dispose of his property

---

1 Regardless of how ambiguous, questionable and difficult it would be to define the term 'Latin civilisation,' the same problem exists with the analogous concepts of the 'Western world' and 'Western civilisation'; cf. Berman Harold Joseph, Law and Revolution. The Formation of the Western Legal Tradition (Cambridge-London: Harvard University Press, 1983), 1–14; Pierre Chaunu, *Le temps des Réformes: histoire religieuse et système de civilisation: la crise de la chrétienté: l'éclatement, 1250–1550* (Paris: Fayard, 1975); Norbert Elias, *Przemiany obyczajów*, 7–16.

2 Jack Goody, *The Development of the Family and Marriage in Europe*, 103–156.

3 The Church gradually extended restrictions not only to marriages between blood relatives, but also between non-related family members and 'spiritual relatives' – godfathers and godmothers. In the sixth century, marriages were prohibited to the third degree of consanguinity, then in the eleventh century the ban was extended to the seventh degree; *ibidem*, 55–59, 73, 144.

4 Which contradicted the primary role of obtaining the family's permission to marry and undermined the authority of the head of the family.

© JAKUB WYSMUŁEK, 2021 | DOI:10.1163/9789004461444_005
This is an open access chapter distributed under the terms of the CC BY-NC-ND 4.0 license.

THE BURGHER FAMILY

by means of a will.[5] These actions by the Church were motivated primarily by theological and moral concerns, but they were also meant to weaken the ties between individuals and their kin and to incorporate them into a new, universal religious community. One important aspect of this phenomenon was the substantial benefits the Church derived from espousing a model of ownership based on private, rather than communal or familial, ownership of goods. The right to freely dispose of one's estate (initially roughly one-third of it)[6] was promoted so that people could 'piously' donate their property to the Church, thus designating, as Saint Augustine observed, "Christ as their heir."[7]

In Polish lands, such pivotal changes began to be introduced only in the thirteenth century, i.e. after the Church's organizational structure and a new legal system based on a Western model had become well-established. Initially, new laws applied only to foreign settlers who moved to Polish lands, but they soon began to regulate the functioning of society at large, which "moved from the notion of community or kin ownership, in which women basically had no rights, to a private, family-controlled system, in which women, unmarried, married and widowed, were given the right to dispose of their private and inherited property."[8] Influenced by these new cultural trends and encouraged by the Church, women began for the first time to finance religious institutions on a large scale; initially these patrons were primarily princesses and duchesses, but women from the noble elite soon followed suit.[9] In the fourteenth century, rich members of the patriciate, both women and men, from the rapidly growing and prospering cities of the Kingdom of Poland, also began to make generous donations to finance new religious institutions. Although exceptional for its time, the earliest surviving Krakow will, made by an affluent burgher woman named Sulisława (*Sulislava civis Cracoviae*) in 1303, provides a perfect example of this process.[10] In the will Sulisława, who shared some sort of a connection

---

5   Michael M. Sheehan, *The Will in Medieval England*, 234–241; Jack Goody, *The Development*, 122.

6   Cf. Chapter 1.

7   Karol Koranyi, *Podstawy średniowiecznego prawa spadkowego*, "Pamiętnik Historyczno-Prawny" 9, 1930, no. 2, 196; cf. Chapter 1.

8   Jack Wiesiołowski, "Zmiany społecznej pozycji kobiety w średniowiecznej Polsce," in *Kobieta w kulturze średniowiecznej Europy. Prace ofiarowane Profesor Alicji Karłowskiej-Kamzowej*, ed. Antoni Gąsiorowski (Poznan: Wydawnictwo Poznańskiego Towarzystwa Przyjaciół Nauk, 1995), 42.

9   E.g. St. Hedwig of Silesia, St. Kinga of Poland, blessed Yolanda and blessed Salomea; cf. *ibidem*, 42–43.

10 KDMK, vol. 3, no. 368, 493–494.

with Albert, the vogt of Krakow,[11] made very generous pious bequests to the Dominican and Franciscan monasteries and to St. Mary's Basilica in Krakow.

In the articles of Magdeburg Law (the *Weichbild* and *Sachsenspiegel*), the family is characterised as a traditional, strong feudal institution.[12] Marriage by contrast is portrayed as a frail institution, a necessary transitional stage, in contrast to the proven strength and permanence of family bonds based on kinship and blood relations. Unlike with the 'Chełmno law,'[13] under Magdeburg Law there was a division of property between the spouses. After the death of one spouse, the couple's common property was divided accordingly between the families of the husband and the wife. Such a solution had serious consequences for the widow, who from the couple's estate only had rights to her dower and – if the late husband made the necessary arrangements – some form of annuity (*vita provisio*).[14] The remaining part of the property was given to the husband's relatives, according to their 'right of expectation.'[15] Likewise, after the death of the widow, her dower (as compensation for her dowry) and vita provisio were not considered her personal estate, but were instead inherited by her late husband's family.[16] Only a portion of her movable property (in Latin *suppellectilia*, in German *gerade*; known also as *wyprawa* under Polish customary law) was inherited by her daughter or, if the widow had no

---

11   He was made both the beneficiary of part of the provisions and their executor; *ibidem*

12   This was affected by, among other things, the nature of the *Sachsenspiegel*, which regulated land law (*Landrecht*) and fief law (*Lehnrecht*). Research has shown that initially the *Sachsenspiegel* had greater significance in the creation of the first Polish city law codes than Magdeburg *Ius civile*; Zygfryd Rymaszewski, *Łacińskie teksty Landrechtu Zwierciadła Saskiego w Polsce: versio Vratislaviensis, versio Sandomiriensis, Łaski* (Wrocław: Zakłas Narodowy Im. Ossolińskich, 1975), 6.

13   *Prawo starochełmińskie 1584 (1394)*, ed. Witold Maisel, Zbigniew Zdrójkowski, trans. Andrzej Bzdęga, Alicja Gaca (Toruń: Uniwersytet Mikołaja Kopernika, 1985).

14   "[...] si aliquis ducit uxorem et si vir de hac luce decesserit, uxor nihil habet in suis bonis nisi dederit sibi pro dotalicio, aut vita provisione pro eius vita in iudicio bannito"; Jan Łaski, *Commune Incliti Poloniae, Libri duo*, part 1, 178.

15   In the mid-sixteenth century, Bartłomiej Groicki recounted the rules of inheritance in Magdeburg Law: "There are four degrees to the inheritance of a deceased person who had not made a will. The first degree is the children. The second, the parents. The third degree includes other individuals mentioned above. The fourth degree is a husband and wife, who inherit from one another when there are no parents, no children, no brothers, no sisters or others down or across the family line. Finally, if there are no individuals belonging to the categories described above, then the inheritance and possessions of the deceased belongs to the royal treasury"; *idem, Porządek sądów i spraw miejskich prawa majdeburskiego w Koronie Polskiej* (Warszawa: Wydawnictwo Prawnicze, 1953), 181.

16   "Nulla mulier potest vite provisione nec dotalicium hereditarie observare et cum de hac luce decedit ad heredes revertitur sui mariti"; Jan Łaski, *Commune Incliti Poloniae, Libri duo*, part 1, 178.

THE BURGHER FAMILY

daughters, by her closest female relative.[17] The unwritten logic behind these provisions was that after the husband's death, the widow should return with her dower (equivalent to her dowry) and gerade to her own family. Male relatives of the late husband took custody of the children. Once all these arrangements were finalized, the marriage was considered dissolved.

Apart from the conservative social system enshrined by Magdeburg Law and the modernizing influences of the Church, a third force that influenced the shape of family relations in late-medieval cities was the changing nature of work and the conditions of everyday life.[18] Cities were populated mostly by first-generation or second-generation immigrants, and the freedom to inherit property and dispose of one's estate allowed to some of them to accumulate capital. In view of these aspects of urban life, the practices of medieval municipal courts, so-called 'living law,'[19] introduced new measures which undermined the severe and archaic system of kin ownership and separate property. Wills played an important role in this process as 'tools of power' because they made individuals active subjects of family relations, also in relation to the law. Wills allowed individuals to shape desirable family relationships, for example to exclude unwanted relatives from inheritance or to include in the group of heirs persons not related to them by ties of blood. This 'power' significantly influenced the evolution of the family institution in the city and the formation of its separate models within the city elite and middle classes of the burgher's *communitas*.

2 New Forms of Bequests for Wives

Despite the existence of generally uniform and unchangeable regulations limiting the widow's right to inheritance, fourteenth-century and fifteenth-century

---

17 Urszula Sowina, "Wdowy i sieroty w świetle prawa w miastach korony w późnym średniowieczu i wczesnej nowożytności," in *Od narodzin do wieku dojrzałego. Dzieci i młodzież w Polsce*, part. 1: *Od średniowiecza do wieku XVIII*, ed. Maria Dąbrowska, Andrzej Klonder (Warszawa: Instytut Archeologii i Etnologii Polskiej Akademii Nauk, 2002), 18–19.

18 Aside from the gradual evolution of urban life in Krakow, another significant factor was the adoption of social and legal remedies already present in other developed cities in the region.

19 The concept of *living law* was adopted by Leopold Pospíšil, an anthropologist of the law, from the work of the nineteenth-century sociologist Eugene Ehrlich: "The living law is not the part of the content of the document that the courts recognize as binding when they decide a legal controversy, but only that part which the parties actually observe in life"; Leopold Pospíšil, *The Ethnology of Law* (New Haven, Conn.: Human Relations Area Files, 1978), 61.

century testators were in fact relatively free to plan for the widow's future and decide what part of the estate she should inherit. Many testators exercised this right to decide about the widow's future – some husbands clearly indicated what part of their movable and immovable property should be used to secure the widow's dower and what household goods should constitute her gerade.[20] Others, in turn, chose to give the wife one-third of the entire estate in exchange for her dower[21] (such as the alderman John Bozemecz in 1394),[22] half of the entire estate (just like the burghers Lawrence, who lived at St. Anna Street, and Theodoric Doring)[23] or even the entire estate (because there were no other heirs, after the death of the widow, the estate was to be donated to opera pietatis).[24] While final bequests contained in fifteenth-century wills vary greatly, reflecting the testator's specific family, financial and social situation, we can distinguish three basic models in them for securing a widow's right to inheritance. In the first, the widow receives her gerade and a dower secured by her late husband's estate, the sum of which was fixed in advance (and often supplemented by an additional sum of money – a so-called *przywianek* in Old Polish). The late husband's children or relatives were obligated to pay the widow what she had been promised, and until they did so, she had the right to make use of her husband's property. One such bequest was made by the shoemaker John Panzira in 1458. His wife Catherine was granted the right to live in their wooden house at St. John Street and retain possession of other movable and immovable goods until she received a dower of 30 grivna.[25] The painter (*pictor*) Martin made a similar bequest in 1463. He bequeathed to his wife Catherine a dower of 50 grivna, supplemented by an additional 20 grivna, secured by his movable and immovable property. Catherine was given the right to make use of her late husband's estate until she was paid the dower owed to her by those appointed as executors of the testament.[26] Apart from the dower to which the wife was entitled by law, some testators also bequeathed their

---

20   SCAB., no. 2070 (1395).
21   The principle of a 1/3 free part of one's possessions had been known in church law since the early Middle Ages, and this is also the source of this principle in Poland.; cf. Berman Harold Joseph, *Law and Revolution*, 230–231; Karol Koranyi, *Podstawy średniowiecznego prawa spadkowego*, 194–195; Urszula Sowina, "Testamenty mieszczan krakowskich o przekazywaniu majątku w późnym średniowieczu i we wczesnej nowożytności," in *Sociální svět středověkého města*, ed. Martin Nodl (Praha: Filosofia, 2006), 177.
22   SCAB., no. 1914.
23   SCAB., no. 1894, 1913.
24   SCAB., no. 1774 (1393), 2069 (1395).
25   LT, fol. 50.
26   LT, fol. 80.

THE BURGHER FAMILY

wives a share of the estate, often one equal in size to that inherited by the children (i.e. the wife was treated on equal terms with the children as an heir). For example, in 1466 Andrew Zyra, a Krakow merchant, bequeathed to his wife a dower of 100 grivna, and also gave her the equivalent of their daughter's inheritance, i.e. half of all remaining property. Many testators did not specify the amount of the dower or gerade, but simply bequeathed a specific real estate property or share of the estate to the widow in lieu of a dower and other goods she had the right to receive. The councillor Hippolyte Spilberger made such a bequest in his will in 1469.[27]

The spouses also provided for one another financially by means of so-called 'subsistence bequests,' i.e. agreements between a husband and wife that provided for the mutual inheritance of their property.[28] In the event of the death of one of the spouses, the surviving spouse had the right to inherit the entire estate.[29] Such contracts clearly stated that all other relatives were disinherited.[30] This not only secured the widow's future financially, it also provided the husband with the assurance that if his wife died, her family would not have the right to her property, which would instead remain with him. Such bequests first began to appear in Krakow's municipal books in the 1350s. They quickly became very popular, as evidenced by the number of similar bequests found in the sources. It appears that in the mid-fourteenth century, Krakow's burghers were given the right to freely dispose of all of their property and to bequeath it to their surviving spouse, at least for the remainder of their lifetime, turning it into a form of annuity, which was permitted under municipal law. These formal changes in the law are evidence of the profound changes burgher family relations were undergoing at that time.

3 The Situation of the Widow

Changes that were gradually introduced into municipal law and the growing popularity of the institution of the will enabled Krakow's burghers to make

---

27   LT, fol. 95.

28   Urszula Sowina, *Wdowy i sieroty*, 19.

29   E.g. "Tilusz cerdo resignavit Margarethe uxori sue omnia bona mobilia et immobilia post mortem, si decesserit absque liberis, et ipsa domina Margaretha econverso resignavit dicto Tilusszio suppellectile et omnia alia bona, que habet"; SCAB., no. 279 (1368).

30   "Paszko Skalka omnia bona sua, que habet aut habiturus est quomodolibet in futurum, Anne uxori sue post mortem suam dedit et ipsa sibi econverso alia littera; reservat maritus dominium et ambo excludunt amicos"; SCAB., no. 2185.

bequests and other plans concerning their property while they were still alive in order to secure the material well-being of their families. At the same time, due to the provisions of municipal law that discriminated against the widow, most testators wished to shield the widow from poverty and from inheritance disputes with the family of the late husband.[31] Naturally, testators used different methods to this end, depending on their familial and financial situation.

A number of wills from the 1390s, whose form (and probably function) was similar to that of pre-nuptial marriage contracts, provide insight into the situation of the widow. It appears that in at least some cases such wills were drafted shortly after the testator married his first or second wife.[32] This is evidenced by the form of the bequest, which includes a detailed description of the wife's future living situation after the death of the husband and her inheritance rights, as well as annotations concerning the inheritance rights of any children they might have. For example, the councillor Nicholas Strelicz left his entire estate to his wife. However, if the couple had any children, they would inherit part of the estate.[33] Similarly, Peter Puczk specified in his will the amount of his wife's dower – she was to receive 81 grivna, but only if their marriage was childless. "However, should God give [Peter Puczk] an heir," the widow was to receive a smaller inheritance.[34] In two bequests, testators explicitly stated that they wished to protect the right to inheritance of the second wife, specifying that the estate should be divided among the second wife, any children from the second marriage, and the children from the first marriage.[35]

Instructions regarding the material well-being of the wife varied. Husbands took into consideration whether the wife would decide to remain a widow, which usually meant looking after the house, raising children and cherishing the memory of the late husband, or whether she would remarry. In other words, husbands based their decisions on whether the wife would remain in his family or remarry and thus enter the family of the new husband.[36] Although we should not underestimate the emotions involved in testators' decisions, i.e. their wish for the wife to remain faithful and dedicated to the memory of the late husband, it seems that such bequests were made predominantly

---

31   Urszula Sowina, *Wdowy i sieroty*, 19.

32   SCAB., no. 1645 (1393), 1654 (1393), 1816 (1393), 1894 (1394), 2042 (1394), 2070 (1395), 2093 (1395), 2210 (1395), 2354 (1396). Probably also: CONS. 428, fol. 231 (1426); CONS. 429, fol. 372 (1466)

33   "[...] si vero pueros ex se procreaverint"; SCAB., no. 1645; cf. Jacek Laberschek, *Mikołaj Strzelicz*, in PSB, vol. 45 (Warszawa–Krakow: Polska Akademia Nauk, Polska Akademia Umiejętności, 2007), 16–17.

34   "[...] ab ich sturbe ane fruchte [...] adir ap vns got fruchte gibt mitenandir"; SCAB., no. 2354.

35   SCAB., no. 1816 (1393), no. 2070 (1395).

36   Brigitte Klosterberg, *Zur Ehre Gottes und zum Wohl der Familie,* 208.

THE BURGHER FAMILY 211

because husbands feared that the wife would squander the inheritance once she remarried. Testators tried to protect their children against such an unfortunate event in various ways. They subjected their wives to the control of the appointed guardians (*tutores*), bequeathed specific parts of the estate to their children, and encouraged their wives to remain widows. For example, in 1390, in the presence of his wife Catherine and before the municipal bench court, Stanisław Grudner[37] made a bequest to Catherine of 40 grivna and half of their household items, which constituted her due dower.[38] Grudner further stated in the contract that if Catherine remained a widow, then she, together with two guardians appointed by Grudner, would have the right to raise any children resulting from the marriage and administer their inheritance until any son they might have turned 24 years old or any daughter married; the children would then be given their separate shares of the estate.[39] If one of the children died, their inheritance should be equally divided between Catherine and the surviving children. Once all the children had received their shares of the estate, the widow would receive 40 grivna as her dower. Thus, while the wife was only entitled to her dower, the amount of which had been determined at the betrothal, as a widow she became the acting head of household, with her late husband's entire estate at her disposal.

A similar contract was made in 1395 by the alderman John Dobschicz. He stated that "if his wife decides to remain a widow, she should take custody of the children and maintain control over the entire estate.[40] However, if she remarries, she should be given 250 grivna as her dower, her gerade and everything else that she is entitled to."[41] Thus, if Dobschicz's wife remained a widow, and if their marriage was childless, she would receive 250 grivna, one-third of the house, and the household items that constituted her gerade. The wife was to manage her late husband's entire estate until her death. Afterwards, it was to be divided equally among the relatives of the late husband, a hospital and charitable bequests.

---

37 He was probably related to the alderman Nicholas Grudner, who held this function in 1385, 1392–1393; KDMK, vol. 3, 52–53.

38 "[...] eidem domine XL mrc. et medietatem suorum suppellectilium, videlicet rade dictorum, racione dothalicii et pro omnibus, que ipsam concernere possent"; SCAB., no. 1267.

39 "[...] si vero vidua permanserit, extunc eadem domina cum infrascriptis tutoribus eorum pueris debent preesse et cum eorum bonis dictos pueros apud se retinere, nec aliquem dictorum puerorum, si masculus fuerit, a se separare, donec ad etatem XXIIII annorum pervenerit, si femina, non prius, nisi marito copuletur"; *ibidem*.

40 "[...] ap se witve blebe, so sal se mit vormunden seyn vnd roten vor ir kinder, vnde behalde der goben hirschaft, dy weyl ich lebe"; cf. SCAB., no. 2093.

41 "[...] ap dy vorgenante Katherin eynen man neme, zo zal man ir geben II½ C mrg. czu tun vnd czu lassen vor morgengabe vnd vor alle ding an ir gerade, dy ir von rechte geborit"; cf. *ibidem*.

However, husbands did not always trust their wives (and future widows) unconditionally. In 1393, John Ederer, an alderman and later member of the Krakow municipal council, authenticated his will, which he had made on a sheet of paper, before the municipal bench court.[42] Like Grudner and Dobschicz, Ederer stated that if his wife remained a widow, she (along with their children) would remain "the mistress of the entire estate until her death."[43] However, the appointed testamentary guardians were to audit the family's finances each year. If they were in good order, the widow would continue to manage the estate. If the opposite was true, the guardians were to step in, take control of the estate, and pay an allowance to the widow and the children to satisfy all their needs.[44]

Childless testators often stated in their wills that their wives should be given their entire estate, or parts of it, in the form of a jointure. They specified that the widow would administer her late husband's estate until her death, but the estate would eventually be inherited by the relatives of the late husband or religious institutions. For example, in 1395, John (*Hanco*) Czartke bequeathed his house at Shoemaker's Street to his wife, instructing the appointed testamentary guardians to sell it after her death and donate the money to selected religious institutions.[45] The affluent burgher John Reichil made a similar bequest in 1442. He left his entire estate to his wife, but after her death the appointed testamentary guardians were to donate everything to fund opera pietatis.[46]

---

42   "[...] eyn czedilpapir, dorin her syn testament vnd lecztin willin yn geschrebin hatte"; SCAB., no 1676; cf. Józef Mitkowski, Jan Ederer, in PSB, vol. 6 (Krakow: Polska Akademia Nauk, Polska Akademia Umiejętności, 1948), 201–202.

43   "[...] sy mynes guttis eyne vrawe bleybin mit sampt mynem kinde bis an ir ende"; SCAB., no. 1676.

44   "[...] alzo daz sy rechenunge tue alle jar den vormunden von dem gutte; is das sy das gut bessert, so sullin is ir dy vormunde lossin, wo sy ys nicht enbessirte, so sullen is dy vormunden nemen czu en vnde sullen de mete des bestin nemen vnd sullin muttir vnd kinde ere notdorf douon gebin"; *ibidem*.

45   "Hanco Czartke gibt noch seyme tode seyn hus gelegin of der Zewgassen, dorynne her wonet, frawen Katherin seyner elichin husfrawen, das se dorynne sal wonen vnd seyn genissen, dy weil se lebit, hengelegt allirley hindernis seyner frunde, vnd noch der frawen tode sullin dy nochgeschrebin vormunden das hus vorkowfen vnde sullin das noch geschrebin gelt geben personen vnde steten, den is beschrebin stet"; SCAB., no. 2069.

46   "[...] alle seyn gut beweglich und unbeweglich das her hot adir ummir haben wirt Dorothee seyner elichen hausfrawen vorrecht und ofgegeben noch seyme tode czu habin mit woller macht czu tuen und czu lossen. Sonder des haws of der Spitler gasse hot her ir gegeben czu irem lebin, und noch irem tode sal is vorkowft werden und das gelt do vor komen in dy werck der barmherczikeyt, wo und wy sy das befelen wirtin irem testament noch irem besten vornemen, und noch undirweysunge irbarrleute"; SCAB. 6, fol. 256.

THE BURGHER FAMILY 213

Testators who had children, especially from a first marriage, sought to ensure that the widow would have a place to live and that the stepchildren would take care of her. The courts generally ruled that the widow could "remain in the estate of the husband" until she received her dower. Once a dotalicium, or dower, was paid, however, the widow was forced to leave the house. In order to prevent such a situation, some wills clearly stated that the widow was to be given a room or chamber in the house of the late husband. The Krakovian patrician Thob Johan made such a bequest in his 1443 will. He stated that if his wife remained a widow, she would receive 700 grivna (constituting her dower and half of the inheritance after the death of their son) and have the right to live in their house until her death. She was to have access to the fireplace and given all that she required.[47] The Krakow alderman John Czarny left even more detailed instructions to his children:

> In addition, my wife is allowed to live in my house until her death. She is to be given the sunny room which overlooks the meat market and one free table in the dining room to sit at that is near the stove and close to the. Moreover, she should also be given all that she requires.[48]

The widow was a vulnerable target for relatives of the late husband who wished to come into possession of the estate. Her situation was especially difficult when she was childless, because she could not dispose of the estate on behalf of non-adult children. Thus, only a will could give her the right to live in the family house and inherit marital property. Of course, even when such a will existed, relatives still actively sought to have their right to inheritance recognized by the court, invoking their rights as family members. Arbitrators ruled on such cases taking into account not only the provisions of the law, but also (and seemingly above all) local customs, a sense of social justice, and a need to avoid lasting conflicts in the local community. For example, we learn from municipal books that in 1462 John Moler, brother of the late Wojtek Moler, made a settlement with Dorothy, the wife of the deceased.[49] The appointed arbitrators, among whom there were two state officials, called *undirwoiwod*,[50] two councillors, and two aldermen, made considerable changes to Moler's will. Instead of the 100 florins her late husband had promised her, the widow

---

47   LT, fol. 7–8.
48   SCAB. 8, fol. 223.
49   CONS. 429, fol. 297.
50   This was probably the position of the deputy voivode (Latin vicepalatinus) – an official responsible primarily for the supervision of prices, measures and weights.

was to be paid 80 florins as her dower.[51] The remaining 20 florins were to be given to John. Valuable *supellectilia*, such as silver cups and spoons, were to be divided evenly between John and the widow. Half of the house, which the widow had received "for her use" (*czu gebrauchen of das*), was to be given to John in exchange for an annual rent. In addition, John was to be given a table, sheets and a silver belt with a cord as a *hergewet* (the hereditary property due to a man). The meat found in the house was also to be divided in half. So, while they respected some of Wojtek Moler's testamentary bequests (for example, a pious bequest of a silver chalice to St. Bernard's Church), in general, the arbitrators adapted them to the traditional inheritance rules of relatives of the late husband and the principle of separate property. Similarly, we learn from a record made in 1432 that Nicholas, a relative of the late Wojtek and a silk embroiderer (*zeydinhafter*), sued Catherine, the widow of Wojtek, demanding the house and hergewet (*arma bellica paramenta vulgariter hergewete*). In this case, however, the court decided that the widow was to receive the compensation of her dower first; only then could the property be divided.[52]

A woman's private property consisted of her dower and everything she had earned while working alongside her husband. In addition, she could also receive a large inheritance after the death of her parents, which often greatly increased her importance in the family and society. The analysed wills show that women often had at their disposal property they inherited from their parents. For example, in 1405, the widow Dorothy Pauswanginne, in disposing of her goods, made bequests to her family worth 160 grivna. In addition, she also stated in her will that she possessed a dower of 200 grivna, 30 grivna in cash, a generous inheritance from her father, and her gerade.[53] Likewise, in her 1461 will, Ursula Grunwaldinne left her husband a house at Shoemaker's Street, which, as she testified, she had inherited from her parents.[54] We can assume that a will or bequest to the other spouse was meant to settle accounts between a husband and wife after the wife had received an inheritance from her parents. For example, in 1451, the armorer (*lorifex*) Thomas and his wife Catherine appeared before the court to legalize a gift *inter vivos* of all their

---

51 This will has not survived to the present day, but its dispositions are mentioned in detail in the analyzed citation.

52 "Sententiatum est Katherine Jostynne relicte Woitkonis Zeydinhafter quod exquo Micolai intromisit se de domo ipsius Woitkonis Zeydenhafter mariti sui et postulat consequenter eciam bellica paramenta vulgariter hergewete, et relicta ipsius defuncti illa habet in sua tenuta wulgariter gewer, tunc ipsa non debet paramenta illa bellica que apud se tenet, alicui dare, nisi facta prius sibi satiffaccione de dote sua de Jure"; SCAB. 6, fol. 32.

53 CONS. 427, fol. 241.

54 LT, fol. 70.

THE BURGHER FAMILY

armamentalia and *paraphernalia*. The remaining part of the estate was to be inherited by the other spouse. After making this bequest, Catherine decided to sell the one-fourth of the house at Grodzka Street that constituted her inheritance.[55] Here, the mutual bequest was meant to secure Catherine's marriage property share after the sale of her inherited property. A similar contract was made in 1451 between Hedwig and her husband Konrad Lang (*Cuncze Lang*), a councillor.[56] Hedwig gave Konrad the rights to all her goods, including those she already owned, those she was to inherit from her father, and those she was to inherit from her grandfather Peter Graser's will.[57] In exchange, Konrad made a bequest to his wife of 400 grivna (as her dower), to be paid out of his estate. In this case, the dower acted as a security for both the wife's dowry and her inheritance.

If a burgher failed to secure his wife's future by means of a will or a mutual bequest, after his death, as mentioned above, a widow who did not have custody of minor children or a widow who decided to remarry had no right to the estate and had to leave the family house.[58] As a result, many widows did not remarry. They chose to honour the will of the husband, manage the estate, and take care of the children. In any case, they chose not to put their material and social position at risk. In view of the fact that women married at an earlier age than men, many widows must have survived their husbands in the medieval city.[59] It thus appears that the wealthiest burghers actively sought to discourage their wives from remarrying. For example, in 1462, the councillor Jarosz Szarlej increased the dower of his wife Margaret so that "she would take care of their children."[60] Poorer burghers, in contrast, realized that after their death, a new marriage could save their wives from poverty. For that reason, in 1458, the shoemaker John Panzira bequeathed 30 grivna to his wife Catherine, which constituted her dower, and allowed her to "benefit from shoemaking" (*uti artem sutoriam*) until she found a new husband.[61]

Testamentary bequests and bequests of similar nature, such as mutual bequests or dower bequests, were meant to effectively undermine the

---

55   SCAB. 7, fol. 160.

56   Marcin Starzyński, *Krakowska rada miejska w średniowieczu*, 278.

57   SCAB. 7, fol. 165.

58   Brigitte Klosterberg, *Zur Ehre Gottes und zum Wohl der Familie*, 209.

59   Jack Goody, *The Development*, 64.

60   "[...] durch des wille das sy dastir fleissiger sal meyne kynder auswartin und dyneryn"; LT, fol. 73.

61   "Item dedit bona voluntate dicte uxori sue quod ipsa debet uti artem Sutoriam et frui Scampnum artes eiusdem et tali condicione scmapnum habere debet donec maritum alium non duxerit"; LT, fol. 50.

traditional system of property division. They helped maintain the integrity of the nuclear family, at the expense of other kin, even after the death of one of the spouses. The spouses inherited not only the property they had earned together, but also their respective private inheritances. Such bequests demonstrate that a new form of the institution of marriage had been strengthened – it was now not only a financial or social union, but also an emotional one, as well. As official documents, fourteenth-century and fifteenth-century wills rarely contained any personal or emotional remarks. However, the fact that the wife often inherited the entire estate at the expense of other relatives speaks for itself. Still, some emotional remarks in wills have survived. For example, in 1438, John Unger (a Hungarian) made a bequest of all his movable and immovable property to his wife, arguing that "he and his wife had earned everything together."[62] The example of the salt merchant (*sallicida*) Michael Godzek is even more telling. In 1494, Godzek left his entire estate to his wife Dorothy, disinheriting all his relatives. He stated that "Dorothy worked with him constantly and faithfully. She nourished, warmed and served him with her guidance and work."[63] In view of formal requirements, such words of gratitude for the hard work shared and property accumulated together could be read as a declaration of love. Such statements were even more common in sixteenth-century and seventeenth-century wills.[64]

4 Children

Most married couples plan to have children and share the hope that raising them will give their future lives special meaning. In the Middle Ages, children were seen as 'guardians of immortality' in a double sense, as they were expected both to pray for their parents' salvation in heaven and preserve their memory on earth.[65] If a testator had children, it was they who would eventually inherit the estate, even if the wife was originally named in the will as the main beneficiary.

---

62   "[...] dixit quidem testator quod ipse eadem bona relicta cum eadem consorte sua laboribus acquisivisset"; LT, fol. 3–4.

63   "In primis dixit quod uxor sua legitima Dorothea fideliter, semper cum eo egit et sua providencia et laboribus eum nutrivisset, foveret et servaret"; LT, fol. 154.

64   "Such remarks are more frequent in the wills of men than in the wills of women, and they usually display such attributes of marital harmony as: love, commitment, fidelity, mutual support in their work and the upbringing of children, care in old age and illness"; Andrzej Karpiński, *Kobieta w mieście polskim w drugiej połowie XVI i w XVII wieku* (Warszawa: Instytut historii PAN, 1995), 197.

65   Brigitte Klosterberg, *Zur Ehre Gottes und zum Wohl der Familie*, 212.

THE BURGHER FAMILY

Although wills often mentioned children, as source materials they do not provide a sound basis for making estimates of the size of a typical medieval burgher family. They are unsuitable for statistical analyses due to variations in the form of the will, the motivations for writing them, and the situation in which they were drafted.[66] In many cases, children were not mentioned in wills because the parents were childless or made the will shortly after they married. In others, a will merely contained a bequest or only addressed the liabilities of the late husband toward his wife and debtors, i.e. it did not provide for the division of the estate among the testator's children and close relatives. In some cases, adult children were not mentioned in the will because they had already come of age and received their share of the estate.[67] In many cases, if children were mentioned in the will, they were only enigmatically referred to by the Latin *pluralis filii* or *liberi*, or, the German, *kinder*.[68]

In wills in which the testator left instructions concerning the division of the estate among all his children, as he stated, in order to avoid family quarrels and feuds, the number of children mentioned is usually between two and four, and rarely five or more. Most studies on medieval urban populations corroborate such an estimate.[69] Affluent burghers probably married more often and thus had more children than the average burgher family.[70] These burghers often

---

66 Such calculations were made in some studies on wills, but they did not provide any new findings, and the authors themselves raised methodological doubts; e.g.: Brigitte Klosterberg, *Zur Ehre Gottes und zum Wohl der Familie*, 212–216; Paul Baur, *Testament und Bürgerschaft*, 205–220; Johannes Schildhauer, *Hansestädtischer Alltag. Untersuchungen auf Grundlage der Stralsunder Bürgertestamente vom Anfang des 14. bis zum Ausgang des 16. Jahrhunderts*, Weimar 1992, 100–113.

67 Sometimes, however, children who had already received their share of the inheritance were mentioned in wills.; cf. CONS. 428, fol. 243 (1428); SCAB. 6, fol. 94 (1434); SCAB. 8, fol. 239–240 (1466).

68 It seems that at this time there was no custom or obligation to list all the descendants in the will under pain of its nullification, as Bartłomiej Groicki wrote in the mid-sixteenth century; cf. *idem, Tytuły prawa majdeburskiego* (Warszawa: Wydawnictwo Prawnicze, 1954), 182.

69 Andrzej Karpiński, *Kobieta w mieście*, 187; Stanisław Waszak, "Dzietność rodziny mieszczańskiej i ruch naturalny ludności miasta Poznania w końcu XVI i XVII w.," *Roczniki Dziejów Społecznych i Gospodarczych* 16 (1954–1955), 365; Brigitte Klosterberg, *Zur Ehre*, 213–214.

70 For example, Margaret Pferdinne, the wealthy widow of goldsmith John Pferd, mentioned her brother's five children in her will: "Item so gebe ich den vonf kyndern meynes gebornen bruders von vatir und muttir Peter Pelczers das haws das ich Inne wone allin gleich eym als dem andern czu gleichim teile"; LT, fol. 52 (1458). Likewise, in her will from 1501, Margaret Czypserowa testified that she had two sons with her first husband, councillor Nicholas Zalcz, and six children with her second husband, Stanisław Czypser, "some of whom survived." At the time of writing her will, Margaret was married to her third husband, John Łowicz, with whom she also had children; cf. LT, fol. 165–166.

even included stepchildren in their wills, which further complicated plans for the division of the estate. Children from a first marriage were seen as a threat to the widow (i.e. the second wife), and wills were often written to avoid disputes between these parties. Evidence from research also confirms that the number of children in the average Krakow family varied depending on its material situation,[71] and whether the head of the family was an immigrant or a local burgher.[72]

According to Magdeburg Law, as it was applied in medieval Krakow, sons and daughters had equal rights to the property of their parents and inherited it in equal parts.[73] This was a departure from traditional Polish land law, according to which daughters received a dowry in cash, while the sons or closest male relatives inherited the estate.[74] The fact that daughters were permitted to inherit real estate property meant a part of the estate could come under the control of the daughter's husband, and thus *de facto* be lost as part of the family assets. Throughout the analysed period, a traditional division was nevertheless maintained in regard to movable property between what was to be inherited by sons or male relatives (*hergewet, arma bellica*) and by daughters or female relatives (*gerade, paraphernalia*). Children born from a second marriage also had the right to receive the same inheritance as children born from the first marriage, a fact that was often stated in wills. For example, in 1393, the affluent burgher Martin Junge decided that if he and his second wife had a child, it would receive the same inheritance as his son born out of his first marriage.[75]

---

71   "Researchers of family structures agree that the actual number of children depended on the financial situation of the parents"; Andrzej Karpiński, *Kobieta w mieście*, 187; Stanisław Waszak, *Dzietność*, 352–353; Brigitte Klosterberg, *Zur Ehre Gottes und zum Wohl der Familie*, 213–215.

72   One theory of historical demographics states that increased mortality and lower fertility rates among immigrants contributed to negative birth rates in medieval cities.; Jan de Vries, *European Urbanization 1500–1800*, Cambridge (Mass.): 1984, 185.

73   It seems that, apart from the regulations provided for in municipal law, Krakowhad its own book of judgements that contained principles providing for the equal inheritance of property regardless of the gender of the children: "omnes quinque liberi seu heredes dicti domini Nycolay Ruteni inter se diuident equalibus virilibus siue paribus porcionibus secundum ius et laudabilem consuetudinem ciuitatis Cracouie, prout est hactenus obseruatum"; NKiRMK, no. 103 (1330).

74   *Statuty Kazimierza Wielkiego*, ed. Otto Balzer, Ludwik Łysiak (Poznan: Nakł. Poznańskiego Tow. Przyjaciół Nauk, 1947), paragraph 131, 132; cf. Wacław Uruszczak, "Statuty Kazimierza Wielkiego jako źródło prawa polskiego," *Studia z Dziejów Państwa i Prawa Polskiego*, 3 (1999), 97–115; Ludwik Łysiak, Statuty Kazimierza Wielkiego w małopolskiej praktyce sądowej XV wieku," *Studia Historyczne* 19, no. 1 (1976), 25–39.

75   "[...] vnde ah ir got eyne frucht bescherte, dy sal auch teilhaft seyn seynis gutis, als vil, als em geborit"; cf. SCAB., no. 1816.

THE BURGHER FAMILY

However, Junge also stated that his stepson Stanisław (Stenczel) was to receive just three grivna. This was because Stanisław belonged to the family of his late father and was thus entitled to receive an inheritence from him. Junge, as his stepfather, was not obliged to share his property with Stanisław, and the bequest of three grivna was made merely to include him symbolically among the heirs. Stepsons, however, could inherit from their parents, thus giving rise to potential conflicts between stepparents and children from a second marriage. It can be assumed that the solution chosen by councillor Martin Chmiel in 1466 was a rather common one. In 1465, Chmiel made a will in which he secured the dower of his second wife, Ursula, bequeathed his house to his son Jacob, and divided the rest of the estate among his other children.[76] However, in 1466, probably due to a family dispute, Chmiel persuaded his son Martin to testify before the court that he had already received the share of the family estate due to him after his mother or father's death. The son was made to swear that he thus had no further rights to his father's estate and would not question the choice of those acting as guardians for his stepmother and stepsiblings after Chmiel's death.[77] A father's second marriage complicated the inheritance rights of children born of the first marriage. Disputes that arose with stepchildren could be risky for the second wife of the testator. The safest solution was to make a will and give children their due parts of the estate while the father was still alive. The situation of minor stepchildren dependent on their stepfather was more complicated. Before going on a pilgrimage in 1450, a Margaret made a mutual bequest to her husband Nicholas Pirich, ensuring that "after her death, he would guard and look after her children and his stepchildren until they came of age [*ad annos pubertatis*]."[78]

However, relations between stepparents and stepchildren were not always problematic. Many different factors influenced the lives of Krakow burghers and, understandably, relations within families varied – it would be impossible to define a single model of family relations. Often, testators who did not have heirs of their own welcomed stepchildren into their family. In his 1435 will, Jost the Bowyer left his wife the house he owned in exchange for her dowry. With the consent of his brother Paul (who had greater rights to his inheritance), Jost also left his tools and workshop (*werggeczew*) to his stepson Hanczel.[79] Another example is provided by the will of the affluent burgher Thob Johan, who bequeathed 400 florins to both his son John (*Hanzel, Hensil*) and his

---

76   SCAB. 8, fol. 204.
77   SCAB. 8, fol. 239–240.
78   SCAB. 7, fol. 80.
79   SCAB. 6, fol. 108.

stepson, a goldsmith, also named John (*Hannus goltsmid*), who also inherited his stepfather's market stall. Both the son and stepson were also given the right of presentation (*ius praesentandi*) to an altar erected by Thob Johan at St. Mary's Basilica.[80] The affluent butcher Peter Crencz, in turn, wrote down that he conducted business with his stepson Matthias, and had an investment of 70 grivna in goods they had purchased together.[81]

Children came of age (*anni discretionis*) when they reached biological maturity, meaning they could have children of their own, and were thus ready to marry and start their own family. A system functioned during the Middle Ages that drew on ancient philosophy and medicine, in which human life was divided into seven-year stages, beginning with infancy (*infantia*), which lasted until the age of seven, followed by childhood (*pueritia*), which continued to the age of fourteen, puberty (*pubertas*), which ended when one reached the age of twenty-one, maturity (*iuventus*) and finally old age (*senectus*).[82] Under Polish land law (as well as ecclesiastical law) boys came of age (*anni discretionis*) at 12, 13, 14 or 15, depending on the region and the time at which the legal provision was introduced, while girls usually came of age at 12.[83] In accordance with the Statutes of Casimir the Great, which regulated the law in Małopolska, both boys and girls were deemed to be of age when they turned 12.[84] In 1423, Władisław Jagiełło stated in the Statute of Warta that boys came of age at 15, while girls did so at 12.[85] It was not until the early sixteenth century that statutes in the Krakow region began to state that children could assume control of their property when they turned 20.[86]

---

80   LT, fol. 7–8.

81   LT, fol. 90.

82   Dorota Żołądź-Strzelczyk, *Dziecko w dawnej Polsce* (Poznan: Wydawnictwo Poznańskie 2006), 16.

83   Małgorzata Delimata, *Dziecko w Polsce średniowiecznej* (Poznan: Wydawn. Poznańskie, 2004), 166–167.

84   "Similiter infantibus ad duodecim annos educatis, si tempore infanciae per quemvispiam iniuria fuerit illata violenciam agitare, pro qua agree non valebat propter defectum etatis, contra ipsos inpedientes seu iniuriantes"; *Statuty Kazimierza Wielkiego*, no. 74.

85   "[...] et quamvis eisdem super etate sit provisum, videlicet maribus ad quintumdecimum et femellis ad duodecimum annos inclusive, quod infra hoc tempus non teneantur respondere"; *Statuta Terrestria in Conventionibus Cracoviensi et Wartensi laudata*, ed. Bolesław Ulanowski, Krakow 1921 (Archiwum Komisji Prawniczej, 4), 457; Dorota Żołądź-Strzelczyk, *Dziecko*, 22; Małgorzata Delimata, *Dziecko*, 167.

86   "If someone who sells or pledges inheritable property to another dies, the sons of the deceased are to receive the inherited property. And if they are not of legal age, they should not be given it until they reach it. Thus, under common law the guardians should give

THE BURGHER FAMILY

221

According to the *Sachsenspiegel*, children became adults at the age of 12,[87] while under Magdeburg Law boys reached legal age at 14, and girls did so at 13.[88] In accordance with the statutes of Krakow from 1342, boys could take control of their share of an inheritance at the age of 15, while girls could do so once they were married (the husband then assumed this responsibility).[89] In the Late Medieval period, the traditional boundary between childhood and maturity, which indicated the age at which one was considered sufficiently mature to undertake legal action, was set at 21 under municipal law.[90] However, in the seventeenth century Polish land law began to consider 24 as the 'age of prudence' (*anni puberum*).[91]

It appears that Krakow's burghers considered a person 15 years of age, the point that marked the beginning of adulthood under Krakow's municipal statutes, to be too young and immature to become an heir. Since the late fourteenth century some testators had explicitly stated in their wills that their children would only assume control of their inherited property at a much later age. The councillor Nicholas Strelicz decided his wife was to give their son his share of the estate when the boy turned 20. The daughter would be given

---

the property to the children when they are fifteen years old, and the children, having taken the inheritance, are to sue him; and yet according to the law, as is customary, the children shalt not sell or pledge the property until they are twenty years old, without the permission of well-benevolant relatives." *Wybór źródeł do historji ustroju i prawa sądowego Polski*, vol. 2: *Spisy prawa zwyczajowego koronnego*, ed. Stanisław Kutrzeba, Adam Vetulani (Krakow: Gebethner i Wolff, 1930), no. 2 (1501 r.); cf. Małgorzata Delimata, *Dziecko*, 167, 199.

87   Jan Łaski, *Commune Incliti Poloniae, Libri duo*, part 1, 189.
88   Andrzej Karpiński, *Kobieta w mieście*, 22–23.
89   KDMK, vol. 1, no. 25; vol. 2, no. 260, §1.
90   In John Łaski's codex, ambiguities stemming from the overlapping of different sources of law are apparent. In book one of *Iuris Maydemburgensis* such a note was made: "Quando puer est duodecim annorum, tunc potest eligere pro sua voluntate tutore. Et qui suus fuerit tutor, hic matri rationem facere habet et adolescent, quod cum bonis factum fuerit. Cum etiam puer fuerit duodecim annorum is mundiburdius, alias sui potens est factus, et potest in eo, iudicium perpetrari, et etiam bona sua a se sive tutore alienare. Sed innatam hereditatem, et proprium debet dare cum consensus heredum. Etiam iste puer de iure ad respondensionem valeat coartari seu compelli"; Jan Łaski, *Commune Incliti Poloniae, Libri duo*, part. 1, 189; in the part containing the articles of the *Saxon Mirror* it was established that: "Vir bonum potest eligere tutorem si necessitas fuerit, et carere potest si voluerit. Ultra viginti et unum annum vor ad annos pubertatis pervenit [...]. Quando adolescens ad annos pubertatis pervenerint extunc sue uxoris tutor esse potest"; *ibidem*, part 2, 208; cf. Urszula Sowina, *Wdowy i sieroty*, 25; Andrzej Karpiński, *Kobieta w mieście*, 22–23.
91   Dorota Żołądź-Strzelczyk, *Dziecko*, 22.

her share of the estate when she married (of course only with the consent of her mother).[92] Strelicz thus precisely defined the moment of his children's 'coming of age' (*cum ad annos debite etatis*). At the turn of the fourteenth and fifteenth centuries, six other influential testators stated that their sons would inherit, and thus have control over, their share of the estate when they turned 24.[93] It is not certain which legal system recognized the age of 24 to be the age of adulthood and prudence, but, surprisingly, such a specific age is only quoted in wills written from 1390 to 1400. In later years, testators employed more generic terms. For example, the municipal notary Eustace uses the phrase 'when he reach his age' (*wenne her czen seynen iaren kompt*),[94] while John Beme in 1465 wrote 'when he will reach a mature age' (*ad matura pervenerit etatem*).[95]

Such a significant raising of the age at which a child in Krakow was considered an adult was probably a reflection of the culture of the urban elite and their professional activity. In such an environment, maturity and independence were associated less with the ability to procreate and obey the wishes of one's elders, as traditionally had been the case, and more on one's knowledge, experience, level of literacy, and capacity to engage in legal acts.

Raising the age at which property could be inherited also affected when people married. Most first marriages were characterized by a considerable age difference – the man was usually at least several years older than the woman. Considering the high rate of maternal mortality, this difference had to be even greater in subsequent marriages.[96] We also need to bear in mind that while women who chose to remain widows for the rest of their lives were treated with respect (for remaining faithful to their late husband), men were usually expected to remarry, since only married men were granted the status of burgher, and thereby received city privileges. Both this fact and social expectations gave

---

92   "[...] si femella, quousque cum voluntate matris maritata fuerit"; SCAB., no. 1645. In 1395 Nicholas Dambraw specified that a daughter reaches legal age when she gives birth to children: "dy mait nicht e, is sey denne, das se fruchte habe"; SCAB., no. 2210.

93   SCAB., no. 1267 (1390), 1676 (1393), 2042 (1394), 2193 (1395), 2210 (1395); CONS. 427, fol. 149 (1400).

94   LT, fol. 61–63 (1459).

95   LT, fol. 86–87.

96   "The law, demographic relations and matrimonial policies often resulted in large differences in age between newlyweds and in situations where minors and the elderly were wedded."; Andrzej Karpiński, *Kobieta w mieście*, 172; Stanisław Waszak, *Dzietność*, 351–352, 365; cf. Krzysztof Mikulski, "Kondycja demograficzna rodziny mieszczańskiej w Toruniu w XVI–XVII wieku (na przykładzie rodziny Neisserów)," in *Kobieta i rodzina w średniowieczu i na progu czasów nowożytnych*, ed. Zenon Hubert Nowak, Andrzej Radzimiński (Toruń: Uniwersytet Mikołaja Kopernika, 1998), 132–137.

THE BURGHER FAMILY

rise to a phenomenon that can be described as a 'rotation of marriages.' In the Middle Ages, men marrying two or three times was more the rule than the exception. Meanwhile, young women who married mature or older men often became widows at a relatively young age and later married younger partners. This was certainly true for young women from affluent burgher and patrician families, who achieved higher social status and increased their wealth through successive marriages to two or more rich burghers. For example, Margaret Czipserinne, a rich Krakow burgher woman who survived two husbands tried in her will to secure the future of her third husband, who was much younger and probably poorer than her.[97]

Once children (especially daughters) reached legal age, preparations began for them to start their own families: suitable candidates were selected, the betrothal was announced, and marriage followed. The first costs associated with moving children out of the house and into adulthood were connected with the wedding ceremony, though these expenses varied greatly depending on the social status of the family. For example, in her 1484 will, an olive oil merchant named Catherine divided her estate equally among her three children – two daughters, Catherine and Barbara, and a son, Bernard. She also stated that Bernard should be given an additional six grivna before the estate is divided, because Catherine and Barbara had already received expensive wedding clothes and accessories (*nupciis necessaria*).[98] The affluent councillor Paul Ber also wished to divide his property in a fair manner. In 1467, all his children were given equal shares of the estate, except for his oldest daughter Barbara, the wife of John Schotcz, who received 200 grivna less. Ber stated that Barbara had been given clothes, belts, spoons and furniture when she married. As a father, Ber had also paid for the wedding.[99] In the same fashion, in his 1469 will councillor Hippolyte Spilberger did not take into consideration the wedding expenses of his stepdaughter Margaret (*Maruscha*), because, as he stated, her husband Ulrich had worked with him, contributing to the family's wealth.[100]

---

97   LT, fol. 165–166.

98   LT, 140–141.

99   "[...] meyne eldiste tochter Barbara Hannus Schotczynne czwehundert gulden mynner nemen sal denne der andern kindern eyns om des willen das ich sy nu ausgericht habe mit cleydern mit gorteln mit leffeln eciam mit alem hausgerethe und mit der hochczeit das foste geldes kostit"; SCAB. 8, fol. 270–271; cf. Krystyna Pieradzka, *Paweł Ber*, in PSB, vol. 1 (Krakow: Wrocław–Warszawa–Krakow: Polska Akademia Nauk, Polska Akademia Umiejętności, 1935), 444.

100   "Item seiner tochtir Maruscha, Ulrichs hausfrawen gibt her ouch gleich teyl, und dy ausrichtungis irer hochczeit sal ir nicht geacht noch abegeslagen werdin, dorumme das

Wedding expenses included not only the costs of the wedding and reception, but also the costs of festive clothes and the things the bride-to-be was to receive in her dowry. For example, in his 1464 will, goldsmith Nicholas Brenner stated that he had manufactured expensive wedding accessories for Łazaria, the wife of Nicholas Slop, including a gilded belt, rings, a cross and a gilded and embroidered *agnus dei*.[101]

The scale and cost of wedding celebrations held by affluent burgher families in Krakow were comparable to those of the rich nobility in Małopolska. In the first version of his will from 1439, John Sweidniczer, one of the richest burghers in Krakow, left 800 grivna to each of his children. His two unmarried daughters were also given an additional 200 grivna for their wedding expenses (*czu ausrichtunge er hochczeit*).[102] Some city statutes tried to regulate 'burgher weddings' and limit the extravagance and lavishness of these events. In order to ensure that burghers knew their rightful place in society, the municipal authorities imposed artificial and rigid restrictions on such things as the number of invited guests, meals and musicians.[103] It seems, however, that wealthy Krakow burghers did not really obey these regulations. The wedding was a social and 'networking' event – one could strengthen the relationship between the families of the bride and the groom and provide for closer relations between the invited guests. A lavish wedding was a display of wealth, power and social status; for example, in 1543 a notary from Poznan wrote down a short epitaph in the municipal chronicle, praising the late physician John Wójcik. As the notary observed, John Wójcik was a renowned burgher, because "he was invited to every important wedding and ceremony in the city."[104] One can imagine that for Krakow burghers the wedding was also an important social event, allowing them to entertain and rub shoulders with prominent figures.

During or immediately after the wedding the husband confirmed the amount of the dower (which had been set at the time of the betrothal). In his 1431 will, Matthias Polak, a tanner at the 'Jewish Gate,' stated that his wife Margaret should receive 20 grivna of her dower, adding that he had promised

---

Ulrich obengenant ir man getrewlich an ym gefarin hat, und getrewlich seine guttir ym hat helfin direrbtin"; LT, fol. 95.

101 "Item so habe uch der frawen Lazarien Niclos Slopottynne of ire hochczeit und ouch der Thachter gemacht gortel of geslagen und forgolt und fingerleyn gemacht Creuczleyn und eyn Agnus dei vorgolt und heftleyn gemacht"; LT, fol. 83.

102 CONS. 428, fol. 402.

103 *Najstarszy zbiór przywilejów i wilkierzy miasta Krakowa*, vol. 2, ed. Stanisław Estreicher, Krakow 1936, no. 15.

104 *Kronika poznańskich pisarzy*, ed. Jacek Wiesiołowski (Poznan: Wydawnictwo Miejskie, 2004), 51.

THE BURGHER FAMILY   225

her this at their wedding. He also left her an additional 20 grivna as a dower in his will.[105]

Unlike in France or Southern Germany, testators in Krakow rarely appointed one of their sons as the primary heir to the entire estate.[106] Merchants usually tried to divide their estate in equal parts among all their children. Only childless testators appointed a main beneficiary, usually one of their relatives, who would inherit their real estate property. A will made in 1462 by Jarosław Szarlej from his prison cell while awaiting execution, is interesting in this respect.[107] This influential member of the Krakow city council had a number of children from two marriages. He refers in his will to four children from his second marriage, who were to receive 150 florins each before the rest of the estate was divided in equal parts among all his children. Szarlej explained that these children were given preferential treatment because the children from his first marriage had already received shares of the estate when they started their own families.[108] Szarlej's will is an interesting example because the testator made it in exceptional circumstances – while awaiting his execution. In it he displays particular favour for his youngest son, bequeathing him a cutlass decorated with silver and a gold ring "to remember him by."[109] These special gifts[110] appear to have signalled the symbolic appointment of a successor and heir to the family business. This seems even more probable in view of the fact that Szarlej's two other sons were probably destined for the priesthood.[111] Interestingly, in his 1459 will the wealthy municipal notary Eustace pays particular attention to a signet ring (*daumen ring*) for the thumb, while listing in detail all the property his only son, also named Eustace, was

---

105   There is no mention of a bequest of the dowry at the time of the marriage of Matthias Polak and Margaret in bench court or council books. This may indicate both that a special book for dowry bequests, which could have been the first Krakowbook of wills, *Liber testamentorum et Dotaliciorum*, was lost, and that the marriage contract was merely a verbal agreement affirmed by witnesses, which was not subsequently certified before the municipal council; cf. CONS. 428, fol. 290.

106   Brigitte Klosterberg, *Zur Ehre Gottes und zum Wohl der Familie*, 216–217.

107   Marcin Starzyński, *Krakowska rada*, 89–96.

108   "[...] iczunt dirczogin habe und ouch gehantlanget mit hulfe"; LT, fol. 73–74.

109   LT, fol. 74.

110   A number of such signet rings have survived to the present day, e.g. a ring with initials, probably belonging to a cloth merchant from Bristol, England was found in 2008 in the vicinity of that city; http://medievalnews.blogspot.com/2009/09/ring-belonging-to-15th-century-mayor-of.html (5 November 2019). The term *thumb ring* is sometimes still used for a signet ring; LT, fol. 61.

111   "Item den andern czween sonen gebe ich meyne gutte cleider also wenne sy prister warden und dorczu man sal en lossen kelliche machen"; LT, fol. 74.

to inherit. Thus, while Krakow merchants usually divided their estate in equal parts among all their children, they also often symbolically appointed one of their sons as the head of the family business.

The custom of designating one primary heir is even more apparent in the wills of Krakovian craftsmen, who made them to bequeath not only their movables and real estate, but also their workshop and the tools of their trade. If the testator had one or more sons, one generally inherited his tools, though they were sometimes divided evenly between two sons, as seen in the wills of the goldsmith Matthias Brenner[112] and the blacksmith Martin Pasternak.[113] However, if the testator was childless, his workshop was usually inherited by one of his closest relatives. The cooper Nicholas Blumental left *alle werggeczew das czu dem hantwerg gehort* to his nephew Matthias,[114] the goldsmith John Polski left his workshop to his nephew Matysko,[115] and the goldsmith Stanisław and goldsmith apprentice Johnny left their businesses to unnamed male relatives.[116] If the testator decided that no relative was worthy of inheriting his workshop, he would sometimes leave it to a member of his wife's family. Nicholas Schobelga left his workshop to his son-in-law Michael;[117] the archer Henczil left his to his brother-in-law;[118] and the aforementioned Jost the Bowyer left his to his stepson.[119] Some testators left their workshops to their wives and daughters, who were to continue running the family business. For example, the belt maker Nicholas Goldener left all his tools to his wife,[120] as did Nicholas Baum, whose wife Barbara inherited *allis werggeczew*. Baum observed in his will that he and Barbara had worked together in his workshop (*das czu unseren hantwerg dynet*).[121] The wills of other craftsmen also imply that wives often worked in workshops alongside their husbands. For example, in his 1458 will, shoemaker John Panzira left his workshop to his wife, allowing her to earn a living as a shoemaker (*uti artem sutoriam*).[122] Similarly, in his 1458 will, shoemaker

---

112 LT, fol. 115 (1476).
113 LT, fol. 55 (1458).
114 LT, fol. 10 (1439).
115 LT, fol. 32 (1453).
116 LT, fol. 88 (1466), 82 (1464).
117 LT, fol. 51 (1458).
118 LT, fol. 29 (1453).
119 SCAB. 6, fol. 108 (1435).
120 LT, fol. 68 (1460).
121 SCAB. 8, fol. 394 (1470).
122 LT, fol. 50.

THE BURGHER FAMILY

Nicholas Mewsil left his workshop and all his tools (*schubang mit allen gerethe*) to his daughter Justine.[123]

Some Krakow testators would discipline their defiant children by threatening to disinherit them. When John Michilwicz married his second wife Catherine in 1395, he explained in detail what part of the estate would be inherited by his daughter Margaret from his first marriage, and what part of the estate would be inherited by Catherine and the children born of his second marriage. In order to settle any potential legal issues and ensure the well-being of all his children, Michilwicz appointed four testamentary guardians (*tutores*). They were to look after the family, but they were also given the right to disinherit Michilwicz's disobedient children.[124] In addition to numerous goods, councillor Franczko Neorze[125] and the affluent pharmacist Paul Tanneman also gave their wives the right to disinherit disobedient children after their death.[126] In practice, such instructions made the widows the family patriarchs. It was they who would decide the fate of their children, either single-handedly or with the help of the appointed testamentary guardians. For example, in her 1441 will, Dorothy Stelmecherinne stated that her daughter would be disinherited if she did not follow her instructions regarding the house. Her share of the estate would be given in equal parts to her brother (Dorothy's son) and in opera pietatis.[127] However, the only Krakow testator known to disinherit his children and relatives was the affluent spice merchant Nicholas Barszcz. In 1449, he testified before the municipal council that he had earned everything through his own hard work (*maximis laboribus aquisita*) and thus decided to disinherit his vagabond (*vagabunda*) daughter and all his relatives.[128]

---

123 LT, fol. 54.

124 "[...] ap der eyns adir me desen nochseschreben vormunden nicht gehorsam wurde seyn, das dy selbin Vormunden irkenten, das meyn guth an em nicht bestat were, so sullen se volle macht haben deme vngehorsamen kinde seyn gut czu entwenden vnde das teil wenden an dy werk der barmherczigkeit noch willin der vormunden"; cf. SCAB., no. 2070.

125 "Item obir das allis, ap meyn son seyner muter nicht fulgen welde, adir welde ir wedirdris tun, so sal her gancz ausgeslossen seyn von alle meym gute czu ewigen tagen"; SCAB. 6, fol. 81 (1434).

126 "Item ap sich der kinder irkeyns wider dy vormunde adir wider dy muter seczen welde, dasselbe kind sal enperen seyns teilis czu ewigen tagen, und dy andern kinder mit der muter sullen desselben kindis teil nemen in dy gemeyne. Ouch gebe ich meyner hawsfrawen folle macht obir meyne kinder und obir allis gut, daz sy dobey tun und lossen mag, mit der vormunde rat und ane dy vormunde sal sy nichtis tuen"; SCAB. 6, fol. 113 (1435).

127 SCAB. 6, fol. 225.

128 LT, fol. 13.

Instructions regarding the division of the estate in the event of the death of one of the children also varied greatly. In his 1497 will, George Lange stated that he wanted to "avoid disputes between his wife and children,"[129] and explained in detail who was to inherit the respective shares of the estate. Lange pointed out that in the event of the death of any of his children who were still minors, their share of the estate would be inherited by the child's mother (*so irkeyn kint storbe so sal sulchs kindis teyl als recht ist komen an dy muttir*). However, if she remarried, then the share of the estate belonging to the late child would be divided equally among her and the remaining children. We find similar dispositions in other wills. Indeed, under municipal law, in the event of the death of a minor, their share of the estate would be inherited by the mother. In turn, in the event of the death of the mother, her share of the estate would be inherited by her children alone.[130] Since child mortality was high, the widow could in fact inherit a majority of the late husband's estate. We know that some husbands tried to avoid such a situation by formulating new inheritance rights in the event of the death of a child. For example, Nicholas Czeginkop, in his 1413 will, stated that in the event of the death of one of his children, their share of the estate would be divided in half. The wife would be given one share and the other half would be donated to opera pietatis.[131] Some husbands included such provisions in separate contracts, as exemplified by an agreement made between the councillor Martin Chmiel, his second wife Ursula, and his son (also named Martin) from his first marriage (Ursula's stepson). The son agreed to honour his father's will, while Ursula agreed that in the event of the death of one of her children, their share of the estate would be divided equally between her, her children and her stepson Martin, even though she had the right to inherit the entire estate belonging to her late child.[132] Some testators decided to divide the part of the estate which belonged to the late child into three parts. For example, Jacob Teudirneudir decided that it was to be divided in equal parts among his wife, his relatives and the Church.[133] Similarly, in 1395, alderman John Dobschicz divided his estate among his relatives, a hospital and the members of the municipal council, who were to donate it to an *opera pietatis* of their choice.[134] It is very probable that some testators were acting on the

---

129   "[...] das noch seinen tode czwischen seynir hawsfrawen und seynen kinder nichtis czwetracht irstunde"; LT, fol. 155.

130   "[...] pars ipsius domine aut pueri defuncti ad ipsam dominam et ad reliquos pueros equaliter dividenda devolvatur"; SCAB., no. 1913 (1394).

131   SCAB. 4, fol. 104–105.

132   SCAB. 8, fol. 240 (1465).

133   That is, 1/3 of the property is transferred to religious foundations to support the Church; cf. SCAB., no. 2042 (1394).

134   SCAB., no. 2093.

THE BURGHER FAMILY

advice of clergymen, who actively encouraged people to donate one-third of their estate to the Church.[135]

5 Grandchildren

Some testators also made bequests to the third generation – their grandchildren. In fact, grandchildren were sometimes treated more favourably than their parents, who had already received their share of the estate when they reached legal age and married. For example, Catherine, the widow of councillor Nicholas Plesner, left 100 grivna to the three sons of her daughter Kasia and 20 grivna to the son of her other daughter Anna, while her remaining money was bequeathed to opera pietatis.[136] Similarly, mine administrator and councillor Gotfrid Fattinante of Genoa left some parts of his estate to his grandson; other family members did not inherit anything.[137] In 1488, Margaret Szolwiczinne made a bequest to her only daughter, but she also left one of her houses in the city to her three grandchildren, because she wished to secure their future.[138] While grandchildren also ensured that the family line would be continued and that testators would be remembered, as minors they were also vulnerable and required special care. While bequests made to one's grandchildren were essentially made to one's children, most wills clearly stated that the grandchildren's property could only be sold or used as security for a loan once the grandchildren reached legal age.

6 Siblings, Nieces and Nephews

In most wills, relatives who were not members of the immediate family played a secondary role.[139] Many of them were referred to not by their name but only briefly and generally as 'relatives' (consanguinei) who were disinherited by means of a testamentary disposition.[140] Nevertheless, the testator's siblings and their children, and sometimes even 'cousins,' were quite often named as

---

135 See Chapter 1, Section 2, p. 36.
136 SCAB., no. 1755.
137 He donated the rest for pious deeds and to his servants and associates; cf. KDWac., vol. 2, no. 396, 182–185 (1393); Józef Garbacik, Gotfrid Fattinante, in PSB, vol. 6 (Krakow: Polska Akademia Nauk, Polska Akademia Umiejętności, 1948), 377–378.
138 LT, fol. 145.
139 Brigitte Klosterberg, Zur Ehre Gottes und zum Wohl der Familie, 226.
140 E.g. SCAB., no. 1816 (1393); SCAB. 5, fol. 158a (1428); SCAB. 6, fol. 55 (1433); CONS. 428, fol. 513 (1448); LT, fol. 146 (1488).

beneficiaries; in fact, testators made willingly the bequests to their nephews and nieces. This was especially true of childless testators, for whom nephews and nieces served in their wills as 'substitute' heirs. In 1393, Stanisław Mochaw left his entire estate to his nephew Hannos vom Salcze. He designated him as his primary heir, and at the same time disinherited all his other relatives.[141] Some childless testators left different sums of money to their various siblings, nieces and nephews.[142] For example, in 1450, the childless coat maker (*mentler*) Nicholas made bequests to his wife (who received her dower) and for opera pietatis. He also made bequests to his niece Katrzyna (who lived with him and his wife) and his nephew (who lived in a monastery in Tyniec). The majority of his estate, however, was left to his siblings, John Walter from Łańcut (*Lanczhuth*), Margaret from Pilzno and Dorothy from Biecz.[143] Siblings were also often treated as 'substitute' heirs. For example, in his 1475 will, the goldsmith (*goltsmid*) Nicholas left ten florins to each of his two brothers and his nephew (who lived with him), but only in the event of the death of his own children.[144] In some cases, more affluent testators helped the children of their poorer siblings by allowing them to live with them and teaching them their trade. As the above examples demonstrate, some childless testators ultimately decided that their siblings, nieces, or nephews should inherit their workshops or market stalls.

7   Other Relatives

Other relatives were rarely named in wills – they usually constituted a threat to a childless testator or his spouse, because they had the right to a share of the estate and to question bequests made by a childless testator. For this reason, Margaret Prewszinne testified before the municipal council that she had obtained all her property through her own hard work or from her husband, as a dower, and had not inherited anything from her relatives.[145] Similarly, in 1491, Barbara, daughter of the late Michael Unger, testified that she had no

---

141   SCAB., no. 1654.

142   SCAB., no. 1676, 1693, 1816, 2093, 2210.

143   SCAB. 7, fol. 81.

144   SCAB. 8, fol. 579.

145   "[...] gutter dy yr got gegeben hat, und nicht von yren frunden anyrstem met noch angekomen, sundir swerlichen dyarbeytet hat und von yrem elichen manne gemorgengobet synt"; LT, fol. 88 (1466).

THE BURGHER FAMILY 231

living relatives who could share in the estate, and thus made Christ her only heir.[146] Most testators used a ready-made formula to disinherit relatives who were not explicitly named in the will. In Latin it read *omnibus aliis amicis suis et consanguineis omni exclusis a percipcionem dictorum bonorum suorum*,[147] and in German *of das testament slisse ich aws alle meyne frunde und nesten*.[148] However, not all testators disinherited relatives who were not next-of-kin, leaving them shares of the estate either to avoid disputes or to honour the family bond. Thanks to the institution of the will, the testator was free to dispose of his estate as he wished. Jacob Teudirneudir and John Dobschicz both decided that in the event of the death of their children, their relatives were to inherit one-third of their estate.[149] Stanisław Mochaw left his relatives no real estate, but he recognized their rights to the traditional hergewet.[150] In 1461, Simon, a needle maker (*noldener*), made a bequest of 20 florins to his relatives "who will come within a year and a day and are indeed next-of-kin."[151] If no relatives came forward, the money was to be donated to St. Mary's Basilica in Krakow. Similarly, in his 1466 will, butcher Peter Krencz left his clothes, personal belongings and armour to his appointed testamentary guardians. They were to either give them to his relatives or, should no relatives come forward, donate them to opera pietatis.[152] Since relatives had the right to the testator's personal belongings (the hergewet) and real estate (if there were no documents certifying its purchase), they sometimes engaged in long-running disputes with the widow. Most testators thus tried to protect their widows by granting them the right to continue living in the family house.[153] Municipal books occasionally inform us that the executors of the will were allowed to act independently, i.e. they did not have to follow the will to the letter. For example, two members of the city council, John Kletner and Jacob Wilkowski, the executors of Dorothy Sweszniczka's will, helped her relative, the shoemaker Bieniak from Wolbrom (*de Wolfram*), even though he was not mentioned in the will. They

---

146 "Item abquociens monita et requisita si amicos sangwine iunctos haberes quod diceret dixit se nullum habere amicum neque consangwineum ideo Christum fecit heredem"; LT, fol. 150.

147 CONS. 428, fol. 198 (1423).

148 SCAB. 6, fol. 181 (1439).

149 SCAB., no. 2042 (1394), 2093 (1395).

150 SCAB., no. 1654 (1393).

151 SCAB. 8, fol. 76.

152 LT, fol. 90.

153 SCAB., no. 1774 (1393), 1894 (1394), 2069 (1395).

232   CHAPTER 3

did so "because he was poor. The man was kindly given three grivna and gave his assurance he would not ask for anything else."[154]

8   Servants and Co-workers

People who lived under the same roof or worked together day-to day in the same workshop or market stall understandably developed strong attachments based on a sense of loyalty and mutual affection. Male and female testators often made bequests to their female servants, male servants, cooks, notaries, teachers and physicians. The amounts and types of goods bequeathed varied. Some testators were more affluent than others, but the emotional bonds that grew between them and their servants differed, depending in part on the latter's tenure and the nature of their work. Only rich burghers could afford to employ numerous servants on a daily basis, or to make bequests to their servants, often at the expense of their closest relatives. Such bequests are first seen in the wills of the Krakow mine administrator Paszko in 1358, councillor Gotfrid Fattinante of Genoa in 1393, and Dorothy Banarika, widow of the alderman and stall-holder Martin, in 1394. It is most likely that none of them had children; thus, they rewarded their servants, who were not their blood relatives. Paszko left 50 grivna to his servant Nicholas, which constituted one third of all the money he bequeathed.[155] In the second of her three surviving wills, Dorothy Banarika gave her two servants, Catherine and Anna, respectively four and two grivna.[156] The third testator, Gotfrid Fattinante of Genoa, demonstrated the keenest interest in his workers. He named his chaplain and notary (in Latin *capellano et notario suo*) Peter prebendary of the altar he established at St. Mary's Basilica. Meanwhile, his physician John was made prebendary of the other altar at All Saints Church (*domino Iohanni presbytero domus sue et medico assignauit*). A separate bequest was made to his servant and household member Niklos, who inherited all of Fattinante's household movables,

---

154   "Item Byenak de Wolfram sutor qui se dicit et dixit amicum et propinquum prefate Dorothee non ex alicuis Iuris debito sed ex mera gratia et benivolencia dominorum intuita pauperitate eis receptis a nobis tribus marcis de prefato testamento recognovit, se iam amplius nullus habere ad illud abernunciat que eidem proximitati, et omni iuri quod habere posset in ewum"; LT, 120–121 (1476).

155   NKiRMK, no. 1693.

156   This bequest was one of many pious bequests made to the Church and the poor; cf SCAB., no. 1893.

THE BURGHER FAMILY

including clothes, furs, coats, tables, chests, sheets and the like.[157] Given how rich Fattinante was, this must have been a very generous bequest. Other servants and workers also received gifts. Rudillon Reger and Nicholas Rothe, who had lost their eyesight working as miners in one of Fattinante's mines, were given 100 grivna. Four of Fattinante's servant-miners injured in the mine in Bochnia were sent to a hospital in this town. The remaining members of his household were given 100 grivna (they were to divide the money among themselves).[158]

Fifteenth-century testators sometimes emphasized that the servants to whom they had made bequests had worked for them for many years, which in practice meant that they were treated like family members. For example, in her 1493 will, Helena, wife of Nicholas Hefter, left her black coat and dress to her servant, Catherine, because she had served her faithfully for many years.[159] Similarly, the municipal notary John Stolle ordered that after his death, in addition to an inheritance of 10 grivna, his faithful servant Margaret was to be given a good new coat.[160] In 1410, Anna, widow of Nicolas Bothener, made a generous bequest of ten grivna as an annuity to her long-time "servant and notary" (*Irem dyner und camirschreiber*) Nicholas Jenyla.[161]

Servants were sometimes more akin to co-workers and factors, and therefore held in very high regard. For example, Burghard, a servant of John Sweidniczer, was referred to in Sweidniczer's will as servant (*dyner*), while in fact he was his master's 'right hand,' buying and selling lead,[162] copper, and cloth worth hundreds of florins in Košice and Levoca. In addition, Burghard was named as an executor of Sweidniczer's will and a guardian of his children, for which, as well as for his faithful service, he received 200 florins.[163] This was a very gener-

---

157 "Preterea res omnes suas videlicet vestes, pelles, pellicia, togas, mensas, cistas, lectisternia ac omnia vniuersaliter et singula, quibuscumque vocitentur nominibus, nullis penitus exceptis, in predicta domo, quam inhabitat, existentes ac existencia, Nicloso cubiculario suo et familiari de presenti earundem cedens possessionem et in ipsum Niclonem transferens, cum omnimoda faciendi et dimittendi facultate legauit"; KDWac., vol. 2, no. 396, 182–185 (1393).

158 "[...] et tercium centum marcas prouidis Rudgloni Reger et Nicolao Rothe lumine oculorum in suo seruicio proch dolor orbato, familiaribus suis diuturnis, quartum centum marcarum inter ceteram suam domus sue familiam secundum maius et minus distribuendum contulit atque dedit"; *ibidem*.

159 "Item yren swarczen mantil und yre kursnen hat sy befolen zu geben Katherine yrer dynerynne wen sy hat ir getrewlich file ior gedynet"; LT, fol. 153.

160 CONS. 429, fol. 27–28.

161 CONS. 427, fol. 365–366.

162 Danuta Molenda, *Polski ołów na rynkach Europy Środkowej*, 104–106.

163 LT, fol. 39–45 (1457).

ous bequest considering that Sweidniczer's two other servants, the notary Paul and teacher Kacper, were given only three and four grivna respectively. Two members of the city council, John Pitczen and John Kletner, also made generous bequests to their servants. In 1457, John Pitczen left his notary (named as 'my bachelor,' in Latin *meinem baccalario*) John his valuable clothes (a gown lined with marten fur, a black coat, and a black dress lined with fur) and, additionally, four grivna for his faithful service. In 1460, John Kletner, in turn, gave his servant (*meynem dyner*) John Newmargten 300 florins "in outstanding payment" (*vor seyn vordint lon*). The servant additionally received 300 florins for his faithful service (*getreulich gedinet und gehantlagent hot*) and was forgiven a debt of 83 florins.[164] John Kletner also left 100 florins to his servant (*meynem knechte*) Staszek as payment and remuneration for his faithful service during Kletner's illness.

In exceptional cases, servants were named by the testator as the main heir. For example, in one version of the will of the municipal notary John Stolle, his housekeeper (*schafferinne*) was given a house at Hospital Street (she could stay in it as long as she lived) and all his movables, including sheets, books and other household items.[165] Similarly, in 1450, before going on a pilgrimage, Dorothy Specfleischinne bequeathed her real estate property, movables and *paraphernalia* to her former servant Stanisław, a painter (*pictor*).[166]

The trust some testators placed in their servants was in some cases apparently reciprocated. This is seen, for example, in a 1439 bequest by John, a long-time servant (*famulus senex*) of Anna Willuschinne, who asked her to donate the wages he was due to the opera pietatis of her choice, because she most likely knew better than he how the money could be put to good use.[167]

Some bequests made to servants may have represented wages due to them, especially when the bequeathed sums were no higher than a few grivna.[168] In most cases, however, such bequests were a testament to a paternalistic relation to the servant that differed from other employer-employee relations. Those employing servants were not only supposed to give them orders, but also to take care of 'their people.' This is most evident in the practice of bequeathing to servants new or used items of clothing. Such gifts were material and practical,

---

164   LT, fol. 67.

165   SCAB. 6, fol. 186 (1439).

166   SCAB. 7, fol. 89.

167   SCAB. 6, fol. 190.

168   This is suggested by, among other things, the execution of the will of Szymek from Jewish Street. The son of the deceased paid five grivna to a Barbara's maid, despite the fact that such a provision was not included in the will; SCAB. 8, fol. 213 (1465).

THE BURGHER FAMILY   235

but also thoughtful, reminding the servant that their former employer was looking after them. For example, Margaret, widow of the miller Sigismund, left her servant Claire two dresses, two coats and two bed sheets.[169] In 1464, Łazaria, the wife of Nicholas Slop, left her servants Catherine and Barbara one dress and one coat each.[170] In 1436, councillor Wilhelm Willand bequeathed to his servant Matthias 24 grivna and his old clothes.[171] Bequests made to servants were often considered charity donations or opera pietatis. At the same time, they also demonstrated that employers cared and felt responsible for their faithful servants and other workers, who very often had lived in their house for years. Some childless testators considered their servants members of the family. This may have been true for Gotfrid Fattinante of Genoa, John Stolle and Dorothy Specfleischinne. Likewise, testators who had children also often treated their servants and workers as valuable additions to their businesses or workshops, or simply as members of the household who took care of the home, worked in the kitchen, and raised the children.

Occasionally, some testators included in their wills people who were neither their relatives nor servants; in such cases, however, they clearly stated that these people were important for them. Many of these beneficiaries were lay people, but it is difficult to determine the exact nature of the relationship between them and the testators. Perhaps some of them belonged to the testator's extended family, while others could have been neighbours or friends from a guild, fraternity or tavern.

9   The Image of the Burgher Family as Presented in Late-Medieval Wills

The wills shed light on many of the family relations in 14–15th c. Krakow. Undoubtedly, wills were 'tools' that were deliberately used to actively shape these relations by changing the traditional rules of inheriting property, including and excluding chosen relatives and friends from heirs, and planning the future of the loved ones. The sum of these individual practices conditioned by

---

169 "Item czwene recke eynen vom bloen gewande den andirn von harris und czwene mentil eynen von harris der andir eyn regen mantil unde czwe par leylach bescheide ich Clare meyner dynerynne"; LT, fol. 79 (1463).

170 "Item gab Katherine irr dinstmayt iren bloen rokund iren swarczen harris mantil [...] Barbare der andern mugen dinstmayt gebit sy iren newenfarben harris rok und eyn alden swarczen mantil den sy iczund hat"; LT, fol. 87.

171 "[...] jopen, hozen swarczen rok der mit fuchsen gefutirt ist"; CONS. 428, fol. 369.

236   CHAPTER 3

very specific relations within different bourgeois families reveals some general trends in the late medieval transformation of this basic social unit. Therefore, wills demonstrate that the institution of family is a changeable concept depending not only on cultural scripts but also on the living conditions, life needs and social position of individuals.

The majority of bequests either took the form of mutual donations or terse instructions meant to secure the well-being of the testator's spouse and children.[172] However, some testators also named in their wills numerous siblings, cousins, grandchildren, business partners, writers, servants and cooks. Even if we take into account the fact that wills were for the most part highly standardized official documents, we can see that they document the existence of two different family models in late-medieval Krakow. On the one hand, we have a classic urban phenomenon, namely the craftsman's small nuclear family. On the other hand, we have evidence of the emergence during this period among members of the patriciate of the model of a large or extended family, which also included servants. As mentioned above, quantitative research does not provide an accurate picture of how popular these two models were due to the limited number and nature of available sources. However, the analysed wills demonstrate that affluent burghers usually developed more complex family relations than moderately rich representatives of the urban municipality. For example, in his 1465 will, councillor John Beme made bequests not only to the Church and the poor, but also to, among others, his wife Ursula, sister Miotka, sister Agnes, nephew Peter from Gdańsk, the poor relatives of his wife Ursula, master John and his sister Margaret, the goldsmith (*aurifabrisse*) Catherine, his nephew Nicholas, his servant's daughter Anna, another servant called Anna, the cook Margaret, the grandchildren born in the marriage between his daughter Anna and Stanisław Graser, and his grandchildren born in the marriage between his daughter Ursula and the future councillor John Turzon.[173] Such a large extended family was not an exception among the richest members of the Krakow patriciate. Councillors John Sweidniczer (in 1452),[174] Konrad Lang (in 1462),[175] and John Czenmark (in 1436)[176] also made bequests to their relatives, in-laws, and friends. It seems that the differences between an affluent patrician family and other members of the urban municipality had to do with social status, the nature of their employment, family history and lifestyle. The extended burgher family was a means for acquiring social and financial

---

172   See introduction, section 1, p. 6.
173   LT, fol. 86–87.
174   LT, fol. 39–45.
175   LT, fol. 72.
176   CONS. 428, fol. 354.

THE BURGHER FAMILY

prominence. Arranged marriages to the daughters and widows of members of the patriciate allowed men to climb the social ladder. Large trading companies were usually family owned and operated – members of Krakow's merchant families therefore tended to live and work in major urban trading hubs somewhere in the vicinity of Krakow, thereby creating branches or trading posts for the family business.[177] Many burghers saw their relatives as 'social capital' that would help them accumulate economic capital.

However, Krakovian artisans and small traders (often first-generation or second-generation immigrants) thought in different terms. Since their personal commitment and skills determined their success, they cared mainly about their nuclear family, about the well-being of their children and spouse, and saw their distant relatives, who often lived in other towns, as a threat. Most wills and 'bequests made in the event of death' demonstrate that testators tried first and foremost to secure the future of their nuclear family, i.e. their spouse, children, and sometimes siblings. In any case, the very concept of the family no longer adhered to the somewhat archaic provisions of municipal law based on the Sachsenspiegel or Magdeburg Law. In the late-medieval city, the burgher family was usually a nuclear family – the strongest family bonds existed between the spouses, children and sometimes siblings. Distant relatives were considered a threat to the well-being of the testator's nuclear family because they were entitled to receive inheritance by default, which often provided the motivation for the testator to make a will in the first place, in order to protect their nuclear family. In both the cases of the artisans and the burghers, however, and depending on individual needs, testators made wills in order to control and protect their estate, and thus their families.

Wills both exemplified and brought about changes in the bonds that existed between members of the late-medieval burgher family. As has been demonstrated, in the late Middle Ages, social bonds, which were often contractual but ultimately derived their strength from the emotional commitment of the parties involved, became more important than kinship.[178] With the support and blessing of the Church, the institution of marriage was also considerably strengthened. Living under the same roof created strong relationships between people – the ancient concept of the *familia*, which included workers, servants and other members of the same household, was reformulated in keeping with that notion.

---

177 For example, the younger brother of Krakow councillor John Sweidniczer moved to Toruń, where Sweidniczer already owned real estate and maintained business relations. John's older son Jorge also moved there; cf. LT, fol. 39–45.

178 Jack Goody, *The Development*, 132.

CHAPTER 4

The Burgher Religiosity

Bequests of last will reflected the nature of urban religiosity. The concepts of Purgatory and the judgment of the soul provided the immediate impetus for the rise of the so-called canonical will, which allowed a person lying on their deathbed to meaningfully influence the duration of their soul's suffering in Purgatory, or whether they would be damned eternally for their sins. The will was the perfect means for testators to use their wealth to secure a place in heaven and guarantee themselves eternal life. Viewed from this perspective, late-medieval urban religiosity was strongly influenced by the institution of the will, seen as a tool for ensuring one's salvation. Works of charity in urban areas, the creation and running of hospitals, the building of churches and parish chapels, clergy supported by pious foundations and altarages, aid to the poor and the infirm – all of these were financed in large part by pious bequests made by burghers in their wills.

The will has long been a symbol of mortality and a means of preparing for one's death. As such, it allows us to analyse the nature and forms of urban piety. The issue of urban religiosity is an extremely complicated one, and wills shed light on merely one key aspect of this topic.[1] While wills contained private, individual dispositions to be carried out in the event of a person's death, in most cases, they drew upon a limited set of general conventions and forms of bequests made for opera pietatis. We might thus ask ourselves here whether it is necessary to look for originality, creativity and individuality in matters concerning religion, which derives its power from collective rituals, the doctrines of canon law, and long-standing, universally recognised customs. A follow-up question here would be: can such bequests tell us something about the testator and his or her social position, family history, personal experience and beliefs,

---

1   This seemingly straightforward term was defined well by Halina Manikowska: "The term "religiosity" is used by researchers commonly, but also quite loosely, interchangeably with others, such as forms of religious life, piety, forms of religious worship. It is used relatively precisely in socio-religious research, but this [definition] does not fully address the issues covered by this concept in historiography. It is understood as a set of religious practices characteristic of a given epoch and particular social groups, and above all, rituals, and, more rarely, internal attitudes, beliefs, knowledge, religious feelings, ideas related to spiritual reality – referred to, especially in the last forty years, as the concept of a religious mentality."; *eadem*, *Religijność miejska*, in *Ecclesia et civitas. Kościół i życie religijne w mieście średniowiecznym*, ed. Halina Manikowska, Hanna Zaremska (Warszawa: Instytut Historii PAN, 2002), 12.

© JAKUB WYSMUŁEK, 2021 | DOI:10.1163/9789004461444_006
This is an open access chapter distributed under the terms of the CC BY-NC-ND 4.0 license.

THE BURGHER RELIGIOSITY

239

even though they usually followed established conventions? In short, can we see the person behind the testamentary bequest?[2] Do the surviving wills of Krakow burghers tell us something about their real religious convictions, or are they just mindless reproductions of religious formulas propagated by the Church and the social elite? And finally, is the model of religiosity found in these wills truly representative of urban society or only that of a certain social group? We need to address these questions if we want to tackle the seemingly obvious question of whether wills can be used to evaluate the nature of urban religiosity in its various forms.[3]

In the late Middle Ages, piety had an important social dimension, reflected in both the rituals and devotional practices associated with the Church, which promoted a traditional conception of the nature and role of community and a mass model of religiosity.[4] Community events filled with religious symbolism provided a break from the routine of burghers' everyday religious practices. Engaging in weighty academic discussions,[5] expressing strong feelings during sermons by renowned itinerant preachers,[6] planning pilgrimages to Rome

---

2 Aron Gurevich, despite his best efforts, remained skeptical about the possibility of seeing traces of individualism in this era: *idem, The Origins of European Individualism* (Oxford: Blackwell, 1995).

3 Martin Nodl very rightly pointed out the different conditions under which the will operated and the role it played in the cities of Central and Eastern Europe compared with those of Western Europe, particularly in the Apennine Peninsula. "However, since this increase [in the number of wills–J.W.] involves a very unrepresentative and clearly a minority group of the urban population, it is very difficult to extend the conclusions of the analysis of the preserved wills to the entire urban population and to base on them conclusions concerning the piety and religious practices of the urban community in the fifteenth century."; *idem,* "Středověký testament jako abnormalita," in *Pozdně středověké testamenty v českých městech. Prameny, metodologie a formy využití. Sborník příspěvků z konference uspořádané 30. listopadu 2005 Archivem hlavního města Prahy a Historickým ústavem Akademie věd České republiky,* ed. Kateřina Jíšová, Eva Doležalová (Praha: Scriptorium, 2006), 158.

4 Jan Drabina, *Wierzenia, religie, wspólnoty wyznaniowe w średniowiecznej Polsce i na Litwie i ich koegzystencja* (Krakow: Nakł. Uniwersytetu Jagiellońskiego, 1994), 58–59.

5 For example, a stir brought about by the visit of Jerome of Prague, accused of heresy, to Kraków in 1413. During his stay in the city, he preached sermons 'causing considerable agitation among the Kraków clergy and burghers, although according to the Krakow bishop Wojciech Jastrzębiec, "common people in Poland are unable to understand the teachings of such a *great philosopher*."; Paweł Kras, *Husyci w piętnastowiecznej Polsce* (Lublin: Towarzystwo Naukowe Katolickiego Uniwersytetu Lubelskiego, 1998), 40–43.

6 John Kapistran's stay in Krakow from August 1453 to May 1454 was particularly significant. The impact of his sermons in the Krakow market was described in detail by Długosz; *Joannis Dlugosssii, Annales seu Cronicae incliti Regni Poloniae,* lib. XII, Cracoviae 2003, 171–172; cf. Jerzy Kłoczowski, *Wspólnoty zakonne w średniowiecznej Polsce* (Lublin: Wydawnictwo KUL, 2010), 261–265.

240   CHAPTER 4

during Jubilee years,[7] and participating in holidays, processions and church fairs[8] were all part of life shared with the larger community. It appears that the emergence in the Kingdom of Poland during the analysed period of new trends promoting a more personal, spiritual approach to religion, referred to in the West (especially in the Netherlands) as *devotio moderna*,[9] had little impact on this state of affairs, with their appeal being limited primarily to social elites. In his timeless book, *The Autumn of the Middle Ages*, Johan Huizinga painted a suggestive picture of the religious attitudes and 'emotional standards' (using Peter Sterns concept[10]) that in his opinion distinguished 'modern' believers from 'traditional' ones, observing that:

> [The] fifteenth century displays this strong religious emotion in a dual form. On the one side, it reveals itself in those vehement moments when an itinerant preacher periodically seizes a whole crowd with his words, igniting all that spiritual fuel like dry tinder. This is the spasmodic expression of that Christological emotion: passionate, intense, but highly transitory. The other aspect is shown by a few individuals who lead their sensitivity into a path of eternal quietude and normalize it into a new life form, that of introspectiveness. This is the pietistic circle of those who, fully conscious of being innovators, call themselves the Modern Devotees, that is contemporary people of piety.[11]

---

7   Halina Manikowska, *Jerozolima – Rzym – Compostela*, 6–8.

8   Aleksandra Witkowska, "Kształtowanie się tradycji pątniczych w średniowiecznym Krakowie," KH, vol. 86 (1979), 965–985.

9   "The general idea uniting all groups involved in the renewal of the spiritual life of the whole of *societatis christianae* was to return to the biblical (evangelical) and sacramental sources of faith in order to reduce the formality of the relationship between a person and God and to make it more individual and direct. This general aspiration consisted of a number of minor tendencies, mainly emphasizing the role of affection in one's spiritual life and its superiority over intellectual reflection (formulated mainly as part of the so-called *schola affectus*), emphasizing religious experience based on personal prayer and contemplation and promoting various forms of individual devotion. The increasing emotionality of the religious mentality of the late Middle Ages was particularly extreme in the phenomenon of dolorism, which is characteristic of mass piety, but also present in the devotion of elites, the origins of which can be found in the socio-economic and cultural circumstances of the fourteenth century"; Alicja Szulc, *Homo religiosus późnego średniowiecza. Bernardyński model religijności masowej* (Studia i Materiały – Uniwersytet im. Adama Mickiewicza w Poznaniu. Wydział Teologiczny, 100) (Poznan: Uniwersytet im. Adama Mickiewicza, 2007), 45.

10   Peter N. Stearns, Carol Zisowitz Stearns, "Emotionology. Clarifying the History of Emotions and Emotional Standards," *The American Historical Review* 90, no. 4 (1985), 813–830.

11   Johan Huizinga, *The Autumn of the Middle Ages*, trans. Rodney Payton, Ulrich Mammitzsch (Chicago: University of Chicago Press, 1996), 221.

THE BURGHER RELIGIOSITY

It seems that, outside of Dutch and northern German cities, this phenomenon did not become a formalized movement or widespread among townspeople. In Central and Eastern Europe, the only example of such an institutionalized new form of religious life, one modelled on the Dutch Congregation of Windesheim, was found in the Hanseatic city of Chełmno.[12]

In Krakow, new forms of worship and devotional practices were largely inspired by the University of Krakow,[13] and three new reformist religious communities: the Order of Canons Regular, a congregation of Czech provenance based at the parish church of Corpus Christi in Kazimierz (which was very popular among Krakow's burghers); the Order of Saint Paul the First Hermit, originally founded in Hungary and adhering both to ermetic and ascetic principles and the Rule of St. Augustine; and the Bernardines, whose first Polish monastery in Stradom (now a part of Krakow) was founded by Zbigniew Oleśnicki in the mid-fifteenth century.[14]

We can assume the religiosity of Krakow's burghers in the late Middle Ages was also shaped by the mosaic of other religious institutions that were founded in the city's environs during this period, and which embodied various religious beliefs and practices. Krakow was praised as a bustling religious centre by the bishop Stanisław Ciołek in his poem *Laus Cracoviae*,[15] and we can assume that the city's wealth of religious institutions was also reflected in the testamentary bequests made there. As part of a complex, multi-layered social reality, urban religiosity assumed different forms depending on the testator's social status and cultural capital, as well as the nature of a given form of religious expression. Therefore, the differences in religious practices reflected to a large extent differences in the social position of particular burghers.

---

12   In the years 1472–1539, a home of the Brethren of the Common Life was brought from Zwolle by the bishop of Chełmno, Wincenty Kiełbasa.; cf. Alicja Szulc, *Homo religiosus*, 37; Zenon Hubert Nowak, *Kultura umysłowa Prus Królewskich w czasach Kopernika* (Toruń: Państw. Wyd. Nauk., 1972), 24–25.

13   "Under the influence of the reformist views of Matthew of Krakow, a significant group of Krakow masters adopted the idea of the Prague version of *devotio moderna*, and expressed it in writings, disputes and sermons, understanding the new movement in the sphere of spirituality and religion as a kind of new theology. The leading representatives of this movement in Krakow circles weren Stanisław from Skalbmierz, Matthias from Łabiszyn, Benedict Hesse, John from Dąbrówka, and above all, the Cistercian (later Carthusian) Jacob from Paradyż, whose rich ascetic and mystical works bear clear signs of a new, deeper understanding of theology and spirituality, similar to the classical *devotio moderna*"; Alicja Szulc, *Homo religiosus*, 42.

14   Stanisław Bylina, "Religijność mieszkańców Europy Środkowo-Wschodniej w późnym średniowieczu," in *Cywilizacja europejska. Wykłady i eseje*, ed. Maciej Koźmiński (Warszawa: Wydaw. Inst. Hist. PAN, 2005), 108.

15   Stanisław Ciołek, *Pochwała Krakowa*, in *Najstarsza poezja polsko-łacińska (do połowy XVI wieku)*, ed. Marian Plezia (Wrocław: Ossolineum, 2005), 30–33.

242   CHAPTER 4

1   A Personal Relationship with God

1.1   *Clergy*

1.1.1   Confessors

The most intimate aspect of Catholic religiosity is one's personal relationship with God, the Virgin Mary and the saints. The sacrament of Holy Confession, the growing practice of Eucharistic adoration, and the awakening of a need for personal communion with the sacred, brought people closer to God and increased the intensity of their religious experiences. Because this relationship was generally a personal and intimate one, we do not have many testimonies that would allow us to assess the significance and scale of this phenomenon of personal communion. It also seems that this type of direct, intimate relationship with God, marked by intense and mystical experiences, was the preserve of a small number of affluent and pious burghers. The prevalence of this type of experience must have also been influenced by the rise in literacy, which more generally brought about transformational changes in people's thinking.[16]

Since the Fourth Council of the Laterans in 1215, in accordance with Church teachings (later confirmed in the synod's statutes), the Catholic Church has obliged all Christians to have their confessions heard at least once a year, during the Easter season.[17] The Church strongly emphasised the necessity of fulfilling this duty, seeing it as a important element of 'the cure of souls' (*cura animarum*) and a prerequisite for receiving Holy Communion. It tied this requirement to a call to heed the teachings of sermons, which were likened to the sowing of the fields, while the sacrament of confession was compared to the reaping of their fruits.[18] Both in the West and in Poland, simple, mnemonic

---

16   "[...] the construction and contemplation of the text constitutes a reflection on the religious life, an invitation not simply to consolidate but to elaborate [...] the construction of the text, which is in any case something other than the transcription of discourse, can lead to its contemplation, to the development of thoughts about thoughts, to a metaphysic that may require its own metalanguage"; Jack Goody, *The Logic of Writing and the Organisation of Society* (Cambridge: Cambridge University Press, 1986), 37–38.

17   "The time of this confession was not specified more precisely, but the imposition of one confession *per annum* in one canon, with the obligation of Communion at Easter meant it happened during Lent, and in principle shortly before receiving the Eucharist."; Izabela Skierska, *Obowiązek mszalny w średniowiecznej Polsce* (Warszawa: Wydawn. Instytutu Historii PAN, 2003), 240; cf. Stanisław Bylina, *Spowiedź jako instrument katechezy i nauki współżycia społecznego w Polsce późnego średniowiecza*, in *Społeczeństwo Polski średniowiecznej*, vol. 5, ed. Stefan.K. Kuczyński (Warszawa: Państw. Wydaw. Naukowe, 1992), 255–265.

18   "Per praedicationem enim seminatur, per confessionem vero colligitur fructus," Humbertus de Romanis, Liber de erudition praedicatorum; za: Krzysztof Bracha, *Nauczanie*

THE BURGHER RELIGIOSITY 243

instructions were given on how to prepare for Confession: "A simple, humble confession is to be pure and faithful, frequent and honest, prudent and voluntary, modest, whole, secret, tearful, imminent, strong and obedient."[19] This message was emphasised in many published sermons that both propagated the instructions of the Council's twenty-first canon (*Omnis utriusque sexus*) and advised believers to have their confessions heard as often as possible (though the question of how often was usually left to the individual, based on their personal needs).[20]

Disputes between parish clergy and mendicant orders about the right to administer the Sacrament of Penance demonstrate not only that Confession was a profitable undertaking, but also the significance of Confession as part of the pastoral care provided to parishioners.[21] Having analysed modern sources on the ritual of confession, Jean Delumeau observed:

> There is no doubt that the forgiveness expressed by God was a source of comfort and strength for the souls of those possessing a genuine religious and ethical sensitivity. Such people therefore turned to their confessor not because they were forced to do so by Church law but because they saw him as a 'guide of the conscience,' a trusted friend and confidant. In the seventeenth century, we can observe a new cultural phenomenon reflecting a deep psychological sensitivity, especially among the wealthy: people having a 'guide of the conscience' in whom they could entrust

---

kaznodziejskie w Polsce późnego średniowiecza. Sermones dominicales et festivales z tzw. kolekcji Piotra z Miłosławia (Kielce: Wydawnictwo Akademii Świetokrzyskiej, 2007), 383–384.

19   "Prosta, pocorna spowyedz ma bycz czysta ywyerna, Cząsta yodcrita, rostropna ydobrowolna, Sromyeslywa, czała, thayemnya, anaszą szalvyącza placzlywa rychla moczna abarszo poslussna," Krzysztof Bracha, *Nauczanie kaznodziejskie*, 384–385.

20   Such behavior was recommended by, among others, Nicholas from Błonie, who referred to a sinner as: "qui semper est in mora." There were only four cases in which one should confess: before receiving Holy Communion, in fear of death, pressed by one's conscience, and if one fears a priest will not be available again; cf. Krzysztof Bracha, *Nauczanie kaznodziejskie*, 387. Nicholas also recommended that believers receive communion at least three times a year: on Easter, Ascension Thursday and Christmas, which, however, does not seem to have been widely practiced; cf. Izabela Skierska, *Obowiązek mszalny*, 249.

21   Pope Clement V sought to regulate this problem at the Council of Vienne of 1311 and 1312. The Mendicants could hear confessions and give communion to the faithful only with the special consent of the parson. They could, however, freely tend to people who lived in their homes and in their hospitals. However, later sources point to disputes and tensions concerning the issue.; Izabela Skierska, *Obowiązek mszalny*, 245–246; Alicja Szulc, *Homo religiosus*, 188–197.

244 CHAPTER 4

their most intimate secrets and who helped their penitents navigate the difficult path to salvation.[22]

These observations also apply to the late Middle Ages, though such practices were limited to a circle of wealthy, pious Krakow burghers. The fact that the confessor was sometimes mentioned in the will alongside other people close to the testator may in itself testify to a deeper level of religious devotion, one not limited to the annual Easter Confession (and probably combined with the frequent taking of Holy Communion).[23] In 1369, upon embarking on a pilgrimage to Rome, Claire, widow of John Hobschbeck, left, among her other pious bequests, one grivna to her confessor Wiślicz.[24] In 1439, the court plenipotentiary Lawrence left his confessor Jacob Stegen six grivna and appointed him as one of the executors of his will, which seems to be evidence of a close bond existing between them.[25] Claire, the pious widow of Jacob Rolle, must have also had a close relationship with her confessor.[26] In her 1419 will, she indicated that since her husband had not left a will, she would make pious bequests as a means of securing the salvation of both spouses' souls.[27] In her bequest, made

---

22   Jean Delumeau, *Wyznanie i przebaczenie. Historia spowiedzi*, trans. Maryna Ochab (Gdańsk: Marabut, 1997), 109–110 (J. Delumeau, *L'aveu et le pardon: Les difficultés de la confession, XIIIe-XVIIIe siècle*, Fayard 2014).

23   "The eucharistic piety movement, which involved the postulate of frequent or even daily Communion by lay people, was quite nonconformist considering the general caution of the Church in this respect and the resulting practice of Easter Communion only... This practice, although it is unclear how widespread it became, was typical of big cities: with the exception of Prague in Wrocław and perhaps Krakow, where the postulates of lay people's frequent participation in the Eucharist met with rather timid echoes in the deliberations of university scholars"; Stanisław Bylina, *Religijność mieszkańców Europy Środkowo-Wschodniej*, 109–110.

24   "[...] unam marcam domino Wislicz suo confessori"; SCAB., no. 414.

25   "Item der sachin aus czu richten alze obin geschreben steet zo kyse ich mir den Erwirdigen prister her Jocob Stegen of dem hause unser beyder beichtvatir und dorczu ouch Stano Apteker Hannus den Bader of dem Zande und kyze ouch dorczu meyne eliche hawsfrawe den vir personen gebe ich macht der sachen ausczurichten alz is oben geschreben steet beyde geystlich und wertlich ydach zo sal under den vir personen eyne an dy ander nichtis tuen"; SCAB. 6, fol. 184.

26   The disposition in the event of Jacob Rolle's death was entered into the book of the bench court in 1392. However, it did not contain any pious bequests.; SCAB., no. 1425.

27   "[...] atque dicti quondam eius mariti, qui decedens testamentum aliud non fecit, nisi quod ipsum disponendum eius fideli reliquit voluntati [...]. In quibus omnibus ac in alijs missis et oracionibus suis, quas consciencie eorum reliquit, offerant memoriam pro salute anime Iacobi Rolle, cuius duris laboribus ea bona sint acquisita, et anime eiusdem Clare, cuius liberali donacione sic eorum quieti et indigencie sit prouisum"; KDMK, vol. 3, no. 406, 532–534 (1419).

THE BURGHER RELIGIOSITY

in the form of a notarial deed, Claire made generous pious bequests of 102 grivna and founded a perpetual altarage at a newly consecrated altar dedicated to Mary Magdalene in St. Mary's Church.[28] The first prebendary was to be Claire's confessor Nicholas von Oyes.[29]

It was the confessor who usually took last confession and administered the sacrament of the anointing of the sick. They thus had a strong influence on the spirituality and religious practices of burghers, and on the manner in which they departed from the earthly world. The roles played by confessors and the bequests made to them indicate that they not only influenced the decision to make a will and how money for opera pietatis should be allocated, but were also later entrusted with caring for the soul of the deceased. In 1433, Margaret widow of the stallholder Jost, left most of her estate to her confessor Nicholas, the altarist of the Altar of St. Anna at St. Mary's Church.[30] Similarly, in 1443, Catherine, widow of the glassmaker Cloze, left most of her estate to her confessor Nicholas Gertner.[31] In 1438, Gertner was referred to in the council book

---

28 "Preterea humiliter obtulit, legauit, dedit et commisit excellentissime celorum Regine, virgini Marie domum suam lapideam cum utensilibus et rebus relinquendis ad prebendam sacerdotalem perpetui altaris, post eius obitum in Ecclesia eiusdem gloriose virginis in Cracouia super altari iam consecrato beate Marie Magdalene comparandam et instituendam per eius executores"; KDMK, vol. 3, no. 406.

29 In a slightly modified version of this will, entered into the book of the bench court a year later, the testator confirmed the foundation of the altar and appointing of Nicholas, her confessor, as its altarist.: "Ich Clara Jacobs Rolle Witwe Widirruffe alle goben die ich vormols benunpt hatte noch meyne tode geben und mache meyn Testament und lecztin willen und zelgerete Alzo, czu erste bescheide ich meyn haus hindir den vlaschbanken do ich iczunt ynne wone und allis gut und gerete mit der gerade nichtis ausgenomen noch ausgeslossen gebe ich und bescheide noch meyme tode, das is Niclos Bastgert und Cuncze Zonnenborn dorin czinse kauffen ewikliche czu beleenunge eynis Altaris in Unsir Liben Frauwen pfarer kirchin ho czu Cracow und ich wil das denselben altir haben sal herre Niclos von Oyes meyn beychtfatir, den die herren Rathmannen der stat Cracow, deine Bischoffe antworten sullen In czu bestetigin czu dinsteben und obir derselben Altir, das her der irste Altir herre als Fare ap her lebit seyn und worden sal, den ich das loen desselben Altires gebe czu ewigen czeyten, auch noch desselbigen herren Niclos meynes beichtfatirs tode eyn andirn czu dirselbin altir deme Bischoffe czu antwortin in eyn zogetaner undirscheit und mosse das sie nymands noch des obgenanten fatir Niclos tode czu eynen Altirherre antwertin sullen deme Bischoffe wennen ey Capplan aus der obgenantes Unser Liben Frawen Pfarrkirchin"; SCAB. 5, fol. 31 (1420).

30 "Item allis das ich lossen werde boben dy gerade, das bescheyde ich meyme beichtvater hern Niclas, elthern das elters sinte Anne czu Unser Liben Frawen, mit befelunge meyner zele, als ich Im getrawe"; SCAB. 6, fol. 59 (1433).

31 "Item alle meyne obrige habe und dy neyge was do bleybet befele ich meynen beychtfater das her das alzo do hin weynde alzo ich im befolen habe mit meynen sele dorch meyner sele und der meyner und meynes selikeyt wille. Ich sunderlich bescheide ich meynem

as the chaplain of the municipal council and the Polish preacher at St. Mary's Church.[32] In both cases, the testators brief bequests asked their beneficiaries to pray for the salvation of their souls (*befelunge meyner zele, meyner sele selikeit*). Although testators' bequests naturally varied in terms of the amounts and types of assets bequeathed, in most cases confessors were given a bequest worth several grivna.[33] Testators sometimes requested that specific actions be taken by confessors on behalf of their soul, such as saying thirty Gregorian Masses for the release of the soul (*pro tricesima legenda*)[34] or donating money for opera pietatis in their name.[35] Some burghers also left clothing to their confessors, which is certainly a sign that a strong bond existed between them. John Czenmark of Košice, husband of a Krakow burgher woman, left his black coat to his confessor Lucas.[36] The patrician burgher John Sweidniczer left his confessor a blue robe (*rog*),[37] while Ursula, daughter of the late councillor George Szwarcz, bequeathed a fur coat (*słymenen pelcz*) to her confessor John Slepkogil.[38] Apart from clothing and money, confessors also received other personal items which, like clothing, was intended to strengthen the bond between the priest and the late benefactor. For example, in 1463, Margaret, widow of the miller Sigismund, left her confessor Martin her best pillow (*eyn kossen das beste*).[39] Barbara, daughter of the late Michael Unger, left her confessor one large silver spoon and one grivna in silver so that he could have a 'pax board' (a small devotional object used during Catholic Mass) made.[40] Interestingly, Anna, widow of the belt maker (*gortlerinne*) Stanisław, left her confessor from Wawel Cathedral (*confessori suo in Castro*) 10 florins and a painting of Saint

---

      beichtfater her Niclos Gertner VI mrc heller das tue ich dorch meyner sele selikeit"; LT, fol. 6 (1443).

32   "Niclas unsir caplan der polnisch prediger czu unsir liben frawen"; CONS. 428, fol. 389; CONS. 428, fol. 442.

33   SCAB. 6, fol. 184 (1439), 313 (1444); LT, fol. 28–29 (1452); SCAB. 7, fol. 361 (1459); LT, fol. 87 (1464) 88–89 (1466); SCAB. 8, fol. 428 (1471), 598–599 (1476).

34   The will of Barbara Putkinne; LT, fol. 11 (1448).

35   In her will, Łazaria, wife of Nicholas Slop, left her confessor, Martin, from St. Barbara's Church, another 150 florins, which he was to dispose of according to her instructions, in addition to the six florins which he was to receive for himself.: "Czum ersten gab sy anderthalb hundert gulden dem herren Mertin irem beichtvatir zu sinte Barbare dy selben sal her haben off allen iren guttern unde Sal dy an wenden und do hyn schicken alzo her wol weis, alz sy ym hette bevolen"; LT, fol. 87 (1464).

36   "[...] swarczen mantel mit bloen leymet"; CONS. 428, fol. 354 (1436).

37   LT, fol. 44 (1457).

38   LT, fol. 56 (1458).

39   LT, fol. 79.

40   "Item unum coclear melius denominavit dandum suo confessori Urbano et cum hoc unam marcam argenti pro pacificali"; LT, fol. 149–150 (1491).

THE BURGHER RELIGIOSITY 247

Veronica (*ymaginem Veronice*), which she may have used as her private altar at home.[41] Anna's bequest seems to confirm the presence of images of saints in the homes of some Krakovian burghers. The existence of such objects of private, personal worship was known earlier from iconography and archaeological research, which indicate that this phenomenon was most likely relatively limited in scope.[42]

1.1.2   Preachers

After confessors, the second most commonly mentioned clergy members in the wills of Krakovian burghers were preachers. They were largely responsible for shaping the eschatological imagination of the faithful and translating complex religious teachings taken from the elite cultural sphere of the written word, into a language understandable by an often-illiterate laity. One of the great preachers of late-medieval Europe, St. Vincent Ferrer, described his mission using the following metaphor:

> [T]he words of the Bible are food for the soul. Who cooks this food? The answer is: the preacher spreading the Word of God. My role is therefore not a minor one in the house of the Lord, but an important one. Like the cook who prepares food while others sleep, the preacher cooks in the kitchen of the Holy Spirit, using the fire of love and devotion and the oil of remembrance while you are asleep and resting in your beds.[43]

Preachers were thus teachers who, by means of their eloquence, charisma and education, were supposed to lead the faithful along the proper path in life and instil in them the appropriate forms of piety. As evidenced by the great preachers of late medieval Europe, some clergy members who performed this function were greatly respected as authority figures by the faithful, and at times even revered as living saints.[44]

Eight of the Krakovian testators whose wills were analysed made pious bequests to preachers. These were often generous bequests to finance perpetual prebends at St. Mary's Church or at nearby St. Barbara's Cemetery Chapel. Wealthy Krakovian burghers gathered in these places of worship to attend

---

41   LT, fol. 98 (1471).

42   Tomasz Borkowski, "Materialne przejawy codziennej religijności w średniowiecznych miastach śląskich. Drobna gliniana plastyka dewocyjna," *Archaeologia Historica Polona* 7 (1998), 47–54.

43   Paweł T. Dobrowolski, *Wincenty Ferrer: kaznodzieja ludowy późnego średniowiecza* (Warszawa: Wydawn. Inst. Historii PAN, 1996), 199.

44   As was the case with St. Vincent Ferrer and St. John of Capestrano.

248   CHAPTER 4

typical religious services or those organised by brotherhoods to which they
belonged (typically Masses for the Dead). In one case, John Sweidniczer made
a bequest of 21 grivna from his large estate to pay for an annuity for a German
preacher who was to celebrate Mass for his soul every day for a year at the altar
Sweidniczer had erected at St. Mary's Church.[45] Stanisław Koczwara, in turn,
made a bequest on behalf of his wife of 16 grivna in annual rent to a Polish
preacher at St. Barbara's Chapel.[46]

---

45   "Item so gebe ich aws meynen guttirn Sechs hundirt ungerische gulden czu stiftunge
      ewiclich und of richtunge eynes Newen Altaris in meyner Capelle czu unsir libin frawen
      alhy in der pfarrekirche, und umb das selbe gelt sollen meyne vormonden kewfen czwen-
      czig marg czinsis ierlichen an eyner sichern stelle of alle Quatuortempora fonf marg czu
      gebin also dassich dasselbe leen alleczeit selbir gebin und vorleyen sal der Dewtschen
      czungen prediger in der obgenanten kirchen der Dewtcz predigen wirt, das der selbe pre-
      diger das obgenante leen mit den czu gehorenden czinsen habin und dy hirschaft doro-
      bir genissen sal alleczeitdy weyle her In eygener persone durch seynen eigenen mitten
      prediger und vorwesir des obgenanten stulis in dewtczer czunge seyn wordeund nicht
      lenger, und merklig ouch in der mosse das derselbe prediger ouch alleczeit forderlich
      von den Ratmannen czu Cracow und von dem pfarrer der obgenanten kirchen irwelit
      und irkorn werden sal, und bey dem stule seyn, und dem selben prediger allewegedy Rat-
      mannen czu Cracow czu dem selbin Altare antworten sollen also lenhern und nemlich
      das iczlichir solchir prediger als vorgeschribin ist vorbunden seyn sal czu bestellen und
      schicken, das alle tage eyne messe obir das gancze iar sal in meyner vorgenanten Capelle
      gelesin werden durch sich und andire prister do Im sollen teglich also gelesin werden
      als am Suntage von dem tage, am Montage vor dy toten, am dinstage von der heiligen
      dreyfaldikeit, an der mitwoch von sinte Stanislao und sinte Bernhardino adir von eynem
      Merterer, am donirstage von dem heiligen leichnam, am freitage von dem leyden Cristi,
      am Sonnobinde von unsir frawen. Wenne sichs abir geburit das heyligetage gefallen an
      welchin tag dy in der wochin komen so lese man dy messe von dem selbin heyligen. Item
      obir dy czwenczig marg czinsis dy vorgeschriben und benant seyn, sal das obgenante
      altare mit eyner besundern marg ierlichis czinsis bewocht werden von meynen guttirn
      dy ich dorczu benume [...]. Item so sollen meyne vormonde kewffen eynen guttirn ornat
      czu meynem altare in meyner Capellen vor den dewtczen prediger"; LT, fol. 43–44 (1457).
46   "Item dixit quod villa Prokoczin domine Elizabeth uxoris sue esset et non sua, et quod
      solum nomine tutele legittime ipsius uxoris sue eam tenuisset et rexisset, sed tamen cum
      presentanes consensu eiusdem uxoris sue voluit super censibus ipsius ville fundari fun-
      dacione perpetua XVI marcas denariorum annui census pro predicatore Polonico pro
      ambone in capella sancte Barbare in cimiterio beate virginis sita et quia id de predicte
      uxoris sue personali consensu et spontanea voluntate fuit et est fundat iam ipso facto, ita
      quod dicta uxor sua, et poste am ipsius ville possessores et heredes de dictis ville censibus
      iam et deinceps singulis annis huiusmodi XVI marcas denariorum census fundacionis
      Domino Doctori moderno et cuilibet poste um in eadem capella predicatori polonico, qui
      cum dominorum Consulum voluntate et consensu et non aliter ad hoc deputatus et elec-
      tus fuit dare solvere et presentare debet et debent in perpetuam eiusdem predicacionis
      officy salariacionem, dotacionem et presentacionem pro sua suorumque ac fidelium ami-
      corum salute"; LT, fol. 70–71 (1461).

THE BURGHER RELIGIOSITY

Poorer burghers made less generous bequests, in accordance with their means. In both versions of his will, Peter, the administrator (*sołtys*) of the village of Filipowicze, bequeathed his house to fund an altarage to support a German preacher at St. Mary's Church.[47] In turn, Stephen Eichorn and his wife Margaret left 100 florins to the acting altarist (*zu dem predigerstule*),[48] while John Raisser of Memmingen made a bequest of one florin in annual rent to his preacher.[49]

Some testators made more symbolic bequests. For example, Ursula, daughter of the councillor George Szwarcz, left two florins to a preacher at St. Mary's Church and one florin to a preacher at an unnamed hospital (probably the hospital of the Holy Spirit).[50] Matthias, a milliner, made a bequest of one florin to a preacher at St. Barbara's,[51] while Margaret Grobniginne instructed the executors of her will to pay for preachers to say a Mass for her soul each year at Krakow churches.[52]

Most of the testators above were members of Krakow's elite, and their pious bequests for preachers were usually part of larger plans to found altarages that

---

47   "Item domum suam sitam on platea Sutorum in qua Hufnayl moratur, confert et dat dominis Consulibus Cracoviensibus, qui plenam proprietatem habere debent vendendi domum ipsam, qua vendita emere debent ipsi domini Consules pro pecuniis exinde provenientibus censum quantum melius possunt pro nova et perpetua fundacione altaris in Ecclesia beate virginis parochiali, ubi ipsum altare ipsis dominis apcius fundandis visum fuit, cuius Altaris ipsi Consules perpetui erunt patroni, convertereque et conferre et appropriare debent domini Consules ipsum censum fundandi altaris pro predicatore Theutonicis iam dicte Ecclesie et non alio pro tali videlicet predicatore Theutonico, qui de assumpcione et voluntate ipsorum dominorum eiusdem Ecclesie pro tempore predicator fuerit Theutonicus, ita quod dum predicator pro tempore existens, vel licenciatus ab ecclesia fuerit aut moreretur, vel alio modo ipsum sedere predicacionis vocare contingerit, alter qui ipsi sede et officio ex dominorum predicatorum susceptione et voluntate prefuit, et quoad predicator extiterit ipsius altaris et census ex Iurepatronatus dominorum et presentacione dominis et possessor erit Predicator autem talis per se vel per alium sacerdotem duas missas super ipso Altari legere sit asstrictus unam pro defunctis, et aliam in honore beate virginis pro anime sue salute"; LT, fol. 28 (1452), 66 (1460).

48   CONS. 429, fol. 557 (1476).

49   "[...] das her ym dy Jorczeyt halden und vorkundige off dem predigestule got vor ym bittende und das lehen des selbigen altaris sullen czu vorleyen haben seyne nehesten frunde czu ewigen tagen, och hot gewolt das der selbige altar eynliczigk sal seyn das ist das der altarista heyn bevesiren merr haben magk wenn das alleyne und ouch das nicht vorwegksiln im der patronen willen und wissen och was seyn wille das alle das oppir das off den altar geoppirt worde das sal des altaristen seyn"; SCAB. 8, fol. 598–599 (1476).

50   LT, fol. 56 (1458).

51   LT, fol. 5 (1440).

52   "[...] und do von sal her in den kirchen dy prediger ausrichten, daz man eyn gancz iar vor ire zele bitte"; LT, fol. 66–67 (1460).

were to be carried out by respected clergymen, which increased the prestige of the foundation and the quality of the pastoral services. The vast majority of these bequests were made to preachers at St. Mary's Church, i.e. to the most important parish church in the city. For example, in the first version of his will from 1439, John Sweidniczer appointed Nicholas of Brzeg,[53] a doctor of theology and preacher at St. Mary's Church, as one of the executors of his will. Stanisław Koczwara, in turn, named in his will a certain *Doctori moderni*, who was a preacher at St. Barbara's Chapel.[54] The fact that the preachers in Krakow's most important Churches were highly educated and well-respected assuredly played an important role in testators deciding to make bequests to these institutions and their clergy.

It should also be noted that Krakovian burghers would clearly indicate whether they wished to support a German or a Polish preacher. This was certainly an indication of a testator's desire to hear sermons in their native tongue. But this decision also reflects the rivalry between the German-speaking and Polish-speaking populations of Krakow that had been ongoing since at least the late fourteenth century.[55]

1.1.3 Other Clergy

There is no doubt that apart from confessors and preachers, other clergy also played an important role in shaping the religious life of Krakovian burghers. Since Krakow parishes were usually large, making it difficult for individuals to identify with the parish community as a whole, an important link between burghers and the Church was the clergymen with whom they had close contact. In making pious bequests, many testators did not fail to include clergymen in their last wills. The very first known Krakovian testator, the burgher woman Sulisława, named in her will priests from two monasteries, making pious donations to both of them. She left half of her market stall to the Dominicans, with whom resided a priest named Michachel, son of Simnikonis;[56] the other half she left to the Franciscans and a resident priest named Minardus.[57] Two other widows, Alusza and Dorothy Banarika, made similar bequests in their wills. Alusza left three grivna to the hospital of the Holy Spirit and one

---

53   "Niclas vom Brige dem doctor der heiligen schrift prediger zu unser liben frawen"; CONS. 428, fol. 402.

54   LT, fol. 70–71 (1461).

55   Hanna Zaremska, *Bractwa w średniowiecznym Krakowie*, 37.

56   "Item de instita sic dispono, quod mediam confero fratribus predicatoribus, in qua Michachel filius simniconis residet"; KDMK, vol. 3, no. 368.

57   "Insuper mediam institam do fratribus minoribus, in qua minardus inhabitat"; *ibidem*.

THE BURGHER RELIGIOSITY   251

grivna to a brother named Nicholas who worked there.[58] Dorothy Banarika specified in one of her wills that a bequest was to be made to a presbyter, also named Nicholas the 'Crusader' (*Cruciferus*) from Kalisz.[59] This presbyter was probably a member of the Order of Canons Regular of the Holy Spirit, which ran the hospital of the Holy Spirit in Kalisz.[60]

The wills of the mine administrator Paszko and councillor Gotfrid Fattinante contained numerous specific bequests. Paszko drafted his last will when he was already very sick, bequeathing some of his clothing to clergymen. His instructions were very specific: "I leave my coat lined with marten fur to brother Bartek. I leave my other brown coat with a lining to brother Gregory and my blue coat and tunic to Bogusław, the parish priest from Osiek. I leave my two silver belts to brother Gregory so that he can turn them into a chalice or two cruet bottles."[61] Such bequests seem to testify to strong bonds existing between the testator and his beneficiaries. Councillor Gotfrid Fattinante also made numerous and generous pious bequests, including the funding of two new altars. He named two close associates as their altarists: a vicar named Peter and a priest named John, who were, respectively, his notary and his doctor.[62] Naturally, it is also possible that some of these bequests were made to priests and monks who were relatives of the testator.[63] However, when priests and monks related to the testator were mentioned in bequests, they were included not only because they were family members, but also because they had been entrusted with securing the testator's immortal soul.[64]

It is worth pointing out here the frequent mistrust shown towards people of the Church, expressed in provisions guaranteeing the future of foundations created in the event of a clergyman's failure to carry out the duties entrusted to him. For example, Catherine, widow of the goldsmith George, stated in her will that Andrew of Wróblewo, permanent resident Vicar (*Vicar*

---

58   "Item Legauit infirmis ad hospitale denariorum grossorum tres marcas et Ibidem ffratri Nycolao vnam marcam"; NKiRMK, no. 616 (1321).

59   "[...] tem domino Nicolao Crucifero in Kalis X mrc"; SCAB., no. 1866.

60   Klara Antosiewicz, "Zakon Ducha Świętego de Saxia w Polsce średniowiecznej," *Nasza Przeszłość* 23, 1966, 175.

61   "Item Palium cum pellibus Marderinis demandauit fratri Bartkoni. Item aliud palium bruneticum cum Subductiua fratri gregorio. Item Palium flaueum cum tunica domino Boguslao plebano in Ossek. Item duos Cingulos argenteos fecit dare fratri Gregorio pro Calice aut pro duabus ampullis"; NKiRMK, no. 1693 (1358).

62   KDWac., vol. 2, no. 396, 182–185 (1393).

63   See chapter Three.

64   For example, Dorothyo Reichelinne left 20 florins to her brother Thomas, a Cistercian monk from Koprzywnica, for the clothes he needed. To make this donation more significant, she also donated 10 florins to the monastery; SCAB. 8, fol. 203 (1465).

252   CHAPTER 4

Perpetuus) of the Krakow cathedral, was to either personally celebrate Mass at the altar she funded or appoint someone in his place, under the threat of excommunication.[65]

1.2   *Religious Objects in Wills*

1.2.1   Rosaries

Private worship, free of intermediaries, was possible only through the practice of individual prayer. Although the Church advised the faithful to kneel and say the Hail Mary whenever they heard a bell ring (usually two or three times a day),[66] in order to instil in them the habit of praying, for the majority of burghers prayer remained a public ritual. Nevertheless, in the fifteenth century, evidence can be seen of a deepening religious awareness among burghers. Improvements in literacy and, as a result, people's knowledge of religious texts, coupled with the wide array of church institutions operating in Krakow, made it possible for conscious choices to be made about how the liturgy was taught and conducted by the Church and for personal preferences to develop. One sign of people's engagement in private, personal forms of religiosity was the habit of praying individually, of which the rosary was a visible symbol in the Middle Ages.

Rosaries, or *Pater Nosters*, are first mentioned in municipal books in the 1430s. However, 'praying the rosary' most likely did not become popular in Krakow until after the mid-fifteenth century, as evidenced by a document dated 1484 in which Pope Innocent VIII offered indulgences to the members of the brotherhood of the Psalter of the Blessed Virgin Mary in Krakow: "According to Alain de la Roche, a brotherhood with such a name should have been devoted to praying the rosary. We can thus assume that this document is the oldest trace of the existence of such a brotherhood affiliated with the Dominican Order in Krakow."[67] The fact that rosaries were frequently mentioned in wills

---

65   "Item rogavit Ipsos dominos Consules et executores qui presentes fuerunt et postnotandos quibus pro hac vice dumtaxat Iuspatronatus donavit ut huiusmodi altare sive ministerium per ipsos pro huiusmodi pecuniis disponendis et emendis primum altaristum presentent honorabilem dominum Andream de Wroblewo vicarium perpetuum in Ecclesia Cathedrali Cracoviensi cuius vitam mores et bonam conversacionem bene noscere asserebat presentandum nominavit et voluit quem sub consciam suam obligatur et obligat ut ad huiusmodi fundacionem altare operam et diligentiam faciat et per se vel per alium huiusmodi missas sicut moris est sub pena excomunicacionis impleat et celebret ac de censibus pro huiusmodi ministerio comparandis gaudet"; LT, fol. 142 (1484).

66   Stanisław Bylina, *Religijność mieszkańców Europy Środkowo-Wschodniej*, 106.

67   Katarzyna Zalewska, *Modlitwa i obraz. Średniowieczna ikonografia różańcowa* (Warszawa: Wydawnictwa Uniwersytetu Warszawskiego, 1994), 17.

THE BURGHER RELIGIOSITY

demonstrates that there was a strong link between wills being written with the intention of securing salvation and the rise of new forms of piety, symbolized by, among other things, praying the rosary, as indicated by relatively frequent references to rosaries in testaments of last will.

The oldest mention of rosaries in a will dates back to at least 1431. Councillor Paul Homan testified before the municipal bench court that his late wife's sister received her coral rosary and golden ring as a gerade.[68] In 1440, as many as three rosaries were listed in the will of the wealthy stallholder Martin Streicher (he was probably related to councillor Stanisław Streicher, who is mentioned in the will).[69] In addition, a silver belt with a pouch containing a coral rosary and a medallion with the image of Saint John the Evangelist were included among Streicher's valuables in his will.[70] The wealthy burghers Martin Pasternak in 1458;[71] Elena, the wife of the embroiderer (*zeidenhafter*) Nicholas in 1476;[72] and the tailor Jarosz in 1492[73] also listed in their wills two coral rosaries as movable property. John Landandis mentions a rosary in his 1472 will.[74]

Testators also specified what material rosaries were made of (they always chose precious coral), which demonstrates that they were valuable objects. In her 1501 will, Margaret Czypserowa, an affluent burgher woman, left her coral rosary (*legibulum alias paternoster de corall*), which she listed alongside her twelve rings, to her children. This demonstrates that rosaries were included in some wills on a par with other valuable objects and movables, and that testators sought to ensure they would be inherited by a worthy heir. On the other hand, as other documents demonstrate, some rosaries were included in the will because they had purely symbolic or emotional value. Testators for whom this was true were predominantly wealthy, religious and most likely literate Krakovian burghers. This is evidenced by Krakow's municipal books: in 1451, Barbara, widow of the deputy prosecutor (*procuratoris*) Henry, testified that the objects she had pledged to councillor Nicholas Zalcz, including four books, a rosary

---

68 SCAB. 6, fol. 29 (1431).

69 "Dy nochgeschreben gerethe hot lossin beschreiben her Mertin Streicher von irsten C gereinte gulden und XXII gulden ist mir scholdig Stana Streicher"; LT, fol. 5; cf. Marcin Starzyński, *Krakowska rada miejska w średniowieczu*, 270.

70 "Item eyn zilberen gurtil von VI marg groschen und zust eyn cleyn selberin gurtil von czwu marg silber mit eyner kaletin und in der Caletin ist eyn korallin potirnoster und czechin Johannes primus"; LT, fol. 5.

71 LT, fol. 28.

72 Advoc. Crac. 83, fol. 8–9; *Cracovia artificum 1300–1500*, ed. Jan Ptaśnik (Krakow: Polska Akademia Umiejętności, 1917), no. 654.

73 LT, fol. 151–152.

74 LT, fol. 101.

254 CHAPTER 4

and a pearl necklace, were returned to her.[75] While we do not know the subject-matter of these books (considering the profession of Barbara's husband, they were probably law books), it is evident that Barbara and her husband were literate. Moreover, the couple must have been both pious (hence the rosary) and of high social status (as evidenced by the pearl necklace).[76] Another interesting example is the will of Nicholas Paternoster. His name suggests that he was either a very pious Christian who prayed the rosary, or someone who manufactured rosaries. In 1450, the year of the great Roman Jubilee, Paternoster drafted a will before embarking on a pilgrimage to Rome.[77] He instructed the executors of his will to sell his house and use the money to make pious bequests to the Church of Corpus Christi in Kazimierz (40 florins), the brotherhood at St. Barbara's Church (20 florins), and one of his relatives (only fifteen florins). The rest of the money was to be donated to opera pietatis.[78] Nicholas must have been very religious, because in addition to making pious bequests and a pilgrimage to Rome, he also specifically stated in his will that all his household items, including his books, should be donated to poor priests and laymen.[79] As with the other examples discussed above, the fact that Nicholas possessed religious books can be seen as proof of his interest in a deeper, more individual form of worship. It also demonstrates that in the late Middle Ages, the rise of literacy and new elite forms of religiosity were interconnected.

1.2.2   Books and Paintings

As mentioned above, increasing levels of literacy were closely connected with more intimate and intentional forms of piety, of which wills were undoubtedly a sign. Writing not only revolutionized trade, governance and social relations within the city, it also helped shape a new mentality, one more accustomed to planning, rational evaluation and intellectual engagement in religion.[80] While

---

75   "Barbara relicta Henrici procuratoris recognovit quod Nicolaus Zalcz quatuor libros, paternoster et collerium margaritheum et ceteros res quasi ipsa una cum viro suo eocem ipso vivente ipsi Nicolao pro censu presesso obligaverat integre et omnimode restituit pronuncians eum de eisdem totaliter liberum et solutum"; CONS. 428, fol. 32.

76   Mentions of rosaries can also be found in the entry concerning its inheritance; CONS. 429, fol. 516 (1474) and in another one in which it was pledged together with other valuables.: "als eyn ledchyn do ynne sint 7 silberene leffil, 3 hauben mit golde gestructit und eyn cleyn obirgolt gortleyn das hot 7 spange ane den senkil, eyn korallen paternoster, eyn cleyne perlen przeniczkyund eyn bendil mit perlen und eyne haube"; SCAB. 8, fol. 428 (1476).

77   SCAB. 7, fol. 43, 47 (1448, 1450).

78   The remaining money was to be divided among the poor, lepers and "czu wege und czu stege"; SCAB. 7, fol. 43 (1448).

79   *Ibidem.*

80   Jack Goody, *The Logic of Writing*, 59–65.

THE BURGHER RELIGIOSITY

the limited number of available sources containing references to literacy among burghers, or the books they read or possessed, do not allow for an accurate determination of the scale of this phenomenon, literacy continued to be increasingly commonplace in the lives of burghers throughout the fourteenth and fifteenth centuries. For reasons of both practicality and prestige, the first *literati* in the burgher community were city officials and merchants, two social groups with strong mutual affiliations. It is estimated that the majority of Krakow officials and merchants were able to read and write by the mid-fourteenth century.[81] As the oldest known Krakow municipal book indicates, literate burghers did not treat reading and writing merely as a practical skill, but also as a means for expanding their intellectual horizons. The book includes an entry showing that the municipal notary Peter lent the alderman (and future councillor) John Puswange the pseudo-Aristotelian book *Secretum Secretorum* and three other works (published in a single volume).[82]

Fourteenth-century bequests of last will generally do not mention valuable or personal items. Books belonging to the testators or their family are mentioned only in two wills. In his 1368 will, Nicholas Essenbach divided his estate, stating that his nephew should be given an annuity, all his books and ten grivna, provided he obey and serve Nicholas's wife, attend school and become a clergyman.[83] The example of a book of accounts that Catherine, widow of alderman Paul Kowal, was to give to her brother-in-law John Bertram (after receiving the money promised to her in the will) expresses a more pragmatic approach to books and literacy.[84]

An inventory of accounts between the merchant Henry Steinmoler and the alderman (and future councillor) Stanisław Morsztyn and his brother George Morsztyn, also a merchant, drawn up in 1451, included three books, the *Katolicon*, a book by Avicenna, and the Bible, which the latter was to reclaim in Antwerp.[85] The selection of books demonstrates that Krakow's elites were indeed

---

81   AgnieszkaBartoszewicz, *Piśmienność mieszczańska w późnośredniowiecznej Polsce*, Warszawa 2012, 34–35.

82   "Petrus notarius concessit librum Secretorum Aristotelis et alios tres in uno volumine Iohanni Puswange"; CONS. 427, fol. 28 (1393).

83   "[...] dicta domina Katherina Petrum filium sororis sue circa se sibi ministrandi vite necessaria pro suo posse in quantum ipsam et scolas sequi voluerit ac sacros presbiteratos ordines mutari et ipsum in libris suis cum X mrc"; cf. SCAB., no. 242.

84   "[...] item promisit librum racionis vel debitorum sui mariti quod velit ipsum fratri sui mariti assignare"; SCAB., no. 1502 (1392).

85   "Ouch bekante her daz dy schulde bey den wirthen czu Magdeburg und Brawnczweig sint Stano und Jorge Mornsteyn und nicht seyn und dorczu allis grethe das in dem lande bey der wirtynne czu Antwerpin ist alz drey bucher Katolicun, Avicenna und eyn Biblia, eyn

256   CHAPTER 4

religious, but also that they had broader intellectual horizons.[86] Naturally, Krakovian burghers also owned practical and 'everyday' books that they could use
to advance their professional knowledge. A list of councillor Stanisław Leymitter's possessions, drawn up by aldermen after his death, included three law
books.[87] The municipal notary Nicholas Knoll (*Schonberg*), who inventoried
the possessions of the late Herman, a physician (*magistri Hermanni Phisici*),
received a chest containing his books and other possessions.[88]

Books were also mentioned in the wills of two important figures in fifteenth-century Krakow, namely one of the city's wealthiest and most influential burghers, John Sweidniczer,[89] and a widely respected municipal notary
and altarist at St Mary's Church, John Stolle of Głogów.[90] In an extremely long
and meticulous listing of all his goods, liabilities and assets, John Sweidniczer
mentions "all my books," including two or three which at the time had possibly
been lent to the parish priest (*dem pfartor*) at St. Mary's Church. Like other
burghers who owned books, John Sweidniczer probably had many books on
different subjects, both secular and religious.[91] A former student of the universities in Prague and Krakow and a municipal notary by profession, John Stolle
had an even larger book collection.[92] Three versions of his will are known to

---

silberynne schale, eyn swarcz mantil mit growerg, eyn swarcz rock mit mardern gefuttirt,
eyn groer rock mit fochsen und ander cleyn gerethe das do frey und unforkommert ist";
CONS. 429, fol. 36 (1451); cf. Adam Kamiński, "Jerzy Morsztyn (żupnik)," in PSB, vol. 21
(Wrocław–Warszawa–Krakow: Polska Akademia Nauk, Polska Akademia Umiejętności,
1976), 816–817.

86   The horizons and intellectual ambitions of the city's elites are evidenced by the fact that
      in the fifteenth century many representatives of the Krakow patricians (including many
      members of the Morsztyn family) were enrolled as students at University of Krakow; cf.
      Krzysztof Boroda, *Studenci Uniwersytetu Krakowskiego w późnym średniowieczu*, 122–124;
      Edward Potkowski, *Książka i pismo w średniowieczu. Studia z dziejów kultury piśmiennej i
      komunikacji społecznej* (Pułtusk: Wyd. Akademia Humanistyczna im. Aleksandra Gieysz-
      tora, 2006), 75–88.

87   "[...] acht margk silber, drey recht bucher, czwe panczer und eyn kolner, das beste hant-
      fas, czwene kasten, drey tysche, czwe bette vunf steyne czenen gefese, schofseln kannen
      scheyben, sechs leichlach, eyne grune tafter decke, czwene tepicht, eyn langen und eynen
      korczen bancfel, eyn banclach mit eynem cleynot"; CONS. 429, fol. 368 (1465).

88   CONS. 428, fol. 520, 534 (1449).

89   LT, fol. 39–45 (1457).

90   SCAB. 6, fol. 186 (1439), 187 (1439), 267 (1442); CONS. 429, S27–28 (1451); KDMK, vol. 3, no.
      439, 574–576 (1454).

91   It is noteworthy that Sweidniczer employed a private tutor and made one of his bequests
      to him; cf. Agnieszka Bartoszewicz, *Piśmienność*, 263.

92   "Born in Głogów, he obtained his bachelor degree in Prague in 1407. In 1414 or 1415, he
      enrolled at the University of Krakow and at the same time was employed in the local
      municipal office (August 1414). However, in 1415 he left Krakow to study in Vienna, but

THE BURGHER RELIGIOSITY   257

have been drafted, two of which were written in both Latin[93] and German.[94] In the first, John Stolle left his impressive book collection (approximately 25 books; ten manuscripts have survived to the present day in the Jagiellonian University Library, including liturgical works, sermons, and books on science and the law)[95] to his housekeeper (*schafferinne*), along with other goods. Stolle further instructed that after the death of his housekeeper the books should be used to fund four altarages at St. Mary's Church.[96] Twelve years later, in 1451, Stolle confirmed the final version of his will on his deathbed. This time he donated all his books on the liberal arts (Latin *in artibus*, German *in der freyen kunsten*) to the University of Krakow, stating, however, that his successor Nicholas Knoll (*Schonberg*) could choose two or three books to keep "for the memory of my soul" (*pro memoria anime mee*). In addition, Stolle left his "old collection of prayers bound in white wood" (in German *Meine alde Collecta in weissen bretin*, in Latin *Collecta mea antique in albis asseribus*) to John, a former deputy notary at the Church of Corpus Christi. Stolle left all his theological books and the *Maius volumen Prisciani*, a textbook of Latin grammar, to St. Mary's Church.[97] It is perhaps not surprising that John Stolle named John

---

     soon returned to the Wawel Castle and the local municipal office. A quarter of a century later, he was very wealthy, associated with the circles of the Krakow patricians. He disposed of his wealth in his will, which he wrote in 1450, not as a municipal notary, but as an alterist at St. Mary's Church"; *ibidem*, 163; cf. Bożena Wyrozumska, *Kancelaria miasta Krakowa w średniowieczu*, 121.

93   SCAB. 6, fol. 187 (1439), 267 (1442); KDMK, vol. 3, no. 439, 574–576 (1454).

94   SCAB. 6, fol. 186 (1439); CONS. 429, fol. 27–28 (1451).

95   AgnieszkaBartoszewicz, *Piśmienność*, 187; Krzysztof Skupieński, *Notariat publiczny w średniowiecznej Polsce* (Lublin: Uniwersytetu Marii Curie-Sklodowskiej, 2002), 128–129; Marcin Starzyński, "Kto był pisarzem Kodeksu Behema?," *Rocznik Krakowski* 73 (2007), 67–69.

96   "Czum ersten bescheyde Ich Dorothee meyner Schafferynne der Bochnerynne swester meyn haws in deme Ich wone of der spitler gasse, czwischen der Felixynne und der faberynne hause czu irem leben, und nicht erblich und dorczu meyne bucher und cleider, und bettegewand, gefolle hawsgerethe, bawierot, geld und alle meyne varende habe keyns ausgenomen, ir czu lone vor ir dinst," "Primo Dorothee dispensatrici mee sorori Bochnerynne lego domum mea in qua habito in platea hospitalensi inter domos Felixynne et Faberynne ad vitam ipsius et non hereditarie possidendam, et cum hoc libros meos et vestes, lacristernia, vasa, supellectilem, utensilia, pecuniam et queque mobilia mea nulle excepto pro ipsius primio deservito"; SCAB. 6, fol. 186–187 (1439).

97   "Item omnes libros meos in artibus do ad Collegium hic in Cracowia, Ita tamen, Quod Nicolaus Schonberg predictus sibi vnum, duos vel tres libros ex ipsis libris qui sibi placebunt, recipere debet, pro memoria anime mee. Eciam lego ad Corpus christi Kazimirie domino Iohanni quondam Vicenotario Collecta mea antique in albis asseribus, Omnesque libros meos in Theologia magnos et parwos, nullo excepto, et maius volumen Prisciani ad laudem et honorem beate virgini ac imperpetuum ei servicium do pro domo

258   CHAPTER 4

Sweidniczer and the aforementioned notary Nicholas Knoll[98] as the executors
of his will, as they had worked together in the city hall, shared a similar social
standing, and probably also shared similar interests.

Stolle's and Sweidniczer's impressive private book collections must have
been exceptional in medieval Krakow. Indeed, Stolle and Sweidniczer were
themselves exceptional individuals, members of the city's intellectual elite, the
highest echelon of a kind of 'fourth estate' – what they would call, in French,
les gens de savoir.[99] However, burghers who possessed less cultural capital also
displayed higher intellectual ambitions.[100] Both Nicholas Paternoster and Margaret, widow of Lawrence Neyser (*Margaretha Lorencz Neysserinne*), neither
of whom were representatives of Krakow's patrician families, also listed books
(probably religious works) in their wills. In Nicholas Paternoster's will, books
were mentioned in a very casual manner, alongside his other movables, including sheets and bedclothes.[101] Margaret's case is also noteworthy. From the note
of agreement between her son Stanisław Slepkogil and daughter Catherine
Dittrichinne we know that among Margaret's movables in the will were listed

---

      sua ad Ecclesiam parrochialem"; CONS. 429, fol. 27–28 (1451); KDMK, vol. 3, no. 439, 574–
      576 (1454).

98   He paid homage to Stolle, calling him "his dearest master' in the obituary he wrote for him
      in the council book."; CONS. 429, fol. 18; Bożena Wyrozumska, *Kancelaria*, 122.

99   Agnieszka Bartoszewicz, *Piśmienność*, 36–41.

100   "The claim that lay people used books primarily for didactic and professional purposes
      seems to be true. But the example of Sweidniczer's will shows that there were also reli-
      gious motives. Many burghers had prayer books, many also showed interest in the life and
      deeds of Jesus, Mary, other figures from the New Testament, and the saints. Burghers may
      have also been interested in some historiographic literature, and *The Alexander Romance*
      was definitely a major one. Latin grammar textbooks, prayer books, and the lives of saints
      were undoubtedly in the greatest demand from booksellers trading in manuscripts and
      printed books. Prognostic calendars with lists of lucky and unlucky days and various
      types of guide books should be added to this list. The library of Anna Kuncz, a Vilnius
      dressmaker who had collected five books, including some chronicle, the prophecies of
      St. Brigid, a book concerning botany and medicine, and a medical book ("ayns Joannis
      paulery, ayns Sante Brigitte, ayns Dy Cronika, das wyrde herbarium, das ffunfte cyrurgia")
      probably quite accurately reflected the interests of the burghers. The book collection of
      John Parzykozeł from Krakow was more ambitious: *Speculum Saxonum*, a book on church
      law, grammar textbooks including the inevitable Donatus and Alexander de Villa De, the
      Adagia by Erasmus of Rotterdam and an edition of *Aesop's Fables*."; Agnieszka Bartosze-
      wicz, *Piśmienność*, 265–266.

101   "Dornoch bescheide ich allen hausrot, bette, leylocher, bucher und allis das man finden
      wirt das sal man geben armen pristern und armen leuten und wo is notdorft wirt"; SCAB.
      7, fol. 43 (1448).

THE BURGHER RELIGIOSITY

259

a painting (*das bilde*) and a 'German book' (*das deutsche buch*).[102]There is no additional information specifying what kind book this was or what the painting depicted. We can assume the painting depicted a saint and was used as a kind of private altar in her home, as was the case with the painting of Saint Veronica that Anna, widow of the belt maker Stanisław, donated to her confessor at the Wawel Cathedral.[103] If we take into consideration Margaret's wealth and social standing, it seems probable that she was literate, and that the book was probably a religious work.

Some wealthy Krakovian burghers not only bought and read (mostly religious) books, but also used them as security and donated them to religious institutions. For example, Bernard Filip of Lubojna states in his will that the parish priest Thomas from Mikanów pledged his book for 36 groszy. The testator stated that the priest had to say thirty Gregorian Masses (*tricesima*) for the release of Bernard's soul to get back his sacramentary (a book containing the sacraments). Should he fail, a different priest should say the Masses, and the sacramentary and Bernard's other books should be given to poor students.[104] We thus know for certain that Bernard Filip owned not only the one sacramentary, but also other books (unfortunately, we do not know what kinds).[105]

Other burghers (including women) who made religious books part of their foundations likewise must have participated at some level in so-called written culture. This is demonstrated by their bequests, which in themselves are expressions both of respect for the written word and evidence of how it was tied to religious activity. Like Bernard Filip, Bartholomeus, a tanner, also left his books to various religious figures and institutions, including a donation to the

---

102   Her son's name indicates that her first husband could have been councillor John Slepkogil or some other member of this wealthy family from Krakow. Catherine's daughter was married to a Krakow alderman and future councillor, Nicholas Dietrich; Marcin Starzyński, *Krakowska rada*, 270, 283.

103   LT, fol. 98 (1471).

104   "Item unum librum dictum Sacramentale quem sibi per dominum Thomam plebanum in Mykanow in vadiatum existit in tribus fertones si et inquantum ipse dominus dictum librum rehabere cupit legit unam tricesimam pro anima sua extunc recipiat librum si ea facere nequit convemat alium legentem pro dicta pecunia et librum recipiat pro se. Item omnes libros legavit propter deum pauperibus scolaribus"; LT, fol. 71 (1461).

105   This is probably how the *Book of the Viaticum* found its way into the hands of a Krakow Jew, Israel. "Ysrahel der Jude hot angeclagit frawe Nethen Hanusynne das her hette eyn buch eyn viaticum bey yr gefunden der ym in dem fewer genomen were. So hot dy frawe Netha gesprochen das yr das buch in eymen phande vorsetczit were von eynen Lithyn der heysit John Lithwyn und den sal sy gestellen czwuschen hyr und Stanislai noch Ostern nehist komende"; CONS. 429, fol. 619 (1478).

260   CHAPTER 4

Bernardines of a new missal, whose "writing had begun" and would be finished using Bartholomeus's money.[106] A similar bequest was made by the wealthy alderman and furrier John Kunisz, who donated a missal worth three florins to the chapel of the furriers' guild at St. Mary's Church.[107] Burgher women were also involved in such 'literary' religious practices. For example, in her 1430 will, Catherine, wife of Henry Schendel, made a bequest (among numerous others) of 20 grivna to the school at St. Mary's Church for the purchase of a book for its students.[108] In the same way, in her 1433 will, Catherine, wife of the glassmaker Nicholas, donated six grivna to St. Mary's Church for the purchase of a new psalter.[109]

Bequests by members of Krakow's elite of missals for private altars played a somewhat different role. Affluent burghers wished to provide all the necessary 'equipment' for the altars they funded to ensure that the priest saying Mass could carry out his duties, but they also wished to display their wealth and demonstrate their piety. Some testators even personally selected the missals and other essential elements (chasubles, chalices, silver cruets) to be used at 'their' altars and chapels as a means of demonstrating their religious knowledge and devotion. For example, the notary John Stolle donated an old Roman missal (in German *eyn gerecht ald romisch messebuch,* in Latin *vetus Romanum missale*) for the altar he funded,[110] while John Sweidniczer donated a missal, chasuble, and other items necessary for 'his' altar.[111] Evidence that Stanisław Plesner donated a missal to support the founding of a new altarage is provided by extant sources from 1437 pertaining to a dispute among his relatives.[112] Salomea, widow of the goldsmith Nicholas Brenner, found it necessary for the altar at St. Mary's Church she funded in her will to be equipped with a

---

106   "Item fratribus ad sanctum Bernhardinum decem marcam pro vestitura et missale quod iniciatu est scribi debet terminari de bonis suis et confirmatum ibidem dari, et si fieri poterit, sive dampno puerorum pro casula octo vel nonem florenorum ibidem eciam tribuentur"; LT, fol. 35 (1455).

107   "Item so bescheide ich of der korszner cappelle zu unsir liben frawen III gulden czu eynen meszbuch czu andirsnichtis anczuwenden"; LT, fol. 127 (1481).

108   "XX czu unsir liben frawen czu eym buche den schulern"; SCAB. 5, fol. 203 (1430).

109   "Item czu den singbuchern czu unser liben frawen vi mrc heller adir wo man is andirs wo bedorffin wirt"; LT, fol. 6 (1443).

110   SCAB. 6, fol. 186, 187 (1439).

111   "Item so sollen meyne vermonde kewffen eynen guttin ornat czu meynem altare in meyner Cappellen vor den dewtczen prediger. Item ouch sal dorczu eyn messebuch das do gancz ist, und drey kazeln dy ich vormols habe"; LT, fol. 44 (1457).

112   "Ouch sal der egenante Hannus Foit so dy voitey czu der Newenstat wedirgehabit wurde durch bote adir durch recht czum ersten dem Testamente seyns ohmen Stano Plesners genugtim und das vor alle andern sachen ausrichten mit XII marken gr ierlichis und ewigis czinsis du mit eyme Messebuche und eyner kazil"; CONS. 428, fol. 377 (1437).

THE BURGHER RELIGIOSITY   261

chasuble, chalice, and missal.[113] Similar bequests were made by others, including Paul Ber, who equipped 'his' altar with a "large new missal";[114] mine administrator Matthias Muscala, who planned to found two altarages for which he had earlier provided missals, chalices and chasubles;[115] and Peter Schepcz, who donated "to his chaplain" Kacper, who was to be the altarist of a new altar: two chasubles (*kasseln*), a chalice, missal, platter (*pater*) and two silver cruets weighing four florins.[116]

In light of the above observations on the rise of literacy and the popularity of religious books (among other types of book) among Krakow's elite, it seems no coincidence that, as wills grew in popularity in fourteenth-century Krakow, most were made by members of the municipal council, aldermen and wealthy merchants. Wills were one manifestation of the close link between the rise of literacy and the spread among the elite of a model of personal religious devotion (which did not exclude participation in traditional communal forms of worship). The fact that wills in some cases were handwritten by testators seems less important than the more general fact that a certain group of people thought it necessary to leave behind a written last will after their death.[117]

1.2.3   Expensive Symbols of Piety: Crosses and *Agnus Dei* Medallions

A person who wished to connect with God through prayer, petitioning Him with words and gestures, most often did so at church, with Christian symbols and signs before his eyes. [...] Gradually, objects of personal devotion, such as home altars, reliquaries and images of saints, became increasingly widespread. They were no longer present only in royal households and on magnates' estates, but also among the lesser nobility and burghers.[118]

---

113   "Item so gebe ich mit der tat und habe gegeben dem obgenanten Hern Mathis alle meyme gerade dy ich mir geczewgt habe, daz her do von kewffe und schaffe allirley gerete das czu eyme Eltir gehoret, also ornat, kelch, messebuch etc."; SCAB. 6, fol. 190 (1439).
114   "Ouch bescheide ich ken Grosglogow yn dy pharkirche zu synte Niclos eyne kamische kasel dy beste undir czween dy ich gereyt habe und das grosse newe Missale das man dy czwestucke alle tagen notczen sal zu eyme gedechtnisse und troste meyner elden und frunde zelen der leychnam derselbiste rasten"; SCAB. 8, fol. 270–271 (1466).
115   LT, fol. 122–124 (1479).
116   LT, fol. 137–139 (1483).
117   Notes specifying that the testator wrote his own will is found, among other places, in the wills of John Reichil, a wealthy staller, SCAB. 6, fol. 196, 256 (1440, 1442), Nicholas Newmeister, a deputy municipal notary of Krakow, SCAB. 7, fol. 120 (1451) and Peter Schepcz, a merchant, LT, fol. 137–140 (1483).
118   Stanisław Bylina, *Religijność późnego średniowiecza. Chrześcijaństwo a kultura tradycyjna w Europie Środkowo-Wschodniej w XIV–XV w.* (Warszawa: Neriton, 2009), 53.

Apart from such devotional objects, small crosses and medallions depicting the Lamb of God (*Agnus Dei*) were also occasionally mentioned in wills. They functioned as religious (Christ depicted on the cross or as a lamb), symbolic (as signs of piety) and perhaps even magical objects that were believed to have protective powers.[119] A silver cross and Agnus Dei medallion were first listed in an inventory of personal possessions taken to the town hall following the death of the wealthy burgher Nicholas Teschner.[120] A silver Agnus Dei medallion was also listed as belonging to Krakow councillor Nicholas Dietrich.[121] Meanwhile, we learn about an image of the Lamb of God owned by Stanisław Weingart (probably a relative of councillor Peter Weingart),[122] from records relating to a dispute over the execution of his will.[123] Another important figure representing both the culture of the written word and the highest echelons of burger society in Krakow was the notary Eustace, whose movables included an expensive Agnus Dei medallion made of gold and mother-of-pearl, which he left to his son.[124] This prestigious symbol of Christianity was also owned by Margaret Czipserowa, who was married three times and widowed twice (her second husband was councillor Nicholas Zalcz).[125] The symbolic power of both crosses and Agnus Dei medallions is evidenced by a bequest made by the goldsmith Nicholas Brenner in his 1464 will. In it Brenner listed all his settlements and accounts, including an order from the bride-to-be Łazaria (wife of Nicholas Slop) for a gilded belt, ring, cross, Agnus Dei and some hook-and-eye closures.[126] This indicates that the Agnus Dei was treated as both an ornament and an important symbol of religious devotion on the bride's dress.

---

119   Aleksandra Witkowska, *Kulty pątnicze piętnastowiecznego Krakowa* (Lublin: Wydawnictwo Towarzystwa Naukowego Katolickiego Uniwersytetu Lubelskiego, 1984), 215–216.

120   "Eyn cleyn crewczchin von silber, 1 silberyn agnus dei"; CONS. 428, fol. 320 (1433).

121   "Item dy frawe hot bey ir eyne kostir und eyne large zeide, und iris mannis cleydir. Item sy hot bey ir silberinne gabilchen Agnus Dei zilberin kapchin zilberin leffil und II zecke mit czwebilzomen und eynen kasten mit buchner manchirlen"; CONS. 429, fol. 344 (1463).

122   Marcin Starzyński, *Krakowska rada*, 248.

123   CONS. 428, fol. 413 (1440).

124   "Item dorczu eyn Agnus Dei vorgolt mit eyner perlen muttir," "Item unum agnus die cum margarita perlen muter"; LT, fol. 61–63 (1459).

125   LT, fol. 165–166 (1501).

126   "Item so habe ich der frawen Lazarien Niclos Sloppottynne of ire hochczeit und ouch der thachter gemacht gortel of geslagen und forgolt und fingerleyn gemacht, creuczleyn und eyn Agnus dei vorgolt und heftleyn gemacht dofon allis czulone ist sy mir scholdig andirthalb marg hellir"; LT, fol. 83–84 (1464).

THE BURGHER RELIGIOSITY   263

1.3 Participation in the sacrum: Personal Belongings Used for Religious Purposes

The division of property into 'movable' and 'immovable,' present in even the oldest codices, was more than just a medieval legal concept, it was also a reflection of a medieval mentality. The difference between movable and immovable property is best reflected in the relationship between these types of property and their owner. While real estate was seen as property that was almost independent of the owner, something held in common with members of the wider social group, movables were considered extensions of their owner's body – *Mobilia ossibus inhaerent*.[127] An identification of testators with the objects they possessed was closest in the case of personal objects, such as clothing and jewellery, but functioned to a lesser extent in relation to their dishes, bedding, tools, armour and weaponry. These things constituted the basic components of specific categories of feminine goods, gerade, and masculine goods, hergewet.[128] Even people today, whose ways of thinking differ greatly from a traditional mentality, tend to identify with certain personal items, believing they in some way express their personality; the value of such objects is assessed in symbolic rather than economic terms. Given our present knowledge of the Middle Ages, both with regard to the realities of everyday life and the prevailing mentality, it seems that the identification of people with their private possessions must have been much stronger than today.

---

127   Karol Koranyi also found an expression close to this ancient maxim in, among other places, a fourteenth-century compilation of Parisian law: "Les bies ensuyvent le corps quanta aux meubles"; *idem*, "Podstawy średniowiecznego prawa spadkowego," *Pamiętnik Historyczno-Prawny* 9, no. 2 (1930), 39.

128   This seemingly anachronistic division is still visible in the dispositions of testators and in disputes regarding wills brought before the courts in Krakow in the late fifteenth century. For example, in her will of 1476, Catherine *glezerynne* ordered that tutors of her choice should donate all the property she left to the work of charity, with the exception of the *gerade*, which should be given to those to who are entitled to it; LT, fol. 114 (1476). The durability of the division into female and male objects is also evidenced by critical remarks made by Bartłomiej Groicki about the *gerade* in the mid-sixteenth century: "I know very well that we should be wary of correcting or contaminating laws, which were established through the hard work of many wise men, and they undoubtedly had merit and proper grounds for the age when they were written. But when other centuries have other customs – alias *vita alios mores* postulate – than scholars of the law, if such need arises or there is a good use for it, it is not a futile task, as they say, that many laws shall change, many of them shall be undone as well. Therefore, there is a new interpretation of conflicting laws concerning the *gerade*, due to the troubles and tensions it brings about among friends, to such injustice that a more distant person is to take, in spite of there being a closer one and to the endless excesses of the female garments"; *idem, Tytuły prawa majdeburskiego*, Warszawa 1954, 13.

The description above is intended to shed light on the reasoning behind a certain kind of donation in which testators bequeathed their personal belongings, such as belts, coats, spoons, pitchers and the like, to the Church. In this way, these objects acquired a religious, mystical and, to some extent, 'magical' significance, i.e. they became liturgical items (usually chalices and chasubles) used to celebrate Holy Mass.[129] Such objects were not important just because they were used during the celebration of Holy Mass, they were considered 'holy' themselves because of their direct participation in the Sacrament of the Eucharist. In the fourteenth and fifteenth centuries, as lay people became more knowledgeable about religion and the cult of the Eucharist became more widespread, their desire to participate more fully in the sacrament grew.[130] In folk religion,[131] the forms of worship accepted by the Church intertwined and overlapped with older, pre-Christian ceremonies and rituals and attitudes toward the sacred.[132] Drawing on numerous testimonies, Johan

---

129   "[...] men most commonly gave vestments, or money to buy vestments, whereas women gave their own clothing such as dresses and kerchiefs, and household linens like sheets and tablecloths – items which held personal meaning but which were also part of their public identity as virtuous, diligent and modest homemakers"; Nicola A. Lowe, "Women's Devotional Bequests of Textiles in the Late Medieval English Parish Church, c. 1350–1550," *Gender & History*, 22 (2010), 408.

130   "The doctrine of Christ's authentic presence in the Eucharist, disseminated among the faithful by the Church and questioned only by the adepts of heretical movements, made it possible to see it as a symbol of worship, but also a the object itself, the very body of Christ within the host. The attitude of devotion promoted by the clergy among believers was based on the natural tendency of people to see a deity present on earth. Therefore, looking at the host became a spiritual need of the followers of Christianity and an important, commonly observed devotional practice. This need in believers, testified to in the sources from the thirteenth century, was reinforced by the development of the Eucharistic cult and lasted until the late pre-Reformation period. It was manifested in the pursuit of frequent and long (as possible) viewing of the host raised during the Mass by the priest. [...] In addition to believing in the mysterious, magical power of the host, looking at it was considered a manifestation of due piety"; Stanisław Bylina, *Religijność późnego średniowiecza*, 54

131   Folk religiousness was defined by Stanisław Bylina as follows: "It includes phenomena involving a substrate of archaic beliefs, manifested even just in traditional attitudes, often with a magical motivation"; *ibidem*, 9.

132   In describing the first stage of the Christianization of the Polish lands in the late thirteenth century, Jerzy Dowiat pointed to the importance of magical thinking for the creation of a kind of syncretic model of Christianity in the lands inhabited by Slavs: "Christians who came to Poland, including clergy [...] also introduced Christian magic: treating objects of liturgical cult as endowed with magical power, and also referring to liturgical texts as a kind of magical spells"; *idem*, "Pogląd na świat," in *Kultura Polski średniowiecznej X–XIII w.*, ed. Jerzy Dowiat (Warszawa: Państwowy Inst. Wydawn., 1985), 174.

THE BURGHER RELIGIOSITY

265

Huizinga demonstrated that in the late Middle Ages the phrase 'to see God'[133] simply referred to the elevation of the host. As such, it straddled the fine line between reverence for the miracle of Holy Communion and profanity. While such an approach to religion prevailed among the uneducated masses, "such traditional attitudes towards religion, expressed in various kinds of rituals and gestures, were also shared by educated members of society, as we learn in theological treatises from the fourteenth and the fifteenth centuries."[134]

The first fourteenth-century bequest to mention the personal belongings of the testator was drafted by the mine administrator Paszek. In 1358, Paszek donated three coats (one made of marten fur, a brown coat with a lining, and a blue coat) and one tunic to clergymen with whom he was friendly.[135] These were undoubtedly expensive gifts, but given the testator's vast wealth, their true value was commemorative. On the one hand, the gifts indicated that Paszek knew the clergymen well; on the other, such a valuable gift demanded some form of reciprocation (praying for Paszek's soul) and would be hard to forget.[136] Paszek also stated in his will that two silver belts should be given to brother Gregory to make a chalice and two silver cruets.[137] Likewise, Barbara, widow of Martin Nimpczer, stated in her will that her belt and spoons should be used to make a gilded chalice for St Mary's Church.[138] Nicholas Topler left two 'big spoons' and a man's belt to St. Bernardine's Church, stating that they should be used to make a chalice and a paten (a type of small plate used in the Eucharist).[139] Many other testators made special dispositions, stating that the silver personal items they possessed should be made into liturgical chalices.[140] For example, Anna, wife of the innkeeper Peter Wolski, bequeathed all of

---

133   Johan Huizinga, *The Autumn of the Middle Ages*, 178.

134   Stanisław Bylina, *Religijność późnego średniowiecza*, 10.

135   "Item Palium cum pellibus Marderinis demandauit fratri Bartkoni. Item aliud palium bruneticum cum Subductiua fratri gregorio. Item Palium flaueum cum tunica domino Boguslao plebano in Ossek"; NKiRMK, no. 1692, 1693.

136   Józef Burszta, *Społeczeństwo daru i dar w społeczeństwie*, in *Do, ut des – dar, pochówek, tradycja* (Funeralia Lednickie, 7), ed. Wojciech Dzieduszycki, Jacek Wrzesiński (Poznan: SNAP. Oddział, 2005), 17–24.

137   "Item duos Cingulos argenteos fecit dare fratri Gregorio pro Calice aut pro duabus ampullis"; SCAB., no. 1692, 1693 (1358).

138   "Item noch meynem tode ap meyne gortil und leffil blebin, so sullen meyne vormunde doraus lossen eynen guten kelch machen und den lossen vorgolden ud sullen den entwerten czu unsir liben frawen am Ringe gelegen"; LT, fol. 27 (1452).

139   "Item so gebe ich czu sinte Bernhardino dy grosten II silberen leffil und eynen mannes gortil das man eyn kelich und eyne patene machen"; LT, fol. 99–100 (1470).

140   For example, Peter, an attorney, recommended: "Item zo hot her gegeben und bescheiden das silbir das her czu Johanne Tendirneudir legin hot czu eyme kelche czu machen und

her movable and immovable property to her husband, except for seven silver spoons and buttons (*nodis*), which were to be made into a chalice that was "as big as possible." The chalice was to be donated to St. Bernadine's Church and the monastery there.[141]

Based on the bequest of Dorothy, wife of Nicholas Kestener, that her valuables be melted down and made into a chalice.[142] A similar bequest was made from the foundation of Claire, the widow of John Hobschbeck, who donated the proceeds from the sale of her meat stall for the purchase of a chalice, chasuble and other liturgical items.[143] In turn, Martin Junge paid for a chalice and a chasuble to commemorate his late wife.[144]We can assume that the testators mentioned above also wished to turn their valuables into liturgical objects that would have direct contact with the sacred.[145] On the one hand, such a gift was another means of commemorating the testator, as their personal belongings – an 'extension' of themselves – were used to celebrate Holy Mass.[146] On the

---

czu sinte Marcus in das Clostir czu geben," CONS. 428, fol. 125 (1419); Margaret Puskinne: "Ouch gebe ich Magistro Johanni czwene slechte cappe silbrin und I cleyn Capchin und IIII leffil czu eyme kelche," SCAB. 5, fol. 114 (1425); Peter Eichler: "Item was von silbrin gerete ist do sal man eyner kelch aws machen," SCAB. 5, fol. 130 (1426); and: LT, fol. 52 (1458), 56 (1458), 68 (1460), 109–110 (1475), 143–144 (1487), 149–150 (1491).

141 "Primo Petro marito suo legitimo legavit effectualiter omnia bona sua mobilia et immobilia debita et utensilia universa nulla penitus exclusis cum plena proprietate faciendi et dimittendi exceptis solum septem cocleariis argenteis et nodis exquibus calix quanto melius fieri potest pro monasterio et ecclesia sancti Bernhardini disponi debet"; LT, fol. 36 (1456).

142 "[...] omnia iocalia ipsius argentea debent fabricari ad calicem et calix ad Ecclesiam in Pilgeramisdorf assignari"; CONS. 427, fol. 74 (1396).

143 "Item quartale macelli, qua vendita [s] debent comparari calix et ornatus cum aliis pertinenciis ad missam"; SCAB., no. 414 (1369).

144 "[...] auch beule ich XVI marg czu sente Stephan czu der kirchen, adir, wirt man bawen eine kirche hy vor der stat, so sal man dy XVI marg dorczu gehen, wenne alzo vil geldis brochte myne frawe czu mir, dy ich vor der hatte, ouch bit ich, das man von der cronen vnde von den schellin, dy do bey sint, sal man I kelch czugen vnd I gancz messegewant dorczu in dy selbe kirche"; SCAB., no. 1816 (1393).

145 "Among these objects, the most important were those paraments that came into direct contact with the sacred during transubstantiation, as well as chasubles, amices, albs, maniples, and other elements of liturgical clothing, which were also becoming key liturgical objects visible throughout the Mass"; Oliński, *Fundacje mieszczańskie w miastach pruskich*, 81.

146 "The psychology of magical thinking lists numerous examples of how the sense of Self of a primitive human did not refer to the model of an integral person. This human saw him or herself rather as a set of independent parts or dispositions. For this reason, the Self also included personal objects and even family goods."; Magdalena Kowalska, *Psychologiczna (prze)moc wzajemności*, in *Do, ut des*, 43.

THE BURGHER RELIGIOSITY   267

other hand, the desire to be in the direct presence of the sacred can be interpreted as a form of 'magical thinking,' a believe in contagious power of the
sacred.[147]

As evidenced by the will of the goldsmith Nicholas Brenner, these valuable
personal belongings were not simply sold to pay for liturgical items. Brenner was a master of his craft, and counted among his clients members of the
uppermost social elite, including the voivode of Krakow, John Tenczyński; the
castellan of Tarnów (*Tharnische herre*); members of Krakow patrician families;
and the canon of Krakow, John Długosz.[148] Because Brenner's will was made
on his deathbed, he listed numerous orders he had not yet fulfilled. These
records clearly show that silver items, such as cups or goblets, were given to
the goldsmith to be melted down and used as raw material for liturgical items.[149]
The donated items, retaining their purity, were thus turned by the goldsmith
into sacred objects, containing, in a symbolic way, the figure of the testator.
For example, gilded chalices donated by Matthias Opoczka, John Odów and
the municipal notary Christopher Rebentcz to St. Mary's Church bore inscrip-
tions clearly stating the names of the donors. The first stated: HIC CALIX COM-
PARATUS EST PER DOMINUM MATHIAM OPOCZKO PRO ECCLESIA BEATE
VIRGINIS; the second: HUNC CALICEM COMPARAVIT IOHANNES ODOW; and
the third: HUNC CALICEM HONORABILIS CHRISTOFORUS NOTARIUS HUIUS
CIVITATIS COMPARAVIT.[150]

Some testators, in turn, donated expensive fabrics for chasubles. In fulfilment of the provisions of John Stolle's will, Sweidniczer donated expensive
damask fabric to St. Mary's Church for a chasuble to be worn by the priest
who celebrated Mass at the altar funded by Stolle. Similarly, Margaret Leipnigerinne donated expensive fabric for a chasuble for 'her altar' at a church

---

147   Stanisław Bylina, *Religijność późnego średniowiecza*, 53–58.
148   LT, fol. 83–84 (1464).
149   Among the interesting entries was one concerning the commission of a new monstrance
       for the Curch of St. Catherine in Kazimierz, Krakow: "Item czu der Monstrancia czu sinte
       Katherina czu Kazmer habe ich entpfangen newnczen marg solber und vonfte halbe
       scot. So habe ich abir entpfangen czwen alde kelche dy haben beide gewegin vir marg
       und sebinczen scot solber ungebrant. Abir entpfangen czwu marg solber und sechs scot
       gebrant. Dornoch habe ich entpfangen drey marg solber minus sechs scot gebrant solber.
       Abir habe ich entpfangen von eynem fusse und eynem koppe ungebrant das wegit fonfte-
       halbe marg und sechstehalbe scot solber. Item so habe ich entpfangen of dy erbit von der
       selben Monstranczia virczen gulden"; LT, fol. 83–84 (1464).
150   *Najdawniejsze inwentarze skarbca kościoła N.P. Maryi w Krakowie z XV wieku*, ed. Fran-
       ciszek Piekosiński, Krakow 1889 (reprint in "Sprawozdania Komisji do Badań Historii
       Sztuki w Polsce" 4, no. 2 (1889), 64–77). Elżbieta Piwowarczyk, *Dzieje Kościoła Mariackiego*
       (*XIII–XVI w.*) (Krakow: Wydaw. Naukowe PAT, 2000), 175–177.

in Bytom. She also donated 12 grivna in silver from her personal silverware to make three chalices for, respectively, St. Bernardine's Church, the monastery in Lechnica, and 'her altar' at the church in Bytom.[151] In his 1492 will, the wealthy tailor Jarosz stated that his expensive damask bedspread (*tectura lectus de kamcho*) should be made into a chasuble for the parish church in his hometown of Zator.[152]

A rare but quite telling bequest was made by the affluent merchant John Reichil. Among his many pious bequests was one for his weapons and armour, including a cuirass, a helmet and visor, and a horse, to be given to the Benedictine monastery of the Holy Cross at Łysa Góra.[153] We do not know how the Krakow merchant came into possession of this military equipment or why he donated it to the Benedictine monks, but we can assume based on the nature of the gift, that its economic value was not as important as its symbolic value – as a kind of votive gift to the sanctuary.[154] It is very possible that the testator made such a gift because he wished to be buried in the monastery.[155] In Polish lands, such bequests were usually made by knights, for whom armour symbolized their function, role and privileged social position.[156] Armour, which was rarely possessed by burghers, constituted part of the hergewet. John Reichil

---

151   LT, fol. 37 (1456).

152   LT, fol. 151–152.

153   "Item so gebe ich den hern czu dem heiligen Crewcze of dem Berge alle meyne Harnosch, panczir, lapke, heubchen etc und eyn pferd"; SCAB. 6, fol. 196–197 (1440).

154   He renewed this disposal two years later in his will of 1442: "und seynen harnisch beschit her czu dem heyligen Crewcze"; SCAB. 6, fol. 256.

155   "Devoting armour *pro remedio animae* was supposedly widespread especially in places where the custom of placing weapons and other objects in graves was abandoned only under the influence of Christianity [...]. Despite Christianization, however, the old belief sometimes manifested itself in acts of last will. By donating certain objects to a church institute, the testator wanted the objects that served him during his lifetime, very often armour in particular, to be placed in his resting place after his death, *où je serai sevelie, ubi corpus meus sepelietur, ubi sepultus fuero, quia ibi expectabit resurrectionem iustorum*. Sometimes this also included objects that the deceased had come into contact with, and therefore were considered his own"; Karol Koranyi, *Podstawy średniowiecznego prawa spadkowego*, 91–92.

156   "The custom of donating armour to the church where the principal was buried is also established in some places in Poland. There are also cases in which the family considered it their duty to donate a part of the deceased's military equipment, such as a horse, to the church. Admittedly, in Polish land law armour did not have a separate legal status among movables as it had in Saxon law. However, there is no denying the possibility that the latter influenced land law in this respect [...]. We can see here the influence of the Church, likely modelled on the practices it developed in other countries, incorporating the aforementioned old religious beliefs that the deceased should be buried close to objects they used during their lifetime."; *ibidem*.

THE BURGHER RELIGIOSITY   269

could thus have made his bequest to the monastery because he lacked male heirs. A potential lack of heirs motivated Catherine, widow of the goldsmith George, to make in her will numerous pious bequests (she also donated two silver cups for chalices to Krakow churches) to be carried out in the event of the death of her only child.[157] The tailor Jarosz decided, in turn, that if one of his sons became a priest, two silver cups (*picarios*) should be made into a chalice and paten.[158]

Testators had different reasons for donating valuable personal belongings, silverware and fabrics to the Church to be turned into liturgical items. The examples listed above generally represent only part of the pious bequests made by these testators. They can be interpreted as yet another means of securing one's salvation, as votive offerings made to gain God's favour (*do ut es*).[159] The decision to turn silver items into chalices, patens and cruets may have been motivated by a scarcity of raw silver 'on the market.' Another factor influencing these dispositions was the specific function played by a burgher's jewellery, silverware and other valuables, which were not only purchased as ostentatious displays of wealth, but also as investments that could be liquidated (sold or melted) if necessary. It is thus difficult to say for certain whether such donations of liturgical items were typical pious bequests or whether they reflected a deeper, unexpressed intention, one reflecting some mix of religious and magical beliefs. Such a mix has been suggested by Aleksandra Witkowska in relation to the votive practices of pilgrims in the Krakovian 'sacred places' i.e. churches storing relics of saints (*loca sacra*):

> Votive practices that treat a saint as a party to a contract are undoubtedly very close to magical practices. The element of magic is especially evident in the custom of offering gifts, which symbolically represent the

---

157   LT, fol. 142–143 (1484).

158   "Item si aliquis dictorum puerorum videlicet Stanislaum vel Jacobum aliqui sacerdotibus conmisit sibi duos argenteos picarios suorum pro bono calice cum patena dandis"; LT, fol. 151–152 (1492).

159   "In the culture of gestures and imagery developed in the late Middle Ages, it seems that the votive gesture – propitiatory, thankful, or, somehow coercing the saint into making a miraculous intervention – served primarily as a visible sign of faith in the power of a 'contract' based on to the principle *do ut des* implicit in the vow. A person approaching the *ad loca sacra* saw their request had been answered or wanted it to be so, and brought a gift symbolizing the relationship established between them and the saint. The contract was made through such a sacrificial gesture, which was suited to a rather primitive religious imagination with a strong element of magical thinking, determinedly seeking the goodwill in the sacred expressed through some kind of transactional exchange of mutual favours";AleksandraWitkowska, *Kulty pątnicze*, 213–214; Marcel Mauss, *The Gift*.

270   CHAPTER 4

donor or the object of his petition for divine intervention. The moment when one appeals for help, motivated undoubtedly by religious convictions, also involves magical thinking. The votive offering symbolising the petition transfers its reality to the symbol or image. Placing it within the nearest sphere of the sacred causes, it is believed, the blessing of the reality that the gift symbolizes.[160]

Due to the popularity of this type of bequest, we have evidence of a confirmed practice and custom found among Krakovian burghers. Due to its specific nature, this custom confirms the hypothesis of a link between these donations and the characteristic need for as direct as possible an experience of the sacred, which was centred around the altar.[161]

2   The Familial Dimension of Piety

Another dimension of burgher religiosity was centred on the family.[162] We can assume that, as with other spheres of burgher community life, religious life also had a syncretic character, insofar as traditional family rituals were saturated with religious symbolism.[163] Such rituals were an important element in

---

160   AleksandraWitkowska, *Kulty pątnicze*, 215.

161   "Apart from the above-mentioned function of the language of communication, votive practices were also considered a chance to prolong the physical presence of a pilgrim at a place of worship. From the point of view of religious anthropology, votive offerings are an important testimony to a special form of participation within the sacred circle. A votive offering is once again used as a substitute. Left in the place of worship, it is equivalent to the physical presence of the vower. The bonds of their contact with the saint are strengthened by this gesture and continue to be maintained"; *ibidem*, 217–218. A similar intention can be seen in the desire to bury the body of the deceased in a church as close to the main altar as possible: "The choicest and most expensive location was the choir, near the altar, where the Mass was said, in the place where the priest recited the *Confiteor*. (The reader will recall that the underlying reason for burial *apud ecclesiam* was the sacrifice of the Mass, rather than the protection of the saints)."; Philippe Ariès, *The Hour of Our Death*, trans. Helen Weaver (New York: Viking, 1981), 79.

162   Marek Słoń, *Religijność komunalna w Europie środkowej późnego średniowiecza*, in *Zbožnost středověku*, ed. Martin Nodl, Krzysztof Bracha, Jan Hrdina, Paweł Kras (Praha: Filosofia, 2007) (Colloquia mediaevalia Pragensia, 6), 21.

163   "Medieval religious practice, whether Christian, Muslim, or Jewish, was intimately connected to family life. Mothers were responsible for basic religious education at virtually all social levels, and personal piety conducted within a domestic environment was a fundamental component of religious practice"; Linda E. Mitchell, *Family Life in the Middle Ages* (Westport: Greenwood Press, 2007), 171.

THE BURGHER RELIGIOSITY 271

family life, greatly influencing the nature and strength of the bonds within this 'basic social unit.' Unfortunately, because so few sources say anything about everyday religious life in the home, this area (like many other aspects of everyday life) will remain for us *terra incognita*.

Another problem we face is the question of the scope of our research and its representativity given the diversity that existed in medieval urban society. In Chapter Three on the family and marriage, an analysis of various bequests allowed us to distinguish two different models of the burgher family. The first, the nuclear family – consisting of parents, children and, sometimes, household servants – was characteristic of the poor and middle class. Family life revolved around the family home, the artisan's workshop, or stall (they were sometimes located in the same building). A characteristic feature of this model was the existence of close emotional bonds existing between the spouses, and a marked distance from (and in some cases even an aversion to) more distant relatives. It can be assumed that this was due to the living situation of many burghers, for whom the success of the individual (often an immigrant) depended primarily on his or her hard work, the support of his spouse and children, and only to a lesser extent, the help of more distant, often poor relatives, who were also potential heirs.

In the second model, that of the extended family, the so-called patrician model characteristic of the city's elite, the bonds between spouses were significantly less marked by a mutual concern for each other's security. The wife of a patrician was not only entitled to a significant dower, she might also receive significant inheritances from members of her family. She was thus relatively independent of her husband, and, it can be assumed, her marriage was more of a 'contract between families' than an expression of true emotions.[164] On the other hand, in the extended family model, mutual bonds connected not only the immediate family, but also adult siblings, nephews, nieces, and the in-law family. This is not surprising, as the success of a merchant's career depended not only on his luck, knowledge and abilities, but also on his social capital, including his family contacts.

The functioning of two such very different family models in the medieval city undoubtedly influenced the religious practices of their members. In this area, the activity of the city's social elite was particularly visible – they engaged in devotional activities not only 'privately,' i.e. directed inward, but also demonstrated their piety 'publicly' to the entire city. As evidenced by the analysed

---

164 Barbara A. Hanawalt, *The Wealth of Wives. Women, Law, and Economy in Late Medieval London* (Oxford: Oxford University Press, 2007), 70–78.

272   CHAPTER 4

sources, an important role was also played here by the culture of the written word, in which patricians participated to the greatest extent. The factors mentioned above were largely responsible for the fact that the family dimension of religiosity visible in the sources is reflective mainly of the wealthiest representatives of urban society rather than of the population of medieval Krakow as a whole.[165]

What we know about religious practices within the family is based on manifestations of these practices outside the family home. The most striking 'external' manifestation of urban religiosity was donations made by Krakow's elite to various churches and religious institutions. Since at least the mid-fourteenth century, affluent Krakovian burghers had been involved in the building and furnishing of St. Mary's Church, and, to a lesser degree, other churches.[166] The information contained in wills provides many examples of commemorative bequests that were meant to ensure the salvation of the testator, as well as of his deceased relatives and ancestors. This was true of a generous foundation from Nicholas Wierzynek (*Wirzing*) the elder to help finance the building of a new presbytery at St. Mary's Church. He was commemorated with a plaque which informed the public who the donor was: FUNDATOR CHORI ISTIUS A. D. 1360 FRANCISCI FESTO DIE SOLIS, DAPIFER WIRZING OBIIT.[167] Nicholas Wierzynek the younger and three other Krakovian burghers, Herman Krancz, Arnold Welker and Nicholas Trutil, also wished to fund private altars at St. Mary's Church. We know this because they wrote to Pope Urban V seeking his permission.[168] Since few sources from this period have survived, it is unclear whether these pious donations were made *inter vivos* or as testamentary bequests. The former seems to be the case, however, as indicated by information pertaining to councillor Herman Krancz's will from 1380 telling us that Krancz had made a bequest to found a new altar, which had been formally

---

165 Although the influence of the elites on the culture of the city as a whole was undeniable, it is certainly not possible to project the presented practices directly into the wider context of the municipality.

166 "The ambition that St. Mary's Church, the parish church for the largest and wealthiest part of the city population, would become an urban cathedral with a status similar to the Wawel Cathedral is visible already in the fifteenth century. These efforts were reflected not only in the altar service, but also in the special patronage of the Krakow burghers, who were working towards its ennoblement through numerous foundations"; Elżbieta Piwowarczyk, *Dzieje*, 123.

167 "According to church records, on the southern wall on the small choir, shielded from view by stalls, was a plaque with the inscription: *Fundator chori istius, A.D. 1360 Francisci festo die solis, Dapifer Wirzing obiit*"; Ambroży Grabowski, *Krakow i jego okolice*, Krakow 1866, 362.

168 Elżbieta Piwowarczyk, *Dzieje*, 131.

THE BURGHER RELIGIOSITY

approved fifteen years earlier.[169] The new altar, dedicated to Corpus Christi, with the altarage of St. Longinus, was placed in the church choir (*a cornu Ewangelii Majoris Altari*) and equipped with the necessary items, purchased with revenue from a farm Krancz had bought in the village of Prądnik.[170] A donation made by councillor Nicholas Edel in 1369, however, was not referred to as a will or testamentary bequest in Krakow's oldest municipal book. In the presence of councillors from the municipal council, Edel left his stall, together with two grivna in annual rent, to the Dominicans. In return, the friars were to say a daily Mass for the salvation of Edel's "ancestors and descendants" in his chapel.[171] However, Edel left further instructions for the councillors, who were to pay the Dominicans rent twice a year and ensure that the friars held up their end of the agreement. Otherwise, the municipal council had the right to spend the money on food for the sick or other acts of charity to ensure the salvation of Edel and his family.[172] As evidenced by his 1393 will, Gotfrid Fattinante of Genoa funded two altars to ensure the salvation of his soul (*in salutare anime sue remedium*).[173] The first altar was erected at St. Mary's Church for the glory

---

169   KDWac., vol. 2, no. 309.

170   "S. Longini 1-ministerij Fundationis Hermani Krancz Civis Cracoviensis. Erectum hoc ministerium Anno D. 1380 d. 13 Januarij ex censu anno f. 80 in Allodio in villa Prąmnik 2000 Reemptionalis, Possesionis Conventus Tynecensis Ordinis S-i Benedicti"; cited in Elżbieta Piwowarczyk, *Dzieje*, 131.

171   "Honorabilis vir Nicolaus Edelingi nobis conconsul, dum simul in pleno sederemus consilio, nobis Magnarum precura instancia intimitis suplicauit, vt assumpta nobis nomine Ciuitatis nostre Instita sua in acie in Medio institarum sita et Duas Marcas polonicales currentis monetę, nos aut qui pro tempore fuerint Consules Ciuitatis constituti, de pretorio singulis annis elemosine perpetue ipsis Religiosis viris fratribus predicatoribus Conuentus dicte nostre Ciuitatis daremus. Cuius elemosine virtute ijdem fratres predicatores ipsorum exigente deuocione ad unam missam cottidie in Capella eiusdem Nicolai Edelingi celebrandam in ipsius predecessorum omnium et posterorum suorum animarum remedium salutare vitro se exhibuerunt firmiter astringendo, prout in eorum literis desuper confectis luculencius continetur"; NKiRMK, no. 1705.

172   This provision from 1369 already indicates the role of the municipal council as an institution that supervised, mediated and supervised the religious life of the Krakow burghers. Initially, this care most likely primarily concerned certain families from urban elite circles.

173   "Primo vero in salutare anime sue remedium Cameram suam pannorum circa cameram Pauli Nutricis et sex marcas census annui et terragij, quem super fundo domus Nicolai Beidner in platea sutorum site, habere dignoscitur, pro altari in honorem sanctorum Anthonij confessoris et alme virginis Dorothee ac martyris ad taxam sedecim marcarum et valorem in ecclesia parochiali sanete Marie Virginis semper gloriose in Cracouia erecturo siue erigendo, feliciter construeturo siue construendo, cuius collacio, presentacio, prouisio seu queuis alia disposicio ad Consules Ciuitatis Cracouiensis nunc et pro tempore existentes, perpetuo pertinere debeat, de quo altari prouidit ad presens domino Petro capellano et notario suo, domum vero suam lapideam in acie circuli circa

274 CHAPTER 4

of St. Anthony, Blessed Dorothy and martyrs (*sanctorum Anthonii confessoris et alme virginis Dorothee ac martyris*). The second altar, dedicated to the same figures, was erected at All Saints Church. Apart from his grandson, whom he mentioned in his will, Gotfrid Fattinante did not have any other close relatives.[174] However, the will of councillor Michael de Czirla, from 1435, explicitly stated that he wished to ensure his own salvation as well as the salvation of his children and ancestors (*pro anime mee et filii mei ac progenitorum meorum suffragio salutary*).[175] This testator funded an altar at St. Mary's Church, "for the glory of God and St. Mary Mother of God" (*ad laudem Dei et eius genitricis honorem*) for this purpose.[176] We can assume that if there was no explicit information in the will about why the testator decided to found new chapels, altars or perpetual altarages, the motivation behind the gift was to commemorate the testators and ensure the salvation of their souls, as well as the salvation of their ancestors, children and grandchildren. In this way, these most generous

---

Powsuange sitam, valido viro domino Spitkoni Palatino ac Capitaneo Cracouiensi, vt per ipsum ac electos presentis testamenti executores infrascriptos alicui ciui vendi debeat, et pro huiusmodi pecunia census sedecim marcarum perpetuus comparari, et de eodem censu sedecim marcarum altare eciam sanctorum Anthonij Confessoris et beate Dorothee Virginis in ecclesia parrochiali Sanctorum Omnium in ciuitate Cracouiensi eciam de taxa sedecim marcarum erigi et construi, cuius collacio seu queuis alia disposicio ipsi domino Spitkoni ac suis posteris legitimisque successoribus perpetuis debet pertinere temporibus, dedit, contulit ac perpetuo assignauit, quod eciam altare domino Iohanni presbytero domus sue et medico assignauit"; KDWac., vol. 2, no. 396, 182–185.

174　It is likely that he was related or associated with the Krakow governor Spytko, known as "Palatinus ac Capitaneus Cracouiensis," to whom he handed over the right of presentment to one of the altars; cf. Józef Garbacik, "Gotfrid Fattinante," in PSB, vol. 6 (Krakow: Polska Akademia Nauk, Polska Akademia Umiejętności, 1948), 377–378.

175　"Primo mencionem faciens capelle, quam in cimiterio beate Marie Virginis contiguam ostio meridionali eiusdem ecclesie citeriori edificandam ipse iam antea disposuit, cuius et iam sunt posita fundamenta, volo inquit, ut compleatur opus illud usque ad plenam ipsius capelle consumacionem, scilicet iuxta eam formam et modum, secundum quod condixi et convencionem feci cum muratore. Et in eadem capella, cum perfecta fuerit, edificari debet altare et consecrari, in quo iugis fiat missarum celebracio ad laudem Dei et eius genitricis honorem, pro anime mee et filii mei ac progenitorum meorum suffragio salutari. Namque ad eiusdem altaris dotacionem, do, lego et assigno 13 mr. census annui et perpetui communis pecunie polonicalis, quorum censuum 8 mr. et 16 scoti sunt in et super teloneo Cracoviensi, quas hucusque annuatim habui et percepi, relique 5 mr. eiusmodi census comparari debent de illis 400 mr. communis pecunie polonicalis, quas michi providus Claus Kezinger, civis Cracoviensis, tenetur, inscriptas in villam suam Trzebinia, ita ut sint 13mr. pro rectore seu altarista dicti altaris et 16 scoti reliqui pro luminibus ad usum eiusdem altaris per ipsum altaristam perpetue convertendi"; CONS. 428, fol. 344.

176　It was to be located in the chapel of St. Mary's Church, which was then under construction, 'by the southern door.'

THE BURGHER RELIGIOSITY   275

pious foundations, which were meant to bring to mind similar bequests made
by noble, secular and spiritual elites, were a testament to the importance and
assumed glory of new Krakow burgher families. This trend was so influential
that expensive foundations were established by both members of long-standing patrician families in Krakow, such as the Wierzyneks (*Wirzings*), Langs and
Morsztyns (*Mornsteyn, Mornstin*), and the 'nouveau riche,' who entered the
elite circles of Krakow through marriage. By the end of the fourteenth century,
burghers had financed eleven new altars at St. Mary's Church, which remained
Krakow's most important religious building. As evidenced by a list made by
John Długosz in *Liber beneficiorum,* in the latter half of the fifteenth century
this number had increased to thirty altars. One, two, or even three Masses were
celebrated before each altar daily.[177] By the end of the fifteenth century, two
new side altars had been erected. Thanks to the joint efforts of the parishioners and numerous testators, a new main altar was built for the church – the
famous St. Mary's Altar by Veit Stoss.[178] As Elżbieta Piwowarczyk aptly noticed:

> At the end of the fifteenth century, chapels began to occupy a special
> place in St. Mary's Church. With time, those possessing them were seen
> as a kind of city's nobility. The families of the founders would often pray
> at the chapel's altars, and in many cases attended Mass more often in the
> chapel than at the main altar... Special stalls were later installed for them.
> In around the mid-fourteenth century, these family chapels began to be
> separated from the main nave with bars placed in the arcades, which
> resulted in their relative isolation from the physical space of the temple.[179]

Krakovian testators did not, however, limit their bequests to St. Mary's Church,
the parish church of many burghers. Similar foundations were established at
other churches in the city and throughout the Krakow urban agglomeration,[180]
as well as at churches in other towns, usually the testators' hometowns.[181] Testators naturally tended to identify most closely with their own parish, which not
only formed a sort of community of prayer, but also comprised a community

---

177   Elżbieta Piwowarczyk, *Dzieje...*, 164–166.
178   Marjan Friedberg, "Ołtarz krakowski Wita Stwosza. Studium archiwalne," *Przegląd Za-
      chodni* 8, no. 7/8 (1952), 673–706.
179   Elżbieta Piwowarczyk, *Dzieje*, 161–162.
180   E.g. the foundation of an altar in All Saints' Church by Gotfried Fattinante; KDWac., vol. 2,
      no. 396.
181   E.g. the foundation of an altar in St. Anne's Church by the councillor Nicholas Zarogowski,
      LT, 129–131 (1482), or an altar owned by Margaret Leipnigerinne in a church in Bytom and
      mentioned in her will, LT, fol. 37 (1456).

276   CHAPTER 4

in the social sense. The participation of a wealthy burgher family in religious rites was likewise usually centred around a particular church, generally the family's parish church, in part due to the increasing popularity of burying lay people on the church grounds (if possible, in the family chapel or the vicinity of an altar funded by the family).[182] However, this privilege and distinction was reserved almost exclusively for the most affluent burghers. According to a fifteenth-century register of people buried in St. Mary's Church (*Registrum sepultorum in ecclesia beate Virginis in Cracovia*), almost all of them were tied to the city's elite.[183] Among the thirty-five people listed in the register, four were members of the Krakow municipal council,[184] and two were aldermen,[185] while others included the spouses, children and grandchildren of municipal councillors.[186] Their being buried in such a prestigious location was often not the result of having made such prior arrangements, but rather due to pious bequests made by their husbands, fathers and grandparents on their behalf.[187]

---

182   As Philippe Ariès noted: "[In wills] the church was almost always chosen for family rea-
      sons, so that one could be buried either beside one's parents or, more often, beside one's
      spouse and children. The practice became widespread in the fifteenth century, and it
      clearly expresses the rise of a feeling that transcended death. Indeed, it may have been the
      moment of death that brought this feeling to full consciousness. [...] The family prevailed
      over the military kinship that had united the Knights of the Round Table in their cemeter-
      ies; their real family had been their fellow warriors. It accommodated itself, on the other
      hand, to the trade brotherhoods, because spouse and children were buried together in the
      chapel of the confraternity."; *idem, The Hour of Our Death*, 75–76.
183   A list of people preserved on a separate sheet of paper, probably written in mid-fifteenth
      century, is certainly not complete, since it ends in 'etc.': "Langmichil metquartus; Petir
      Ffetttir; Iohannis Sweydniczers due filie; Herman Wolff; Paulus Homan; Martinus Leyp-
      niger; Stano Rockinberg; Morsteynynne; Pavel Bemynne; Stano Plesner cum uxore; De....
      preterita; Orientynne; Kaltherberginne; Paulus Fetter; Hedwigis uxor Maly; Petrus filius
      Fettir; Hannus Wynkonis filia; Claus Kesling filia; Crokerynne; Stano apotecarius; Agne
      Cromerynne; Langniclas filia; Petri Hirsberg filius cum filia; Bernharth vom Brige; Bern-
      hardus notarius civitatis; Sweydniczer filius; Ffornal; Petri Grazer filius; Beeczsky filia;
      Thewdernewderynne; Mater domini Nicolaj Gortner; Bochnerynne; Neorzynne rotman-
      nene etc."; *Najdawniejsze inwentarze*, 76–77.
184   "Langmichil, Paulus Homan, Petir Ffetttir, Bernharth vom Brige"; *ibidem*.
185   "Herman Wolff, Paulus Fetter"; *ibidem*.
186   "Iohannis Sweydniczers due filie, Martinus Leypniger, Morsteynynne, Pavel Bemynne,
      Orientynne, Kaltherberginne, Petrus filius Fettir, Hannus Wynkonis filia, Claus Kesling
      filia, Langniclas filia, Petri Hirsberg filius cum filia, Sweydniczer filius, Petri Grazer filius,
      Beeczsky filia, Bochnerynne, Neorzynne rotmannene"; *ibidem*.
187   There are examples of women also being involved in foundation activities in Krakow and
      other cities; cf. Oliński, *Fundacje i legaty religijne kobiet świeckich w wielkich miastach pru-
      skich*, in *Kobieta i rodzina w średniowieczu i na progu czasów nowożytnych*, ed. Zenon Hubert
      Nowak, Andrzej Radzimiński (Toruń: Uniwersytet Mikołaja Kopernika, 1998), 143–160.

THE BURGHER RELIGIOSITY   277

For example, in his 1440 will, councillor Peter Hirszberg made a bequest of ten *grivna* of rent to pay for a *ministerium* at the altar of St. Agnes he had funded at St. Mary's Church.[188] Other testators, including Paul Homan,[189] Michael Lang (*Langmichel*)[190] and Stanisław Morsztyn[191] also funded *ministeria* at St. Mary's Church. Other members of the patriciate listed in the register had their own 'private' chapels, altars or prebends at St. Mary's Church and other churches in Krakow.[192] Burials of patricians on the grounds of a church, with their tombstones embedded in the church floor, was another manifestation of the ongoing 'privatization' of the physical space inside churches.[193]

The family dimension of urban religiosity also manifested itself in the paternalistic relation of some patricians to their servants. For example, after

---

188   "Ich Peter Hirsberg der Cromer mache meyn testament und schickunge meyns leczten willens also. Meyn haus in deme ich wone in der Schugasse an der ecke, czu nest bey Stane Gortelers hause gelegen, das bescheide ich und gebe czu gotis dinste, und czu eyme ewigen zelegerethe in sulchir weyze, daz meyne vormunde hy noch geschreben, das haws noch meyme tode vorkewffen sullen noch der Stat recht, und sullen umb das geld czinse kewffen czeen mark, adir wy vil man mag, und dy czinse vorreichen und geben czu dem Elter sinte Agniten, den ich gebawt und angericht habein der pfarkirchen unser frawen hy czu Cracow, in eyne ewige belenunge desselben Eltirs, und denselben Eltir vorleyeich und gebe, czum irsten den irben pristir hern Mathis Peyser der denselben Elter iczunt belist und vorwest von meyner Schickunge, und noch seyme tode so gebe ich das loen desselben eltirs meyme Swoger Peter Olslager dem Cromen und noch im seynen erben und elichen nochkomelingen czu ewigen tagen, also mit namen, daz sy dy czinse als obene czu dem Eltir schicken sullen, und dy nummer lossen abegeen durch keyne ablozunge adir wedirkowfft in keyner weyze"; SCAB. 6, fol. 205.
189   "Czu dem erstin gebe ich IIC mrg breyter groschin czu eynen Altare czu unser liben frawen wo man daz dirkennen wirt, wo ist notdorfft ist"; SCAB. 5, fol. 79 (1423).
190   "Primo mencionem faciens capelle, quam in cimiterio beate Marie Virginis contiguam ostio meridionali eiusdem ecclesie citeriori edificandam ipse iam antea disposuit, cuius et iam sunt posita fundamenta, volo inquit, ut compleatur opus illud usque ad plenam ipsius capelle consumacionem, scilicet iuxta eam formam et modum, secundum quod condixi et convencionem feci cum muratore. Et in eadem capella, cum perfecta fuerit, edificari debet altare et consecrari, in quo iugis fiat missarum celebracio ad laudem Dei et eius genitricis honorem, pro anime mee et filii mei ac progenitorum meorum suffragio salutari"; CONS. 428, fol. 344 (1435); cf. Sławomira Pańków, "Lang (de Czirla)," in PSB, vol. 16 (Wrocław–Warszawa–Krakow: Polska Akademia Umiejętności, 1971), 481–482.
191   SCAB. 7, fol. 82 (1450); cf. Maria Michalewicz, "Stanisław Morsztyn," in PSB, vol. 21, Wrocław–Warszawa–Krakow 1976, 821–822.
192   E.g. John Sweidniczer, Paul Homan, Paul Beme, Peter Graser or Martin Beczky.
193   Information about the tombstones of the alderman Stanisław Czipser, the councillors John Schultis, Nicholas Kreidler, John Sebenwirt and probably also three councillors beheaded for the murder of Andrew Tęczyński (Stanisław Leymitter, Kuncze Lang and Jarosz Szarlej), as well as, perhaps, John Szyling and Wojciech Malarz, have survived to this day; Elżbieta Piwowarczyk, *Dzieje*, 162–164; Marcin Starzyński, *Krakowska rada*, 92–94.

278   CHAPTER 4

the death of his servant Martin, councillor Nicholas Dambraw acted as executor of his last will, ensuring that Martin's distant relatives from the outskirts of Wrocław received his belongings.[194] John, an aged servant of Anna Williuschinne, asked her in his will to donate his wages to opera pietatis.[195] We also know that some wealthy burghers joined religious brotherhoods together with both members of their immediate family and their servants.[196] Wealthy patricians looked after their servants' interests even after their death. As evidenced by the 'register of the dead' maintained by the Brotherhood of the Blessed Virgin Mary, some burghers paid for Masses and obituaries for their deceased servants. In one such case, the name of Nicholas Dambraw's servant Martin appears in the register shortly before Dambraw's own name.[197] The register also lists the names of many servants employed by the municipal council,[198] various brotherhoods[199] and patrician families in Krakow.[200]

Some testamentary bequests also show us the importance of family tombs and the family rituals that revolved around them. Testators generally made bequests in order to make donations to churches in which they either wished to be buried or in which their ancestors or late spouses were laid to rest. For example, Margaret Glezerinne, widow of councillor Nicholas Glezer, left 30 grivna to the Dominican order to pay for a perpetual Mass for her soul. She also donated two chasubles and a chalice to the Dominican church in Krakow,

---

194   "Martinus czirnyk de suburbio civitatis Wratislaviensis nomine tutorio sue conthoralis legitime ac suorum puerorum recepit decem marcas gr. prg. num. pol. a provido Nicolao Dambraw nostri collega consilii, executore testamenti Martini pie memorie sui famuli, de omnibus bonis ac universis rebus ipsum Czirnyk, uxorem eius pueros que ipsorum, quomodolicet concernere valentibus prefatum Dambrow dimisit liberum penitus et solutum"; CONS. 427, fol. 69 (1396).

195   "Johannes famulus senex Anne Willischynne constituit eandem dominam suam ad precium suum deservitum, quod is apud eam habet in opera pietatis, secundum quod ipsa salubrius fore cognoverit convertendum, exclusitque omnes suos consangwineos et propinquos"; SCAB. 6, fol. 190 (1439).

196   "At this point we should note that employees would customarily join the organization together with their employers, as confirmed by the register of the Kleparz Brotherhood. In 1503, Anna Mandzina and her deceased relative were entered in the afore-mentioned book. The next entry concerns Valentine, referred to as the *servus* of Anna Mandzina. In 1504, John Szczyrba and his wife joined the brotherhood, followed by Catherine, *uxor fabri Jacobi qui apud Szczyrba moratur et laborat.*"; Hanna Zaremska, *Bractwa*, 162.

197   Józef Mitkowski, "Księga zmarłych bractwa kościoła Panny Marii w Krakowie (wiek XIV–XVIII)," *Studia Historyczne* 11, no. 1 (1968), 83.

198   Cf. "Vor Andris stat dyner"; *ibidem*, 82.

199   Cf. "Vor Cuncze eyn dyner der brueder"; *ibidem*, 83.

200   Cf. "Vor Maczko Stane Wirsings dyner"; *ibidem*, 82.

THE BURGHER RELIGIOSITY   279

asking to be buried in the church alongside her husband.[201] Ursula, widow of
the municipal notary Eustace, wanted to be buried in St. Mary's Church next
to the tomb of her mother, which was located between the altar of the Blessed
Virgin Mary and the altar of St. Catherine.[202] Councillor Hippolyte Spilberger
also asked in his will to be buried in St. Mary's Church, including a bequest
of 20 grivna to the church.[203] The noblewoman Anna Obulczowa, daughter
of councillor George Orient, donated all of her clothing (including an expensive coat listed in the will), jewellery, and household items for her burial and
'works of mercy.' She asked to be buried in her family's chapel, the so-called
Weynrich's chapel,[204] which contained an altar dedicated to the Annunciation
of the Blessed Virgin Mary.[205] In her 1458 will, Margaret Pferdinne set aside 50
grivna for her funeral (stating that the rest of the estate should be used to buy
clothing for the poor) and instructed that her body should be buried wrapped
in a black shroud.[206] As evidenced by the will of alderman and councillor Paul
Ber, family tombs helped maintain strong bonds between an individual and
the parish church of their former home. In 1467, Ber instructed the executors of
his will to donate to St. Nicholas's Church in Głogów, among other things, "the

---

201   "Item czu den paulern do meyne elden leggen und do ich leggen wil sal man XXX marg
       werunge geben czu eyner ewigen messe, und czwu kasiln dy ich habe lossen machen und
       eynen kelch"; CONS. 428, fol. 243 (1428).
202   "Item man zal nich begrabinn do meyne mutter leyt tczwenschinn Unser liben frawen
       alter und sante Katherine alter"; LT, fol. 148–149 (1489).
203   "Item zu unser liben frawen kirchin am Ringe gibt her zu gebewde XX mrc und dorumme
       sal hero uch in der selbin kirchin begrabin werdin"; LT, fol. 95 (1469). In 1501, the widow of
       Nicholas Zalcz and Stanisław Czipser and the wife of John Łowicz gave only 10 florins for
       burial in the St. Mary's Church: "Sepultura vero elegit in ecclesia Beate Marie Virginis in
       circulo pro qua dat decem florenum"; LT, fol. 166 (1501).
204   "Item omnes vestes, schubas, clenodia et utensilia domus commisit domino Stanislao
       vendendas et cum pecunia honestam sepulturam et pro salute anime sue disponendas...
       Item elegit sibi sepulturam in capella sua Weynrich etc."; LT, fol. 147 (1489).
205   The altar was originally founded in the last will and testament from 1449 of Theodoric
       Weinrich, a Krakow presbyter. In 1462, the altar ministry was endowed again by Weynrich's
       relative, Duchess Barbara of Racibórz, mother of the future Duchess Machna of Zator and
       Anna Obulczowa, mentioned here.; KDMK, vol. 3, no. 432 (1449); Elżbieta Piwowarczyk,
       Dzieje, 146; Katalog Archiwum Aktów Dawnych Miasta Krakowa, vol. 1: Dyplomy pergami-
       nowe (Krakow: Archiwum Aktów Dawnych Miasta Krakowa, 1907), 102, 165.
206   "Item von den obrigen fonczig marken sal man mir dy beygraft ausrichtin, und was do obir
       bleben lewten czu cleydern. Item ouch von den genanten fonfczig marken sal man In alle
       Clostir lossen lesen dreyssig selemessin vor meyne sele. Item so hab ich eynen grossen
       selbereynen kop aus dem selben sollen meyne vormonden lossen machen czwene kellich
       und das machlon sal man nehmen von den vonfczig marken und das beczalen und dy selben
       czwene kellich sollen meyne vormonden gabin noch irem dirkentnis [...]. Item ich begere
       das man mich undir swarczen gewande losse czu grabe tragen dorbey vir korczen"; LT, fol. 52.

better of two silk (*kamcha*) chasubles he had ordered"[207] and a new missal so "that these two things would help preserve the memory and ensure the salvation of his parents and relatives buried there."[208] We also learn from the will that at the time his sister was still living in Głogów. This will demonstrates that, even as a burgher of Krakow, who had lived in the city for many years, Paul Ber did not break his ties with his old parish church. The ties between Ber and St. Nicholas's Church were also influenced by his family history: Ber's ancestors were buried in that church.

3   The Corporate Dimension of Burghers' Piety

Among the features defining an urban community (which clearly differed from a traditional agrarian community) was the diversity of the people comprising it and the complexity of its social structure. While in the countryside a relatively small and homogeneous local community was bound together by the local parish church, an urban community featured more diverse social relations, suited to the needs of the burghers who lived there. As urban populations grew, the inhabitants of cities looked beyond their local parish or commune for ways to satisfy their natural need for belonging and their desire to participate in social life. A unique 'urban culture' developed, comprised of smaller, more homogenous (and initially informal) burgher communities. Urban municipalities developed their own internal social structures, including city offices, councils and bench courts, as well as professional organizations such as guilds and corporations, and religious organizations such as brotherhoods and, to some degree, communities of unmarried or widowed lay religious women, known as beguinages.[209] These developments reflected both a natural human need for social belonging suited to the modern relations of production and social relations taking shape at that time, and the adoption (and adaptation to local conditions) of German municipal organizational forms. The role of the Church was significant in this respect because it exerted a tremendous influence on culture, eschatology and social relations.[210] An equally important role was played by German settlers who immigrated to Krakow from Silesia. They

---

207   "[...] eyne kamiche kasel dy beste undir czween dy ich gereyt habe"; SCAB. 8, fol. 270–271.

208   "[...] das man dy czwestucke alle tage notczen sal zu eyme gedechtnisse und troste meyner elden und frunden zelen, der leythnam dorselbist rasten"; SCAB. 8, fol. 270–271.

209   Jerzy Wyrozumski, *Korporacje zawodowe i religijne w średniowiecznym Krakowie*, in *idem*, *Cracovia mediaevalis*, ed. Marcin Starzyński (Krakow: Avalon, 2010), 213–221.

210   Hanna Pátková, *Bractwa w czeskich miastach katolickich i utrakwistycznych*, in *Ecclesia et civitas*, 219.

THE BURGHER RELIGIOSITY   281

first helped Krakow receive its charter, and then essentially took control of the
city's power structures.[211] Two common features of all these more or less formalised communities were their tendency to function as corporations and – in
spite of theoretically being open to everyone – the practice of admitting into
their ranks only members of specific burgher social groups.[212] Despite their
many differences, the authorities, guilds and brotherhoods in a city functioned
as both secular and religious organizations (distinguishing between the two
was impossible in the Middle Ages). While the purposes of these communities differed, none of them could have come into existence or performed their
function without rituals to 'sanctify' the role they played in society. This created a great deal of historiographical confusion in the description and classification of urban communities by historians, who attempted to demarcate
the boundaries between the spheres of the *sacrum* and *profanum* in the medieval city. Meanwhile, the burgher wills (like the statutes and legal privileges of
these organizations) demonstrate that the sacred and the profane were closely
interconnected.[213] Councillors and aldermen acted in the religious sphere
not only as representatives and guardians of burgher interests (as will be discussed further on), but also of those of their own corporation.[214] Craftsmen

---

211   Feliks Kiryk. *Migracje z miast małopolskich do elity władzy Krakowa w XIV–XVI wieku*, in
       Elita władzy miasta Krakowa, 181–190; Jerzy Wyrozumski, *Lokacja 1257 roku na tle rozwoju
       krakowskiego zespołu osadniczego*, in *idem, Cracovia mediaevalis*, 181–204.

212   Women, especially wives and widows of guild craftsmen, can also be considered mem-
       bers of these corporations; cf. Janusz Tandecki, *Kobieta w rzemiośle miast pruskich na
       przełomie średniowiecza i czasów nowożytnych*, in *Kobieta i rodzina*, 161–174.

213   "The corporate character of the social life of medieval towns was reflected in the cor-
       porate style of devotion at that time. When the dominance of the councillors and their
       circles in the municipality is considered, the question of their relationship with the parish
       church arises. A list of the guilds that were forming then should be aligned with a map of
       the churches in which their chapels were placed. The emergence of journeymen's associa-
       tions is accompanied by the creation of corresponding centres of worship, distinct from
       those serving the city's guilds in general. When the council established a beggars' confra-
       ternity, it looked for a spiritual guardian and a church for them. The same is true of ethnic
       groups, each of which strived for a separate area to satisfy their devotional needs"; Hanna
       Zaremska, *Bractwa*, 37.

214   The numerous manifestations of this activity include the creation of the council's chapel
       in the town hall or benches in St. Mary's Church dedicated to councillors and aldermans.
       "In the Middle Ages, there were no permanent church benches filling the entire interior
       of the church. Sitting at Mass was a privilege of the few. Not only possessing decorative
       stalls, but even the fact of sitting in the church was a demonstration of power. Initially,
       representatives of the clergy, rulers and church patrons had the right to sit on benches
       during Mass; by the end of the Middle Ages they were joined by patricians and members
       of fraternities and guilds;"; Katarzyna Cieślak, *Między Rzymem, Wittenbergą a Genewą.
       Sztuka Gdańska jako miasta podzielonego wyznaniowo* (Wrocław: Fundacja na Rzecz

282   CHAPTER 4

who were members of guilds and brotherhoods cared not only about their own businesses and material well-being, but also attended the funerals of their deceased 'brothers' and prayed for their souls.[215] After all, as one fifteenth-century preacher stated, "you are considered damned, if no one lights a candle for you."[216] It seems, therefore, that in the medieval city every community was,[217] technically speaking, a Christian community and acting on its behalf was thus considered a pious act.

Although few lists of the members of brotherhoods in late-medieval Krakow have survived,[218] we can examine the relations between burghers and brotherhoods by analysing testamentary bequests. Forty people (out of 457 testators) specifically made bequests to guilds or brotherhoods in their wills, but we should assume that such organizations were often the beneficiaries of wills in which the spouse, family members or other executors of the will were authorized by the testator to donate money to opera pietatis. It should be emphasized that Krakow wills also demonstrate that medieval burghers did not distinguish between religious brotherhoods and professional organizations. Both were usually referred to by the Latin *fraternitas*, or the German *bruderschaft*,[219] indicating that they were seen as both secular and religious communities:

     Nauki Polskiej, 2000), 296; cf. Michał Rożek, *Przewodnik po zabytkach Krakowa*, 2nd ed. (Krakow: Wydawnictwo WAM, 2010), 144; Krzysztof J. Czyżewski, "Siądź mi po boku prawym.' O zasiadaniu w kościele słów kilka," in *Mecenat artystyczny a oblicze miasta. Materiały LVI Ogólnopolskiej Sesji Naukowej Stowarzyszenia Historyków Sztuki, Krakow 8–10 XI 2007*, ed. Dariusz Nowacki (Krakow: Stowarzyszenie Historyków Sztuki. Oddział Krakowski, 2008), 57–76.

215   "Collective forms of fraternal piety are primarily preoccupied with matters of the next life. While examining efforts to obtain indulgences, organise proper burial ceremonies, and the power of a supplicatory procession, it is difficult to distinguish between concern for one's eternal life and striving to comply with God's commandments in one's life on Earth. The eschatological imagination is closely intertwined with the concern for the everyday dimension of the worldly present."; Hanna Zaremska, *Bractwa*, 137; *eadem*, "Żywi wobec zmarłych. Brackie i cechowe pogrzeby w Krakowie w XIV–pierwszej połowie XVI w.," KH, vol. 81, 1974, no. 4, 733–749.

216   Aleksander Brückner, "Kazania i pieśni: szkice literackie i obyczajowe," in *Literatura religijna w Polsce średniowiecznej*, vol. 1 (Warszawa: Gebethner i Wolff, 1902), 72.

217   It seems that as a consequence of this juxtaposition, the individual was ideologically degraded to a sinful being, and a community of such sinners made sacred for being endowed with the will of God and His mission.

218   Only lists from the Krakow Brotherhood of the Blessed Virgin Mary from St. Mary's Church from 1481 and 1484 have survived since the Middle Ages.; Hanna Zaremska, *Bractwa*, 67–75.

219   E.g. SCAB., 2168 (1395); SCAB. 5, fol. 72 (1423).

THE BURGHER RELIGIOSITY

283

These guilds, city council corporations, and shooting confraternities, from the point of view of the clergy, were liturgical congregations that required the services of priests to provide them with spiritual and religious guidance. The shared practice of regularly attending Mass together and the centering of social life around devotional activities created more or less permanent spiritual bonds between their members.[220]

In 1447, the elders of the Brotherhood of Millers at the Church of the Holy Trinity (*seniores fraternitatis molendinatorum ad sanctam Trinitatem*) appeared before the municipal council as witnesses to the will of the late Catherine, a weaver (*textrix*). They testified that she had died at the home of John Kuchler,[221] and left all her movables to Jacob, the church prior, to be spent on charitable acts and to pay for her funeral, and John Kuchler, to repay him for his kindness towards her.[222] It should be noted here that in the Middle Ages there was no millers' guild in Krakow,[223] and thus this (rather enigmatic) brotherhood affiliated with the Dominican Church must have acted as a 'substitute' congregation.[224]

The 1458 will of Agnes Lossinne is also interesting. She appointed as executors of her will a journeyman from the Tailors' Guild, Peter Bogener,[225] who owed her 50 florins, and two master craftsmen from the Cutlers' Guild, John Neisser and John Haze.[226] Lossinne disinherited all of her relatives, and instructed the executors of her will to donate her assets as an act of charity to Krakow's hospitals and leper houses. The only specific dispositions found in the will are instructions concerning the money that Peter Bogener owed her:

---

220 Hanna Zaremska, *Bractwa*, 41.

221 In 1418 and 1424, John Kuchler (Luchler) was listed as the master of the bakers' guild on the list of senior guild members, and in 1444 his son, who shared his name and surname, was probably an elder of the carpenter's guild.; CONS. 428, fol. 108, 207, 470 (1418, 1424, 1444).

222 "Pyotr, Woyteg Roszani halfarze, Domenig murars et Micolay seniores fraternitatis molendinatorum ad sanctam Trinitatem recognoverint quod Katherina textrix bone memorie in domo Johannis Kuchler defuncta ad huc dum in humanis viveret omnia sua bona mobilia que habuit eisdem commisit distribuit pro amore dei et salute anime sue ad Ecclesiam sancte Trinitatis et etiam pro sepulture religiosumque fratri Jacobum priori eiusdem Ecclesie, Johannem Kuchler ab omnibus si ingruerint infestacionibus intercedere et evintere racione bonorum et iterum per eum datorum etc. que fuerit ipsius Katherine etc."; CONS. 428, fol. 500.

223 A millers' guild is not mentioned in any surviving medieval list of older guilds in Krakow.

224 E.g. CONS. 428, fol. 497 (1447), 511 (1448), 523, 524 (1449).

225 He acted as a master of the tailor's guild in 1459.; CONS. 429, fol. 226.

226 Neisser held this position in 1458 and Haze in the following year; CONS. 429, fol. 196, 227 (1458, 1459).

ten florins were to be donated for the *fabrica* of St. Bernardine's Church and another ten florins used to buy a shroud (*leichtuche*) for the Cutlers' Guild.[227] There are no surviving sources indicating that the Cutlers' Guild was associated with any specific church in Krakow;[228] however, the structure of the bequest suggests that it may have been affiliated with the newly founded observant Franciscan monastery in 1453. The funding of the shroud, however, indicates that the Guild undoubtedly organized funerals, the importance of which is emphasised in the statutes of all of Krakow's guilds and brotherhoods.[229]

The third professional corporation mentioned in the analysed Krakow wills was the Brotherhood of Goldsmiths (*goltsmede bruderschaft*). In 1460, Margaret Grobniginne instructed the executors of her will to sell half of her house and use the money to finance her pious bequests. In contrast to Catherine and Agnes Lossinne, Margaret chose to make numerous small bequests (from five to ten florins each) to different churches (St. Mary's Church and St. Bernardine's Church), hospitals, leper houses and the poor. In her last donation, she left a mere one grivna to the Brotherhood of Goldsmiths. Here again, we do not know whether this Brotherhood was affiliated with any specific church in Krakow. However, given the prestige of the profession, the wealth of the testatrix, and the bequest she made to St. Mary's Church, it is probable that the Krakovian goldsmiths took part in religious services there. The bequest of one grivna made to the Brotherhood was probably meant to cover the costs of the funeral, in which the members of the Brotherhood were to take part.[230]

---

227   "Czum irsten gebe ich czeen gulden czu dem gebewde der kirchen sinte Bernhardin. Item czeen gulden czu eynen leichtuche der Bruderschaft des hanthwergis der Messirsmede alhy czu Cracow und dese czwenczig gulden obgenant sollen genomen werden von der schult der funfczig gulden ungerisch, dy mir Petir Bogener obgenant schuldig ist"; LT, fol. 50 (1458).

228   Hanna Zaremska did not mention cutlers in her list of connections between the guilds of Krakow and city churches; *eadem, Bractwa*, 40.

229   "The funeral ceremony in fraternal circles was one of the most prominent forms of commemorating the dead. Participation in the final farewell for a companion became a duty, which stemmed to a large extent from the conviction that the ceremony was important for the future fate of the deceased. Participation in funerals was an inherent obligation of brothers and sisters in religious associations from the fourteenth to the sixteenth century."; *ibidem*, 140.

230   "The second group among the members of the brotherhood [of Blessed Virgin Mary – J.W.] in 1481 were craftsmen. There were 32 of them, including 15 senior guild members. The most numerous groups were butchers, goldsmiths and furriers. The corporation associated all senior representatives of the professional circles of that time."; *ibidem*, 68–70; Jerzy Pietrusiński, *Złotnicy krakowscy*, 55–77.

THE BURGHER RELIGIOSITY 285

Most bequests, however, were made to brotherhoods with no clear professional affiliations. The majority of bequests was made to two of the most prestigious corporations, namely the Brotherhood of the Blessed Virgin Mary (eleven bequests) and the Brotherhood of St. Barbara, named after St. Barbara's Cemetery Chapel (fifteen bequests). Both fraternities were affiliated with Krakow's main parish – St. Mary's Church. The Brotherhood of the Blessed Virgin Mary was probably the oldest and the most prestigious confraternity in Krakow. It was established no later than the early 1370s.[231] From its inception, it played a special role in Krakow, bringing together representatives of the municipal authorities and affluent burghers. We find the names of some of those affiliated with this corporation in the so-called *Book of the Dead*,[232] and from a list of brothers and sisters from the time of its reactivation in 1481.[233] In her analysis of the most credible list of the Brotherhood's members, Hanna Zaremska observed that during that period the corporation's membership comprised the city's elite, which was closely connected through *professional and family ties*: "The brotherhood affiliated Germans, many of whom were newly-arrived immigrants, whose representatives began to gain dominance over 'old' families such as the Wierzyneks or the Gleywiczs in the latter half of the fifteenth century."[234] With many members of Krakow's richest burgher families among its ranks, the organization was not surprisingly generously endowed by them. For example, in her 1440 will, Salomea, wealthy widow of goldsmith Nicholas Brenner, donated 200 florins from the sale of part of her house located on the main market square to fund an altarage at the altar dedicated to the "*Omnipotentis Dei et Visitationis B.M.V.*"[235] This altar was located in the chapel of the Brotherhood of the Blessed Virgin Mary, near the choir by the main entrance to the church, between its two towers.[236] She passed on her patronage of this altarage to the Brotherhood after her death.

---

231 Because the first people entered in the obituary of the Brotherhood of Blessed Virgin Mary had died.; cf. Józef Mitkowski, *Księga zmarłych*, 77; Hanna Zaremska, *Bractwa*, 48.

232 Józef Mitkowski, *Księga zmarłych*, 71–95.

233 Biblioteka Jagiellońska, ms 2365, Reformacio fraternitatis S. Marie in circulo Cracoviensi facta est anno incarnacionis Domini 1481, 10–13.

234 Hanna Zaremska, *Bractwa*, 70.

235 Elżbieta Piwowarczyk, *Dzieje*, 134–135.

236 "Et pro eisdem ducentis florenis ungaricalibus in auro, census quantos et ubi tute petent amat, in dotacionem altaris ipsius fraternitatis quod est in capella ipsorum super ingressum ipsius ecclesie inter duas turres, eiusque altaris iuspaternatus et presentandi reservo michi ad tempora vite mee, post mortem vero meam idem Juspaternatus et presentandi do fraternitati predicte iure perpetuo possidendum"; SCAB. 6, fol. 215.

We can deduce from surviving sources that the Brotherhood of St. Barbara was an equally prestigious organization. It was founded by the Bishop of Krakow Peter Wysz in 1404. Although its establishment may have initially resulted from a rivalry between the bishop and the Krakow municipal council,[237] in the following decades, its members and benefactors, like those of its Marian counterpart, included affluent Krakovian patricians. This specific aspect of the brotherhood, which it shared with St. Mary's Church, was emphasized by the name by which it was referred to in a diploma received by Zbigniew Oleśnicki in 1444: The Brotherhood of Merchants (*Fraternitas Mercatorum*).[238]

The third most important brotherhood in Krakow in terms of the number of testamentary bequests made to it was the brotherhood affiliated with the so-called Hungarian chapel at the mendicant church of St. Francis (which received eight bequests). The name of the chapel and some written sources indicate a link between the corporation, and the chapel with which it was affiliated, with Krakovian burghers of Hungarian origin.[239] However, the wealthy testators who made bequests to it do not appear to have had any ties with Hungary; all of them were, in fact, affluent representatives of the handicrafts in Krakow.[240]

Somewhat fewer bequests were made to the Brotherhood of the Holy Spirit, which was affiliated with the church and the hospital of the same name. The brotherhood must have had strong ties to the hospital, because testators usually made bequests to the 'brotherhood in the hospital' (*czard bruderschaft in dem Spetil*) or to the brotherhood in the hospital of the Holy Spirit (*dy bruderschaft czum Spital alhy czu Krakow czu der Heiligen Geiste*).[241] As many as four out of six individuals who made bequests to this confraternity also made bequests to other brotherhoods. We can thus assume that such bequests were seen as donations to the city hospital.

Two bequests of a similar nature were made to the oldest and the most important confraternity in the city of Kazimierz, the Brotherhood of Corpus Christi, based in the church of the same name. Founded some time before

---

237   Hanna Zaremska, *Bractwa*, 76–77.

238   *Ibidem*, 77.

239   The Hungarian chapel served Hungarian students of the University of Krakow. In 1507, King Zygmunt granted them eight barrels of salt a year, on condition that on holidays they would sing *Gaude Dei genitrix*; cited in *ibidem*, 83.

240   John Lode, LT, fol. 10 (1439); Peter Eichler, a tailor, LT, fol. 12 (1448); Catherine Michelinne, CONS. 429, fol. 54 (1452); Wincenty Czanser, a fustian weaver, LT, fol. 47 (1457); Simon Noldener, a bowyer, LT, fol. 55 (1458); Margaret Prewszinne, a bowyer, LT, fol. 59–60 (1459); Stanisław Kulek, a stallholder, LT, fol. 93 (1468); Łazarz a cutler, LT, fol. 109–110 (1475).

241   SCAB. 6, fol. 59, 313 (1433, 1444).

THE BURGHER RELIGIOSITY 287

the mid-fourteenth century, it had strong ties with the Kazimierz municipal council, indicating that it, like the Brotherhood of the Blessed Virgin Mary in Krakow, most likely attracted members of the social elite.[242] John Zindram and the cutler Łazarz both made testamentary bequests to the Brotherhood of Corpus Christi, while at the same time also making bequests to, respectively, the confraternity of the Blessed Virgin Mary[243] and the brotherhood connected with the so-called Hungarian chapel.[244] It is possible that these burghers belonged to both confraternities, but the Brotherhood of Corpus Christi in Kazimierz was probably an additional affiliation to the two Krakow brotherhoods.

Other fraternities, two in Krakow (the Brotherhood of the Eleven Thousand Virgins at St. Stephen's Church and the Brotherhood of St. Sophia at St. Mark's Church), one in Kazimierz (the Brotherhood of St. Catherine) and one in the Krakow's suburb (the Brotherhood of St. Nicholas), were each mentioned in the analysed wills once. In 1457, Elizabeth, daughter of the late Philip, a tailor, made a bequest of two grivna to the brotherhood at St. Stephen's Church and of one grivna to the brotherhood at St. Mark's Church.[245] Apart from these modest bequests, there is little more that can be said about these rather unimportant congregations until the late fifteenth century.[246] The confraternity of St. Catherine at the church of the Augustinians in Kazimierz and the brotherhood of St. Nicholas at the suburban parish church were probably more important. In 1464, before going to war against the Turks, the bricklayer Martin made a bequest of five grivna to both St. Nicholas's Church and the Polish brotherhood in this church (*fraternitati polonorum in ecclesia predicta*).[247] It is worth noting that, since its founding in the early fifteenth century, the confraternity of St. Catherine at the church of the Augustinians had been referred to as the Polish Brotherhood (*Fraternitas Polonorum*).[248] In 1459, the wealthy widow Anna Florianinne made a bequest of ten florins to this brotherhood. However, because this bequest was only one of many similar donations made by this testatrix, we cannot determine the nature of the relation between her and the brotherhood.[249] Nevertheless, the fact that these religious fraternities were referred

---

242 This is evidenced by a document from 1347 which granted indulgences to brotherhood members; Hanna Zaremska, *Bractwa*, 85–86.
243 LT, fol. 9 (1446).
244 LT, fol. 109–110 (1475).
245 SCAB. 7, fol. 312.
246 Hanna Zaremska, *Bractwa*, 79–82.
247 LT, s 82.
248 Hanna Zaremska, *Bractwa*, 88.
249 LT, fol. 64–65.

to as either Polish or German indicates that there existed religious, social and linguistic divisions in medieval Krakow.

Krakovian testators made bequests to two other fraternities outside of the Krakow agglomeration. One was in Krosno and the other "in Prussia." In the first, the above-mentioned Anna Florianinne made a bequest of ten florins to the brotherhood at the parish church in Krosno.[250] In the second, in addition to a bequest of ten florins to the brotherhood at the Krakow hospital of Holy Spirit, Margaret Leipnigerinne made a bequest of ten florins to the brotherhood at the Carthusian monastery "in Prussia ... to which she belonged."[251] These donations appear to demonstrate that the testatrices maintained strong ties with religious communities in their former hometowns.

A characteristic feature of the analysed donations to lay religious fraternities was their relatively modest size. The vast majority of bequests did not exceed a couple of grivna and were one of many bequests made by the testator. For example, in addition to his bequest of five grivna to the Brotherhood of the Blessed Virgin Mary at St. Mary's Church "to maintain the service" (*czu stewir des dinstis*), the court plenipotentiary Lawrence made analogous bequests to the Franciscans (for the *fabrica* of the church), to lepers near Krakow (at St. Valentine's church and hospital) to purchase foodstuffs, and to lepers near Kazimierz (at St. Leonard's church and hospital) "for construction work and other needs."[252] In his 1435 will, the pharmacist Paul Tanneman made a bequest of five grivna to the Brotherhood of Saint Barbara. He also made similar bequests to the Church of Corpus Christi in Kazimierz, to the poor at two hospitals (of the Holy Spirit and of St. Hedwig), and to other poor men and women.[253] More generous bequests were made by John Frolich in his 1395 will. If he, his wife, and his son died, Frolich's estate was to be divided into two parts, with one part to be donated to the Brotherhood of the Blessed Virgin Mary and the other to the poor and the sick (*pauperibus infirmis*).[254] In turn, the stallholder Margaret Jostinne donated her gerade to her confessor, an altarist at the altar of Saint

---

250   *Ibidem.*

251   "Den karthewsern in Prewssen czu den ich bruderschaft habe czen gulden"; LT, fol. 36 (1456).

252   SCAB. 6, fol. 213 (1440).

253   KLK6, 113.

254   "[...] si autem pueri morirentur, extunc pars ipsorum omnium ad ipsam dominam devolvatur, prefatis vero personis, tam domina, quam pueris omnibus sublatis de medio, debet medietas bonorum residuancium ad fraternitatem ecclesie sancte Marie et reliqua medietas pauperibus infirmis dari tam per fratres, quam per procuratores eius, Nicolaum Morrensteyn et Petrum Weidochse: reservat dominium"; SCAB., no. 2168.

THE BURGHER RELIGIOSITY   289

Anna at St. Mary's Church. Should he die, "because we are all mortal,"[255] the
gerade was to be divided into four parts and donated to St. Mary's Church,
the Brotherhood of the Blessed Virgin Mary at the same church, the altarists'
home, and the brotherhood at the hospital (of the Holy Spirit).[256]

It should be emphasized that nine people made simultaneous bequests to
two fraternities, without favouring either one – both fraternities were given
the same sum of money. The councillor John Sweidniczer made two bequests
of ten grivna each to both the Brotherhood of the Blessed Virgin Mary and to
the Brotherhood of St. Barbara. He also made identical bequests to the lepers
at the hospitals of St. Leonard and St. Valentine, to St. Mary's Church, to the
Dominicans, to the Franciscans, to St. Catherine's Church, and to the church
of Corpus Christi. The bequests to the fraternities were thus one of many
other identical bequests made to religious institutions located in the Krakow
agglomeration.[257] While this may indicate that John Sweidniczer was a member of all of these organizations, it may also demonstrate a characteristic desire
among medieval burghers to make bequests to as many institutions and people as possible. The possibility also exists that both tendencies are reflected in
this case. Nevertheless, these multiple bequests show that being a member of
a brotherhood constituted an important aspect of the social and religious life
of some medieval burghers.

It can also be assumed that the bequests made to brotherhoods were often a
form of payment for funeral ceremonies and memorial Masses in the brotherhood's chapel, for the salvation of a testator's soul:

> The fact that responsibility for the organisation of funerals rested in the
> hands of lay fraternities appears to shed new light on the role they played
> in the social life of the local community. The corporation's memory of

---

255 "Geschege is ader als wir alle totlich seyn, daz derselbe her Niclas ee vorschide wenn ich";
     SCAB. 6, fol. 59 (1433).
256 "Item allis das ich lossen werde boben dy gerade, das bescheyde ich meyme beichtvater
     hern Niclas, elthern das elters sinte Anne czu Unser Liben Frawen, mit befelunge meyner
     zele, als ich Im getrawe. Geschege is ader als wir alle totlich seyn, daz derselbe her Niclas
     ee vorschide wenn ich, so sullen meyne vormunde das geben in dy werk der barmherc-
     zikeyt, als eyn teyl czu unser liben frawen czur kirchen, und eyn teyl czur bruderschaft
     deselbist, eyn teyl den Elterhern doselbist czum hawse in dy gemeynem eyn teyl czur
     bruderschaft in dem Spetil, und czur heiligen befelen"; SCAB. 6, fol. 59 (1433).
257 The testator also assessed the value of the institutions, because he bequeath 20 *grivna* for
     the construction of St. Bernard's Church as well as to the sick both in the hospital of the
     Holy Spirit and St. Hedwig, and 5 *grivna* each to St. Mark's Church, 'the New Convent' (the
     Carmelites) and to St. Ann.; LT, fol. 39–45 (1457).

their deceased brother was not limited to ceremonially sending them off on a solemn journey. The chapels of guilds and fraternities essentially served as a place for holding funeral services and praying for souls in Purgatory. Masses for the dead (*Missa pro defunctis*) were also periodically held in them, during which long lists of the names of those who had died in recent years were read out loud. This was an expression of their efforts to ensure that their prayers were properly 'addressed' with the names of the individuals whom those in the terrestrial *communitas* wished to support in their efforts to attain eternal peace.[258]

This is evidenced by the will made by Wilhelm Megirszheimer of the Nurembergian town of Thunkilspul (Dinkelsbühl) in 1482.[259] Each of his pious bequests, regardless of place and purpose, were for ten Rhenish florins. He donated ten Rhenish florins for the new altarpiece (*hohen altar*) on which Veit Stoss was working, and for the *fabrica* (*zum gebaude*) of St. Mary's Church, his final resting place. Megirszheimer also made bequests of ten florins to the Franciscans and to the Carmelites (for a new church and for Gregorian Masses for the release of his soul). In addition, Megirszheimer also made a bequest of ten florins to the Brotherhood of St. Barbara, on condition that its members "provide all the things needed for his funeral, including a shroud and other things in accordance with the custom of the brotherhood."[260] He also stated that "all funeral costs should be properly accounted for."[261] Moreover, he left his brother 400 florins, instructing him to pay for a perpetual Mass for his soul in his home town of Thunkilspul. Wilhelm Megirszheimer appointed three executors of his will – they were to ensure that all his instructions regarding bequests made to Krakow churches and institutions were carried out properly. This will is very interesting because of the testator's background. A merchant by profession, he came to Krakow on a business trip. A sudden illness or some other unforeseen misfortune forced him to plan his funeral and secure his salvation far away from home. Since transporting his body back to his distant hometown in Germany was impossible, he decided to organize his funeral at Krakow's most important church. He made bequests to the long-standing

---

258 Hanna Zaremska, *Żywi wobec zmarłych*, 748.

259 LT, fol. 135–136.

260 "Item X reynische gulden hat her bescheiden zu der brudirschaft alhir zu sinte Barbare und dy sal alle gerete z udem begrebnisse dar zu geben als leychtuch und sust noch gewonheit der brudirschaft"; LT, fol. 135.

261 "Item was of das begrebnisse wirt gehen sal man och awsrichten zu guttir rechenunge"; LT, fol. 136.

THE BURGHER RELIGIOSITY   291

Franciscan order and to the Carmelites, whose convent was being built at the time, because they 'specialized' in praying for the souls of the dead. In turn, he chose the Brotherhood of St. Barbara, which was affiliated with the cemetery chapel of St. Mary's Church, because he wanted to have an adequate funeral ceremony. While we cannot determine why the foreigner chose this specific brotherhood, it seems probable that his business partners in Krakow offered their advice in this matter. However, Megirszheimer undoubtedly made such a generous bequest to this brotherhood not as a member, but as a 'client' who wished to pay for the funeral services it provided.[262]

The bequest made by cloth maker Wincenty Czanser in 1457 was similar in nature.[263] Czanser left his entire estate to his wife, Dorota, provided that she pay for a psalter to be said for the sake of his soul at St. Stephen's Church, which was probably his parish church. He also stated that a Gregorian Mass should be sung at his grave by the Brotherhood of St. Francis.[264] In this case, the brotherhood at the so-called Hungarian chapel provided not only for burial in the church, but also for prayers during a Mass celebrated by the brotherhood's priest.[265] The fact that fraternities offered funeral services and were tasked with commemorating their dead is also evidenced by the so-called *Book of the Dead* maintained by the Brotherhood of the Blessed Virgin Mary.[266] Hanna Zaremska, who has analysed the names listed in the register, points out that the *Book of the Dead* only lists people whose mourning relatives (widows, widowers, children, etc.) paid for a Mass for their soul. The register includes

---

262   "From the very beginning, or at least since the fifteenth century, religious confraternities considered funeral services a form of communal activity outside the corporation. This is probably why they were called funeral fraternities in literature"; Hanna Zaremska, *Bractwa*, 141.

263   LT, fol. 47.

264   "Item Dorothea uxor iam dicti Vincencii debet et promisit de bonis ipsius mariti disponendo unum psalterium ad legendum pro anima sua apus sanctum Steffanum. Item unum Tricesimam decantare mittere debet apud sanctum Franciscum in fraternitate et sepulturam ibidem faciendo"; *ibidem*.

265   "It seems that burying bodies in parish churches was not a result of agreements between corporations or their initiative, and the decision depended instead on the position and financial standing of the family of the deceased. Sometimes burial in a church was provided for in the will. The matter of burying the dead in monasteries was completely different. In Poland, from the early Middle Ages, monasteries enjoyed *liberam sepulchram* – the right to accommodate the corpses of those who had chosen them as their final resting place. This legal custom was reinforced in the struggle between parish clergy and mendicant congregations. Therefore, there is no reason to believe that the burials of members of corporations associated with monasteries did not take place on their grounds."; Hanna Zaremska, *Bractwa*, 142–143.

266   Józef Mitkowski, *Księga zmarłych*, 76.

not only members of the brotherhood, but also their relatives[267] For example, the patrician Jacob Borneysen increased his wife's dower in his very short will,[268] which he drafted on his deathbed, but he did not instruct the members of the municipal council who came to visit him during his illness to make any other pious bequests. Nevertheless, his name (*Vor Jacob Bornayzen*) is included in the *Book of the Dead* of the Brotherhood of the Blessed Virgin Mary.[269] Perhaps Borneysen was a member of this brotherhood or perhaps he had made some sort of donation to it during his life.[270] It seems more probable, however, that it was his wife and children, to whom he left his entire estate, who paid the Brotherhood to organize a proper funeral for him. Such a wish was expressed directly by another member of the patriciate, councillor Peter Lang, in 1479. Lang left his entire estate to his wife and children, but he ordered them to make pious bequests on his behalf after his death (*werg der barmherczikeit*). One donation was to be made to St. Mary's Church and the other to pay for the altarpiece (on which Veit Stoss was working at the time) "in accordance with [Lang's] wish."[271] It is not known whether Lang's family followed his instructions. Peter Lang's name is not listed in the *Book of the Dead*, unlike his wife, Agnes's.[272]

By the end of the fifteenth century, nearly 700 people were listed in the *Book of the Dead* kept by the Brotherhood of the Blessed Virgin Mary. This demonstrates the popularity of the brotherhood and the funeral services it provided, especially in the late fifteenth century. No less important were the special indulgences that all of these brotherhoods received.[273] The sheer number

---

267 Hanna Zaremska, *Bractwa*, 71.

268 CONS. 428, fol. 437 (1441).

269 Józef Mitkowski, *Księga zmarłych*, 85.

270 This may be evidenced by a record in the inventory of the St. Mary's Church vault.: "Item eyne kamchen kasel von slechten blumen, gemeyne, Borneisyn dedit"; *Najdawniejsze inwentarze*, 76.

271 "Ouch was her yn bevolen hat awsczurichten in werg der barmherczikeit alhir zurr Unsir lieben frawen zu der kirchen und ouch zu der toffil, das sullen sy mit fleysse awsrichten alse her yn hat bevolen und wol vortrawet"; LT, fol. 125.

272 Józef Mitkowski, *Księga zmarłych*, 87.

273 "Indulgences were an opportunity offered by the church to believers. Fraternities helped to seize this opportunity. They also ensured the memory of their members would be honoured after they passed away. The chapels of the corporations served as places of mourning and supplication for souls in purgatory. There, *pro defunctis* Masses were celebrated every quarter, during which the custom was to read out long lists of those who had died in recent years; this was an expression of the care taken to ensure that prayers 'sent' to heaven were 'addressed' accurately, thanks to listing the names of those with whom the earthly *communitas* was united in their efforts to gain eternal peace"; Hanna Zaremska, *Bractwa*, 140.

THE BURGHER RELIGIOSITY 293

of religious and professional fraternities affiliated with parish and monastic churches (including such popular organizations as the Brotherhood of St. Barbara) demonstrates just how popular and influential such confraternities were in the religious and social life of Krakovian burghers.

4 Parish Identity and Ties to Other Religious Institutions in the Medieval City

The observation that a person in the Middle Ages was, first of all, a member of their parish community, while true of those living in the countryside, is less applicable to parish life in a large medieval city: "Unlike the rural parish, large parishes like those in the city no longer functioned as a homogeneous social community. The urban parish offered fewer opportunities for interaction and collective participation, elements necessary for the creation of a true community in the psychological and social sense."[274] Nevertheless, despite both the wide-ranging religious 'offering' in Krakow, manifested in the activities of mendicant orders and various fraternities, as well as the growing popularity of private and family-oriented means of worship, the parish church remained the primary reference point in the city's social and religious life. It was where burghers married, baptized their children, and often sought to be buried. As mentioned earlier, the wealthiest families had strong ties to their parish church and often acted as patrons of the church, both because the pious bequests of their predecessors required them to do so, and because the church was the site where the mortal remains of their kin lay. These strong ties are particularly visible in the case of testators who had moved to Krakow from other towns, because their bequests tended to reflect their beliefs and emotions rather than local customs. As noted above, Wilhelm Megirszheimer allocated 400 florins to found a perpetual Mass for his soul in his hometown Thunkilspul.[275] The will of another foreigner, John Raisser from the Bavarian town of Memmingen (Mammyngen), is also interesting in this context: "For the love of God and his most excellent mother Mary and for the salvation of his soul and the consolation of his relatives,"[276] he donated 500 Rhenish florins to found a perpetual altarage in the parish church of St. Gallen (about 100 km from Memmingen). Like Wilhelm Megirszheimer, John Raisser made bequests to Krakow's churches to pay

---

274 *Ibidem*, 155.
275 LT, fol. 135–136 (1482).
276 "Czum irsten hot her czum lobe gotis und seynir hochwirdigen mutter Marie czu seynir zelen zelickeit und seynir frunden czu troste"; SCAB. 8, fol. 598 (1476).

for his funeral ceremony. Raisser bequeathed five grivna to St. Mary's Church (for his funeral), another five grivna for a monstrance at the Church of the Holy Cross,[277] and three grivna "to St. Hedwig," probably in the hope that the poor at this hospital would attend the funeral and pray for his soul. For this same reason he donated 24 grivna "for his funeral and for the poor." This money was most likely to be given to the poor as alms during the funeral.[278]

The 1443 will of the wealthy Krakovian merchant Thob Johan is also notable. In addition to generous bequests to St. Mary's Church and to fund various "works of charity," Johan also instructed that the money from the sale of his house be used to fund an altarage in his private chapel at St. Mary's Church.[279] In addition, he made several smaller bequests to Krakow's hospitals. Moreover, his donations were not limited to religious institutions in Krakow, and included leaving a considerable sum of money to various churches in his home town of Brzeg. Among these were an annuity of the amount of ten grivna each for the suburban church of St. Anthony in Strzelniki, the parish church in Brzeg, and the Order of Saint John, located in the parish courtyard (*Pharhoff den Creuczigern*). Johan also allocated 36 grivna in annual rent for a perpetual Mass at the parish church in the city.[280]

---

277 He followed the same procedure as many of Krakow patricians, who, before their death, donated liturgical objects to clergymen, fraternities or churches in Krakow. These objects were simultaneously a kind of votive offering and obliged, in this case, a convent of clergy responsible for the largest hospital in Krakow, to participate in the funeral ceremony.

278 "Item alhy czu Crakow czu unsir liben frawen kirchen funf margk czu seynen begrebnisse, Item do selbist czu dem heiligen crewcze czu der monstrancia funf marg. Item czu sinte Hedwig den armen sichen drey margk. Item sust czu seynir beygraft und armen lewten fier und czwenczig margk"; SCAB. 8, fol. 599.

279 "Ite, czu seyner Capellen und Elter czu unser frawen beschit her dy helfte und eyn achteteyl sejnes hausis of der brudergassen das man das vorkeuffen sal und czinse dor von keuffen und gibt das selbe altare Nicolao Asschirhaus seyner diner und noch des tode sal das leen an Hannus seynen stifson und Henseln seynen son sterben und noch der tot ap si ane erbe storben sal das salbe leen sterben an dy hern Ratman und noch Asschirhaus tode sullen di abgenanten sone ader di hern Ratman ap is an si storbe das leen geben deme wachern der of dy selbe czeit wirt seyn in der pfarkirchen"; LT, fol. 7.

280 "Item von den LXVI marg czinse dy her czu Breslaw hot gebt her X mrc czinse ken Brige czu seinte Antonien kirche. Item czr pfarkirchen ouch czum Brige in der stat gibt her ouch X marg von dem obgenante czinse czu Bresla. Item X marg doselbist czum Brige of den pfarhoff den Creuczigern ouch dem czinse czu Bresla. Item czu Bresla czu dem heiligen Leichnom dy oberige XXXVI marg und XXXII bemesche groschen czu eyner stiftunge eyner ewigen messen do selbist czu seyner selen selikeit czu singen czu wilchen messe sy eyner sunderlichen eltir benumen sullen of deme si gesungen sal werden"; LT, fol. 7–8.

THE BURGHER RELIGIOSITY   295

Other Krakovian burghers also felt a strong connection to their former parishes, and made testamentary bequests to them. The Krakow alderman and councillor Serwatius not only donated 30 grivna to St. Mary's Church, but also made bequests of 100 grivna to the parish church in Nowy Sącz. He also donated 30 grivna each to the hospital of the Holy Spirit and the Franciscan church in Nowy Sącz.[281] The councillor Paul Ber donated, among other things, a chasuble and a missal to the parish church of St. Nicholas in Głogów, in which, as he stated, his parents and other family members were buried.[282] Krakovian burghers who were not counted among the city's patrician elite and whose ancestors were probably not buried in their former or present parish churches, still made generous donations to them. The maltster Nicholas Kmitta left four grivna each to the Corpus Christi parish church in Kazimierz and to the parish church of St. Stephen in Krakow, which might indicate that he had moved from Kazimierz to Krakow.[283] Bernard Philippi de Luboyna left his fish farm to the parish church in Mikanów in order to fund a weekly Mass for the dead.[284] The tailor Jarosz not only made generous bequests to St. Mary's Church, the Brotherhood of the Blessed Virgin Mary, and four Krakow monasteries (those of the Bernardines, the Dominicans, the Carmelites and the Franciscans), but also donated his expensive damask bedspread (to be turned into a chasuble) and some silverware to the parish church in Zator, which was most likely his former parish church.[285]

Although parish churches in Krakow had to 'compete' with many other religious institutions, and thus did not have a monopoly on the teaching of Christian doctrine to the faithful, they remained the most important places of worship for the majority of medieval burghers. Most burghers had well-established personal and family ties with their parish churches and regularly attended Sunday Mass there. In spite of a lack of evidence in the analysed wills, we can assume that shared participation in religious services and the social bonds formed by this common experience must have been an important factor integrating the medieval burgher community. While in the fourteenth and

---

281   SCAB. 6, fol. 139 (1437).
282   SCAB. 8, s 270–271 (1467).
283   CONS. 428, fol. 21 (1412).
284   "Primo piscinam meam ante villam Luboyna do et assigno plebano Ecclesie parochiali in Mikanow et omnibus aliis ipsius Ecclesie sequencibus id est rectoribus dicte Ecclesie dictam piscinam pro se habendam utifruendam temporibus perpetuis ita tamen quod dicti Rectores Eclesie presentes et futuri omnia septimana unam missam pro defunctis legendam"; LT, fol. 71 (1461).
285   LT, fol. 151–152 (1492).

fifteenth centuries religious confraternities provided an attractive option for a small group of pious burghers, most city residents preferred the social and religious community formed by their parish church. Indeed, most pious bequests in that period were made to five parish churches in Krakow (St. Mary's Church, the church of the Holy Cross, St. Stephen's Church, All Saints Church, St. Anne's Church) and a number of parish churches in Kazimierz (the Church of Corpus Christi, St. James's Church, St. Michael's Church and St. Stanislaus's Church), Kleparz (St. Florian's Church) and Wesoła (St. Nicholas's Church).[286] In the fifteenth century, nearly 60% of all testamentary bequests were made to parish churches and over 75% of such bequests were made to St. Mary's Church – Krakow's most important religious building.[287] These numbers not only show that people wished to ensure their salvation, but also demonstrate the high social status of most testators, who were parishioners of St. Mary's Church. While wills in which no pious bequests were made were not taken into account in this study, we can still observe a clear convergence between the number of bequests made to St. Mary's Church and the number of wealthy and very wealthy testators in Krakow.[288]

In terms of form and structure, bequests made to other parish churches in Krakow were similar to those made to St. Mary's Church. However, such donations were clearly secondary to other dispositions and usually a matter of convention, as the practice of donating small amounts to as many religious institutions as possible was common in the Middle Ages. Testators wanted to ensure that as many lay people and clergymen as possible would pray for their soul, delivering them from Purgatory or shortening the time spent there through "the power of mass prayer." For example, the purse maker (*beuteler*) Stephen donated one grivna each to three parish churches in Kazimierz (the Church of Corpus Christi, St. James's Church and St. Catherine's Church), three parish churches in Krakow (All Saints Church, St. Mary's Church, St. Anne's Church), four orders (the Franciscans, the Dominicans, the Carmelites, and the order of St. Mark), and two hospitals (the hospital of the Holy Spirit and St. Hedwig's Hospital). Thus, this moderately rich Krakow burgher spent only

---

286 Elżbieta Piwowarczyk, *Legaty testamentowe ad pias causas*, 101–136; Aleksandra Witkowska, *Przestrzeń sakralna późnośredniowiecznego Krakowa*, in *Ecclesia et civitas*, 39–41; Jakub Wysmułek, "Przejawy religijności mieszczan krakowskich na podstawie XIV-wiecznych testamentów i zapisów pobożnych," *Odrodzenie i Reformacja w Polsce* 54 (2010), 90–94.

287 Elżbieta Piwowarczyk, *Legaty testamentowe*, 103, 114–115.

288 See chapter 2, section 5, p. 152.

THE BURGHER RELIGIOSITY 297

twelve grivna in ensuring that as many as twelve different religious institutions in the Krakow agglomeration would pray for his soul.[289]

The wealthy widow Anna Florianinne left similar instructions in her 1459 will. Although it contains elements that can be found in many other bequests of last will, it stands out in terms of the religious commitment of the testator and the degree of thought she put into the dispositions she made. For these reasons, it is reproduced here in its entirety:

> I, Anna Florianinne, a burgher woman of Kraków, declare this to be my last will and testament. First of all, I ask the executors of my will [*vormunde*] to prepare my funeral in such a way as to ensure the salvation of my soul, to which end I leave 10 florins. Thirty Masses for my soul should be said in each of the following churches in Kraków: St. Mary's Church, at the hospital, St. Barbara's Church, the Dominican Church, All Saints Church, St. Francis's Church, St. Anna's Church, St. Stephen's Church, St. Bernardine's Church, the Church of Corpus Christi and St. Catherine's Church. The priests who will celebrate the Masses should be given 30 groszy. In addition, I leave 10 florins for the *fabrica* of St. Mary's Church in Kraków. I likewise donate 10 florins for the *fabrica* of St. Bernardine's Church in Stradom. To St. Catherine's I bequeath 10 florins for the brotherhood. For the Brotherhood of St Bernardine I order the purchase of two warps of fabric for clothing. To the poor in three hospitals, St. Hedwig's, St. Valentine's, and St. Leonard's beyond Kazimierz, I leave five florins for clothing and shoes. The executors of my will should carry out [these dispositions] in accordance with current needs, acting on their own judgment. In addition, I bequeath 20 florins to the poor at the hospital in Kraków, for the executors of my will to buy meat, fish and beer each week until all the money is spent. I bequeath 10 florins to the brotherhood at the parish church in Krosno. I leave five florins to the Franciscans in Krosno so they can renovate their monastery. I give five florins to the poor at Krosno's hospital. I give five florins for the building of a hospital for poor students at Hospital Street in Kraków. To the poor brothers [the Carmelites] from the New Monastery I bequeath 30 groszy to say 30 Gregorian Masses for

---

289 "[...] czu desen nochgeschrebenen kirchen, alse czum Heiligen Leichnam, czu sinte Jocob und czu sinte Katherin czu Kazmer, Czu der Barfussen, czu der Allen Heiligen, Czu der Pawlern, Czu unser liben frawen hy in der Stat, Czu der Hornechten, czu sinte Annen, und czum Newencloster czu iczlicher kirchen besundir eyne marg czu dem gebewde, und das geld sal man geben den kirchenbitern und nicht den pristern. Item den sichen Im Spital hy czu Cracow eyne marg und czu sinte Hedwig ouch eyne marg"; CONS. 428, fol. 379 (1437).

the release of my soul. I give same to St. Stanislas's Church and St. Florian's Church to pay for 30 Gregorian Masses for the release of my soul. I bequeath three florins, a down quilt and one set of bed linen to John, a mansionary at St. Barbara's Church, who replaced Stanisław Geweitfewer. To Jaczke and Jacob, two priests at the castle, I give three florins each. I give five florins to the Franciscan Observants [the Bernardines] from Stradom to purchase clothing. I leave two quilts, *eyn pfel*, four bed sheets and one chest to my servant Dorota. I donate small pieces of linen that are to be found around the house to Magdalene at St. Bernardine's so that she can make a corporal and give it to the priest, as I have instructed. All my fabrics (*fechil, dromleyn etc.*) should be given to the Bernardine sisters. I leave 50 elbows of linen for making albs to be given to churches in need of them. To the shoemaker Lawrence, who has a blessed daughter [*seligen tochter*], I leave three florins to use for whatever he needs. I leave my royal dress [*koniglyn korssche*] and my tablecloth [*decke*] to Benigna, wife of John Meisner. I give my old dress and the coat I wear every day to my servant Dorothy. The yarn that will be found around the house, both small and large, should be given to Benigna, wife of John Meisner. The linen canvas made by her should be used to make shirts for the poor who need them. I also give two florins to John and Lucas. Moreover, so that this will is executed properly, I ask the executors of my will to sell all my household items and all other remaining goods and donate the money for works of charity. I also disinherit all my family members and relatives whom I do not know and do not. I name John Meisner, a butcher, and Stanisław Czipser, a furrier, as the executors of this will. They have the right to execute this will and perform works of charity, as stated in the will. This notwithstanding, I have the right to dispose of my estate as long as I live.[290]

In this will, Anna Florianinne demonstrates her religious commitment and her understanding of how to effectively perform 'works of charity.' This will distinguishes her from many other testators, who generally made less thoughtful and more schematic bequests. However, like Stephen, a purse maker,[291] Anna Florianinne wished to ensure that as many people as possible would pray for her soul. She assumed that a Gregorian Mass was worth 30 groszy each, but she ordered them in as many as fourteen houses of worship, including parish

---

290   LT, fol. 64–65.
291   CONS. 428, fol. 379 (1437).

THE BURGHER RELIGIOSITY

churches, monasteries and hospitals in Krakow, Kazimierz, Kleparz, Skałka and Piasek. The testatrix also planned her funeral ceremony (Krakow's testators rarely included such instructions in their wills) and left specific instructions as to how her money should be distributed among the poor. She did not forget about her parish church, the hospital in the city or the Franciscan monastery in her hometown Krosno. Last but not least, she also made bequests to her female servant and close friends, including a very interesting bequest to a certain Krakow shoemaker who had a "blessed daughter" (*die selige tochter*). Anna Florianinne also demonstrated that she had ties to her parish church – she donated 10 florins for the construction of St. Mary's Church. However, she donated the same amounts to St. Bernardine's Church, which was still under construction in 1459, and to the religious brotherhood at St. Catherine's Church in Kazimierz.[292] Anna's husband, the merchant Florian, who became a Krakow burgher in 1432, also left a will,[293] but he did not make bequests to religious institutions, and probably delegated this task to his wife.

In terms of piety, Anna Florianinne's will also demonstrates that Krakovian burghers differed in regards to their level of religious commitment. The form of the bequest itself reflects the material situation and social position of a widow of a wealthy merchant,[294] though it is notable that the will does not particularly privilege her parish church, and instead includes numerous bequests to various religious institutions and clerics with whom the testatrix was acquainted. This is probably tied to the fact that she had arrived in Krakow relatively recently and actively participated in the spiritual life of various religious communities, both in the Krakow agglomeration and in her home town of Krosno.

A survey of these wills gives one the impression that donations for the building of new churches was the preferred form of bequest for most burghers. Perhaps by donating money for the construction of a symbolic, but also very real, 'house of God' they wished to personally participate in the sacred.[295] Con-

---

292   An interesting aspect of this bequest was the fact that the brotherhood at St. Catherine's Church had been identified as a Polish brotherhood from its very beginning: 'Fraternitas Polonorum.' Anna's Polish identity may also be indicated by the fact that she came from Krosno. Therefore, it seems characteristic that there was no bequest for other Krakow religious fraternities, including the most important 'German' brotherhood – NMP; cf. Hanna Zaremska, *Bractwa*, 88–92.

293   SCAB. 6, fol. 172 (1439).

294   She received from her husband a significant sum of 300 *grivna* as her dowry; *ibidem*.

295   This phenomenon was first observed by Kateřina Jíšová. She quoted a vivid opinion from the period, according to which "stone will eventually win as a more durable and tangible witness of time, which cannot be easily destroyed"; cf. *eadem*, "Testamenty pražských

300   CHAPTER 4

sidering that fourteenth-century Krakow was a vast building site with many churches under construction, its citizens had a wide array of choices. This is evidenced by the *pro fabrica ecclesiae* bequests appearing in many wills. For example, Margaret, wife of Peter Wilrich, asked that her estate and movables be donated either "to the poor" or "for construction [of a church]."[296] A similar bequest was made by Martin Jung, in which he left sixteen grivna to be given either to St. Stephen's Church or a different church "under construction outside the city."[297]

A characteristic feature of some donations made by Krakovian burghers were bequests to pay for the construction of specific parts of a church or elements of its furnishings. This shows that burghers felt responsible for taking care of, decorating, and furnishing their local churches and wished to personally participate in the construction of a new church, or at least some part of it. For example, burghers made donations *pro fabrica ecclesiae*[298] or specific bequests to pay for a new roof,[299] windows,[300] tower roof,[301] pipe organ,[302] church bell[303] or main altarpiece.[304] It is also possible that priests or preachers instructed the faithful as to what they should buy or finance for a specific church.

5   *Religion Civique* – Communal Religiosity

The relative weakness of parish communities (due to the large number of religious institutions active in the city) and the ongoing formation of a civic

---

      měšťanů v pozdním středověku. Religiozita, sociální rozvrstvení, majetkové a rodinné poměry novoměstských měšťanů (1421–1533)," in *Pierwsze polsko-czeskie forum młodych mediewistów. Materiały z konferencji naukowej, Gniezno 27–29 września 2005 r.*, ed. Józef Dobosz (Poznan: Instytut Historii UAM, 2007), 299.

296   "[...] das se erbe vnd beweglich gut, was se noch ir lossen wirt, sullin in dy werk der barmherczikeit wenden armen leuthen, adir, wy se en her noch wurde beuelen"; SCAB., no. 1773–1774 (1393).

297   "[...] beuele ich XVI marg czu sente Stephan czu der kirchen, adir, wirt man bawen eine kirche hy vor der stat, so sal man dy XVI marg dorczu gehen"; SCAB., no. 1816 (1393).

298   For example, in the note on the will of Gertrude, widow of Nicholas of Kluczbork: "Henricus Schere petitor ecclesie sancte Marie Resignauit vnum Bancum panis, qui pro parte dimidia ad fabricam ecclesie sancte Marie per Dominam Gerdrudim quondam Relictam Nicolai de Cruceburc erat legatus"; NKiRMK, no. 1548 (1345).

299   LT, fol. 31 (1451); SCAB. 8, fol. 270–271 (1467); LT, fol. 154 (1494).

300   SCAB., no. 2092 (1395); SCAB. 6, fol. 338 (1445); LT, fol. 68 (1460).

301   LT, fol. 27 (1452).

302   CONS. 428, fol. 243(1428); LT, fol. 154 (1494), 165–166 (1501).

303   SCAB. 6, fol. 184 (1439), 188 (1439).

304   LT, fol. 92–93 (1467), 108–109 (1473), 120–121 (1476), 119–120 (1477).

THE BURGHER RELIGIOSITY   301

identity – conceived of as a local patriotism and sense of community delimited by the boundaries of Krakow's sphere of influence as an urban centre[305] – were important causal factors in shaping the nature of burgher religiosity. This included not only the phenomena discussed above, related to religion in its private, familial, corporate and parish dimensions, but also by the urban milieu and factors outside of parish life. This can be seen in the tendency described earlier for testators to make pious bequests to churches located throughout the Krakow agglomeration. This indicates that they must have identified with a wider community, i.e. the city organism as a whole. The pious bequests they made (whether to the Church or to the 'poor') were in the interest of this wider community, and in return they expected this community to respond to their needs, remember them and pray for their souls.

To understand this urban model of religiosity we have to consider two interrelated phenomena. The first is the burghers' function within the wider urban community, including religious life (manifested most clearly during annual Corpus Christi processions);[306] the other is the way in which the municipal authorities shaped these relations from above. It is worth examining the latter phenomenon here, as it also influenced the institution of the will.

Western historiography has long been aware of the phenomenon of municipal authorities assuming 'patronage' over religious life in the community, coining the terms *religion civique* in French, *bürgerliche Religiosität* in German and *civic religion* in English to refer to it.[307] André Vauchez defines it as essentially being "the appropriation of values of the religious life by urban powers

---

305   Halina Manikowska, *Religijność miejska*, 19–24; Roman Czaja, "Tożsamość mieszczaństwa hanzeatyckiego w średniowieczu," in *Aetas media, aetas moderna. Studia ofiarowane profesorowi Henrykowi Samsonowiczowi w siedemdziesiątą rocznicę urodzin*, ed. Agnieszka Bartoszewicz, Wojciech Fałkowski, Halina Manikowska, Antoni Mączak, Karol Modzelewski (Warszawa: Instytut Historyczny Uniwersytetu Warszawskiego, 2000), 182–191.

306   An important testimony to the importance of the Corpus Christi procession is the bequest from Paul Gortler's testament of 1474, in which he donated, according to the will of his father, half of the stall towards the organization of this procession "with flags and candles as before and forever and ever," "Czum irsten zo hat her bescheiden seinen halben krom als oben des vor dy ander helffte her Marcus ist zu dem testament das seyn vatir gemacht hat zu ere des heiligen leichnams ouff seyn teyl, das sulche processio vor dem Heiligen Leichnam mit fanen mit lichten alsus denum bis do her gehalden isteynen ewigen vorgang, und bestehn habe"; LT, fol. 106 (1474); cf. Hanna Zaremska, "Procesje Bożego Ciała w Krakowie w XIV–XVI wieku," in *Kultura elitarna a kultura masowa w Polsce późnego średniowiecza*, ed. Bronisław Geremek (Wrocław: Zakład Narodowy im. Ossolińskich, 1978), 25–40.

307   Marek Słoń, *Religijność komunalna*, 9–10; Andrew Brown, *Civic Ceremony and Religion in Medieval Bruges c. 1300–1520* (Cambridge: Cambridge University press, 2011); Trevor Dean, *The Towns of Italy*, 63–71.

302   CHAPTER 4

for the purposes of legitimation, celebration and public well-being."[308] Polish
historians have coined their own terms and definitions in recent years. For
example, Halina Manikowska has translated the French term into Polish. She
writes about 'urban religiosity,' emphasizing the role played by the municipal authorities in shaping this phenomenon.[309] Marek Słoń, in turn, suggests
that the term 'communal religiosity' describes "the semantic field in question"
more accurately.[310] Previous studies have identified several major areas of
urban religiosity. These included the cult of the patron saint of the city, support from the municipal council in the creation and functioning of religious
fraternities, funding provided by the municipal council for various religious
institutions in the city, governance over hospitals and schools, the participation of councillors in processions and other forms of public worship, the
patronage of municipal authorities over churches, chapels, altars and prebends financed by burghers, and commemorating deceased members of the
urban community.[311] When seen in such terms, the municipal authorities' participation in the sphere of the sacred can be considered an additional dimension of urban religiosity.

The analysed wills illustrate the links between power and religion in the
medieval city and how the institution of the will comprised an element of
religion civique. We first see signs of the municipal authorities' involvement
in the authentication and execution of pious bequests in the early fourteenth
century. This tendency is evident in Sulisława's will from 1303: pious bequests
of a butcher stall, market stall and bread stall (*Brotbank*) were to be made by
Albert, the vogt of Krakow, as the executor of her will. The butcher stall was to
be sold for 24 grivna and the money given to the Franciscans. Albert was also

---

308   André Vauchez, *La religion civique à l'époque médiévale et moderne. Chrétienté et islam:
       actes du colloque*, Rome 1995, 1, cited in Trevor Dean, *The Towns of Italy*, 63.
309   "*Religion civique* means more than just burghers' religiosity, and is distinct especially in its
       forms of worship and devotional practices from rural religiousness. It is defined as a set of
       religious phenomena – connected with worship, piety and urban institutions - in which
       secular governance and local authorities subjugated to it to various degrees (city master,
       city council, guild authorities) played an essential role. Through organising municipal
       festivities and manifestations of public order, these authorities appropriated the val-
       ues associated with religious life (e.g. for purposes of legitimacy)."; Halina Manikowska,
       Religijność miejska, 15.
310   Marek Słoń, *Religijność komunalna*, 9–21.
311   Jörg Oberste, "Macht und Memoria. Religiöses Leben und soziale Netzwerke des Regens-
       burger Patriziates im später Mittelalter," in *Regensburg im Spättmittelalter. Bestands-
       aufnahme und Impulse*, ed. Schmid (Regensburg: Schnell & Steiner, cop., 2007), 25–48;
       Trevor Dean, *The Towns of Italy*, 63–71; Halina Manikowska, *Religijność miejska*, 11–34.

THE BURGHER RELIGIOSITY

303

to buy half of the market stall on similar terms for a fair market price.[312] The vogt was also tasked with donating the income from the bread stall for the *fabrica* of St. Mary's Church. He was also given the option to purchase this stall for himself and his heirs (with the consent of the municipal council).[313] Albert was thus the executor of the will, and at the same time, one of its beneficiaries. The municipal council, whose official written consent he needed to purchase the stall and whose seal was affixed to the will,[314] played a secondary role.

The role of the municipal council in the execution of wills grew in importance after a rebellion led by the vogt Albert in 1311–1312.[315] For example, we learn from a 1317 entry pertaining to the will of the first wife of the alderman Henry Srolle that the provincial vogt Wilhelm, acting on behalf of a Dominican friar named John, passed on the donation in question to the municipal council and the city.[316] In 1318, Marusza, widow of Wilhelm of the Orient,[317]

---

312 The other half was supposedly given to a man named Minardus, a Franciscan.: "Item de instita sic dispono, quod mediam confero fratribus predicatoribus, in qua Michachel filius simniconis residet, tali interposita condicione, quod prefatus dominus albertus eandem medietatem instite aput prescriptos fratres pro se et ipsius posteris redimat, sicut tunc taxata fuerit, iure hereditario conseruando. Insuper mediam institam do fratribus minoribus, in qua minardus inhabitat, tali caucione intermedia, quod ipse minardus aput ipsos fratres eandem medietatem (s) instite emat pro se et suis successoribus, prout tunc estimata fuerit, ipsam inperpetuum possidendo"; KDMK, vol. 3, no. 368.

313 "Item vsum vnius banci panis concedo ad opus beate virginis marie, cousque antedictum opus consumatum fuerit ex integro, constituens sepedictum dominum albertum procuratorem et exsecutorem eiusdem banci; consumato opere eiusdem ecclesie ipse dominus albertus pro se et suis successoribus cum consensu consulum exsoluat, si sibi visum fuerit et consultum, pecuniam vero, quam pro ipso banco dederit, ponet ad vsum eiusdem ecclesie et conuertat"; *ibidem.*

314 Most likely, it was councilors who were being ambiguously referred to as "honorabilium virorum civium cracoviensium"; *ibidem.*

315 "Just as the location privilege of Krakow opened the way to the creation of the institution of the council, the fall of Albert made it possible for the Krakow patricians who formed this council to assume real power over the city. In the first forty years of its existence, the Council of Krakow evolved from a body that originally supervised trade in the city to a body that determined the shape of the city's politics."; Marcin Starzyński, *Krakowska rada*, 57–58.

316 Two or three words were scratched out, so it is not possible to determine what the donation concerned, but due to the similarity to other provisions from that time it was probably a stall, a bench or a slaughterhouse: "Item in eodem Iudicio Vilhelmus aduocatus prouincialis sub nomine fratris Iohannis predicatoris de ordine predicatorum vnum ___ ___ ___, quod Henricus Srolle legauerat fratribus predicatoribus pro testamento prime uxoris sue, Consulibus et Ciuitati Crachouie resignauit"; NKiRMK, no. 411 (1317).

317 Jerzy Rajman distinguishes between Wilhelm, the councilor and provincial mayor, and Wilhelm of Orient, who lived at the same time, "'Unsere libe Fraue.' Wspólnota miasta i kościoła w Krakowie w XIV wieku," *Średniowiecze Polskie i Powszechne* 4 (8), 155–156.

304   CHAPTER 4

stated that her husband had made a will when he was still alive, donating one grivna in annual rent to St. Mary's Church (specifically to buy candles).[318] The municipal council then advised Marusza to sell the rent of eight grivna and donate the money to St. Mary's Church.[319] The growing role of the municipal council is also evidenced by other wills. In the 1325 will of Konrad the maltster, councillors acted as executors of his will, donating Konrad's house to St. Mary's Church.[320] In turn, the burgher widow of Otton, in her 1340 will,[321] chose councillors as the 'patrons' of one of her testamentary dispositions. The widow donated to the city half of a stall, with the condition that she could continue using it as long as she lived; after her death, however, the councillors would run her stall and use the profits to benefit the poor and for the salvation of her and her husband's souls. The widow emphasised in the bequest that "all this should be done with the advice of the councilors."[322] The municipal council thus not only guaranteed the execution of the will's dispositions, but because the body was permanent and collegial in nature, it also ensured something highly sought after by pious burghers – that their legacy funding would continue for many years (and, according to the testators' intentions, indefinitely).

Such a guarantee of permanence was indeed important, especially in the case of generous pious foundation, which were meant to continue 'working'

---

318 "Item in eodem iudicio bannito domina Marussa relicta Wilhelmi protestata fuit et publicavit coram predictis advocatis et scabinis, quod ipse Vilhelmus maritus eius faciens testamentum, unam marcam grossorum censualem super fundum et mediam curiam Lexandri in platea sutorum annis singulis ecclesie sancte Marie Virginis dedit et legavit pro luminibus in eadem ecclesia conparandis et pro salute anime sue ordinandis"; NKiRMK, no. 477 (1318).

319 "Item in eodem Iudicio domina Marussa relicta Vilhelmi de Consilio dominorum Consulum vendidit vnam marcam Censualem que iacuit super Curiam Lexandri in platea sutorum pro octo marcis Grossorum, que pecunia data est et donata ad fabricam Ecclesie sancte Marie virginis. Et ipsa domina Marussa eandem marcam censualem dicto Lexandro resignauit"; NKiRMK, no. 478 (1318).

320 "Item predicti Consules mediam Curiam cum fundo ad opus Ecclesie sancte marie assignatam pro testamento Conrado braseatori vendiderunt et in predicto iudicio iure hereditario resignauerunt, que iacet in platea sancti ffloriani prope Curiam relicte Sere in acie"; NKiRMK, no. 750 (1325).

321 She may have been Alusha, a testator from 1321, a widow of an alderman Otto; NKiRMK, no. 616 (1321).

322 "Eodem Anno et die resignauit Relicta Ottonis medium Cramum ciuitati, ita quod interea quando uixerit, debet in Cramo stare, et post mortem suam Consules loco ciuitatis debent se intromittere et censum dare infirmis; Si autem venderetur Cramus, pecunia non alias, quam pro infirmis et utilitate ipsorum est conuertenda pro animabus mariti eius et uxoris iamdicte, et hoc totum fieri debet cum consilio dominorum Consulum ciuitatis"; NKiRNK, no. 1407.

THE BURGHER RELIGIOSITY 305

indefinitely to ensure the salvation of the testator and their family (i.e. by making sure that someone would always pray for them) and commemorate their achievements among the living. This is why burgher testators who founded chapels, altars and perpetual Masses chose councillors as patrons of these bequests. This solution seems natural because the wealthiest testators usually had strong ties to the municipal authorities, and it was only natural to entrust one's relatives or friends from the same social circles to act as the executors of one's will. For example, in his 1369 will, councillor Nicholas Edel (*Edeling*) donated his stall and two grivna in rent to the Dominicans, asking them in exchange to celebrate a daily Mass for the souls of all his ancestors and descendants.[323] As the executors of the will, the municipal council administered the rent and ensured that the Dominicans carried out their end of the deal. The money was to be paid twice a year, but in the event that the Dominicans breached the contract, the municipal council had the right to withdraw from it and donate the money to the sick at a hospital or for other 'works of mercy.'[324]

In setting up a foundation for two altars – one in St. Mary's Church and one in All Saints Church (both dedicated to St. Anthony, blessed Dorothy and martyrs), the wealthy mine administrator Gotfrid Fattinante of Genoa appointed Krakow city councillors and Spytko of Melsztyn, the second voivode and starost

---

323 "Honorabilis vir Nicolaus Edelingi nobis conconsul, dum simul in pleno sederemus consilio, nobis Magnarum precura instancia intimitis suplicauit, ut assumpta nobis nomine Ciuitatis nostre Instita sua in acie in Medio institarum sita et Duas Marcas polonicales currentis monetę, nos aut qui pro tempore fuerint Consules Ciuitatis constituti, de pretorio singulis annis elemosine perpetue ipsis Religiosis viris fratribus predicatoribus Conuentus dicte nostre Ciuitatis daremus. Cuius elemosine virtute idem fratres predicatores ipsorum exigente devocione ad vnam missam cottidie in Capella eiusdem Nicolai Edelingi celebrandam in ipsius predecessorum omnium et posterorum suorum animarum remedium salutare salutare vitro se exhibuerunt firmiter astringendo, prout in eorum literis desuper confectis luculencius continetur"; NKiRMK, no. 1705; cf. Józef Mitkowski, « Mikołaj Edeling, » in PSB, vol. 6 (Krakow: Polska Akademia Nauk, Polska Akademia Umiejętności, 1948), 201.

324 "Nos vero Consules predicti nostro ac memorate Uniuersitatis Ciuitatis nomine antedictam nobis assumpsimus et assumimus Institam premissis ipsius Nicolai Edlingi pijs ac iustis affeccionibus amicabiliter annuentes, volumus et spondemus dictis fratribus predicatoribus eandem elemosi-nam annuam et perpetuam puta vnam marcam super Aduentum domini et aliam Marcam super Quadragesimam occasionibus omnibus atque dilacionibus propulsatis, de ipso nostro pretorio, uel qui pro tempore fuerint Consules, annis singulis elargiri. Si autem dicti fratres in dicte celebracione misse non continuarent, seu ipsam Missam, quod non credimus, quoquomodo postergarent, extunc a pretactis fratribus predicatoribus deinceps nolumus pro elemosina huiusmodi aliqualiter amoneri, Sed esse liberi ad ipsam elemosinam dandam pro refeccione langwidorum hospitalis aut in alia conuertere opera pietatis"; NKiRMK, no. 1705.

306   CHAPTER 4

of Krakow, as the patrons and guardians of the two altars.[325] In addition, Gotfrid Fattinante appointed the Bishop of Krakow Peter Wysz of Radolin, Spytko and members of the Krakow municipal council as the executors of his will. This demonstrates that burghers who did not have close relatives often asked the municipal authorities to serve as patrons of chapels, altars, and altarages they had founded, usually for two reasons; namely, to ensure their continuation and increase their prestige. And while for the majority of burghers, the council symbolized the primary municipal authority, in some cases, as in that of Fattinante (probably because he was a mine administrator), this function could be performed by the starost or voivode.

In 1401, councillor John Bartfal appointed members of the Krakow municipal council as patrons of his generous pious bequest, explicitly linking his choice with his desire to ensure the perpetual fulfilment of its provisions.[326]

---

325   "Primo vero in salutare anime sue remedium Cameram suam pannorum circa cameram Pauli Nutricis et sex marcas census annui et terragij, quem super fundo domus Nicolai Beidner in platea sutorum site, habere dignoscitur, pro altari in honorem sanctorum Anthonij confessoris et alme virginis Dorothee ac martyris ad taxam sedecim marcarum et valorem in ecclesia parochiali sanete Marie Virginis semper gloriose in Cracouia erecturo siue erigendo, feliciter construeturo siue construendo, cuius collacio, presentacio, prouisio seu queuis alia disposicio ad Consules Ciuitatis Cracouiensis nunc et pro tempore existentes, perpetuo pertinere debeat, de quo altari prouidit ad presens domino Petro capellano et notario suo, domum vero suam lapideam in acie circuli circa Powsuange sitam, valido viro domino Spitkoni Palatino ac Capitaneo Cracouiensi, vt per ipsum ac electos presentis testamenti executores infrascriptos alicui ciui vendi debeat, et pro huiusmodi pecunia census sedecim marcarum perpetuus comparari, et de eodem censu sedecim marcarum altare eciam sanctorum Anthonij Confessoris et beate Dorothee Virginis in ecclesia parrochiali Sanctorum Omnium in ciuitate Cracouiensi eciam de taxa sedecim marcarum erigi et construi, cuius collacio seu queuis alia disposicio ipsi domino Spitkoni ac suis posteris legitimisque successoribus perpetuis debet pertinere temporibus, dedit, contulit ac perpetuo assignauit, quod eciam altare domino Iohanni presbytero domus sue et medico assignauit, superfluum vero pecunie domus predicte, si que vltra empeioriem sedeeim marcarum census annui predicti superfuerit, ipsius Spitconis consciencie recommendat. Preterea res omnes suas videlicet vestes, pelles, pellicia, togas, mensas, cistas, lectisternia ac omnia vniuersaliter et singula, quibuscumque vocitentur nominibus, nullis penitus exceptis, in predicta domo, quam inhabitat, existentes ac existencia, Nicloso cubiculario suo et familiari de presenti earundem cedens possessionem et in ipsum Niclonem transferens, cum omnimoda faciendi et dimittendi facultate legauit"; KDWac., vol. 2, no. 396, 182–183 (1393).

326   "Johannes Bartfal volbedocht als her sprach und mit gutir vornumft mit seynis selbimunt redinde, hot wedirrufin al seyn testament und lecztin willen und auch dy vormundschaft von den vormunden, das her gemacht hatte und ader dy her gekorn hatte neulich vorgehegtin dinge, wen her habe nicht vornomyn noch eren enweys wy is gemacht sey wordin, is sey seyn wort nicht sundir das ist sey seyn wille das man von alle seyme gute und gelde saleyn eltir stiften von XLII marken gemaynir muncze und nicht prag. gr., alzo mogin

THE BURGHER RELIGIOSITY   307

Similarly, in 1439, the municipal notary and clergyman John Stolle appointed
members of the municipal council as 'patrons' of four altarages he funded
in his will.[327] Similar instructions were given by other wealthy burghers who
made very generous perpetual foundation bequests to finance chapels, altars
or prebends at an existing altar, asking the municipal council to act as patrons
of these bequests. It seems that such a choice was most often made by members of the city's elite who did not have children – those who lacked heirs who
could look after and continue to fund chapels, altars or prebends, and thereby
commemorate the testator – and were therefore more likely to ask the municipal council for help in this matter. Gotfrid Fattinante, John Bartfal, John Stolle,

---

dy czinse gefolgin off den erbin dy her hot in der stat adir beusin, zo sal man sy der off
gebin das leyt ander Rathmannen Wille mochte das nicht geseyn zo sulde man als obin ist
geschrebin, von allern seynen gute und gelde andir czinse keufin und dorczu gebin und
das lehen des eltirs sullin dy Rathmann habin und dis obingeschrebin gemechte sal czu
mole ewiklich, als is gemacht ist alzo bleybin und gibt distiftunge und das lehen iczunt
den Rathmannen in di hende, Sundir um alle seyn gut, das do oberig bleibit das will her
beschrebin gebin adir usweysin ab man das seynen vrunden obir czu stegen und wegin
gebin sal adir wy man is domite haldin sal"; CONS. 427, fol. 167; cf. Krystyna Pieradzka, "Jan
Bartfal," in PSB, vol. 1 (Krakow: Polska Akademia Nauk, Polska Akademia Umiejętności,
1935), 311.

327   "[...] befele ich dasselbe haws meynen hern den Ratmannen der Stat Cracow, daz sy das
vorkewffen, noch seyner wirde, und unis das geld czinse kewffen czu newer belenunge,
des eltirs sinte Marie Magdalene, in der kirchen unser frawen hy czu Cracow, czu newhir
stiftunge pristerliches amechts steter und ewigen messe abgesundirt von allir czuge-
horunge der vorgen belenunge desselben eltirs und seynes vorgen eltirheren; Item das
leen desselben eltirs gebe ich meynen hern den Ratmanen der Stat Cracow czu ewigen
tagen, also daz sy den eltir derselben meyner newer belenunge geben sullen dem eldisten
Caplan am dinste derselben kirchen unser frawen, und nimande andirs, und dorumme
wenne is dorczu kompt, daz dy Ratmanne das obgenante haws vorkewffen sullen, so sal
der eldiste Caplan, der of dy czeit seyn wirt am dinste der obgenanten kirchen mete wissen und raten, helffen und sorge tragen czu derselben vorkewffunge des hawsis, und czu
bewarunge des geldis derselben beczalunge, und czu dem kawffe des czinses umb dasselbe geld, dorczu kyze ich in iczunt hy, wer der seyn wirt. Item dy virczig marg ierlichis
czinsis dy ich hy habe of der Stat Cleynen woge und crome und brotbenke bescheide ich
czu belenunge dreyen eltir in derselben pfarkirchen unser frawen hy czu Cracow, als czu
des Heylgen Crewczis eltir eyn dritteyl, czu sinte Annen eltir eyn dritteyl, und czu sinte
Peters und pavels elter an her Lucas Capelle steende eyn dritteyl, czu stiftunge dreyen
newen pristirlichen amecht stetirund ewigir messe, dreyen newen eltirhern, abgesundirt
von den czinsen und eltirhern und allir czugeherunge, dy dyselben elter vormols haben,
von andirr leute belenunge und vorgar stiftunge. Item das leen derselben dreyen eltir
meyner newen obgenanten belenunge und stiftunge gebe ich ouch meynen hern den
Ratmanen der Stat Cracowczu ewigen tagen in sulchir weyze, als obene, daz sy dorczu
iczlich mol als sich das geboren wirt entwirten sullen den eldisten Caplan am dinste der
derselben kirchen am lengisten gedint hot und nymande andirs"; SCAB. 6, fol. 186.

308   CHAPTER 4

the village administrator Peter Filipowski,[328] and Salomea, widow of Nicholas
Brenner, were all childless.[329] Some testators who had children, in turn, stated
that in the event of the death of all their descendants the municipal council
should act as the patron of the altars they had built. In her 1484 will, Catherine left her house (valued at 800 florins and located at Grodzka Street) to her
grandson John. However, should John die childless, this house was to be sold
and the money used to finance an altar or prebend, and the municipal council was to serve as its patron. Two Masses a week were to be celebrated at the
altar. One Mass was to be dedicated to the Assumption of the Virgin Mary, and
the other to Catherine's deceased relatives and all believers.[330] Similar instructions were left by Thob Johan,[331] Peter Schepcz[332] and Michael Lang.[333] They

---

328   In the provisions of his testaments of 1452 and 1460, the village administrator Peter Fili-
       powski (Philippowsky) gave his house in Shoemaker's Street to the councillors, asking
       them to sell the rent and use it to establish a ministry for a German preacher in St. Mary's
       Church.; LT, fol. 28 (1452), 66 (1460).

329   "Czum irsten kyze ich mir czu vormunde und czu vorwezer dy erben manne Johannes
       Syndram und Michel Goltsmed, den befele ich noch meym tode, meym haws und alle
       meyn gut erblich und farnde das ich iczunt habe adir hernochmols haben werde und
       noch meym tode lossen werde, in sulchir weyze, daz sy dasselbe haus und gut vorkewffen
       sullen noch seyme wirden und sullen do von czinse kewffen czu belenung eyns Eltirs in
       der kirchen unsir liben frawen hy czu Cracow, czu newer stiftunge pristirlichis amechts
       stetir und ewigen messe und denselben Eltir, so der mit der hulffe gotis vorbrocht wirt,
       vorleye ich und gebe dem erben prister hern Mathis dem vicario czu unsir liben frawen
       hy czu Cracow, und noch Im dem Eldsten vicario und Caplan am dinste der derselben
       kirchen am lengisten gedint hot, und das leen desselben Eltirs gebe ich den hern Rat-
       manen der Stat Cracow czu ewigen tagen, alzo das sy den eltir derselben newen bele-
       nunge geben sullen dem eldisten Caplan am dinste derselben kirchen und nymande
       anders"; SCAB. 6, fol. 190.

330   "Primo lapideam suum domum eius in platea Castrensis inter Johannis Kromsch et Lazari
       domos iacentis quam ad octingentos florenorum existimat dedit puero Johannis filio olim
       Byali Jan sartoris ex filia ipsius nato tali conditione si vivet, Si autem sine prole morire-
       tur extunc voluit et commisit ut eandemdomum executores sive tutores per eam nomi-
       nandos vendant et altare in Ecclesia sancte Marie in circulo seu ministerium fundant et
       erigant circa quod altare volt habere unum lectorem qui leget duas missas septimanatim
       unam de assumpcionem sancte marie et aliam pro mortuis suum amicabus, propinquo-
       rum et consangwineorum suorum ac omnium fidelium, Cuius altaris sive ministerii dom-
       inos Consules Cracoviensis pro tempore existentes voluit esse patronos"; LT, fol. 142–143.

331   LT, fol. 7–8 (1443).

332   LT, fol. 137–139 (1483).

333   Councillor Michael de Czirla alias Langmichel had already obtained permission to build
       his own chapel in St. Mary's Church, where the founded altar was probably placed: "Primo
       mencionem faciens capelle, quam in cimiterio beate Marie Virginis contiguam ostio
       meridionali eiusdem ecclesie citerioriedificandam ipse iam antea disposuit, cuius et iam

THE BURGHER RELIGIOSITY

all established perpetual Mass funds and appointed altarists responsible for celebrating Mass, stating that the municipal council should exercise patronage over their foundations if their heirs died childless. Paul Gortler donated 300 florins to fund one perpetual altarage at St. Mary's Church (stating that two Masses a week should be celebrated at the altar). He appointed the "deputy notary John" (*Johann undirstatschreiber*) as the first altarist, stating that that after John's death the next altarist should be appointed by the municipal council. Later, however, that privilege was to be passed on to Gortler's distant relatives.[334] In the first version of her will, Salomea Brennerinne, a childless burgher woman, asked the Krakow municipal council to act as patron for an altar she had funded. A year later, however, in a second version of her will, she granted this right to the Brotherhood of the Blessed Virgin Mary, to which she probably belonged. She seemed to have had reasons to think the brotherhood was better suited to perform this function.[335]

Other fourteenth-century and fifteenth-century wills also demonstrate that the municipal council exercised patronage over and supervised the performance of works of charity. For example, in 1405, Dorothy, widow of the councillor John Pauswang, gave almost her entire estate (including a generous dower, gerade, cash, and part of the inheritance she had received from her father) to the municipal council. The councillors were to decide which 'works of charity'

---

    sunt posita fundamenta, volo inquit, ut compleatur opus illud usque ad plenam ipsius capelle consumacionem, scilicet iuxta eam formam et modum, secundum quod condixi et convencionem feci cum muratore. Et in eadem capella, cum perfecta fuerit, edificari debet altare et consecrari, in quo iugis fiat missarum celebracio ad laudem Dei et eius genitricis honorem, pro anime mee et filii mei ac progenitorum meorum suffragio salutary [...]. Deinde descendens memoratus fundator ad institutionem ministri et patronorum: Volo, inquit, ut iste presens hic Nicolaus Schreiberdorff de Brega primus sit predicti altaris altarista qui ad provisionem meam, quam ei dedi iam cepit ad sacros ordines promoveri, post illum vero deinceps, quociens idem altare vacaverit, domini consules civitatis Cracovie, qui pro tempore fuerint, presentare ad ipsum debent unum ex vicariis ecclesie beate Virginis predicte senioribus, qui ipsis consulibus magis idoneus videatur. Ipsis enim dominis consulibus do et confero ius patronatus ipsius altaris et presentandi ad ipsum, ut predictum est ab his perpetuis temporibus possidendum"; CONS. 428, fol. 344 (1435); cf. Sławomira Pańków, "Michał Lang (de Czirla)," in PSB vol. 16, 481–482.

334   "Item zo hot her benumet bescheiden und gegeben IIIc ungaricales gulden zu einir stiftunge eynes ewigen altarum yn unser lieben frawen kirchen dor ouff man II messen dy woche sal lesen eyne vom Heiligen geistis dy ander von unser lieben frawen zum welchen altaris her itczunder gepuntiret hat Johannem unsir undirstatschreyber, noch welchis tode her den hern Rothmanne von Croke ouch eyn vorleyen eynes altaristen vorlegen und gegeben ffort sal sulch lehen an seyne frunde bekomen"; LT, fol. 105–107 (1484).

335   cf. SCAB. 6, fol. 190 (1439), 213, 215 (1440); SCAB. 7, fol. 7–8 (1447).

310   CHAPTER 4

to support for the salvation of Dorothy's soul.[336] In some cases, the fact that
the testator left money to the municipal council meant that the council had
to first collect the money for the works of charity from debtors, as was the
case with the will of Thob Johan,[337] or liquidate valuables.[338] For example, the
tailor Jarosz testified that he possessed 34 silver spoons, three silver belts, four
gold rings, two coral rosaries, two dagger scabbards decorated with silver ornaments, a silver belt, four silver mugs and 250 florins in gold in his chests. "He
entrusted all of this to councillors to spend on works of charity, upon determining where the need was greatest, according to their will."[339]

In Krakow, as in other cities, the municipal council assumed oversight of
the city's hospitals.[340] This is visible in many wills in which donations were
made to benefit the poor in general or to one of the hospitals within the Krakow agglomeration. In 1413, Elizabeth, widow of Nicholas Rozler, donated 20
grivna she was owed to the Hospital of the Holy Spirit. As the executors of her
will, she appointed Nicholas Schultis and Matthias, an administrator (*prow-
izor*) responsible for the poor, "or any other councillor selected in his place."[341]
The councillor Wilhelm Willand made a bequest of 25 grivna to a hospital in

---

336 "Item allis ir oberig gelt und gut, alz IIc marg ire morgengobe, XXX marg bereytis geldis,
     alle ir teyl ires vetirlichen angevellis, und alle ire gerade, dy ir mit rechte geboren mag was
     doran oberig bleibit, obir das vorgeschrebene bescheidere gelt, das hat se den Ersamen
     weysen dem ganczen Rate, und den Ratmannen allin czu Cracovia bescheiden und be-
     volhen noch irem trewen und besten vornemen czuwenden wo das allir notdurftigiste
     wirt seyn, in dy werk der heilgen barmherczikeit, durch zelikeit willen irer zele"; CONS.
     427, fol. 241.

337 He ordered that 900 florins from Koszyce and Bardejov he was entitled to should be
     reclaimed by his son and stepson, and given to the councillors, so that they could use it
     for works of charity to help the poor; LT, fol. 7–8 (1443).

338 Alderman Matthias Opoczko donated 21 silver spoons, a silver gold-plated cup (*picarium
     alias kubeck*), two silver women's belts, all his receivables, supellectilia, garlands (*vittas*),
     four carpets (*tapeta*), all his other household items and tools (*apparatus*) and a chalice
     (*calix*) made of three marks of silver to the St. Mary's Church; LT, fol. 108–109 (1473).

339 "Que omnia pro operibus misericordie commisit post mortem suam distribuenda et
     danda ex manibus dominorum consulum pro libitu et voluntate eorum ubi melius et
     divius videbitur expeditum"; LT, fol. 151–152 (1492).

340 Marek Słoń, "Fundacje szpitalne władz komunalnych jako centra kultu miejskiego," in
     Ecclesia et civitas, 361–373.

341 "Elizabeth Niclos Rozlers witwe, durch Niclos Schultis ir doselbist czu vormunde
     nemende, hat der LV mrc dy ir Thomas Spiczschirch eyn fleyscher schuldig ist, der sie
     vorderunge Nicolaum Platener vormols mechtig gemacht hat XX mrc den Armen sichen
     in dem hospitali czum Heiligengeiste legenden und dreyssig mrc czur den Paulern czum
     gebeude des Clostirs noch irem tode bescheiden czu gebin. Alzo dasman dy XX mrc sal
     gebin Niclos Schultis und Mathie der Armen Sichen obgenanten Bitter, adir dy denne czu
     der czeyt denselbin Armen von den Ratleuten gesaczt werden und dy oberigen V mrc

THE BURGHER RELIGIOSITY   311

Krakow, asking the municipal council to distribute the money.[342] Similarly, in his 1452 will, the village administrator Peter Filipowski donated ten grivna to a hospital in Krakow. The money was to be given to the municipal council, which, in turn, was to use it to benefit the poor and fund the maintenance of the hospital building.[343] In 1487, Hedwig Granoszowa explicitly designated the municipal council as guardians (*vorweser*) of the poor and the sick at the Hospital of the Holy Spirit, asking them to donate her house to the hospital.[344] In 1435, Peter of Tenczyn, an altarist from Sącz, donated valuable items to the Krakow municipal council, in this way carrying out the will of a burgher from Sącz. Councillors, who are referred to in the document as 'guardians of the poor' (*vorwesern der armen sichen*)[345] recorded that they had spent four grivna to buy fabrics for the poor, while the rest of the money was to be used to buy other necessary items for them.[346]

The municipal council did not only act as 'guardians' and 'patrons' of chapels, altars or prebends funded by testators. As part of the municipal authorities, councillors were often asked to act as executors of all the testamentary bequests in a will. For example, alderman Erhart Eigilwart (a Krakow burgher who originally hailed from Augsburg) named two councillors, George Szwarcz and Wilhelm Willand as the executors of his will.[347] In his 1439 will, another alderman, John Briger, stated that after his death his widowed daughter and her two sons would be left unsupported, and asked that councillors, with the aid of God and the Virgin Mary, act as guardians and executors of his will, and

---

     wil sie selbir von deme obgenanten Thoma offhebin und nemen dorobir behelt sie in dy herschafft dy weyle się lebit"; CONS. 428, fol. 46.

342 CONS. 428, fol. 369 (1436).

343 "Item executores ipsi vendere debent domum suam in platea sancti Johannis et pecuniam exinde pro edificiis Ecclesiarum subscriptarum convertere et distribuere scilicet pro pauperibus hospitalis in Cracovia et ipsorum necessitate X marg et ille debent dominus consulibus presentari qui eam in usum pauperum vel ipsorum edificacionem dispendere debebunt"; LT, fol. 28.

344 "Hedwigis Granoschowa mit gutter vornunft wesinde sitczende off den stule in der stobe yn yren hawse unbetwungen mit gutten freyen willen hat yre haws off der twergassen kegen bursa pauperorum czwuschen her Clethner und Casper Parchwicz gelegen mit allen den rechten als sy das bis do her gehat hat und mit 1 marg czins erdczins czinsinde alle jor den armen sichin in den Spital zum heiligen geisten den selben armen sichen offgegeben also das dy herren Rathmanne als vorwesir der selben mit den selben zu thuen noch yren besten vornemen ydoch wil sy frey wonne yn den selben hawse dy weile sy lebet"; LT, fol. 145.

345 CONS. 428, fol. 350.

346 "Item von dem gelde habe wir gegeben IIII marg czu czichen den armen kraken und das obirge ist komen czu andirr notdorft der armen"; *ibidem*.

347 CONS. 428, fol. 305 (1431).

administrators of his estate.[348] Some testators, such as Barbara, daughter of Michael Unger, appointed two or three specific people as executors of her will (in most cases at least one was a member of the municipal council). However, Barbara also stated that councillors should carry out her will if the people she had appointed refused.[349] Testators sometimes asked the municipal council to manage their estate because they feared it would be squandered. For example, in his 1459 will, goldsmith John Beme asked the municipal council to make an inventory of goods he kept in a chest and then seal it so that nothing went missing.[350] Interestingly, it seems that it was around that time that the municipal council also began to compile inventories of late burghers' possessions.

Funding a chapel, altar or prebend, which was practically speaking an act of 'buying a place in a church,' was usually very expensive. It could even cost as much as one's entire estate. However, such generous bequests were seen as a gift for God, the urban community and, above all, the testator's family. This gift was not only meant to ensure testators' eternal life, but also glorify them among the living. Such a bequest was meant to render the testator 'immortal' and bring them benefits until the Final Judgment, which is why childless or heirless testators often renounced their right of patronage, asking municipal authorities to act as guardians for the chapels, altars and prebends they financed.

Indeed, instructions pertaining to the execution of the will and the need of guardianship are mostly connected with the 'patronage' over the will that the municipal council began to exercise in the late fourteenth century. In practice, this meant that two members of the municipal council visited the testator on his deathbed in order to officially draw up and authenticate the will. The

---

348 "Ich sterbe meyne hawsfraw, meyne tachtir Katherina mit iren czween sonen, so bite ich dy erben hern Ratmanne daz sy meyne vormunde und ausrichter seyn sullen umb gotis willen und unser liben frawen des testamentis und meyner guter farnde und unfarnde was do bleiben wirt"; SCAB. 6, fol. 188.

349 "Elegit in tutores huius testamenti Jacobum Glaser et Thomam Bastgert, si se submittere vellent et suscipere omnis nollent suscipere Quic dominos consules Cracoviensi denominavit et petivit propter deum ut ipsi susciperent tutelam et fidei commissiam et distribuerent bona sua ut super expressum est, cum omnia proprietate et facultate quam tutoriam et executiorem testamenti cum dicti Jacobum Glaser et Thomam Bastgert Eciam requisiti et petiviti suscipere noluerent nos enim Consules suscepimus et illud testamentum expediendis nos submisimus et submittimus commisionem testatricis prout pro concive nostra facere tenetur"; LT, fol. 149–150 (1491).

350 "Libin herren meyne gutter dy ich habe bete ich und begere das dy beseen werden und vorsegilt, das dy nicht vorrockit worden, das dy ouch in eynem kasten eyngeslossen und vorsegilt werden"; LT, fol. 58.

THE BURGHER RELIGIOSITY

Krakow municipal council also began to keep the first *Book of Wills*.[351] Both actions demonstrate the wider phenomenon of *religion civique*. As an embodiment of power, authority and permanence, the municipal council assumed many of the responsibilities that had been traditionally the domain of the Church (pursuant to canon law) or the municipal bench court (pursuant to Magdeburg Law).

5.1 Beguinages

The municipal council's patronage over beguinages is another aspect of *religion civique*. Beguinages were small informal groups of single (unmarried or widowed) women, who pledged to abide by a set of rules guiding their religious and community life. They were often established by means of testamentary foundation bequests, with the municipal council acting as their guardians and administrators.[352] The provisions of a beguinage's rules required them to participate in commemorative services (prayers for the souls of donors),[353] perform charity work (care for the poor and the sick),[354] and undertake skilled crafts (in keeping with the Christian work ethic).[355] Scholars link the popularity of beguinages in the Middle Ages to the growing number of unmarried, and thus often poor, women who had difficulty supporting themselves.[356] The limited number of convents and their unwillingness to accept such women into their ranks led some impoverished commoners to establish their own religious communities or to join other such groups. It seems, however, that at least their founders were primarily inspired by their religious beliefs, their aspirations to dedicate themselves more fully to devotional activities, and a desire to live a life modelled on those of the saints (the *vita apostolica*).

The presence of beguinages in Polish lands dates back to the latter half of the thirteenth century, while in the fourteenth century, their numbers grew

---

351 Cf. Chapter 1, Section 6.

352 On the basis of available sources, it is very difficult to distinguish between third-order convents, Beguines and so-called 'soul houses' (*Seelhäuser*). In the sources they are referred to collectively as *conventus* or *Haus*, and their inhabitants as *sorores devotae*, *moniales* or *mulieres* (*Seelhäuser*); Jarosław Szymański, *Ruchy heretyckie na Śląsku w XIII i XIV wieku* (Katowice: Instytut Książki, 2007), 90–91; Jerzy Wyrozumski, "Beginki i begardzi w Polsce," *Zeszyty Naukowe Uniwersytetu Jagiellońskiego. Prace Historyczne*, 35 (1971), 7–22, 15.

353 Jarosław Szymański, *Ruchy heretyckie*, 90.

354 *Ibidem*, 95; Jerzy Wyrozumski, *Beginki i begardzi*, 12.

355 Jerzy Wyrozumski, *Beginki i begardzi*, 12.

356 *Ibidem*, 15–16; Jarosław Szymański, *Ruchy heretyckie*, 79.

substantially in many urban areas,[357] especially in Silesia, but also in the Małopolska (Sandomierz, Krakow) and the Wielkopolska (Toruń, Poznan) regions.[358] While there are only a few mentions of beguinages in fourteenth-century sources from the Krakow agglomeration, we can assume that beguinages had been common in Krakow since at least the 1350s.[359] The oldest sources confirming the presence of beguines in Krakow are two records in books of the bench court from 1336 and 1338 respectively, in which "Benka, a nun" (*Benka monialis*), is mentioned.[360] In 1344, the "nun Pauline" (*Paulina monialis*) was mentioned in the bench court book as a second beguine. We also know of a transaction that took place between Pauline and Peter, the superior of the Franciscan monastery. "With the consent of the king and the convent" (*de voluntate domini Regis et consensu Tocius Conuentus fratrum Minorum*), Peter sold her, for 40 grivna, a plot of land located next to the house of Tichon Snelli and opposite the cemetery. Pauline instructed in her eternal will (*perpetuum testamentum*) that after her death the municipal council was to use and manage the land to ensure the salvation of Pauline and her soul.[361] Since the transaction was carried out with the consent of the king and since, as in the case of the nun Benka, the plot was located next to the house of the councillor Tichon Snell, we can assume that this was the founding act of a beguinage, whose members were to pray for the salvation of their benefactors and guardians.

---

357 Jerzy Kłoczowski, *Wspólnoty zakonne*, 200–201.

358 Jerzy Wyrozumski, *Beginki i begardzi*, 14. The first mention of their presence in Wrocław dates back to 1285. There is information about the existence of 61 such congregations in Wrocław in the years 1373–1508, and Halina Manikowska estimates the number of their members at about 150 people; *eadem*, "Klasztor żeński w mieście średniowiecznym," *Roczniki Dziejów Społecznych i Gospodarczych* 42 (2002), 45; cf. Jarosław Szymański, *Ruchy heretyckie*, 91–92.

359 "[...] the presence of the Beguines in Krakow in the latter half of the fourteenth century is confirmed by sources. They enjoyed special protection from the municipal council and occupied several houses near the Dominican and Franciscan churches, as well as the no longer existing All Saints" Church; Jerzy Wyrozumski, *Beginki i begardzi*, 14; cf. *idem*, Produkcja sukiennicza w zgromadzeniach religijnych Polski średniowiecznej, *Zeszyty Naukowe UJ. Prace Historyczne*, 12 (1963), 16–17.

360 The first one concerns Benka keeping the inheritance of her father and mother, which had been claimed by the Franciscans, the parson of the All Saints' Church and a man named Dirsko Mandroska. Perhaps this suggests that a will had been made for these people, but was later invalidated by one of Benka's parents. In the second entry, she sells part of the plot next to councillor Ticzon Snelli's house to him, under the condition that a channel for rainwater from both properties is installed; NKiRMK, no. 1188, 1241

361 NKiRMK, no. 1524.

THE BURGHER RELIGIOSITY
315

In a bequest dated April 4, 1352, Elizabeth de Dornburg asked the municipal council to exercise patronage over the house she had inherited from her parents, in which lived a convent of sisters (*Conventus Sororum*). After Elizabeth's death, the members of the Krakow municipal council were to become the eternal guardians and plenipotentiaries of the sisters, who devoted their lives to God and praying for the salvation of their ancestors (*devotarum deo serviencium temporibus perpetuis in remedium animarum predecessorum suorum*).[362] A similar transaction took place in the same year when Claire, daughter of the *magister* Martin likewise asked the municipal council to exercise patronage over a house located at the Franciscan monastery.[363] In 1354, there is mention of two nuns, Agnes and Hedwig, who donated a house in which there was a beguinage (*Conventus pro Monialibus et Sororibus Beginis*), located opposite the Dominican monastery, to councillor Peter Weinrich and his successors, provided he agreed to act as its guardian. The analysed sources demonstrate that in the mid-fourteenth century, the municipal council actively tried to assume guardianship over such houses, inhabited by "informal female associations." This may have been related, to some extent, to the persecution Beghards (lay religious male communities) were experiencing in Europe at that time, and the charges of heresy levelled at some Beguine congregations.[364] It seems, however, that the councillors' desire to support these communities derived primarily from their interest in reaping the financial benefits, in accordance with the notion of the 'economy of salvation.'[365]

In the late fourteenth century, Dorothy Banarika, the widow of the stallholder Martin, made numerous pious bequests to Krakow's beguinages. In her three wills made between 1394 and 1395, she mentioned three convents, even providing the names of sisters who resided in two of them (Wartinberginne and Langekethe). The first beguinage was said to be located opposite the Dominican monastery. It was probably the same house over which Peter Weinrich earlier exercised his patronage. The second beguinage was probably that founded by Elizabeth de Dornburg or Claire, the daughter of the *magister*

---

362   NKiRMK, no. 1643.

363   Józef Szujski writes about it in the introduction to the NKiRMK, LV.

364   Jarosław Szymański, *Ruchy heretyckie*, 84.

365   *Ibidem*, 94. Piotr Oliński also writes about such phenomena occurring in Prussia since the late thirteenth century: "They arose out of the private initiative of the burghers, in agreement with municipal councils and often later were placed under their jurisdiction. [...] Foundations for houses for women, widows and the poor were often made by widows and bound to the *memoria* of the owner of the donated property. [...] In terms of religion, they were placed under the care of monks from the mendicant orders or the local parish priest"; *idem*, *Fundacje mieszczańskie*, 61–62.

Martin, and affiliated with the Franciscans. The third beguinage was said to be located at the Bishop's Palace, i.e. also near the Franciscan monastery.[366] The beguinages mentioned in all three cases were located between St. Florian Street and the Dominican Church of the Holy Trinity. Such a concentration of houses inhabited by beguines was rather typical. For example, we know that in Świdnica, Legnica and Kłodzko, beguinages were all located in streets of the same name, i.e. Nuns Street (*Nonnengasse*). In Wrocław, all beguinages were located near the Dominican Monastery (St. Adalbert's Church) and the monastery of The Knights of the Cross with the Red Star (St. Matthias's Church).[367] These locations also demonstrate that beguinages were affiliated with specific orders, which provided Beguines with religious guidance and perhaps even inspired them to establish new beguinages.[368] For example, Dorothy Banarika also made a bequest to a girl (*puelle*) named Barbara, who worked as a servant for the Poor Clares at St. Andrew's Church.[369] Both Dorothy Banarika and Barbara were probably Beguines, because we know that in 1306 the Poor Clares in Wrocław were given permission by the Pope to keep one or two female companions.[370]

The above-mentioned sources allow us to determine the material status of some Krakow Beguines. It seems that the Beguines mentioned in municipal books were relatively affluent. We know that Pauline could afford to buy a plot of land for 40 grivna and that Elizabeth de Dornburg donated a house she had inherited from her parents. We also know that Dorothy Banarika was married to the alderman and stallholder Martin and that Claire was the daughter of the *magister* Martin. These women thus belonged to relatively rich burgher families. If Pauline, Elizabeth de Dornburg, Dorothy Banarika, and Claire were also the founders of these convents (at least some of them), they would thus exemplify the religious passion and devotion characteristic of some medieval burgher women. We should also remember that most of these women were

---

366   "Item ad conventum monialium, ubi moratur Wartinberginne ex opposito Fratrum Predicatorum IIII mrc, item ad conventum monialium, ubi moratur Langekethe II mrc, item ad conventum penes curiam domini episcopi II mrc."; SCAB., no. 1893, 1866, 2092.

367   Jarosław Szymański, *Ruchy heretyckie*, 92.

368   Halina Manikowska considers this phenomenon in terms of the 'spiritual' safeguarding of the city: "The nuns, committed to purity and living in the holiness of virginity, founded a holy monastery city. [...] This accumulated 'power of virginity' reflected the power of the city, which was able to maintain and sustain them."; Halina Manikowska, *Klasztor żeński*, 24–25.

369   In the second version of the will, the same amount of two *grivna* was allocated to the father of this girl; SCAB., no. 1893.

370   Cited in Szymański, *Ruchy heretyckie*, 94.

THE BURGHER RELIGIOSITY   317

(and decided to remain) widows. Testamentary bequests confirm that many burghers preferred for their wives to remain widows, and bestowed on them numerous privileges. They were seen as devoted guardians of their minor children, but also as providing the best means for cultivating the memory (*memoria*) of their late husband, honouring him and praying for his soul. Beguinages thus offered widows an attractive arrangement: they could live together as a community with fellow burgher women in a shared home.

6   Christian Duty

A feeling of connectedness with the wider, abstract community of all Christians, an important element of Church teaching, was slowly forming in the secular community, as well.[371] Since there was no actual social community embodying the Christian community as a whole, one had to imagine one, which required a religious awareness and intellectual horizons that exceeded the boundaries of one's own municipality. Apart from proselytism, the foundations for the construction of such a community were provided by travel: the itinerant craftsmen's journeys, merchants' travels, military expeditions (especially against the Saracens) and, perhaps above all, pilgrimages, which became increasingly popular in the Middle Ages.

Like other aspects of urban religiosity, the pilgrimage had existed for generations. However, as a result of the intensive changes taking place in urban culture in the fourteenth and fifteenth centuries, pilgrimages during this period acquired a new significance and previously unmatched level of popularity.[372] Pope Boniface VIII's plenary indulgence of 1300 (which actually dated from Christmas 1299), granted to pilgrims travelling to the great Jubilee in Rome, was one of the most important factors in the rise of pilgrimages in medieval Europe. During the analysed period, the official dates of the Jubilees which

---

371   One example of this phenomenon in the subject literature is the negligible participation of the inhabitants of the Polish lands between the eleventh and thirteenth centuries in the crusade movement, while another is the absence of any traces of anti-Jewish incidents until the late 13th century.; cf. Jerzy Dowiat, *Normy postępowania i wzory osobowe*, in *Kultura polski średniowiecznej*, 319–321.

372   "The history of the first two centuries of jubilees illustrates well their role in the development of late-medieval piety and the rapidly growing importance of indulgences in religious life. This is especially visible during the pontificate of Boniface IX (1389–1404), who started selling various types of indulgences on a massive scale, and jubilees became the main incentive for pilgrims to travel to sanctuaries endowed with the privilege of granting them"; Halina Manikowska, *Jerozolima – Rzym – Compostela*, 6–8.

attracted pilgrims to Rome were the years 1350, 1390, 1400, 1423,[373] 1450, 1475 and 1500.[374] Undoubtedly, however, as evidenced by the analysed sources, the faithful made pilgrimages to visit holy places in other years, as well.

The popularity of pilgrimages to holy places in Europe seems to have been less dependent on wealth or social position than other more elite forms of piety.[375] A larger role must have been played by personal motivations, religious zeal and the wish to be involved with other highly devout believers, who placed piety above personal gain, comfort and a sense of security. In terms of religious motivations, the desire to visit the tombs of saints, see holy relics and gain plenary indulgences all played an important role. Before setting out on a pilgrimage, Nicholas of Cieszyn transferred his entire property to his wife, stating that he was going on this journey in order to attain eternal life (*profecturus ad limina beatorum intendens saluti sue*).[376]

Indulgences could also be granted to those in whose name a sacred pilgrimage was being made. The belief spread that indulgences could 'erase' punishment for sins, or even the sins themselves, and thus ensure salvation. Those testators who, for various reasons, were unable to go on a pilgrimage themselves and thereby gain indulgences, sometimes asked their family members to do so on their behalf. The widow Nela Folmosin left her house and cloth stall to her son, asking him, among others, to order a pilgrimage to Rome for her sake after her death.[377] In his will of 1400, Andrew Melczer ordered two pilgrimages (one to Rome and one to Aachen).[378] John Czenmark, among other dispositions, made a bequest of 40 florins to pay "for a pilgrimage to Rome" (*of eyne Romfard*). It was to be made by an appointed person in the name of Czenmark's salvation.[379] A similar motivation led Bartholomeus, a wealthy tanner (and, as evidenced by his will, a steel and lead merchant), to instruct the executors of his will to send a religious man, "or any other good man," to Rome, and

---

373 "The next jubilee, which, according to Urban VI's decision, was due to take place in 1423, was probably never officially announced, but still attracted crowds of pilgrims to Rome, although numerous testimonies document their presence rather in 1424"; *ibidem*, 7.

374 *Ibidem*.

375 This is clearly expressed in Geoffrey Chaucer's *Canterbury Tales*; cf. "The pilgrimage itself could have cost very little and was accessible to the truly poor"; Halina Manikowska, *Jerozolima – Rzym – Compostela*, 369.

376 NKiRMK, no. 1189 (1336).

377 "Domina Nela Folmosin condam Stanislai relicta, Hannus Monacho pro tutore recepto, domum suam, cimiterio sancte Anne contiguam, cum scampno panum, Stenoni filio suo post mortem ipsius resignavit taliter, quod idem Steno viam Romanam unam et unum stamen griseum cum IIII mrc. debiti solucione debet ordinare"; SCAB., no. 884 (1373).

378 "[...] ich bevele asczurichten eyn fusgengir czu eynir Romfart und eyn czu eynir ochfart"; CONS. 427, fol. 157.

379 "Item of eyne Romfard XL rote golden"; CONS. 428, fol. 354 (1436).

THE BURGHER RELIGIOSITY   319

cover the costs associated with the pilgrimage.[380] Another entry in the book of
the bench court appears to be evidence of an attempt to carry out a testator's
instructions. Hano Hesse, a burgher from Krakow, swore under the penalty of
ten grivna that a man called Cuncze Rudila would present proof of his journey
to Rome and Aachen by the feast day of John the Baptist.[381] Cuncze Rudila was
to go on these pilgrimages "for his brother Michael Czobot" (*di Romfart und
ochfart, di Cuncze vor synne brudir tun sal, eczwen Nichil Czobot*).[382] In another
entry, we see someone vouching for a pilgrim about to set out on his journey
(possibly not entirely willingly); here Peter Peszko agrees to go to Rome and
bring back a letter as a proof of his journey (*quod Romam debeat transire et lit-
eras reportare*).[383] A pilgrimage was more than just an act of penance, a quest
for indulgence, or a journey to seek aid from a patron saint (or thank them for
help one had already received). In view of the risks and costs involved, a pilgrimage was also a means of redeeming oneself, even after having committing
a grave crime.[384] For example, murderers or other serious criminals were given
a chance to redeem themselves and thus regain the status of burgher. Jörg
Steinkeller, a convicted coin forger, or the people who took part in the Wrocław
rebellion of 1418, were given such a chance as well.[385] Perhaps the aforementioned Peter Peszko was also a convicted criminal who redeemed himself by
going on a pilgrimage. Such a situation is described in a letter written by John,
a parish priest from Bystrzyca (*de Wystricz*), that was attached to the Kazimierz municipal books. John writes that Bartholomeus, a butcher and burgher
of Bystrzyca, killed Nicholas, a stonemason. Bartholomeus was convicted and
sentenced to death. However, as a result of numerous pleas and guarantees
given by priests, pious wives and widows, the murderer was given a chance to
redeem himself by going on a pilgrimage to the tombs of Saint Peter and Saint

---

380   "Item si decesserit ipse tunc executores huius testamenti expedire debet in curiam
Romanam unum sacerdotem vel alium probium virum cum expensis competentibus";
LT, fol. 35 (1455).

381   "Das Hano Hesse ist burge wordin vor Concze Rudil umben di Romfart und ochfart, di
Cuncze vor synne brudir tun sal, eczwen Nichil Czobot, ab der obgen[annten] Cuncze
Rudil nicht beweisunge czwischin synte Iohannis tage baptiste brengit von Rome und oche
so sal Hano Hesse X marcas grossorum vor di hirren legin, brengit her abir beweisunge, so
sollin dem vorgenanten Cunczen volgin di X marcas grossorum"; CONS. 427, fol. 11 (1393).

382   Name of Nicholas Czobot was also found in the *Book of the Dead* of the Brotherhood of
the Blessed Virgin Mary.; cf. Józef Mitkowski, *Księga zmarłych*, 83.

383   CONS. 427, fol. 46 (1394).

384   cf. Hanna Zaremska, "Pielgrzymka jako kara za zabójstwo: Europa Środkowa XIII–XV w.,"
in *Peregrinationes. Pielgrzymki w kulturze dawnej Europy*, ed. Halina Manikowska, Hanna
Zaremska (Warszawa: Instytut Historii Polskiej Akademii Nauk, 1995), 147–151.

385   Halina Manikowska, *Jerozolima – Rzym – Compostela*, 237.

320   CHAPTER 4

Paul in Rome.[386] John Tuesgerne, a convicted murderer, was also pardoned in this way – he was ordered to make a pilgrimage to Rome, join a brotherhood in Wieluń and pay for a hundred Masses for the soul of the man he had killed.[387]

Fourteenth-century and fifteenth-century sources mostly document the fact that Krakovian burghers went on pilgrimages to Rome. However, some sources demonstrate that they also visited two other very important sanctuaries in the Christian world: the holy city of Jerusalem, to visit the tomb of Christ (*ad limina sepulcri dominici*),[388] and to the tomb of the Apostle Saint James the Greater (*ad sanctum Jacobum*) in Compostela.[389] Apart from these important *peregrinationes maiores*, pilgrims also travelled to Aachen to see the famous holy relics (often combining this trip with a pilgrimage to Rome) and to Wilsnack in Brandenburg, which became a pilgrimage destination in 1384, when three bleeding hosts (*via ad sanguinem Christi*)[390] were found in the ruins of a local church.

Krakow municipal books from the fourteenth and fifteenth centuries show that during that period at least 68 burghers planned to go on a pilgrimage far from home. The number of such testators is undoubtedly much higher, however, as the reasons for drafting a will were not always stated. Sometimes the testamentary document was not a typical will, but merely a form of a mutual donation, a bequest of property to be made in the event of one's death, or a letter in which guardians for the wife and children were named. Such instructions or bequests were often recorded one after another and were indeed quite similar in terms of form and structure. It can thus be assumed that many other Krakovian burghers also wished to go on a pilgrimage, most probably to Rome, even though they did not explicitly state this in the analysed sources.[391]

---

386 *Księgi radzieckie kazimierskie 1369–1381 i 1385–1402. Acta consularia Casimiriensia 1369–1381 et 1385–1402*, ed. Adam Chmiel, Krakow 1932 (Wydawnictwo Aktów Dawnych miasta Krakowa, 2), 140.

387 "Hannus tuesgerne promisit pergere Romam et fraternitatem invenire et lucrari in Welun causa homicidii perpetrati et hoc debet facere post festum S. Ih. Bpt. Indilate et debet acquirere C missas"; CONS. 427, fol. 151 (1400).

388 Nicholas Rutenus was planning a pilgrimage to Jerusalem; NKiRMK, no. 1036 (1330).

389 Elian, a burgher from Kazimierz, was travelling there; *Księgi radzieckie kazimierskie*, 447 (1398).

390 Stanisław Bylina, *Religijność późnego średniowiecza*, 55.

391 Such a situation can be observed, for example, in the bequests of Chunad de Tost and Chunad Wolf. They are immediately adjacent to records from the same day concerning Margaret, Nicholas Wronche's mother-in-law, and Catherine, widow of Hankon from Gliwice, who made bequests in the event they did not return from a pilgrimage to Rome. Although there is no mention of the pilgrimage in the records on either Chunad, the

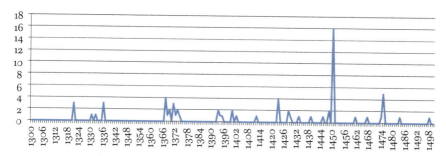

GRAPH 16   The number of testators who made wills before going on a pilgrimage

The data contained in the chart below (Graph 16) illustrates the documented number of Krakovian burghers participating in the pilgrimage movement throughout the Western World. Unfortunately, it is not representative of the entire population, but only of the city's elite. However, some less-wealthy people are also included, such as Irmtruda (who owned a house in front of the Szewska Gate),[392] Paul Korcze, a tanner,[393] or Margaret, mother-in-law of Nicholas Wronche, who left behind two children and only seven grivna.[394]

The chart shows that the number of wills made before going on a pilgrimage correlates closely with the dates of the great Roman Jubilees. Indeed, Krakovian burghers knew that the Jubilee years were special years, during which thousands of pilgrims would set out for Rome in pursuit of plenary indulgences, and they too wished to participate in this special event. The Jubilees in the years 1423, 1475 and above all 1450 (most of the surviving wills from the analysed period were made in 1450) are all clearly visible in the chart. The Jubilee of 1500 is not included in it due to the loss of bench court books from the end of fifteenth century. However, a number of wills that had probably been made in connection with this Jubilee were recorded in Krakow's municipal books in the years that followed.

Going on a pilgrimage was an expression of deep and profound piety. It was an exceptional and glorious act which required significant financial resources and great sacrifice. A pilgrim wished to be rewarded after death, but could also count on some rewards while still alive. Indeed, in a society whose value system

---

numerous pious bequests included there and the expression *inquantum moriretur in via* in the record concerning Chunad Wolf are indicative of such a motivation; cf. SCAB., no. 218–221.

392   NKiRMK, no. 1088 (1332).
393   SCAB., no. 548 (1371).
394   SCAB., no. 218 (1367).

was based on the preaching of the Church, going on a pilgrimage or financing an altar or a chapel was a source of pride and prestige. We can assume that making pilgrimages, like being a member of the elite Brotherhood of the Blessed Virgin Mary at St. Mary's Church, allowed one to achieve and maintain a strong position within the social hierarchy of the urban municipality, especially in patrician circles. As the historian Halina Manikowska put it: "Apart from collecting indulgences, especially private indulgences, a long pilgrimage, especially to Jerusalem to see the Holy Sepulcher, was an important element of the urban lifestyle and one of the determinants of social prestige."[395] This is exemplified by the wealthy councillor Nicholas Rutenus, who decided to go on a dangerous and expensive pilgrimage to Jerusalem in 1330 (and most probably never returned to Krakow).[396]

7   Summary

When we study religiosity, we are often forced to focus only on external manifestations of people's inner religious life, limiting ourselves to the study of social relations and declarations. We rarely gain insight into what lies 'inside' a person. Yet, religiosity is not only conceived of in terms of mysticism and internalised articles of faith; it should be seen, first and foremost, as a communal and public phenomenon, involving outward manifestations – symbols and concrete actions – of one's religious belief. Such external and analysable manifestations of faith allow us to observe the existence of a strong connection between the manner in which society is organized and its religious practices. Every society has its own unique religious practices, which help unite it, alleviate its fears, and provide its members with a means of coming into contact with the sacred. On the one hand, in the Middle Ages, the ritualization of life within the family, guild, parish, and even the city itself, helped unify social groups. On the other hand, as a result, society's internal hierarchy became more fixed. In the context of the family, this meant honouring the memory

---

395   Halina Manikowska, *Jerozolima – Rzym – Compostela*, 16.

396   "[...] dominus Nycolaus Rutenus ad limina sepulcri dominici se aptando"; NKiRMK, no. 1036. Based on the notes of the Wrocław burgher Peter Rindfleisch from his pilgrimage to the Holy Sepulcher in 1496, it can be calculated that he spent the significant amount of 222 florins on the entire journey, including all the necessary purchases made on the way. It can be assumed that the journey of Nicholas Rutenus, made 166 years earlier, must have involved an equally significant, if not greater, financial investment; cf. Halina Manikowska, *Jerozolima – Rzym – Compostela*, 78–79.

THE BURGHER RELIGIOSITY 323

of one's ancestors and emphasizing the dominant role of the father. In the context of the city of Krakow (for example during the annual Corpus Christi procession), this involved emphasizing the dominant role of the municipal council and acknowledging the place occupied in the municipal hierarchy by every corporation, guild and brotherhood.[397]

The examples discussed in this chapter certainly do not represent all the spheres of life in which Krakovian burghers participated, be they public or religious.[398] They also do not exhaust the list of ways in which Krakow's inhabitants tried to secure their salvation.

They represent, however, the variety of religious practices in which wills played an important role. Although devotional practices and pious records existed alongside and in the absence of wills, it was the institution of the will that provided them with a special power and protection, and it seems that it contributed significantly to their dissemination among the townspeople. The first chapter explains the genesis of the medieval will, created primarily as a tool for the efficient transfer of material goods to the institution of the church. Then, however, after its dissemination in the urban environment, the testamentary practice was adapted to the urban needs. Especially the needs of the upper classes of the bourgeoisie. Wills made the posthumous future of wealthy burghers independent of the good will of their relatives. They allowed testators to take care of their eternal life by themselves i.e. by transforming their economic capital accumulated during lifetime into 'eschatological capital.' For this purpose salvation specialists were used, such as mendicant congregations or urban poor. Efforts were also made to maintain the memory and provide prayers for the soul of the deceased in parish churches, among religious brotherhoods or by trusted clergy. Finally, by the power of testamentary bequest, testators could plan and supervise their own memorial activities for which spouses, children or distant relatives were responsible.

---

397 "For fraternities, as for other corporations, the celebrations, apart from proving their position in the social structure of the municipality, were an opportunity for the members of their community to meet people from outside the organization. Their intention to demonstrate their power to others and emphasize their wealth and rank explains to a large extent why the members were obliged to participate in the celebrations. Competition for a place in the Corpus Christi procession, which is testified to by sources from the early sixteenth century concerning guilds, and from the end of the century in terms of fraternities, are proof that these corporations understood well that this opportunity to present themselves to the city should not be ignored"; Hanna Zaremska, *Bractwa*, 153.

398 E.g. the existence of communities established on the basis of language, as manifested, for example, in affiliating in 'Polish fraternities' or in bequests to pay for Polish and German preachers.

Wills, sometimes written many years before death, due to their revocability until the end of their lives, gave wealthy testators power over the living, whom they could appreciate in their records or condemn and practically disinherit. Similarly, generous contributions made to religious institutions allowed them to enjoy their favor even during the testator's lifetime. While the prestige and glory associated with costly religious foundations served as the accumulation of symbolic capital by members of city's elite.

In the medieval city, the religious and the social intertwined. Indeed, as Johan Huizinga observes: "Life was permeated by religion to the degree that the distance between the earthly and the spiritual was in danger of being obliterated at any moment. While on the one hand all of ordinary life was raised to the sphere of the divine, on the other, the divine was bound to the mundane in an indissoluble mixture with daily life."[399] 'Internal' religious needs went hand-in-hand with the desire for self-presentation; the personal intertwined with the social. As Manikowska observes: "In the late Middle Ages, we are dealing with a complicated and dynamic arrangement: individualism—actions benefiting the community; privacy—actions benefiting the public sphere."[400] The analysed wills from the fourteenth and fifteenth centuries demonstrate how Krakovian burghers patronised both long-established and newly-founded churches and monastic communities, and how their preferences changed over time.[401] But they also show how burghers both perceived and exhibited newly emergent types of religious bond. Despite reasonable doubts as to whether wills and testamentary bequests accurately represent the entire urban society,[402] my analysis demonstrates that we can observe here two models of religiosity: (i) communal religiosity that was characteristic of the majority of urban society, and (ii) private worship that was practiced by pious individuals who wished to acquire a deeper understanding of their faith. The latter was not a mass phenomenon and it was largely tied to the rise of literacy. Such social and religious differences and the supposed opposition between the elite and mass models of religiosity do not, however, undermine the fundamental unity of religious beliefs[403] in late medieval Krakow: "Different cultural spheres coexisted in one and the same consciousness and they must have coexisted even

---

399   Johan Huizinga, *The Autumn of the Middle Ages*, 178.

400   Hanna Manikowska, *Religijność miejska*, 26.

401   This was one of the main subject areas analysed by Elżbieta Piwowarczyk in her work *Legaty testamentowe ad pias causas w XV-wiecznym Krakowie*.

402   Martin Nodl, *Średniowieczny testament*, 149–160.

403   Aleksandra Witkowska, *Kulty pątnicze*, 218.

THE BURGHER RELIGIOSITY 325

in the educated minds of theologians, scholastics, university professors and church officials. Although these people were both educated and dogmatic, mythical, poetical and folklore images and thought patterns were nevertheless buried deep within their psyche."[404]

404 Aron J. Gurevich, "Kultura elitarna i kultura ludowa w średniowiecznej Europie," in *Biedni i bogaci. Studia z dziejów społeczeństwa i kultury ofiarowane Bronisławowi Geremkowi w sześćdziesiątą rocznicę urodzin* (Warszawa: Wydawn. Nauk. PWN, 1992), 211.

Conclusion

Few historical sources are as complex and multifaceted as the medieval will. The complex nature of this legal instrument is often obscured by its perception through the lenses of the *ars moriendi* genre. According to it, the will was an indispensable element of a proper Christian departure from this earthly life. A dying man was to divide his accumulated wealth among his children, list his outstanding debts and allocate a generous share of his wealth for 'works of piety' (*opera pietatis*), which was to ease the torments he would suffer in purgatory for his sins and provide him with a path to eternal life. However, if we analyse the will's long history solely from the perspective of didactic literature, we limit our research perspective, resulting in one-sided, static observations. Ultimately, the wealth of information contained in wills cannot be properly interpreted without analysing the crucial role these instruments played within their changing social and cultural context.

The history of the will represents one aspect of the process by which the traditional ties binding individuals to their kinship group weakened and private property came to be distinguished from that held within the family. The medieval world was undergoing a process of modernisation that involved dynamic social transformations – land could be bought and sold, women obtained the right to inherit real estate, and alongside the previous binary division of property into movables and real estate, a third category emerged, namely inherited property. Understandably, these changes were particularly momentous in cities, since these were the leading economic and commercial centres in the medieval world, places where money, and not honours and titles, determined one's place in the social hierarchy.

A fundamental role in this process was played by the Church, whose activities as an institution can be analysed in terms of both ideology and practice. In terms of ideology, the Church preached that everyone was equal before God at the moment of their death (reflected artistically in the motif of the *danse macabre*) and shaped people's image of the judgement of the soul (portrayed in ars moriendi prints and paintings), creating grounds for the belief that one could actively work to secure both worldly and eternal life. The Church also deserves credit for its role in propagating the concept of marital unity and love, which gave rise to the formation of a new model, the nuclear family, which became dominant in the late medieval city. Moreover, the Church promoted equal rights for sons and daughters in inheriting property from their parents, thereby undermining the tradition of property being inherited by male

CONCLUSION

relatives. This change meant that assets could be transferred to individuals outside the family line, weakening its material position.

These actions brought measurable benefits both to the Church as an institution and to its representatives. Radical limitations on consanguineous marriage, and prohibitions on adoption and cohabitation eliminated both the traditional means by which the strength of the family line was maintained and weakened the individual's ties to his family community. Instead of kinship, a new community of believers (*congregatio fidelium*) became the most important social group. What is more, since men were expected to secure their own salvation, usually by 'designating Christ as their heir,' the Church could accumulate wealth quickly. The institution of the will, reintroduced and transformed in the mid-twelfth century, allowed the Church to inherit property from laymen. The rules for drafting wills in accordance with canon law were simplified and bishops were entrusted with their execution.

For the greater part of the fourteenth century, the wills of Krakovian burghers were conceived of solely as religious acts. They contained mostly pious dispositions intended to secure the salvation of the testator and his family. However, apart from documents referred to as *testamentum seu ultima voluntatis* "testaments or last will," city books also listed wills that were free of such dispositions, and were instead written as a means for an individual to dispense of his property to his loved ones in the event of his death. Such wills, referred to in German as *geschefte Testament*, were drafted in accordance with municipal law, which distinguished the concept of 'acquired goods.' In late-fourteenth-century Krakow, the *geschefte Testament* type of records merged with the form of canonical will. This marked the emergence of the modern urban will, which contained both secular and pious bequests. These dispositions, regardless of whether they contained opera pietatis or only included legacies for lay people, were endowed with the title of 'testament.'

The Krakow municipal council played an important role in this process, especially at the turn of the fourteenth and fifteenth centuries. Councillors would visit burghers on their deathbeds to draft their wills. Consequently, the Krakow municipal council began to maintain its first book of wills in 1396. From that point on, the municipal council and bench court took an active part in drafting and recording wills. Wills were made either in person (in front of a municipal official) or in writing as a 'closed will' (authenticated by a municipal official after the death of the testator). Municipal books contain many wills written by healthy individuals, people who planned to go on a pilgrimage or a trade mission, or who had married or come into an inheritance and simply wished to settle their financial affairs, as well as dispositions of last will made by people 'on their deathbed,' who in accordance with the notion of a 'good death,' wished to 'part with this world as good Christians.'

In this study, I propose the use of the term 'communal will' to indicate how the institution of the will came to fall within the scope of responsibility of the municipal authorities and how its form was adapted to the needs of affluent members of the urban municipality.

Further changes in testamentary practices did not take place in Krakow until the latter half of the fifteenth century. Since many burghers wished to participate in the upcoming 1450 Jubilee, the municipal council began to maintain a second book of wills (which lists the majority of all surviving medieval wills). Yet since the 1470s, bench courts had become increasingly involved in the drafting and execution of wills. This is evidenced by the fact that the number of wills listed in municipal books and in the *Liber Testamentorum* declined. By contrast, the number of wills listed in the books maintained by the bench court rose. This change may have resulted from the growing popularity of wills in the urban milieu. It is also possible that the municipal council, whose task it was to visit the testator on his deathbed, may have been overburdened with such requests. It is likewise possible that councillors were afraid of contracting an infectious disease. We should also bear in mind that Magdeburg Law became the dominant source of law in the late fifteenth century, and according to its provisions all transactions concerning goods in the city should be handled by the bench court.

An analysis of the social structure of late-medieval Krakow demonstrates the tensions that existed between the ideal of a homogenous urban community and the actual divisions that existed within it, related among others to informal limits in access to municipal offices, and to divisions between those who worked as merchants, stall owners and craftsmen. The analysis of the testators' wealth statuses, social positions and origins demonstrates that one social group was particularly interested in drafting wills, and therefore popularizing this legal instrument – the urban elites, especially councillors and aldermen and their families, constituted at least 25% of all known testators from the analysed period. As wills became increasingly popular during the fifteenth century as a proper means for settling accounts with one's earthly life, other inhabitants of the urban municipality also began to appear with increasing frequency as testators. My analysis demonstrates that tradesmen were particularly active in this field, although a precise determination of a testator's profession was often difficult (even in the case of elders or masters of a given guild). However, we are certain that most craftsmen who drafted a will were employed in prestigious, well-paid professions, including goldsmiths,

CONCLUSION 329

belt makers, food professionals (brewers, maltsters, innkeepers, butchers and bakers), tailors, furriers, weapon makers, notaries and court proxies.

Further research on the financial position of testators was carried out on the basis of the sums included in the dower bequests found in about one-fourth of all wills, estimated values of the goods listed in wills and prosopographic research. Apart from the above-mentioned dower bequests, the wealth of burghers was assessed in keeping with the following criteria: cash and annuity donations made in wills, the number of houses owned and their location (in or outside the city), municipal duties performed, family and territorial origin, occupation and other sources of income. The analysis demonstrates that 60–70% of all burghers belonged to the upper class, 25–30% belonged to the middle class and only a few percent of all testators belonged to the lower class.

The origins and family connections of Krakovian burghers were established in various ways: some people were given nicknames connected with their places of origin; municipal books sometimes listed the place of origin of a new citizen; most testators mentioned in their wills parents or siblings from other cities, as well as donations made to hospitals and parish churches outside of Krakow. The analysis demonstrates that at least one-third of all Krakovian testators were immigrants. Since many wealthy newcomers from large Silesian, German or Italian cities quickly became successful in Krakow, we believe that they had had established business relationships with Krakovian burghers prior to settling in the city. Such immigrants also possessed significant cultural capital, which made it easier for them to be accepted by Kraków's social elites.

The analysis of dower bequests made by the wealthiest burghers demonstrates that urban elites differed in terms of wealth and social prestige. The municipal council, like urban society in general, had its own social structure. The leading group consisted of the most influential, wealthy, and recognizable individuals. Other Krakow councillors were less diversified in terms of wealth, and their status was comparable to that of very wealthy Krakovian citizens. This demonstrates that wealth (economic capital) was an important factor in determining a testator's social position, but it was certainly not the only criterion for admitting a burgher to the municipal council. Cultural capital was also influential: For example, preliminary research on the educational background of some testators in the latter half of the fifteenth century demonstrates that members of the urban elite had generally received a university education.

Social prestige was first and foremost connected with municipal authority – that is, being a councillor, an alderman or a master craftsman. Many wealthy testators performed such honourable functions, which was the best indication of their social status in the municipal hierarchy. However, other, less obvious public functions were also connected with high social status. Such civic functions as quarter captains, tower commanders or church keeper were usually performed by people from the middle class, but they were nevertheless connected with high social status.

An analysis of the biographies of those burghers who left two or more versions of their will also provide interesting results. While many elusive factors could influence the position occupied by a given person in the urban social structure, marriages were undoubtedly the most important in this respect. Arranged and 'strategic' marriages must have been regarded as especially important among the representatives of the higher class (as evidenced by, for example, the amounts of dowers listed in municipal books), but even less-wealthy citizens accumulated wealth and increased their social status through a carefully planned marriage.

The family model in the late-medieval city was shaped by three basic legal and cultural factors: (i) conservative municipal law, which protected the rights of relatives; (ii) the modernizing influence of the Church, which protected and sanctified the institution of marriage in its affective dimensions, thus weakening kinship ties; and (iii) the changing nature of work and everyday life in a large medieval city, whose citizens were mostly first- or second-generation immigrants, wishing to accumulate wealth through inheritance.

The will and the changes gradually introduced into municipal law allowed Krakovian burghers to dispose of their estates and provide for their families. In most cases, testators focused the concern primarily on the well-being of their spouse and children. However, we also know of numerous wills in which testators made bequests to relatives, servants and co-workers. Indeed, wills document the existence of two different family models in late-medieval Krakow. On the one hand, we have a small nuclear family, typical of craftsmen and tradesmen. On the other hand, there existed the patrician model of an extended family. The patrician family and the average burgher family differed as regards their history, lifestyle, origin and status. The patrician family was instrumental in achieving high social and financial status. New people entered urban elite primarily thanks to arranged marriages with daughters and widows of wealthy patricians. Big trade companies were usually family owned and operated – the members of merchant families settled in business hubs around Krakow, thus creating branches of the family business. Therefore, patricians treated their relatives as social capital, which, in turn, allowed them to accumulate economic capital. The situation of less wealthy tradesmen and craftsmen (often first- or second-generation immigrants) was different. They had earned their success through individual work, rather than relying on accumulated economic capital and a kinship network. For this group, the thought of distant

CONCLUSION   331

relatives made them fear for the well-being of their nuclear family – their children and the widowed spouse. In both family models, however, wills played an important role in controlling social relations. In the case of the patrician family, the extensive regulations regarding the inheritance of property allowed the head of the family to discipline and control their family members even after death. For example, affluent burghers could dispose of their estate and designate the next head of the family business in their will.

On the other hand, the majority of Krakovian burghers, i.e. moderately wealthy families, used wills to secure the well-being of the nuclear family and disinherit relatives. Wills are thus an important testimony to the fact that the bonds holding together members of the burgher family in the late Middle Ages were evolving. Social bonds, often sanctioned in the form of a contract, became more important than kinship ties. However, we also learn that even this new type of family was primarily based on emotional ties. The best example of such a new family model was marriage, as it was also sanctified by the Church. People who lived in the same household together also understandably grew closer to one another, marking a return to the Roman concept of *familia*, which included co-workers, family members and servants.

Late-medieval urban religiosity was inextricably linked to the notion of the will. The notion of purgatory and of the soul of the dying being judged at the moment of their death inspired the emergence of the canonical will. A person on their deathbed could use a will as a 'tool' in order to shorten their suffering in purgatory and avoid eternal damnation. The economic capital one had acquired in life became eschatological capital – money could be used to make pious bequests. This age-old reciprocal exchange, made in the spirit of the principle of do ut des "I give so you may give," was mediated by 'specialists in salvation' – the clergy and the poor – whose prayers could deliver a sinner's soul from hell. By such means, in large cities numerous churches, monasteries, hospitals, altars and clergymen were financed by testamentary bequests.

In the late Middle Ages, both in terms of church rituals and devotional activities, piety was conceived of as a social phenomenon. The traditional conception and role of community and the postulated dominant model of mass religiosity both played a role in this process. Although some new religious trends became popular in the Kingdom of Poland in the late Middle Ages among elites, including an increased focus on the inner, spiritual dimension of religiosity and the spread of the *devotio moderna* movement, so popular in Western Europe, these changes did not exert a significant influence on society at large. Still, an analysis of expressions of piety among testators indicates a growing preference for individual forms of worship, which manifested itself in, among other things, frequent confession and taking of Holy Communion, praying the Rosary and reading religious literature. These manifestations of 'elitist' religiosity, however, functioned alongside more traditional religious practices, which bordered on magical thinking. Testators would also often donate clothing and valuables to the Church so that they could be made into liturgical objects. We can interpret such donations as attempts at direct participation in the sacred, which was centred around the altar.

Testamentary bequests also demonstrate how the organization of society and religious practices were interconnected. Religious rituals, which were meant to consolidate a given community, alleviate its eschatological fears, and assure its members contact with the sacred existed at every level of society. The ritualization of family, guild, parish and communal life both brought these social groups closer together and reinforced their internal hierarchies. In terms of the family, this meant honouring one's ancestors and emphasizing the authority of the father. In terms of urban life, for example, during the Corpus Christi procession, this meant asserting the authority of the municipal council and acknowledging the place occupied by various convents, guilds and fraternities.

While a correlation between an increase in the number of wills in a given year and important social events or natural phenomena exists, people usually decided to make a will for personal reasons. Testators, for example, rarely expressed a fear of death or eschatological doubts in their wills. Much more often, they expressed their fear of greedy or quarrelsome relatives and dishonest clergy. Some testators did openly express their fear of oblivion, in the form of concerns that their descendants would die, their relatives would ignore their dispositions or their wills would be destroyed. In surviving Krakovian wills we can see an expression, rarely stated explicitly, of the eternal human desire to defy the passing of time and somehow preserve – no matter what the cost – the memory of oneself. This was a striving to secure one's future life, both in heaven and in the memories of one's loved ones on earth. These desires, to secure one's place in heaven and in the memories of successive generations, found form in the eternal principle of *do ut des*, the reason and justification for a testator's generosity and charity.

The main argument of the book is that we should look at the wills as instruments providing individuals power to actively shape their social position, family relationships and manage the endeavors for eternal life. Wills were created by church as the efficient legal tools for transferring material goods into religious institutions. In consequence, however, large sums of money donated by wills and prestige of the institutions supervising and guaranteeing their execution made them the subject of competition between the church and city authorities, which successfully sought to include these acts within their

CONCLUSION 333

own jurisdiction. In this process the form and content of wills were adapted to the needs of the city elite and the wealthy middle class. Wills allowed them to extend their individual control over material world in terms of the legal alienation of goods both during the owner's lifetime and after death. Based on the principle of revocation of a will and the principle of reciprocity of the gift wills became also an instrument of power over one's relatives, friends and co-workers, the clergy, and others. As a consequence, the shape of an urban family was transformed and adapted to the needs of different social classes living in the city. Through the power of testamentary bequest the accumulated material goods were transformed into social, symbolic and eschatological' capital, i.e. the shape of social relations, the individual prestige and community's memory and the testators chances for eternal life.

APPENDIX

Catalogue of Krakow Wills from Fourteenth and Fifteenth Centuries

No.	Year	Name	Language	Source
1.	1303	Sulisława	Latin	KDMK, vol. 3, no. 368
2.	1306	Peczold of Rożnow (19)[a]	German	NKiRMK, no. 34
3.	1310	Frederick of Olkusz	Latin	NKiRMK, no. 106
4.	1313	Henry of Racibórz	Latin	NKiRMK, no. 286
5.	1313	Ekel the old butcher	Latin	NKiRMK, no. 284, 285
6.	1316	Tymo the old	Latin	NKiRMK, no. 358
7.	1317	First wife of Henry Srolle	Latin	NKiRMK, no. 411
8.	1318	Wilhelm (31)	Latin	NKiRMK, no. 477, 487
9.	1320	Herman called Kopka	Latin	NKiRMK, no. 589
10.	1321	Alusza widow of Otton	Latin	NKiRMK, no. 616
11.	1323	Heineman Edel the older (51) [I][b]	Latin	NKiRMK, no. 673
12.	1325	Heineman Edel sthe older (51) [II]	Latin	NKiRMK, no. 760
13.	1325	Konrad the maltster	Latin	NKiRMK, no. 750
14.	1326	Martin the brewer called *Cavercianus*	Latin	NKiRMK, no. 858
15.	1326	Ulrich Tatar (48)	Latin	NKiRMK, no. 847
16.	1327	John (*Hanco*) of Kietrz	Latin	NKiRMK, no. 897
17.	1330	Elizabeth widow of Paul	Latin	NKiRMK, no. 1030
18.	1331	Arnold Sunprister	Latin	NKiRMK, no. 1045, 1059, 1064
19.	1332	Irmtruda	Latin	NKiRMK, no. 1088
20.	1333	Nicholas Ruthenus (49)	Latin	NKiRMK, no. 1036-139

a   Arabic numerals in round brackets denote the number occupied by a person in the "Chronological List of Krakow Councilors of the 13th–15th Centuries," contained as an annex in the work of Marcin Starzyński, Marcin Starzyński, Krakowska rada, 217–301.

b   Roman numerals in square brackets which stand next to the names of testators, denote cases when more than one version of their will has survived.

336 APPENDIX

(*cont.*)

No.	Year	Name	Language	Source
21.	1333	Nicholas of Zawichost (43)	Latin	NKiRMK, no. 1141, 1177
22.	1336	Herman of Żary	Latin	NKiRMK, no. 1190, 1325
23.	1336	Nicholas of Cieszyn	Latin	NKiRMK, no. 1189
24.	1336	Widow of John Gelhor a stallholder	Latin	NKiRMK, no. 1196
25.	1337	John of Muchow	Latin	NKiRMK, no. 1227–1230
26.	1338	Fryczko Kurtzwurst	Latin	NKiRMK, no. 1243, 1244
27.	1338	Wilhelm called Silwerworcht	Latin	NKiRMK, no. 1260
28.	1340	Widow of Otton	Latin	NKiRMK, no. 1407
29.	1340	Sydelman of Głogów [I]	Latin	NKiRMK, no. 1352
30.	1341	Sydelman of Głogów [II]	Latin	NKiRMK, no. 1397
31.	1344	Hedwig (*Heze*) the stallholder	Latin	NKiRMK, no. 1537
32.	1345	Gertrude widow of Nicholas of Kluczbork	Latin	NKiRMK, no. 1548
33.	1347	Martin the stallholder	Latin	NKiRMK, no. 1578
34.	1350	Anna daughter of Nicholas Ruthenus (49)	Latin	NKiRMK, no. 1616
35.	1358	Paszko (*Paulino Cavallo*) (89)	Latin	NKiRMK, no. 1692, 1693
36.	1366	Frenczlin of Prague a goldsmith (103)	Latin	SCAB., no. 41
37.	1367	Margaret mother-in-law of Nicholas Wronche	Latin	SCAB., no. 218
38.	1367	Nicholas Rese	Latin	SCAB., no. 150
39.	1367	Tyczko Crutanfleisch	Latin	SCAB., no. 157
40.	1367	Catherine widow of John Gliwicz	Latin	SCAB., no. 219
41.	1367	Chunad Wolf	Latin	SCAB., no. 221
42.	1367	Chunad de Tost	Latin	SCAB., no. 220
43.	1368	Alex of Racibórz (125)	Latin	SCAB., no. 240
44.	1368	Nicholas Essenbach	Latin	SCAB., no. 242
45.	1369	Nicholas Edeling (85) and Catherine daughter of Paul Wierzynek (*Wirzing*)	Latin	NKiRMK, no. 1705
46.	1369	Staszek Czajka	Latin	SCAB., no. 440
47.	1369	Konrad the miller	Latin	SCAB., no. 446

APPENDIX   337

(*cont.*)

No.	Year	Name	Language	Source
48.	1369	Claire widow of John Hobschbecke	Latin	SCAB., no. 414
49.	1370	Tilo the small (*Parvus*)	Latin	SCAB., no. 463
50.	1371	Paszko Fladir	Latin	SCAB., no. 646
51.	1371	Bertold Freyberk	Latin	SCAB., no. 645
52.	1371	John Swop	Latin	SCAB., no. 614
53.	1372	Kisvetir	Latin	SCAB., no. 665
54.	1373	Hensil Schoenbil	Latin	SCAB., no. 798
55.	1373	John Czetirwange	Latin	SCAB., no. 812
56.	1390	John Wise	Latin	SCAB., no. 1288
57.	1390	Stanisław Grudner	Latin	SCAB., no. 1267
58.	1391	Catherine (*Kascha*) widow of John Hunil	Latin	SCAB., no. 1365
59.	1391	Nicholas Polak	Latin	SCAB., no. 1322
60.	1392	Jacob Rolle	Latin	SCAB., no. 1425
61.	1392	John Weinant	Latin	SCAB., no. 1441
62.	1392	Nicholas Meye	Latin	SCAB., no. 1436
63.	1393	Peter Wilrichthe a capmaker and his wife Margaret	German	SCAB., no. 1773, 1774
64.	1393	Stanisław Mochaw (164)	German	SCAB., no. 1654
65.	1393	John Ederer (*Oderer*) (166) [1]	German	SCAB., no. 1676
66.	1393	Anna widow of Peter the blacksmith	Latin	SCAB., no. 1777
67.	1393	Nicholas Strelicz (170)	Latin	SCAB., no. 1645
68.	1393	Anna Helmsmedynne	German	SCAB., no. 1641, 1642
69.	1393	Martin Junge	German	SCAB., no. 1816
70.	1393	John Hulczner (154)	Latin	SCAB., no. 1770
71.	1393	Catherine widow of Nicholas Plesner (106)	German	SCAB., no. 1755
72.	1393	Gotfrid Fattinante of Genua (the councilor)c	Latin	KDWac., vol 2, no. 396
73.	1394	Lawrence of St. Anna street	German	SCAB., no. 1894
74.	1394	Nicholas Hungerkaste	Latin	SCAB., no. 1967, 1968
75.	1394	John Bozemecz	Latin	SCAB., no. 1914

---

c   Gotfrid Fattinante was not mentioned by Marcin Starzyński in his list of Krakow councilors. The office was mentioned in his will "Ceterum quia pretactus Gotfridus quondam distributor peccuniarum Ciuitatis Cracouiensis et legalis Consul extiterat...," KDWac., t. 2, no. 396.

338　　　　　　　　　　　　　　　　　　　　　　　APPENDIX

(*cont.*)

No.	Year	Name	Language	Source
76.	1394	Jacob Teudirneudir	German	SCAB., no. 2042, 2043
77.	1394	Nicholas Remstil	Latin	SCAB., no. 1953, 1954
78.	1394	Theodoric Doring	Latin	SCAB., no. 1913
79.	1394	John Gotschalk	German	SCAB., no. 2041
80.	1394	Dorothy Banarica widow of Martin the stallholder [I]	Latin	SCAB., no. 1866
81.	1394	Dorothy Banarica widow of Martin the stallholder [II]	Latin	SCAB., no. 1893
82.	1394	Kunil Geluke	German	SCAB., no. 1931
83.	1394	John Willusch of Zator	Latin	CONS. 427, fol. 46
84.	1395	Dorothy Banarica widow of Martin the stallholder [III]	Latin	SCAB., no. 2092
85.	1395	John Dobszicz	German	SCAB., no. 2093
86.	1395	John Saxo a goldmisth	Latin	SCAB., no. 2193
87.	1395	Matthias Breunchin	Latin	SCAB., no. 2155
88.	1395	John (*Hanco*) Czartke (69)	Niemieci	SCAB., no. 2069
89.	1395	John Birwain	Latin	SCAB., no. 2111
90.	1395	Nicholas Weidnow	Latin	SCAB., no. 2209
91.	1395	John Michilwicz	German	SCAB., no. 2070
92.	1395	Nicholas Dambraw (153)	German	SCAB., no. 2210
93.	1395	John Frolich	Latin	SCAB., no. 2168
94.	1395	Jacob of Opole	Latin	SCAB., no. 2086
95.	1396	John Degin	Latin	SCAB., no. 2349
96.	1396	Peter Puczk	German	SCAB., no. 2354
97.	1398	George Dubrawka	Latin	CONS. 427, fol. 106
98.	1398	Świątek (*Swantaq*) Polak	Latin	CONS. 427, fol. 106
99.	1400	Catherine daughter of Kachan	German	CONS. 427, fol. 149
100.	1400	Henry Woger and his wife Ursula	German	CONS. 427, fol. 151
101.	1400	Andrew Melczer	German	CONS. 427, fol. 157
102.	1401	John Bartfal (155)	German	CONS. 427, fol. 167
103.	1402	Widow of Libiskind	German	CONS. 427, fol. 172
104.	1402	Stanisław Gryfik	Latin	CONS. 427, fol. 171
105.	1405	Anna Treutelinne	German	CONS. 427, fol. 228
106.	1405	Lucas Bochner (177)	German	CONS. 427, fol. 240
107.	1406	Dorothy Puswanginne widow of John Puswange (163)	German	CONS. 427, fol. 241

APPENDIX

(*cont.*)

No.	Year	Name	Language	Source
108.	1408	John Beme	German	CONS. 427, fol. 306
109.	1408	John Stelmecher	Latin	CONS. 427, fol. 328
110.	1409	Nicholas of Nowa Wieś (*Neudorff*)	German	CONS. 427, fol. 334–335
111.	1409	John Spicymir the younger (137)	Latin	SCAB. 4, fol. 17
112.	1409	Young Peter a tanner	German	CONS. 427, fol. 354
113.	1410	Nicholas Popiolka	German	CONS. 427, fol. 364
114.	1410	Adam Czech	Latin	CONS. 427, fol. 376
115.	1410	Anna widow of Nicholas Botner the older (143)	German	CONS. 427, fol. 365
116.	1411	Catherine wife of Peter Bedlka	Latin	SCAB. 4, fol. 41
117.	1412	John Ederer (*Oderer*) (166) [11]	German	CONS. 428, fol. 4
118.	1412	Dorothy wife of Stanisław Homan	German	SCAB. 4, fol. 71
119.	1412	Nicholas Glezer (220) [1]	German	SCAB. 4, fol. 66b
120.	1412	Nicholas Kmitta	Latin	CONS. 428, fol. 21
121.	1412	Stanisław Leitman the younger, grandson of Peter Fochsczagil (148)	German	CONS. 428, fol. 23
122.	1413	Nicholas Czeginkop	German	SCAB. 4, fol. 104–105
123.	1413	Elizabeth widow of Nicholas Rozler	German	CONS. 428, fol. 46
124.	1414	Peter Fochsczagil (148)	German	SCAB. 5, fol. 15
125.	1416	Sophie widow of Nicholas Polczer	Latin	CONS. 428, fol. 94
126.	1416	Nicholas Morsztyn (*Niczko Mornstin*)	German	SCAB. 4, fol. 143
127.	1416	Peter son of John Schultis	German	CONS. 428, fol. 90
128.	1416	John (*Hanko*) Tile	German	SCAB. 4, fol. 144d
129.	1418	Michael of Nowa Wieś (*Neudorff*) (188)	German	CONS. 428, fol. 126
130.	1419	Martin Smersneider	Latin	CONS. 428, fol. 131
131.	1419	Claire Rolle widow of Jacob Rolle [1]	Latin	KDMK, vol. 3, no. 406
132.	1419	Martin of Biecz (*Betschsky*) (224)	Latin	CONS. 428, fol. 130
133.	1419	Nicholas Smersneyder	Latin	CONS. 428, fol. 120
134.	1419	Barbara widow of John Polak (*Polan*)	Latin	SCAB. 5, fol. 8
135.	1419	Anna widow of John Bartfal (155)	Latin	CONS. 428, fol. 123
136.	1419	Peter the lawyer (*prolocutor*)	German	CONS. 428, fol. 125
137.	1420	Claire Rolle widow of Jacob Rolle [11]	German	SCAB. 5, fol. 31
138.	1420	Sophie mother-in-law of John Messingsloer	Latin	CONS. 428, fol. 143
139.	1420	Peter Fetter (198) [1]	Latin	CONS. 428, fol. 137

APPENDIX

(cont.)

No.	Year	Name	Language	Source
140.	1420	Agnes widow of Miczko	Latin	SCAB. 5, fol. 19–20
141.	1421	Little (*wenige*) Jelge	Latin	SCAB. 5, fol. 43
142.	1421	Nicholas of Bytom	Latin	CONS. 428, fol. 161
143.	1423	Paul Homan (195)	German	SCAB. 5, fol. 79
144.	1423	Nicholas the stallholder	German	SCAB. 5, fol. 72
145.	1423	John Pferd a goldsmith [I]	Latin	CONS. 428, fol. 198
146.	1423	Jokusz Hokenbecke	Latin	SCAB. 5, fol. 80
147.	1423	John the bath owner of Piasek [I]	Latin	SCAB. 5, fol. 77
148.	1423	Stephen the pursemaker (*beuteler*) [I]	Latin	SCAB. 5, fol. 78
149.	1423	John son of Martin a goldsmith	Latin	SCAB. 5, fol. 80
150.	1423	Nicholas the founder (*cremator*)	Latin	SCAB. 5, fol. 79
151.	1424	Paszko Smolcz [I]	German	SCAB. 5, fol. 99
152.	1425	John Pferd a goldsmith [II]	Latin	SCAB. 5, fol. 109
153.	1425	Margaret Puskinne	German	SCAB. 5, fol. 114
154.	1425	Hedwig daughter of Nicholas the goldsmith	Latin	SCAB. 5, fol. 110
155.	1425	Francis the maltster (*melczer*)	Latin	SCAB. 5, fol. 113
156.	1426	Nicholas Glezer (220) [II]	Latin	SCAB. 5, fol. 121
157.	1426	Nicholas Wierzynek (*Wirzing*) (217) [I]	Latin	CONS. 428, fol. 231
158.	1426	Lawrence Hirszberg a cooper	Latin	SCAB. 5, fol. 116
159.	1426	Peter Eicheler [I]	German	SCAB. 5, fol. 130
160.	1427	Paszko Smolcz [II]	German	SCAB. 5, fol. 137
161.	1427	John Schorenbrant	German	SCAB. 5, fol. 136
162.	1427	John Wanser	Latin	SCAB. 5, fol. 148
163.	1427	Martin Beme	German	LT, fol. 3
164.	1428	Francis Nieorza (200) [I]	Latin	SCAB. 5, fol. 158a
165.	1428	Margaret widow of Nicholas Glezer (220)	German	CONS. 428, fol. 243
166.	1428	Dorothy widow of John of Bedzin	German	SCAB. 5, fol. 173
167.	1428	Andrew of Cieszyn	Latin	SCAB. 5, fol. 157a
168.	1428	Peter Hafer	German	SCAB. 5, fol. 167
169.	1428	Matthias the capmaker (*hutter*) [I]	German	SCAB. 5, fol. 157b
170.	1430	Catherine widow of Henry Schendel	German	SCAB. 5, fol. 203
171.	1430	Dorothy widow of Little Jelge [I]	Latin	SCAB. 5, fol. 208
172.	1430	Dorothy widow of Little Jelge [II]	German	SCAB. 5, fol. 210
173.	1430	Herman Meisner	German	SCAB. 5, fol. 203

APPENDIX

341

(*cont.*)

No.	Year	Name	Language	Source
174.	1430	Peter „with the mother" (*mit de muter*) the carpenter	German	CONS. 428, fol. 273
175.	1431	Erhart Eigilwart of Augsburg	German	CONS. 428, fol. 305
176.	1431	Matthias Polak, a tanner at the 'Jewish Gate'	German	CONS. 428, fol. 290
177.	1432	George Szwarcz (210) [I]	German	CONS. 428, fol. 305
178.	1432	Peter Scharf, a poor stallholder	Latin	LT, fol. 3
179.	1433	Paul Ostroszka	German	CONS. 428, fol. 321
180.	1433	Agnes widow of Francis Leimitter	German	SCAB. 6, fol. 55
181.	1433	Peter Tarnow (243)	German	CONS. 428, fol. 319
182.	1433	John Stochse, a gunsmith [I]	Latin	CONS. 428, fol. 317
183.	1433	Margaret widow of Jost the stallholder	German	SCAB. 6, fol. 59
184.	1433	Margaret widow of Lecheler [I]	Latin	SCAB. 6, fol. 65
185.	1433	Nicholas Fridil, an armorer	Latin	CONS. 428, fol. 317
186.	1434	Francis Nieorza (200) [II]	German	SCAB. 6, fol. 81
187.	1434	Catherine widow of Friczko the armorer [I]	German	SCAB. 6, fol. 74
188.	1434	Hedwig widow of John the pipelines administrator (*rurmistrz*)	Latin	SCAB. 6, fol. 94
189.	1434	Margaret Sadowniczka	German	SCAB. 6, fol. 81
190.	1435	Peter Fetter (198) [II]	German	SCAB. 6, fol. 100
191.	1435	Paul Tanneman, an apothecary [I]		SCAB. 6, fol. 113
192.	1435	Michael Lang (*von der Czirla, Langmichel*) (174) [I]	German	CONS. 428, fol. 341
193.	1435	Michael Lang (*von der Czirla, Langmichel*) (174) [II]	Latin	CONS. 428, fol. 344
194.	1435	Nicholas Opoczka [I]	Latin	SCAB. 6, fol. 110
195.	1435	Nicholas Opoczka [II]	Niemecki	SCAB. 6, fol. 111
196.	1435	Dorothy widow of Andrew Polner	German	SCAB. 6, fol. 103
197.	1435	Jost the crossbow maker (*bogner*)	German	SCAB. 6, fol. 108
198.	1436	George Swarcz (210) [II]	German	CONS. 428, fol. 365
199.	1436	John Czenmark of Koszyce	German	CONS. 428, fol. 354
200.	1436	John Briger [I]	German	SCAB. 6, fol. 126
201.	1436	Wilhelm Willand (213)	German	CONS. 428, fol. 369
202.	1436	Matthias Engil a goldsmith	Latin	LT, fol. 3

APPENDIX

(*cont.*)

No.	Year	Name	Language	Source
203.	1436	Lawrence Scherer	German	SCAB. 6, fol. 136
204.	1437	John the bad owner of Piasek [II]	German	SCAB. 6, fol. 140
205.	1437	Stephan the purse maker (*beuteler*) [II]	German	CONS. 428, fol. 379
206.	1437	Servatius (245)	German	SCAB. 6, fol. 139
207.	1437	Nicholas Tunkel, a capmaker	Latin	SCAB. 6, fol. 149
208.	1438	Matthias the capmaker (*hutter*) [II]	German	SCAB. 6, fol. 167–168
209.	1438	John Briger [II]	German	SCAB. 6, fol. 162
210.	1438	John Briger [III]	German	SCAB. 6, fol. 188
211.	1438	John Slepkugil the younger (232)	German	CONS. 428, fol. 397
212.	1438	Peter Putko [I]	German	SCAB. 6, fol. 158
213.	1438	Nicholas Rustab	German	SCAB. 6, fol. 154
214.	1438	John Unger from St. Stephen cemetary	Latin	LT, fol. 3–4
215.	1438	John Strich	German	SCAB. 6, fol. 159
216.	1439	John Pferd, a goldsmith [III]	Latin	CONS. 428, fol. 403
217.	1439	Margaret widow of Lecheler [II]	German	SCAB. 6, fol. 183
218.	1439	John Weinke (237)	German	SCAB. 6, fol. 188
219.	1439	Stanisław Weingarte	Latin	CONS. 428, fol. 406
220.	1439	John Stolle of Głogów, the municipal notary [I]	German	SCAB. 6, fol. 186
221.	1439	John Stolle of Głogów, the municipal notary [II]	Latin	SCAB. 6, fol. 187
222.	1439	John Swidniczer (223) [I]	German	CONS. 428, fol. 402
223.	1439	Florian	German	SCAB. 6, fol. 172, 173
224.	1439	Świętochna Bentkowska	Latin	CONS. 428, fol. 403
225.	1439	Margaret widow of Nicholas Slepkugil	Latin	CONS. 428, fol. 398
226.	1439	Stanisław Streicher (233)	German	SCAB. 6, fol. 174
227.	1439	Gobelinne	German	SCAB. 6, fol. 172
228.	1439	Catherine widow of Prager	Latin	SCAB. 6, fol. 181
229.	1439	Salomea widow of Nicholas Brenner [I]	German	SCAB. 6, fol. 190
230.	1439	Lawrence the court plenipotentiary [I]	German	SCAB. 6, fol. 184
231.	1439	John Lode [I]	German	LT, fol. 10
232.	1439	John stepson of Jost the bowyer (*bogner*)	German	SCAB. 6, fol. 184
233.	1439	Nicholas Blumental, a cooper	German	LT, fol. 10

APPENDIX

343

(*cont.*)

No.	Year	Name	Language	Source
234.	1439	Henry Krancz, a goldsmith	German	CONS. 428, fol. 402
235.	1440	Matthias the cap maker (*hutter*) [III]	Latin	LT, fol. 5
236.	1440	Salomea widow of Nicholas Brenner [II]	German	SCAB. 6, fol. 213
237.	1440	Salomea widow of Nicholas Brenner [III]	Latin	SCAB. 6, fol. 215
238.	1440	Lawrence the court plenipotentiary [II]	German	SCAB. 6, fol. 213
239.	1440	Peter Hirszberg, a stallholder (244)	German	SCAB. 6, fol. 205
240.	1440	John Baumgart, a furrier [I]	German	SCAB. 6, fol. 215
241.	1440	Dorothy Stelmecherinne [I]	German	SCAB. 6, fol. 202
242.	1440	Martin Streicher	German	LT, fol. 5–6
243.	1440	John Reichil [I]	German	SCAB. 6, fol. 196
244.	1440	John Wole of Kamień [I]	Latin	SCAB. 6, fol. 195
245.	1440	Erasmus Strich	Latin	SCAB. 6, fol. 209
246.	1440	Michael Molner [I]	German	LT, fol. 8
247.	1440	Nicholas Schultis, an innkeeper from St. Florian street	Latin	SCAB. 6, fol. 198
248.	1441	Dorothy Stelmecherinne [II]	German	SCAB. 6, fol. 225
249	1441	Jacob Borneisen	German	CONS. 428, fol. 437
250.	1441	Martin the stallholder	Latin	LT, fol. 6
251.	1441	Nicholas of Bełz	German	SCAB. 6, fol. 246
252.	1441	Michael the goldsmith	German	SCAB. 6, fol. 228
253.	1441	Peter Rogosz (*Naraszny*), a councillor of Kleparz	German	CONS. 428, fol. 430
254.	1441	John Tifnaw, a tailor and his wife Agnes	German	SCAB. 6, fol. 226
255.	1442	Peter Putko [II]	German	SCAB. 6, fol. 263–264
256.	1442	John Stolle of Głogów, a municipal notary [III]	Latin	SCAB. 6, fol. 267
257.	1442	John Reichil [II]	German	SCAB. 6, fol. 256
258.	1442	Peter the tailor of the queen (Peter of Pyzdry) (246)	Latin	LT, fol. 4
259.	1442	Nicholas Karmnik	Latin	SCAB. 6, fol. 262
260.	1442	Peter *smersneider* Krzywagłowa	German	SCAB. 6, fol. 261
261.	1442	Stanisław Motyka [II]	Latin	SCAB. 6, fol. 263
262.	1443	John Baumgart, a furrier [II]	Latin	CONS. 428, fol. 466

(*cont.*)

No.	Year	Name	Language	Source
263.	1443	John Schultis (Thob Johan) [I]	German	LT, fol. 7–8
264.	1443	Catherine widow of Nicholas Glazer [I]	German	LT, fol. 6
265.	1444	Michael Molner [II]	German	SCAB. 6, fol. 321
266.	1444	Nicholas Kizeweter	German	SCAB. 6, fol. 306
267.	1444	Catherine widow of Sigismund the vogt of the Higher court of Magdeburg Law	Latin	LT, fol. 8
268.	1444	Martin Molle, a minter	German	SCAB. 6, fol. 312
269.	1444	Catherine widow of Philip Botner	German	SCAB. 6, fol. 313
270.	1445	John Pferd, a goldsmith [IV]	German	SCAB. 6, fol. 338
271.	1445	John Pferd, a goldsmith [V]	German	SCAB. 6, fol. 342
272.	1445	Peter Ossuch, a baker	Latin	LT, fol. 9
273.	1445	Dorothy Zawirbirin	Latin	SCAB. 6, fol. 324
274.	1446	Catherine widow of Friczko the armorer [II]	German	SCAB. 6, fol. 361
275.	1446	John Zyndram (249)	German	LT, fol. 9
276.	1447	Salomea widow of Nicholas Brenner [IV]	German	SCAB. 7, fol. 7–8
277.	1447	Catherine the weaver	Latin	CONS. 428, fol. 500
278.	1447	John Strzesich alias Smed	Latin	LT, fol. 11
279.	1448	Peter Eicheler [II]	German	LT, fol. 12
280.	1448	John Wole of Kamień [II]	German	SCAB. 7, fol. 32
281.	1448	Stanisław Motyka [I]	Latin	SCAB. 7, fol. 46
282.	1448	Barbara Putkinne [I]	German	LT, fol. 11
283.	1448	Agnes Petrzikowa	Latin	SCAB. 7, fol. 32
284.	1448	Paszko the servant from the castle	Latin	CONS. 428, fol. 514
285.	1448	Ludmiła the herring seller	Latin	CONS. 428, fol. 513
286.	1448	Nicholas Paternoster [I]	German	SCAB. 7, fol. 43
287.	1448	Nicholas Paternoster [II]	German	SCAB. 7, fol. 49
288.	1448	Nicholas Nicz, an innkeeper and a baker	German	LT, fol. 10
289.	1449	Nicholas Wierzynek (*Wirzing*) (217) [II]	German	SCAB. 7, fol. 74
290.	1449	Nicholas Barszcz	Latin	LT, fol. 13
291.	1449	Koczwara the old	German	LT, fol. 12–13

APPENDIX   345

(*cont.*)

No.	Year	Name	Language	Source
292.	1450	Catherine widow of Nicholas Glezer [II]	German	SCAB. 7, fol. 88
293.	1450	Stanisław Morsztyn (*Mornstein*) (258)	German	SCAB. 7, fol. 86
294.	1450	Thomas the armorer (*Zarwechter*) (257)	Latin	SCAB. 7, fol. 81
295.	1450	Peter Chromy, a stallholder	German	CONS. 429, fol. 16–17
296.	1450	Peter Warzygarnek	Latin	SCAB. 7, fol. 100
297.	1450	Simon the needle maker [I]	German	CONS. 429, fol. 16
298.	1450	John Morsztyn (*Mornstein*)	Latin	CONS. 429, fol. 12
299.	1450	Nicholas the coat tailor (*mentler*) [I]	Latin	SCAB. 7, fol. 81
300.	1450	Nicholas Zarogowski (296) [I]	Latin	CONS. 429, fol. 15–16
301.	1450	Nicholas Dietrich (272)	German	SCAB. 7, fol. 86
302.	1450	Matthias Kościeński	Latin	SCAB. 7, fol. 105–106
303.	1450	Elizabeth *Slechczyanka*, a shoemaker	German	CONS. 429, fol. 15
304.	1450	Margaret Mundelinne	Latin	SCAB. 7, fol. 82
305.	1450	Catherine called Mechowska widow of Paszko the shoemaker	German	CONS. 429, fol. 15
306.	1450	Dorothy Spekfleischinne	Latin	SCAB. 7, fol. 89
307.	1450	John Beme, a harnessmaker	German	SCAB. 7, fol. 82–83
308.	1450	Nicholas Klingsor	Latin	SCAB. 7, fol. 82
309.	1450	John Specht [I]	Latin	SCAB. 7, fol. 81
310.	1450	Martin Pasternak, a blacksmith [I]	Latin	SCAB. 7, fol. 81
311.	1450	Nicholas Topler [I]	Latin	CONS. 429, fol. 16
312.	1450	Stephen Eichhorn [I]	Latin	SCAB. 7, fol. 83
313.	1451	John Stolle of Głogów, a municipal notary [IV]	German	CONS. 429, fol. 27–28
314.	1451	John Schultis (Thob Johan) [II]	Latin	LT, fol. 31
315.	1451	John Noldenfesser, customs collector	German	LT, fol. 27
316.	1451	Ambrose Czockeling	German	LT, fol. 26
317.	1451	Nicholas Newmeister, a deputy municipal notary	German	SCAB. 7, fol. 120
318.	1452	Sylvester Swidniczer	German	LT, fol. 28–29
319.	1452	Jacob the old stallholder	Latin	SCAB. 7, fol. 155
320.	1452	Catherine Michelinne	German	CONS. 429, fol. 54
321.	1452	Elizabeth widow of Philip the tailor	Latin	CONS. 429, fol. 55
322.	1452	Barbara widow of Martin Nimpczer from Grodzka street [I]	German	LT, fol. 27

No.	Year	Name	Language	Source
323.	1452	John Milde, a tanner	German	LT, fol. 25
324.	1452	Peter Filipowski, a village administrator (*sołtys*) [I]	Latin	LT, fol. 28
325.	1453	John Stochse, a gunsmith [II]	German	LT, fol. 30
326.	1453	John Teschner, the older (242)	German	CONS. 429, fol. 71
327.	1453	Polski John, a goldsmith	Latin	LT, fol. 32
328.	1453	Anna Mazerinne, a cap maker	Latin	LT, fol. 30
329.	1453	Nicholas the Jewish bad owner	German	LT, fol. 29
330	1453	Henczil the bowyer	Latin	LT, fol. 29
331.	1454	Nicholas Wierzynek (*Wirzing*) (217) [III]	Latin	LT, fol. 32
332.	1454	John Stochse, a gunsmith [III]	Latin	LT, fol. 33
333.	1454	John Stolle of Głogów, a municipal notary [V]	Latin	KDMK, vol. 3, no. 339
334.	1454	David of Kamień (*von Steyne*)	German	LT, fol. 32
335.	1454	Anna widow of Henil Weidelich	German	LT, fol. 33
336.	1455	Michael Graser	German	LT, fol. 34
337.	1455	Bartholomeus the tanner	Latin	LT, fol. 35
338.	1456	John Lode [II]	German	LT, fol. 37
339.	1456	Barbara Putkinne [II]	German	LT, fol. 38
340.	1456	Margaret Leipnigerinne	German	LT, fol. 37
341.	1456	Anna wife of Peter Wolski, an innkeeper	Latin	LT, fol. 36
342.	1457	Paul Tanneman, an apothecary [II]	German	SCAB. 7, fol. 303–304
343.	1457	John Swidniczer (223) [II]	German	LT, fol. 39–45
344.	1457	John Piczczin the younger (247)	German	LT, fol. 45
345.	1457	Oswald Schorenbrand	German	LT, fol. 47
346.	1457	Catherine Pocklerinne	German	SCAB. 7, fol. 309
347.	1457	Vincent Czanser, a fustian maker	Latin	LT, fol. 47
348.	1457	Elizabeth widow of Philip the taylor	German	SCAB. 7, fol. 312
349.	1457	Anna widow of Jacob Nirchen	Latin	LT, fol. 46
350.	1458	John Stochse, a gunsmith [IV]	German	LT, fol. 51
351.	1458	Simon the needle maker [II]	German	LT, fol. 55
352.	1458	Martin Pasternak, a blacksmith [II]	German	LT, fol. 55
353.	1458	Ursula daughter of George Szwarcz (210)	German	LT, fol. 56

APPENDIX

347

(*cont.*)

No.	Year	Name	Language	Source
354.	1458	Nicholas Niempcze	German	LT, fol. 57
355.	1458	Nicholas Seyfrid (227)	German	LT, fol. 48–49
356.	1458	Johan Thob, son of Johan Thoba the older	German	LT, fol. 53–54
357.	1458	Nicholas Mewsil, a shoemaker	German	LT, fol. 54
358.	1458	John Panzira, a shoemaker	Latin	LT, fol. 50
359.	1458	Margaret Pferdinne	German	LT, fol. 52
360.	1458	Anna Gregorinne	German	LT, fol. 48
361.	1458	*nobilis* Helena Leszczyńska	German	LT, fol. 53
362.	1458	Agnes Loszinne	German	LT, fol. 50
363.	1458	Nicholas Schramme, a harnessmaker	German	LT, fol. 57
364.	1458	Nicholas Scholbelga	German	LT, fol. 51
365.	1459	Barbara widow of Martin Nimpczer from Grodzka street [II]	German	SCAB. 7, fol. 361
366.	1459	Margaret Prewszinne, a bowyer [I]	German	LT, fol. 59–60
367.	1459	Eustace, a municipal notary	German	LT, fol. 61–63
368.	1459	Peter the barber	German	LT, fol. 58
369.	1459	Anna widow of Florian	German	LT, fol. 64–65
370.	1459	George Beme, a goldsmith	German	LT, fol. 58–59
371.	1459	Jacob Glaser and Margaret Caliszinne his sister in law	German	SCAB. 7, fol. 363–364
372.	1459	Agnes Pferdinne called *Goldenerynne*	German	LT, fol. 59
373.	1460	Peter Filipowski a village administrator (*sołtys*) [II]	Latin	LT, fol. 66
374.	1460	John Kletner (299)	German	LT, fol. 67
375.	1460	Gregory of Nowy Sącz	German	SCAB. 8, 29
376.	1460	John Igiełka	German	SCAB. 8, 59
377.	1460	Anna wife of John the stallholder, before wife of Philip the stallholder	Latin	LT, fol. 65
378.	1460	Margaret Grobniginne	German	LT, fol. 66–67
379.	1460	Nicholas Goldener, a belt maker	German	LT, fol. 68
380.	1460	Peter the bowyer	Latin	LT, fol. 63–64
381.	1461	Simon the needle maker [III]	German	SCAB. 8, 69
382.	1461	Nicholas Topler [II]	Latin	LT, fol. 69
383.	1461	Stanisław Koczwara (267)	Latin	LT, fol. 70–71
384.	1461	Martin Weiner	German	LT, fol. 68–69

348 APPENDIX

(*cont.*)

No.	Year	Name	Language	Source
385.	1461	Bernard of Lubojna	Latin	LT, fol. 71
386.	1461	Dorothy Farberinne	Latin	LT, fol. 75
387.	1461	Ursula Grunwaldinne	German	LT, fol. 70
388.	1462	Konrad Lang (*Cuncze Lange*) (256)	German	LT, fol. 72–73
389.	1462	Jarosz Scharlej (266)	German	LT, fol. 73–74
390.	1462	Stanisław Leymiter (277)	German	LT, fol. 81
391.	1462	Peter May, an innkeeper	Latin	LT, fol. 74–75
392.	1462	John Reinczka of Olkusz	German	LT, fol. 76
393.	1462	Sophie widow of John *smersneider*	German	LT, fol. 75
394.	1463	Kuncze the furrier (230)	German	LT, fol. 78–79
395.	1463	John Raczek	German	SCAB. 8, 145
396.	1463	Margaret widow of Sigismung Molner	German	LT, fol. 79–80
397.	1463	Michael Faber	German	LT, fol. 77
398.	1463	Martin Pictor	German	LT, fol. 80
399.	1464	John Unger	Latin	LT, fol. 85
400.	1464	John journeyman of the goldsmiths guild	German	LT, fol. 82
401.	1464	Martin the bricklayer	Latin	LT, fol. 82
402.	1464	Lazaria wife of Nicholas Slop	German	LT, fol. 87
403.	1464	Stanisław the glover	Latin	LT, fol. 81
404.	1464	Nicholas Brenner, a goldsmith	German	LT, fol. 83–84
405.	1464	John Noga, an oiler	Latin	SCAB. 8, 177
406.	1464	Nicholas Scholtiszek	Latin	SCAB. 8, 197
407.	1465	John Beme (261)	Latin	LT, fol. 86–87
408.	1465	Martin Chmiel (236) [I]	Latin	SCAB. 8, 204
409.	1465	John Mazancz	German	LT, fol. 93–94
410.	1465	Simon from Jewish street	Latin	SCAB. 8, 202
411.	1465	Dorothy Reichelinne	German	SCAB. 8, 203
412.	1465	Black (*Czarny*) John	German	SCAB. 8, 223
413.	1465	Świętochna the bell founder	Latin	LT, fol. 85
414.	1466	Martin Chmiel (236) [II]	German	SCAB. 8, 239–240
415.	1466	John Specht [II]	Latin	LT, fol. 88
416.	1466	Margaret Prewszinne, a bowyer [II]	German	LT, fol. 88–89
417.	1466	Martin Chmiel (236) [III]	German	CONS. 429, fol. 382
418.	1466	Bartholomeus Graudencz	German	SCAB. 8, 246
419.	1466	Jacob Wilkowski (284)	Latin	CONS. 429, fol. 372

APPENDIX

349

(*cont.*)

No.	Year	Name	Language	Source
420.	1466	Duchon [I]	German	CONS. 429, fol. 382
421.	1466	Andrew Zyra, a merchant	Latin	LT, fol. 90–91
422.	1466	Peter Krencz, a butcher	Latin	LT, fol. 90
423.	1466	Catherine Bochsenmeisterinne	German	LT, fol. 89
424.	1466	Stanisław (*Stenczil*) the goldsmith	German	LT, fol. 88
425.	1467	Anna widow of Hartlip the Krakow vogt (263)	Latin	LT, fol. 91–92
426.	1467	Hartlip Parchwicz (263)	Latin	SCAB. 8, 269
427.	1467	Paul Ber (301)	German	SCAB. 8, 270–271
428.	1467	Klimek the stallholder	German	SCAB. 8, 286
429.	1467	Bienisz the stallholder	German	SCAB. 8, 272
430.	1467	John Kunisz, a furrier [I]	German	SCAB. 8, 273
431.	1467	John Gartner (*Gerstman*) (287)	German	SCAB. 8, 269
432.	1467	John Czarny (Black)	Latin	SCAB. 8, 300–301
433.	1467	Nicholas Wishube	German	SCAB. 8, 250
434.	1467	Elizabeth Piotrowa	German	SCAB. 8, 286
435.	1467	Dorothy widow of Peter Masztalerz (*Marstelle*)	Latin	LT, fol. 92–93
436.	1468	Nicholas Klausnicz, a fustian maker of Toruń	German	LT, fol. 94
437.	1468	Stanisław Kulek	Latin	LT, fol. 93
438.	1468	Magdalene Sauerfintinna	Latin	SCAB. 8, 326
439.	1469	Nicholas the coat maker (*mentler*) [II]	German	SCAB. 8, 384
440.	1469	John Specht [III]	German	SCAB. 8, 373
441.	1469	Hippolytus Spilberger (274)	German	LT, fol. 95
442.	1470	Nicholas Topler [III]	German	LT, fol. 99–100
443.	1470	Margaret Miotkinne	Latin	LT, fol. 96–97
444.	1470	Nicholas Baum	German	SCAB. 8, 394
445.	1470	John Stresnel the older	German	SCAB. 8, 393
446.	1471	Margaret Prewszinne, a bowyer [III]	German	SCAB. 8, 428
447.	1471	Anna widow of Stanisław the belt maker (292)	Latin	LT, fol. 98
448.	1471	Margaret Czailstinkinne	Latin	SCAB. 8, 442
449.	1471	Agnes Kitliczinne	Latin	LT, fol. 98
450.	1471	John Koler	Latin	SCAB. 8, 435
451.	1472	Paul Tanneman, an apothecary [III]	German	SCAB. 8, 466

APPENDIX

(*cont.*)

No.	Year	Name	Language	Source
452.	1472	Andrew Zastowski	German	LT, fol. 102–104
453.	1472	John Landandis	German	LT, fol. 101
454.	1472	Dorothy widow of John Tuchler	Latin	SCAB. 8, 485
455.	1472	Catherine Grapperinne	German	LT, fol. 100
456.	1472	Margaret Schoffinne	German	LT, fol. 99
457.	1472	Dorothy widow of Stanisław the apothecary and wife of Andrew (*Dosza Andriszinne*)	German	LT, fol. 105
458.	1472	Nicholas Zarogowski (296) [II]	Latin	Cod. Dipl. UJ, vol. 3, no. 236
459.	1473	Paul Tanneman, an apothecary [IV]	German	SCAB. 8, 501–502
460.	1473	Matthias Opoczko	Latin	LT, fol. 108–109
461.	1473	Matthias Paszko (290)	German	LT, fol. 108
462.	1474	Paul the belt maker	German	LT, fol. 105–107
463.	1474	Jacob Preust, journeyman of fustian makers guild	Latin	CONS. 429, fol. 501
464.	1474	Dorothy Kościołkowa	Latin	CONS. 429, fol. 519
465.	1474	Margaret widow of George the butcher (*Jorge Fleyscherinne*)	German	SCAB. 8, 532
466.	1475	Duchon [II]	German	LT, fol. 111–113
467.	1475	Lazarus nożownik	German	LT, fol. 109–110
468.	1475	John Teschner the younger, a tailor (286)	German	SCAB. 8, 577
469.	1475	Peter Romanus	Latin	CONS. 429, fol. 544
470.	1475	Anna Thilischinne	German	SCAB. 8, 580
471.	1475	Nicholas the goldsmith	German	SCAB. 8, 579
472.	1476	Stephen Eichhorn [II]	German	CONS. 429, fol. 557
473.	1476	John Raisser of Memmingen	German	SCAB. 8, 598–599
474.	1476	Stanisław Lang (282)	Latin	LT, fol. 117
475.	1476	Peter Tarras	Latin	LT, fol. 113
476.	1476	Matthias Brenner, a goldsmith	Latin	LT, fol. 115
477.	1476	Kuncze Kannengiser	German	LT, fol. 116
478.	1476	Dorothy Broszlinne	German	LT, fol. 116
479.	1476	Catherine widow of Thomas Glaser	German	LT, fol. 114
480.	1476	Dorothy Świeczniczka	German	LT, fol. 120–121

APPENDIX   351

(*cont.*)

No.	Year	Name	Language	Source
481.	1476	Elena wife of Nicholas the silk embroider	Latin	Advoc. Crac. 83, fol. 8–9
482.	1477	Barbara widow of Michael Szwarcz	German	LT, fol. 118
483.	1477	Barbara widow of Mark Donerwolf	Latin	LT, fol. 120
484.	1477	Świętosław the herring seller	German	LT, fol. 118–119
485.	1477	Lawrence the fustian maker	German	LT, fol. 124
486.	1477	Stanisław Fischberk	German	LT, fol. 119–120
487.	1477	Michael Rot	German	LT, fol. 114
488.	1479	Peter Lang (289)	German	LT, fol. 125
489.	1479	John Felix	Latin	LT, fol. 125
490.	1479	Matthias Muscala, a salter of Szczepańska street	Latin	LT, fol. 122–124
491.	1479	Stanisław Czollek	Latin	LT, fol. 121
492.	1480	Bernard Szarlej	German	CONS. 429, fol. 676
493.	1481	John Kunisz, a furrier [11]	German	LT, fol. 126
494.	1481	Christopher Rebentcz, the municipal notary	German	CONS. 429, fol. 693
495.	1482	Nicholas Zarogowski (296) [111]	Latin	LT, fol. 129–131
496.	1482	Stephen Eichhorn [111]	German	LT, fol. 133
497.	1482	Catherine Romerinne, daughter of Graser	German	LT, fol. 132–133
498.	1482	Wilhelm Megirszheimer of Dinkelsbühl (*von Thunkilspul*)	German	LT, fol. 135–136
499.	1482	Paul Newburger (280)	German	LT, fol. 132
500.	1482	Stanisław Przedbor (297) [1]	German	LT, fol. 127
501.	1482	John Biały, a tailor	Latin	LT, fol. 133–134
502.	1482	Matthias Szelwa	Latin	LT, fol. 132
503.	1482	Hedwig widow of Nicholas Biały	Latin	LT, fol. 132
504.	1482	Martin Białek	Latin	LT, fol. 132
505.	1482	Nicholas Graudencz	German	LT, fol. 128
506.	1482	Margaret Koruchilinne	Latin	LT, fol. 127
507.	1482	Susan widow of Matthias Beck	German	LT, fol. 135
508.	1483	John Odoj	Latin	LT, fol. 136
509.	1483	Peter Szepcz	German	LT, fol. 137–140
510.	1483	Peter Giemiolek, a fustian maker	Latin	LT, fol. 136

352   APPENDIX

(*cont.*)

No.	Year	Name	Language	Source
511.	1484	Catherine widow of George the goldsmith	Latin	LT, fol. 142–143
512.	1484	Catherine the oiler	Latin	LT, fol. 140–141
513.	1487	Nicholas Dolski	Latin	LT, fol. 143–144
514.	1487	Hedwig Granoszowa	German	LT, fol. 145
515.	1487	Wojtek płatnerz	Latin	LT, fol. 143
516.	1488	Margaret Szolwiczinne	German	LT, fol. 145
517.	1488	Paul Flek	Latin	LT, fol. 146
518.	1489	*nobilis* Anna Obulczowa, daughter of George Orient (226)	Latin	LT, fol. 147
519.	1489	Ursula widow of Eustace the municipal notary	German	LT, fol. 148–149
520.	1491	Barbara daughter of Michael Unger	German	LT, fol. 149–150
521.	1492	Jarosz the tailor	Latin	LT, fol. 151–152
522.	1492	Hedwig Fiwegerinne	Latin	LT, fol. 150–151
523.	1493	Helen widow of Nicholas the embroider	German	LT, fol. 153
524.	1493	George Monczer	Latin	LT, fol. 153
525.	1494	Hedwig widow of George the belt maker (*Gortlerinne*)	German	LT, fol. 154–155
526.	1494	John Włosaty, a salter	Latin	LT, fol. 154
527.	1494	Michael Godzek, a salter	Latin	LT, fol. 154
528.	1495	Stanisław Przedbor (297) [11]	Latin	LT, fol. 155
529.	1497	George Lang (309)	German	LT, fol. 155–156
530.	1497	John Wiewiórka (314)	Latin	LT, fol. 156
531.	1498	Ulrich Jeczimberger (306)	German	LT, fol. 157–158
532.	1498	Catherine Kitliczinne	German	LT, fol. 158–159
533.	1499	Erhard Schlacker	German	LT, fol. 159–160
534.	1500	George Morsztyn (*Mornstein*) (307)	German	LT, fol. 161–164
535.	1500	Anna widow of John Gobel	German	SCAB. 9, fol. 7
536.	1500	Catherine Danczkowa	Latin	SCAB. 9, fol. 9
537.	1500	Klemens Opoczka	Latin	SCAB. 9, fol. 20

APPENDIX

FIGURE 1   The oldest woodcut picture of Krakow, Kazimierz and Kleparz, by Hartmann Schedl, *Liber Cronicarum* (1493)

FIGURE 2   Map of Wacław Grodecki (1535–1591). It was included in the first modern world atlas, *Theatrum Orbis Terrarum*, published by Abraham Ortelius in 1570 (1579) in Antwerp. "Cracovia" is depicted in the lower left corner of the map, in the Lesser Poland Voivodeship.

APPENDIX

FIGURE 3   Plan of the city of Krakow by Filip Lichocki, issued in 1787. The plan includes Krakow within the walls, together with Wawel hill, Stradom, Kazimierz and a fragment of Podgórze (called Jozefstadt at that time).

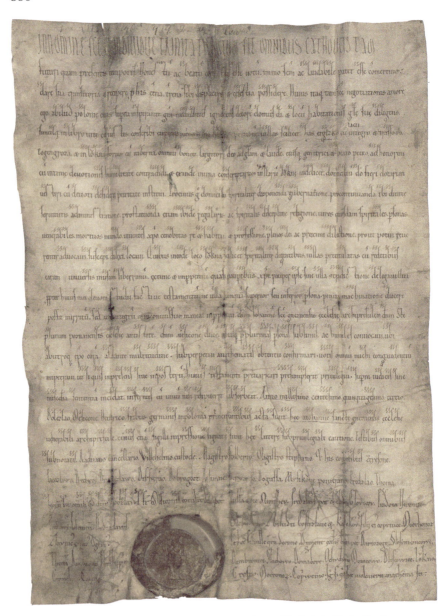

FIGURE 4 Document of foundation as a 'testament,' issued by knight Zbylut for the Cistercian monastery in Łekno in 1153

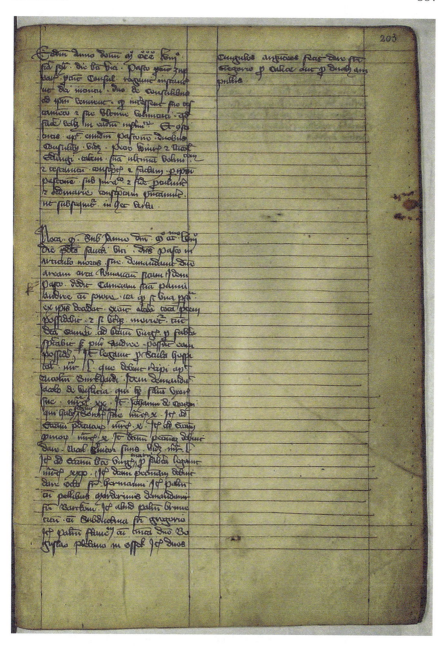

FIGURE 5   Will of Paszko vel Paulino Cavallo (1358), a Genoese-born councillor in Krakow and administrator of the Bochnia salt mines

FIGURE 6   Will of Nicholas Dambraw (1395), councilor of Krakow. Card with a will was pasted between the pages of the bench book.

APPENDIX

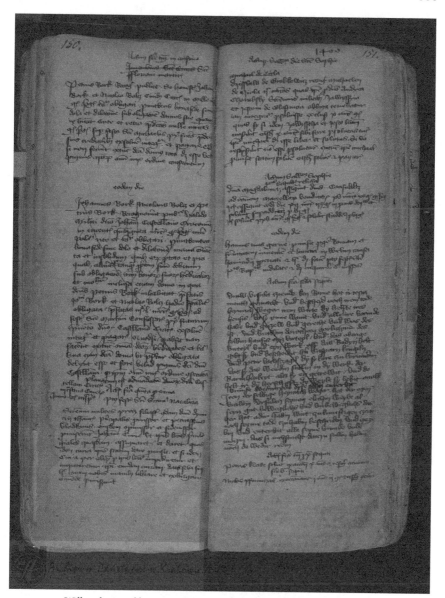

FIGURE 7   Will and mutual bequest of Henry Woger and his wife Ursula (1400)

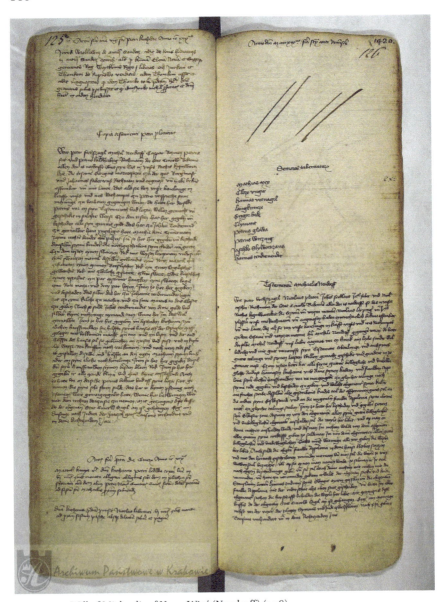

FIGURE 8   Will of Michaelis of Nowa Wieś (Neudorff) (1418)

APPENDIX

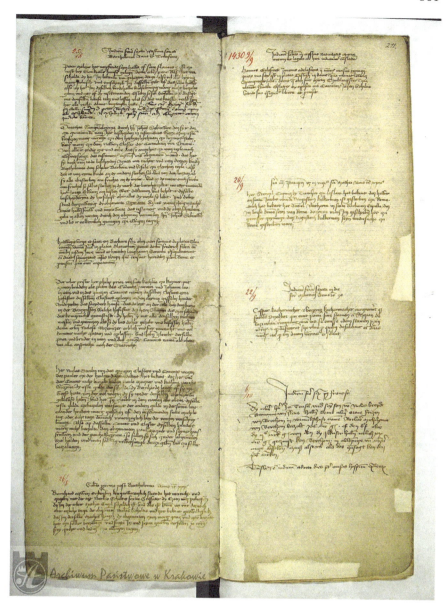

FIGURE 9   Will of Dorothy, widow of Little Jelge (1430)

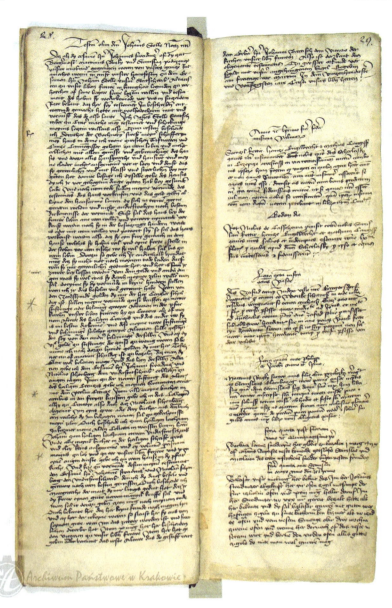

FIGURE 10   Will of Johannes Stolle of Głogów, the municipal notary (1451)

APPENDIX 363

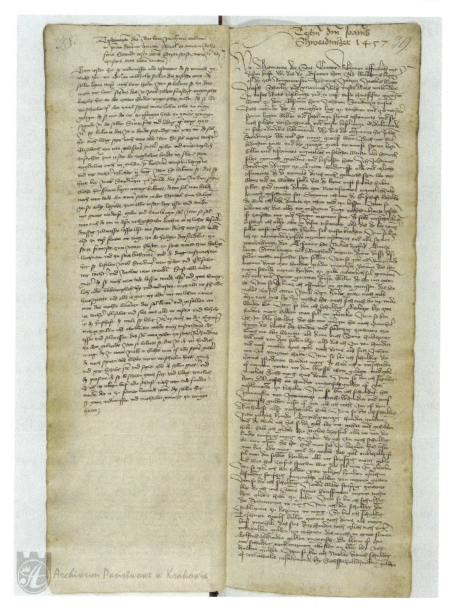

FIGURE 11   Will of Barbara Putkinne (1456) and the first part of the will of John Swidniczer (1457) from *Liber Testamentorum*

Glossary

Bench court* (Lat. *iudicium bannitum, iudicium civile*; Pol. *wiec, sąd gajony, sąd wiecowy*; Ger. *gehegte bang, gehegetes ding*). The principal tribunal in cities based on Magdeburg Law composed of the eligible aldermen (Ger. *scabini iurati; scheppen, schöffen*) under the presidency of the mayor/Vogt.

Court sessions were divided into ordinary and extraordinary. To the first group belonged standard sessions (Lat. *iudicium particulare, iudicium parvum, iudicium bannitum civile, iudicum expositum*; Pol. *powiatek, sąd powieśny*) and the great courts held three times a year with an accelerated procedure (Lat. *iudicium bannitum generale, colloquium generale, iudicium magnum, magnum plebiscitum*; Pol. *sąd wielki, wielki wiec*).

Extraordinary sessions were divided into necessary courts (Lat. *iudicium necessarium, iudicium opportunum*; Pol. *sądy konieczne*) dealing with civil issues, quarrels and criminal cases, hospitable courts (Lat. *iudicium hospitum*; Pol. *sąd gościnny*) dealing with all disagreements between citizens and newcomers and bought courts (Lat. *iudicium emptum*; Pol. *sąd wykupiony*) i.e. a paid court hearing convened at someone's private request.

Castellan (Lat. *castellanus*; Pol. *kasztelan*). Initially, a functionary of high royal administrator on a given territory, later on a member of the royal council.

Dower (Lat. *dotalicio*; Pol. *wiano*; Ger. *morgengabe*). A sum of money or a goods given or promised to the bride by the groom at the start of the marriage. The dower was a response to a dowry.

Although all the property of the spouses was managed by the husband, dower was perceived as the wife's property and come back to her in the event of his death.

Dowry (Lat. *dos*, Pol. *posag*). A sum of money or goods that wife brought into marriage after wedding

Gerada (Ger.; Lat. *paraphernalia*). According to Magdeburg Law a personal property of woman passed from one generation to the next in the female line. It included such objects as clothing, jewelry, various home textiles, dishes as well as prayer books and flock animals.

Village administrator (Lat. *scultetus*; Pol. *sołtys*; *Scholcz*, G. *Scholtes*). A foreman in villages organized according to Magdeburg Law, similar to the Vogt in towns. As a subordinate of the owner of the village was obliged both to military service as

---

* These entries were described on the basis of a glossary prepared by Agnieszka Bartoszewicz in *Urban Literacy in Late Medieval Poland*, Brepols 2017, 413–418

GLOSSARY

well as collecting of tributes. He served also a function the chairman of the village court, composed of peasant aldermen.

Hergewet. (Ger.; Lat. *arma bellica*) According to Magdeburg Law a personal equipment and belongings of man passed from one generation to the next in the male line. It included such objects as weapons, armor, clothes, and private textiles.

Vogt (Lat. *advocatus*; Pol. *wójt*; Ger. *voyt*). Initially (late thirteenth and first half of fourteenth c.), a hereditary administrator of the town and foreman of the bench court on behalf of town's owner. He was usually remunerated with various proprieties and privileges, assigned to him in the locatio-charter. The office of mayor/Vogt, with its legal, financial, and material prerogatives, could be sold with consent of the owner of the town. In such a case his prerogatives passed into hands of the city councilors, and the office of Vogt a foreman of city courts began to be elected.

Municipal council (Lat. *consulatus*; Pol. *rada miejska*). Eligible body of the self-government of the urban community composed of councillors (Lat. *consules*; Pol. *rajcy*; Ger. *rathmänner*) under the presidency of the mayor (Lat. magister civium, proconsul, prothoconsul; Pol. *burmistrz*; Ger. *burgermeister*). The chief municipal office responsible for the legal, financial and public order issues and regulations in the city.

Starosta (Lat. *capitaneus*). A royal official exercised judicial and military power as well as collector of royal taxes within a given district

Urban statutes (Lat. *laudum civitatis;* Pol. *wilkierz*, Ger. *Willkür*). Legal regulations concerning various matters of urban life and public order, issued by the municipal council.

Urteil (Ger.; Lat. *privilegium*; Pol. *ortyl*). Court sentences and legal counsels issued by the so-called higher courts of Magdeburg Law, initially given by the aldermen of Magdeburg. From 1356 onwards, their competences were officially taken over by the highest court of German law at Krakow castle (*ius supremum Magdeburgensis castri Cracoviensis*)

Vice-Vogt (Lat. *viceadvocatus*; Pol. *podwójci*). Deputy Vogt assisting him in legal duties and sometimes acting as Vogt's scribe

Bibliography

Archival Sources

The National Archives in Krakow, Department III – Files of the City of Krakow (Archiwum Narodowe w Krakowie, Akta miasta Krakowa)

Advocatalia Cracoviensia, ms 83.

Consularia Cracoviensia. Inscriptiones, ms 427–431.

Scabinalia Cracoviensia. Inscriptiones, ms 3–9.

Liber Testamentorum. Testamenta in officio consulari Cracoviensi, ms 772.

Testamenta, ms 779.

Jagiellonian Library

Reformacio fraternitatis S. Marie in circulo Cracoviensi facta est anno incarnacionis Domini 1481…, ms 2365.

Łaski Jan, *Commune Incliti Poloniae regni privilegium constitutionum et indultuum publicitus decretorum approbatorumque*, Krakow, 1506.

Edited sources

Balzer, Oswald. *Statuty Kazimierza Wielkiego*. Poznań: Nakł. Poznańskiego Tow. Przyjaciół Nauk , 1947.

Bartoszewicz, Agnieszka, Andrzej Karpiński and Katarzyna Warda (eds.). *Testamenty mieszczan warszawskich od XV do końca XVII wieku. Katalog*. Warszawa: Semper, 2010.

Behrend, Jacob-Friedrich (ed.). *Die Magdeburger Fragen*. Berlin: Guttentag, 1865.

Borkowska, Małgorzata (ed.). *Dekret w niebieskim ferowany parlamencie: wybór testamentów z XVII – XVIII wieku*. Krakow: Znak, 1984.

Brückner, Alexander (ed.). *Kazania i pieśni: szkice literackie i obyczajowe, in Literatura religijna w Polsce średniowiecznej*, vol. 1. Warszawa: Gebethner i Wolff, 1902.

Ciołek, Stanisław, "Pochwała Krakowa." In *Codex Epistolaris Vitoldi Magni Ducis Lithuanie 1376–1430*, ed. Antoni Prochaska. Krakow: Sumptibus Acad. Literarum Cracoviensis 1882, 1057–1058.

Danowska, Ewa (ed.). *Dług śmiertelności wypłacić potrzeba. Wybór testamentów mieszczan krakowskich z XVII-XVIII wieku*. Krakow: Polska Akademia Umiejętności, 2011.

Długosz, Jan. *Annales Seu Cronicae Incliti Regni Poloniae: Lib. 11 Et Lib. 12., 1431–1444*. Warszawa: Wydawn. Nauk. PWN, 2001

BIBLIOGRAPHY

367

Dybaś, Bogusław and Janusz Tandecki (eds.). *Księga cechowa złotników krakowskich 1462–1566*, in *Złotnicy krakowscy XIV-XVI wieku i ich księga cechowa*, ed., Bogusław Dybaś, Janusz Tandecki. Warszawa: Instytut Sztuki PAN, 2000.

Dymmel, Piotr (ed.). *Testamenty mieszczan wojnickich 1599–1809*. Wojnicz: Tow. Przyjaciół Ziemi Wojnickiej, 1997.

Estreicher, Stanisław (ed.). *Najstarszy zbiór przywilejów i wilkierzy miasta Krakowa.* Krakow: Polska Akademia Umiejętności, 1936.

Fabiański, Marcin (ed.). *Miniatury z Kodeksu Baltazara Behema*, ed. Krakow: Wydawnictwo Karpaty, 2000.

Falniowska-Gradowska, Alicja (ed.). *Testamenty szlachty krakowskiej XVII – XVIII w. Wybór tekstów źródłowych z lat 1650–1799*. Krakow: Polska Akademia Umiejętności, Secesja, 1997.

Fijałek, Jan and Adam Vetulani (eds.). *Statuty synodalne wieluńsko-kaliskie Mikołaja Trąby z r. 1420. Z materiałów przysposobionych przez B. Ulanowskiego*. Krakow: Polska Akademia Umiejętności, 1951.

Gąsiorowski, Antoni, Tomasz Jurek and Izabela Skierska (eds.). *Najstarsza księga promocji Wydziału Sztuk Uniwersytetu Krakowskiego z lat 1402–1541*. Warszawa: Instytut Historii PAN, 2011.

Gąsiorowski, Antoni, Tomasz Jurek, Izabela Skierska and Ryszard Grzesik (eds.). *Metryka Uniwersytetu Krakowskiego z lat 1400–1508*, vol. 1. Krakow: Towarzystwo Naukowe "Societas Vistulana," 2004.

Grodecki, Roman (ed.). *Liber Fundationis claustre Sancte Marie Virginis in Henrichow. Księga henrykowska*. Poznań: Instytut Zachodni, 1949.

Groicki, Bartłomiej. *Artykuły prawa majdeburskiego. Postępek sądów około karania na gardle. Ustawa płacej u sądów*. Warszawa: Wydawnictwo Prawnicze, 1954.

Groicki, Bartłomiej. *Porządek sądów i spraw miejskich prawa majdeburskiego w Koronie Polskiej*, Warszawa 1953.

Groicki, Bartłomiej. *Tytuły prawa majdeburskiego*. Warszawa: Wydawnictwo Prawnicze, 1954.

Heyzmann, Udalricus (ed.). *Statuta synodalia episcoporum Cracoviensium XIV et XV saeculi e codicibus manu scriptis typis mandata additis statutis Vielunii et Calisii a. 1420 conditis (et ex rarissimis editionibus – etiam authenticis – nunc iterum editis)*. In *Starodawne prawa polskiego pomniki*, vol. 4. Krakow: Academiae Literarum, 1875, 51–261.

Chmiel, Adam (ed.). *Księgi radzieckie kazimierskie 1369–1381 i 1385–1402. Acta consularia Casimiriensia 1369–1381 et 1385–1402*. Krakow: W drukarni Uniwersytetu Jagiellońskiego, 1932.

Jelicz, Antonina (ed.). *Antologia poezji polsko-łacińskiej: 1470–1543*. Szczecin: Glob, 1985.

Judit, Majorossy and Katalin Szende (eds.). *Das Pressburger Protocollum Testamentorum 1410 (1427) – 1529*, vol. 1: 1410–1487. Wien: Bohlau Verlag, 2010.

368 BIBLIOGRAPHY

Kaczmarczyk, Kazimierz (ed.). *Księgi przyjęć do prawa miejskiego w Krakowie 1392–1506. Libri iuris civilis Cracoviensis 1392–1506.* Krakow: Filipowski, 1913.

Katalog Archiwum Aktów Dawnych Miasta Krakowa, vol. 1. *Dyplomy pergaminowe.* Krakow: Archiwum Aktów Dawnych Miasta Krakowa, 1907.

Kovachich, Martin Georg (ed,). *Codex authenticus iuris tavernicalis.* Buda: Kilian, 1803

Král, Pavel (ed.). *Mezi životem a smrtí: testamenty české šlechty v letech 1550 až 1650.* České Budějovice: Historický Ústav Jihočeské Univ., 2002.

Krzyżanowski, Stanisław (ed.). *Księgi ławnicze krakowskie 1365–1376 i 1390–1397. Acta scabinalia Cracoviensia 1365–1376 et 1390–1397.* Krakow: Filipowski, 1904.

Kuraś, Stanisław (ed.). *Zbiór dokumentów katedry i diecezji krakowskiej*, vol. 1: 1063–1415, vol. 2: 1416–1450, Lublin: Towarzystwo Naukowe Katolickiego Uniw. Lubelskiego, 1965–1973.

Kuraś, Stanisław and Irena Sułkowska-Kuraś (eds.). *Zbiór dokumentów małopolskich*, vol. I–VIII. Wrocław-Warszawa-Krakow-Gdańsk: Zakład Narodowy im. Ossolińskich, 1962–1975.

Kutrzeba, Stanisław and Adam Vetulani (eds.). *Wybór źródeł do historji ustroju i prawa sądowego Polski*, nr. 2: *Spisy prawa zwyczajowego koronnego.* Krakow: Księgarnia Gebethnera i Wolffa, 1930.

Laband, Paul (ed.). *Das Magdeburger-Breslauer systematische Schöffenrecht aus der Mitte des XIV. Jahrhunderts.* Berlin: Dümmlers Ferd. Verlagsbuchhandlung, Harrwitz und Gossmann, 1863

Lewański, Julian (ed.). *Dramaty staropolskie. Antologia*, vol. 1. Warszawa: Państ. Instytut Wydawniczy, 1959.

Lubczyński, Mariusz, Jacek Pielas and Henryk Suchojad (eds.). *Cui contingit nasci, restat mori. Wybór testamentów staropolskich z województwa sandomierskiego.* Warszawa: Semper, 2005.

Łysiak, Ludwik (ed.). *Decreta iuris supremi Magdeburgensis castri Cracoviensis. Rechtssprüche des Oberhofs des deutschen Rechts auf der Burg zu Krakau*, vol. 1: 1456–1481, vol. 2: 1481–1511. Frankfurt am Main: V. Klostermann, 1995–1997.

Mack, Dietrich (ed.). *Testamente der Stadt Braunschweig*, vol. 1–5. Göttingen: Göttingen Goltze, 1988–1990.

Maisel, Witold (ed.). *Ortyle sądów wyższych miast wielkopolskich XV i XVI wieku*, Wrocław: Zakład Narodowy im. Ossolińskich, 1959.

Maisel, Witold (ed.). *Poznańska księga prawa magdeburskiego i miśnieńskiego. Das Posener Buch des Magdeburger und Meissner Rechts.* Wrocław: Zakład Narodowy im Ossolińskich, 1964.

Maisel, Witold (ed.). *Wilkierze poznańskie*, vol. 1–2. Wrocław-Warszawa-Krakow: Zakład Narodowy im. Ossolińskich, 1966–1968.

Maisel, Witold and Zbigniew Zdrójkowski (eds.). *Prawo starochełmińskie 1585 (1394)*, trans. Andrzej Bzdęga, Alicja Gaca. Toruń: Uniwersytet Mikołaja Kopernika, 1985.

BIBLIOGRAPHY

369

Matuszewski Józef and Jacek Matuszewski (eds.). *Najstarszy zwód prawa polskiego.* Łódź: Wyd. Uniwersytetu Łódzkiego, 1995.

Mitkowski, Józef. "Księga zmarłych bractwa kościoła Panny Marii w Krakowie (wiek XIV–XVIII)." *Studia Historyczne* 11, no. 1 (1968): 71–95.

Niwiński, Mieczysław, Krystyna Jelonek-Litewka and Aleksander Litewka (eds.). *Księga wójtowska krakowska 1442–1443. Registrum domini advocati Cracoviensis 1442–1443. Ze zbiorów Archiwum Państwowego w Krakowie.* Krakow: Wojewódzkie Archiwum Państwowe, 1995.

Piekosiński, Franciszek (ed.). *Codex Diplomaticus Universitatis Studii Generalis Cracoviensis*, vol. 1–3. Krakow: sumptibus Universitatis, 1870–1880.

Piekosiński, Franciszek (ed.). *Kodeks dyplomatyczny katedry krakowskiej św. Wacława*, vol. I–II. Krakow: Akademia Umiejętności, 1874–1883.

Piekosiński, Franciszek (ed.). *Kodeks dyplomatyczny Małopolski*, vol. I–IV. Krakow: Akademia Umiejętności, 1874–1905.

Piekosiński, Franciszek (ed.). *Kodeks dyplomatyczny miasta Krakowa*, vol. I–IV. Krakow: Akademia Umiejętności, 1879–1882.

Piekosiński, Franciszek (ed.). *Najdawniejsze inwentarze skarbca kościoła N. P. Maryi w Krakowie z XV wieku.* Krakow 1889; repr.: "Sprawozdania Komisji do Badań Historii Sztuki w Polsce," vol. 4, no. 2 (Krakow, 1889), 64–77.

Piekosiński, Franciszek (ed.). *Prawa, przywileje i statuta miasta Krakowa (1507–1795)*, vol. 1. Krakow: Akademia Umiejętności, 1885.

Piekosiński, Franciszek (ed.). *Registra perceptorum et distributorum civitatis Cracoviensis annorum 1390–1393, 1395–1405 nec non 1407–1410.* In *Libri antiquissimi civitatis Cracoviae saeculi decimi quinti*, pars posteriori, Krakow 1877, 224–343.

Piekosiński, Franciszek and Józef Szujski (eds.). *Liber actorum, resignationum nec non ordinationum civitatis Cracoviae 1300–1375* In *Libri antiquissimi civitatis Cracoviae saeculi decimi quinti*, pars posteriori, eds. Piekosiński, Franciszek. Józef Szujski. Krakow: 1878, 1–247.

Plezia, Marian (ed.). *Najstarsza poezja polsko-łacińska (do połowy XVI wieku).* Wrocław: Ossolineum, 2005.

Przeździecki, Aleksander (ed.). *Jana Długosza kanonika krakowskiego Dziejów polskich ksiąg dwanaście*, trans. Karol Mecherzyński. Krakow: Drukarnia W. Kirchmayera, 1869.

Przybyszewski, Bolesław (ed.). *Cracovia artificum. Supplementa 1462–1475.* Krakow: Zakład Narodowy Im. Ossolińskich, 2000.

Przybyszewski, Bolesław (ed.). *Cracovia artificum. Supplementa. Teksty źródłowe do dziejów kultury i sztuki z najdawniejszych oficjaliów krakowskich, lata 1410–1412 oraz 1421–1424.* Wrocław: Zakład Narodowy im. Ossolińskich, 1985.

Przybyszewski, Bolesław (ed.). *Cracovia artificum. Supplementa. Teksty źródłowe do dziejów kultury i sztuki z archiwów kurialnych i kapitulnych w Krakowie 1441–1450.* Krakow: Secesja, 1993.

Ptaśnik, Jan (ed.). *Cracovia artificum 1300–1500*. Krakow: Polska Akademia Umiejętności, 1917.

Raczek, Józef and Wacław Twardzik (eds.). *Najstarsze staropolskie tłumaczenie ortyli magdeburskich według rękopisu nr 50 Biblioteki Zakładu Narodowego im. Ossolińskich*, vol. 1–2. Wrocław: Zakład Narodowy im. Ossolińskich, 1970–1972.

Reinhardt, Uta (ed.). *Lüneburger Testamente des Mittelalters 1323 bis 1500*. Hannover: Hahn, 1996.

Rzepka, Wojciech Ryszard, and Wiesław Wydra *Cały świat nie pomieściłby ksiąg. Staropolskie opowieści i przekazy apokryficzne*, ed.. Warszawa: Wydawnictwo Naukowe PWN, 2008

Rzyszczewski, Leon, Antoni Muczkowski, Antoni Zygmunt Helcel and Julian Bartoszewicz (eds.). *Codex Diplomaticus Poloniae*, vol. 1, no. 6. Warszawa: Stabski, 1847

Sokołowski, August and Józef Szujski (eds.). *Codex epistolaris saeculi decimi quinti*, vol. I. Krakow 1876, vol. II, ed. Antoni Lewicki. Krakow: Akad. Umiejętności, 1876, 1891, 1894.

Szczerbic, Paweł, *Ius municipale, to jest prawo miejskie majdeburskie, nowo z łacińskiego i Germanego na polski język z pilnością i wiernie przełożone*. ed. Grzegorz Maria Kowalski. Krakow: Księgarnia Akademicka, 2011.

Szujski, Józef (ed.). *Acta consularia nec non proscriptiones ab anno 1392 ad annum 1400*. In *Libri antiquissimi civitatis Cracoviae saeculi decimi quinti*, pars posteriori, eds. Piekosiński, Franciszek. Józef Szujski. Krakow: 1877, 77–223.

Tacitus, Publius, Cornelius, *Germania*. trans. Tomasz Płóciennik. Poznań: Wydawnictwo Naukowe UAM, 2008

Ulanowski, Bolesław (ed.). *Libri Formularum saeculi XVmi*. In *Starodawne Prawa Polskiego Pomniki*, vol. X. Krakow: Nakł. Księgarni G. Sennewalda, 1888.

Ulanowski, Bolesław. *Acta capitulorum Cracoviensis et Plocensis selecta: (1438–1523, 1438–1525)*. Krakow: Akademia Umiejętności, 1891.

Ulanowski, Bolesław. *Acta capitulorum nec non iudiciorum ecclesiasticorum selecta 1–3*. Krakow: Nakł. Akad. Umiejetności, 1894–1908.

Wiesiołowski, Jacek (ed.). *Kronika poznańskich pisarzy*. Poznań: Wydawnictwo Miejskie, 2004.

Wisłocki, Władysław (ed.). *Kodex Pilźnieński ortylów magdeburskich. Odbitka z II tomu Sprawozdań Wydz. Hist. Fil. Akad. Umiejętn.* Krakow: Akademia Umiejętności, 1874.

Wiszniewski, Michał. *Historya literatury polskiej*, vol. V. Krakow: 1843.

Włodarski, Maciej (ed.). *Polska poezja świecka XV wieku*. Wrocław: Biblioteka Narodowa, 1998.

Wyrozumska, Bożena (ed.). *Księga proskrypcji i skarg miasta Krakowa 1360–1422: ze zbiorów Archiwum Państwowego w Krakowie. Liber proscriptionum et querelarum civitatis Cracoviensis 1360–1422*. Krakow: Secesja, 2001.

BIBLIOGRAPHY 371

Wyrozumska, Bożena, "Zapiski z księgi radzieckiej krakowskiej 1393–1400. Uzupełnienie do wydawnictwa Najstarsze księgi i rachunki miasta Krakowa," *Studia Historyczne* 35, no. 4 (1992), 110–189.

Zakrzewski, Ignacy (ed.). *Kodeks dyplomatyczny Wielkopolski*, vol. 1. Poznań: Państwowe Wydawnuctwo Naukowe, 1877.

Zathey, Jerzy and Jerzy Reichan (eds.). *Indeks studentów Uniwersytetu Krakowskiego w latach 1400–1500*. Wrocław: Zakład Narodowy im. Ossolińskich, 1974.

Literature

Aders, Günter. *Das Testamentsrecht der Stadt Köln im Mittelalter*. Köln: Verlag des Kölnischen Geschichtsvereins e.V. in Kommission bei Creutzer & Company, 1932.

Aleksandrowicz-Szmulikowska, Małgorzata. *Radziwiłłówny w świetle swoich testamentów. Przyczynek do badań mentalności magnackiej XVI-XVII wieku*. Warszawa: Semper, 1995.

Antosiewicz, Klara. "Zakon Ducha Świętego de Saxia *w* Polsce średniowiecznej." *Nasza Przeszłość*, 23 (1966), 167–198.

Cichowicz, Stanisław and Jakub M. Godzimirski (eds.) *Antropologia śmierci. Myśl francuska*, trans. Stanisław Cichowicz, Jakub M. Godzimirski. Warszawa: Wydawn. Naukowe PWN, 1993.

Ariès, Philippe. *The Hour of Our Death*, trans. Helen Weaver. New York: Viking, 1981.

Attreed, Lorraine. "Urban Identity in Medieval English Towns." *The Journal of Interdisciplinary History* 32, no. 4 (2002): 571–592.

Augustyniak, Urszula. *Testamenty ewangelików reformowanych w Wielkim Księstwie Litewskim*. Warszawa: Semper, 1992.

Augustyniak, Urszula. "Wizerunek Krzysztofa II Radziwiłła jako magnata-ewangelika w świetle jego testamentów." *Przegląd Historyczny* 81, no. 3–4 (1990), 461–477.

Bach, Udalrich,. *Das Testament als Literarische form. Versuch einer Gattungsbestimmung auf der Grundlage eglischer Texte*. Düsseldorf: Stern-Verlag Janssen, 1977.

Bardach, Juliusz. *Historia państwa i prawa Polski do połowy XV wieku*. Warszawa: Państwowe Wydawnictwo Naukowe, 1957.

Bardach, Juliusz, Bogusław Leśnodorski, Michał Pietrzak. *Historia ustroju i prawa polskiego*. Warszawa: Lexis Nexis, 2000.

Bartoszewicz, Agnieszka. *Czas w małych miastach. Studium, z dziejów kultury umysłowej późnośredniowiecznej Polski*. Warszawa-Pułtusk: Inst. Historyczny Uniw. Warszawskiego, 2003.

Bartoszewicz, Agnieszka. "Języki wernakularne w testamentach mieszczan krakowskich XIV–XV w.," *KHKM* 61, no 2 (2013), 251–261.

Bartoszewicz, Agnieszka, *Pauperes litterati w polskich miastach późnego średniowiecza.* In *Europejczycy Afrykanie inni – Studia ofiarowane profesorowi Michałowi Tymowskiemu,* edited by Bronisław Nowak, Mirosław Nagielski, Jerzy Pysiak, 93–112. Warszawa: Wydawnictwo Uniwersytetu Warszawskiego, 2011.

Bartoszewicz, Agnieszka. *Piśmienność mieszczańska w poźnośredniowiecznej Polsce.* In *Historia społeczna późnego średniowiecza. Nowe badania,* edited by Sławomir Gawlas, 275–292. Warszawa: DiG, 2011.

Bartoszewicz, Agnieszka. *Piśmienność mieszczańska w późnośredniowiecznej Polsce.* Warszawa: Wydawnictwo Uniwersytetu Warszawskiego, 2012.

Bartoszewicz, Agnieszka. *Urban Literacy in Late Medieval Poland.* Turnhout: Brepols, 2017.

Bartoszewicz, Agnieszka. "Testament jako źródło do badań nad piśmiennością mieszczańską w późnym średniowieczu." *KHKM* 59, no. 2 (2011): 293–304.

Bartoszewicz, Agnieszka. *Warta, społeczeństwo miasta w II połowie XV i na początku XVI wieku.* Warszawa: Wydawn. Fundacji Historia pro Futuro, 1997.

Bauman, Zygmunt. *Socjologia,* trans. Jerzy Łoziński. Poznań: Zysk i S-ka, 1990.

Baur, Paul. *Testament und Bürgerschaft, Alltagsleben und Sachkultur im spätmittelalterlichen Konstanz.* Sigmaringen: Jan Thorbecke Verlag, 1989.

Benadusi, Giovanna. "Investing the Riches of the Poor: Servant Women and Their Last Wills." *The American Historical Review* 109, no. 3 (2004): 805–826.

Berman, Harold Joseph. *Law and Revolution. The Formation of the Western Legal Tradition.* Cambridge-London: Harvard University Press, 1983.

Biancalana, Joseph. "Testamentary cases in fifteenth-century Chancery." *The Legal History Review* 76, no. 3–4 (2008): 283–306.

Bieberstedt, Andreas. *Textstructur, Textstrukturvariation, Textstrukturmuster. Lübecker mittelniederdeutsche Testamente des 14. Und 15. Jahrhunderts.* Wien: Praesens Verlag, 2007.

Bieda, Justyna. "Utrata mocy testamentu w świetle ustawodawstwa obowiązującego na ziemiach Królestwa Polskiego." *Studia z Dziejów Państwa i Prawa Polskiego* 10 (2007): 195–203

Bieślarzewska, Małgorzata. "Szlacheckie pożegnanie z życiem. Testamenty z wielkopolskich ksiąg grodzkich z lat 1702–1723." *Genealogia* 18 (2006): 37–97.

Biłous, Natalia. "Testamenty mieszkańców Kijowa z XVI - pierwszej połowy XVII wieku." *KHKM* 58, no. 2 (2010): 245–258.

Biłous, Natalia. *Testamenty mieszkańców miasta Ołyki z lat 1660–1670. KHKM* 59, no. 2 (2011): 347–362.

Bobowski, Bogdan. *Kultura materialna mieszczan Świdnicy i rycerstwa Weichbildu świdnickiego w świetle testamentów (od I połowy XIV do końca I ćwierci XVII wieku).* Zielona Góra: Uniwersytet Zielonogórski, 2011.

Bobowski, Bogdan. "Testament w średniowiecznym prawie polskim." *Zeszyty Historyczne* 10, no. 10 (2009): 83–90.

BIBLIOGRAPHY

Bogdan, Danuta. "Testamenty szlacheckie i mieszczańskie z XVII wieku jako przejaw kultury prawnej Warmii." *Komunikaty Mazursko-Warmińskie* 4 (2004): 463–473.

Bogucka, Maria. "Rodzina w polskim mieście XVI-XVII wieku: wprowadzenie w problematykę." *Przegląd Historyczny* 74, no. 3 (1983): 495–505.

Bogucka, Maria and, Henryk Samsonowicz, *Dzieje miast i mieszczaństwa w Polsce przedrozbiorowej*. Wrocław-Warszawa- Krakow: Zakład Narodowy im. Ossolińskich, 1986.

Bogucka, Maria. "Testament burmistrza gdańskiego Hansa Speymana z 1625 r." In *Kultura średniowieczna i staropolska. Studia ofiarowane Aleksandrowi Gieysztorowi w pięćdziesięciolecie pracy naukowej*, edited by Danuta Gawinowa, 587–597. Warszawa: Państwowe Wydawnictwo Naukowe, 1991.

Boockmann, Hartmut. *Leben und Sterben in einer spätmittelalterlichen Stadt. Über ein Göttinger Testament des 15. Jahrhunderts*. Göttingen: Hartmut Boockmann. Vandenhoeck & Ruprecht, 1983.

Borkowski, Tomasz. "Materialne przejawy codziennej religijności w średniowiecznych miastach śląskich. Drobna gliniana plastyka dewocyjna." *Archaeologia Historica Polona* 7 (1998): 47–54.

Boroda, Krzysztof. *Studenci uniwersytetu krakowskiego w późnym średniowieczu*. Krakow: Avalon, 2010.

Bourdieu, Pierre. *The Logic of Practice*. Cambridge: Cambridge University Press, 1990.

Bourdieu, Pierre. "The Forms of Social Capital." In *Education, Culture, Economy and Society*, eds. A. H. Halsey, Hugh Lauder, Phillip Brown, Amy Stuart Wells, 46–58. Oxford: Oxford University Press, 1997.

Bracha, Krzysztof, ""De ymaginibus sanctorum, quibus utitur ecclesia et cruce" w traktacie De superstitionibus (1444/1445) Jana z Wünschelburga." In *Peregrinationes. Pielgrzymki w kulturze dawnej Europy*, edited by Halina Manikowska and Hanna Zaremska, 64–71. Warszawa: Instytut Historii Polskiej Akademii Nauk, 1995.

Bracha, Krzysztof. *Nauczanie kaznodziejskie w Polsce późnego średniowiecza*. Kielce: Wydawnictwo Akademii Świętokrzyskiej w Kielcach, 2007.

Brown, Andrew. *Civic Ceremony and Religion in Medieval Bruges c. 1300–1520*. Cambridge: Cambridge University Press, 2011.

Bukowska, Krystyna. *Orzecznictwo krakowskich sądów wyższych w sporach o nieruchomości miejskie (XVI-XVIII w.)*. Warszawa: Państwowe Wydawnictwo Naukowe, 1997.

Burges, Clive. "'By Quick and by Dead': wills and pious provision in late medieval Bristol." *The English Historical Review* 102, no. 405 (1987): 837–858.

Burke, Peter. *Popular Culture in Early Modern Europe*. Aldershot: Ashgate Publishing House, 2009.

Burszta, Józef. "Społeczeństwo daru i dar w społeczeństwie." In *Do, ut des – dar, pochówek, tradycja*, edited by Wojciech Dzieduszycki and, Jacek Wrzesiński, 17–24. Poznań: SNAP Oddział, 2005.

BIBLIOGRAPHY

Buss, Harm. *Letztwillige Verfügungen nach ostfriesischen Recht*. Göttingen: Verlag Ostfriesische Landschaft, 1963.

Bylina, Stanisław. *Człowiek i zaświaty. Wizje kar pośmiertnych w Polsce średniowiecznej*. Warszawa: Instytut Historii PAN, 1992.

Bylina, Stanisław. "Jednostka i zbiorowość w pobożności ludowej Europy środkowowschodniej w późnym średniowieczu." In *Człowiek w społeczeństwie średniowiecznym*, edited by Roman Michałowski, 119–134. Warszawa: DiG, 1997.

Bylina, Stanisław. "Religijność mieszkańców Europy Środkowo-Wschodniej w późnym średniowieczu." In *Cywilizacja Europejska. Wykłady i eseje*, edited by Maciej Koźmiński, 103–120. Warszawa: Instytut Historii PAN, 2005.

Bylina, Stanisław. *Religijność późnego średniowiecza. Chrześcijaństwo a kultura tradycyjna w Europie środkowo-wschodniej w XIV-XV w.* Warszawa: Neriton, 2009.

Bylina, Stanisław. "Spowiedź jako instrument katechezy i nauki współżycia społecznego w Polsce późnego średniowiecza." In *Społeczeństwo Polski średniowiecznej 5*, edited by Stefan Krzysztof Kuczyński, 255–265. Warszawa: Państwowe Wydawnictwo Naukowe, 1992.

Chaunu, Pierre. *Le temps des Réformes: histoire religieuse et système de civilisation: la crise de la chrétienté: l'éclatement, 1250–1550*, Paris: Fayard, 1975.

Chiffoleau, Jacques. *La comptabilite de l'audela: les hommes, la mort et la religion dans la region d'Avignon a la fin du Moyen Age (vers 1320 - vers 1480)*. Rome: École française de Rome, 1980.

Cieślak, Edmund. *Walki ustrojowe w Gdańsku i Toruniu oraz niektórych miastach hanzeatyckich w XV w.* Gdańsk: Gdańskie Towarz. Nauk, 1960.

Cieślak, Katarzyna. *Między Rzymem, Wittenbergą a Genewą. Sztuka Gdańska jako miasta podzielonego wyznaniowo*, Wrocław: Fundacja na Rzecz Nauki Polskiej, 2000.

Cohn, Samuel Kline. *The Cult of Remembrance and the Black Death: Six Renaissance Cities in Central Italy*. Baltimore: Johns Hopkins University Press, 1992.

Czacharowski, Antoni. "Ze studiów nad strukturą społeczną mieszczaństwa toruńskiego na przełomie XIV/XV wieku." *Acta Universitatis Nicolai Copernici: Historia 9* (1973): 89–96.

Czaja, Roman. *Grupy rządzące w miastach nadbałtyckich w średniowieczu*. Toruń: Wydawnictwo Naukowe Uniwersytetu Mikołaja Kopernika, 2008.

Czaja, Roman. *Socjotopografia miasta Elbląga w średniowieczu*. Toruń: Wydawnictwo Adam Marszałek, 1992.

Czaja, Roman. "Społeczna mobilność jako paradygmat badań nad patrycjatem i grupami kierowniczymi w średniowieczu." In *Elita władzy miasta Krakowa i jej związki z miastami Europy w średniowieczu i epoce nowożytnej (do połowy XVII wieku). Zbiór studiów*, edited by Zdzisław Noga, 9–21. Krakow: Antykwa, 2011.

BIBLIOGRAPHY 375

Czaja, Roman. "Spór cechów chełmińskich z radą miejską. Przyczynek do konfliktów społecznych w miastach pruskich w średniowieczu." In *Prusy – Polska – Europa. Studia z dziejów średniowiecza i czasów wczesnonowożytnych. Prace ofiarowane Zenonowi Hubertowi Nowakowi w sześćdziesiątą piątą rocznicę urodzin i czterdziestolecie pracy naukowej*, edited by Andrzej Radzimiński, Janusz Tandecki, 327–337. Toruń: Wydawn. Uniw. Mikołaja Kopernika, 1999,

Czaja, Roman. "Tożsamość mieszczaństwa hanzeatyckiego w średniowieczu." In *Aetas Media Aetas Moderna. Studia ofiarowane profesorowi Henrykowi Samsonowiczowi w siedemdziesiątą rocznicę urodzin*, edited by Agnieszka Bartoszewicz, Wojciech Fałkowski, Halina Manikowska, Antoni Mączak, Karol Modzelewski, 182–191. Warszawa: Instytut Historyczny Uniwersytetu Warszawskiego, 2000.

Czyżewski, Krzysztof J. "'Siądź mi po boku prawym.' O zasiadaniu w kościele słów kilka." In *Mecenat artystyczny a oblicze miasta. Materiały LVI Ogólnopolskiej Sesji Naukowej Stowarzyszenia Historyków Sztuki, Krakow 8–10 XI 2007*, edited by Dariusz Nowacki, 57–76. Krakow: Stowarzyszenie Historyków Sztuki. Oddział Krakowski, 2008.

Dąbkowski, Przemysław. *Prawo prywatne polskie*, vol. 2. Lwów: Drukarnia Uniwersytetu Jagiellońskiego, 1911.

Dąbrowski, Jan. "Krakow a Węgry w wiekach średnich." *Rocznik Krakowski* 13 (1911): 187–250.

Dean, Trevor. *The Towns of Italy in the Later Middle Ages*. Manchester: Manchester University Press, 2000.

Dekker, Rudolf. "Jacques Presser's Heritage: Egodocuments in the Study of History." *Memoria y Civilización* 5 (2002): 13–37.

Delimata, Małgorzata. *Dziecko w Polsce średniowiecznej*. Poznań: Wydawn. Poznańskie, 2004.

Delumeau, Jean, *Wyznanie i przebaczenie*, trans. Maryna Ochab. Gdańsk: Marabut, 1997. (J. Delumeau, *L'aveu et le pardon: Les difficultés de la confession, XIIIe-XVIIIe siècle*, Fayard 2014)

Dembska, Róża. "O testamencie w polskim prawie średniowiecznym." In *Studia z historii ustroju i prawa. Księga dedykowana profesorowi Jerzemu Walachowiczowi*, edited by Henryk Olszewski, 57–71. Poznań: Printer, 2002.

Denecke, Dietrich. Sozialtopographie und sozialräumliche Gliederung der spätmittelalterlichen Stadt." In *Über Bürger, Stadt und stadtische Literatur im Spätmittelalter*, edited by Josef Fleckenstein, Karl Stackmann. Göttingen: Vandenhoeck & Ruprecht, 1980.

Derwich, Marek. "Zakonnicy a rozwój religijności na ziemiach polskich." In *Animarum cultura. Studia nad kulturą religijną na ziemiach polskich w średniowieczu*, vol. 1: *Struktury kościelno-publiczne*, edited by Halina Manikowska, Wojciech Brojer, 329–352. Warszawa: Instytut Historii PAN, 2008.

Derwich, Marek. "Mnisi w polskim mieście średniowiecznym." In *Ecclesia et civitas. Kościół i życie religijne w mieście średniowiecznym*, edited by Halina Manikowska, Hanna Zaremska, 143–160. Warszawa: Instytut Historii PAN, 2002.

Długołęcki, Wiesław. *Elita władzy miasta Malborka w średniowieczu*. Malbork: Malbork Muzeum Zamkowe w Malborku, 2004.

Dobrowolski, Paweł T. *Wincenty Ferrer kaznodzieja ludowy późnego średniowiecza*. Warszawa: Instytut Historii PAN, 1996.

Dowiat, Jerzy. "Normy postępowania i wzory osobowe." In *Kultura polski średniowiecznej X-XIII w.*, edited by Jerzy Dowiat, 301–374. Warszawa: Państwowy Instytut Wydawniczy, 1985.

Dowiat, Jerzy. "Pogląd na świat." In *Kultura Polski średniowiecznej X-XIII w.*, edited by Jerzy Dowiat, 169–192. Warszawa: Państwowy Instytut Wydawniczy, 1985.

Drabina, Jerzy. *Wierzenia, religie, wspólnoty wyznaniowe w średniowiecznej Polsce i na Litwie i ich koegzystencja*. Krakow: Nakł. Uniwersytetu Jagiellońskiego, 1994.

Duffy, Eamon. *The Stripping of the Altars: Traditional Religion in England, 1400–1580*. New Haven, London: Yale University Press, 2005.

Dumanowski, Jarosław. "'Pompa funebris?' Z testamentów szlachty wielkopolskiej XVIII w." In *Wesela, chrzciny i pogrzeby w XVI – XVIII wieku. Kultura życia i śmierci*, edited by Henryk Suchojad, 315–322. Warszawa: Semper, 2001.

Dumanowski, Jarosław. "Torunianin z wyboru. Z testamentu biskupa Stanisława Dąbskiego." *Rocznik Toruński* 26 (1999): 91–105.

Ehrhardt, Rafael. *Familie und Memoria in der Stadt. Eine Fallstudie zu Lübeck im Spätmittelalter*. PhD diss., Georg-August-Universität Göttingen, 2001.

Elias, Norbert. *Przemiany obyczajów w cywilizacji Zachodu*, trans. Tadeusz Zabłudowski, Warszawa: Państwowy Instytut Wydawniczy, 1980.

Epstein, Steven. *Wills and Wealth in Medieval Genoa, 1150–1250*. Cambridge (Mass.), London: Harvard University Press, 1984.

Fischer, Stanisław. *Dzieje bocheńskiej żupy solnej*. Warszawa: Wydawnictwo Geologiczne, 1962.

Fulbrook, Mary and, Ulinka Rublack. "In Relation: The 'Social Self' and Ego-Documents." *German History* 28 no. 3 (2010): 263–272.

Frank, Thomas. "Confraternities, Memoria, and Law in Late Medieval Italy." *Confraternitas* 17, no. 1 (2006): 1–19.

French, Katherine L. "Loving Friends. Surviving Widowhood in Late Medieval Westminster." *Gender & History* 22 no. 1 (2010): 21–37.

Friedberg, Marjan. "Ołtarz krakowski Wita Stwosza. Studium archiwalne." *Przegląd Zachodni* 8, no. 7/8 (1952): 673–706.

Friedberg, Marjan. "Założenie i początkowe dzieje kościoła N. Panny Marji w Krakowie (XIII-XV w.)." *Rocznik Krakowski* 22 (1929): 1–31.

BIBLIOGRAPHY

Schultz, Gabriele. *Testamente des späten Mittelalters aus dem Mittelrheingebiet. Eine Untersuchung in rechts- und kulturgeschichtlicher Hinsicht.* Mainz: Selbstverlag der Gesellschaft für Mittelrheinische Kirchengeschichte, 1976.

Garbacik, Józef. "Gotfryd Fattinante." PSB 6 (1948): 377–378.

Gąsiorowski, Antoni. "Ludność napływowa w strukturze społecznej późnośredniowiecznego Poznania." *Studia i Materiały do Dziejów Wielkopolski i Pomorza* 11, no. 2 (1975): 11–25.

Gąsiorowski, Antoni. "O mieszczanach studiujących na Uniwersytecie Krakowskim w XV wieku." In *Aetas Media Aetas Moderna. Studia ofiarowane profesorowi Henrykowi Samsonowiczowi w siedemdziesiątą rocznicę urodzin,* edited by Agnieszka Bartoszewicz, Wojciech Fałkowski, Halina Manikowska, Antoni Mączak, Karol Modzelewski, 653–663. Warszawa: Instytut Historyczny UW, 2000.

Gąsiorowski, Antoni. "Skąd pochodził krakowski pisarz miejski Mikołaj Jaskier?" In *Miasta, ludzie, instytucje, znaki. Księga jubileuszowa ofiarowana Profesor Bożenie Wyrozumskiej w 75. rocznicę urodzin,* edited by Zenon Piech, 361–367. Krakow: Towarzystwo Naukowe Societas Vistulana, 2008.

Gąsiorowski, Antoni. "Walki o władzę w Poznaniu u schyłku wieków średnich." *Kwartalnik Historyczny* 82, no. 2 (1975): 255–266.

Geremek, Bronisław. *Litość i szubienica. Dzieje nędzy i miłosierdzia.* Warszawa: Czytelnik, 1989.

Gierszewski, Stanisław. *Obywatele miast Polski przedrozbiorowej.* Warszawa: Państwowe Wydawn. Naukowe, 1973.

Głowacka-Penczyńska, Anetta, "Testamenty mieszkańców małych miast wielkopolskich z XVII w." KHKM 59, no. 2 (2011): 381–394.

Główka Dariusz, "Legaty pieniężne i rzeczowe na rzecz instytucji kościelnych w testamentach duchownych z diecezji płockiej w XVII w." KHKM 59, no. 2 (2011): 409–414.

Główka, Dariusz. *Majątek osobisty duchowieństwa katolickiego w Koronie w XVII i XVIII wieku.* Warszawa: Wydawnictwo Instytutu Archeologii i Etnologii PAN, 2004.

Główka, Dariusz. "Między prawem i konwencją a osobistą refleksją. Ze studiów nad testamentami duchowieństwa diecezji płockiej w XVII i XVIII w." KHKM 58, no. 2 (2010): 259–266.

Główka, Dariusz. "Podstawy prawne testamentów i inwentarzy pośmiertnych duchowieństwa katolickiego w Polsce w epoce potrydenckiej." *Archeologia Historica Polona* 5 (1997): 203–210.

Główka, Jan. "Testamenty mieszczan kieleckich z końca XVIII w. zwierciadłem epoki (w świetle księgi rady miejskiej Kielc 1789–1792)." In *Wesela, chrzciny i pogrzeby w XVI-XVIII wieku. Kultura życia i śmierci,* edited by Henryk Suchojad, 323–332. Warszawa: Semper, 2001.

Goliński, Mateusz. "Relacje patrycjatu krakowskiego z Wrocławiem w średniowieczu." In *Elita władzy miasta Krakowa i jej związki z miastami Europy w średniowieczu i epoce nowożytnej (do połowy XVII wieku). Zbiór studiów*, edited by Zdzisław Noga, 33–47. Krakow: Antykwa, 2011.

Goliński, Mateusz. *Socjotopografia późnośredniowiecznego Wrocławia*. Wrocław: Wydawnictwo Uniwersytetu Wrocławskiego, 1997.

Gołąb, Marcin. "Testament Stanisława Tarnowskiego, pisarza żup wielickich." *KHKM* 59, no. 2 (2011): 327–332

Goody, Jack. *The development of the family and marriage in Europe*, Cambridge: Cambridge University Press, 1983.

Goody, Jack. *The Logic of Writing and the Organisation of Society*, Cambridge: Cambridge University Press, 1986.

Górny, Marek. "W sprawie badania rodziny staropolskiej na podstawie testamentów." *Studia Historyczne* 30, no. 3 (1987): 487–494.

Grabowski, Ambroży. *Krakow i jego okolice*. Krakow 1866.

Grace, Philip. "Family and familiars. The concentric household in late medieval penitentiary petitions." *Journal of Medieval History* 35 (2009): 189–203.

von Greyerz, Kaspar. "Ego-Documents: The Last Word?" *German History* 28, no. 3 (2010): 273–282.

Grzelczak-Miłoś, Iwona. *Mieszczaństwo poznańskie w świetle Libri testamentorum*. PhD Diss. Poznań: Uniwersytet Adama Mickiewicza, 2011.

Gurevich, Aron J. *The Origins of European Individualism*. Oxford: Oxford University Press, 1995.

Gurewich, Aron J. "Kultura elitarna i kultura ludowa w średniowiecznej Europie." In *Biedni i bogaci. Studia z dziejów społeczeństwa i kultury ofiarowane Bronisławowi Geremkowi w sześćdziesiątą rocznicę urodzin*, edited by Maurice Aymard, 207–212. Warszawa: Wydawn. Nauk. PWN, 1992.

Gurevich, Aron J. "Kupiec." In *Człowiek średniowiecza*, edited by Jacques Le Goff, 305–351. Warszawa-Gdańsk: Świat Książki, 1996. (Aron J. Gurevich, *Le Marchand*, "L'Homme medieval," ed. Jacques Le Goff, Seuil 1989)

Gurevich, Aron J. *Kultura i społeczeństwo średniowiecznej Europy. Exempla XIII wieku*. Warszawa: Oficyna Wydawnicza Volumen, 1997.

Guzzetti, Linda. *Venezianische Vermächtnisse, Die soziale und wirtschaftliche Situation von Frauen im Spiegel spätmittelalterlichen Testamente*. Weimar: Verlag J. B. Metzler, 1998.

Hanawalt, Barbara A. *The Wealth of Wives. Women, Law, and Economy in Late Medieval London*. Oxford: Oxford University Press, 2007.

Hedemann, Otton. *Testamenty brasławsko-dziśnieńskie XVII-XVIII wieku jako źródło historyczne*. Wilno: Księgarnia św. Wojciecha, 1935.

BIBLIOGRAPHY

Helmholz, Richard H. "Marriage Contracts in Medieval England." In *To Have and to Hold. Marrying and Its Documentation in Western Christendom, 400–1600*, edited by Philip L. Reynolds, John Witte, 260–286. Cambridge: Cambridge University Press, 2007.

Herbst, Stanisław. *Toruńskie cechy rzemieślnicze: zarys przeszłości*. Toruń: Nakładem Cechów toruńskich, 1933.

Hledíková, Zdeňka. "Charakter i przejawy religijności mieszczaństwa praskiego na przełomie XIV i XV w." In *Ecclesia et civitas. Kościół i życie religijne w mieście średniowiecznym*, edited by Halina Manikowska, Hanna Zaremska, 297–314. Warszawa: Instytut Historii PAN, 2002.

Hoffman, Walter. "Deutsch und Latein im spätmittelalterlichen Köln. Zur äußeren Sprachgeschichte des Kölner Geschäftsschriftums im 14. Jahrhundert." *Rheinsche Vierteljaharblätter* 44 (1980): 117–147.

Hołdys, Sybilla. "Więzi rodzinne w świetle mieszczańskich testamentów z pierwszej połowy XVII wieku." *Studia Historyczne* 29, no. 3 (1986): 347–357.

Houlbrooke, Ralph A. *Death, Religion, and the Family in England 1480–1750*. Oxford: Oxford University Press, 1998.

Huckstadt, Gerhard. *Der Testamentvollstrecker im deutschen Recht des Mittelalters*. PhD diss., Kiel, 1971.

Hughes, Diane Owen. "Urban Growth and Family Structure in Medieval Genoa." *Past & Present* 66 (1975): 3–28.

Huizinga, Johan. *The Autumn of the Middle Ages*, trans. Rodney Payton, Ulrich. Mammitzsch, Chicago: University of Chicago Press, 1996.

Huszał, Grzegorz. "Przygotowanie do śmierci w XVII w." *Roczniki Humanistyczne* 31, no. 2 (1983): 105–150.

Jaritz, Gerhard. "Osterreichische Burgertestamente als Quelle zur Erforschung stadtischer Lebensformen des Spatmittelalters." *Jahrbuch für Geschichte des Feudalismus* 8 (1984): 249–264.

Jasiński, Kazimierz. "Kielich płocki z pateną – dar księcia mazowieckiego Konrada I." In Człowiek w społeczeństwie średniowiecznym." Edited by Roman Michałowski, 283–298. Warszawa: DiG, 1997.

Jasiński, Tomasz. "Z zagadnień topografii społecznej średniowiecznego Torunia, vol. 1: Stare Miasto." *Zapiski Historyczne*, 48, no. 3 (1983): 5–47.

Jišová, Kateřina. "Charita, milosrdenstvi a spása duše v pozdně středověké Praze." In *Kaci, Święci, Templariusze*, edited by Błażej Śliwiński, 139–190. Malbork: Muzeum Zamkowe, 2008.

Jišová, Kateřina. "Die Testamente der Elite von Krakau und Prag im Spätmittelalter." In *Elita władzy miasta Krakowa i jej związki z miastami Europy w średniowieczu i epoce nowożytnej (do połowy XVII wieku). Zbiór studiów*, edited by Zdzisław Noga, 447–459. Krakow: Antykwa, 2011.

Jišová, Kateřina. *Religiozita novoměstského měšťanstva ve druhé polovině 15. století.* PhD diss., Univerzita Karlova, 2008.

Jišová Kateřina, "Testamenty pražských měšťanů v pozdním středověku. Religiozita, sociální rozvrstvení, majetkové a rodinné poměry novoměstských měšťanů (1421–1533)." In *Pierwsze polsko-czeskie forum młodych mediewistów. Materiały z konferencji naukowej, Gniezno 27–29 września 2005 r.*, edited by Józef Dobosz, 295–309. Poznań: Instytut Historii UAM, 2007.

Jones, Neil G. "Wills, Trusts and Trusting from the Statute of Uses to Lord Nottingham." The *Journal of Legal History* 31, no. 3 (2010): 273–298.

Jurek, Tomasz. "Pismo w życiu społecznym Polski późnego średniowiecza." In *Historia społeczna późnego średniowiecza. Nowe badania,* edited by Sławomir Gawlas, 203–232. Warszawa: DiG, 2011.

Justyniarska-Chojak, Katarzyna. "Spadkobranie w rodzinach mieszczańskich lewobrzeżnej części województwa sandomierskiego w XVII wieku." In *Rodzina i gospodarstwo domowe na ziemiach polskich w XV-XX wieku. Struktury demograficzne, społeczne i gospodarcze,* edited by Cezary Kuklo, 283–294. Warszawa: DiG, 2008.

Justyniarska-Chojak, Katarzyna. *Testamenty i inwentarze pośmiertne z ksiąg miejskich województwa sandomierskiego (XVI-XVIII wiek).* Kielce: Wydaw. Uniwersytetu Humanistyczno-Przyrodniczego Jana Kochanowskiego, 2010.

Justyniarska-Chojak, Katarzyna. *Testamenty mieszkańców Krzyżanowic z XVI-XVIII wieku,* in *Między Wisłą a Pilicą. Studia i materiały historyczne,* edited by Beata Wojciechowska, Lidia Michalska, Krzysztof Bracha, vol. 3, 327–340. Kielce: Wyższa Szkoła Pedagogiczna im. Jana Kochanowskiego, 2002.

Justyniarska-Chojak, Katarzyna. "Wydziedziczenie w testamentach mieszczańskich z województwa sandomierskiego (w XVI-XVIII wieku)." *Almanach Historyczny* 11 (2009): 17–20.

Kaliszuk, Jerzy. "Przemiany społecznych funkcji pisma w późnym średniowieczu. Programy badawcze i ich rezultaty." In *Historia społeczna późnego średniowiecza. Nowe badania,* edited by Sławomir Gawlas, 169–188. Warszawa: DiG, 2011.

Kamińska, Krystyna. "Summa Rajmunda Partenopejczyka jako zabytek średniowiecznego prawa polskiego." *Czasopismo Prawno-Historyczne* 26, no. 1 (1974): 147–157.

Kamiński, Adam. "Jerzy Morsztyn (rajca)." PSB 21 (1976): 817.

Kamiński, Adam. "Jerzy Morsztyn (żupnik)." PSB 21 (1976): 816–817.

Kapral, Miron. "Kontakty patrycjatu krakowskiego i lwowskiego w średniowieczu i w epoce nowożytnej (XV-XVI wiek)." In *Elita władzy miasta Krakowa i jej związki z miastami Europy w średniowieczu i epoce nowożytnej (do połowy XVII wieku). Zbiór studiów,* edited by Zdzisław Noga, 201–219. Krakow: Antykwa, 2011.

Kaps, Johannes. Das Testamentsrecht der Weltgeistlichen und Ordenspersonen in Rechtsgeschichte, Kirchenrecht und Bürgerlichem Recht Deutschlands, Österreichs und der Schweiz. München: Verlag Christ Unterwegs, 1958.

BIBLIOGRAPHY

Karczewski, Dariusz. "Miejsce krakowskiego klasztoru franciszkanów w strukturze czesko-polskiej prowincji zakonnej." In *Mendykanci w średniowiecznym Krakowie*, edited by Krzysztof Ożóg, Tomasz Gałuszka, Anna Zajchowska, 83–96. Krakow: Esprit, 2008.

Karpiński, Andrzej. *Kobieta w mieście polskim w drugiej połowie XVI i w XVII wieku.* Warszawa: Instytut Historii PAN, 1995.

Karpiński, Andrzej. *Pauperes. O mieszkańcach Warszawy XVI i XVII wieku.* Warszawa: Państwowe Wydawnictwo Naukowe, 1983.

Karpiński, Andrzej. *W walce z niewidzialnym wrogiem. Epidemie chorób zakaźnych w Rzeczypospolitej w XVI-XVIII wieku i ich następstwa demograficzne, społeczno-ekonomiczne i polityczne.* Warszawa: Neriton, 2000.

Karpiński, Andrzej. "Zapisy pobożne i postawy religijne mieszczanek polskich w świetle testamentów z drugiej połowy XVI i XVII wieku." In *Tryumfy i porażki. Studia z dziejów kultury polskiej XVI-XVIII wieku*, edited by Maria Bogucka, 204–233. Warszawa: Państwowe Wydawnictwo Naukowe, 1989.

Karpiński, Andrzej. *Dobroczynne i religijne legaty lwowskich mieszczan w świetle ich testamentów z lat 1550–1700, KHKM* 59, no. 2 (2011): 363–381.

Kętrzyński, Stanisław. *Zarys nauki o dokumencie polskim wieków średnich.* Poznań: Wydawnictwo Poznańskie, 2008.

Kiryk, Feliks. "Etos pracy (podstawy gospodarcze formowania się Krakowa lokacyjnego 1257–1333)." In *Krakow – dziedzictwo lokacji. Materiały sesji naukowej odbytej 21 kwietnia 2007 roku*, edited by Jan M. Małecki, 51–73. Krakow: Towarzystwo Miłośników Historii i Zabytków Krakowa, 2008.

Kiryk, Feliks. "Migracje z miast małopolskich do elity władzy Krakowa w XIV-XVI wieku." In *Elita władzy miasta Krakowa i jej związki z miastami Europy w średniowieczu i epoce nowożytnej (do połowy XVII wieku). Zbiór studiów*, edited by Zdzisław Noga, 181–190. Krakow: Antykwa, 2011.

Kiryk, Feliks. "Porządek cechowy w lokacyjnym Krakowie." In *Krakow. Studia z dziejów miasta*, edited by Jerzy Rajman, 76–86. Krakow: Wydawn. Nauk. Akademii Pedagogicznej, 2007.

Kiryk, Feliks. "Zarys dziejów osadnictwa." In *Dzieje Olkusza i regionu olkuskiego*, vol. 1, edited by Feliks Kiryk, Ryszard Kołodziejczyk, 41–142. Warszawa: Państwowe Wydawnictwo Naukowe, 1978.

Kiryk, Feliks. "Związki Krakowa z Lwowem w późnym średniowieczu." In *Lwów. Miasto, społeczeństwo, kultura*, vol. II, edited by Henryk W. Żaliński, Kazimierz Karolczak, 9–39. Krakow: Wydawnictwo Naukowe Wyższej Szkoły Pedagogicznej, 1998.

Kittell, Ellen E., "Testaments of two cities: A comparative analysis of the wills of medieval Genoa and Douai." *European Review of History* 5, no. 1 (1998), 47–84.

Klimecka, Grażyna. "Model społeczeństwa w retorykach uniwersyteckich." In *Społeczeństwo Polski średniowiecznej*, vol. 8, edited by Stefan Krzysztof Kuczyński, 255–268. Warszawa: Państwowe Wydawnictwo Naukowe, 1999.

Klint, Paweł. "Testament Zofii ze Smoszowskich Pogorzelskiej z 1658 roku." *Genealogia. Studia i Materiały Historyczne,* 13 (2001): 117–128.

Klint, Paweł. *Testamenty szlacheckie z ksiąg grodzkich wielkopolskich 1657–1680.* Wrocław: Wydawnictwo Uniwersytetu Wrocławskiego, 2012.

Klonder, Andrzej. "Koszty pogrzebu w testamentach oraz inwentarzach pośmiertnych mieszczan w dawnej Rzeczypospolitej." *KHKM* 59, no. 2 (2011): 415–422.

Klonder, Andrzej. *Wszystka spuścizna w Bogu spoczywającego. Majątek ruchomy zwykłych mieszkańców Elbląga i Gdańska w XVII wieku,* Warszawa: Wydawnictwo Instytutu Archeologii i Etnologii PAN, 2000.

Klosterberg, Brigitte. *Zur Ehre Gottes und zum Wohl der Familie – Kölner Testamente von Laien und Kleriken im Spätmittelalter.* Köln: SH-Verlag, 1995.

Kłoczowski, Jerzy. *Wspólnoty zakonne w średniowiecznej Polsce,* Lublin: Wydawnictwo KUL, 2010.

Koczerska, Maria. "Testamenty kanonika tarnowskiego i plebana Wszystkich Świętych w Krakowie." In *Ludzie, kościół, wierzenia. Studia z dziejów kultury i społeczeństwa Europy Środkowej (średniowiecze – wczesna epoka nowożytna),* edited by Wojciech Iwańczak, 237–254. Warszawa: DiG, 2001.

Koczerska, Maria. "Związki kanoników katedry krakowskiej z mieszczaństwem Krakowa w XV w." In *Ecclesia et civitas. Kościół i życie religijne w mieście średniowiecznym,* edited by Halina Manikowska, Hanna Zaremska, 161–174. Warszawa: Instytut Historii PAN, 2002.

Kolańczyk, Kazimierz. "Studia nad reliktami wspólnej własności ziemi w najdawniejszej Polsce. Rozporządzenia własnością ziemską do końca XIV wieku." In *Studia nad historią prawa polskiego* 20, no. 2 (1950): 125–150.

Kolmer, Lothar. "Spatmittelalterliche Regensburger testamente. Forschungsergebnisse und Forschungsziele. Regensburger Testamente im Vergleich." *Zeitschrift für Bayerische Landesgeschichte* 52 (1989): 475–500.

Koranyi, Karol. "Podstawy średniowiecznego prawa spadkowego." *Pamiętnik Historyczno-Prawny* 9, no. 2 (1930): 165–520.

Korpiola, Mia and, Anu Lahtinen, "Introduction." In *Planning for Death. Wills and Death-Related Property Arrangements in Europe, 1200–1600,* edited by Mia Korpiola, Anu Lahtinen, Leiden: Brill 2018.

Kowalczyk, Maria. "Testament biskupa krakowskiego Floriana z Mokrska." *Studia Źródłoznawcze* 41 (2003): 65–70.

Kowalska, Magdalena. "Psychologiczna (prze)moc wzajemności." In *Do, ut des – dar, pochówek, tradycja,* edited by Wojciech Dzieduszycki, Jacek Wrzesiński, 43–46. Poznań: SNAP Oddział, 2005.

BIBLIOGRAPHY

Kowalski, Marek D. "Piętnastowieczne statuty kapituły katedralnej w Krakowie." In *Polska i jej sąsiedzi w późnym średniowieczu*, edited by Krzysztof Ożóg, Stanisław Szczur, 233–253. Krakow: Towarzystwo Naukowe Societas Vistulana, 2000.

Kowalski, Waldemar. "Testament daleszyckiego rajcy z 1637 roku." *Studia Kieleckie* 45, no. 1 (1985): 129–135.

Krakowski, Stefan. "Mieszczanie *Częstochowy w* XVII wieku *w* świetle testamentów." *Ziemia* Częstochowska 5 (1965): 115–125.

Kras, Paweł. *Husyci w piętnastowiecznej Polsce*. Lublin: Towarzystwo Naukowe Katolickiego Uniwersytetu Lubelskiego, 1998.

Krasnowolski, Bogusław. "Lokacje i rozwój Krakowa, Kazimierza i Okołu. Problematyka rozwiązań urbanistycznych." In *Krakow. Nowe studia nad rozwojem miasta*, edited by Jerzy Wyrozumski, 355–426. Krakow: Tow. Miłośników Historii i Zabytków Krakowa, 2007.

Krochmal, Jacek. "Przemyskie testamenty staropolskie." *Rocznik Historyczno-Archiwalny* 6 (1989): 133–160.

Krzenck, Thomas. *Böhmische Bürgertestamente des 15. Jahrhunderts. Das Beispiel der Prager Neustadt*, in *Husitví Reformace Renesance. Sborník k 60. Narozeninám Františka Šmahela*, ed. Jaroslav Pánek, Miroslav Polívka, Noemi Rejchrtová, Praha 1994, 627–648.

Krzenck Thomas, "Pražské a vídenské testamenty pozdního středovĕku - pokus o komparaci." In *Pozdnĕ středovĕké testamenty v českých mĕstech. Prameny, metodologie a formy využití. Sbornik příspĕvků z konference uspořádané 30. listopadu 2005 Archivem hlavního mĕsta Prahy a Historickým ústavem Akademie vĕd České republiky*, edited by Kateřina Jíšová, Eva Doležalová, 87 -94. Praha: Scriptorium, 2006.

Kubicki, Rafał. "Kultura materialna w testamentach elbląskich z XV-początku XVI w." *KHKM* 58, no. 2 (2010): 197–210.

Kubicki, Rafał. "Testamenty elbląskie z XIV - początków XVI w. Charakterystyka wraz z listą testatorów w układzie chronologicznym." *Rocznik Elbląski* 20 (2006): 199–208.

Kurtyka, Janusz. *Tęczyńscy. Studium z dziejów polskiej elity możnowładczej w średniowieczu*. Krakow: Secesja, 1997.

Kutrzeba, Stanisław. *Finanse i handel średniowiecznego Krakowa*, edited by Marcin Starzyński, Krakow: Wydawnictwo Avalon, 2009.

Kutrzeba, Stanisław and, Jan Ptaśnik. "Dzieje handlu i kupiectwa krakowskiego." *Rocznik Krakowski* 14 (1910).

Laberschek, Jacek. "Mikołaj Strzelicz." PSB 45 (2007): 16–17.

Laberschek, Jacek. "Mikołaj z Zawichostu." PSB 21 (1976): 152.

Le Goff, Jacques. *Money and the Middle Ages*. Cambridge: Cambridge University Press, 2012.

Lee, Robert. "Early Death and Long Life in History: Establishing the Scale of Premature Death in Europe and its Cultural, Economic and Social Significance." *Historical Social Research* 34, no. 4 (2009): 23–60.

Lentze, Hans. "Das Wiener Testamentsrecht des Mittelalters." *Zeitschrift der Savigny-Stiftung für Rechtsgeschichte, Germanische Abteilung* 69/70 (1952/1953): 98–154/159–229.

Loening, Otto. *Das Testament im Gebiet des Magdeburger Stadtrechtes*, Breslau: M&G Marcus, 1906.

Loose, Hans-Dieter. *Hamburger Testamente, 1351 bis 1400. Veröffentlichungen aus dem Staatsarchiv der Freien und Hansestadt Hamburg.* Hamburg: Christians, 1970.

Lowe, Nicola A. "Women's Devotional Bequests of Textiles in the Late Medieval English Parish Church, c. 1350–1550." *Gender & History* 22 no. 2 (2010): 407–429.

Łosowska, Anna. *Kolekcja "Liber legum" i jej miejsce w kulturze umysłowej późnośredniowiecznego Przemyśla.* Warszawa–Przemyśl: Archiwum Państwowe, Przemyśl; Naczelna Dyrekcja Archiwów Państwowych, 2007.

Łysiak, Ludwik. "Statuty Kazimierza Wielkiego w małopolskiej praktyce sądowej XV wieku, *Studia Historyczne*, 19, 1976, no. 1, 25–39.

Maine, Henry Sumner. *Ancient Law*, London: Oxford University Press, (1861) 1931.

Maisel, Witold. Poznański rękopis Summy Rajmunda Partenopejczyka, *Czasopismo Prawno-Historyczne* 12, no.2 (1960): 135–149.

Maisel, Witold. *Sądownictwo miasta Poznania do końca XVI w.* Poznań: Państwowe Wydawnictwo Naukowe, 1961.

Majorossy, Judit. "Archives of the Dead: Administration of Las Wills in Medieval Hungarian Towns." *Medium Aevum Quotidianum* 48 (2003): 13–28.

Majorossy, Judit. *Church in Town: Urban Religious Life in Late Medieval Pressburg in the Mirror of Las Wills*, PhD diss. Central European University, 1997.

Manikowska, Halina. *Jerozolima-Rzym-Compostela. Wielkie pielgrzymowanie u schyłku średniowiecza.* Wrocław: Wydawnictwo Uniwersytetu Wrocławskiego, 2008.

Manikowska, Halina. "Klasztor żeński w mieście średniowiecznym." *Roczniki Dziejów Społecznych i Gospodarczych* 42 (2002), 7–46.

Manikowska, Halina. "Religijność miejska." In *Ecclesia et civitas. Kościół i życie religijne w mieście średniowiecznym*, edited by Halina Manikowska, Hanna Zaremska, 11–37. Warszawa: Instytut Historii PAN, 2002.

Manikowska, Halina. "Wpływ środowiska uniwersyteckiego na kulturę religijną w modelu recepcji kultury." In *Animarum cultura. Studia nad kulturą religijną na ziemiach polskich w średniowieczu*, vol. 1: *Struktury kościelno-publiczne*, edited by Halina Manikowska, Wojciech Brojer, 441–458. Warszawa: Instytut Historii PAN, 2008.

Marriage, Property and Succession, edited by Lloyd Bonfield. Berlin: Duncker & Humblot, 1992.

Marquardt, Uta. "Görlitzer Testamente des 16. Jahrhunderts als Quelle sozialgeschichtlicher Untersuchungen." *Neues Lausitzisches Magazin* 123, no.4 (2001): 35–55.

Materielle Kultur und Religiöse stiftung im Spätmittelalter. Internationales Round-Table-Gespräch Krems an der Donau, 26 September 1988, edited by Jaritz Gerhard. Wien: Verlag der österreichischen Akademie der Wissenschaften, 1990.

BIBLIOGRAPHY

Mauss, Marcel. *The Gift: The Form and Reason for Exchange in Archaic Societies*, trans. W.D. Halls. New York: W. W. Norton & Company, 1990.

Mecherzyński, Karol. *O magistratach miast polskich a w szczególności miasta Krakowa.* Krakow: D. E. Friedlein, 1845.

Michalewicz, Maria. "Stanisław Morsztyn." PSB 21 (1976): 821–822.

Mikulski, Krzysztof. "Kondycja demograficzna rodziny mieszczańskiej w Toruniu w XVI–XVIIS wieku (na przykładzie rodziny Neisserów)." in *Kobieta i rodzina w średniowieczu i na progu czasów nowożytnych*, edited by Zenon Hubert Nowak, Andrzej Radzimiński, 115–142. Toruń: Wydawnictwo Uniwersytetu Mikołaja Kopernika, 1998.

Mikulski, Krzysztof and, Kopiński Krzysztof. "Z Westfalii przez Toruń i Krakow za węgierską miedzią (rodzina von der Linde od XIV do pierwszej połowy XVI wieku)." In *Miasta, ludzie, instytucje, znaki. Księga jubileuszowa ofiarowana Profesor Bożenie Wyrozumskiej w 75. rocznicę urodzin*, ed. Zenon Piech, 263–288. Krakow: Tow. Naukowego Societas Vistulana, 2008.

Mikulski, Krzysztof. *Przestrzeń i społeczeństwo Torunia od końca XIV do początku XVIII wieku*. Toruń: Wydaw. Uniwersytetu Mikołaja Kopernika, 1999.

Mikuła, Maciej. *Prawodawstwo króla i sejmu dla małopolskich miast królewskich (1386–1572)*. Krakow: Wydawnictwo Uniwersytetu Jagiellońskiego, 2014.

Mikuła, Maciej. *Prawo miejskie magdeburskie (Ius municipale Magdeburgense) w Polsce XIV-pocz. XVI w. Studium o ewolucji i adaptacji prawa*, Krakow: Wydawnictwo Uniwersytetu Jagiellońskiego, 2019.

Mikuła, Maciej. "Statuty prawa spadkowego w miastach polskich prawa magdeburskiego (do końca XVI wieku)." *Z Dziejów Prawa* 7 (2014): 33–63.

Miller, Maureen C., "Donors, Their Gifts, and Religious Innovation in Medieval Verona." *Speculum* 66, no.1 (1991): 27–42.

Mitchell, Linda E. *Family Life in The Middle Ages*, Westport: Westport: Greenwood Press, 2007.

Mitkowski, Józef. "Hejnman Edeling." PSB 6 (1948): 200.

Mitkowski, Józef. "Jan Ederer." PSB 6 (1948): 201–202.

Mitkowski, Józef. "Mikołaj Edeling." PSB 6, 1948: 201.

Modzelewski, Karol. *Barbarian Europe*, trans. Ewa Macura. Frankfurt am Main: Peter Lang, 2015.

Molenda, Danuta. *Polski ołów na rynkach Europy Środkowej w XIII-XVII wieku*. Warszawa: Instytut Archeologii i Etnologii PAN, 2001.

Molenda, Danuta. "Dzieje Olkusza do 1795 roku." In *Dzieje Olkusza i regionu olkuskiego*, 1, edited by Feliks Kiryk, Ryszard Kołodziejczyk, 147–226. Warszawa: Państwowe Wydawnictwo Naukowe, 1978.

Moslerß-Cristoph, Susanne. *Die materielle kultur in den Lüneburger Testamenten 1323 bis 1500*. PhD diss., Georg-August-Universität Göttingen, 1998.

Możejko, Beata. "Gdański mieszczanin w obliczu śmierci. Zapisy testamentowe z II połowy XV w. (na podstawie księgi ławniczej)." In *Mieszczanie, wasale, zakonnicy. Studia z dziejów średniowiecza* no. 10, edited by Błażej Śliwiński, 127–162. Malbork: Muzeum Zamkowe w Malborku, 2004.

Możejko, Beata. *Rozrachunek z życiem doczesnym. Gdańskie testamenty mieszczańskie z XV i początku XVI wieku.* Gdańsk: Wydawnictwo Uniwersytetu Gdańskiego, 2010.

Mrozowski, Krzysztof. "Religijność mieszczan późnośredniowiecznej Warszawy w świetle najstarszych zachowanych testamentów." *KHKM* 58, no.2 (2010): 191–196.

Murray, Jacqueline., "Kinship and Friendship: The Perception of Family by Clergy and Laity in Late Medieval London." *Albion: A Quarterly Journal Concerned with British Studies* 20, no. 3 (1988), 369–385.

Muszyńska, Jadwiga. "Testamenty mieszczan szydłowieckich z lat 1638–1645." In *Szydłowiec – z dziejów miasta*, edited by Jacek Wijaczka, 133–160. Szydłowiec: Muzeum Ludowych Instrumentów Muzycznych, 1999.

Neschwara, Christian. *Rechtsformen Letzwilligerverfügungen in den wiener Stadtbüchern (1395–1430). Eine Bilanz aufgrund der vorliegenden Edition bis 1417, Testamente aus der Habsburgermonarchie Alltagskultur, Recht, Überlieferung.* Wien: Böhlau, 2009.

Niewiński, Andrzej. *Przestrzeń kościelna w topografii średniowiecznego Krakowa. Próba syntezy.* Lublin: Towarzystwo Naukowe Katolickiego Uniwersytetu Lubelskiego, 2004.

Nodl, Martin. "Středověký testament jako abnormalita." In *Pozdně středověké testamenty v českých městech. Prameny, metodologie a formy využití. Sborník příspěvků z konference uspořádané 30. listopadu 2005 Archivem hlavního města Prahy a Historickým ústavem Akademie věd České republiky*, edited by Kateřina Jíšová, Eva Doležalová, 73–86. Praha: Scriptorium, 2006.

Noga, Zdzisław. "Geografia imigracji do krakowskiej elity władzy w średniowieczu i epoce nowożytnej (do połowy XVII wieku)." In *Elita władzy miasta Krakowa i jej związki z miastami Europy w średniowieczu i epoce nowożytnej (do połowy XVII wieku). Zbiór studiów*, edited by Zdzisław Noga, 23–32. Krakow: Antykwa, 2011.

Noga, Zdzisław. "Grupy zawodowe i przepływy międzygrupowe w Krakowie i miastach województwa krakowskiego w średniowieczu." In *Człowiek w średniowieczu*, edited by Alicja Szymczakowa, 253–263. Łódź: Wydawnictwo Uniwersytetu Łódzkiego, 2009.

Noga, Zdzisław. *Krakowska rada miejska w XVI wieku. Studium o elicie władzy*, Krakow: Wydawnictwo Naukowe Akademii Pedagogicznej, 2003.

Noga, Zdzisław. "Między oligarchią a reprezentacją. Uwagi o ewolucji władz miejskich Krakowa w okresie przedrozbiorowym." In *Krakow. Studia z dziejów miasta*, edited by Jerzy Rajman, 101–109. Krakow: Wydawn. Nauk. Akademii Pedagogicznej, 2007.

Noga, Zdzisław. *Urzędnicy miejscy Krakowa*, vol. 2: *1500–1794*. Krakow: Wydawnictwo Naukowe Uniwersytetu Pedagogicznego, 2008.

BIBLIOGRAPHY

Nowak, Zdzisław. *Kultura umysłowa Prus Królewskich w czasach Kopernika*, Toruń: Państwowe Wydawnictwo Naukowe, 1972.

Oberste, Jörg. "Macht und Memoria. Religiöses Leben und soziale Netzwerke des Regensburger Patriziates im später Mittelalter." In *Regensburg im Spättmittelalter. Bestandsaufnahme und Impulse*, edited by Peter Schmid, 25–48. Regensburg: Schnell & Steiner, cop, 2007.

Obyczaje w Polsce: od średniowiecza do czasów współczesnych: praca zbiorowa, edited by Andrzej Chwalba. Warszawa: Państwowe Wydawnictwo Naukowe, 2004.

Ocker, Christopherm. *Johannes Klenkok. A Friar's Life c. 1310–1374*, Philadelphia: American Philosophical Society, 1993.

Oexle, Otto Gerhard. "Die Gegenwart der Lebenden und der Toten. Gedanken über Memoria." *Gedächtnis, das Gemeinschaft stiftet*, edited by Karl Schmid. München-Zürich: Verl. Schnell & Steiner, 1985.

Oexle, Otto Gerhard, "Memoria und Memorialüberlieferung im frühen Mittelalter." *Frühmittelalterliche Studien* 10 (1976): 70–95.

Oliński, Piotr. "Mieszczanin w trosce o zbawienie. Uwagi o memoratywnych funkcjach fundacji mieszczańskich w wielkich miastach pruskich." In *Ecclesia et civitas. Kościół i życie religijne w mieście średniowiecznym*, edited by Halina Manikowska, Hanna Zaremska, 347–359. Warszawa: Instytut Historii PAN.

Oliński, Piotr. "Fundacje i legaty religijne kobiet świeckich w wielkich miastach pruskich." In *Kobieta i rodzina w średniowieczu i na progu czasów nowożytnych*, edited by Zenon Hubert Nowak, Andrzej Radzimiński, Toruń: 143–160. Wydawnictwo Uniwersytetu Mikołaja Kopernika, 1998.

Oliński, Piotr. *Fundacje mieszczańskie w miastach pruskich w okresie średniowiecza i na progu czasów nowożytnych (Chełmno, Toruń, Elbląg, Gdańsk, Królewiec, Braniewo)*. Toruń: Wydawnictwo Naukowe Uniwersytetu Mikołaja Kopernika, 2008.

Oliński, Piotr. "Społeczne uwarunkowania zapisów testamentowych w średniowiecznym Elblągu." In *In memoriam honoremque Casimiri Jasiński*, edited by Jarosław Wenta, Piotr Oliński, 181–192. Toruń: Wydawnictwo Naukowe Uniwersytetu Mikołaja Kopernika, 2010.

Olszewski, Wojciech. "Testament jako źródło do badań życia miasta w średniowieczu." *Archaeologia Historica Polona* 7 (1998): 79–92.

Ożóg, Krzysztof. "Studia krakowian na praskim uniwersytecie do początku XV wieku." In *Miasta, ludzie, instytucje, znaki. Księga jubileuszowa ofiarowana Profesor Bożenie Wyrozumskiej w 75. rocznicę urodzin*, edited by Zenon Piech, 637–651. Krakow: Towarzystwo Naukowe Societas Vistulana, 2008.

Ożóg, Krzysztof. "Wpływ środowiska uniwersyteckiego na kształtowanie i rozwój kultury religijnej w Polsce średniowiecznej." In *Animarum cultura. Studia nad kulturą religijną na ziemiach polskich w średniowieczu*, vol. 1: *Struktury kościelno-publiczne,* edited by Halina Manikowska, Wojciech Brojer, 407–440. Warszawa: Instytut Historii PAN, 2008.

Pańków, Stanisława. "Friczko płatnerz." PSB 7 (1948–1958): 137.

Pańków, Stanisława. "Michał Lang (de Czirla)." PSB 16 (1971): 481–482.

Pańków, Stanisława. "Stanisław Leymitter." PSB 17 (1971): 263.

Patkaniowski, Michał. *Krakowska rada miejska w średnich wiekach*, Krakow: Towarzystwo Miłośników Historii i Zabytków Krakowa, 1934.

Pátková, Hanna. "Bractva w czeskich miastach katolickich i utrakwistycznych." In *Ecclesia et civitas. Kościół i życie religijne w mieście średniowiecznym*, edited by Halina Manikowska, Hanna Zaremska, 217–222. Warszawa: Instytut Historii PAN, 2002.

Pawlikowska, Wioletta. "Testamenty mieszkańców małych miast wielkopolskich z XVII w. prawo i praktyka" *KHKM* 59, no.2 (2011): 395–408.

Petersen, Frederik. "Marriage Contracts and the Church Courts of Fourteenth-Century England." In *To Have and to Hold. Marrying and Its Documentation in Western Christendom, 400–1600*, edited by Philip L. Reynolds, John Witte, 287–331. Cambridge: Cambridge University Press, 2007.

Petryshak, Bohdana. "Sporządzanie testamentów we Lwowie w późnym średniowieczu — pisarze, ceny, okoliczności," *KHKM* 62, no. 3 (2014): 329–336.

Pieradzka, Katarzyna. "Jan Bartfal." PSB 1 (1935): 311.

Pieradzka, Katarzyna. "Paweł Ber." PSB 1 (1935): 444.

Pierer, Heinrich August. *Das Universal-Lexikon der Gegenwart und Vergangenheit*. Altenburg: Pierer, 1857–1865.

Piotrowicz, Józef. "Żupy krakowskie w pierwszych wiekach rozwoju, od połowy XIII do połowy XVI wieku." In *Dzieje żup krakowskich*. Wieliczka: Muzeum Żup Krakowskich Wieliczka, 1988.

Piper, Henning. *Testament und Vergabung von Todes wegen im braunschweigischen Stadtrecht des 13 bis 17 Jh.*. Braunschwig: Waisenhaus-Buchdruckerei und Verlag, 1960.

Piwowarczyk, Elżbieta. *Dzieje Kościoła Mariackiego (XIII-XVI w.)*, Krakow: Wydaw. Naukowe PAT, 2000.

Piwowarczyk, Elżbieta. "Legaty na kościół i klasztor oo. Dominikanów w Krakowie (XIV-XV w.). Z badań nad pobożnością miejską." In *Mendykanci w średniowiecznym Krakowie*, edited by Krzysztof Ożóg, Tomasz Gałuszka, Anna Zajchowska, 485–503. Krakow: Esprit, 2008.

Piwowarczyk, Elżbieta. "Legaty na kościół Panny Marii (Mariacki) w Krakowie (XIV-XV w.). Przyczynek do badań nad religijnością miejską." *Rocznik Krakowski* 72 (2006): 5–23.

Piwowarczyk, Elżbieta. *Legaty testamentowe ad pias causas w XV-wiecznym Krakowie*. Krakow: Drukarnia Akcydensowa, 2010.

BIBLIOGRAPHY

Piwowarczyk, Elżbieta. "Legaty testamentowe na kościół św. Anny (1400–1530). Z krakowskich ksiąg miejskich." In *Studia z dziejów kościoła św. Anny w Krakowie*, edited by Zdzisław Kliś, Tomasz Węcławowicz, 73–89. Krakow Wydawnictwo UNUM, 2009.

Piwowarczyk, Elżbieta and, Piotr Tyszka, "Przyczynek do pobożności mieszczan krakowskich na podstawie XV – wiecznych legatów w Liber testamentorum (rkps 772)." *Nasza Przeszłość* 105 (2006): 7–42.

Popiołek, Bożena. "Krakow i jego mieszkańcy w świetle testamentów mieszczan krakowskich z XVII-XVIII wieku." In *Krakow. Studia z dziejów miasta*, edited by Jerzy Rajman, 120–132. Krakow: Wydawnictwo Naukowe Akademii Pedagogicznej, 2007.

Pospišil, Leopold. *Anthropology of Law. A comparative theory*. New Haven: Harper & Row, 1974.

Pospíšil, Leopold. *The Ethnology of Law*. New Haven: Human Relations Area Files, 1978.

Postles, Dave. "Small gifts, but big rewards: the symbolism of some gifts to the religious." *Journal of Medieval History* 27 (2001): 23–42.

Pośpiech, Andrzej. *Pułapka oczywistości. Pośmiertne spisy ruchomości szlachty wielkopolskiej z XVII wieku*. Warszawa: Wydawn. Adam Marszałek, 1992.

Potkowski, Edward. "Autorytet prawa w średniowieczu." In *Kultura prawna w Europie Środkowej*, edited by Antoni Barciak, 15–34. Katowice: Instytut Górnośląski, 2006.

Potkowski, Edward. *Książka i pismo w średniowieczu. Studia z dziejów kultury piśmiennej i komunikacji społecznej*. Pułtusk: Wyd. Akademia Humanistyczna im. Aleksandra Gieysztora, 2006.

Pozdně středověké testamenty v českých městech. Prameny, metodologie a formy využití. edited by Kateřina Jíšová, Eva Doležalová, Praha: Scriptorium, 2006.

"Praktyka w sprawach małżeńskich w sądach duchownych djecezyi krakowskiej w wieku XV," edited by Bolesław Ulanowski. In *Archiwum Komisji Historycznej*, vol. 5, 87–195. Krakow: Nakładem Akademii Umiejętności, 1888.

Ptaśnik, Jan. *Kultura włoska wieków średnich w Polsce*. Warszawa: Państwowe Wydawn. Naukowe, 2002.

Ptaśnik, Jan. *Miasta i mieszczaństwo w dawnej Polsce*. Warszawa: Państwowy Instytut Wydawniczy, 1949.

Ptaśnik, Jan. "Studia nad patrycjatem krakowskim wieków średnich." *Rocznik Krakowski* 15 (1913): 23–95.

Rafacz, Józef. *Zastępcy stron w dawnym procesie polskim*. Krakow: Gebethner & Wolff, 1923.

Rajman, Jerzy. "Gmina miasta lokacyjnego w XIII i początkach XIV wieku." In *Krakow. Studia z dziejów miasta*, edited by Jerzy Rajman, 61–75. Krakow: Wydawn. Nauk. Akademii Pedagogicznej 2007.

Rajman, Jerzy. *Krakow – zespół osadniczy, proces lokacji, mieszczanie do roku 1333*, Krakow: Wydawnictwo Naukowe Akademii Pedagogicznej, 2004.

Rajman Jerzy, "Mieszczanie z Górnego Śląska w elicie władzy Krakowa w XIV w." In *Elita władzy miasta Krakowa i jej związki z miastami Europy w średniowieczu i epoce nowożytnej (do połowy XVII w.). Zbiór studiów*, edited by Zdzisław Noga), 49–63. Krakow: Antykwa, 2011.

Reyerson, Kathryn L. "Changes in Testamentary Practice at Montpellier on the Eve of the Black Death." *Church History* 47 no. 3 (1978): 253–269.

Riethmüller, Marianne. *To troste miner sele, Aspekte spätmittelalterlicher Frömmigkeit im Spiegel Hamburger Testamente (1310–1400)*. Hamburg: Verlag Verein für Hamburgische Geschichte, 1994.

Rosa, Agnieszka. "Testamenty fordońskie jako egodokumenty mieszczańskie." *Kronika Bydgoska* 29 (2006): 41–72.

Rosenbaiger, Kazimierz. *Dzieje Kościoła OO. Franciszkanów w Krakowie w wiekach średnich*. Krakow: Towarzystwo miłośników historii i zabytków Krakowa, 1933.

Rossiaud, Jacques. *Mieszczanin i życie w mieście, in Człowiek średniowiecza*, edited by Jacques Le Goff, trans. Maria Radożycka-Paoletti, 179–227. Warszawa-Gdańsk: Świat Książki, 1996. (J. Rossiaud, *Le Citadin*, "L'Homme medieval," ed. Jacques Le Goff, Seuil 1989)

Rożek, Michał. *Przewodnik po zabytkach Krakowa*, 2nd ed. Krakow: Wydawnictwo WAM, 2010.

Rymaszewski, Zygfryd. *Łacińskie teksty Landrechtu Zwierciadła Saskiego w Polsce: versio Vratislaviensis, versio Sandomiriensis, Łaski*. Wrocław: Zakład Narodowy im. Ossolińskich, 1975.

Rymaszewski Zygfryd, *Łacińskie teksty Landrechtu Zwierciadła Saskiego w Polsce: Jaskier – tekst główny i noty marginesowe*. Wrocław: Zakład Narodowy im. Ossolińskich, 1985.

Rymaszewski, Zygfryd. "Miejskość czy wiejskość prawa niemieckiego w Polsce." *Zeszyty Naukowe Uniwersytetu Łódzkiego*. Seria I 69 (1970): 65–87.

Rymaszewski, Zygfryd. *Prawo bliższości krewnych w polskim prawie ziemskim do końca XV wieku*. Wrocław-Warszawa-Krakow: Zakład Narodowy im. Ossolińskich, 1970.

Samsonowicz, Henryk. *Badania nad kapitałem mieszczańskim Gdańska w II połowie XV wieku*. Warszawa: Uniwersytet Warszawski, 1960.

Samsonowicz, Henryk. "Cechy rzemieślnicze w średniowiecznej Polsce. Mity i rzeczywistość." *Przegląd Historyczny* 75, no. 2 (1984): 551–567.

Samsonowicz, Henryk. "Mieszczańska dobroczynność prywatna w Polsce późnego średniowiecza." In *Cultus et cognitio. Studia z dziejów średniowiecznej kultury*, edited by Stefan K. Kuczyński, Aleksander Gieysztor, 505–511. Warszawa: Państwowe Wydawnictwo Naukowe, 1976.

Samsonowicz, Henryk. "Społeczeństwo w Polsce ok 1400 r." In *Polska około roku 1400. Państwo, społeczeństwo, kultura*, edited by Wojciech Fałkowski, 9–40. Warszawa: Neriton, 2001.

BIBLIOGRAPHY

Samsonowicz, Henryk. "Struktura społeczna późnego średniowiecza Polski w badaniach historycznych." In *Społeczeństwo Polski Średniowiecznej*, vol. 7, edited by Stefan Krzysztof Kuczyński, 267–282. Warszawa: Państwowe Wydawnictwo Naukowe, 1996.

Samsonowicz, Henryk. "Studia nad rentą miejską w Prusach w XV wieku." *Zapiski Historyczne* 25, no. 2 (1960): 35–55.

Samsonowicz, Henryk. "Zagadnienia demografii historycznej w rejonie Hanzy w XV-XVI w." *Zapiski Historyczne* 28, no. 4 (1963), 523–554.

Schildhauer, Johannes. Hans*estädtischer Alltag: Untersuchungen auf der Grundlage der Stralsunder Bürgertestamente vom Anfang des 14. bis zum Ausgang des 16. Jahrhunderts*. Weimar: Hermann Böhlaus Nachfolger, 1992.

Schindler, Norbert. *Ludzie prości, ludzie niepokorni... kultura ludowa w początkach dziejów nowożytnych*. Warszawa: Wiedza Powszechna, 2002.

Schulte-Beckhausen, Otto. *Das Ehe- und Familienrecht im Sachsenspiegel*. PhD diss. Rheinische Friedrich-Wilhelms-Universität Bonn, 1957.

Schulze Winfried, "Ego-Dokumente: Annäherung an den Menschen in der Geschichte? Vorüberlegungen für die Tagung "Ego-Dokumente." In *Ego-Dokumente: Annäherung an den Menschen in der Geschichte*, ed. Winfried Schulze, 11–31. Berlin: Berlin Akademie Verlag, 1996.

Seelenheil und irdischer Besitz. Testamente als Quellen für den Umgang mit den "letzten Dingen," edited by Markwart Herzog, Cecilie Hollberg. Konstanz: UVK-Verl.-Ges, 2007

Seredyka, Jan. "Testament Krzysztofa Moniwida Dorohostajskiego," in Aere *perennius. Profesorowi Gerardowi Labudzie dnia 28 XII 2001 w hołdzie*, edited by Marceli Kosman, 115–129. Poznań-Wrocław: Forum Naukowe, 2001.

Sheehan, Michael M. *Marriage, Family and Law in Medieval Europe. Collected Studies*, edited by James K. Farge. Cardiff: University of Toronto Press, 1996.

Sheehan, Michael M. *The Will in Medieval England. From the Conversion of the Anglo-Saxons to the End of the Thirteen Century*. Toronto: Pontifical Institute of Mediaeval Studies, 1963.

Sikora, Franciszek. "Testament Przedbora z Koniecpola z roku 1460." *Studia Historyczne* 26, no. 2 (1983): 297–314.

Skierska, Izabela. *Obowiązek mszalny w średniowiecznej Polsce*. Warszawa: Instytut Historii PAN, 2003.

Skierska, Izabela. "Miasto w kościele. Obowiązek mszalny w wielkich miastach średniowiecznej Polski." In *Ecclesia et civitas. Kościół i życie religijne w mieście średniowiecznym*, edited by Halina Manikowska, Hanna Zaremska, 389–414. Warszawa: Instytut Historii PAN, 2002.

Skupieński, Krzysztof. *Notariat publiczny w średniowiecznej Polsce*. Lublin: Uniwersytet Marii Curie-Sklodowskiej, 2002.

Skupieński, Krzysztof. "Notariusze i notariat w średniowiecznej Polsce." In *Kultura piśmienna średniowiecza i czasów nowożytnych. Problemy i konteksty badawcze*, edited by Piotr Dymmel, Barbara Trelińska, 165–181. Lublin: Wydawn. Uniwersytetu Marii Curie-Skłodowskiej, 1998.

Slezáková, Miroslava. "The Relationship between Elites of Krakow and Košice (Kaschau) in Late Middle Ages." In *Elita władzy miasta Krakowa i jej związki z miastami Europy w średniowieczu i epoce nowożytnej (do połowy XVII wieku). Zbiór studiów*, ed. Zdzisław Noga, 149–158. Krakow: Antykwa, 2011.

Słoń, Marek. "Fundacje szpitalne władz komunalnych jako centra kultu miejskiego." In *Ecclesia et civitas. Kościół i życie religijne w mieście średniowiecznym*, edited by Halina Manikowska, Hanna Zaremska, 361–374. Warszawa: Instytut Historii PAN, 2002.

Słoń, Marek. "Religijność komunalna w Europie środkowej późnego średniowiecza" In *Zbožnost středověku*, edited by Martin Nodl, Krzysztof Bracha, Jan Hrdina, Paweł Kras, 9–21. Praha: Filosofia, 2007.

Słoń, Marek. *Szpitale średniowiecznego Wrocławia*. Warszawa: Instytut Historii PAN, 2000.

Sowina, Urszula. "Najstarsze sieradzkie testamenty mieszczańskie z początku XVI w. Analiza źródłoznawcza." *KHKM* 39, no. 1 (1991), 3–25.

Sowina, Urszula and, Kazimierz Pacuski. "Testamenty mieszczan krakowskich jako źródła do badań nad stronami rodzinnymi imigrantów w krakowskiej elicie władzy (Przykład Jana z Reguł na Mazowszu)." In *Elita władzy miasta Krakowa i jej związki z miastami Europy w średniowieczu i epoce nowożytnej (do połowy XVII wieku). Zbiór studiów*, edited by Zdzisław Noga, 433–446. Krakow: Antykwa, 2011.

Sowina, Urszula. "Testament pewnego kmiecia. Przyczynek do badań nad relacjami międzystanowymi w późnym średniowieczu i wczesnej nowożytności." In *Civitas & villa. Miasto i wieś w średniowiecznej Europie środkowej*, edited by Cezary Buśko, 209–214. Wrocław-Praha: Instytut Archeologii i Etnologii PAN, 2002.

Sowina, Urszula. "Testamenty mieszczan krakowskich o przekazywaniu majątku w późnym średniowieczu i we wczesnej nowożytności." In *Sociální svět středověkého města*, edited by Martin Nodl, 173–183. Praha: Scriptorium, 2006.

Sowina, Urszula. "Wdowy i sieroty w świetle prawa w miastach korony w późnym średniowieczu i wczesnej nowożytności." In *Od narodzin do wieku dojrzałego. Dzieci i młodzież w Polsce*, vol. 1: *Od średniowiecza do wieku XVIII*, edited by Maria Dąbrowska, Andrzej Klonder, 15–28. Warszawa: Instytut Archeologii i Etnologii PAN, 2002.

Sowina, Urszula. "Testamenty krakowskie z przełomu średniowiecza i nowożytności wobec zasad dziedziczenia według prawa magdeburskiego." *KHKM* 58, no. 2 (2010): 185–190.

BIBLIOGRAPHY

Spence, Cathryn. "Women and business in sixteenth-century Edinburgh: Evidence from their Testaments." *Journal of Scottish Historical Studies* 28, no. 1 (2008): 1–19.

Sroka, Stanisław A. "Klęski elementarne w Krakowie." *Rocznik Krakowski* 67 (2001), 13–18.

Starczewska, Ewa. "Testamenty kobiet z księgi konsystorza pułtuskiego z 1509 roku." *KHKM* 59, no.2 (2011): 313–318.

Starzyński, Marcin. *Krakowska rada miejska*, Krakow: Tow. Naukowe "Societas Vistulana," 2010.

Starzyński, Marcin. "Kto był pisarzem *Kodeksu Behema?*" *Rocznik Krakowski* 73 (2007): 61–71.

Starzyński, Marcin. "Nad średniowiecznymi księgami rachunkowymi miasta Krakowa." *Roczniki Historyczne* 74 (2008): 165–178.

Starzyński, Marcin. Patrycjat krakowski w aktach Kamery Papieskiej z XIV w. (ze studiów nad udziałem kupiectwa krakowskiego w międzynarodowym transferze finansów)." In *Elita władzy miasta Krakowa i jej związki z miastami Europy w średniowieczu i epoce nowożytnej (do połowy XVII wieku). Zbiór studiów*, edited by Zdzisław Noga, 333–378. Krakow: Antykwa, 2011.

Stomma, Ludwik. *Antropologia kultury wsi polskiej XIX wieku oraz wybrane eseje*, 13–40. Łódź: P. Dopierała, 2002.

Strocchia, Sharon T., "Remembering the Family: Women, Kin, and Commemorative Masses in Renaissance Florence." *Renaissance Quarterly* 42, no. 4 (1989): 635–654.

Suchojad, Henryk. "Rozstanie ze światem doczesnym księdza Jakuba Grometiusa (1572–1651), plebana w Gnojnie (w świetle testamentu i towarzyszących mu dokumentów)." In *Wesela, chrzciny i pogrzeby w XVI – XVIII wieku. Kultura życia i śmierci*, edited by Henryk Suchojad, 303–313. Warszawa: Semper, 2001.

Suchojad, Henryk. "Wyposażenie siedzib duchownych i szlacheckich w świetle testamentów z XVII – XVIII wieku na terenie województwa sandomierskiego." In *Dwór polski. Zjawisko historyczne i kulturowe*, edited by Jerzy baranowski, 449–457. Warszawa: Stowarzyszenie Historyków Sztuki, 2000.

Szczygieł, Ryszard. "Konflikty społeczne w miastach Królestwa Polskiego w XV i XVI wieku związane z dostępem do władz miejskich." *Socium* 7 (2007): 35–42.

Szczygieł, Ryszard. "Wpływ konfliktów wewnętrznych w miastach polskich XV–XVI wieku na zmiany struktur społecznych." In *Stare i nowe struktury społeczne w Polsce*, vol. 1: *Miasto*, edited by Irena Machaj i Józef Styk, 39–50. Lublin: Uniwersytet Marii Curie-Skłodowskiej, 1994.

Szelińska, Wacława. "Dwa testamenty Jana Dąbrówki. Z dziejów życia umysłowego Uniwersytetu Krakowskiego w połowie XV wieku." *Studia i materiały z dziejów nauki polskiej*, seria A, no. 5 (1962): 1–40.

Szende, Katalin. "Testaments and Testimonies: Orality and Literacy in Composing Last Wills in Late Medieval Hungary." In *Oral history of the Middle Ages: the spoken word in context*, edited by Gerhard Jaritz, Michael Richter, 49–66. Krems: Medium Aevum Quotidianum; Budapest: Dept. of Medieval Studies, Central European University, 2001.

Sztetyłło, Janusz. "Rzemiosła metalowe wraz z uzbrojeniem." In *Historia kultury materialnej Polski w zarysie*, vol. 2 *od XIII do XV w.*, edited by Anna Rutkowska-Płachcińska, 73–108. Wrocław-Warszawa-Krakow-Gdańsk: Zakład Narodowy im. Ossolińskich, 1978.

Sztumski, Janusz. *Elity, ich miejsce i rola w społeczeństwie*. Katowice: Śląsk, 1997.

Szulc, Alicja. *Homo Religiosus późnego średniowiecza. Bernardyński model dewocji masowej*. Poznań: Uniwersytet im. Adama Mickiewicza, 2007.

Szymański, Jarosław. *Ruchy heretyckie na Śląsku w XIII i XIV wieku*. Katowice: Instytut Książki, 2007.

Szymczak, Jan. "Od samostrzelników do grzebieniarzy w Krakowie, czyli rzecz o zmierzchu znaczenia kuszy na przełomie XV i XVI wieku." In *Aetas Media Aetas Moderna. Studia ofiarowane profesorowi Henrykowi Samsonowiczowi w siedemdziesiątą rocznicę urodzin*, edited by Agnieszka Bartoszewicz, Wojciech Fałkowski, Halina Manikowska, Antoni Mączak, Karol Modzelewski, 122–128. Warszawa: Instytut Historyczny UW, 2000.

Szymczak, Alicja and, Jan Szymczak. "Legaty testamentowe kanonika krakowskiego Adama z Będkowa z 1451 roku dla rodziny." In *Księga Jubileuszowa Profesora Feliksa Kiryka*, edited by Andrzej Jureczko; Franciszek Leśniak; Zdzisław Noga, 421–430. Krakow: Wydawnictwo Naukowe Akademii Pedagogicznej, 2004.

Szymczak, Alicja and, Jan Szymczak. "Procesy w konsystorzu gnieźnieńskim o legaty mieszczan z Polski środkowej dla Kościoła w XV wieku." In *Miasta, ludzie, instytucje, znaki. Księga jubileuszowa ofiarowana Profesor Bożenie Wyrozumskiej w 75. rocznicę urodzin*, edited by Zenon Piech, 307–318. Krakow: Towarzystwo Naukowe Societas Vistulana, 2008.

Tandecki, Janusz. "Dzieje kaplicy i ołtarza Bożego Ciała w katedrze św. Jana Chrzciciela i św. Jana Ewangelisty w Toruniu w świetle zachowanych archiwaliów." In *Studia nad dziejami miast i mieszczaństwa w średniowieczu. Studia ofiarowane Antoniemu Czacharowskiemu w sześćdziesiątą piątą rocznicę urodzin i czterdziestolecie pracy naukowej*, edited by Roman Czaja, Janusz Tandecki, 179–192. Toruń: Uniwersytet Mikołaja Kopernika, 1996.

Tandecki, Janusz. "Kobieta w rzemiośle miast pruskich na przełomie średniowiecza i czasów nowożytnych." In *Kobieta i rodzina w średniowieczu i na progu czasów nowożytnych*, edited by Zenon Hubert Nowak, Andrzej Radzimiński, 161–174. Toruń: Wydawnictwo Uniwersytetu Mikołaja Kopernika, 1998.

Tandecki, Janusz. "Pozazawodowe źródła dochodów mieszkańców miast pruskich w średniowieczu." In *Miasta, ludzie, instytucje, znaki. Księga jubileuszowa ofiarowana*

BIBLIOGRAPHY

Profesor Bożenie Wyrozumskiej w 75. rocznicę urodzin, edited by Zenon Piech, 161–171. Krakow: Towarzystwo Naukowe Societas Vistulana, 2008.

Tandecki, Janusz. *Struktury administracyjne i społeczne oraz formy życia w wielkich miastach Prus Krzyżackich i Królewskich w średniowieczu i na progu czasów nowożytnych*. Toruń: Wydawnictwo Uniwersytetu Mikołaja Kopernika, 2001.

Tandecki, Janusz. *Szkice z dziejów Torunia i Prus w średniowieczu i na progu czasów nowożytnych*. Toruń: Wydawnictwo Adam Marszałek, 2008.

Tandecki, Janusz. "Średniowieczne korporacje mieszczańskie w pruskich miastach hanzeatyckich." In *Prusy – Polska – Europa. Studia z dziejów średniowiecza i czasów wczesnonowożytnych. Prace ofiarowane Zenonowi Hubertowi Nowakowi w sześćdziesiątą piątą rocznicę urodzin i czterdziestolecie pracy naukowej*, ed. Andrzej Radzimiński, Janusz Tandecki, 313–326. Toruń: Wydawnictwo Uniwersytetu Mikołaja Kopernika, 1999.

Tandecki, Janusz. *Średniowieczne księgi wielkich miast pruskich jako źródła historyczne i zabytki kultury mieszczańskiej (organizacja władz, zachowane archiwalia, działalność kancelarii)*. Warszawa-Toruń: IS PAN, 1990.

Tęgowski, Jan. "Testament ostatniego Piasta mazowieckiego." *Przegląd Historyczny* 96, no. 1 (2005): 77–90.

Trajdos, Tadeusz M. Testament Stanisława Moniaka, *Rocznik Babiogórski* 4 (2002): 215–223.

Trelińska, Barbara. "Szlachectwo Romerów mieszczan krakowskich." In *Miasta, ludzie, instytucjem znaki. Księga jubileuszowa ofiarowana Profesor Bożenie Wyrozumskiej w 75. rocznicę urodzin*, edited by Zenon Piech, 301–306. Krakow: Towarzystwo Naukowe Societas Vistulana, 2008.

Tönnies, Ferdinand. *Community and Civil Society*, edited by Jose Harris. Cambridge: Cambridge University Press, 2001.

Tyszka, Piotr. "Mieszczanie, instytucje kościelne i pieniądze. Zapisy pobożne w przestrzeni późnośredniowiecznego Krakowa." In *Ecclesia et civitas. Kościół i życie religijne w mieście średniowiecznym*, edited by Halina Manikowska, Hanna Zaremska, 53–63. Warszawa: Instytut Historii PAN, 2002.

Tyszka, Piotr. *Obraz przestrzeni miejskiej Krakowa XIV-XV wieku w świadomości jego mieszkańców*, Lublin: Wydawnictwo Uniwersytetu Marii Curie-Skłodowskiej, 2001.

Uruszczak, Wacław. "Statuty Kazimierza Wielkiego jako źródło prawa polskiego." *Studia z dziejów państwa i prawa polskiego* 3 (1999): 97–115.

Vauchez, André. *La religion civique a` l'époque médiévale et moderne: chrétienté et islam: actes du colloque*. Rome: École Française de Rome, 1995.

Vetulani, Adam. *Fragment Summy Rajmunda w rękopisie warszawskim, Czasopismo Prawno-Historyczne* 14 no. 2 (1962): 165–172.

Vetulani, Adam. *Z badań nad kulturą prawniczą w Polsce piastowskiej*. Wrocław: Zakł. Nar. im. Ossolińskich, 1976.

Vovelle, Michel. *Śmierć w cywilizacji Zachodu od roku 1300 po współczesność*. trans. Tomasz Swoboda. Warszawa: "Słowo/Obraz Terytoria," 2008.

de Vries, Jan. *European Urbanization 1500–1800*. Cambridge (Mass.): Cambridge University Press, 1984.

Waszak, Stanisław. "Dzietność rodziny mieszczańskiej i ruch naturalny ludności miasta Poznania w końcu XVI i XVII w." *Rocznik Dziejów Społecznych i Gospodarczych* 16 (1954–1955): 316–380.

Weber, Max. *Economy and Society*, trans. Keith Tribe. Harvard: Harvard University Press, 2019.

Wiesiołowski, Jacek. "Biedni, bogaci, przeciętni. Stratyfikacja społeczeństwa polskiego w końcu XV w." In *Biedni i bogaci. Studia z dziejów społeczeństwa i kultury ofiarowane Bronisławowi Geremkowi w sześćdziesiątą rocznicę urodzin*, edited by Maurice Aymard, 145–154. Warszawa 1992.

Wiesiołowski, Jacek. *Jak poznańska burmistrzowa ze swą krawcową do Rzymu na jubileusz 1500 r. pielgrzymowała*. Poznań: Poznańskie Tow. Przyjaciół Nauk, 2010.

Wiesiołowski, Jacek. "Pielgrzymowanie Polaków do Rzymu na przełomie XV i XVI w. (1478–1526). Komunikat." In *Peregrinationes. Pielgrzymki w kulturze dawnej Europy*, edited by Halina Manikowska, Hanna Zaremska, 157–160. Warszawa: Instytut Historii PAN, 1995.

Wiesiołowski, Jacek. *Socjotopografia późnośredniowiecznego Poznania*, Poznań: Państwowe Wydawn. Nauk, 1997.

Wiesiołowski, Jacek. "Stratyfikacja mieszczaństwa polskiego w późnym średniowieczu" In *Struktura feudální společnosti na území Československa a Polska do přelomu 15. a 16. stoleti*, edited by Ján Čierny, František Hejl, Antonín Verbík, 277–319. Praha: Ústav československých a světových dějin Československé akademie věd, 1984.

Wiesiołowski, Jacek. "Zmiany społecznej pozycji kobiety w średniowiecznej Polsce." In *Kobieta w kulturze średniowiecznej Europy. Prace ofiarowane Profesor Alicji Karłowskiej-Kamzowej*, ed. Antoni Gąsiorowski, 41–46. Poznań: Wydawnictwo Poznańskiego Towarzystwa Przyjaciół Nauk, 1995.

Wiktorowicz, Jacek. *Krakauer Kenzleisprache. Forschungsperspektiven und Analysemethoden*. Warszawa: Zakład Graficzny Uniwersytetu Warszawskiego, 2011.

Wilczek-Karczewska, Magdalena. *Testamenty szlachty wielkopolskiej z XVII w.*, KHKM 59, no. 2 (2011): 333–346.

Wiślicz, Tomasz. *Zarobić na duszne zbawienie. Religijność chłopów małopolskich od połowy XVI do końca XVIII wieku*. Warszawa: Neriton 2001.

Witkowska, Aleksandra. *Kulty pątnicze piętnastowiecznego Krakowa*, Lublin: Wydawnictwo Towarzystwa Naukowego Katolickiego Uniwersytetu Lubelskiego, 1984.

Witkowska, Aleksandra. "Ośrodki kultowe w geografii sakralnej średniowiecznego Krakowa." In *Animarum cultura. Studia nad kulturą religijną na ziemiach polskich w średniowieczu*, vol. 1: *Struktury kościelno-publiczne*, edited by Halina Manikowska, Wojciech Brojer 133–148. Warszawa: Instytut Historii PAN, 2008.

BIBLIOGRAPHY 397

Witkowska, Aleksandra. "Peregrinatio religiosa w średniowiecznej Europie." In *Peregrinationes. Pielgrzymki w kulturze dawnej Europy*, edited by Halina Manikowska, Hanna Zaremska, 9–16. Warszawa: Instytut Historii PAN, 1995.

Witkowska, Aleksandra. "Przestrzeń sakralna późnośredniowiecznego Krakowa." In *Ecclesia et civitas. Kościół i życie religijne w mieście średniowiecznym*, edited by Halina Manikowska, Hanna Zaremska, 37–48. Warszawa: Instytut Historii PAN, 2002.

Witkowska, Aleksandra, "Kształtowanie się tradycji pątniczych w średniowiecznym Krakowie." *Kwartalnik Historyczny* 86 (1979): 965–985.

Włodarski, Maciej. *Ars moriendi w literaturze polskiej XV i XVI w.* Krakow: Znak, 1987.

Woolgar, Chris M. "Gifts of food in late medieval England." *Journal of Medieval History* 37 (2011): 6–18.

Wółkiewicz, Ewa. "Formy dobroczynności w miastach śląskich w średniowieczu." *KHKM*, 58, no. 2 (2010): 211–230.

Wółkiewicz, Ewa. "Migracje do miast średniowiecznych w świetle ksiąg przyjęć do prawa miejskiego" In *Miasto czyni wolnym. W 790 lat lokacji Opola (ok.1217–2007)*, edited by Anna Pobóg-Lenartowicz, 43–52. Opole: Polskie Towarzystwo Historyczne, 2008.

Wółkiewicz, Ewa. "Testament Anny Isenecher jako źródło do badań mikrohistorycznych. Próba ustalenia kręgu towarzyskiego śląskiej mieszczanki z XIV wieku" *Zeszyty Historyczne WSP w Częstochowie* 6 (2000): 385–399.

Wółkiewicz, Ewa. *Testament księcia opolskiego Mikołaja II,* in M*iasto czyni wolnym. W 790. rocznicę lokacji Opola*, edited by Anna Pobóg-Lenartowicz, 85–103. Opole: Polskie Towarzystwo Historyczne, 2008.

Wyrozumska, Bożena. *Kancelaria miasta Krakowa w średniowieczu.* Krakow: Wydawnictwo Uniwersytetu Jagiellońskiego, 1995.

Wyrozumski, Jerzy. "Beginki i Begardzi w Polsce." *Zeszyty Naukowe Uniwersytetu Jagiellońskiego. Prace Historyczne*, 35 (1971): 7–22.

Wyrozumski, Jerzy. *Cracovia Mediaevalis*, edited by Marcin Starzyński. Krakow: Avalon, 2010.

Wyrozumski, Jerzy. *Dzieje Krakowa. Krakow do schyłku wieków średnich.* Krakow: Wydawnictwo Literackie, 1992.

Wyrozumski, Jerzy. "Miejsce Krakowa w średniowiecznej Europie." In *Krakow i Praga – dwie stolice Europy Środkowej*, edited by Jacek Purchla, 11–18. Krakow: Międzynarodowe Centrum Kultury, 2002.

Wyrozumski, Jerzy. "Produkcja sukiennicza w zgromadzeniach religijnych Polski średniowiecznej" *Zeszyty Naukowe Uniwersytetu Jagiellońskiego. Prace Historyczne* 12 (1963): 7–24.

Wyrozumski, Jerzy. "Lokacja czy lokacje Krakowa na prawie niemieckim?" In *Krakow. Nowe studia nad rozwojem miasta*, edited by Jerzy Wyrozumski, 121–151. Krakow: Tow. Miłośników Historii i Zabytków Krakowa 2007.

Wysmułek, Jakub. "Family from a Perspective of Dying – Evaluating Power of Testaments." In *Law and Private Life in Middle Ages*, edited by Per Andersen, Mia Münster-Swendsen & Helle Vogt, 219–229. Copenhagen: DJØF, 2011.

Wysmułek, Jakub. "Formen der Frömmigkeit der Bürger von Krakau. Testamente und Vermächtnisse des vierzehnten Jahrhunderts." In *Breslau und Krakau im Hoch- und Spätmittelalter Stadtgestalt - Wohnraum – Lebensstil*, edited by Eduard Mühle, 337–372. Köln: Böhlau 2013.

Wysmułek, Jakub. *Katalog testamentów z krakowskich ksiąg miejskich do 1550 roku*. Warszawa: Semper, 2017.

Wysmułek, Jakub. "Krakowska Liber Testamentorum jako źródło do badań społeczeństwa miasta późnośredniowiecznego (zarys problematyki)." *KHKM* 59, no. 2 (2011), 305–312.

Wysmułek, Jakub. "Last Wills as Tool of Power: Development of Testamentary Practice in Krakow during Late Middle Ages." *Planning for Death: Wills and Death-Related Property Arrangements in Europe, 1200–1600*, edited by Mia Korpiola, Anu Lahtinen, 213–238. Leiden: Brill, 2018.

Wysmułek, Jakub. "Przejawy religijności mieszczan krakowskich na podstawie XIV-wiecznych testamentów i zapisów pobożnych." *Odrodzenie i Reformacja w Polsce* 54 (2010): 85–126.

Wysmułek, Jakub. *Testamenty mieszczan krakowskich (XIV-XV w.)*. Warszawa: Neriton, 2015.

Wysmułek, Jakub. "Urban Testaments in Medieval Poland: Researches Present and Future." In "Medieval Urban Literacy I," edited by Marco Mostert, 299–312. Turnhout: Brepols, 2014.

Wysmułek, Jakub. "Wills as Testimony of Marriage Contracts in Late Medieval Krakow." In *Law and Marriage in Medieval and Early Modern Times, Proceedings of the Eight Carlsberg Academy Conference on Medieval Legal History 2011*, edited by Per Andersen, Kirsi Salonen, Helle Møller Sigh, Helle Vogt, 181–190. Copenhagen: DJØF, 2012.

Zahnd, Urs Martin. "Spätmittelalterliche Bürgertestamente als Quellen zu Realienkunde und Sozialgeschichte." *Mitteilungen des Instituts für österreichische Geschichtsforschung* 96 (1988): 55–78.

Zalewska, Katarzyna. *Modlitwa i obraz. Średniowieczna ikonografia różańcowa*. Warszawa: Wydawnictwo Uniwersytetu Warszawskiego, 1994.

Zaremska, Hanna. *Bractwa w średniowiecznym Krakowie. Studium form społecznych życia religijnego*. Wrocław-Warszawa-Krakow-Gdańsk: Instytut Historii PAN, 1977.

Zaremska, Hanna. "Człowiek wobec śmierci: wyobrażenia i rytuały" In *Kultura Polski średniowiecznej, XIV- XV w.*, edited by Bronisław Geremek, 485–510. Warszawa: Semper, 1997.

BIBLIOGRAPHY

Zaremska, Hanna. "Pielgrzymka jako kara za zabójstwo: Europa Środkowa XIII-XV w." In *Peregrinationes. Pielgrzymki w kulturze dawnej Europy*, ed. Halina Manikowska, Hanna Zaremska, 147–156. Warszawa: Instytut Historii PAN, 1995.

Zaremska, Hanna. "Procesje Bożego Ciała w Krakowie w XIV-XVI wieku." In *Kultura elitarna a kultura masowa w Polsce późnego średniowiecza*, edited by Bronisław Geremek, 25–40. Wrocław: Zakład Narodowy im. Ossolińskich, 1978.

Zaremska, Hanna. *Żydzi w średniowiecznej Polsce. Gmina krakowska*. Warszawa: Instytut Historii PAN, 2011.

Zaremska, Hanna. "Żywi wobec zmarłych brackie i cechowe pogrzeby w Krakowie w XIV- pierwszej połowie XVI w." *Kwartalnik Historyczny* 81, no. 4 (1974): 733–749.

Zielecka, Wioletta. "Testamenty prawosławnych i unitów jako źródło do badań nad dziejami konfesji wschodnich w Rzeczypospolitej XVI-XVIII wieku (stan badań, postulaty badawcze)" *KHKM* 58, no. 2 (2010): 237–244.

Zielińska, Katarzyna. "Więzi społeczne w połowie XVII wieku w świetle testamentów konsystorza pułtuskiego." *Przegląd Historyczny* 77, no. 1 (1986): 45–59.

Pietrusiński, Jerzy. *Złotnicy krakowscy XIV-XVI wieku i ich księga cechowa*. Warszawa: Instytut Sztuki PAN, 2000.

Zyglewski, Zbigniew. "Religijność w miastach kujawskich późnego średniowiecza" In *Ecclesia et civitas. Kościół i życie religijne w mieście średniowiecznym*, edited by Halina Manikowska, Hanna Zaremska, 327–347. Warszawa: Instytut Historii PAN, 2002.

Żerek-Kleszcz, Hanna. "Testamenty mieszczan pabianickich w XVII-XVIII wieku." *Pabianiciana* 1 (1992): 37–50.

Żerelik, Rościsław. "Testament Franciszka Koeckritza zwanego Faberem, pisarza miasta Wrocławia w latach 1542–1565." *Archaeologia Historica Polona* 7 (1998): 93–102.

Żmigrodzka, Bożena. *Testament jako gatunek tekstu*. Katowice: Wydawnictwo Uniwersytetu Śląskiego, 1995.

Żołądź-Strzelczyk, Dorota. *Dziecko w dawnej Polsce*. Poznań: Wydawnictwo Poznańskie, 2006.

Index of Places

Aachen   318, 319, 320
Augsburg   90, 136, 172, 182, 188, 311, 341
Avignon   46

Bochnia   67, 68, 233, 357
Brzeg   168, 181, 182, 188, 191, 250, 294
Bystrzyca   319

Chełmno   241
Cieszyn   176
Cologne   16, 192
Compostella   320

Dornburg   14, 315, 316

Ebląg   19, 155, 156

Gdansk   17, 19, 183, 236
Głogów   14, 66, 86, 172, 176, 180, 182, 256, 279,
   280, 295, 336, 342, 343, 345, 346, 362

Jerusalem   35, 320, 322

Kalisz   251
Kazimierz   137, 148, 158, 185, 241, 254, 267,
   286, 287, 288, 295, 296, 297, 299, 319,
   320, 353, 355
Kleparz   278, 296, 299, 343, 353
Kłodzko   316
Kluczbork   176, 300, 336
Košice   90, 188, 233, 246
Krosno   288, 297, 299

Legnica   316
Levoča   186, 233
Lübeck   156–157
Lviv   19, 158, 188

Magdeburg   50, 51, 82, 93
Mazovia   88
Memmingen   92, 135, 172, 182, 249, 293, 350

Nowy Sącz   176, 295, 347

Nuremberg   120, 136, 290

Olkusz   62, 158, 176, 179, 181, 189, 335

Piasek   148, 299, 340, 342
Pilzno   182, 230
Plzeň   201
Poznań   52, 59, 88, 93, 116, 132, 158, 160,
   183–185, 224, 314
Prague   35, 239, 241, 244, 256, 336
Prussia   18, 156, 288, 315
Przemyśl   52

Racibórz   65, 68, 176, 182, 279, 335, 336
Robczyce   182
Rome   65, 68, 73, 74, 79, 85, 100, 105, 112, 115,
   120, 140, 170, 171, 199, 200, 239, 244, 254,
   317–321
Rostock   156–157
Rożnów   176, 335

Sandomierz   38, 182, 314
Silesia   44, 48, 140, 176, 182, 198, 280, 314, 329
Skałka   299
Stralsund   15, 156
Strzelniki   294
Świdnica   180, 316

Thunkilspul (*Dinkelsbuhl*)   110, 136, 290, 293
Toruń   135, 156, 176, 180, 237, 314, 349

Wesoła   296
Wieliczka   68
Wilsnack   320
Wolbrom   231
Wróblewo   251, 252
Wrocław   43, 44, 45, 48, 86, 94, 100, 134, 141,
   154, 155, 156, 176, 180–182, 188, 244, 278,
   314, 316, 319, 322

Ząbkowice Śląskie (*Frankinsteyn*)   182
Żary   176, 336
Zator   176, 181, 268, 279, 295, 338

Index of Names

Albert, vogt of Krakow   64, 206, 302, 303
Alexander iii, pope   31
Andrew Tęczyński   121, 128, 129, 130, 277

Bartłomiej Groicki   28, 58, 59, 98, 160, 206,
   217, 263
Benedict Hesse   241
Bolesław the Pious   35
Bolesław v the Chaste   35, 38

Casimir the Great   80, 220

Florian Mokrski, bishop   40

Gregory xi, pope   45–47, 55

Innocent iv, pope   37
Innocent viii, pope   252

Jacob from Paradyż   241
Jacob, bishop of Płock   41
John Długosz   112, 172, 239, 267, 275
John from Dąbrówka   241
John from Reguły   191
John Grot, bishop   39
John Łaski, archbishop   26, 28, 45, 46, 48, 51,
   52, 53, 55, 56, 206, 221
John Tęczyński, voivode of Krakow   121, 172

St. Kinga   35, 37, 205
Konrad of Sandomierz   44

Louis Decius   183

Martin v, pope   100
Matthew of Krakow   3, 241
Matthias from Łabiszyn   241
Mieszko iii the Old   33

Nanker, bishop   38
Nicholas Jaskier   58
Nicholas of Kurów, archbishop   41
Nicholas Trąba, archbishop   41

Peter Wysz of Radolin, bishop   40, 69, 86,
   191, 306
Philip of Fermo, bishop   38
Przemysł ii   35

Raymund Parthenopeus   51–56, 59

Salomea of Krakow   35, 36, 37, 205
Sigismund i the Old, king of Poland   57, 60,
   183
Spytko of Melsztyn   69, 305
Stanisław Ciołek, bishop   116, 241
Stanisław from Skalbmierz   241

Tacitus   30

Wincenty Ferrer   247
Wincenty Kiełbasa, bishop   241
Władysław Odonic   35

Zbigniew Oleśnicki   241, 286
Zbylut   32, 34, 356

Index of Subjects

All Saints Church in Krakow 137, 197, 232, 274, 275, 296, 297, 305, 314
ars moriendi 2, 3, 326

beguinages 280, 313–317
Benedictine abbey in Mogilno 33
Benedictine abbey in Tyniec 230
Benedictine Abbey of the Holy Cross at Łysa Góra 268
Bernardines 130, 137, 199, 200, 241, 259
brotherhoods 88, 89, 137, 148, 151, 189, 195, 201, 248, 252, 254, 276, 278, 280–293, 295, 297, 299, 309, 319, 320, 322, 323

canon law 5, 30, 31, 32, 36, 38, 41, 43, 51, 54, 59, 66, 67, 70, 79, 80, 82, 191, 238, 313, 327
canonical will 5, 32, 36, 60, 64, 67, 70, 86, 114, 238, 327, 331
Canons Regular 242, 251
of the Holy Sepulchre monastery in Miechów 48
Carmelites 289, 290, 291, 295, 296, 297
Carthusians 241, 268, 288
Chełmno law 44, 206
Cistercians 32, 36, 241, 251, 356
abbey in Łekno 32, 34
abbey in Mogiła 71, 130
Code of Justinian 51
common law 5, 7, 43, 44, 58, 59, 220
communal will 5, 7, 70, 80, 110, 126, 128, 328
Corpus Christi Church in Kazimierz 137, 147, 241, 254, 257, 273, 286, 287, 288, 289, 295, 296

Decretum Gratiani 31
devotio moderna 240, 241, 331
Dominicans 37, 64, 65, 148, 197, 206, 250, 252, 273, 278, 283, 289, 295, 296, 297, 303, 305, 314, 315, 316
donationes mortis causa 7, 8, 29, 109, 111

ecclesiastical court (*iudicium spirituale*) 42, 59

Franciscans 37, 64, 66, 148, 180, 201, 206, 284, 291, 295, 298, 299, 303, 314, 315, 316
free portion (*freiteil*) 29

gemechte acts– 8, 102, 142, 307
gerada 27–29, 77, 153, 364
grave gifts (*totenteil, totengabe*) 27

hergewet (*arma bellica*) 27, 131, 153, 214, 218, 231, 263, 268, 365
Higher court of Magdeburg Law at the Castle of Krakow 106, 148, 344
Holy Cross Church and Monastery in Świdnica 180
Holy Cross Church at Łysa Góra 268
Holy Cross Church in Krakow 294, 296
hospitals 65, 67, 79, 87, 92, 129, 137, 148, 176, 180, 181, 184, 189, 195, 196, 199, 201, 211, 228, 238, 243, 249, 250, 251, 283, 284, 288, 289, 294–297, 299, 302, 305, 310, 311, 329, 331
Holy Spirit's Hospital in Kalisz 251
Holy Spirit's Hospital in Krakow 65, 67, 79, 87, 129, 137, 148, 195, 196, 199, 200, 201, 249, 250, 286, 288, 289, 295, 296, 310, 311
hospital in Bochnia 233
hospital in Brzeg 181
hospital in Krosno 297
St. Barbara's Hospital in Wrocław 181
St. Hedwig's Hospital in Stradom 129, 137, 189, 199, 200, 288, 289, 294, 296, 297
St. Leonard's leper hospital near Kazimierz. *See* St. Leonard's Church and leper hospital near Kazimierz
St. Valentine's leper hospital near Krakow. *See* St. Valentine's Church and leper hospital near Krakow

indulgences 73, 100, 252, 282, 287, 292, 317, 318, 319, 321, 322

Jubilee years 73, 100, 105, 112, 137, 199, 240, 254, 317–318, 321, 328

INDEX OF SUBJECTS 403

Knights of St. John of Jerusalem (Knights Hospitaller) Monastery in Korytowo 35

leper houses 129, 137, 148, 254, 283, 284, 288, 289

Magdeburg Law 15, 28, 43–46, 48, 50, 51, 58, 59, 60, 82, 89, 93, 94, 98, 106, 148, 154, 206, 207, 218, 221, 237, 255, 313, 328, 344, 364, 365
Monastery of the Knights of the Cross with Red Star in Wrocław 180, 316
municipal statutes 57, 58, 59, 76, 183, 221

Norbertine abbey in Busko 33
Norbertine abbey in Witowo 33

Order of St. John 294
Order of St. Paul the First Hermit 241

Pauline Monastery in Częstochowa 130
pilgrimages 24, 65, 68, 74, 79, 80, 85, 93, 100, 105, 112, 114, 115, 128, 137, 140, 169, 170, 171, 199, 200, 219, 234, 239, 244, 254, 317–322, 327
plagues 57, 89, 92, 94, 106, 107, 110, 112, 128, 132, 199
Poor Clares 35, 36, 316
    monastery in Skała 36
processions 117, 152, 240, 282, 301, 302, 323, 332

religion civique 24, 196, 300–313
Roman law 30–32, 51–54, 59, 69, 191

salt mines 56, 65, 67, 68, 192, 357
Saxon Mirror (*Sachsenspiegel*) 26, 44–48, 51, 206, 221, 237

St. Andrew's Church in Krakow 316
St. Anne's Church in Krakow 275, 296
St. Anthony's Church in Brzeg 181
St. Anthony's Church in Strzelniki 294
St. Barbara's Church 246–250, 254, 285, 286, 289, 290, 291, 293, 297, 298
St. Bernardine's Church in Krakow 265, 268, 284, 297, 298, 299
St. Florian's Church in Krakow 296, 298
St. James Church in Krakow 296
St. Leonard's Church and leper hospital near Kazimierz 129, 137, 148, 189, 199, 200, 288, 289, 297
St. Mark's Church and Monastery in Krakow 137, 149, 190, 201, 287, 289, 296
St. Mary's Church in Krakow 14, 64, 65, 66, 68, 71, 87, 88, 91, 102, 144, 148, 188, 195, 201, 206, 220, 231, 232, 245, 246, 247, 248, 249, 250, 256, 260, 267, 272, 273, 274, 275, 276, 277, 279, 281, 282, 284, 285, 286, 288, 289, 290, 291, 292, 294, 295, 296, 297, 299, 303, 304, 305, 308, 309, 310, 322
St. Michael's Church in Krakow 296
St. Nicholas Church in Głogów 180, 279, 280, 295
St. Nicholas Church in Krakow 112, 151, 287, 296
St. Stanislaus at Wawel Church in Krakow 65, 296
St. Stephen Church in Krakow 137, 201, 287, 291, 295, 296
St. Valentine's Church and leper hospital near Krakow 129, 137, 148, 189, 199, 200, 288, 297

University of Krakow 51, 192, 241, 256, 257, 286

Printed in the United States
by Baker & Taylor Publisher Services